CONTENTS

A NOTE ABOUT COPYRIGHT

Dear Customer

What does the little © mean and why does it matter?

Your market-leading BPP books, course materials and e-learning materials do not write and update themselves. People write them: on their own behalf or as employees of an organisation that invests in this activity. Copyright law protects their livelihoods. It does so by creating rights over the use of the content.

Breach of copyright is a form of theft – as well as being a criminal offence in some jurisdictions, it is potentially a serious breach of professional ethics.

With current technology, things might seem a bit hazy but, basically, without the express permission of BPP Learning Media:

- Photocopying our materials is a breach of copyright

- Scanning, ripcasting or conversion of our digital materials into different file formats, uploading them to facebook or emailing them to your friends is a breach of copyright

You can, of course, sell your books, in the form in which you have bought them – once you have finished with them. (Is this fair to your fellow students? We update for a reason.)

And what about outside the UK? BPP Learning Media strives to make our materials available at prices students can afford by local printing arrangements, pricing policies and partnerships which are clearly listed on our website. A tiny minority ignore this and indulge in criminal activity by illegally photocopying our material or supporting organisations that do. If they act illegally and unethically in one area, can you really trust them?

AAT

Qualifications and Credit Framework (QCF)

LEVEL 2 CERTIFICATE IN ACCOUNTING

TEXT

Basic Accounting II

2012 Edition

First edition July 2010

Third edition June 2012

ISBN 9781 4453 9457 2 (previous edition 9780 7517 9727 5)

British Library Cataloguing-in-Publication Data
A catalogue record for this book is available from the British
Library

Published by

BPP Learning Media Ltd
BPP House
Aldine Place
London
W12 8AA

www.bpp.com/learningmedia

Printed in the United Kingdom

INTRODUCTION

Since July 2010 the AAT's assessments have fallen within the **Qualifications and Credit Framework** and most papers are now assessed by way of an on demand **computer based assessment**. BPP Learning Media has invested heavily to ensure our ground breaking materials are as relevant as possible for this method of assessment. In particular, our **suite of online resources** ensures that you are prepared for online testing by allowing you to practise numerous online tasks that are similar to the tasks you will encounter in the AAT's assessments.

The BPP range of resources comprises:

- **Texts**, covering all the knowledge and understanding needed by students, with numerous illustrations of 'how it works', practical examples and tasks for you to use to consolidate your learning. The majority of tasks within the texts have been written in an interactive style that reflects the style of the online tasks we anticipate the AAT will set. Texts are available in our traditional paper format and, in addition, as ebooks which can be downloaded to your PC or laptop.

- **Question Banks**, including additional learning questions plus the AAT's practice assessments and a number of other full practice assessments. Full answers to all questions and assessments, prepared by BPP Learning Media Ltd, are included. Our question banks are provided free of charge in an online environment containing tasks similar to those you will encounter in the AAT's testing environment. This means you can become familiar with being tested in an online environment prior to completing the real assessment.

- **Passcards**, which are handy pocket-sized revision tools designed to fit in a handbag or briefcase to enable you to revise anywhere at anytime. All major points are covered in the Passcards which have been designed to assist you in consolidating knowledge.

- **Workbooks**, which have been designed to cover the units that are assessed by way of project/case study. The workbooks contain many practical tasks to assist in the learning process and also a sample assessment or project to work through.

- **Lecturers' resources**, providing a further bank of tasks, answers and full practice assessments for classroom use, available separately only to lecturers whose colleges adopt BPP Learning Media material. The practice assessments within the Lecturers' resources are available in both paper format and online in e format.

This Text for Basic Accounting II has been written specifically to ensure comprehensive yet concise coverage of the AAT's learning outcomes and assessment criteria. It is fully up to date as at June 2012 and reflects both the AAT's unit guide and the practice assessments provided by the AAT.

Each chapter contains:

- Clear, step by step explanation of the topic

- Logical progression and linking from one chapter to the next

- Numerous illustrations of 'how it works'

- Interactive tasks within the text of the chapter itself, with answers at the back of the book. In general, these tasks have been written in the interactive form that students can expect to see in their real assessments

- Test your learning questions of varying complexity, again with answers supplied at the back of the book. In general these test questions have been written in the interactive form that students can expect to see in their real assessments

The emphasis in all tasks and test questions is on the practical application of the skills acquired.

If you have any comments about this book, please e-mail paulsutcliffe@bpp.com or write to Paul Sutcliffe, Senior Publishing Manager, BPP Learning Media Ltd, BPP House, Aldine Place, London W12 8AA.

A NOTE ON TERMINOLOGY

On 1 January 2012, the AAT moved from UK GAAP to IFRS terminology. Although you may be used to UK terminology, you need to now know the equivalent international terminology for your assessments.

The following information is taken from an article on the AAT's website and describes how the terminology changes impact on students studying for each level of the AAT QCF qualification.

What is the impact of IFRS terms on AAT assessments?

The list shown in the table that follows gives the 'translation' between UK GAAP and IFRS.

UK GAAP	IFRS
Final accounts	Financial statements
Trading and profit and loss account	**Income statement or Statement of comprehensive income**
Turnover or Sales	Revenue or Sales Revenue
Sundry income	Other operating income
Interest payable	Finance costs
Sundry expenses	Other operating costs
Operating profit	Profit from operations
Net profit/loss	Profit/Loss for the year/period
Balance sheet	**Statement of financial position**
Fixed assets	Non-current assets
Net book value	Carrying amount
Tangible assets	Property, plant and equipment
Reducing balance depreciation	Diminishing balance depreciation
Depreciation/Depreciation expense(s)	Depreciation charge(s)
Stocks	Inventories
Trade debtors or Debtors	Trade receivables
Prepayments	Other receivables
Debtors and prepayments	Trade and other receivables
Cash at bank and in hand	Cash and cash equivalents

UK GAAP	IFRS
Trade creditors or Creditors	Trade payables
Accruals	Other payables
Creditors and accruals	Trade and other payables
Long-term liabilities	Non-current liabilities
Capital and reserves	Equity (limited companies)
Profit and loss balance	Retained earnings
Minority interest	Non-controlling interest
Cash flow statement	**Statement of cash flows**

This is certainly not a comprehensive list, which would run to several pages, but it does cover the main terms that you will come across in your studies and assessments. However, you won't need to know all of these in the early stages of your studies – some of the terms will not be used until you reach Level 4. For each level of the AAT qualification, the points to bear in mind are as follows:

Level 2 Certificate in Accounting

The IFRS terms do not impact greatly at this level. Make sure you are familiar with 'receivables' (also referred to as 'trade receivables'), 'payables' (also referred to as 'trade payables'), and 'inventories'. The terms sales ledger and purchases ledger – together with their control accounts – will continue to be used. Sometimes the control accounts might be called 'trade receivables control account' and 'trade payables control account'. The other term to be aware of is 'non-current asset' – this may be used in some assessments.

Level 3 Diploma in Accounting

At this level you need to be familiar with the term 'financial statements'. The financial statements comprise an 'income statement' (profit and loss account), and a 'statement of financial position' (balance sheet). In the income statement the term 'revenue' or 'sales revenue' takes the place of 'sales', and 'profit for the year' replaces 'net profit'. Other terms may be used in the statement of financial position – eg 'non-current assets' and 'carrying amount'. However, specialist limited company terms are not required at this level.

Level 4 Diploma in Accounting

At Level 4 a wider range of IFRS terms is needed, and in the case of Financial statements (FNST), are already in use – particularly those relating to limited companies. Note especially that an income statement becomes a 'statement of comprehensive income'.

Note: The information above was taken from an AAT article from the 'assessment news' area of the AAT website (www.aat.org.uk).

ASSESSMENT STRATEGY

Basic Accounting II (BAII) is the second of two financial accounting assessments at level 2. The AAT recommend that Basic Accounting I is studied and taken before BAII.

The assessment is normally a two hour computer based assessment.

The BAII assessment consists of 14 tasks, six in Section 1 and eight in Section 2.

Section 1 is about the trial balance. Tasks will involve making adjustments through the journal and redrafting the initial trial balance.

Section 2 is about the cash book, petty cash book and the reconciliation of control accounts. Tasks will involve processing transactions through the cash book and petty cash book and carrying out reconciliation procedures.

Competency

Learners will be required to demonstrate competence in both sections of the assessment. For the purpose of assessment the competency level for AAT assessment is set at 70 per cent. The level descriptor in the table below describes the ability and skills students at this level must successfully demonstrate to achieve competence.

QCF Level descriptor	Summary
	Achievement at level 2 reflects the ability to select and use relevant knowledge, ideas, skills and procedures to complete well-defined tasks and address straightforward problems. It includes taking responsibility for completing tasks and procedures and exercising autonomy and judgement subject to overall direction or guidance.
	Knowledge and understanding
	■ Use understanding of facts, procedures and ideas to complete well-defined tasks and address straightforward problems
	■ Interpret relevant information and ideas
	■ Be aware of the types of information that are relevant to the area of study or work
	Application and action
	■ Complete well-defined, generally routine tasks and address straightforward problems
	■ Select and use relevant skills and procedures
	■ Identify, gather and use relevant information to inform actions
	■ Identify how effective actions have been
	Autonomy and accountability
	■ Take responsibility for completing tasks and procedures
	■ Exercise autonomy and judgement subject to overall direction or guidance

AAT UNIT GUIDE

Basic Accounting II (BAII)

Introduction

Basic Accounting II is the second of two financial accounting assessments at level 2.

Once Basic Accounting II has been achieved five full QCF units are gained, and the final part of a sixth unit:

- Maintaining petty cash records
- Maintaining and reconciling the cash book
- Maintaining the journal
- Maintaining control accounts
- Banking procedures
- *Principles of recording and processing financial transactions (part)

*The first part of this QCF unit is tested in Basic Accounting I.

The purpose of the learning area

This learning area comprises the QCF units stated above and is designed to build on Basic Accounting I which focuses on the double entry bookkeeping system up to an initial trial balance. Basic Accounting II looks in more detail at the cash book and petty cash book and introduces the reconciliation of control accounts. The learner is also required to make adjustments through the journal and re-draft the initial trial balance once adjustments have been made.

Learning objectives

This learning area enables candidates to further develop their understanding of the double entry bookkeeping system.

Candidates will develop the necessary knowledge and skills to use the journal to record a variety of transactions. They will need to know how to process transactions through the ledgers, cash book and petty cash book, and carry out reconciliation procedures.

Candidates will be able to re-draft the initial trial balance, following adjustments.

Learning outcomes

There are five full QCF units involved. Each is divided into component learning outcomes. There are 15 learning outcomes for this learning area.

QCF Unit	Learning Outcome	Covered in Chapter
Maintaining petty cash receipts	1. Complete a petty cash voucher	1
	2. Maintain an analysed petty cash book	1
	3. Maintain a petty cash balance	1
Maintaining and reconciling the cash book	4. Maintain a three column analysed cash book	2
	5. Reconcile a bank statement with the cash book	3
Maintaining the journal	6. Understand the use of the journal	6
	7. Open a new set of double entry bookkeeping records using the journal	6
	8. Use the journal to correct errors disclosed and not disclosed by the trial balance	7
	9. Create and clear a suspense account using the journal	7
	10. Use the journal to record other transactions	6, 7
Maintaining control accounts	11. Understand control accounts	4
	12. Prepare sales and purchases ledger and tax control accounts	4, 5
	13. Reconcile sales and purchases ledger and tax control accounts	5
Banking procedures	14. Understand the banking process	8
	15. Understand document retention and storage requirements	8

Delivery guidance

The topics which will be tested in this learning area are:

- Preparing petty cash vouchers, including calculating the VAT content of VAT inclusive amounts where appropriate

- Preparing petty cash reimbursement documentation to restore the imprest amount

- Making entries in an analysed petty cash book to record expenses, with or without VAT

- Making entries in a petty cash book to record the reimbursement of cash to restore the imprest amount

- Totalling and balancing the petty cash book

- Reconciling the petty cash book with the amount of cash held in the petty cash box

- Understanding the use of the petty cash book as part of the double entry system or a book of prime entry

- Making entries in a three column analysed cash book to record receipts and payments, using relevant primary records.

  - In this instance the three columns are bank, cash and settlement discount, with VAT being part of the analysis columns

  - Primary records may include paying in slip stubs, cheque book stubs, automated payment records, remittance advice notes, receipts, bank statement, sales invoices and purchase invoices

  - Entries include cash sales, cash purchases, discounts received and discounts allowed, payments to suppliers, receipts from customers, dishonoured cheques and other payments and receipts.

- Making entries in customer and supplier accounts to record settlement discounts

- Totalling and balancing the cash book

- Updating the cash book using the bank statement and direct debit and standing order schedules

- Reconciling the bank statement with the cash book and preparing a bank reconciliation statement

- Understanding the use of the cash book as part of the double entry system or a book of prime entry

- Understanding the purpose and use of the journal including correction of errors that are, and are not, disclosed by the trial balance

- Preparing journal entries and subsequently posting them to the general ledger:

  - Opening entries

  - Irrecoverable debt write off, including VAT

  - Payroll transactions including gross pay, income tax, employers' and employees', NIC, employers' and employees' pension and voluntary deductions

  - Opening and clearing a suspense account

- Identifying errors and types of errors, preparing journal entries, and subsequently posting them to the general ledger to correct errors not disclosed by the trial balance: errors of omission, commission, principle, original entry, reversal of entries, or compensating error

- Identifying errors and types of errors, preparing journal entries and subsequently posting them to the general ledger to correct errors disclosed by the trial balance: calculation errors in ledger accounts, single entry transactions, recording two debits or two credits for a transaction, errors transferring balances to the trial balance or omission of a general ledger account in the trial balance

- Balancing the trial balance using a suspense account

- Redrafting a trial balance following the correction of errors and elimination of the suspense account

- Understanding the purpose of control accounts (sales and purchases ledger control accounts and VAT control account), and the importance of regular reconciliation to identify and deal with discrepancies quickly and professionally

- Understanding the use of an aged trade receivables analysis for monitoring debts

- Preparing, balancing and reconciling control accounts (sales ledger control account, purchases ledger control account, VAT control account)

- Understanding the main services offered by banks and building societies, and the bank clearing system

- Understanding different forms of payment and the checks to be made on each: cash, cheques, credit cards, debit cards, automated payments

- Understanding the bank processing and security procedures of cash, cheques, dishonoured cheques, credit cards and debit cards

- Understanding document retention requirements in relation to banking
    - Types of documents retained
    - Importance of document retention policy

Note:

This learning area **does** require the learner to understand the double entry bookkeeping system and be able to perform double entry bookkeeping tasks.

For assessment purposes sales and purchases ledger control accounts will be contained in the general ledger forming part of the double entry. The terms sales and purchases ledger control accounts will be used throughout the assessment for consistency. The individual accounts of trade receivables and trade payables will be in the subsidiary ledgers and will therefore be regarded as subsidiary accounts.

chapter 1:
PETTY CASH PROCEDURES

chapter coverage 📖

In Basic Accounting I we learned how to calculate and record payments to credit and cash suppliers. The payments of most organisations will usually be by cheque or automated payment, but they will on occasion require small amounts of cash 'in hand' to make various types of payment, especially for reimbursement of employees who have paid out their own cash on behalf of the organisation. This 'cash in hand' is known as petty ('small') cash. In Basic Accounting I we saw how to post from the petty cash books to the general ledger. In Basic Accounting II we build on this knowledge and consider all the procedures necessary for dealing with petty cash and recording it in the petty cash book. The topics covered are:

✍ The need for petty cash in a business

✍ How a petty cash claim is made

✍ The meaning of an imprest petty cash system

✍ The details of a petty cash voucher

✍ The layout of the analysed petty cash book

✍ Accounting for VAT incurred on petty cash purchases

✍ Writing-up the analysed petty cash book

✍ Reconciling the petty cash book balance to the cash amount in the petty cash box

✍ Topping-up the petty cash box amount to the imprest amount

✍ The petty cash book as part of the double entry system

THE NEED FOR PETTY CASH

Most business expenses are paid for by cheque or automated payment. However, most organisations find that they need small amounts of cash on the premises in order to:

- make low value cash purchases and
- reimburse employees for valid business expenses.

Examples of typical reasons for needing cash for purchases might include:

- Purchase of stationery or small items (eg milk, coffee) required in the office

- Postage payments

- Payment of casual, non-payroll wages, eg the window cleaner

- Payment of taxi and bus fares needed for business travel by relevant staff

It would be inappropriate to draw up a cheque or authorise an automated payment each time these types of expense are incurred so, instead, a small amount of cash is kept for these purposes, known as the PETTY CASH FLOAT.

In outline, the way that it works is that a cheque is written out for a certain amount of cash and this is taken out of the bank and put into a lockable PETTY CASH BOX (we saw how the double entry for this worked in Basic Accounting I: debit petty cash book, credit cash book).

This 'cash in hand' is then the responsibility of the PETTY CASHIER. The petty cashier ensures that every payment has a valid PETTY CASH VOUCHER and deals with all PETTY CASH CLAIMS. The petty cashier also writes up the PETTY CASH BOOK.

PETTY CASH CLAIMS

Before looking at the details of recording and accounting for petty cash we will consider the overall process of an employee being reimbursed for expenditure by making a claim for petty cash.

HOW IT WORKS

Your name is P Norris and you work in the accounts department of Southfield Electrical. You have been asked to go out to the local shop, called Corner Stores, to buy more coffee for the office kitchen. This is how the petty cash claim process would work:

BPP
LEARNING MEDIA

you go to the shop and buy a jar of coffee
with your own money for £3.59

you return to the office with the coffee
and a shop till receipt for £3.59

you go to the petty cashier and fill out a petty cash voucher
with the shop receipt attached

you take the petty cash voucher to the person who told you
to buy the coffee for authorisation

you take the authorised petty cash voucher to the petty cashier
and you are given £3.59 in return

the petty cashier puts the petty cash voucher in the petty cash box
and eventually records this in the petty cash book

We will now consider this system in more detail.

AN IMPREST SYSTEM FOR PETTY CASH

An IMPREST SYSTEM for petty cash is a common method of dealing with petty cash as it provides a fairly simple way of controlling the cash and payments.

The principle of an imprest system is that when the system is set up a certain sum of cash, say £100, is put into the petty cash box. This is the IMPREST AMOUNT. In order for any money to be paid out of the petty cash box a valid, authorised petty cash voucher must be created. These vouchers, once the money that they represent has been paid out, are also kept in the petty cash box. Therefore, at any point in time, the amount of cash in the box plus the total of the vouchers should equal the imprest amount:

3

| CASH | + | VOUCHERS | = | £100 |

At the end of a period of time (such as a week or month, or when the cash falls below a certain level) the cash in the petty cash box is topped-up to the imprest amount. This is done by withdrawing cash from the organisation's bank account (by writing a cheque payable to cash and presenting this at the bank). The amount needed to top-up the petty cash box to the imprest amount is the total of the vouchers for the period:

	£
Imprest amount at start of period	100.00
Petty cash paid out = vouchers	(64.00)
Cash remaining in box	36.00
Cash withdrawn from bank to restore imprest amount	64.00
Cash at start of next period = imprest amount	100.00

Other non-imprest petty cash systems may be used by some organisations where, for example, a fixed amount is paid into the petty cash box at the start of each week or month.

PETTY CASH VOUCHERS

The key internal document for the proper functioning of a petty cash system is the PETTY CASH VOUCHER. This must be completed and authorised before any cash can be paid out of the petty cash box.

The petty cash voucher for your coffee purchase from Corner Stores is given below:

PETTY CASH VOUCHER

Number: *0463*   Date: *1 June XX*

Details	Amount
Coffee for office kitchen	*3 - 59*
Net	*3 - 59*
VAT	—
Total	*3 - 59*

Claimed by: *P. Norris*

Authorised by: *J. Smith*

There are a number of important points to note about this petty cash voucher:

- It is prepared by the petty cashier in response to a request from an employee who has a valid receipt – in this case it would be a till receipt – for expenditure to be reimbursed

4

- It has a sequential number entered by the petty cashier – '0463' – which ensures that all petty cash vouchers are accounted for

- The details of the expense are clear – 'coffee for office kitchen' – and a receipt (from the shop) should be attached

- The amount of the expense is shown both net of VAT and gross, with VAT at 20% separated out where appropriate – in this case there is no charge for VAT because the purchase was of food (see later in the chapter)

- The voucher is signed by you, the employee claiming the petty cash – 'P Norris'

- Most importantly the voucher is authorised by an appropriate member of staff – 'J Smith'

If money had been taken out of the box by you and taken to Corner Stores to pay for the purchase, so you did not have to pay out your own cash at all, then the petty cash voucher would be completed in the same way, except that instead of 'Claimed by P Norris' it would be marked 'Paid to Corner Stores'. The till receipt would need to be authorised and attached in both cases.

Task 1

Stationery has been purchased for £4.00 plus VAT at 20%. Insert the amount that will be included as the total figure on the petty cash voucher.

£

PETTY CASH BOOK

Once payments have been made out of the petty cash box and petty cash vouchers have been placed back in the box, they must be recorded in the petty cash book, which is the book of prime entry. We saw in Basic Accounting I that as well as being a book of prime entry the payments side of the petty cash book may also itself be the credit side of a general ledger account and, therefore, part of the double entry system.

The petty cash book can therefore be thought of as the petty cash general ledger account:

- the DEBIT side is for receipts
- the CREDIT side is for payments

This is what a typical petty cash book might look like:

RECEIPTS			PAYMENTS				ANALYSIS COLUMNS				
Date	Details	Total £	Date	Details	Voucher number	Total £	VAT £	Travel £	Post £	Stationery £	Office supplies £

Note the following points about this layout:

- The receipts side of the petty cash book is not analysed, as all that will be recorded here is the receipt of cash from the bank into the petty cash box

- The payments side is analysed into the types of petty cash expenditure incurred by the organisation (there may well be more columns than are illustrated here)

- The payments side includes a column for VAT as this must be analysed out if any of the payments include a VAT element (see below)

VAT

If a payment is made out of the petty cash box for an item that has had VAT charged on it:

- The total amount paid out is recorded in the total column

- The VAT paid is analysed in the VAT column

- The net of VAT amount is analysed in the relevant analysis column (eg stationery, office supplies)

The VAT laws are fairly complex but for the purposes of writing-up the petty cash book the following guidelines should help. There is no VAT on:

- Postage costs
- Bus or rail fares
- Food or drink

Where the seller is registered for VAT there is VAT on:

- Stationery
- Taxi fares

When goods are purchased in a shop a till receipt is given to the customer. When a claim for petty cash is made this receipt is used to determine any VAT on the purchase. Very often this till receipt shows only the total price of the goods and the VAT is not analysed out. However, provided:

- The total is less than £250, and
- The retailer's name, address and VAT registration number, and
- The date of supply and a description of the goods

are shown on the till receipt, the VAT can be reclaimed from HM Revenue & Customs. In this instance the VAT can be calculated from the total amount (using the 20/120 or 1/6 VAT fraction) and recorded in the petty cash book.

In an assessment you may assume that a valid till receipt for VAT is held unless you are specifically told otherwise.

HOW IT WORKS

A typical till receipt for a pack of printer paper is shown below:

```
F G SMITH
VAT 446 7265 31

1 Manchester Road
London, W1 3PZ

PAPER          3.60
TOTAL          3.60

CASH           5.00
CHANGE         1.40

CASHIER 2
10.26AM 8/12/XX
```

- The receipt contains the shop's name, address and VAT registration number
- The receipt shows the total cost of the paper as £3.60
- The receipt contains a date and description of the goods purchased
- The cash given to pay for it was £5.00 and the change was £1.40
- The total includes VAT so the amount of the VAT must be calculated using the VAT fraction (rounding down the VAT):

  £3.60 × 20/120 (or 1/6) = £0.60
- The net cost of the paper is therefore:

  £3.60 – 0.60 = £3.00

Task 2

A taxi fare of £9.36 has been paid from petty cash. The receipt issued by the taxi driver is dated and contains his VAT registration number and name and address, and includes VAT.

Calculate:

The VAT included in this fare

£ [   ]

The net amount of the fare

£ [   ]

WRITING UP THE PETTY CASH BOOK

At regular intervals the petty cashier will write up the petty cash book from the petty cash vouchers that have been kept in the petty cash box, and will then file the vouchers in numerical sequence. When the petty cash float is reimbursed or 'topped-up' to the imprest amount there will also be an entry in the receipts side of the petty cash book for the cash paid in.

HOW IT WORKS

One of your duties at Southfield Electrical is to write up the petty cash book each week. At the start of the week, 4 October, the petty cash box was empty and the imprest amount of £100.00 was withdrawn from the bank in cash and placed in the petty cash box.

The petty cash vouchers for the week show the following details:

Voucher 0465	Stationery costing £5.64 including VAT
Voucher 0466	Train fare of £15.80 (no VAT)
Voucher 0467	Postage costs of £15.60 (no VAT)
Voucher 0468	Coffee and biscuits for the office costing £3.85 (no VAT)
Voucher 0469	Copy paper £7.50 including VAT
Voucher 0470	Postage costs of £8.30 (no VAT)
Voucher 0471	Envelopes costing £2.82 including VAT
Voucher 0472	Train fare of £12.30 (no VAT)

The petty cash book will now be written up.

RECEIPTS			PAYMENTS								
								ANALYSIS COLUMNS			
Date	Details	Total £	Date	Details	Voucher number	Total £	VAT £	Travel £	Post £	Stationery £	Office supplies £
4/10	Cash	100.00	8/10	Stationery	465	5.64	0.94			4.70	
			8/10	Train fare	466	15.80		15.80			
			8/10	Postage	467	15.60			15.60		
			8/10	Coffee	468	3.85					3.85
			8/10	Copy paper	469	7.50	1.25			6.25	
			8/10	Postage	470	8.30			8.30		
			8/10	Envelopes	471	2.82	0.47			2.35	
			8/10	Train fare	472	12.30		12.30			

Once the petty cash vouchers have been written up in the petty cash book they are filed in numerical sequence. The petty cash book is then totalled and balanced.

Step 1   Total the total receipts column and underline it.

Step 2   Total the total payments column but do not underline the total.

Step 3   Total each of the payments analysis columns and rule them off. Cross-cast these totals to ensure that they add back to the total of the total payments column.

Step 4   Put the receipts total as the final total in the payments column and calculate the difference between the receipts total and the total payments total – this is the balance on the petty cash book that should be carried down (c/d) from the payments side and brought down (b/d) as the opening balance on the receipts side.

RECEIPTS			PAYMENTS								
								ANALYSIS COLUMNS			
Date	Details	Total £	Date	Details	Voucher number	Total £	VAT £	Travel £	Post £	Stationery £	Office supplies £
4 Oct	Cash	100.00	8 Oct	Stationery	465	5.64	0.94			4.70	
			8 Oct	Train fare	466	15.80		15.80			
			8 Oct	Postage	467	15.60			15.60		
			8 Oct	Coffee	468	3.85					3.85
			8 Oct	Copy paper	469	7.50	1.25			6.25	
			8 Oct	Postage	470	8.30			8.30		
			8 Oct	Envelopes	471	2.82	0.47			2.35	
			8 Oct	Train fare	472	12.30		12.30			
						71.81	2.66	28.10	23.90	13.30	3.85
				Balance c/d		28.19					
		100.00				100.00					
Balance b/d		28.19									

RECONCILING THE PETTY CASH BOOK WITH PETTY CASH

Whenever a balance is calculated on the petty cash book it is usual to ensure that it agrees with the actual amount of cash in the petty cash box at that time. This is done by counting the cash, totalling it on the PETTY CASH SCHEDULE and checking that it agrees to the balance on the petty cash book – a process known as RECONCILIATION.

HOW IT WORKS

Having written up and balanced the petty cash book, one of your duties at Southfield Electrical is to reconcile the balance with the contents of the petty cash box.

Step 1   Empty the petty cash box and list out the notes and coins it contains on the petty cash schedule (there will not be any petty cash vouchers as you have just written them all up in the petty cash book and filed them away).

Step 2   Calculate the total of the notes and coins.

Step 3   Enter the balance calculated on the petty cash book and sign the schedule to show that the total and the balance reconcile.

PETTY CASH SCHEDULE		Date: 8/10/XX
	In petty cash box	
Denomination	Number	£
£20	0	0.00
£10	1	10.00
£5	2	10.00
£2	3	6.00
£1	1	1.00
50p	2	1.00
20p	0	0.00
10p	1	0.10
5p	1	0.05
2p	1	0.02
1p	2	0.02
Total		28.19
Balance per petty cash book		£28.19
Amounts reconcile?		Yes
Signature		P Norris

When the reconciliation of the cash in the petty cash box to the vouchers is carried out and the two amounts do not agree back to the imprest amount, it is clear that something has gone wrong with the system or procedure.

Too little cash in the petty cash box

If the reconciliation shows that there is not enough cash in the petty cash box then there are a number of possible reasons for this:

- Probably the most obvious is that cash has been removed from the petty cash box without being supported by an authorised petty cash voucher

- Too much cash may have been given to a petty cash claimant and not noticed by either the petty cashier or the claimant

- A petty cash voucher may be missing – this can be checked as the petty cash vouchers should be sequentially numbered

- A top-up has been recorded but the cash was not placed in the petty cash box

Too much cash in the petty cash box

If the reconciliation shows that there is more cash in the petty cash box than there should be, this could also be for a number of possible reasons:

- Too little cash may have been given to a petty cash claimant and not noticed by either the petty cashier or the claimant

- A petty cash voucher has been placed in the petty cash box but no cash has yet been paid out

- The amount paid into the petty cash box at the start of the period brought it up to an amount that was greater than the imprest amount

- Some cash has been placed in the petty cash box and this has not been recorded

---

Task 3

The petty cash box is totalled and reconciled at the end of the week and it is discovered that there are petty cash vouchers totalling £103.69 and actual cash of £36.31. The imprest amount is £150. Does the petty cash reconcile with the vouchers?   Yes/No

If not, suggest possible reasons why not.

These matters must be fully investigated and rectified before the next stage in the process – topping-up the petty cash – can be performed.

TOPPING-UP PETTY CASH: RESTORING THE IMPREST

The final stage in the process is to bring the petty cash amount back to the imprest amount and to record this in the petty cash book.

HOW IT WORKS

We have already seen that to bring the petty cash amount back to the imprest amount the cash required is the total of all of the petty cash vouchers. Therefore, in this case, £71.81 in cash is required. A CHEQUE REQUISITION FORM for this amount must be completed, as shown below:

CHEQUE REQUISITION FORM
Southfield Electrical

Requested by: _Petty cashier_   **Date:** _8 Oct XX_

Payable to: _Cash_

Amount: _£71.81_

Send to: _Petty cashier_

Reason: _Petty cash imprest_

Invoice/receipt attached: _____

Other documentation: _____

Authorised by: _____ **Date:** _____

The cheque requisition form will now be authorised by a more senior person in the accounts department and a cheque written out made payable to 'cash' of £71.81. This will be presented at the bank, together with an extended form of the petty cash schedule listing the denominations of notes and coin that the organisation would like the bank to hand over. The mix of notes and coin will be decided by the petty cashier based on:

- What is in the box already
- Their experience of how often each denomination is used

An extended petty cash schedule is set out next.

PETTY CASH SCHEDULE				Date: 8/10/XX
	In petty cash box		Required in top-up	
Denomination	Number	£	Number	£
£20	0	0.00	2	40.00
£10	1	10.00	2	20.00
£5	2	10.00	1	5.00
£2	3	6.00	1	2.00
£1	1	1.00	3	3.00
50p	2	1.00	1	0.50
20p	0	0.00	5	1.00
10p	1	0.10	3	0.30
5p	1	0.05	0	0.00
2p	1	0.02	0	0.00
1p	2	0.02	1	0.01
Total		28.19		71.81
Balance per petty cash book		£28.19		
Amounts reconcile?		Yes		
Signature		P. Norris		

When the cash is obtained from the bank and put into the petty cash box it will contain £100 in notes and coin as follows:

PETTY CASH SCHEDULE			Date: 8/10/XX			
	In petty cash box		Top-up		Final	
Denomination	Number	£	Number	£	Number	£
£20	0	0.00	2	40.00	2	40.00
£10	1	10.00	2	20.00	3	30.00
£5	2	10.00	1	5.00	3	15.00
£2	3	6.00	1	2.00	4	8.00
£1	1	1.00	3	3.00	4	4.00
50p	2	1.00	1	0.50	3	1.50
20p	0	0.00	5	1.00	5	1.00
10p	1	0.10	3	0.30	4	0.40
5p	1	0.05	0	0.00	1	0.05
2p	1	0.02	0	0.00	1	0.02
1p	2	0.02	1	0.01	3	0.03
Total		28.19		71.81		100.00

The receipts side of the petty cash book will be written up to show the receipt of the top-up cash (remember from Basic Accounting I that the credit side of this transaction is the bank general ledger account):

RECEIPTS			PAYMENTS								
									ANALYSIS COLUMNS		
Date	Details	Total £	Date	Details	Voucher number	Total £	VAT £	Travel £	Post £	Stationery £	Office supplies £
4 Oct	Cash	100.00	8 Oct	Stationery	465	5.64	0.94			4.70	
			8 Oct	Train fare	466	15.80		15.80			
			8 Oct	Postage	467	15.60			15.60		
			8 Oct	Coffee	468	3.85					3.85
			8 Oct	Copy paper	469	7.50	1.25			6.25	
			8 Oct	Postage	470	8.30			8.30		
			8 Oct	Envelopes	471	2.82	0.47			2.35	
			8 Oct	Train fare	472	12.30		12.30			
						71.81	2.66	28.10	23.90	13.30	3.85
			Balance c/d			28.19					
		100.00				100.00					
Balance b/d		28.19									
8 Oct	Bank	71.81									

The petty cash book now has an opening balance of £100.00 (£28.19 + £71.81), the imprest amount, ready for the start of the following week.

Task 4

A business has a petty cash system with an imprest amount of £50.00. During the week petty cash was paid out of the petty cash box totalling £41.30 and the remaining balance in the box was £8.70. How much cash is required to bring the petty cash box back to the imprest amount?

£ [   ]

POSTING THE PETTY CASH BOOK

We covered posting both sides of the analysed petty cash book to the general ledger in Basic Accounting I.

PETTY CASH BOOK AND THE GENERAL LEDGER

It is normal practice for the petty cash book to be not only the book of prime entry for petty cash vouchers but also part of the double entry in the general ledger. This means that other than writing up the petty cash book, the only necessary entries are to debit the various expense accounts with the totals of the analysis columns on the payments (credit) side of the petty cash book, and to credit Bank with the amount of the top-up entered on the receipts (debit) side of the petty cash book.

In some businesses the petty cash book is simply the book of prime entry and is not part of the double entry system in the general ledger. In such an accounting system there will be a separate general ledger account for petty cash, often called the PETTY CASH CONTROL ACCOUNT.

- The total of petty cash receipts will be debited to the petty cash control account

- The total of petty cash payments for the period will be credited to the petty cash control account

The VAT and analysed payments will be debited from the petty cash book to the general ledger as usual.

CHAPTER OVERVIEW

- Most businesses will require small amounts of cash on the premises for the purchase of low value items and the reimbursement of employees for business expenses

- This cash is known as the petty cash float and is kept in the petty cash box by the petty cashier

- If an employee incurs a business expense and pays for it themselves then this can be reclaimed by presenting evidence of the expense to the petty cashier, who prepares the petty cash voucher, has the voucher authorised and then reimburses the employee for the amount spent out of the petty cash float

- An imprest system for petty cash is where the petty cash box is always topped-up to the same amount, the imprest amount, at the end of each week or month

- Claims can only be paid by the petty cashier if they are supported by a properly authorised petty cash voucher plus a receipt

- The petty cash vouchers must then be written up in the petty cash book

- The petty cash book has a receipts side and a payments side and is normally part of the general ledger as well as being a book of prime entry – the payments side is analysed into columns for VAT and all of the types of petty cash expense that the organisation normally deals with

- When the petty cash vouchers have been written up into the petty cash book it must then be totalled and balanced

- The amount of notes and coin in the petty cash box is counted and agreed to the balance on the petty cash book using a petty cash schedule

- Finally the petty cash box must be reimbursed back to the imprest amount by means of a receipt of note and coin taken out from the bank, and this is recorded on the receipts side of the petty cash book

- The double entry for the cash being paid into the petty cash box is a credit entry in the Bank account and a debit entry in the petty cash book

- The analysed payments side of the petty cash book is posted to the general ledger by debiting the VAT and analysis column totals to the relevant accounts in the general ledger

- Other non-imprest petty cash systems may be used by some organisations where, for example, a fixed amount is paid into the petty cash box at the start of each week or month

CHAPTER OVERVIEW CONTINUED

- If the petty cash book is just a book of prime entry and not part of the double entry system then a separate petty cash control account must be kept in the general ledger to record the receipts into the petty cash box and the total payments made; the VAT and analysis amounts are posted as usual

Keywords

Petty cash float – the amount of cash held in the petty cash box at any one time

Petty cash box – a secure lockable box in which the petty cash float and petty cash vouchers are kept

Petty cashier – the person in the organisation who is responsible for the petty cash

Petty cash voucher – the document that must be completed and authorised before any cash can be paid out to an employee from the petty cash box

Petty cash claims – a claim from an employee for reimbursement from the petty cash box

Petty cash book – the primary record used to record the petty cash vouchers and any money paid into the petty cash box

Petty cash control account – the general ledger account for petty cash when the petty cash book acts only as a book of prime entry

Imprest system – a petty cash system whereby the petty cash box is always topped-up to the same amount at the end of each week or month

Imprest amount – the amount to which the petty cash float is topped-up at the end of a period of time

Credit side of the petty cash book is used to record the total amount of each payment and to analyse that payment into its VAT and expense components

Debit side of the petty cash book is used to record the total amount of each receipt into petty cash

Petty cash schedule – a list of the different denominations of notes and coin contained in the petty cash float. It can be extended to include an analysis of the actual notes and coin that the organisation wants the bank to provide as the top-up

Reconciliation – the process by which a check is carried out that two amounts agree

Cheque requisition form – an internal document used to request a cheque to be raised

TEST YOUR LEARNING

Test 1

Complete the following explanation of how an imprest petty cash system works by selecting the appropriate choices in each case.

1.1 An imprest petty cash system is one where the amount of the topped-up petty cash float at the start of each period is:

Always the same

Sometimes the same

Never the same

1.2 Amounts that have been paid out for authorised expenditure are represented in the petty cash box by:

Notes and coin

Petty cash vouchers

Till receipts

1.3 At the end of the period the total of the

> Notes and coin
> Petty cash vouchers
> Till receipts

in the petty cash box is the amount needed to restore the petty cash box to the imprest amount.

Test 2

A petty cash claim has been made by Janis Williams for the purchase of paper costing £5.40 and envelopes costing £2.82 for use in the office (both including VAT).

Complete the petty cash voucher showing all of the details for this claim. The last petty cash voucher used was number 0623 and today's date is 20 October.

PETTY CASH VOUCHER		
Number:		
Date:		
	Details:	
Paper	£	
Envelopes	£	
Net	£	
VAT	£	
Total	£	

Test 3

A petty cash system is run on the basis of £150 in the petty cash box at the start of each week. At the end of one week the total of the vouchers in the petty cash box was £89.46. For how much should the cheque requisition form be made out to restore the petty cash box to its imprest amount?

£	

Test 4

The petty cash system in your organisation is run on an imprest system with an imprest amount of £150.00. The petty cash float at the start of the week beginning 20 October was £150.00 and eight petty cash vouchers were completed, authorised and paid on 24 October. The petty cash book analyses payments into VAT, postage, travel, sundry office expenses, and miscellaneous expenses.

The details of the petty cash vouchers are given below:

Voucher 771   Train fare (no VAT) £14.00
Voucher 772   Postage (no VAT) £18.60
Voucher 773   Envelopes (VAT receipt) £16.80
Voucher 774   Window cleaner (no VAT receipt) £20.00
Voucher 775   Pens and paper (VAT receipt) £18.90
Voucher 776   Postage (no VAT) £5.46
Voucher 777   Taxi fare (VAT receipt) £9.60
Voucher 778   Rewritable CDs for computers (VAT receipt) £28.20

You are required to:

(a)   Write up the petty cash book for these vouchers

(b)   Total and balance the petty cash book, bringing down the balance

(c) Record the amount of cash paid into the petty cash box to restore it to the imprest amount

RECEIPTS			PAYMENTS								
Date	Details	Amount £	Date	Details	Voucher number	Total £	VAT £	Post £	Travel £	Sundry office £	Misc £
20 Oct	Bank	150.00									
						——	——	——	——	——	——
						——	——	——	——	——	——
		——	Balance c/d			——					
Total		——	Total			——					
Balance b/d											
Cash top-up											

Test 5

This is a summary of petty cash payments made by a business.

Post Office paid	£12.60 (no VAT)
Motor Repair Workshop paid	£72.60 including VAT
Great Eastern Trains paid	£32.00 (no VAT)

Use the appropriate narrative from the picklist to complete the details column:

(a) Enter the above transactions in the petty cash book.
(b) Total the petty cash book and show the balance carried down.

Petty cash book

Debit side		Credit side					
Details	Amount £	Details	Amount £	VAT £	Postage £	Travel £	Motor expenses £
Balance b/d	180.00						

Picklist:

Amount
Balance b/d
Balance c/d
Details
Great Eastern Trains
Motor expenses
Motor Repair Workshop
Postage
Post Office
Travel
VAT

Test 6

Two amounts have been paid from petty cash:

- Office cleaning for £62.90 plus VAT
- Printer paper for £17.40 including VAT

(a) Complete the petty cash vouchers.

Petty cash voucher		
Date: 14/09/XX Number: PC453		
Carpet clean in office area		
Net	£	
VAT	£	
Gross	£	

Petty cash voucher		
Date: 14/09/XX Number: PC454		
5 reams A4 printer paper		
Net	£	
VAT	£	
Gross	£	

Part way through the month the petty cash account had a balance of £78.60. The cash in the petty cash box was checked and the following notes and coins were there.

Notes and coins	£
1 × £20 notes	20.00
3 × £5 notes	15.00
6 × £2 coins	12.00
21 × £1 coins	21.00
19 × 50p coins	9.50
13 × 10p coins	1.30
13 × 5p coins	0.65

(b) Reconcile the cash amount in the petty cash box with the balance on the petty cash account.

Amount in petty cash box	£	
Balance on petty cash account	£	
Difference	£	

At the end of the month the cash in the petty cash box was £12.32.

(c) Complete the petty cash reimbursement document below to restore the imprest amount of £150.

Petty cash reimbursement		
Date: 30/09/20XX		
Amount required to restore the cash in the petty cash box	£	

chapter 2:
MAINTAINING THE CASH BOOK

── **chapter coverage** 📖 ──

The cash book is the main book of prime entry as it is vital for any business to ensure control over its cash, both when it is held on the premises (such as by a shop) and when it is in the bank account. Maintaining a cash book so that there is tight control of recording is therefore vital. The topics covered are:

✍ The two-column cash book
✍ The three-column cash book
✍ Primary records for the cash book
✍ Writing up and maintaining the cash book
✍ Totalling and posting the cash book
✍ Balancing the cash book

THE CASH BOOK

In Basic Accounting I (BAI) we looked at:

- How the cash book is posted to the general ledger

- How it can be (and usually is in practice) both a book of prime entry and part of the double entry system in the general ledger:

    - Receipts are entered in the cash book as the DEBIT side of the Bank account, so only CREDIT entries are posted in respect of receipts from the cash book (except for the double posting from the discounts allowed column)

    - Payments are entered in the cash book as the CREDIT side of the Bank account, so only DEBIT entries are posted in respect of payments from the cash book (except for the double posting from the discounts received column)

- How there is only a separate Bank ledger account in the general ledger (sometimes called the Bank control account) if the cash book is just acting as a book of prime entry. In this case debit and credit postings need to be made from both sides of the cash book

The CASH BOOK can therefore be thought of as the Bank general ledger (GL) account.

THE TWO-COLUMN CASH BOOK

A typical cash book, based on the two sides that we studied in BAI, would look like this:

Cash Book – Debit Side

Date	Details	Discounts allowed £	Bank £	VAT £	Cash sales £	Trade receivables £	Sundry £
10/5	Grigsons Ltd		124.55			124.55	
10/5	Sukie Ltd	22.00	1,651.00			1,651.00	
10/5	Cash sale		360.00	60.00	300.00		
10/5	Capital introduced		1,000.00				1,000.00
	Totals	22.00	3,135.55	60.00	300.00	1,775.55	1,000.00

Cash Book – Credit Side

Date	Details	Discounts received £	Bank £	VAT £	Cash purchases £	Trade payables £	Petty cash £	Sundry £
10/5	Haley Ltd		35.25			35.25		
10/5	Shipley & C0	200.00	4,465.00			4,465.00		
10/5	Cash purchase		204.00	34.00	170.00			
10/5	Drawings		300.00					300.00
10/5	Petty cash		150.00				150.00	
	Totals	200.00	5,154.25	34.00	170.00	4,500.25	150.00	300.00

What we have just seen is known as an analysed TWO-COLUMN CASH BOOK:

- The first column is the **discounts column**, which is not part of the cash book double entry and is therefore not included in the cross casting – it is a memorandum column only

- The second is part of the double entry, being the total or **Bank column**

- All the other columns, including the VAT column, are analysis columns

- The column for postings to credit customers' accounts in the sales ledger may be headed '**Sales ledger**' or '**Trade receivables**'

- The column for postings to credit suppliers' accounts in the purchases ledger may be headed '**Purchases ledger**' or '**Trade payables**'

It is clearer to see this if we slightly rearrange the columns:

Cash Book – Debit Side

		TWO COLUMNS		ANALYSIS COLUMNS			
Date	Details	Discounts allowed £	Bank £	VAT £	Cash sales £	Sales ledger £	Sundry £
	Totals	22.00	3,135.55	60.00	300.00	1,775.55	1,000.00
		Post DEBIT to Discounts allowed in GL	= DEBIT side of GL account	Post CREDIT entries to relevant GL accounts			
		Post CREDIT to Sales ledger control in GL					

Cash Book – Credit Side

		TWO COLUMNS		ANALYSIS COLUMNS				
Date	Details	Discounts received £	Bank £	VAT £	Cash purchases £	Purchases ledger £	Petty cash £	Sundry £
	Totals	200.00	5,154.25	34.00	170.00	4,500.25	150.00	300.00
		Post DEBIT to Purchases ledger control in GL	= CREDIT side of GL account	Post DEBIT entries to relevant GL accounts				
		Post CREDIT to Discounts received in GL						

THE THREE-COLUMN CASH BOOK

In BAII we look at the cash book in more detail, in particular, seeing how to write it up to record receipts and payments. However, before we do so we need to introduce an important amendment to how the cash book is presented, required by the BAII assessment: the THREE-COLUMN CASH BOOK.

As well as cash held in the bank account and in petty cash, many businesses – especially retailers – have cash sales settled in notes and coin or by cheque, and also receive many cheques from credit customers through the post. They may use some of the notes and coin to make purchases in cash, and may also only bank the cheques and notes and coin occasionally, say on one day of the week. Having 'cash in hand' on the business's premises like this may cause security risks, but what we are more interested in here is that the recording of cash and cheques as they come in and go out must be complete.

The three-column cash book allows businesses to record all transactions properly and, therefore, have more control over them. In a three-column cash book an additional, third column headed 'Cash' is included on each side of the cash book. This acts as a Cash general ledger account that is separate from the Bank general ledger account. When there are transfers between the two accounts it is therefore easier to ensure they are fully reflected in the double entry system.

- In the Cash column on the DEBIT side we record receipts of cash from cash sales or from credit customers, and analyse these as usual (so that the relevant credit entries can be posted to the general ledger and the sales ledger)

- In the Cash column on the CREDIT side we record:

  - Payments of cash as cash purchases or (rarely) to credit suppliers, and analyse these as usual (so the relevant debit entries can be posted to the general ledger and the purchases ledger)

  - Payments of cash into the Bank account – the corresponding debit entry for this in the general ledger is in the Bank column on the DEBIT side of the cash book

The Bank columns on either side are therefore effectively the same as in the two-column cash book.

Before we look at how such a cash book is maintained it is helpful to see how it will look:

Cash Book – Debit Side

		THREE COLUMNS			ANALYSIS COLUMNS			
Date	Details	Discounts allowed £	Cash £	Bank £	VAT £	Cash sales £	Sales ledger £	Sundry £
		Post DEBIT to Discounts allowed in GL Post CREDIT to Sales ledger control in GL	= DEBIT side of GL account for Cash	= DEBIT side of GL account for Bank	Post CREDIT entries to relevant GL accounts			

Cash Book – Credit Side

		THREE COLUMNS			ANALYSIS COLUMNS			
Date	Details	Discounts received £	Cash £	Bank £	VAT £	Cash purchases £	Purchases ledger £	Petty cash £	Sundry £
		Post DEBIT to Purchases ledger control in GL Post CREDIT to Discounts received in GL	= CREDIT side of GL account for Cash	= CREDIT side of GL account for Bank	Post DEBIT entries to relevant GL accounts				

29

MAKING ENTRIES IN THE THREE-COLUMN CASH BOOK

Before we can complete the double entry from the cash book of course we must first record transactions in it as a book of prime entry. All receipts and payments of cash must be separately recorded and then analysed.

Using the three-column cash book means that we record separately:

- Receipts into and payments out of the business's bank account, and
- Receipts of and payments out of cash by the business

Note that the cash transactions that are recorded are **not** those related to petty cash (see Chapter 1).

HOW IT WORKS

Zoe runs her own business and is registered for VAT. She banks all her cash and cheques at the end of each day. Zoe makes the following transactions in one day:

- Receives a cheque for £450 from Antoine, a credit customer

- Sells some goods to Bazzer for £282 cash including VAT

- Buys some goods for resale from a market for £56.40 including VAT and pays in cash

- Sends a cheque for £60 to Charlie, a credit supplier

- Pays Desmond, a credit supplier, £200 in cash, taking advantage of a £10 settlement discount

- Receives an automated payment from Ellie, a credit customer, into the bank account for £750. Ellie has taken £30 settlement discount

- Makes a payment of £40 by standing order for business rates

- Banks all the cash and cheques at the end of the day

Let's take each transaction in turn.

- **Receives a cheque for £450 from Antoine, a credit customer**

This is not a receipt of cash so it should be recorded in the **Bank** column of the cash book (debit side) and analysed to Sales ledger.

Cash Book – Debit Side

Details	Discounts allowed £	Cash £	Bank £	VAT £	Cash sales £	Sales ledger £	Sundry £
Antoine			450.00			450.00	

- **Sells some goods to Bazzer for £282 cash including VAT**

This is not a receipt straight into the bank account so it is recorded in the **cash** column, and analysed to sales (£282 × 100/120 = £235) and VAT (£282 × 20/120 = £47)

Cash Book – Debit Side

Details	Discounts allowed £	Cash £	Bank £	VAT £	Cash sales £	Sales ledger £	Sundry £
Antoine			450.00			450.00	
Bazzer		282.00		47.00	235.00		

- **Buys some goods for resale from a market for £56.40 including VAT and pays in cash**

This cash comes out of the amount of cash that Zoe has received from Bazzer so it is recorded in the **cash** column of the credit side of the cash book, and analysed to purchases (£56.40 × 100/120 = £47.00) and VAT (£56.40 × 20/120 = £9.40).

Cash Book – Credit Side

Details	Discounts received £	Cash £	Bank £	VAT £	Cash purchases £	Purchases ledger £	Petty cash £	Sundry £
Market		56.40		9.40	47.00			

- **Sends a cheque for £60 to Charlie, a credit supplier**

Writing out a cheque means that the money will come straight out of Zoe's bank account and will bypass the cash system entirely. Thus it is recorded in the **bank** column.

Cash Book – Credit Side

Details	Discounts received £	Cash £	Bank £	VAT £	Cash purchases £	Purchases ledger £	Petty cash £	Sundry £
Market		56.40		9.40	47.00			
Charlie			60.00			60.00		

- **Pays Desmond, a credit supplier, £200 in cash, taking advantage of a £10 settlement discount**

This is again a payment out of the cash that Zoe has collected in the day. By taking a £10 settlement discount she pays £200 in cash to settle a debt of £210. We record this in the **cash** column on the credit side and analyse it to the purchases ledger. We record the discount in the **discounts received** column.

Cash Book – Credit Side

Details	Discounts received £	Cash £	Bank £	VAT £	Cash purchases £	Purchases ledger £	Petty cash £	Sundry £
Market		56.40		9.40	47.00			
Charlie			60.00			60.00		
Desmond	10.00	200.00				200.00		

- **Receives an automated payment from Ellie, a credit customer, into the bank account for £750. Ellie has taken £30 settlement discount**

The automated payment means that the money will come straight into Zoe's bank account and bypasses the cash system entirely. Thus it is recorded in the **bank** column on the debit side and analysed to the sales ledger. We record the discount in the **discounts allowed** column.

Cash Book – Debit Side

Details	Discounts allowed £	Cash £	Bank £	VAT £	Cash sales £	Sales ledger £	Sundry £
Antoine			450.00			450.00	
Bazzer		282.00		47.00	235.00		
Ellie	30.00		750.00			750.00	

- **Makes a payment of £40 by standing order for business rates**

A standing order payment means that the money will come straight out of Zoe's bank account and will bypass the cash system entirely. Thus it is recorded in the **Bank** column on the credit side and analysed in the Sundry column.

Cash Book – Credit Side

Details	Discounts received £	Cash £	Bank £	VAT £	Cash purchases £	Purchases ledger £	Petty cash £	Sundry £
Market		56.40		9.40	47.00			
Charlie			60.00			60.00		
Desmond	10.00	200.00				200.00		
Rates			40.00					40.00

- **Banks all the cash that it holds at the end of the day**

To calculate and record this we follow a three-step process:

Step 1   Calculate a balance on Zoe's cash account by totalling both Cash columns and deducting the cash on the credit side from the cash on the debit side (£282.00 – £256.40 = £25.60)

Cash Book – Debit Side

Details	Discounts allowed £	Cash £	Bank £	VAT £	Cash sales £	Sales ledger £	Sundry £
Antoine			450.00			450.00	
Bazzer		282.00		47.00	235.00		
Ellie	30.00	_____	750.00			750.00	
Total		**282.00**					

Cash Book – Credit Side

Details	Discounts received £	Cash £	Bank £	VAT £	Cash purchases £	Purchases ledger £	Petty cash £	Sundry £
Market		56.40		9.40	47.00			
Charlie			60.00			60.00		
Desmond	10.00	200.00				200.00		
Rates		_____	40.00					40.00
Total		**256.40**						
Balance		**25.60**						

Step 2   Keep the amount of the cash balance in the **Cash** column on the credit side as the 'Banking' amount, since it is a payment of the balance of cash out of the cash account and into the bank account. This reduces the cash balance to zero. (For clarity, you should also delete the total calculated in the other cash column.)

Cash Book – Credit Side

Details	Discounts received £	Cash £	Bank £	VAT £	Cash purchases £	Purchases ledger £	Petty cash £	Sundry £
Market		56.40		9.40	47.00			
Charlie			60.00			60.00		
Desmond	10.00	200.00				200.00		
Rates			40.00					40.00
~~Total~~		~~256.40~~						
~~Balance~~ Banking		25.60						

Step 3 Enter the same amount in the **Bank** column on the debit side as it is a receipt into the bank account. (For clarity, you should also delete the total calculated in the cash column on this side.)

Cash Book – Debit Side

Details	Discounts allowed £	Cash £	Bank £	VAT £	Cash sales £	Sales ledger £	Sundry £
Antoine			450.00			450.00	
Bazzer		282.00		47.00	235.00		
Ellie	30.00		750.00			750.00	
~~Total~~		~~282.00~~					
Banking			25.60				

PRIMARY RECORDS FOR THE CASH BOOK

Most businesses like Zoe's do not record each transaction immediately in the cash book. Instead they maintain PRIMARY RECORDS which are financial documents that are used to update the cash book on a regular basis. These primary records include:

For receipts	For payments
Invoices issued to cash customers and marked as paid	Invoices issued by cash suppliers and marked as paid
Remittance advice notes from credit customers	Remittance advice notes sent to credit suppliers
Receipts issued to cash customers (usually till receipts)	Receipts issued by suppliers paid in cash (usually till receipts)
Paying-in slip stubs	Cheque book stubs
Automated receipts – bank statement and remittance advice note from customers	Automated payments – bank giro credit forms, and BACS, standing order and direct debit schedules, plus remittance advices sent to suppliers
Bank statements issued by the bank	

Till receipts

If Zoe was a retailer she would almost certainly have a computerised till which would produce receipts for cash customers. As Zoe is VAT registered this would show the same information as we saw on the supplier's till receipt in Chapter 1:

```
Z SMITH
VAT 446 7265 31

56 Smith Street
London, Sw3 6PZ

PAPER        3.60
TOTAL        3.60

CASH         5.00
CHANGE       1.40

CASHIER 2
10.26AM 8/12/XX
```

Zoe will retain the till receipts for any purchases she makes in cash so they can be recorded in the Cash column on the cash book's credit side (assuming they are paid for out of cash received from customers rather than from petty cash).

Paying-in slip stubs

When opening an account with a bank a business will be issued with a paying-in book which will contain pre-printed, sequentially numbered PAYING-IN SLIPS. A typical paying-in slip plus the PAYING-IN SLIP STUB (to the left) is shown below – note how both front and back are shown as both sides need to be completed in detail.

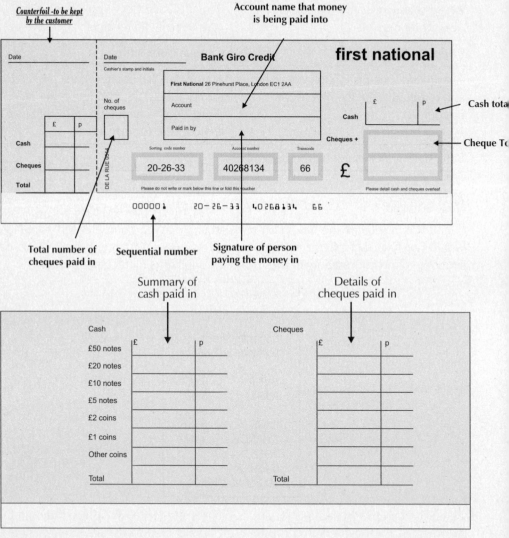

When cash and cheques received by a business are ready to be paid into the bank, the paying-in slip must be carefully and accurately completed.

Cash

- The cash must be first sorted into each denomination of notes and coins.

- Each denomination must then be counted and the total entered in the appropriate box on the back of the paying-in slip.

Cheques

- These are each listed separately on the back of both the paying in slip itself (which will be handed over to the bank with the cash and cheques) and on the back of the stub (which will be retained as the business's primary record of cash and cheques paid in).

- A total for cheques is calculated and transferred to the front of the paying in slip.

We see in Chapter 8 the checks that must be made to ensure that cheques received are valid and correctly completed.

HOW IT WORKS

It is 21 October 20XX and you are preparing the paying-in slip for your organisation. The following amounts of cash have been sorted and counted:

£50 notes	2
£20 notes	6
£10 notes	17
£5 notes	13
£2 coins	0
£1 coins	28
50p coins	16
20p coins	37
10p coins	18
5p coins	9
2p coins	25
1p coins	42

These amounts must now be entered onto the back of the paying-in slip.

Cash	£	p		Cheques	£	p
£50 notes	100	00				
£20 notes	120	00				
£10 notes	170	00				
£5 notes	65	00				
£2 coins	0	00				
£1 coins	28	00				
Other coins	18	57				
Total	501	57		Total		

There are also three cheques from customers to be paid in. They have each been checked as valid and correct.

Customer	Amount
	£
C Kelly	157.80
L Clifton	85.69
F Gingham	142.74

These must now be entered on the back of the paying-in slip and on the back of the paying-in slip stub.

Cash	£	p		Cheques	£	p	
£50 notes	100	00			157	80	C Kelly
£20 notes	120	00			85	69	L Clifton
£10 notes	170	00			142	74	F Gingham
£5 notes	65	00					
£2 coins	0	00					
£1 coins	28	00					
Other coins	18	57					
Total	501	57		Total	386	23	

Now the front of the paying-in slip must be completed:

- Fill in the date
- Enter the business's name as the bank account name that the money is to be paid into
- Enter the amount of cash in total taken from the back of the paying-in slip
- Enter the total of the cheques taken from the back of the paying-in slip
- Total the cash and cheques
- Enter the number of cheques paid in in the box provided

- Complete the stub with the date, total cash, total cheques and grand total
- Sign the paying-in slip

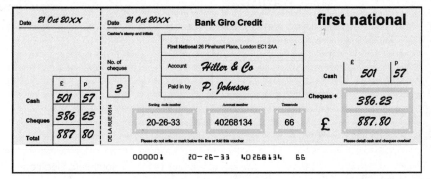

The paying-in slip is now complete and can be taken to the bank together with the cash and cheques. The stub is retained in the paying-in book and is the primary record for what is entered in the cash book.

Cheque book stubs

When opening an account with a bank a business will be issued with a cheque book which will contain pre-printed, sequentially numbered CHEQUES. When a business writes out a cheque made payable to a supplier it is instructing its bank to pay the supplier the amount of the cheque from the business's bank account.

A CHEQUE may be defined as 'a written order to the bank, signed by the bank's customer to pay a certain amount, specified in words and figures, to another specified person'.

There are three parties involved in a cheque:

- The DRAWEE – the bank who has issued the cheque and will have to pay the cheque
- The PAYEE – the person to whom the cheque is being paid (ie the supplier)
- The DRAWER – the person who is writing and signing the cheque in order to make a payment (ie the customer)

Increasingly, retailers and a business's regular suppliers are reluctant to accept cheques as a form of payment, and indeed many businesses prefer to make automated payments. However, cheques are still regularly used so you need to be aware of the procedures that relate to them.

A typical cheque and its CHEQUE BOOK STUB (the part of the document that is retained by the business writing out the cheque as its primary record, also known as a counterfoil) is shown below, together with an indication of what each of the details on the face of the cheque means.

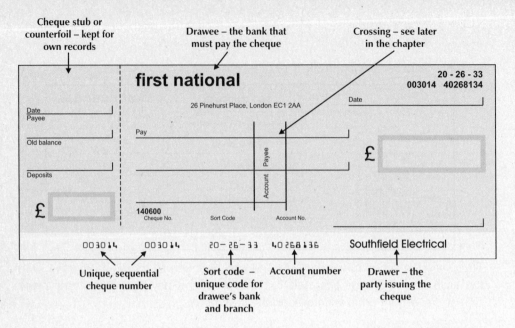

Cheque stub or counterfoil – kept for own records

Drawee – the bank that must pay the cheque

Crossing – see later in the chapter

Unique, sequential cheque number

Sort code – unique code for drawee's bank and branch

Account number

Drawer – the party issuing the cheque

A cheque must be filled out properly as illustrated below and we detail the checks that should be carried out.

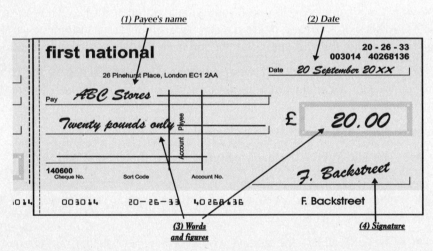

(1) Payee's name

(2) Date

(3) Words and figures

(4) Signature

(1)   The payee's name, ie your supplier, must be correct. For many shops this is not relevant as their customers' cheques are stamped with the organisation's name rather than the customer having to write it out.

(2)   The date must be today's date. A cheque should not be dated later than today's date as it cannot be paid into the supplier's account until the date on the cheque. Also the cheque must not have an earlier date on it. A cheque has a limited life and is out of date or "stale" after six months.

(3) The words and figures for the amount of the cheque must be the same. If they do not agree then the bank may return or 'dishonour' the cheque and your supplier will not be paid from your account.

(4) The cheque must be signed by a person who has been authorised to do so (an authorised signatory). Most organisations have a written agreement with their bank regarding who is allowed to sign the organisation's cheques. The bank will only accept cheques that have been signed by the correct people. In many organisations there will be monetary limits set on cheque signatures. For example, a business operating as a company may have a policy where the signature of just one director is required for cheques up to a value of £8,000, but if the cheque is for more than this amount then two directors' signatures are required.

(5) The date, supplier and amount must be written onto the cheque book stub for the cheque, as this is the primary record from which the cash book will be written-up.

The two parallel vertical lines on a cheque with **Account payee** written between them are known as a CROSSING. This means that the cheque can only be paid into the bank account of the payee on the cheque, ie into ABC Stores' bank account.

HOW IT WORKS

Southfield Electrical is making a payment to a supplier, Grangemouth Supplies, of £783.60 after deducting a settlement discount of £23.50. The cheque and stub are shown below:

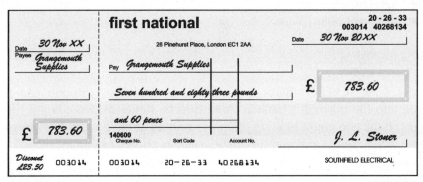

Note that where there are any blank spaces on the cheque, for example after the writing of the amount in words, a line is drawn through the space in order to minimise the chances of the cheque being fraudulently altered. If an error is made when writing out the cheque this should be amended and then initialled by an AUTHORISED SIGNATORY.

We shall see in Chapter 8 that there is a special type of cheque called a bank draft which a bank draws on itself at the request of its customer, provided the customer has sufficient funds to cover the payment. Both the drawer and the drawee of a bank draft is the bank. Drafts are used to give the recipient an absolute guarantee that they will receive payment for the amount of the draft, as they cannot be cancelled or dishonoured.

Automated transfers

Customers are increasingly keen to make automated transfers to their suppliers, in which case there are normally two primary records for the business receiving the payment:

- The remittance advice note sent by the customer, which shows the amount of the payment and any settlement discount being taken (it should also show which specific invoices are being paid).

- The business's bank statement, which shows the amount of the payment actually received (we shall come back to this).

In some circumstances, such as when the business is in regular receipt of rental income, instead of a remittance advice note there may be a payment schedule for perhaps the year ahead. This schedule will list out when each amount will be received into the business's bank account. The actual receipt can then be checked on the business's bank statement.

Automated transfers may take one of several forms:

- A bank giro credit (BGC)
- A BACS transfer
- A CHAPS transfer
- A standing order
- A direct debit

Bank giro credit

A BANK GIRO CREDIT (BGC) is a method by which a customer can pay a cheque into the business's bank account directly rather than sending it through the post. Bank giro credit slips are often pre-printed at the bottom of invoices and statements for credit cards and for utilities such as phone, electricity etc.

HOW IT WORKS

Southfield Electrical has received an invoice for phone charges and wishes to pay this by bank giro credit.

Step 1   A cheque is written out for the amount of the invoice

Step 2   The bank giro credit slip at the bottom of the invoice is detached
         and the amount of the cheque written in, together with the date
         and an authorised signature:

Step 3   The cheque and bank giro credit slip are handed in at Southfield's
         bank and the payment leaves Southfield's bank account in due
         course and reaches that of the phone company

BACS

BACS stands for Bankers Automated Clearing System. This is a system for making
transfers between one bank account and another via the banks' computer
systems. Unlike a bank giro credit it means that, to make a payment to another
party's bank account, there is no need to physically go to the bank itself with a
cheque.

The details of each supplier's bank account and the amount to be paid are
submitted to the BACS Clearing Centre by computer and the payments are then
taken directly from the business's bank account and paid in to each supplier's
bank account.

CHAPS

A CHAPS transfer is an instruction by the business to its bank to move money to
the recipient's account at another bank so that the funds are available the same
working day. Unlike with a cheque, the funds transfer is performed
instantaneously so there is no chance for the business to stop the payment, and
the bank cannot refuse payment once it has been made due to insufficient funds.
CHAPS transfers are commonly used for large amounts such as transferring funds
to solicitors for the purchase of property.

Standing order schedule

A STANDING ORDER is a method of making regular payments directly from the business's bank account to the bank account of a third party. This is organised through the bank by filling in a STANDING ORDER SCHEDULE – an example is shown below:

STANDING ORDER SCHEDULE

To: First National Bank

Please make the payments detailed below and debit my account:

Name of account to be debited _____

Account number _____

Payee details _____

Name of payee _____

Bank of payee _____

Sort code of payee _____

Account number of payee _____

Amount of payment (in words) _____ £ _____

STANDING ORDER SCHEDULE

Date of first payment _____

Frequency of payment _____

Continue payments until _____

Signature _____ Date _____

This standing order schedule is an order to the bank to make a payment of a fixed amount out of the business's bank account and into that of the payee on a regular basis.

You will note that the following details are included on the schedule:

- It is addressed to the business's bank

- Details of the business's bank account

- Details of the payee and their bank account ie, account number, sort code, bank

- The amount of the payment

- The date of the first payment

- The frequency of the payment thereafter, usually monthly or quarterly

- The date that the payments cease

- The authorised signatory for the account

As a standing order is for a fixed amount it is not particularly useful for paying credit suppliers, but can be of use for making fixed payments such as rent, insurance premiums or loan repayments.

Direct debits

A DIRECT DEBIT is a further method of making a payment directly from the business's bank account to that of another party. However, it operates in a different manner to a standing order.

HOW IT WORKS

Suppose that Southfield Electrical wish to pay National Water for its water rates by direct debit. The steps in the process are as follows:

Step 1 National Water sends Southfield Electrical a Direct Debit mandate which it has prepared – an example is given below

NATIONAL
WATER

Please fill in the whole form including 'the official use' box using a ball point pen and send the form to us at the address below in the envelope provided. Please do not send this instruction direct to your bank.

National Water plc
PO Box 284
Donchurch
South Yorkshire
DN4 5PE

Name(s) of Account Holder(s)

Bank/Building Society account number

Branch Sort Code

Name and full postal address of your Bank or Building Society
To: The Manager   Bank/Building Society

Address

Postcode

Reference Number (as shown on your water services bill)

| 2 | 2 | 3 | 0 | 1 | 7 | 4 | 0 | 1 | 2 | 0 | 1 | 6 |

Instruction to your Bank or Building Society to pay by Direct Debit

Originator's Identification Number

| 6 | 2 | 4 | 8 | 3 | 2 |

FOR NATIONAL WATER PLC OFFICIAL USE ONLY
This is not part of the instruction to your Bank or Building Society
To be completed by customer
Please tick required option:

☐ Annually ☐ Half Yearly ☐ Monthly April to January

☐ 1st of the month ☐ 15th of the month

Instruction to your Bank or Building Society
Please pay National Water plc Direct Debits from the account detailed in this Instruction subject to the safeguards assured by the Direct Debit Guarantee. I understand that this Instruction may remain with National Water plc and if so, details will be passed electronically to my Bank/Building Society.

Signature(s)

Date

Banks and Building Societies may not accept Direct Debit Instructions from some types of account

The Direct Debit Guarantee

■ This Guarantee is offered by all Banks and Building Societies that take part in the Direct Debit Scheme. The efficiency and security of the Scheme is monitored and protected by your own Bank or Building Society.

■ If the amounts to be paid or the payment dates change National Water plc will notify you 10 days in advance of your account being debited or as otherwise agreed.

■ If an error is made by National Water plc or your Bank or Building Society, you are guaranteed a full and immediate refund from your branch of the amount paid.

■ You can cancel a Direct Debit at any time by writing to your Bank or Building Society. Please also send a copy of your letter to us.

Step 2 Southfield Electrical completes the Direct Debit mandate instructing its bank to pay the amounts that National Water ask for on the dates that National Water requests payment

Step 3   Southfield Electrical return the Direct Debit mandate to National Water who then send this to its bank

Step 4   When a payment is required from Southfield Electrical to National Water this is requested by National Water and Southfield's bank will pay the amount requested

The usefulness of a direct debit compared to a standing order is that:

- It can be for variable rather than fixed amounts
- It can be used for payments to be made at varying time intervals

BANK STATEMENTS

At regular intervals a business's bank will send out a BANK STATEMENT showing movements on the bank account since the date of the last bank statement. A business current account which has many payments and receipts may require a weekly bank statement whereas a deposit account with less movement may only warrant a monthly statement. Many businesses will in addition make use of the ability to view their statements online.

A typical bank statement for Southfield Electrical is shown below.

STATEMENT

first national
30 High Street
Benham
DR4 8TT

SOUTHFIELD ELECTRICAL

CHEQUE ACCOUNT

Account number: 20-26-33 40268134

Sheet 023

Date	Sheet 023	Paid out	Paid in	Balance
20XX 17 Oct	Balance brought forward			2,595.23 CR
18 Oct	Cheque No 003067	424.80		
	Cheque No 003069	122.60		2,047.83 CR
19 Oct	DD Benham District Council	450.00		
	CR Paid in		1,081.23	2,679.06 CR
20 Oct	Cheque No 003073	1,480.20		
	Cheque No 003074	1,865.67		666.81 DR
21 Oct	CR Paid in		1,116.20	449.39 CR
	Balance carried forward			449.39 CR

There are various points to note about this bank statement:

- Each sheet of a bank statement is sequentially numbered so a business can tell if any statements are missing

- After each day's transactions the balance on the account is shown

- Sometimes each type of transaction is given a code:
  - CHQ is a cheque payment from the account in the process of being paid
  - DD is a direct debit payment
  - SO is a standing order payment
  - CR is an amount paid into the account

- Note that on 20 October the account went into an overdraft balance which is denoted by DR standing for Debit

You may have noticed something strange about the debit and credit terminology on the bank statement.

- Money paid into the bank account and a positive balance at the bank are credits and

- Payments out of the bank account are a debit, as is an overdraft balance.

This is the opposite way round to the way in which debits and credits are treated when writing up the cash and bank account in the organisation's own books – money in is a debit and money out is a credit!

The reason for this is that the bank is looking at the accounting from the opposite side to how the business is looking at it. To the bank, money paid into the account is an increase in the amount that the bank owes back to the customer, and cheques paid out of the account decreases the amount the bank owes to the customer.

Task 1

If money is paid into a bank current account this will appear on the bank statement as (please tick)

A debit ☐

A credit ☐

When a business is writing up its cash book it will check its bank statement to ensure that all the transactions that go through the account held by the bank are legitimate, and are recorded in the cash book. We shall come back to this in Chapter 3.

Dishonoured cheques

It is usually only by examining the bank statement that a business receives its first notice of a DISHONOURED CHEQUE. This means that a cheque has not been accepted as payable by the bank on which it is drawn, usually because the drawer of the cheque has insufficient funds in their bank account to cover payment of the cheque.

There are two situations that may occur for a business:

- A cheque that it has received from a customer and paid into its bank account may be dishonoured. In this case the original entry was:

  - Debit Bank column on the debit side of the cash book

  - Credit Sales ledger (or Sales/VAT if it was a cheque received in settlement of a cash sale) from the analysis column(s) of the cash book

  On notice of dishonour these entries must be reversed:

  - Credit Bank column on the credit side of the cash book

  - Debit Sales ledger (or Sales/VAT) from the cash book (as cheques are not often dishonoured, the analysis in the cash book would usually be in the Sundry column)

- A cheque that it has sent to a supplier has been paid into its bank account by the supplier, but it has been dishonoured. The business would usually be informed of this by its bank by letter. In this case the original entry was:

  - Credit Bank column on the credit side of the cash book

  - Debit Purchases ledger (or Purchases/VAT if it was a cheque paid in settlement of a cash purchase) from the analysis column(s) of the cash book

  On notice of dishonour these entries must be reversed:

  - Debit Bank column on the debit side of the cash book

  - Credit Purchases ledger (or Purchases/VAT if it was a cheque paid in settlement of a cash purchase) from the analysis column(s) of the cash book

WRITING UP AND MAINTAINING THE CASH BOOK

We are now ready to go through the full process of writing up and maintaining the cash book from primary records, including:

- Cash and bank balances brought forward
- Writing up transactions from primary records
- Making the entry for banking cash and cheques received
- Identifying the postings from the cash book
- Casting and cross-casting the cash book
- Calculating and carrying down the balances for Cash and for Bank

HOW IT WORKS

We will use examples of receipts and payments that Southfield Electrical received and made during the week ended 28 September 20XX. Before we start it may be useful for you to see the cash book as it will eventually be written up:

Cash Book – Debit Side

Details	Ref	Discounts allowed £	Cash £	Bank £	VAT £	Cash sales £	Sales ledger £
Bal b/f			900.00	12,940.00			
Dagwell	SL15	14.02		336.50			336.50
Polygon	SL03			158.20			158.20
Hayward				227.40	37.90	189.50	
G Thomas	SL30	11.23		269.43			269.43
Whitehill	SL24	28.07		673.58			673.58
Weller	SL18			225.49			225.49
Cash sale			75.60		12.60	63.00	
Treseme	SL42	40.00		2,910.00			2,910.00
Banking				200.00			
Totals		93.32	975.60	17,940.60	50.50	252.50	4,573.20
Bal b/d			**7.30**	**14,115.96**			

Cash Book – Credit Side

Details	Cheque number	Ref	Discounts received £	Cash £	Bank £	VAT £	Cash purchases £	Purchases ledger £
Seeban	003102	PL46	67.62		1,284.90			1,284.90
Electric	003103	PL13			440.00			440.00
Comtec	003104	PL19	34.23		650.37			650.37
Chiller	003105	PL03			849.37			849.37
Cash purchase				267.90		44.65	223.25	
Cash purchase				500.40		83.40	417.00	
Benham	STO	PL12			400.00			400.00
Gas	DD	PL04			200.00			200.00
Banking				200.00				
Bal c/d				7.30	14,115.96			
Totals			101.85	968.30 / 975.60	3,824.64 / 17,940.60	128.05	640.25	3,824.64

Southfield Electrical started the week with £900.00 held in cash and £12,940.00 held in the bank account. As we saw in Basic Accounting I, and also in Chapter 1 of this Text in respect of petty cash, brought down balances of assets are shown on the DEBIT side of a general ledger account, that is on the RECEIPTS side of the cash book.

Cash Book – Debit Side

Details	Ref	Discounts allowed £	Cash £	Bank £	VAT £	Cash sales £	Sales ledger £
Bal b/f			Bal b/f	12,940.00			

Receipts of cheques and cash for the week, together with information on settlement discounts taken as set out in the customer's remittance advice notes, were as follows:

CASH AND CHEQUES RECEIVED	
	£
Dagwell Enterprises, cheque	336.50 (£14.02 discount taken)
Polygon Stores, cheque	158.20
Peter Hayward, cheque (customer without credit account)	227.40 including VAT
G Thomas & Co, cheque	269.43 (£11.23 discount taken)
Whitehill Superstores, cheque	673.58 (£28.07 discount taken)
Weller Enterprises, cheque	225.49
John Cooper, cash (customer without credit account)	75.60 including VAT

Customer codes (being the sales ledger account codes) are as follows:

Polygon Stores	SL03
Dagwell Enterprises	SL15
Weller Enterprises	SL18
Whitehill Superstores	SL24
G Thomas	SL30
Treseme Ltd	SL42

A remittance advice from Treseme Ltd indicates a receipt of £2,910.00 with discount taken of £40. This is to be received directly into the bank account by BACS transfer on 28 September.

Cheques completed and sent in the week together with supplier codes (purchase ledger account codes), and receipts for cash purchases made, were as follows:

CHEQUES SENT

Cheque number	Payee	Supplier code	Amount £	Discount £
003102	Seeban	PL46	1,284.90	67.62
003103	Elec. North Ltd	PL13	440.00	
003104	Comtec Ltd	PL19	650.37	34.23
003105	Chiller Supplies	PL03	849.37	

RECEIPTS FOR PURCHASES MADE IN CASH

P J Harvey (inc VAT)	Cash purchase	267.90
W G Supplies (inc VAT)	Cash purchase	500.40

The relevant information from the business's automated payments schedules is as follows:

25th of each month	Benham District Council – business rates PL12
	£400.00 STO
27th of each month	English Gas – gas bill PL04
	£200.00 DD

Finally the paying-in book stub shows that £200.00 of cash physically held by Southfield at the end of the week was paid into the bank account on the Friday afternoon.

We can now complete both sides of the cash book.

As regards **receipts**:

- All the receipts of cash by Southfield will be entered in the Cash column (we are not including dates for reasons of space).

- All the receipts of cheques will be entered individually in the Bank column.

- The automated payment received is entered in the Bank column (we shall see how to check the bank statement for this in a later chapter). Each receipt then needs to be analysed.

- The payment of cash into the bank account is recorded in the Bank column on the debit side.

Cash Book – Debit Side

Details	Ref	Discounts allowed £	Cash £	Bank £	VAT £	Cash sales £	Sales ledger £
Bal b/f			900.00	12,940.00			
Dagwell	SL15	14.02		336.50			336.50
Polygon	SL03			158.20			158.20
Hayward				227.40	37.90	189.50	
G Thomas	SL30	11.23		269.43			269.43
Whitehill	SL24	28.07		673.58			673.58
Weller	SL18			225.49			225.49
Cash sale			75.60		12.60	63.00	
Treseme	SL42	40.00		2,910.00			2,910.00
Banking				200.00			

Remember that when cash sales are made the VAT element must be analysed out:

Peter Hayward	VAT = £227.40 × 20/120	=	£37.90
John Cooper	VAT = £75.60 × 20/120	=	£12.60

As regards **payments**:

- The cheques, standing order and direct debit payments will be entered in the Bank column on the credit side. Each payment then needs to be analysed.

- The purchases made in cash will be entered in the Cash column. Each payment then needs to be analysed.

- The payment of cash into the bank account is recorded in the Cash column

Cash Book – Credit Side

Details	Cheque number	Ref	Discounts received	Cash	Bank	VAT	Cash purchases	Purchases ledger
			£	£	£	£	£	£
Seeban	003102	PL46	67.62		1,284.90			1,284.90
Electric	003103	PL13			440.00			440.00
Comtec	003104	PL19	34.23		650.37			650.37
Chiller	003105	PL03			849.37			849.37
Cash purchase				267.90		44.65	223.25	
Cash purchase				500.40		83.40	417.00	
Benham	STO	PL12			400.00			400.00
Gas	DD	PL04			200.00			200.00
Banking				200.00				

The cash purchases include VAT so must be analysed out into the VAT column:

| P J Harvey | VAT = £267.90 × 20/120 | = | £44.65 |
| W G Suppliers | VAT = £500.40 × 20/120 | = | £83.40 |

TOTALLING AND POSTING THE CASH BOOK

At this stage the cash book should be cast and cross-cast, and the relevant amounts posted to the general ledger.

HOW IT WORKS

We cast each column and ensure that, for each side of the cash book, the analysis columns added together are the same as the totals for the two cash and bank columns, **ignoring any balance brought forward.**

Step 1 Cast each column in the debit side of the cash book.

Cash Book – Debit Side

Details	Ref	Discounts allowed £	Cash £	Bank £	VAT £	Cash sales £	Sales ledger £
Bal b/f			900.00	12,940.00			
Dagwell	SL15	14.02		336.50			336.50
Polygon	SL03			158.20			158.20
Hayward				227.40	37.90	189.50	
G Thomas	SL30	11.23		269.43			269.43
Whitehill	SL24	28.07		673.58			673.58
Weller	SL18			225.49			225.49
Cash sale			75.60		12.60	63.00	
Treseme	SL42	40.00		2,910.00			2,910.00
Banking		——	——	——	——	——	——
Totals		93.32	975.60	17,940.60	50.50	252.50	4,573.20

Step 2 Cross-cast the entries for the week in the cash book, making sure:

- Both the brought forward balances and the banking figure are deducted from the Cash and Bank totals

- The discounts allowed column is not included

	£
Cash total	975.60
Less: cash balance b/f	(900.00)
Bank receipts total	17,940.60
Less: bank balance b/f	(12,940.00)
Less: receipt of cash banked	(200.00)
	4,876.20
VAT	50.50
Cash sales	252.50
Sales ledger	4,573.20
	4,876.20

Step 3   Cast each column in the cash book on the credit side.

Cash Book – Credit Side

Details	Cheque number	Ref	Discounts received £	Cash £	Bank £	VAT £	Cash purchases £	Purchases ledger £
Seeban	003102	PL46	67.62		1,284.90			1,284.90
Electric	003103	PL13			440.00			440.00
Comtec	003104	PL19	34.23		650.37			650.37
Chiller	003105	PL03			849.37			849.37
Cash purchase				267.90		44.65	223.25	
Cash purchase				500.40		83.40	417.00	
Benham	STO	PL12			400.00			400.00
Gas	DD	PL04			200.00			200.00
Banking				200.00				
Totals			101.85	968.30	3,824.64	128.05	640.25	3,824.64

Step 4   Cross-cast the entries for the week in the cash book on the credit side, making sure:

- Any brought forward balances (there are none here) and the banking figure are deducted from the Cash and Bank totals

- The discounts received column is not included

	£
Cash total	968.30
Less: payment of cash into bank	(200.00)
Bank total	3,824.64
	4,592.94
VAT	128.05
Cash purchases	640.25
Purchases ledger	3,824.64
	4,592.94

Step 5   Make the postings from the analysis columns of the debit side of the cash book. Remember that the cash book here is both a book of prime entry and a general ledger account. Therefore on the **receipts** side of the cash book:

- Entries in the Cash and the Bank columns are the **debit** entries in the general ledger

- The analysis columns are posted to the **credit** sides of the relevant general ledger accounts (individual entries in the sales

ledger column are also credited to each relevant account in the sales ledger)

- The discounts allowed column total is:
  - **Debited** to Discounts allowed
  - **Credited** to the Sales ledger control account

Cash Book – Debit Side

		Discounts allowed £	Cash £	Bank £	VAT £	Cash sales £	Sales ledger £
Totals		93.32	975.60	17,940.60	50.50	252.50	4,573.20
General ledger	Debit	Discounts allowed					
	Credit	Sales ledger control			VAT	Sales	Sales ledger control

Step 6 Make the postings from the analysis columns of the **credit** side of the cash book:

- Entries in the Cash and the Bank columns are the **credit** entries in the general ledger

- The analysis columns are posted to the **debit** sides of the relevant general ledger accounts (individual entries in the purchases ledger column are also debited to each relevant account in the purchases ledger)

- The discounts received column total is:
  - **Debited** to the Purchases ledger control account
  - **Credited** to Discounts received

Cash Book – Credit Side

		Discounts received £	Cash £	Bank £	VAT £	Cash purchases £	Purchases ledger £
Totals		101.85	968.30	3,824.64	128.05	640.25	3,824.64
General ledger	Debit	Purchases ledger control			VAT	Purchases	Purchases ledger control
	Credit	Discounts received					

BALANCING THE CASH BOOK

In a three-column cash book there are two balances: for Cash in hand on the premises and for the Bank account.

The procedure for finding the balances on the cash book is the same as for any other general ledger account. Let us look first at the Bank columns:

Step 1	For the totals on the two Bank columns, deduct the lower total from the higher total
Step 2	Write in this difference as the balance carried down in the column with the lower total
Step 3	Amend the total in that column so it casts properly
Step 4	Enter the balance in the Bank column on the other side as the balance brought down

Unless it has a nil balance, the Bank column may have either a debit or a credit balance brought down:

- A **debit balance** brought down means that the business has an **asset** at the bank, that is it has a **positive bank balance**

- A **credit balance** brought down means that the business has a **liability** to the bank, that is it has a negative or **overdrawn bank balance,** or **overdraft**

The same procedure applies for the Cash columns, but note that as we are dealing with actual notes and coin on the premises, there will only ever be either no balance for the Cash columns, or a debit balance.

HOW IT WORKS

Returning to Southfield Electrical Ltd you need to write in the closing balances on the cash book at 28 September 20XX.

- For the Bank columns, the debit side total (£17,940.60) is greater than the credit side (£3,824.64), so the balance of £14,115.96 is carried down from the credit side to the debit side, where it is a **debit balance**.

- For the Cash columns, the debit side total (£975.60) is greater than the credit side (£968.30), so the balance of £7.30 is carried down from the credit side to the debit side, where it is again a **debit balance**.

Cash Book – Debit Side

Details	Ref	Discounts allowed £	Cash £	Bank £	VAT £	Cash sales £	Sales ledger £
Bal b/f			900.00	12,940.00			
Dagwell	SL15	14.02		336.50			336.50
Polygon	SL03			158.20			158.20
Hayward				227.40	37.90	189.50	
G Thomas	SL30	11.23		269.43			269.43
Whitehill	SL24	28.07		673.58			673.58
Weller	SL18			225.49			225.49
Cash sale			75.60		12.60	63.00	
Treseme	SL42	40.00		2,910.00			2,910.00
Banking				200.00			
Totals		93.32	975.60	17,940.60	50.50	252.50	4,573.20
Bal b/d			**7.30**	**14,115.96**			

Cash Book – Credit Side

Details	Cheque number	Ref	Discounts received £	Cash £	Bank £	VAT £	Cash purchases £	Purchases ledger £
Seeban	003102	PL46	67.62		1,284.90			1,284.90
Electric	003103	PL13			440.00			440.00
Comtec	003104	PL19	34.23		650.37			650.37
Chiller	003105	PL03			849.37			849.37
Cash purchase				267.90		44.65	223.25	
Cash purchase				500.40		83.40	417.00	
Benham	STO	PL12			400.00			400.00
Gas	DD	PL04			200.00			200.00
Banking				200.00				
Bal c/d				**7.30**	**14,115.96**			
Totals			101.85	968.30 / **975.60**	3,824.64 / **17,940.60**	128.05	640.25	3,824.64

CHAPTER OVERVIEW

- A three-column cash book includes a Cash column and a Bank column on each side and enables a business to fully record all transactions involving cash or the bank account

- The cash book (debit side) is written up from cheques, and cash received plus automated receipts, usually summarised in the remittance list

- The cash book (credit side) is written up from the cheque book stubs (counterfoils) or from the cheque listing and automated payments list

- The standing order schedule must also be consulted to ensure that all standing order and direct debit payments are recorded in the cash book on the correct date

Keywords

Cash book – name given to the Cash and Bank general ledger accounts, both the debit (receipts) and the credit (payments) side

Two-column cash book – An analysed cash book where the first column is the discounts column and the second is the Bank column

Three-column cash book – Like a two-column cash book but with a third column for Cash

Primary records – receipts, invoices, remittances and other documents which are retained and used to update the cash book on a regular basis

Paying in slip – a pre-printed, sequentially numbered document for paying cash and cheques into the bank

Paying in slip stub – the part of the paying in slip that is retained by the business as its primary record of cash and cheques paid into the bank

Cheque – a written order to the bank, signed by the bank's customer to pay a certain amount, specified in words and figures, to another specified person

Drawee – the bank who has issued the cheque and will have to pay the cheque

Payee – the person to whom the cheque is being paid (ie the supplier)

Drawer – the person who is writing and signing the cheque in order to make a payment (ie the customer)

Cheque book stub – the part of the cheque that is retained by the drawer as its primary record

Keywords

Crossing – The two parallel vertical lines on a cheque with 'Account payee' written between them to ensure that the cheque can only be paid into the bank account of the payee

Authorised signatory – a person authorised to sign a cheque

Bank Giro Credit (BGC) – payment method whereby a customer pays a cheque directly into the supplier's bank account rather than sending it through the post

BACS (Bankers Automated Clearing System) – a system for making payments directly between bank accounts

CHAPS – an instruction by the business to its bank to move money to the recipient's account at another bank so the money is available the same working day

Standing order – method of making regular payments directly from the bank account of the customer to the bank account of the supplier

Standing order schedule – listing showing all of the standing order and direct debit payments that a business has

Direct debit – a method of making payments direct from the bank where payments are for variable amounts and/or varying time intervals

Bank statement – shows movements on the bank account since the date of the last bank statement

Dishonoured cheque – a cheque that has not been accepted as payable by the bank

TEST YOUR LEARNING

Test 1

You work for Natural Productions. One of your duties is to write up the cash book. Natural Productions makes sales on credit to a number of credit customers and also has some cash sales from a small retail outlet attached to the factory.

The cash and cheques received for the last week in January 20XX are given below.

23 Jan	£545.14 cheque from Hoppers Ltd – settlement discount £16.86
23 Jan	£116.70 cheque from Superior Products
24 Jan	£128.46 from cash sales including VAT
24 Jan	£367.20 cheque from Esporta Leisure – settlement discount £11.36
25 Jan	£86.40 from cash sales including VAT
27 Jan	£706.64 cheque from Body Perfect – settlement discount £21.86
27 Jan	£58.80 from cash sales including VAT
27 Jan	£267.90 cheque from Langans Beauty

You are required to:

(a) Record these receipts in the cash book given below
(b) Total the cash book and check that it cross-casts

Cash Book – Debit Side

Date	Details	Discounts allowed £	Cash £	Bank £	VAT £	Cash sales £	Sales ledger £

Test 2

What is the double entry required for discounts allowed to customers?

Debit

Credit

Test 3

Most of the payments by Natural Productions are to credit suppliers but there are some cash purchases of materials from small suppliers which include VAT.

The cheque payments and cash purchases (all of which include VAT) for the week ending 27 January 20XX are given below:

Date	Cheque number	Supplier	Amount	Discount
			£	£
23 Jan	002144	Trenter Ltd	1,110.09	28.47
23 Jan		Cash purchase	105.60	
24 Jan	002145	W J Jones	246.75	
24 Jan	002146	P J Phillips	789.60	
24 Jan		Cash purchases	125.40	
25 Jan	002147	Packing Supplies	305.45	8.04
26 Jan	002148	O & P Ltd	703.87	18.72
27 Jan		Cash purchases	96.00	

You are required to:

(a) Record these payments in the analysed cash book (credit side) given below

(b) Total the credit side of the cash book and check that it cross-casts

Date	Details	Cheque No	Discounts received £	Cash £	Bank £	VAT £	Cash purchases £	Purchases ledger £

Test 4

At the beginning of the week ending 27 January 20XX Natural Productions had cash of £142.60 and an overdraft of £1,290.00. At the end of the week it banked £50.00. With reference to your answers to Tests 1 and 3, what are the Cash and Bank balances at the end of the week?

Cash	£	
Bank	£	

Test 5

There are five payments to be entered in Isdain Co's cash book.

Receipts from suppliers for Isdain Co's cash purchases

Supplier: Klimt Supplies	**Supplier: Patel Trading**	**Supplier: TWE Ltd**
Received cash with thanks for goods bought.	Received cash with thanks for goods bought.	Received cash with thanks for goods bought. Net £83 (No VAT)
Net £75 VAT £15 Total £90	Net £285 VAT £57 Total £342	

Stubs from Isdain Co's cheque book

Payee: Western Industries (Purchases ledger account PL725) £4,278 (Note: We have taken £80 settlement discount) Cheque number 256387	Payee: Mountebank Co For marketing leaflets (Isdain Co has no credit account with this supplier) £564 including VAT Cheque number 256388

(a) Enter the details of the three receipts from suppliers and two cheque book stubs into the credit side of the cash book shown below. Total each column.

Cash Book – Credit Side

Details	Discounts £	Cash £	Bank £	VAT £	Purchases ledger £	Cash purchases £	Marketing £
Balance b/f			3,295				
Klimt Supplies							
Patel Trading							
TWE Ltd							
Western Industries							
Mountebank Co							
Total							

There are two cheques from credit customers to be entered in the cash book:

Vantage Ltd   £1,278

Marbles Co   £2,183 (this customer has taken a £15 discount)

(b) Enter the above details into the debit side of the cash book and total each column.

Cash Book – Debit Side

Details	Discounts £	Cash £	Bank £	Sales ledger £
Balance b/f		792		
Vantage Ltd				
Marbles Co				
Total				

(c) Using your answers to (a) and (b) above, calculate the cash balance.

£	

(d)   Using your answers to (a) and (b) above, calculate the bank balance.

£	

(e)   Is the bank balance calculated in (d) above a debit or credit balance?

	✓
Debit	
Credit	

chapter 3:
BANK RECONCILIATIONS

chapter coverage 📖

The cash book is one of the main books of prime entry and it is vital for any business to ensure control over its cash held at the bank. A key means of control is through the bank reconciliation process. The topics covered are:

✍ The procedure for comparing the cash book to the bank statement and the types of discrepancy that might arise

✍ Preparing the bank reconciliation statement

COMPARING THE BANK STATEMENT TO THE CASH BOOK

When all the receipts for a period plus all the cash and cheque payments, BACS payments, standing orders, direct debits and other transactions have been entered into the cash book, before completing the casting and balancing process that we saw in Chapter 2 it is usual to check that the entries in the Bank columns agree with the entries on the bank statement.

Procedure for checking the bank statement to the cash book

When the bank statement for the period is received the following steps should be followed for comparison with the cash book:

Step 1   Work through all of the receipts shown on the bank statement comparing each one to entries in the Bank column on the debit side. When each receipt has been agreed to the Bank column the entry on the bank statement and in the cash book should be ticked.

Step 2   Work through all of the payments shown on the bank statement comparing each one to entries in the Bank column on the credit side. When each payment has been agreed to the Bank column the entry on the bank statement and in the cash book should be ticked.

Step 3   Any unticked items on the bank statement must be checked to ensure that the bank has not made a mistake.

Step 4   If the unticked items on the bank statement are valid the bank statement can then be used to adjust the Bank columns in the cash book, whichever is relevant, and eventually to prepare the bank reconciliation statement.

HOW IT WORKS

Southfield's cash book, prior to being cast etc, for the week ending 28 September 20XX is as follows:

Cash Book – Debit Side

Details	Ref	Discounts allowed £	Cash £	Bank £	VAT £	Cash sales £	Sales ledger £
Bal b/f			900.00	12,940.00			
Dagwell	SL15	14.02		336.50			336.50
Polygon	SL03			158.20			158.20
Hayward				227.40	37.90	189.50	
G Thomas	SL30	11.23		269.43			269.43
Whitehill	SL24	28.07		673.58			673.58
Weller	SL18			225.49			225.49
Cash sale			75.60		12.60	63.00	
Treseme	SL42	40.00		2,910.00			2,910.00
Banking				200.00			

Cash Book – Credit Side

Details	Cheque number	Ref	Discounts received £	Cash £	Bank £	VAT £	Cash purchases £	Purchases ledger £
Seeban	003102	PL46	67.62		1,284.90			1,284.90
Electric	003103	PL13			440.00			440.00
Comtec	003104	PL19	34.23		650.37			650.37
Chiller	003105	PL03			849.37			849.37
Cash purchase				267.90		44.65	223.25	
Cash purchase				500.40		83.40	417.00	
Benham	STO	PL12			400.00			400.00
Gas	DD	PL04			200.00			200.00
Banking				200.00				

Its bank statement for the week ending 28 September 20XX is shown below.

	FIRST NATIONAL BANK			
	30 High Street, Benham, DR4 8TT			
	STATEMENT			
	Account Name:			
	Southfield Electrical Ltd			
	Account No: 20-26-33 40268134			
Date 20XX	**Details**	**Payments £**	**Receipts £**	**Balance £**
21/09	Balance b/f			12,940.00 CR
21/09	Dagwell Enterprises		336.50	13,276.50 CR
22/09	Polygon Stores		158.20	
22/09	Peter Hayward		227.40	13,662.10 CR
23/09	G Thomas & Co		269.43	13,931.53 CR
24/09	BGC – B B Berry Ltd		442.19	
24/09	Whitehill Superstores		673.58	15,047.30 CR
25/09	STO – BDC	400.00		14,647.30 CR
26/09	Weller Enterprises		225.49	14,872.79 CR
27/09	Bank charges	15.80		
	DD – English Gas	200.00		14,656.99 CR
28/09	Cheque 003102	1,284.90		
	BGC – Treseme		2,910.00	
	Cheque 003104	650.37		
	BACS – wages	1,804.80		
	Cash paid in		200.00	14,026.92 CR

Now we need to compare the entries on the bank statement to the entries in the cash book.

Step 1 Compare the receipts on the bank statement to the Bank column on the debit side. As each receipt on the bank statement (a further copy is shown after the cash book) is agreed to the Bank column then both the cash book (debit side) and the bank statement are ticked.

Remember that the receipts in the bank statement are shown in the credit column on the bank statement.

Cash Book – Debit Side

Details	Ref	Disc allowed £	Cash £	Bank £	VAT £	Cash sales £	Sales ledger £
Bal b/f			900.00	12,940.00			
Dagwell	SL15	14.02		✓336.50			336.50
Polygon	SL03			✓158.20			158.20
Hayward				✓227.40	37.90	189.50	
G Thomas	SL30	11.23		✓269.43			269.43
Whitehill	SL24	28.07		✓673.58			673.58
Weller	SL18			✓225.49			225.49
Cash sale			75.60		12.60	63.00	
Treseme	SL42	40.00		✓2,910.00			2,910.00
Banking				✓200.00			

Step 2 Compare the payments in the bank statement to the Bank column on the credit side of the cash book. When each payment from the bank statement is agreed to the Bank column, tick the item in both the cash book and the bank statement.

Use the descriptions of the entries and any cheque numbers to help you locate the items in the cash book.

Cash Book – Credit Side

Details	Cheque number	Ref	Discounts received £	Cash £	Bank £	VAT £	Cash purchases £	Purchases ledger £
Seeban	003102	PL46	67.62		✓1,284.90			1,284.90
Electric	003103	PL13			440.00			440.00
Comtec	003104	PL19	34.23		✓650.37			650.37
Chiller	003105	PL03			849.37			849.37
Cash purchase				267.90		44.65	223.25	
Cash purchase				500.40		83.40	417.00	
Benham	STO	PL12			✓400.00			400.00
Gas	DD	PL04			✓200.00			200.00
Banking				200.00				

FIRST NATIONAL BANK

30 High Street, Benham, DR4 8TT

STATEMENT

Account Name:

Southfield Electrical Ltd

Account No: 20-26-33 40268134

Date 20XX	Details	Payments DR £	Receipts CR £	Balance £
21/09	Balance b/f			12,940.00 CR
21/09	Dagwell Enterprises		✓336.50	13,276.50 CR
22/09	Polygon Stores		✓158.20	
22/09	Peter Hayward		✓227.40	13,662.10 CR
23/09	G Thomas & Co		✓269.43	13,931.53 CR
24/09	BGC – B B Berry Ltd		442.19	
24/09	Whitehill Superstores		✓673.58	15,047.30 CR
25/09	STO – BDC	✓400.00		14,647.30 CR
26/09	Weller Enterprises		✓225.49	14,872.79 CR
27/09	Bank charges	15.80		
	DD – English Gas	✓200.00		14,656.99 CR
28/09	Cheque 003102	✓1,284.90		
	BGC – Treseme		✓2,910.00	
	Cheque 003104	✓650.37		
	BACS – wages	1,804.80		
	Cash paid in		✓200.00	14,026.92 CR

Step 3 We now need to consider the items on the bank statement that are still unticked.

Unticked items

Starting with the receipt – there is a bank giro credit receipt from B B Berry Ltd of £442.19 on 24 September which, as it is not ticked, needs to be included in the Bank column on the debit side of the cash book. You discover that the sales ledger code for this customer is SL41 and, on finding the customer's remittance advice note, that no settlement discount was taken.

When this has been entered into the cash book both the cash book and the bank statement should be ticked.

Cash Book – Debit Side

Details	Ref	Disc allowed £	Cash £	Bank £	VAT £	Cash sales £	Sales ledger £
Bal b/f			900.00	12,940.00			
Dagwell	SL15	14.02		✓336.50			336.50
Polygon	SL03			✓158.20			158.20
Hayward				✓227.40	37.90	189.50	
G Thomas	SL30	11.23		✓269.43			269.43
Whitehill	SL24	28.07		✓673.58			673.58
Weller	SL18			✓225.49			225.49
Cash sale			75.60		12.60	63.00	
Treseme	SL42	40.00		✓2,910.00			2,910.00
Banking				✓200.00			
B B Berry	SL41			✓442.19			442.19

Now for the bank payments – there are more unticked items here:

- 27/9 Bank charges £15.80 – these have not yet been entered into the Bank column on the credit side as they would only have been known about when the bank statement was received. Therefore the cash book must be adjusted to show these bank charges.

- 28/9 BACS wages payment £1,804.80 – there must have been an error in not entering this in the Bank column. Southfield would have authorised and scheduled the wages payment through BACS and this should have been entered into the cash book. Again an adjustment must be made for this.

In both cases the 'Sundry' column is the only one that can be used for analysis.

Cash Book – Credit Side

Details	Cheque number	Ref	Discounts received £	Cash £	Bank £	VAT £	Cash purchases £	Sundry £	Purchases ledger £
Seeban	003102	PL46	67.62		✓1,284.90				1,284.90
Electric	003103	PL13			440.00				440.00
Comtec	003104	PL19	34.23		✓650.37				650.37
Chiller	003105	PL03			849.37				849.37
Cash purchase				267.90		44.65	223.25		
Cash purchase				500.40		83.40	417.00		
Benham	STO	PL12			✓400.00				400.00
Gas	DD	PL04			✓200.00				200.00
Banking				200.00					
Bank charges	Chgs				✓15.80			15.80	
Wages					✓1,804.80			1,804.80	

The bank charges and wages should be ticked in both the cash book and the bank statement when they have been entered into the Bank column.

Every item on the bank statement has now been ticked.

FIRST NATIONAL BANK

30 High Street, Benham, DR4 8TT

STATEMENT

Account Name:

Southfield Electrical Ltd

Account No: 20-26-33 40268134

Date 20XX	Details	Payments DR £	Receipts CR £	Balance £
21/09	Balance b/f			12,940.00 CR
21/09	Dagwell Enterprises		✓336.50	13,276.50 CR
22/09	Polygon Stores		✓158.20	
22/09	Peter Hayward		✓227.40	13,662.10 CR
23/09	G Thomas & Co		✓269.43	13,931.53 CR
24/09	BGC – B B Berry Ltd		✓442.19	
24/09	Whitehill Superstores		✓673.58	15,047.30 CR
25/09	STO – BDC	✓400.00		14,647.30 CR
26/09	Weller Enterprises		✓225.49	14,872.79 CR
27/09	Bank charges	✓15.80		
	DD – English Gas	✓200.00		14,656.99 CR
28/09	Cheque 003102	✓1,284.90		
	BGC – Treseme		✓2,910.00	
	Cheque 003104	✓650.37		
	BACS – wages	✓1,804.80		
	Cash paid in		✓200.00	14,026.92 CR

You will note, however, that there are two unticked items in the Bank column on the credit side of the cash book. These are cheques that have been written and sent out to suppliers but that have not yet been paid into the supplier's account. These are known as UNPRESENTED CHEQUES and will be dealt with later in the chapter.

Other possible discrepancies

So far we have come across a bank giro credit receipt not recorded in the Bank column on the debit side and bank charges and a BACS payment not recorded in the Bank column on the credit side.

There are a few other types of difference that might be discovered:

- **Bank interest received** – some accounts earn interest when the account is in credit and therefore instead of bank charges there might be a receipt for bank interest being added to the balance on the bank account.

- **Standing order or direct debit** – we saw in Chapter 2 how the standing order schedule should be consulted when writing-up the Bank column on the credit side and any automated payments for the period put through. However, if this procedure was omitted or a new standing order or direct debit was not included in the schedule, then the bank statement would be the first evidence of the payment.

- **Bank errors** – banks make errors and, in particular, you must check carefully the amount and date of payment of standing orders and direct debits, and the validity of any automated payments and receipts.

- **Dishonoured cheque paid in** – as we saw in Chapter 2, sometimes the business will not actually receive the money from a cheque it has paid in as it is returned by the drawer's bank. This might be due either to the fact that the drawer has "stopped" or cancelled the cheque or because the cheque has "bounced" or been returned "refer to drawer", usually because the drawer has insufficient funds in its account. In either case the money will not be received on this cheque and an adjustment is required in the cash book. The adjustment is made by crediting the Bank column, and analysing the entry to either Sales ledger or Sales/VAT (as cheques are not often dishonoured, the analysis would usually be in the Sundry column). The entries on the bank statement for a dishonoured – sometimes called a 'returned' – cheque from a supplier would appear as follows:

FIRST NATIONAL BANK				
30 High Street, Benham, DR4 8TT				
STATEMENT				
Account Name:				
Southfield Electrical Ltd				
Account No: 20-26-33 40268134				
Date 20XX	Details	Payments DR £	Receipts CR £	Balance £
1/10	Cheque paid in		160.00	
7/10	Cheque returned unpaid	160.00		

- **Dishonoured cheque paid out** – if the business sends out a cheque that its bank refuses to pay, this will not usually appear on the bank statement at all, as the bank will simply not process the payment. The business still needs to adjust the cash book however once either the bank or the supplier inform it of a problem. The entry will be to debit Bank and to analyse this to the Purchases ledger or Purchases/VAT (as this is a rare occurrence the analysis will generally be to Sundry in the debit side of the cash book).

Task 1

If a figure for bank interest appeared in the credit column of the bank statement, this would be adjusted for in the (please tick)

Debit side of the cash book

Credit side of the cash book

Task 2

A standing order from the standing order schedule has been omitted from the cash book. This should be adjusted for in the (please tick)

Debit side of the cash book

Credit side of the cash book

BANK RECONCILIATION STATEMENT

We shall now recalculate the balance on Southfield Electrical's cash book as at 28 September 20XX:

Cash Book – Debit Side

Details	Ref	Disc allowed £	Cash £	Bank £	VAT £	Cash sales £	Sales ledger £
Bal b/f			900.00	12,940.00			
Dagwell	SL15	14.02		✓336.50			336.50
Polygon	SL03			✓158.20			158.20
Hayward				✓227.40	37.90	189.50	
G Thomas	SL30	11.23		✓269.43			269.43
Whitehill	SL24	28.07		✓673.58			673.58
Weller	SL18			✓225.49			225.49
Cash sale			75.60		12.60	63.00	
Treseme	SL42	40.00		✓2,910.00			2,910.00
Banking				✓200.00			
B B Berry	SL41	____	____	✓442.19	____	____	442.19
Totals		93.32	975.60	18,382.79	50.50	252.50	5,015.39
Bal b/d			7.30	12,737.55			

Cash Book – Credit Side

Details	Cheque number	Ref	Discounts received £	Cash £	Bank £	VAT £	Cash purchases £	Sundry £	Purchases ledger £
Seeban	003102	PL46	67.62		✓1,284.90				1,284.90
Electric	003103	PL13			440.00				440.00
Comtec	003104	PL19	34.23		✓650.37				650.37
Chiller	003105	PL03			849.37				849.37
Cash purchase				267.90		44.65	223.25		
Cash purchase				500.40		83.40	417.00		
Benham	STO	PL12			✓400.00				400.00
Gas	DD	PL04			✓200.00				200.00
Banking				200.00					
Bank charges	Chgs				✓15.80			15.80	
Wages					✓1,804.80			1,804.80	
Bal c/d				7.30	12,737.55				
Totals			101.85	975.60	18,382.79	128.05	640.25	1,820.60	3,824.64

We now have the correct balance for the bank account in the cash book at 28 September of £12,737.55. However, if you return to the bank statement you will see that this does not agree with the bank's closing balance of £14,026.92.

This will nearly always be the case and the reasons are TIMING DIFFERENCES. There is a time lag between recording receipts and payments in the cash book and their appearance on the bank statement.

Cash and cheques paid in are recorded in the Bank column on the debit side but there is a three-day delay, caused by the banks' clearing system, before they appear on the bank statement. Such amounts are known as OUTSTANDING LODGEMENTS.

When cheques are written to suppliers they are entered into the Bank column immediately. The cheques are then sent to the supplier, the supplier must take them to the bank and then there is the three-day clearing period before they appear on the bank statement. Those cheque payments that are in the cash book but not on the bank statement yet are known as UNPRESENTED CHEQUES, as we saw earlier.

HOW IT WORKS

We can now produce a BANK RECONCILIATION STATEMENT for Southfield which will reconcile the corrected cash book balance for the bank account on 28 September with the bank statement balance on the same date.

We start with the bank statement balance.

Bank reconciliation statement at 28 September 20XX

	£	£
Balance per bank statement		14,026.92

By examining the Bank column in the debit side of the cash book we can see that there are no outstanding lodgements, but there are still two unticked items in the Bank column on the credit side, which are cheques that have not yet been paid out by the bank. These are UNPRESENTED CHEQUES, and if they had been presented they would make the bank statement figure smaller. Therefore we deduct these in the bank reconciliation statement in order to come back to the cash book balance for the bank account of £12,737.55.

Bank reconciliation statement at 28 September 20XX

	£	£
Balance per bank statement		14,026.92
Less: unpresented cheques		
003103	440.00	
003105	849.37	
Total to subtract		(1,289.37)
Balance as per amended cash book		12,737.55

SUMMARY

We will now just summarise the procedure for carrying out a bank reconciliation before working through a further example.

Step 1   Compare the Bank column in the debit side of the cash book to the receipts shown on the bank statement (the credits on the bank statement) – for each receipt that agrees, tick the item in both the cash book and the bank statement.

Step 2   Compare the Bank column in the credit side of the cash book to the payments shown on the bank statement (the debits on the bank statement) – for each payment that agrees, tick the item in both the cash book and the bank statement.

Step 3   Any unticked items on the bank statement (other than errors made by the bank) will be items that should have been entered into the cash book but have been omitted for some reason. Enter these into the cash book and then the amended balance on the cash book can be found as usual.

Step 4   Finally, any unticked items in the cash book will be timing differences – outstanding lodgements and unpresented cheques – that will be used to reconcile the bank statement closing balance to the corrected cash book closing balance.

HOW IT WORKS

Given below is a summary of the cash book of a sole trader, Dawn Fisher, for February (note that we are just showing the bank columns – the discount, analysis and cash columns of a three-column cash book are not relevant for preparing a bank reconciliation).

Cash Book – Debit Side

Date	Details	Bank £
2 Feb	Balance b/f	387.90
2 Feb	G Hollings	1,368.48
7 Feb	S Dancer	368.36
14 Feb	K C Ltd	2,004.37
20 Feb	F W Painter	856.09
26 Feb	J J Hammond	648.34
28 Feb	L Minns	257.50
		5,891.04

Note that Dawn pays in each cheque to her bank account as it is received.

Cash Book – Credit Side

Date	Details	Cheque number	£
3 Feb	Long Associates	103567	1,007.46
5 Feb	Harland Bros	103568	524.71
5 Feb	L and P Timms	103569	1,035.76
8 Feb	Peter Thomas	103570	663.45
15 Feb	English Gas	103571	480.50
20 Feb	F P Travel	103572	1,233.80
24 Feb	K Riley	103573	246.58
26 Feb	Farman Ltd	103574	103.64
			5,295.90

Dawn has just received her bank statement for the month of February.

STATEMENT

first national
30 High Street
Benham
DR4 8TT

DAWN FISHER

CHEQUE ACCOUNT

Account number: 20-26-33 40268134

Sheet 011

Date		Paid out	Paid in	Balance
1 Feb	Balance b/f			387.90
6 Feb	Credit		1,368.48	1,756.38
9 Feb	Cheque No 103568	524.71		1,231.67
11 Feb	Credit		368.36	
	Bank giro credit		208.34	
	Cheque No 103567	1,107.46		700.91
13 Feb	Cheque No 103570	663.45		37.46
18 Feb	Credit		2,004.37	
	SO - FC Property	400.00		1,641.83
19 Feb	Cheque No 103571	480.50		1,161.33
24 Feb	Credit		856.09	
	Cheque No 103569	1,035.76		981.66
28 Feb	Bank interest		4.84	986.50
28 Feb	Balance c/f			986.50

The bank reconciliation will now be prepared:

- Compare the receipts and payments in the cash book to the bank statement – for each one that agrees, tick both the bank statement and the cash book entry.

Cash Book – Debit Side

Date	Details	Bank £	
2 Feb	Balance b/f	387.90	
2 Feb	G Hollings	1,368.48	✓
7 Feb	S Dancer	368.36	✓
14 Feb	K C Ltd	2,004.37	✓
20 Feb	F W Painter	856.09	✓
26 Feb	J J Hammond	648.34	
28 Feb	L Minns	257.50	
		5,891.04	

Cash Book – Credit Side

Date	Details	Cheque number	Bank £	
3 Feb	Long Associates	103567	1,007.46	
5 Feb	Harland Bros	103568	524.71	✓
5 Feb	L and P Timms	103569	1,035.76	✓
8 Feb	Peter Thomas	103570	663.45	✓
15 Feb	English Gas	103571	480.50	✓
20 Feb	F P Travel	103572	1,233.80	
24 Feb	K Riley	103573	246.58	
26 Feb	Farman Ltd	103574	103.64	
			5,295.90	

STATEMENT

first national
30 High Street
Benham
DR4 8TT

DAWN FISHER

Account number: 20-26-33 40268134

CHEQUE ACCOUNT

Sheet 011

Date		Paid out	Paid in	Balance
1 Feb	Balance b/f			387.90
6 Feb	Credit		1,368.48 ✓	1,756.38
9 Feb	Cheque No 103568	524.71 ✓		1,231.67
11 Feb	Credit		368.36 ✓	
	Bank giro credit		208.34	
	Cheque No 103567	1,107.46		700.91
13 Feb	Cheque No 103570	663.45 ✓		37.46
18 Feb	Credit		2,004.37 ✓	
	SO - FC Property	400.00		1,641.83
19 Feb	Cheque No 103571	480.50 ✓		1,161.33
24 Feb	Credit		856.09 ✓	
	Cheque No 103569	1,035.76 ✓		981.66
28 Feb	Bank interest		4.84	986.50
28 Feb	Balance c/f			986.50

- Deal with each of the unticked items in the bank statement:

Payments

- Cheque number 103567 has been recorded in the Bank column as £1,007.46 whereas the bank statement shows it as an amount of £1,107.46. Assuming this is correct, the cash book must be adjusted by including an extra £100 payment in the Bank column on the credit side

- The standing order of £400.00 on 18 February has not been recorded in the Bank column – the cash book must be corrected

Receipts

- The bank giro credit of £208.34 on 11 February has not been recorded in the Bank column – the cash book must be corrected
- On 28 February an amount of £4.84 bank interest has been credited to the account by the bank, ie it is a payment in of bank interest – this must be entered into the cash book

- Now the cash book must be amended to find the corrected bank balance. Tick the items that have been written in to tie up with the bank statement. The items that remain unticked are timing differences that will appear on the bank reconciliation, so it is good practice to mark these items in the cash book with an R (for 'reconciling').

Cash Book – Debit Side

Date	Details	Bank £	
2 Feb	Balance b/f	387.90	
2 Feb	G Hollings	1,368.48	✓
7 Feb	S Dancer	368.36	✓
14 Feb	K C Ltd	2,004.37	✓
20 Feb	F W Painter	856.09	✓
26 Feb	J J Hammond	648.34	R
28 Feb	L Minns	257.50	R
11 Feb	BGC	208.34	✓
28 Feb	Bank interest received	4.84	✓
Total		6,104.22	

Cash Book – Debit Side

Date	Details	Cheque number	Bank £	
3 Feb	Long Associates	103567	1,007.46	✓
5 Feb	Harland Bros	103568	524.71	✓
5 Feb	L and P Timms	103569	1,035.76	✓
8 Feb	Peter Thomas	103570	663.45	✓
15 Feb	English Gas	103571	480.50	✓
20 Feb	F P Travel	103572	1,233.80	R
24 Feb	K Riley	103573	246.58	R
26 Feb	Farman Ltd	103574	103.64	R
11 Feb	Correction cheque	103567	100.00	✓
18 Feb	FC Property	STO	400.00	✓
28 Feb	Bal c/d		308.32	
Total			6,104.22	

- Now the bank statement balance must be reconciled with this amended balance on the cash book – this is done by listing the items marked 'R' in the cash book as the reconciling items (timing differences).

Bank reconciliation statement at 28 February 20XX

	£	£
Balance per bank statement		986.50
Add: outstanding lodgements		
J J Hammond	648.34	
L Minns	257.50	
Total to add		905.84
		1,892.34
Less: unpresented cheques		
103572	1,233.80	
103573	246.58	
103574	103.64	
Total to subtract		(1,584.02)
Balance as per cash book		308.32

The bank statement and the cash book have now been reconciled and the figure that will appear in the trial balance for the Bank account is the amended cash book balance of £308.32.

Task 3

A cheque in the Bank column on the credit side of the cash book is unticked after the bank statement and cash book have been compared.

How should this be dealt with in the bank reconciliation statement (please tick)?

As an unpresented cheque   ☐

As an outstanding lodgement   ☐

Opening balances on the cash book and bank statement

In both examples you may have noted that the opening balance on the cash book agreed with that of the bank statement – there were no unpresented cheques or outstanding lodgements at the end of the previous period.

This will not always be the case. If there were timing differences at the end of the previous period then you would have prepared a bank reconciliation statement at that date. When comparing this period's bank statement and cash book you therefore need to have the previous period's bank reconciliation statement to hand in order to tick off last period's timing differences when they appear on the bank statement in this period.

HOW IT WORKS

When Dawn is preparing her bank reconciliation at the end of March she will find that the unpresented cheques at the end of February, cheque numbers 103572 to 103574, appear on the bank statement in March. When they are found on the bank statement in March then they should be ticked on that bank statement and on the opening bank reconciliation statement. The same will happen with the two outstanding lodgements at the end of February when they appear on the bank statement in March.

Task 4

A business's bank statement shows bank charges deducted. This has not been recorded in the cash book.

How would this be recorded in the bank ledger account?

Debit

Credit

Overdraft balances

Take care when calculating the balance on the cash book to identify whether its opening balance is a debit balance (often called CASH AT BANK on a trial balance) or a credit balance – an OVERDRAFT.

HOW IT WORKS

Suppose that the opening balance on Southfield's cash book on 2 May was a credit balance of £225.68. The total receipts for the week ending 9 May are £4,246.73 and the total payments £4,114.98. What is the closing balance on the cash book?

As the opening balance is an overdraft it should appear in the Bank column on the credit side of the cash book.

	£
Opening balance (balance b/f in the Bank column on the credit side)	(225.68)
Total bank payments for week	(4,114.98)
Total bank receipts for week	4,246.73
Closing balance (balance c/d in the Bank column on the debit side)	(93.93)

Task 5

The opening overdrawn balance on a business's cash book is £1,367.34. Bank receipts for the period are £7,336.49 and bank payments for the period are £4,527.22.

What is the closing balance on the cash book?

£ [   ] | overdraft/debit balance

CHAPTER OVERVIEW

- To ensure the accuracy of the bank columns in the cash book, they must be checked at regular intervals to bank statements received

- The debit and credit entries and balances on the bank statement are the opposite to the entries in the ledger accounts as the bank is considering the accounting from its own perspective

- When checking the bank statement to the cash book, check each of the receipts and payments from the bank statement to the Bank columns on the debit and credit sides of the cash book respectively, and tick each agreed item in both the cash book and the bank statement

- Any valid unticked items on the bank statement must be entered into the relevant Bank column, either receipts or payments

- Unticked items in the cash book are timing differences which are used to prepare the bank reconciliation statement

- Once the relevant corrections have been made to the cash book the bank columns must be totalled

- To find the Bank balance for the trial balance the cash book must be balanced

- If the opening balance on the cash book is an overdraft then this must appear in the Bank column on the credit side

- The closing balance on the bank statement is reconciled to the corrected cash book balance in the bank reconciliation statement. The reconciling items will be the outstanding lodgements and unpresented cheques in the cash book

Keywords

Unpresented cheques – cheque payments that have been recorded in the cash book but that do not yet appear on the bank statement

Bank reconciliation statement – a statement reconciling the bank statement balance to the corrected cash book balance

Cash at bank – Debit balance in cash book (term used in trial balance)

Timing differences – the reasons why the bank statement balance rarely agrees with the balance on the cash book, as receipts and payments recorded in the cash book appear later on the bank statement due to how the clearing system operates

Outstanding lodgements – cheques that have been received and recorded in the Bank column on the debit side of the cash book but that do not yet appear on the bank statement

Bank reconciliation statement – an exercise to reconcile the cash book balance on a given date with the bank statement on the same date

Overdraft – this is where the business effectively owes the bank money – it appears as a debit balance in the bank statement and a credit balance in the cash book

TEST YOUR LEARNING

Test 1

You are the cashier for Thames Traders and you have on your desk lists for the week ending 30 November showing cheques received and cheques sent, plus the standing order schedule. Each of these documents is reproduced below.

LIST OF CHEQUES RECEIVED			
	SL code	Amount £	Discount allowed £
Burser Ltd	SL14	147.89	6.49
Crawley Partners	SL23	448.36	18.79
Breon & Co	SL15	273.37	
Kogart Supplies	SL06	552.68	42.67
Alex & Bros	SL09	273.46	
Minicar Ltd	SL22	194.68	

LIST OF CHEQUES SENT TO CREDIT SUPPLIERS				
		PL code	Amount £	Discount received £
001367	Waterloo Partners	PL21	336.47	12.47
001368	Central Supplies	PL16	169.36	
001369	General London Trade	PL23	268.38	10.58
001370	Eye of the Tiger	PL19	84.50	
001371	Chare & Cope	PL27	447.39	19.86

Extract from standing order schedule

27th of each month – standing order to Loan Finance Repayment Reference ML 23 £250.00

Write up the cash book for all these bank transactions.

Cash Book – Debit Side

Date	Details	Ref	Discounts allowed £	Bank £	Sales ledger £

Cash Book – Credit Side

Date	Details	Ref	Discounts received £	Bank £	Purchases ledger £	Sundry £

Test 2

You are now given the bank statement for Thames Traders for the week ending 30 November. Compare this to the Cash Book.

Make a note of the treatment required in either the Cash Book or the bank statement for any items that cannot be agreed.

STATEMENT

NATIONAL DIRECT

THAMES TRADERS

CHEQUE ACCOUNT

Account number: 15-20-40 10267432

Date	Sheet 136	Paid out	Paid in	Balance
23.11	Balance b/f			1489.65 CR
26.11	Bank Giro Credit - Burser Ltd		52.00	1541.65 CR
27.11	SO-Loan Finance Repayment	250.00		1291.65 CR
28.11	Cheque No 001367	336.47		
	Credit		147.89	1103.07 CR
29.11	Cheque No 001368	196.36		
	Credit		448.36	1355.07 CR
30.11	Credit		552.68	
	Bank charges	34.53		1,873.22 CR

Test 3

Adjust the Cash Book for any items that appear to be relevant (assume that the bank statement is correct) and total it.

Test 4

You discover from the records of Thames Traders that the balance on the Cash Book at 23 November was £1,489.65, a debit balance.

What figure will appear in the trial balance for the bank account at 30 November?

£ [   ]

Test 5

Reconcile the closing bank statement balance to the corrected cash book balance for Thames Traders.

	£
Balance per bank statement	
Add:	
Total to add:	
Less:	
Total to subtract:	
Balance as per cash book	

Test 6

On 26 February Bremner Ltd received the following bank statement from Northpoint Bank as at 23 February.

Assume today's date is 28 February.

	Northpoint Bank PLC				
	17 Market Square, Axford, AX56 2HJ				
To: Bremner Ltd	Account No 92382222		23 February 20XX		
	Statement of Account				
Date 20XX	**Detail**	**Paid out £**	**Paid in £**	**Balance £**	
03 Feb	Balance b/f			6,230	C
03 Feb	Cheque 003252	2,567		3,663	C
03 Feb	Cheque 003253	333		3,330	C
03 Feb	Cheque 003254	1,006		2,324	C
04 Feb	Cheque 003257	3,775		1,451	D
09 Feb	BGC Branthill Co		1,559	108	
11 Feb	Cheque 003255	966		858	D
13 Feb	DD AxDC	250		1,108	D
18 Feb	DD Trust Insurance	325		1,433	D
20 Feb	Bank charges	14		1,447	D
22 Feb	Interest charge	56		1,503	D
23 Feb	Paid in at Northpoint Bank		2,228	725	C

D = Debit   C = Credit   BGC = Bank Giro Credit   DD = Direct Debit

The cash book as at 23 February is shown below.

(a) Check the items on the bank statement against the items in the cash book.

(b) Using the picklist below for the details column, enter any items in the cash book as needed.

(c) Total the cash book and clearly show the balance carried down at 23 February and brought down at 24 February.

(d) Using the picklist below complete the bank reconciliation statement as at 23 February.

Cash Book

Date 20XX	Details	Bank £	Date 20XX	Cheque number	Details	Bank £
01 Feb	Balance b/f	6,230	01 Feb	003252	Jeggers Ltd	2,567
20 Feb	Straightens Co	2,228	01 Feb	003253	Short & Fell	333
21 Feb	Plumpers	925	01 Feb	003254	Rastop Ltd	1,006
22 Feb	Eastern Supplies	1,743	01 Feb	003255	A & D Trading	966
			02 Feb	003256	Jesmond Warr	2,309
			02 Feb	003257	Nistral Ltd	3,775
			13 Feb	003258	Simpsons	449
			13 Feb		AxDC	250

Bank reconciliation statement as at 23 Feb 20XX

Balance per bank statement		£	
Add:			
Name:		£	
Name:		£	
Total to add		£	
Less:			
Name:		£	
Name:		£	
Total to subtract		£	
Balance as per cash book		£	

Picklist:

A & D Trading
AxDC
Balance b/d
Balance c/d
Bank charges
Branthill Co
Closing balance
Eastern Supplies
Interest charge
Jeggers Ltd
Jesmond Warr
Nistral Ltd
Opening balance
Plumpers
Rastop Ltd
Short & Fell
Simpsons
Straightens Co
Trust Insurance

chapter 4:
INTRODUCTION TO CONTROL ACCOUNTS

chapter coverage 📖

In this chapter we look first at the overall purpose of control accounts and at the three most important control accounts: for trade receivables, trade payables and VAT. We then revise the postings to the sales ledger, purchases ledger and VAT control accounts and to the relevant accounts in the subsidiary sales and purchases ledger. The topics covered are:

✍ The purpose of control accounts

✍ Types of control account

✍ The accounting system for trade receivables, trade payables and VAT

THE PURPOSE OF CONTROL ACCOUNTS

In BAI we followed through the double entry required in the general ledger for transactions relating to a business's credit sales and purchases. We saw that:

- Totals for all the numerous individual credit sales and purchases transactions in the various day books were posted to 'control' accounts for the sales and purchases ledgers in the general ledger, and it was in this ledger that the other sides of the transactions were posted

- Individual transactions were entered from the various day books into separate accounts for individual customers (trade receivables) in the sales ledger, and for individual suppliers (trade payables) in the purchases ledger

Once all the ledger accounts – in both the general ledger and the subsidiary ledgers – are balanced then we should have:

- Balances for total trade receivables and total trade payables in the general ledger, from the two control accounts

- Balances for individual trade receivables and trade payables in the subsidiary ledgers which are essentially a breakdown of each total in the general ledger

The control account system therefore means that:

- Transactions posted to the general ledger are kept to a minimum so there is less room for error in the general ledger double entry system

- It is easy at any point in time to identify how much in total the business owes and is owed

- It is possible at any point in time to see in the subsidiary ledgers how much is owed by/to individual trade receivables/trade payables

- The accuracy of the general ledger and the subsidiary ledgers can be checked by reconciling the balance on the control account in the former to the total of the balances on the latter (we see how to do this in Chapter 5). This helps us to identify and deal with discrepancies quickly.

TYPES OF CONTROL ACCOUNT

CONTROL ACCOUNTS for trade receivables – the sales ledger control account – and for trade payables – the purchases ledger control account – operate as a form of control over the balances owed by the many trade receivables and to the many trade payables that a business may have.

In addition to these there are three other types of control account that are often seen:

- Cash control and Bank control accounts – used where the cash book (see Chapter 2) is just a book of prime entry, so total receipts and total payments are posted to the Cash control and the Bank control accounts at the same time as the postings are made from the analysis and discounts columns. It is on these general ledger accounts that a balance can be calculated (as a book of prime entry the cash book would not need to contain balances)

- Petty cash control account – again this is used where the petty cash book (see Chapter 1) is just a book of prime entry, and it operates in the same way as the Cash and Bank control accounts. Again, it is on this account that a balance can be calculated (as a book of prime entry the petty cash book would not need to contain a balance)

- VAT control account – this is the account to which output and input VAT, plus payments to and from HM Revenue & Customs (HMRC), are posted. It is on this account that a balance of VAT owed or refundable can be calculated. Like the Cash, Bank and Petty cash control accounts, the VAT control account does not 'control' the accuracy of subsidiary ledgers in the same way as the sales and purchases ledgers are 'controlled' by their control accounts. Unlike the Cash, Bank and Petty cash control accounts however the business has no option but to maintain a VAT control account: HMRC require it. It cannot be replaced by day books doubling up as general ledger accounts.

For the rest of this chapter we shall concentrate on how the control account system operates for trade receivables, trade payables and VAT.

THE ACCOUNTING SYSTEM FOR TRADE RECEIVABLES

In BAI we considered the sales and sales returns day books, plus the full double entry process for trade receivables, and in Chapter 2 we looked in detail at the maintenance of the cash book. In this chapter we bring together the operation of the whole system.

The process of accounting for trade receivables is as follows:

- Sales invoices are sent to credit customers and recorded in the sales day book

- The total of the sales day book is debited to the sales ledger control account in the general ledger

- The individual sales invoices in the sales day book are debited to the individual trade receivables' accounts in the sales ledger

- Credit notes sent to customers are recorded in the sales returns day book

- The total of the sales returns day book is credited to the sales ledger control account in the general ledger

- The individual credit notes are credited to the individual trade receivables' accounts in the sales ledger

- Receipts from trade receivables are recorded in the cash book (debit side)

- The total of the sales ledger column in the cash book is credited to the sales ledger control account in the general ledger

- The individual receipts are credited to the individual trade receivables' accounts in the sales ledger

- Discounts allowed to trade receivables are recorded in the cash book (debit side)

- The total of the discounts allowed column in the cash book is credited to the sales ledger control account in the general ledger, and debited to the discounts allowed account

- The individual discounts are credited to the individual trade receivables' accounts in the sales ledger

HOW IT WORKS

Ben Charles has recently set up in business and he currently has just three credit customers: A, B and C. He operates both a general ledger and a sales ledger. His sales day book and cash book (debit side) for the month of May are given (he has no sales returns day book):

Sales Day Book

Date	Customer	Invoice no.	Ref	Invoice total £		VAT £	Net £
3/05	A	0045	SL01	240.00		40.00	200.00
5/05	C	0046	SL03	144.00		24.00	120.00
8/05	B	0047	SL02	180.00		30.00	150.00
15/05	C	0048	SL03	264.00		44.00	220.00
20/05	B	0049	SL02	120.00		20.00	100.00
28/05	A	0050	SL01	216.00		36.00	180.00
				1,164.00		194.00	970.00

The total of the invoice totals (£1,164.00) must be debited to the sales ledger control account and the individual invoice totals must be debited to the individual trade receivables' accounts in the sales ledger:

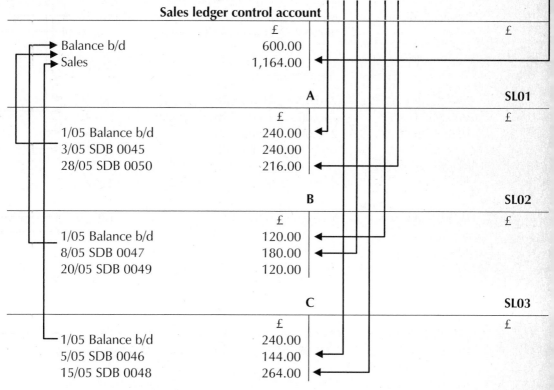

Sales ledger control account

	£		£
Balance b/d	600.00		
Sales	1,164.00		

A — SL01

	£		£
1/05 Balance b/d	240.00		
3/05 SDB 0045	240.00		
28/05 SDB 0050	216.00		

B — SL02

	£		£
1/05 Balance b/d	120.00		
8/05 SDB 0047	180.00		
20/05 SDB 0049	120.00		

C — SL03

	£		£
1/05 Balance b/d	240.00		
5/05 SDB 0046	144.00		
15/05 SDB 0048	264.00		

Cash Book – Debit Side

Date	Details	Ref	Bank £	VAT £	Cash sales £	Sales ledger £	Discounts allowed £
6/05	B	SL02	120.00	——		120.00	
10/05	A	SL01	230.60	——		230.60	9.40
13/05	C	SL03	200.00	——		200.00	
20/05	A	SL01	230.60	——		230.60	9.40
28/05	C	SL03	100.00	——		100.00	
30/05	B	SL02	180.00	——		180.00	
			1,061.20			1,061.20	18.80

This must now also be posted to the general ledger and the sales ledger.

Sales ledger control account

	£		£
Balance b/d	600.00	Bank	1,061.20
Sales	1,164.00	Discounts allowed	18.80

A   SL01

	£		£
1/05 Balance b/d	240.00	10/05 CRB	230.60
3/05 SDB 0045	240.00	10/05 CRB – discount	9.40
28/05 SDB 0050	216.00	20/05 CRB	230.60
		20/05 CRB – discount	9.40

B   SL02

	£		£
1/05 Balance b/d	120.00	6/05 CRB	120.00
8/05 SDB 0047	180.00	30/05 CRB	180.00
20/05 SDB 0049	120.00		

C   SL03

	£		£
1/05 Balance b/d	240.00	13/05 CRB	200.00
5/05 SDB 0046	144.00	28/05 CRB	100.00
15/05 SDB 0048	264.00		

Finally, at the end of May each of the accounts should be balanced:

Sales ledger control account

	£		£
Balance b/d	600.00	Bank	1,061.20
Sales	1,164.00	Discounts allowed	18.80
		Balance c/d	684.00
	1,764.00		1,764.00
Balance b/d	684.00		

A   SL01

	£		£
1/05 Balance b/d	240.00	10/05 CRB	230.60
3/05 SDB 0045	240.00	10/05 CRB – discount	9.40
28/05 SDB 0050	216.00	20/05 CRB	230.60
		20/05 CRB – discount	9.40
		Balance c/d	216.00
	696.00		696.00
Balance b/d	216.00		

B   SL02

	£		£
1/05 Balance b/d	120.00	6/05 CRB	120.00
8/05 SDB 0047	180.00	30/05 CRB	180.00
20/05 SDB 0049	120.00	Balance c/d	120.00
	420.00		420.00
Balance b/d	120.00		

C   SL03

	£		£
1/05 Balance b/d	240.00	13/05 CRB	200.00
5/05 SDB 0046	144.00	28/05 CRB	100.00
15/05 SDB 0048	264.00	Balance c/d	348.00
	648.00		648.00
Balance b/d	348.00		

Balances carried down

Note how the total of each of the individual receivable balances equals the balance on the sales ledger control account.

	£
A	216.00
B	120.00
C	348.00
Sales ledger control account balance	684.00

If the double entry in the general ledger and the entries in the subsidiary ledger have all been correctly carried out then the total of the list of receivable balances in the sales ledger will always equal the balance on the sales ledger control account.

This whole process of accounting for credit sales in the general ledger and in the sales ledger, ignoring credit notes for now, can be illustrated in a diagram:

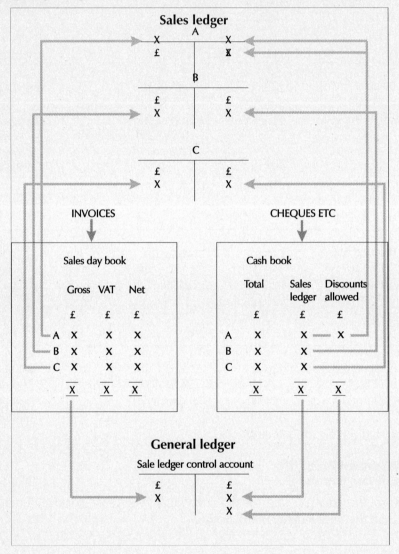

Task 1

What is the double entry in the general ledger for sales on credit?

Debit

Credit

THE ACCOUNTING SYSTEM FOR TRADE PAYABLES

The accounting process for trade payables is precisely the same as for trade receivables except that the entries in the accounts are the other way around.

- Purchase invoices received are recorded in the purchases day book

- The total of the purchases day book is credited to the purchases ledger control account in the general ledger

- The individual invoices in the purchases day book are credited to the individual trade payables' accounts in the purchases ledger

- Credit notes from trade payables are recorded in the purchases returns day book

- The total of the purchases returns day book is debited to the purchases ledger control account in the general ledger

- The individual credit notes are debited to the individual trade payables' accounts in the purchases ledger

- Payments to trade payables are recorded in the cash book (credit side)

- The total of the purchases ledger column in the cash book is debited to the purchases ledger control account in the general ledger

- The individual payments are debited to the individual trade payables' accounts in the purchases ledger

- Discounts received from trade payables are recorded in the cash book (credit side)

- The total of the discounts received column in the cash book is debited to the purchases ledger control account in the general ledger, and credited to the discounts received account

- The individual discounts are debited to the individual trade payables' accounts in the purchases ledger

Again this can be shown in a diagram, ignoring credit notes once again:

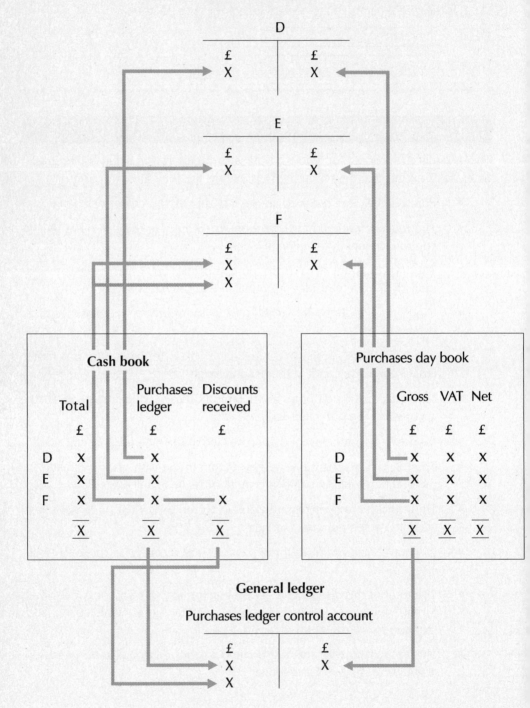

Balances carried down

In just the same way as with the accounting system for trade receivables, if the double entry has been correctly performed in the general ledger and the entries have been correctly made in the subsidiary ledger, the balances carried down on the individual payable accounts in the purchases ledger should total back to the balance carried down on the purchases ledger control account in the general ledger.

HOW IT WORKS

If Ben Charles has three credit suppliers, D, E and F then the sum of the final balances on their accounts should agree with the purchases ledger control account:

D

	£		£
		Balance b/d	115.60

E

	£		£
		Balance b/d	220.00

F

	£		£
		Balance b/d	150.00

Purchases ledger control account

	£		£
		Balance b/d	485.60

	£
D	115.60
E	220.00
F	150.00
Purchases ledger control account balance	485.60

Task 2

What is the double entry in the general ledger for purchases on credit?

Debit   [   ]

Credit   [   ]

THE ACCOUNTING SYSTEM FOR VAT

As we saw in BAI, VAT is a tax on consumers that is collected on behalf of HM Revenue and Customs (HMRC) by VAT registered businesses. At the end of each three month period the business will usually pay over to HMRC the excess of (output) VAT collected from customers over the amount of (input) VAT paid to suppliers, or more rarely it will receive a refund from HMRC of the excess VAT paid over that collected.

VAT is accounted for at the same time as we account for trade receivables and trade payables, but then we must also account for payments of VAT owed to HMRC and receipts of VAT from them:

- The VAT amounts on sales and purchase invoices and credit notes, and on cash sales and purchases, are recorded in the day books and then totals are posted to the VAT control account

- Payments to HMRC in respect of VAT owed is recorded in the Bank column of the cash book (credit side) and debited to the VAT control account

- Receipts of VAT refunds from HMRC are recorded in the Bank column of the cash book (debit side) and credited to the VAT control account

- The balance on the VAT control account is the amount owed to (credit balance) or refundable by (debit balance) HMRC

CHAPTER OVERVIEW

- The sales ledger control account in the general ledger is debited with sales invoices from the sales day book and credited with credit notes from the sales returns day book, plus receipts and settlement discounts from the cash book (debit side)

- The individual accounts for each receivable in the sales ledger are also debited with each invoice total and credited with the credit notes, receipts and discounts

- If all of the entries are correctly carried out then the total of the closing balances on the individual trade receivables' accounts from the sales ledger should agree to the balance on the sales ledger control account in the general ledger

- The same system applies to accounting for trade payables, although the entries are all on the opposite sides

- Cash, Bank and Petty cash control accounts in the general ledger are only used in businesses where the cash book and petty cash book operate as day books only

- The VAT control account is used for all transactions (cash and credit) related to VAT, and allows the business to identify clearly how much is owed to HM Revenue and Customs in respect of VAT in a period, or how much is due from them

Keyword

Control accounts – general ledger accounts that include totals for the books of prime entry. These give no indication of individual balances

TEST YOUR LEARNING

Test 1

Assuming they all include VAT where relevant, identify the double entry for the following transactions.

	Bank DR/CR	SLCA DR/CR	PLCA DR/CR	VAT DR/CR	Sales DR/CR	Purchases returns DR/CR	Discounts received DR/CR	Discounts allowed DR/CR
Gross sales								
Gross purchases returns								
Discounts allowed								
Discounts received								
Gross payments from cash customers								
Payments to credit suppliers								

Test 2

DP Printing is a small company that has currently only four credit customers. The opening balances on the trade receivables' accounts in DP's sales ledger at the start of May 20XX were as follows:

	£
Virgo Partners	227.58
McGowan & Sons	552.73
J J Westrope	317.59
Jacks Ltd	118.36

The opening balance on the sales ledger control account at the start of May was £1,216.26.

The Sales Day Book and Cash Book (debit side) for May are given below:

Sales Day Book

Date	Customer	Gross £	VAT £	Net £
3 May	J J Westrope	167.40	27.90	139.50
10 May	Virgo Partners	96.72	16.12	80.60
12 May	Jacks Ltd	107.64	17.94	89.70
15 May	J J Westrope	277.32	46.22	231.10
20 May	McGowan & Sons	595.08	99.18	495.90
23 May	Jacks Ltd	177.60	29.60	148.00
30 May	Virgo Partners	214.44	35.74	178.70
		1,636.20	272.70	1,363.50

Cash Book – Debit Side

Date	Details	Bank £	VAT £	Cash sales £	Sales ledger £	Discounts allowed £
	Cash sales	486.96	81.16	405.80		
4 May	Virgo Partners	117.38			117.38	
10 May	Cash sales	451.80	75.30	376.50		
12 May	J J Westrope	308.86			308.86	8.73
15 May	McGowan & Sons	552.73			552.73	
17 May	Cash sales	512.28	85.38	426.90		
20 May	Jacks Ltd	100.00			100.00	
30 May	Cash sales	582.24	97.04	485.20		
		3,112.25	338.88	1,694.40	1,078.97	8.73

(a) Write up the sales ledger control account for the month and the individual trade receivables' accounts in the sales ledger.

(b) Agree the control account balance to the total of the sales ledger account balances at the end of the month.

General ledger

Sales ledger control account

	£		£

Sales ledger

Virgo Partners

	£		£

McGowan & Sons

	£		£

J J Westrope

	£		£

Jacks Ltd

	£		£

Reconciliation

	£
Sales ledger control account balance as at 31 May	
Total of sales ledger accounts as at 31 May	
Difference	

Test 3

DP Printing has three credit suppliers and the opening balances on its trade payables' accounts in the purchases ledger at the start of May were:

	£
Jenkins Suppliers	441.56
Kilnfarm Paper	150.00
Barnfield Ltd	247.90

The opening balance on the purchases ledger control account at the start of May was £839.46.

The purchases day book and cash book (credit side) for the period are given below:

Purchases Day Book

Date	Supplier	Gross £	VAT £	Net £
5 May	Kilnfarm Paper	153.12	25.52	127.60
10 May	Jenkins Suppliers	219.96	36.66	183.30
12 May	Barnfield Ltd	317.16	52.86	264.30
20 May	Kilnfarm Paper	153.12	25.52	127.60
27 May	Jenkins Suppliers	451.32	75.22	376.10
30 May	Barnfield Ltd	312.24	52.04	260.20
		1,606.92	267.82	1,339.10

Cash Book – Credit Side

Date	Details	Bank £	VAT £	Cash purchases £	Purchases ledger £	Discount received £
5 May	Cash purchases	230.52	38.42	192.10		
10 May	Jenkins Suppliers	423.89			423.89	17.67
12 May	Kilnfarm Paper	150.00			150.00	
15 May	Cash Purchases	321.84	53.64	268.20		
20 May	Barnfield Ltd	235.50			235.50	12.40
27 May	Kilnfarm Paper	150.00			150.00	
30 May	Cash purchases	214.92	35.82	179.10		
		1,726.67	127.88	639.40	959.39	30.07

(a) Write up the purchases ledger control account for May and the individual trade payables' accounts in the purchases ledger.

(b) Agree the control account balance at the end of May to the total of the list of individual balances in the purchases ledger.

General ledger

Purchases ledger control account

	£		£

Purchases ledger

Jenkins Suppliers

	£		£

Kilnfarm Paper

	£		£

Barnfield Ltd

	£		£

Reconciliation

	£
Purchases ledger control account balance as at 31 May	
Total of purchases ledger accounts as at 31 May	
Difference	

chapter 5:
PREPARING AND RECONCILING CONTROL ACCOUNTS

───── **chapter coverage** 📖 ─────

In this chapter we cover in more detail how to prepare control accounts using the books of prime entry, and how to reconcile them to the subsidiary ledgers. In the process we consider how to account for irrecoverable debts in regard to trade receivables, and how to use an aged trade receivable analysis. The topics covered are:

✍ The detailed entries to the sales ledger control account including accounting for irrecoverable debts

✍ The sales ledger control account reconciliation

✍ Using an aged trade receivable analysis to monitor the age of trade receivables

✍ The detailed entries to the purchases ledger control account

✍ The purchases ledger control account reconciliation

✍ The detailed entries to the VAT control account

ENTRIES IN THE SALES LEDGER CONTROL ACCOUNT

We now look in more detail at the figures that are likely to appear in the sales ledger control account, as so far we have only considered the basic entries for invoices, credit notes, payments received and discounts allowed.

A typical sales ledger control account (SLCA) might have the following types of entry:

Sales ledger control account

	£		£
Balance b/d	X	Credit sales returns	X
Credit sales	X	Payments received	X
Dishonoured cheques	X	Discounts allowed	X
		Irrecoverable debts written off	X
	_	Balance c/d	X
	X		X
Balance b/d	X		

These entries need a little more explanation:

Balance b/d – the brought down balance on the account at the beginning and at the end of the period is a (large) debit balance as credit customers owe the business money. In some circumstances an individual credit customer may have a credit balance at the start of the period, for instance if they overpay their account, but the SLCA is a total account for all trade receivables and therefore has a debit balance.

Credit sales – this is the total figure that is posted from the invoice total column in the Sales Day Book. The credit entry is to Sales, and also to VAT control.

Dishonoured cheques – if a customer has paid for goods then the SLCA would be credited with the payment. If the bank then returns the cheque as unpaid, ie the cheque has been dishonoured, the original entry must be reversed by debiting the SLCA. The credit entry is in the cash book (credit side).

Credit sales returns – this is the posting of the credit note total column in the sales returns day book. The credit entry is to Sales returns, and also to VAT control.

Payments received – this is the posting from the sales ledger column total in the cash book (debit side). The debit entry is in the cash book (debit side).

Discounts allowed – this is the posting from the memorandum discounts allowed column in the cash book (debit side). The debit entry is in the Discounts allowed account.

Irrecoverable debts written off – when a sale is made on credit to a customer it is assumed that the customer will eventually pay the amount due. However, on occasion, it may become clear that a customer is not going to pay the amount owing. This may be due to the fact that they have become insolvent or have simply disappeared. Whatever the reason, if it is thought that the customer will not pay then this is known as an IRRECOVERABLE DEBT. The debit entries are in the Irrecoverable Debts account (see below) and the VAT control account.

Balance c/d – the closing balance on the SLCA is carried down from the credit side.

Accounting for irrecoverable debts

The accounting treatment for an irrecoverable debt is that it must be removed from the accounting records as it is no longer a valid trade receivable. The double entry is:

DR   Irrecoverable debts (an expense account) with the net amount of the sale

DR   VAT control account with the VAT element

CR   SLCA with the invoice total

The trade receivable for the full, VAT-inclusive amount is removed by crediting the SLCA. The lost sale is treated as an expense of the business, by debiting the net amount to the separate irrecoverable debts expense account: the debit entry is never made in the sales account even though the effect is to reverse the sale. The VAT element of the original invoice is removed by debiting the VAT control account.

The total irrecoverable debt must also be removed from the individual account in the sales ledger by crediting the individual trade receivable account with the full amount of the irrecoverable debt.

Task 1

What is the double entry for writing off an irrecoverable debt?

Debit   [   ]

Debit   [   ]

Credit   [   ]

SALES LEDGER CONTROL ACCOUNT RECONCILIATION

If all the double entry in the general ledger, and entries in the sales ledger, are correctly carried out, then the totals of the balances on the sales ledger should be equal to the balance on the control account.

Control account balance

The balance on the SLCA is the figure that will appear in the trial balance for trade receivables so it is important to ensure that the figure is correct. This is done by carrying out a SALES LEDGER CONTROL ACCOUNT RECONCILIATION.

The purpose of this reconciliation is to compare the balance on the control account to the total of the balances of the individual accounts in the sales ledger. If the two totals do not agree then there are discrepancies and errors that have arisen EITHER in the control account OR in the sales ledger OR both. These must be discovered, investigated and corrected.

Some of the errors might have been made in the double entry in the general ledger so they affect the control account. Other errors may have been made when posting entries to the individual accounts in the sales ledger or in calculating and listing the balances in the sales ledger.

Errors affecting the control account

Typical types of error that may have been made in the double entry in the general ledger include the following:

- The books of prime entry have been undercast or overcast so the incorrect total is posted to the control account

- Postings have been made to the wrong side of the control account

- The discounts allowed recorded in the cash book may be incorrectly posted

- An irrecoverable debt may not have been recorded in the general ledger although it was written off in the sales ledger

Sales ledger balances

Each individual account in the sales ledger must be totalled and balanced for the reconciliation to go ahead. The types of transaction that affect these accounts are exactly the same as we saw above for the control account, including irrecoverable debts and dishonoured cheques. An added complication is that there may be some credit customers who end up as trade payables rather than trade receivables because they have a credit balance on their sales ledger account rather than a debit balance. Possible reasons for credit balances in the sales ledger might be:

- If by mistake the customer paid too much for the goods owing. This would then turn them from being a trade receivable into being a trade payable ie, the business owes the money back to the customer

- If the customer had returned goods after paying for them then the credit note would create a credit balance on the account, as the business owes the cost of the returned goods back to the customer

When listing out the balances on the sales ledger in order to total them and reconcile them to the SLCA, it is very important that any credit balances are clearly marked as such, so they are deducted from the total.

Errors affecting the list of sales ledger balances

Some errors will not affect the double entry in the general ledger but will mean either that the individual balances in the sales ledger are not correct, or that these balances are listed and totalled incorrectly. Typical of these are:

- An entry from the books of prime entry not posted to the sales ledger at all

- Entries posted to the wrong side of the sales ledger account

- An entry posted as the wrong amount to the sales ledger account

- A balance on an account in the sales ledger included in the list of balances as the wrong amount or as the wrong type of balance, eg a debit rather than a credit balance.

Task 2

If the sales day book total for a week is overcast by £1,000 this would affect (please tick)

The sales ledger control account	
The individual accounts in the sales ledger	

Preparing the sales ledger control account reconciliation

A sales ledger control account reconciliation is a comparison of the balance on the sales ledger control account to the total of the list of balances from the sales ledger. This should be carried out on a regular basis, usually monthly, so that errors and discrepancies can be identified and dealt with quickly.

HOW IT WORKS

Southfield Electrical is carrying out its sales ledger control account reconciliation at the end of October 20XX. The debit balance on the sales ledger control account is £14,382.

Sales ledger control account

	£		£
Balance b/d	14,382		

The total of the list of trade receivables account balances from the sales ledger comes to £13,777.

Step 1   Calculate the difference between the control account balance and the total of the sales ledger balances.

	£
Control account balance	14,382
Total of the list of balances	13,777
Difference	605

This difference must be investigated.

Step 2   Check the control account and the individual accounts and balances and note any errors or omissions.

In Southfield's case the following errors were noted:

(a)   The total column on a page of the cash book (debit side) had been overcast by £100

(b)   The total from the sales day book for a week had been posted as £3,675 instead of £3,765

(c)   An irrecoverable debt of £240 has been written off in the individual sales ledger account but not in the general ledger

(d)   An invoice to Weller Enterprises for £478 had been entered into the account of Dagwell Enterprises instead

(e)   A cash receipt from B B Berry Ltd has been entered into the account in the sales ledger as £256 instead of the correct figure from the cash book of £265

(f)   A balance of £604 on one sales ledger account had been omitted from the list of balances

(g)   A credit balance of £20 on a sales ledger account had been included in the list of sales ledger balances as a debit balance

Step 3   The sales ledger control account must be adjusted for any of the errors that affect it:

Sales ledger control account

	£		£
Balance b/d	14,382		
(a) Bank	100	(c) Irrecoverable debts	240
(b) Sales	90	Balance c/d	14,332
	14,572		14,572
Balance b/d	14,332		

(a) The total from the cash book would have been credited to the sales ledger control account. Therefore if it was overcast by £100 the SLCA must be debited with £100, to reduce the amount of the original entry

(b) The total from the sales day book is debited to the sales ledger control account. The original entry was for £90 too little (£3,675 instead of £3,765) so an extra debit entry of £90 is required to correct the error

(c) To write off an irrecoverable debt the sales ledger control account must be credited as the debt is no longer receivable

Therefore the amended net balance on the control account is £14,332.

Step 4 Adjust the total of the list of balances from the sales ledger by adding or deducting the errors that affect this total.

	£
Original total	13,777
Less: additional cash receipt (265–256) (e)	(9)
Add: balance omitted (f)	604
Less: credit balance included as debit balance (g)	(40)
	14,332

(d) The two sales ledger accounts will need to be adjusted in the sales ledger to correct the error but this type of error does not affect the overall total of the balances on the sales ledger accounts

(e) The additional receipt of £9 that should have been recorded reduces the total of the sales ledger balances

(f) The balance omitted must be added in to the total of the list of balances

(g) The £20 credit balance that was included as a debit balance would have reduced the total balance if it had been correctly included – however, twice the amount of the balance must be deducted as the balance has not been omitted but included on the wrong side and this must be cancelled out

The amended total of the list of balances now agrees to the amended sales ledger control account total and the general ledger and sales ledger are therefore reconciled.

Task 3

If the total of the discounts allowed column from the cash book of £300 was not posted for a period, this would be adjusted for in the sales ledger control account reconciliation by adding £300 to/subtracting £300 from the SLCA

balance/total of list of balances .

THE AGED TRADE RECEIVABLE ANALYSIS

All businesses need cash in order to survive and so they are keen to monitor their trade receivables and make sure that they pay what is owed when, or even before, it is due. (This is the purpose after all of allowing settlement discount; although the discount is an expense to the business, it helps to ensure that the debt is not only settled but is settled early.)

The business can easily tell from the sales ledger that a particular customer owes, say, £1,000 as that is the balance on their account. What the balance alone does not tell the business is how 'old' that debt is. If the sale was recent then the business will be unconcerned that there is a trade receivable for £1,000. If the sale took place six months ago then the business would be very worried at the 'age' of the debt, and may have cause to doubt whether it will be paid at all. It may be an irrecoverable debt.

These are aspects of what is known as 'cash management and credit control' and they are covered in detail elsewhere in your studies. One aspect is relevant here however: the AGED TRADE RECEIVABLE ANALYSIS. For BAII you do not need to be able to prepare an aged trade receivable analysis, simply to understand how to use one in monitoring trade receivables.

Once all the correcting entries have been made in the sales ledger, it is common practice to produce an aged trade receivable analysis in the form of a schedule showing, for each trade receivable, how long the balance has been unpaid.

HOW IT WORKS

Given below is an extract from the aged trade receivable analysis for Southfield Electrical at 31 October 20XX. In it, each balance is split as follows:

- The part of each balance that is analysed as 'current' are invoices etc that have been sent out in the last 30 days (the credit period offered by Southfield) and so are 'not yet due' for payment.

- All the other analysis columns represent invoices etc that are 'overdue', in this case being two (30–59 days), three (60–89 days) or more than three (>90 days) months old.

		BALANCE	ANALYSIS			
				30–59	60–89	> 90
Customer code	Account name		Current	days	days	days
		£	£	£	£	£
SL03	Polygon Stores	2,593.29	2,593.29	0.00	0.00	0.00
SL15	Dagwell Ent	2,254.67	1,356.26	898.41	0.00	0.00
SL18	Weller Ent	2,154.72	1,118.36	637.28	399.08	0.00
SL30	G Thomas & Co	3,425.47	3,116.35	0.00	0.00	309.12
		10,428.15	8,184.26	1,535.69	399.08	309.12

AGED TRADE RECEIVABLE ANALYSIS

Date: 31 October 20XX

The aged trade receivable analysis can be used to monitor these trade receivables and decide whether any action needs to be taken with each of them.

- Polygon Stores – the entire balance is current which shows that Polygon is a regular payer of the amounts due within the stated 30-day credit period.

- Dagwell Enterprises – although some of the debt owed by Dagwell is current there is a large amount of £898.41 which has been outstanding for more than 30 days. It may be that Dagwell always pays in this manner or, if not, the 30–59 day amount may need to be investigated and a telephone call made or letter sent to Dagwell Enterprises.

- Weller Enterprises – as well as the current element some of this balance is more than 60 days old and some is more than 30 days old. Southfield should write to Weller Enterprises encouraging payment of the overdue amounts.

- G Thomas & Co – the vast majority of this balance is current with only a fairly small amount more than 90 days old. This old debt should be investigated as there may be a problem with the invoice or goods – perhaps G Thomas & Co returned these goods and are awaiting a credit note.

ENTRIES IN THE PURCHASES LEDGER CONTROL ACCOUNT

A typical purchases ledger control account (PLCA) might look like this:

Purchases ledger control account

	£		£
Credit purchases returns	X	Balance b/d	X
Payments to suppliers	X	Credit purchases	X
Discounts received	X		
Balance c/d	X		
	X		X
		Balance b/d	X

Credit purchases returns – this is the posting of the credit notes total column from the purchases returns day book.

Payments to suppliers – this is the posting from the purchases ledger column total in the credit side of the cash book.

Discounts received – this is the posting from the memorandum discounts received column total in the cash book.

Balance c/d – the closing balance on the account is carried down from the debit side.

Balance b/d – the balance brought down at the beginning of the period and again at the end will be on the credit side of the account. Occasionally, there may be a small debit balance brought down on an individual account with a supplier because of items such as over-payment, but the total PLCA will always have a credit balance.

Credit purchases – this is the posting from the invoice total column in the purchases day book.

PURCHASES LEDGER CONTROL ACCOUNT RECONCILIATION

A purchases ledger control account reconciliation works in exactly the same manner and for the same purpose as a sales ledger control account reconciliation, although there will **not** be complications related to:

- Dishonoured cheques (we will assume that our business does not write out cheques that the bank does not honour)
- Irrecoverable debts written off

If all the double entry in the general ledger, and entries in the purchases ledger, are correctly carried out, then the totals of the balances on the purchases ledger should be equal to the balance on the control account.

Control account balance

The balance on the purchases ledger control account is the figure that will appear in the trial balance for trade payables so it is important to ensure that it is correct, by carrying out a PURCHASES LEDGER CONTROL ACCOUNT RECONCILIATION.

The purpose of this reconciliation is to compare the balance on the control account to the total of the balances of the individual accounts in the purchases ledger. If the two totals do not agree then there are discrepancies and errors that must be discovered, investigated and corrected in either the control account or the purchases ledger or both.

Errors affecting the control account

Typical types of error that might have been made in the double entry in the general ledger include the following:

- The books of prime entry have been undercast or overcast so the incorrect total is posted to the control account

- Postings have been made to the wrong side of the control account

- The discounts received recorded in the cash book may be incorrectly posted

Purchases ledger balances

Each individual account in the purchases ledger must be totalled and balanced for the reconciliation to go ahead. The types of transaction that affect these accounts are exactly the same as we saw above for the control account. An added complication is that there may be some credit suppliers who end up as trade receivables rather than trade payables because they have a debit balance on their purchases ledger account rather than a credit balance. Possible reasons for debit balances may be:

- The business paid too much for the goods owing so the supplier owes the money back to the business

- The business returned goods after paying for them and the credit note then created a debit balance on the account, as the supplier owed the cost of the returned goods back to the business

When listing out the balances on the purchases ledger in order to total them and reconcile them to the PLCA, it is very important that any debit balances are clearly marked as such, so they are deducted from the total.

Errors affecting the list of purchases ledger balances

Some errors will not affect the double entry in the general ledger but will mean either that the individual balances in the purchases ledger are not correct, or that these balances are listed and totalled incorrectly. Typical of these are the following:

- An entry from the books of prime entry not posted to the purchases ledger at all

- An entry from the books of prime entry posted to the wrong account in the purchases ledger

- Entries posted to the wrong side of the purchases ledger account

- An entry posted as the wrong amount to the purchases ledger account

- A balance on an account in the purchases ledger included in the list of balances as the wrong amount or as the wrong type of balance, eg a credit rather than a debit balance

---

Task 4

If the purchases day book total for a week is undercast by £800 this would affect (please tick)

The purchases ledger control account

The individual accounts in the purchases ledger

HOW IT WORKS

Whitehill Superstores is currently preparing its purchases ledger control account reconciliation at the end of October 20XX. The balance on the purchases ledger control account is £17,240 and the total of the list of balances on the purchases ledger is £16,720.

The following discrepancies have been noted:

(a) One page of the Purchases Day Book has been overcast by £200

(b) An invoice has been posted to an individual account in the purchases ledger as £957 instead of the correct figure from the Purchases Day Book of £597

(c) The total for discounts received of £250 has been credited to the purchases ledger control account

(d) One of the credit balances in the purchases ledger has been included in the total at a figure of £468 instead of £648

Step 1 Amend the control account balance for any errors that affect it.

Purchases ledger control account

	£		£
(a) Purchases	200	Balance b/d	17,240
(c) Discounts received	250		
Discounts received	250		
Balance c/d	16,540		
	17,240		17,240
		Balance b/d	16,540

(a) The total from the purchases day book is credited to the purchases ledger control account, and therefore if it was overcast by £200 then the PLCA must be debited by £200

(c) The discounts received should have been debited to the PLCA – instead they were credited and therefore there should be two debits in the PLCA for £250, one to cancel out the credit and one to enter the debit entry

Step 2 Amend the total of the list of balances to adjust for any errors that affect the individual balances or their total.

	£
Original total	16,720
(b) Less: invoice misposting (957 – 597)	(360)
(d) Add: balance misstated (648 – 468)	180
	16,540

(b) An invoice would be posted to the credit side of the purchases ledger account – in this case it was posted at a figure £360 too high and therefore the purchases ledger balances will be reduced when the account is amended

(d) The balance that was misstated was shown as £180 too little – therefore the balances need to be increased by £180

Task 5

An invoice for £200 was entered into the individual account in the purchases ledger on the wrong side of the account. This would be adjusted for in the purchases ledger control account reconciliation by ⌈adding £400 to/⌋ ⌈subtracting £400 from the purchases ledger control account/the list of purchases⌋ ⌈ledger balances⌋ .

ENTRIES IN THE VAT CONTROL ACCOUNT

We will now look in more detail at the figures that are likely to appear in the VAT CONTROL ACCOUNT.

A typical VAT control account for a business which has a liability to HM Revenue and Customs (HMRC) in respect of VAT will receive postings from more books of prime entry than either the sales or the purchases ledger control accounts, as follows:

VAT control account

	£		£
VAT on credit purchases	X	Balance b/d	X
VAT on cash purchases	X	VAT on credit sales	X
VAT on sales returns	X	VAT on cash sales	X
VAT on irrecoverable debts written off	X	VAT on purchases returns	X
VAT paid to HMRC	X		
Balance c/d	X		
	X		X
	X	Balance b/d	X

- **VAT on credit purchases** – this is the VAT figure posted from the Purchases Day Book. It represents input VAT incurred on purchases which is recoverable from HMRC.

- **VAT on cash purchases** – this is the VAT figure posted from the cash book (credit side). It represents input VAT incurred on purchases which is recoverable from HMRC.

- **VAT on sales returns** – this is VAT from the sales returns day book.

- **VAT on irrecoverable debts written off** – this is the VAT element of the amount that is written off by crediting the sales ledger/sales ledger control account. The remainder of the debit entry is to the irrecoverable debts expense account.

- **VAT paid to HMRC** – this is the amount that settles the liability of the business to HMRC. It is posted from the Cash Book (credit side). The amount due at the time a VAT RETURN is prepared for HMRC is the balance on the VAT control account at the date to which the return is prepared. This will be covered further later in your studies.

- **Balance c/d** – the closing balance on the account is usually carried down from the debit side, though if the business is due a refund of VAT from HMRC this amount will appear on the credit side.

- **Balance b/d** – the brought down balance on the account at the beginning or end of the period is usually, but not always, a credit balance as most businesses record more output VAT (on sales) than input VAT (on purchases). A credit balance means that some money will

have to be paid over at some stage to HMRC. A debit balance would mean that the business is due a repayment of VAT by HMRC.

- **VAT on credit sales** – this is the VAT figure posted from the sales day book. It represents output VAT charged on sales which is payable to HMRC.

- **VAT on cash sales** – this is the VAT figure posted from the cash book (debit side). It represents output VAT charged on sales which is payable to HMRC.

- **VAT on purchases returns** – this is VAT from the purchases returns day book.

It may also receive entries from the petty cash book in respect of purchases made from petty cash.

It is very important that the VAT control account is accurately and promptly prepared, as VAT Returns and payments to HMRC must always be made on time in order to avoid penalties.

HOW IT WORKS

DP Printing has calculated that its output tax for May is £611.58 and its input tax for May is £395.70. It had a credit balance brought forward on its VAT account at 1 May of £250.00. The business's sales day book, purchases day book and cash book for the month of May are set out below (there are no returns day books), and we need to (a) prepare a VAT control account for May and (b) ensure that the final balance reconciles to the calculation prepared by the business.

Sales Day Book

Date	Customer	Gross £	VAT £	Net £
3 May	J J Westrope	167.40	27.90	139.50
10 May	Virgo Partners	96.72	16.12	80.60
12 May	Jacks Ltd	107.64	17.94	89.70
15 May	J J Westrope	277.32	46.22	231.10
20 May	McGowan & Sons	595.08	99.18	495.90
23 May	Jacks Ltd	177.60	29.60	148.00
30 May	Virgo Partners	214.44	35.74	178.70
		1,636.20	272.70	1,363.50

Purchases Day Book

Date	Supplier	Gross £	VAT £	Net £
5 May	Kilnfarm Paper	153.12	25.52	127.60
10 May	Jenkins Suppliers	219.96	36.66	183.30
12 May	Barnfield Ltd	317.16	52.86	264.30
20 May	Kilnfarm Paper	153.12	25.52	127.60
27 May	Jenkins Suppliers	451.32	75.22	376.10
30 May	Barnfield Ltd	312.24	52.04	260.20
		1,606.92	267.82	1,339.10

Cash Book – Debit Side

Date	Details	Bank £	VAT £	Cash sales £	Sales ledger £	Discounts allowed £
	Cash sales	486.96	81.16	405.80		
4 May	Virgo Partners	117.38			117.38	
10 May	Cash sales	451.80	75.30	376.50		
12 May	J J Westrope	308.86			308.86	8.73
15 May	McGowan & Sons	552.73			552.73	
17 May	Cash sales	512.28	85.38	426.90		
20 May	Jacks Ltd	100.00			100.00	
30 May	Cash sales	582.24	97.04	485.20		
		3,112.25	338.88	1,694.40		8.73
					1,078.97	

Cash Book – Credit Side

Date	Details	Bank £	VAT £	Cash purchases £	Purchase ledger £	Sundry £	Discount received £
5 May	Cash purchases	230.52	38.42	192.10			
10 May	Jenkins Suppliers	423.89			423.89		17.67
12 May	Kilnfarm Paper	150.00			150.00		
14 May	HMRC re VAT	250.00				250.00	
15 May	Cash Purchases	321.84	53.64	268.20			
20 May	Barnfield Ltd	235.50			235.50		12.40
27 May	Kilnfarm Paper	150.00			150.00		
30 May	Cash purchases	214.92	35.82	179.10			
		1,976.67	127.88	639.40	959.39	250.00	30.07

The VAT control account is prepared by:

- inserting the VAT column totals from all four day books provided
- inserting the amount paid to HMRC on 14 May in settlement of the opening credit balance due
- carrying down a balance

VAT control account

	£		£
VAT on credit purchases	267.82	Balance b/d	250.00
VAT on cash purchases	127.88	VAT on credit sales	272.70
VAT paid to HMRC	250.00	VAT on cash sales	338.88
Balance c/d	215.88		
	861.58		861.58
		Balance b/d	215.88

	£
Output tax (on sales)	611.58
Input tax (on purchases)	(395.70)
Net VAT due to HMRC for May	215.88

As this amount agrees with the VAT control account balance at the end of May, we can be confident that we have the correct figures.

CHAPTER OVERVIEW

- If all of the entries in the general ledger are correctly carried out then the total of the closing balances on the sales and purchases ledgers should agree to the balance on the relevant control accounts

- The sales ledger control account will potentially have entries for credit notes, dishonoured cheques and irrecoverable debts written off as well as the basic entries for invoices, receipts from customers and discounts allowed

- The double entry for writing off an irrecoverable debt is to debit both the irrecoverable debts expense account and the VAT control account, and credit the sales ledger control account

- The purchases ledger control account will potentially have entries for credit notes as well as the basic entries for invoices, payments made to suppliers and discounts received

- If all of the entries in the general ledger and subsidiary ledger have not been properly performed, and/or if the lists of subsidiary ledger balances have been inaccurately prepared, then the subsidiary ledger balances total will not agree to the balance on the control account – in which case the causes of the difference must be discovered

- A sales ledger control account reconciliation compares the balance on the sales ledger control account to the total of the trade receivables' account balances in the sales ledger – both are amended for any errors that have been made and the total and balance should agree after putting through the amendments

- An aged trade receivables analysis is used to monitor how slowly customers are paying their debts

- A purchases ledger control account reconciliation works in exactly the same way as the sales ledger control account reconciliation, although all of the entries and balances are on the opposite sides

- The VAT control account potentially receives postings from all the books of prime entry, and is the means by which the business keeps track of what it owes HMRC (or what it is owed by HMRC)

Keywords

Irrecoverable debt – a debt which it is believed will never be recovered

Sales ledger control account reconciliation – an exercise which agrees the balance on the sales ledger control account to the total of the list of balances in the sales ledger

Aged trade receivable analysis – a schedule showing, for each trade receivable, how long the component parts of the balance have been unpaid

Purchases ledger control account reconciliation – an exercise which agrees the balance on the purchases ledger control account to the total of the list of balances in the purchases ledger

VAT control account – the account which shows how much VAT the business owes HMRC (credit balance) or is owed by HMRC (debit balance)

VAT return – a report to HMRC by registered businesses showing sales and services transacted on which VAT is due

TEST YOUR LEARNING

Test 1

Write up the sales ledger control account for the month of July from the following information:

	£
Opening balance 1 July	16,339
Credit sales for the month	50,926
Cash sales for the month	12,776
Sales returns (all for credit sales) for the month	3,446
Amount received from credit customers in the month	47,612
Settlement discounts allowed to credit customers in the month	1,658
Irrecoverable debt to be written off (total)	500
Cheque returned by the bank 'refer to drawer'	366

Sales ledger control account

	£		£

Test 2

Write up the purchases ledger control account for the month of July from the following information:

	£
Opening balance 1 July	12,587
Cash purchases for the month	15,600
Credit purchases for the month	40,827
Purchases returns (all for purchases on credit)	2,568
Cheques paid to trade payables in the month	38,227
Settlement discounts received from supplier in the month	998

Purchases ledger control account

	£		£

Test 3

The balance on a business's sales ledger control account at the end of June was £41,774 and the total of the list of trade receivable balances from the sales ledger came to £41,586.

The following errors were discovered:

(a) The sales day book was undercast by £100 on one page

(b) A page from the sales returns day book with a total of £450 had not been posted to the control account although the individual returns had been recorded in the sales ledger

(c) An invoice from the sales day book had been posted to the individual account of the trade receivable as £769 instead of the correct figure of £679

(d) A discount allowed to one customer of £16 had been posted to the wrong side of the customer's account in the sales ledger

(e) An irrecoverable debt of £210 had been written off in the customer's individual account in the sales ledger but not in the general ledger

(f) A credit balance in the sales ledger of £125 had been included in the list of balances as a debit balance

Write up the sales ledger control account and reconcile to the total of the list of balances from the sales ledger after taking account of the errors noted.

Sales ledger control account

	£		£

	£
Original total of list of balances	
Error 1	
Error 2	
Error 3	
Amended list of balances	
Amended control account balance	

Test 4

The balance on a business's purchases ledger control account at the end of June is £38,694 and the total of the list of balances in the purchases ledger came to £39,741.

The following errors were noted for the month:

(a) A page in the purchases returns day book was overcast by £300

(b) A total from the cash book of £3,145 was posted in the general ledger as £3,415

(c) Settlement discounts received from suppliers of £267 were omitted from both the general ledger and the purchases ledger

(d) A credit note from a supplier for £210 was entered into the supplier's account in the purchases ledger as £120

(e) A debit balance on a supplier's account in the purchases ledger of £187 was omitted from the list of balances

(f) A credit balance in the purchases ledger should have been included in the list as £570 but instead was recorded as £770

Write up the purchases ledger control account and reconcile to the total of the list of balances in the purchases ledger after taking account of these errors.

Purchases ledger control account

	£		£

	£
Original total of list of balances	
Error 1	
Error 2	
Error 3	
Error 4	
Amended list of balances	
Amended control account balance	

Test 5

This is a summary of transactions with suppliers during the month of August.

(a) Show whether each entry will be a debit or credit in the purchases ledger control account in the general ledger.

Details	Amount £	Debit ✓	Credit ✓
Amount due to credit suppliers at 1 August	42,394		
Payments to credit suppliers	39,876		
Purchases on credit	31,243		
Purchases returned to credit suppliers	1,266		
Discounts received	501		

(b) What will be the balance brought down on 1 September on the above account?

	✓
Dr £ 31,994	
Cr £ 31,994	
Dr £ 34,526	
Cr £ 34,526	
Dr £ 32,996	
Cr £ 32,996	

The following credit balances were in the purchases ledger on 1 September.

	£
Robinson Kate	8,239
Livesley Ltd	6,300
Townsend and Douglas	1,204
Miles Better Co	10,993
Strongarm Partners	4,375
Ambley Brothers	1,079

(c) Reconcile the balances shown above with the purchases ledger control account balance you have calculated in part (b).

	£
Purchases ledger control account balance as at 31 August	
Total of purchases ledger accounts as at 31 August	
Difference	

(d) What may have caused the difference you calculated in part (c)?

	✓
A debit balance in the subsidiary ledger may have been included as a credit balance when calculating the total of the list of balances	
A credit balance in the subsidiary ledger may have been included as a debit balance when calculating the total of the list of balances	
A credit note may have been omitted from the purchases returns day book total	
Discounts received may only have been entered in the subsidiary ledger	

Test 6

The following is an extract from a business's books of prime entry.

Totals for three month period			
Sales day book		**Purchases day book**	
Net:	£145,360	Net:	£71,840
VAT:	£29,072	VAT:	£14,368
Gross:	£174,432	Gross:	£86,208
Sales returns day book		**Purchases returns day book**	
Net:	£4,290	Net:	£2,440
VAT:	£858	VAT:	£488
Gross:	£5,148	Gross:	£2,928
Cash book			
Net cash sales:	£1,660		
VAT:	£332		
Gross cash sales:	£1,992		

(a) Using the picklist of account names to complete the details columns, make the required entries in the VAT control account to record the VAT transactions in the period.

VAT control

Details	Amount £	Details	Amount £

Picklist of account names:

Cash book	Sales
Cash sales	Sales day book
Purchases	Sales returns
Purchases day book	Sales returns day book
Purchases returns day book	

The VAT return has been completed and shows an amount owing from HM Revenue and Customs of £14,666.

(b) Is the VAT return correct?

	✓
Yes	
No	

chapter 6:
THE JOURNAL

chapter coverage 📖

In this chapter we introduce the final book of prime entry with which you are concerned: the journal. We see the format of a journal entry, and how the journal is used for making non-standard entries in the general and subsidiary ledgers, such as writing off irrecoverable debts. We also look at journal entries for entering opening balances in a new set of accounts, and for entering payroll transactions.

The topics covered are:

- ✍ The journal as a book of prime entry
- ✍ Preparing and posting journal entries
- ✍ Uses of the journal
- ✍ Entering opening balances in a new set of accounts
- ✍ The journal and payroll transactions

THE JOURNAL AS A BOOK OF PRIME ENTRY

So far we have looked at a number of books of prime entry, in which transactions are initially recorded from primary records and from which postings are made to the general ledger and the memorandum sales and purchases ledgers.

The JOURNAL is the final book of prime entry that we need to look at. It is used to record transactions that do not appear in any of the other books of prime entry, so that they can then be posted to the ledgers. Often these are non-regular entries such as writing off irrecoverable debts.

The journal consists of a series of JOURNAL ENTRIES. A single journal entry is a written instruction to the person maintaining the general ledger to make a double entry.

PREPARING AND POSTING A JOURNAL ENTRY

A typical journal entry that you would see in practice is given below:

Journal number:	0225		
Date:	5 April 20XX		
Authorised by:	D Fisher		
Account	*Reference*	*Debit* *£*	*Credit* *£*
Irrecoverable debts expense	GL023	700.00	
VAT control	GL009	140.00	
Sales ledger control	GL100		840.00
Total		840.00	840.00
R Sanderson	*SL072*		*840.00*
Narrative: Being the write-off of R Sanderson's debt			

The key points to be noted about the journal entry, intended to write off an irrecoverable debt, are:

- Each journal has a sequential number (0225) to ensure that all are entered into the ledger accounts

- Each journal must be dated and authorised – the authorisation is vital as this is an adjustment to the ledger accounts

- The general ledger accounts that are to be debited and credited are named and coded (GL023 etc)

- The amounts to be entered in each ledger account are set out, together with an indication of whether they are to be debited or credited

148

- A total is calculated for debits and for credits, to check that the amounts are the same and so the double entry is correct

- If the entries also affect one of the subsidiary ledgers then the effect on them should also be set out, to ensure that they do not go out of line with the control accounts. This has been done in italic type here to make it clear that this part of the journal is separate from the general ledger one, and it includes the account name, the sales ledger/customer code, the amount and whether the entry is a debit or a credit

- A narrative is included to describe what the journal entry is for

In your assessment the style of journal entry that you will be required to prepare will not include a narrative. It will look like this:

Account name	Amount £	Debit ✓	Credit ✓

You choose the account name from a given picklist of names, you enter the figures in the 'amount' column, and then you place a tick in the debit or credit column as appropriate.

HOW IT WORKS

To prepare the journal for the irrecoverable debt write-off that we saw above, the following information is required:

- The names and ledger codes for the accounts affected (both in the general ledger and in the sales ledger)

- The amounts to be entered in each ledger account

- Whether each account needs to be debited or credited

- The authorisation for the transaction – all postings to the ledgers need to be authorised. Since most journal entries are non-standard it is particularly important that they are valid

Journal number:	0225		
Date:	5 April 20XX		
Authorised by:	D Fisher		
Account	*Reference*	*Debit* *£*	*Credit* *£*
Irrecoverable debts expense	GL023	700.00	
VAT control	GL009	140.00	
Sales ledger control	GL100		840.00
Total		840.00	840.00
R Sanderson	*SL072*		*840.00*
Narrative: Being the write-off of R Sanderson's debt			

In your assessment you would show the above journal as far as it affects the general ledger as follows:

Account name	Amount £	Debit ✓	Credit ✓
Irrecoverable debts expense	700.00	✓	
VAT control	140.00	✓	
Sales ledger control	840.00		✓

In the assessment you may also need to prepare a memorandum journal for the sales ledger:

Account name	Amount £	Debit ✓	Credit ✓
R Sanderson	840.00		✓

The journal entries can now be posted to the four accounts that they affect:

General ledger

Sales ledger control   **GL100**

Date	Ref	Folio	£	Date	Ref	Folio	£
				5/4/XX	Irrecoverable debts expense	J225	840.00

Irrecoverable debts expense   **GL023**

Date	Ref	Folio	£	Date	Ref	Folio	£
5/4/XX	Sales ledger control	J225	700.00				

VAT control   **GL009**

Date	Ref	Folio	£	Date	Ref	Folio	£
5/4/XX	Sales ledger control	J225	140.00				

Sales ledger

R Sanderson   **SL072**

Date	Ref	Folio	£	Date	Ref	Folio	£
				5/4/XX	Irrecoverable debts expense	J225	840.00

Note that for each entry, the Ref column contains the name of the main account that takes the other side of the entry, and the Folio column contains the journal number. Since journal entries are non-standard it is particularly important that all this information is complete.

USES OF THE JOURNAL

Journal entries are most often used to correct errors, which we shall look at in Chapter 7, but you will also see them in your assessment in relation to:

- Writing off irrecoverable debts (see above)
- Entering opening balances in a new set of ledger accounts
- Recording payroll transactions

ENTERING OPENING BALANCES IN A NEW SET OF ACCOUNTS

For a new business, the journal is used to enter opening balances into its accounting system.

Entering opening asset and liability balances

It is a straightforward matter to enter the business's assets, liabilities and capital in the new set of accounts.

- Asset accounts are debit balances
- Liability and capital accounts are credit balances

Entering opening expense and income balances

Even before it has started its accounts a new business is likely to make some transactions. These will not only be to take out a loan, for instance, and pay the money into a business bank account (a liability and an asset, as we have just

seen). It may also, for instance, pay rent in advance, get an inventory of stationery in, receive a down-payment from a credit customer, and have a phone line installed.

It is just as straightforward a matter to enter the business's expenses and income in the new set of accounts as it is to enter assets, liabilities and capital.

- Expenses accounts are debit balances
- Income accounts are credit balances

HOW IT WORKS

Sarah Clifford is starting a business on 1 November 20XX with the following balances:

	£
Bank loan	22,000
Capital	9,100
Cash at bank	6,550
Expenses	300
Non-current assets	25,000
Petty cash	450
Sales	1,200

We need to create a journal to enter the appropriate opening balances in Sarah's accounts as at 1 November 20XX.

Step 1   Draw up a journal entry to enter the opening balances in the new accounts. We just work through the list identifying balances.

Journal

Account name	Debit	Credit
	£	£
Bank loan		22,000
Capital		9,100
Cash at bank	6,550	
Expenses	300	
Non-current assets	25,000	
Petty cash	450	
Sales		1,200
Totals	32,300	32,300

Step 2 The second step is to enter the journal in the new set of accounts.

Bank loan account

			£				£
				1 Nov	Journal		22,000

Capital account

			£				£
				I Nov	Journal		9,100

Cash at bank account

			£				£
1 Nov	Journal		6,550				

Expenses account

			£				£
1 Nov	Journal		300				

Non-current assets account

			£				£
1 Nov	Journal		25,000				

Petty cash account

			£				£
1 Nov	Journal		450				

Sales account

			£				£
				1 Nov	Journal		1,200

THE JOURNAL AND PAYROLL TRANSACTIONS

To understand the entries in the accounting system that are made for payments to employees in respect of salaries (or wages) – known as PAYROLL TRANSACTIONS – you need to have a basic understanding of the way in which individuals are taxed in the UK.

Most employees receive an annual wage (or salary) which is paid in regular intervals over the year, eg paid monthly. Some employees receive wages paid weekly. For our purposes salary and wages are the same so we will refer just to 'wages' from now on.

The amount that the employer owes the employee each month/week is known as their GROSS PAY.

Income tax and employee's NIC

An individual must pay INCOME TAX to HMRC on all sources of income. The only income that we are concerned about is the wages that an employee earns, and we are not concerned with how the tax calculations are made.

Employees pay their income tax under the PAYE system, which stands for Pay-As-You Earn. This means that each time an employee is paid by their employer the income tax for that month is deducted from their wages by the employer, and the employer then pays the income tax over to HMRC on the employee's behalf.

Employees must also pay employees' NATIONAL INSURANCE CONTRIBUTIONS (NIC) to HMRC. NIC are just another form of tax, calculated differently from income tax. An individual's employees' NIC are deducted from the employee's wages and paid over to HMRC together with the employee's income tax.

PAYE income tax and employees' NIC are known as STATUTORY DEDUCTIONS from gross pay, because the law (statute) requires employers to make these deductions.

There may be other (voluntary) deductions from gross pay as well. Once all deductions have been made the amount paid to the employee is called NET PAY.

In the most simple of cases:

Gross pay – statutory deductions = net pay

HOW IT WORKS

Let's suppose that Ian is employed by Southfield. He earns £48,000 a year which is paid monthly. This means that each month his gross pay is (£48,000/12) = £4,000. Remember gross pay is the amount an employee earns before any deductions from pay.

The payroll department of Southfield has calculated that the income tax due by Ian for this month, October, is £770, and that his employees' NIC payment for the month should be £320.

Therefore, so far, Ian's monthly net pay is calculated as follows:

	£	
Gross wages	4,000	
PAYE Income tax	(770)	Paid to HMRC by Southfield
NIC	(320)	Paid to HMRC by Southfield
Net pay	2,910	Paid to Ian by Southfield

This means that although Ian will receive a smaller amount each month than his gross pay he does not have to worry about paying any income tax or employees' NIC on his earnings to HMRC as it has already been done on his behalf by Southfield.

Employer's NIC

We have seen that at each pay day the employee must pay EMPLOYEES' NIC. The employer is also required to pay an additional amount of NIC for each employee, known as the EMPLOYER'S NIC. This is yet another form of tax, but the difference is that it is only suffered by the employer; there is no deduction from the employee's gross pay for employer's NIC.

HOW IT WORKS

When Southfield pay Ian each month they are also required to pay employer's NIC to HMRC.

Suppose that the employer's NIC for Ian is calculated as £415. In total, Southfield must pay HMRC in respect of Ian:

	£
PAYE deducted from gross pay	770
Employees' NIC deducted from gross pay	320
Employer's NIC suffered by Southfield	415
Total payable by Southfield to HMRC	1,505

VOLUNTARY DEDUCTIONS

There may also be other types of deduction from an employee's pay which are not required by the law but which have been chosen by the employee and employer. These are VOLUNTARY DEDUCTIONS. The most common of these are pension contributions.

Pension contributions

Many employees elect to pay a certain percentage of their gross pay into the business's pension scheme or into a scheme run by an external provider. PENSION CONTRIBUTIONS accumulate to provide a pension for the employee on their retirement. Like income tax and NIC, the employee's pension contribution is deducted from the employee's gross pay by the employer and paid into the pension scheme on the employee's behalf. Often the employer will itself pay an amount into the pension scheme for that employee on each pay day, usually calculated as a certain percentage of the employee's gross pay. Like employer's NIC, the employer's pension contribution is not deducted from the employee's gross pay in arriving at net pay.

Give-as-you-earn scheme – GAYE

Employees can choose to pay money to an approved charity directly from their gross wages under the Give-As-You-Earn scheme, GAYE. The employee is allowed to pay any amount without limit per tax year and the employer deducts the money from the employee's gross pay and pays it over to the stated charity.

Other deductions

There are also other deductions that can be made from an employee's gross pay, for example a regular subscription to the employee's trade union or the business's social club. If the employer makes a loan to an employee, say to help pay for an annual season ticket on public transport, regular repayments of this loan by the employee will be deducted by the employer in arriving at net pay.

GROSS PAY TO NET PAY

Once all of the deductions, both statutory and voluntary, have been made from an employee's gross pay, what is left is the amount that the employee will actually receive – the net pay.

HOW IT WORKS

When Ian joined Southfield Electrical it was agreed that each month he would pay 5% of his gross pay into the company pension scheme, that is £200 per month. Southfield agree to make a further contribution to the pension scheme of 7.5% of Ian's gross pay.

We will now see all the elements of Ian's monthly pay and see who pays what to whom:

	£		
Gross pay	4,000.00		
PAYE Income tax	(770.00)	⟶	HMRC
Employees' NIC	(320.00)	⟶	HMRC
Pension contribution	(200.00)	⟶	Pension scheme
Net pay	2,710.00	⟶	Ian

So of the original gross wages of £4,000 per month Ian only receives £2,710. However his income tax liability has been settled as has the amount of NIC due from him, and he has also paid into his pension fund.

There are two further payments by Southfield to be made:

Employer's NIC	£415	⟶	HMRC
Employer's pension	£300	⟶	Pension scheme
(£4,000 × 7.5%)			

Task 1

Joan also works for Southfield and is paid on a weekly basis. Her gross pay is £400 per week. The payroll department has calculated that for this week the PAYE income tax payable is £69 and Joan's NIC for the week is £34. Joan also pays a weekly subscription to her trade union through the payroll of £2.50.

What is Joan's net pay?

£ [   ]

PAYING EMPLOYEES

Once the payroll department has made all of the calculations required for each employee for that pay day then the employees must be actually paid.

Methods of payment

Cash

It is possible to pay employees in cash. However, the practical and security arrangements required mean that this is very rarely done.

Cheque

It is also possible to pay each employee's net pay with a cheque. Again, however, this is a time-consuming process as a cheque must be written out for each

individual's net pay. Payment by this method would normally only be in an organisation with a small number of employees or for one-off payments for work carried out.

BACS

The most common method of making payroll payments is automated payment by BACS, Bankers Automated Clearing System. This ensures that the net pay for each employee is paid directly into that employee's bank account. The total payment for all employees is taken from the business's bank account by its bank.

ACCOUNTING FOR PAYROLL PAYMENTS

The entries into the general ledger accounts for the payroll payments may seem fairly complex but if you bear in mind the system that has just been considered they can be followed through logically:

- The full cost of employing an employee is:

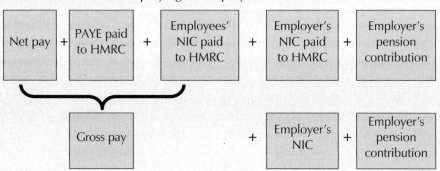

Therefore gross pay plus employer's NIC plus employer's pension contribution is the cost of employing employees and must be what appears as the wages expense for the business.

- The PAYE and NIC that is deducted from the employees' gross pay plus the employer's NIC must normally be paid over to HMRC by the 19th of the month following pay day. Therefore these amounts are payables until they are paid and must appear in a liability account. The total is not normally classified as a 'trade payable' since the entity to which money is owed is HMRC, not a supplier with which the business trades. Sometimes instead it is referred to as an 'other payable'.

- The pension contribution that is deducted from the employee's gross pay plus the employer's pension contribution must be paid over to the pension scheme. Again, the total is an 'other payable' until it is paid and must appear in a liability account.

The double entry reflects these factors and uses four main accounts:

- The WAGES CONTROL ACCOUNT
- The wages expense account
- The PAYE/NIC payable account
- The pension payable account

(There may be other payable accounts if further voluntary deductions are made, say in respect of GAYE, trade union and social club subscriptions. If there is an employee loan outstanding, the repayments deducted in arriving at net pay are entered in the loan account, which is an asset account, since the employee is the business's receivable.)

There are four double entries to be made:

- Gross pay:

  - **Debit** entry in the wages expense account
  - **Credit** entry in the wages control account

- Net pay paid to employees:

  - **Debit** entry in the wages control account
  - **Credit** entry in the Bank column of the cash book (credit side)

- PAYE and employees' NIC deducted from gross pay

  - **Debit** entry in the wages control account
  - **Credit** entry in the PAYE/NIC payable account

- Employees' pension contributions deducted from gross pay

  - **Debit** entry in the wages control account
  - **Credit** entry in the pension payable account

- Employer's NIC

  - **Debit** entry in the wages expense account
  - **Credit** entry in the wages control account

and

  - **Debit** entry in the wages control account
  - **Credit** entry in the PAYE/NIC payable account

- Employer's pension contributions

  - **Debit** entry in the wages expense account
  - **Credit** entry in the wages control account

and

  - **Debit** entry in the wages control account
  - **Credit** entry in the pension payable account

HOW IT WORKS

We return to Ian's wages payment which is summarised below:

	£
Gross wages	4,000
PAYE Income tax	(770)
Employees' NIC	(320)
Pension contribution	(200)
Net pay	2,710
Employer's NIC	415
Employer's pension	300

The entries in the ledger accounts would be as follows:

- Gross pay

Wages expense account

	£		£
Wages control	4,000		

Wages control account

	£		£
		Wages expense	4,000

- Net pay paid to employee

Wages control account

	£		£
Bank	2,710	Wages expense	4,000

Bank account

	£		£
		Wages control	2,710

- PAYE and NIC deducted from gross pay

Wages control account

	£		£
Bank	2,710	Wages expense	4,000
PAYE/NIC payable	1,090		
(770 + 320)			

PAYE/NIC payable account

	£		£
		Wages control	1,090

- Employee's pension contribution deducted from gross pay

Wages control account

	£		£
Bank	2,710	Wages expense	4,000
PAYE/NIC payable	1,090		
Pension payable	200		

Pension payable account

	£		£
		Wages control	200

- Employer's NIC

Wages control account

	£		£
Bank	2,710	Wages expense	4,000
PAYE/NIC payable	1,090	Wages expense	415
Pension payable	200		
PAYE/NIC payable	415		

Wages expense account

	£		£
Wages control	4,000		
Wages control	415		

PAYE/NIC payable account

	£		£
		Wages control	1,090
		Wages control	415

- Employer's pension contributions

Wages control account

	£		£
Bank	2,710	Wages expense	4,000
PAYE/NIC payable	1,090	Wages expense	415
Pension payable	200	Wages expense	300
PAYE/NIC payable	415		
Pension payable	300		
	4,715		4,715

Wages expense account

	£		£
Wages control	4,000		
Wages control	415		
Wages control	300		

Pension payable account

£		£
	Wages control	200
	Wages control	300

- The wages control account is a clearing account which helps to ensure that the double entry is made correctly. If so, the account should balance to zero at the end of each period (see above)

- The wages expense account shows the cost of employing Ian, ie gross pay plus employer's NIC plus employer's pension contribution

- The PAYE/NIC payable account shows how much must be paid over to HMRC by the 19th of the following month

- The pension payable account shows how much should be paid into the pension scheme

Task 2

Joan works for Southfield and is paid on a weekly basis. Her gross pay is £400 per week. Her PAYE income tax payable is £69 and her NIC for the week is £33. Joan also pays a weekly subscription to her trade union through the payroll of £2.50. Southfield's NIC contribution for Joan for this week is £41. What are the balances on the following accounts (before any payments are made to HMRC)?

The PAYE/NIC payable account

£ [   ]

The wages expense account

£ [   ]

The payroll and the payroll journal entry

In practice, the double entry considered above would not be made for each individual employee. Instead the details of gross pay, deductions, net pay and employer's NIC and pension for each employee would be recorded in what is known as a 'payroll'. From this primary record a payroll journal entry would be prepared on each pay day, summarising the required double entry. It is the journal, therefore, that is the book of prime entry for recording payroll transactions. The summary journal for Southfield's payroll (in relation to Ian) would be as follows:

Journal

Account name	Debit £	Credit £
Wages expense	4,715	
Pension payable		500
PAYE/NIC payable		1,505
Bank		2,710
Totals	4,715	4,715

Alternatively, the business could prepare a more detailed journal that contained all the double entry involving the wages control account that we followed through earlier.

PAYMENTS TO HMRC AND THE PENSION SCHEME

The PAYE and NIC deducted from the employees' gross pay and the employer's NIC must be paid over to HMRC each month by the employer. The payment must normally be made within fourteen days of the tax month end, which is the 5th of each month. So payment must reach HMRC by the 19th of each month. Similarly, the contributions to the pension scheme must be paid over in line with the relevant agreement.

When the payments are made, the relevant payable account is debited and bank account is credited.

CHAPTER OVERVIEW

- The journal is the book of prime entry for all non-standard transactions to be recorded in the accounting system, including the recording of:

  - Opening balances for assets, liabilities and capital at the beginning of a new business

  - Payroll transactions

- In the UK individuals pay income tax on all of their income at various rates depending upon the amount of that income

- If a person is employed then they will pay their income tax through the PAYE system

- A further statutory deduction from the employee's gross pay is employees' National Insurance Contributions (NIC)

- The employer must also pay employer's NIC for each employee who earns more than a stated amount per week

- The PAYE deducted, the employees' NIC deducted and the employer's NIC will all be paid over to HMRC by the employer

- There are also other, non-statutory amounts that may be deducted from an employee's gross pay – pension contributions, GAYE payments, trade union and social club subscriptions, loan repayments etc

- Wages may be paid in cash or by cheque but the most common method is by BACS

- The ledger entries for payroll transactions take place in three main general ledger accounts – the wages control account, the wages expense account and the PAYE/NIC payable account

- In practice, the journal is used as the book of prime entry for the summary figures from the payroll in which details of gross pay, deductions and net pay will be recorded for each employee each month. The PAYE and NIC due must be paid to HMRC normally by the 19th of the month following the pay day.

Keywords

Journal – the book of prime entry that is used to record transactions that do not appear in any of the other books of prime entry

Journal entry – a written instruction to the bookkeeper to make a double entry into the general and/or subsidiary ledgers

Payroll transactions – payments to employees in respect of salaries and wages

Gross pay – the salary/wage payable to an employee before any statutory or voluntary deductions

Income tax – a tax that is paid by individuals on all sources of income, including salaries and wages

PAYE system – the system which allows the employer to pay employees their salaries net of income tax (and NICs), and to pay it to HMRC on the employees' behalf

National insurance contributions (employees' NIC) – a tax on employees' income

Statutory deductions – deductions made by the employer from an employee's pay in respect of income tax and employees' NIC

Net pay – the amount of the employee's wages actually paid to the employee, net of statutory and voluntary deductions

National insurance contributions (employer's NIC) – an additional tax, suffered by the employer, based on an employee's gross pay,

Voluntary deductions – non-statutory amounts deducted from employees' pay with their consent eg give-as-you-earn (GAYE) and trade union subscriptions

Pension contribution – a form of voluntary deduction from employees, and a contribution from employers in addition, which builds up in the hands of the pension administrator to provide a pension for the employee on retirement

Wages control account – a clearing account used to ensure that the double entry for payroll transactions is correct

TEST YOUR LEARNING

Test 1

Prepare a journal entry for recording the following opening balances in a new set of accounts: capital £7,500, trade receivables £2,000, trade payables £2,500, cash at bank £8,000.

Account name	Amount £	Debit ✓	Credit ✓

Test 2

State whether the following deductions from gross pay are statutory or non-statutory deductions:

	Statutory deduction ✓	Non-statutory deduction ✓
Pension contributions		
Income tax		
Employee's NIC		
Trade union fees		

Test 3

An employee earns a gross wage of £27,000 and is paid on a monthly basis. For the month of October the payroll department has calculated a PAYE income tax deduction of £418.16 and NI contributions due of £189.00 from the employee and £274.50 from the employer.

(a) What is the employee's net pay?

£ [   ]

(b) Record the payroll transactions for this employee in the ledger accounts.

Wages control account

	£		£

Wages expense account

	£		£

PAYE/NIC payable account

	£		£

Bank account

	£		£

Test 4

One of Grangemouth Ltd's credit customers, Markham Co, has ceased trading, owing Grangemouth Ltd £1,290 plus VAT.

(a) Using the picklist of account names, record the journal entries needed in the general ledger to write off the net amount and the VAT.

Account name	Amount £	Debit ✓	Credit ✓

Picklist of account names:

Irrecoverable debts
Grangemouth Ltd
Markham Co
Purchases
Purchases ledger control
Sales
Sales ledger control

(b) A new business, Carswell & Sons, is opening a new set of accounts. A partially completed journal to record the opening entries is shown below.

Record the journal entries needed in the accounts in the general ledger of Carswell & Sons to deal with the opening entries.

Account name	Amount £	Debit ✓	Credit ✓
Capital	18,410		
Cash at bank	3,270		
Heat and light	300		
Loan from bank	5,000		
Machinery	10,000		
Motor vehicle	7,800		
Petty cash	200		
Rent	1,300		
Stationery	190		
Vehicle expenses	350		
Journal to record the opening entries of new business			

Test 5

A business pays its employees by BACS every month and maintains a wages control account. A summary of last month's payroll transactions is shown below:

Item	£
Gross wages	12,756
Employer's NIC	1,020
Employees' NIC	765
Income tax	1,913
Loan repayment	100

Using the picklist of account names, record the journal entries needed in the general ledger to:

(a)   Record the wages expense

Account name	Amount £	Debit ✓	Credit ✓

(b)   Record the HM Revenue and Customs liability

Account name	Amount £	Debit ✓	Credit ✓

(c)   Record the net wages paid to the employees

Account name	Amount £	Debit ✓	Credit ✓

(d)   Record the loan repayment

Account name	Amount £	Debit ✓	Credit ✓

Picklist of account names:

Bank
Employees' NIC
Employer's NIC
HM Revenue and Customs
Income tax
Net wages
Loan
Wages control
Wages expense

chapter 7:
ERRORS AND THE TRIAL BALANCE

chapter coverage 📖

In BAI we saw how to prepare an initial trial balance. This chapter considers a trial balance that does not balance. This indicates that the double entry has not operated properly so there are errors in the ledger accounts. You are expected to identify errors, correct them using a suspense account and the journal, and then re-draft the trial balance. In order to identify the errors you need to be aware of the different types of error that exist, both those that are shown up by the trial balance and those that are not. The topics covered are:

✍ Types of error

✍ The procedure to follow to identify the error or errors made when the trial balance does not balance

✍ Correcting errors

✍ Creation of a suspense account

✍ Correction of errors using the journal

✍ Redrafting the trial balance

TYPES OF ERROR

In any accounting system there are several types of error that can be made when making entries in the ledger accounts. Some of these errors will be identified when a trial balance is extracted but a number of types of error can take place and the trial balance will still balance.

Errors leading to an imbalance on the trial balance

Several types of error will mean that the debit balances on the trial balance will not equal the credit balances.

Single entry transactions – if only one side of the double entry has been made in the ledger accounts, eg the debit and not the credit, then the trial balance will not balance

Two debits/two credits error – instead of posting a transaction as a debit in one account and a credit in another, a common error is to post both accounts with debit entries, or both with credit entries. This means that one account will be correct but the other will be out of balance by twice the amount of the posting. For instance, when recording discounts received of £500, the correct entry is to debit Purchases ledger control with £500 and credit Discounts received with £500, so there would be a debit balance of £500 on PLCA and a credit balance of £500 on Discounts received. If instead a credit entry was made in each account, both would have credit balances of £500. To bring the PLCA to the correct balance we would have to debit it with £500 to correct the error, and then debit it again to make the correct entry:

Purchases ledger control account

	£		£
Correct incorrect posting	500	Incorrect posting	500
Make correct posting	500	Balance c/d	500
	1,000		1,000
Balance b/d	500		

Transposition error – a TRANSPOSITION ERROR is where the digits in a number are transposed (swapped round), eg a transaction for £435 is recorded correctly as a debit entry in one account, but the credit entry is made at £345. It is also possible for the balance on an account to be transposed when it is taken to the trial balance, eg a debit balance of £1,268 is recorded in the trial balance as a debit balance of £1,628. Both these errors will mean that the trial balance does not balance. If a transposition error has been made – and is the only error – then the difference between the total debits and the total credits in the trial balance will be exactly

divisible by 9. This is a very useful trick to know when trying to track down errors.

Calculation error – if a mistake is made in calculating the balance on a ledger account then an incorrect balance will be included in the trial balance, so it will not balance.

Balance omission – if a balance on a general ledger account is omitted from the trial balance this means that the debits will not equal the credits.

Task 1

A sales invoice recorded in the sales day book at £1,678 has been correctly recorded in the sales ledger control account but has been entered into the sales account as £1,768. This is a single entry/transposition/balancing/balance omission error.

Errors which do not cause an imbalance on the trial balance

Unfortunately, there are also some types of error that do not cause an imbalance on the trial balance and therefore cannot be shown up through the trial balance process – though they must still be found of course!

Error of original entry – here both entries into the general ledger, debit and credit, have been made using the wrong amount. This may be because:

- The transaction was recorded in the primary record or the book of prime entry at the incorrect amount, or

- The wrong figure was picked up from the primary record (eg a transposition error was made) and this incorrect figure was used for both the debit and the credit entry in the general ledger.

As long as both the debit and the credit entry are equal this error will not cause an imbalance in the trial balance.

Error of omission – an entry is completely omitted from the ledger accounts. If the transaction is not recorded as either a debit or a credit then it cannot affect the trial balance.

Error of reversal of entries – this type of error is where the correct figure has been used and a debit and a credit entry made but the debit and the credit are on the wrong sides of the respective accounts. The trial balance will still balance but the two accounts will have incorrect balances.

Error of commission – the double entry is arithmetically correct but a wrong account of the **same type** has been used. For example, if the phone bill is paid the bank account will be credited and an expense account, the phone

account, should be debited. If, instead, the electricity account is debited this is an error of commission. It does not affect the trial balance but it does mean that both the phone account and electricity account show the wrong balance.

Error of principle – an error of principle is similar to an error of commission in that the double entry is arithmetically correct but the **wrong type** of account has been used. For example, if computer disks are purchased, the bank account should be credited and the computer expenses or office expenses account debited. If, instead, the cost of the disks is debited to a non-current asset account (ie it is treated as capital expenditure rather than revenue expenditure), this is an error of principle but, again, it does not affect the balancing of the trial balance.

Compensating errors – these are probably rare in practice but it is where two errors are made which exactly cancel each other out. For example, if the sales ledger control account is debited with £100 too much in respect of a sales transaction and the purchases returns account is credited with £100 too much in respect of a purchases transaction, the two errors will cancel each other out. The errors are unrelated but the fact that they both occurred will mean that there is no imbalance in the trial balance to help identify them.

Task 2

A sales invoice to J K Reynolds was recorded in the sales ledger in the account of T M Reynolds. This is (please tick)

An error of original entry	☐
An error of principle	☐
A commission error	☐
An omission error	☐

IMBALANCE ON THE TRIAL BALANCE

If the trial balance does not balance then the reason or reasons for this must be discovered. As we have seen there are several types of error that could cause the total of the debits not to equal the total of the credits in the general ledger. Rather than going back to each ledger account and checking each entry to find the cause of the imbalance it makes sense, both in practice and in assessments, to take a logical approach to finding the causes of any imbalance.

The problem might be arithmetical or it may be to do with the double entry, but it makes sense to check the more obvious and simpler errors before getting involved with detailed checking of the ledger accounts.

Procedure for finding the error/errors

Step 1 Check the totalling of the debit column and the credit column on the trial balance. It is very easy to make an error when totalling a long column of figures so this is an obvious place to start.

Step 2 Calculate the difference between the debit and credit total – this may come in useful later in the checking exercise if the difference cannot be found easily (see Steps 6 and 7).

Step 3 Check that each balance in the general ledger has been correctly copied into the trial balance and that each has been included on the correct side, debit or credit.

Step 4 Check that all the balances in the general ledger have been included in the trial balance. In particular, ensure that the cash and bank balances and the petty cash balances have been included as these are generally kept physically separate from the general ledger since the cash book and petty cash book are usually both books of prime entry and part of the general ledger.

Step 5 Check the calculation of the balance on each ledger account is correct.

Step 6 Look in the ledger accounts for any entry that is for the same amount as the difference on the trial balance. If this amount is found, check that the double entry for the relevant transaction has been correctly carried out.

Step 7 Look in the ledger accounts for any entry that is for half the amount of the difference on the trial balance. If this is found, check that the double entry for the relevant transaction has been correctly carried out.

If all else fails you have to:

Step 8 Check all the bookkeeping entries from the books of prime entry since the date of the last trial balance, and then

Step 9 Check that all the books of prime entry have been written up from primary documents and totalled correctly

Number tricks to look out for

We have already seen that if the difference on the trial balance is divisible exactly by 9 then the error is likely to be a transposition error. This means that two digits in a figure have been reversed, eg £654 is entered as £564 – the difference of £90 is exactly divisible by 9.

If the difference on the trial balance is a round number, eg £10, £100, £1,000 etc then it is likely that the error made is arithmetical rather than a double entry error. Therefore take great care when checking account balance calculations.

CORRECTING AN ERROR THAT DOES NOT CAUSE AN IMBALANCE

Each error or omission must be corrected and this is done using a journal entry. We shall concentrate first on errors that do not cause an imbalance on the trial balance.

HOW IT WORKS

In a business which does not charge VAT on sales, the sales day book for a period had been undercast by £1,000. This means that both the sales ledger control account and the sales account have been understated by £1,000. It is likely that this error would have been picked up when the SLCA did not reconcile with the total of the sales ledger balances. Because the postings to the individual sales ledger accounts are of the individual invoice totals, they are unaffected by the calculation of a wrong overall total in the sales day book, whereas the two general ledger accounts will both be posted with the incorrect total.

Both general ledger accounts must have an additional entry. This is done by writing out a journal to make the right entries. As there is only one debit amount and one credit amount we do not need to calculate a total to double check that the general ledger postings will be correct.

Date	Ref	Debit	Credit
20XX			
		£	£
Sales ledger control account	GL94	1,000	
Sales account	GL02		1,000
Being correction of the undercasting of the sales day book			

CORRECTING AN ERROR THAT DOES CAUSE AN IMBALANCE – THE SUSPENSE ACCOUNT

If the debit total does not equal the credit total when the trial balance is initially drafted then the reasons for this must be investigated and eventually corrected. Until the reasons for the imbalance on the trial balance have been discovered and corrected a SUSPENSE ACCOUNT is opened in order to make the trial balance totals equal.

HOW IT WORKS

A business drafted its initial trial balance and found the totals of the debit and credit columns were as follows:

	Debit £	Credit £
Total	157,600	157,900

The difference of £300 is initially dealt with by opening a suspense account in order to create a balanced trial balance.

	Debit £	Credit £
Original total balances	157,600	157,900
Suspense account	300	
Trial balance totals	157,900	157,900

The trial balance now balances but there is also a new general ledger account, the suspense account, with a debit balance.

Suspense account			
	£		£
Balance b/d	300		

This balance must **not** remain in the ledger accounts. The reasons for the imbalance on the trial balance must be investigated and corrections must be made using journal entries. Once the corrections have been put through the suspense account will be cleared to a balance of zero.

CORRECTING ERRORS

In an assessment you will need to identify errors from information given to you and then draft the journal entries to correct them. The procedure to follow is:

- Work out what the incorrect double entry was, *then*
- Determine what the correct double entry is, *then*
- Prepare the journal entry:
  - Reversing the incorrect double entry, *and*
  - Making the correct double entry.

(Note that it is also possible in practice to make net journal entries, which reverse and correct only the incorrect original entries, leaving the parts of the entries that were made correctly the first time unaffected. In the AAT assessment, however, you need to follow the 'reverse and correct' approach, as we shall see from now on.)

Not all errors affect the balancing of the trial balance so when you draft journals to correct errors you will not always have to make an entry in the suspense account.

The only time there will be a suspense account entry in the journal is when the original double entry broke down in some way. This means there will be one reversing double entry in a normal general ledger account and the suspense account, followed by a correcting double entry in the normal general ledger accounts.

HOW IT WORKS

Continuing with the previous example where there is a debit balance of £300 on the suspense account, you are now told that the business does not account for VAT and the following errors have been discovered:

(1) Discounts received of £175 have been omitted from the general ledger accounts

(2) Sales returns were correctly recorded as £1,500 in the sales returns account but as only £1,000 in the sales ledger control account

(3) When the rent account was balanced it was undercast by £1,000

(4) A purchase invoice for £460 was omitted from the Purchases Day Book

(5) Purchases returns of £580 were recorded in the general ledger as £850

(6) Discounts allowed of £200 were only entered in the discounts allowed account

(7) A receipt from a credit customer of £140 was entered on the wrong side of the trade receivable's account in the sales ledger

We will deal with each of these errors in turn.

(1) Discounts received of £175 have been omitted from the general ledger accounts

As this has been omitted from the general ledger totally there is no need for a reversing double entry. We just need to make the full double entry for discounts received.

Account name	Amount £	Debit	Credit
Purchases ledger control	175	✓	
Discounts received	175		✓

(2) Sales returns were correctly recorded as £1,500 in the sales returns account but as only £1,000 in the sales ledger control account

First of all we must identify the original incorrect double entry. The sales returns account was debited with £1,500 and the SLCA was credited with £1,000. Where was the other £500 credited? While the entry was not physically made, in effect £500 was credited to the suspense account. These incorrect entries must therefore be reversed, and then the correct entries can be made. This is all done using one journal:

Account name	Amount £	Debit	Credit
Sales returns	1,500		✓
Sales ledger control	1,000	✓	
Suspense	500	✓	
Sales returns	1,500	✓	
Sales ledger control	1,500		✓

The effect on the suspense account is as follows:

Suspense account

	£		£
Balance b/d	300		
Sales returns	500		

(3) When the rent account was balanced it was undercast by £1,000

The rent balance in the trial balance has to be increased by £1,000, but as this is the only entry required the other side of the entry must be to the suspense account.

Account name	Amount £	Debit	Credit
Rent	1,000	✓	
Suspense	1,000		✓

The effect on the suspense account is as follows:

Suspense account

	£		£
Balance b/d	300	Rent	1,000
Sales returns	500		

(4) A purchase invoice for £460 was omitted from the purchases day book

As the invoice was not entered in the purchases day book it has not been entered in the general ledger. Therefore the full double entry is required.

Account name	Amount £	Debit	Credit
Purchases	460	✓	
Purchases ledger control	460		✓

(5) Purchases returns of £580 were recorded in the general ledger as £850

Both sides of the entry for purchases returns are too high by £270, which as it is divisible by 9 suggests that a transposition error has been made. The original double entry must be reversed and the correct double entry made.

Account name	Amount £	Debit	Credit
Purchases ledger control	850		✓
Purchases returns	850	✓	
Purchases ledger control	580	✓	
Purchases returns	580		✓

(6) Discounts allowed of £200 were only entered in the discounts allowed account

If the discount was only entered in the discounts allowed account then the missing credit entry was effectively made to the suspense account when it should have been made to the sales ledger control account. We must reverse the original incorrect double entry then make the correct ones.

Account name	Amount £	Debit	Credit
Discounts allowed	200		✓
Suspense	200	✓	
Discounts allowed	200	✓	
Sales ledger control	200		✓

The effect on the suspense account is as follows:

Suspense account

	£		£
Balance b/d	300	Rent	1,000
Sales returns	500		
Discounts allowed	200		

(7) A receipt from a credit customer of £140 was entered on the wrong side of the trade receivable's account in the sales ledger

As this error was made in the sales ledger it does not affect the double entry so there is no requirement for any alteration to the general ledger accounts (though the sales ledger should of course be corrected, otherwise the totals of the balances will not agree with the balance on the sales ledger control account).

Clearing the suspense account

Once all of the errors have been dealt with via journal entries, there should be no remaining balance on the suspense account.

Suspense account

	£		£
Balance b/d	300	Rent	1,000
Sales returns	500		
Discount allowed	200		
	1,000		1,000

Task 3

A receipt from a credit customer of £1,250 was entered on the debit side in both the cash book and the sales ledger control account.

What are the journal entry required to reverse the original entries and make the correct ones in the ledger accounts?

Account name	Amount £	Debit ✓	Credit ✓

REDRAFTING THE TRIAL BALANCE

Once the suspense account has been opened and cleared the trial balance can be redrafted.

HOW IT WORKS

Harry Naylor runs a small business and he has handed you the following balances on his ledger accounts that he has prepared.

Cash book

	Cash £	Bank £		Cash £	Bank £
Bal b/d	1,000	2,390			

Capital account

	£		£
		Bal b/d	10,000

Non-current assets account

	£		£
Bal b/d	20,000		

Purchases account

	£		£
Bal b/d	13,100		

Purchases ledger control account

	£		£
		Bal b/d	550

Rent account

	£		£
Bal b/d	600		

Sales account

	£		£
		Bal b/d	33,291

Sales ledger control account

	£		£
Bal b/d	5,925		

Petty cash

	£		£
Bal b/d	135		

Stationery account

	£		£
Bal b/d	200		

Drawings account

	£		£
Bal b/d	500		

Discounts allowed

	£		£
Bal b/d	50		

Discounts received

	£		£
		Bal b/d	100

Harry is aware that he has made two mistakes as follows:

(a) He entered one sales day book total correctly as £1,298 in the sales ledger control account but as £1,289 in the sales account.

(b) He omitted the posting to the purchases ledger control account when recording discounts received of £50.

These are the steps to follow:

- Draw up an initial trial balance, calculating and inserting a suspense account balance if this is needed to make it balance.

Account name	Debit £	Credit £
Cash in hand	1,000	
Cash at bank	2,390	
Capital		10,000
Non-current assets	20,000	
Purchases	13,100	
PLCA		550
Rent	600	
Sales		33,291
SLCA	5,925	
Petty cash	135	
Stationery	200	
Drawings	500	
Discounts allowed	50	
Discounts received		100
Suspense	41	
Totals	43,941	43,941

- Open up the suspense ledger account.

Suspense account

	£		£
Bal b/d	41		

- Prepare journal entries to make the necessary corrections to the ledger accounts

(a) The original entry should have been debit SLCA £1,298 and credit sales £1,298. Too little (£1,298 – £1,289 = £9) was credited to sales, so as this creates an imbalance on the trial balance we know that effectively

£9 was credited to the suspense account. We need to reverse the original entries and make the correct ones:

Account name	Amount £	Debit	Credit
Sales account	1,289	✓	
Suspense account	9	✓	
SLCA	1,298		✓
SLCA	1,298	✓	
Sales	1,298		✓

(b) The original entry should have been debit PLCA £50 and credit discounts received £50. The PLCA posting was omitted entirely, so effectively £50 was debited to the suspense account. We need to reverse the original entries and make the correct ones.

Account name	Amount £	Debit	Credit
Discounts received	50	✓	
Suspense account	50		✓
PLCA	50	✓	
Discounts received	50		✓

■ Process the journal entries in the ledger accounts and balance them.

Sales account

	£		£
SLCA	1,289	Bal b/d	33,291
Bal c/d	33,300	SLCA	1,298
	34,589		34,589
		Bal b/d	33,300

Sales ledger control account

	£		£
Bal b/d	5,925	Sales/suspense	1,298
Sales	1,298	Bal c/d	5,925
	7,223		7,223
Bal b/d	5,925		

Discounts received

	£		£
Suspense	50	Bal b/d	100
Bal c/d	100	PLCA	50
	150		150
		Bal b/d	100

Purchases ledger control account

	£		£
Discounts received	50	Bal b/d	550
Bal c/d	500		
	550		550
		Bal b/d	500

Suspense account

	£		£
Bal b/d	41	Discounts received	50
SLCA	9		
	50		50

■ Redraft the trial balance

Account name	Debit £	Credit £
Cash in hand	1,000	
Cash at bank	2,390	
Capital		10,000
Non-current assets	20,000	
Purchases	13,100	
PLCA		500
Rent	600	
Sales		33,300
SLCA	5,925	
Petty cash	135	
Stationery	200	
Drawings	500	
Discounts allowed	50	
Discounts received		100
~~Suspense~~	~~41~~	-
Revised totals	**43,900**	**43,900**

CHAPTER OVERVIEW

- Some errors in the accounting records will result in an imbalance on the trial balance – these include single entry rather than double entry, a transposition error, a calculation error and a balance being omitted from the trial balance

- There are other errors in the accounting records which will not cause an imbalance on the trial balance – error of original entry, error of omission, error of reversal, error of commission, error of principle, compensating errors

- To find the error or errors when total debits do not agree with total credits on the trial balance: carry out the basic arithmetical checks before examining the detailed double entry

- Calculate the difference on the trial balance and look for this amount or half this amount in the ledger accounts, and check the double entry of this transaction

- If the trial balance does not balance, set up a suspense account to make the debits equal to the credits

- Once the errors have been determined:

    - Work out what the original, incorrect double entry was (including effective entries in the suspense account)

    - Draft journal entries to (i) reverse the incorrect entries, including those to the suspense account and (ii) make the correct entries

    - Enter the journals to clear the suspense account then

    - Redraft the trial balance

Keywords

Transposition error – the digits in a number are transposed (swapped round)

Calculation error – a mistake is made in calculating the balance on a ledger account

Error of original entry – both the debit and credit entries in the ledgers have been made at the wrong amount

Error of omission – both the debit and credit entries have been omitted from the ledger accounts

Error of reversal – the debit and credit entries have been reversed in the ledger accounts

Error of commission – the double entry is arithmetically correct but one of the entries has been made to the wrong account, though an account of the correct type

Error of principle – the double entry is arithmetically correct but one of the entries has been to the wrong type of account

Compensating error – two separate errors that completely cancel each other out

Suspense account – opened in order to make the balances on a trial balance equal while the reason for the imbalance is discovered and corrected

TEST YOUR LEARNING

Test 1

A payment for rent of £4,300 has been entered into the cash book and the rent account as £3,400. What type of error is this?

Test 2

The sales returns for a period of £1,276 have been entered into the ledger accounts as:

DR   Sales ledger control
CR   Sales returns

What type of error has taken place?

Test 3

A credit note from supplier Hamish & Co has been debited to the account of C Hamish. What type of error is this?

Test 4

The total of the debit balances on a trial balance are £325,778 and the total of the credit balances are £326,048. What would be one of the first types of error that you might look for?

Test 5

The total of the debit balances on a trial balance was £452,362 and the credit side totalled £450,241. What is the balance on the suspense account?

£		Credit balance/ Debit balance

Test 6

The total of the debit balances on a trial balance was £184,266 and the credit side totalled £181,278. The following errors were discovered:

(a) A receipt of £3,250 from a customer was recorded in the Cash Book correctly but in the sales ledger control account as £2,350

(b) When the discounts allowed account was being balanced prior to its entry in the trial balance (TB) it was overcast by £1,000

(c) Discounts received of £450 were debited to the discounts received account and credited to the purchases ledger control account

(d) Purchases returns of £1,088 had been correctly entered in the purchases ledger control account but had been omitted from the purchases returns account

Draft journal entries for each of these errors and show how the suspense account is cleared.

Account name	Amount £	Debit ✓	Credit ✓

Suspense account

	£		£
	———		———
	———		———

Test 7

Alvescot Co's trial balance was extracted and did not balance. The debit column of the trial balance totalled £52,673 and the credit column totalled £61,920.

(a) What entry would be made in the suspense account to balance the trial balance?

Account name	Amount £	Debit ✓	Credit ✓
Suspense			

It is important to understand the types of error that are disclosed by the trial balance and those that are not.

(b) Show which of the errors below are, or are not, disclosed by the trial balance.

Error in the general ledger	Error disclosed by the trial balance ✓	Error NOT disclosed by the trial balance ✓
Calculating the balance on a ledger account incorrectly by £100		
Recording a supplier's credit note for £800 at £80 in the purchases returns day book.		
Forgetting to include the £200 balance on the petty cash book in the trial balance		
Making the debit entry for a cash sale of £150 but not the credit entry		
Failing to record a petty cash purchase of food for £20 (no VAT)		
For a purchase of stationery on credit, debiting the PLCA and crediting the stationery account		

Test 8

The initial trial balance of a business includes a suspense account with a balance of £1,000.

The error has been traced to the purchases day book shown below.

Purchases Day Book

Date 20XX	Details	Invoice number	Total £	VAT £	Net £
31 Oct	Hughson Ltd	1902	1,740	290	1,450
31 Oct	Rundle Co	43902	432	72	360
31 Oct	Westcot Jenks	6327	2,562	427	2,135
	Totals		4,734	789	4,945

(a) Identify the error and, using the picklist of account names, record the journal entries needed in the general ledger to:

(i) Remove the amount entered incorrectly

Account name	Amount £	Debit ✓	Credit ✓

(ii) Record the correct entry

Account name	Amount £	Debit ✓	Credit ✓

(iii) Remove the suspense account balance

Account name	Amount £	Debit ✓	Credit ✓

Picklist of account names:

Hughson Ltd
Purchases
Purchases day book
Purchases ledger control
Purchases returns
Purchases returns day book
Rundle Co

Sales
Sales day book
Sales ledger control
Sales returns
Sales returns day book
Suspense
VAT
Westcot Jenks

(b) An entry to record purchases of goods on credit for £980 (no VAT) has been reversed. Using the picklist of account names, record the journal entries needed in the general ledger to:

(i) Remove the incorrect entries

Account name	Amount £	Debit ✓	Credit ✓

(ii) Record the correct entries

Account name	Amount £	Debit ✓	Credit ✓

Picklist of account names:

Bank
Cash
Purchases
Purchases ledger control
Sales
Sales ledger control
Suspense
VAT

Test 9

The initial trial balance of a business included a suspense account. All the bookkeeping errors have now been traced and the journal entries shown below have been recorded.

Journal entries

Account name	Debit £	Credit £
Discounts allowed	149	
Discounts received		149
Suspense	256	
Purchases		256
Motor expenses	893	
Suspense		893

Post the journal entries to the general ledger accounts. Dates are not required.

Purchases

Details	Amount £	Details	Amount £

Motor expenses

Details	Amount £	Details	Amount £

Suspense

Details	Amount £	Details	Amount £
Balance b/d	637		

Discounts received

Details	Amount £	Details	Amount £

Discounts allowed

Details	Amount £	Details	Amount £

Picklist of account names:

Balance b/d
Discounts allowed
Discounts received
Motor expenses
Purchases
Suspense

Test 10

On 31 March a business extracted an initial trial balance which did not balance, and a suspense account was opened. On 1 April journal entries were prepared to correct the errors that had been found, and clear the suspense account. The list of balances in the initial trial balance, and the journal entries to correct the errors, are shown below. The journals had not yet been entered when the account balances were extracted.

Taking into account the journal entries, which will clear the suspense account, re-draft the trial balance by placing the figures in the debit or credit column.

	Balances extracted on 31 March £	Balances at 1 April	
		Debit £	Credit £
Machinery	52,910		
Fixtures and fittings	17,835		
Computers	9,920		
Cash at bank	2,367		
Petty cash	250		
Sales ledger control	115,438		
Purchases ledger control	34,290		
VAT owing to HM Revenue and Customs	2,337		
Capital	52,254		
Sales	270,256		
Purchases	78,309		
Purchases returns	3,203		
Wages	54,219		
Maintenance expenses	3,445		
Administration expenses	10,254		
Marketing expenses	6,287		
Premises expenses	15,244		
Discounts received	4,278		
Discounts allowed	1,288		
Suspense account (credit balance)	1,148		
Totals			

Journal entries

Account name	Debit £	Credit £
Discounts allowed		1,359
Suspense	1,359	
Discounts allowed	1,539	
Suspense		1,539

Account name	Debit £	Credit £
Purchases ledger control		664
Suspense	664	
Purchases ledger control		664
Suspense	664	

chapter 8:
THE BANKING PROCESS

chapter coverage 📖

In this final chapter we cover how the banking system works and the way in which receipts are checked. The topics covered are:

- ✍ Banking services
- ✍ How the clearing system works
- ✍ Banking documentation
- ✍ Checking payments received
- ✍ Paying in cash and cheques to the bank
- ✍ Automated payments and receipts

BANKING SERVICES

Most people and businesses have a bank account so that they do not have to keep all their money only as cash. The problems with cash are that:

- It poses a security risk
- It earns no interest
- It is difficult to use as a means of payment except in face-to-face transactions

Due to immense competition between the retail banks in recent years they now offer a vast array of services to customers. These services fall into four main categories:

HOLDING money for customers	Making PAYMENTS for customers
Providing LOANS	OTHER services

Competition in all banking services comes from mutual building societies, which historically had concentrated only on:

- Holding money for customers in savings accounts, and
- Providing mortgage loans

While some smaller building societies still focus only on these areas, perhaps providing foreign currency and insurance services in addition, the bigger ones are in all areas of banking services, including overdrafts, personal loans credit cards, business banking and safe custody.

Holding of money

Most banks offer a variety of different types of bank account to suit all customers' needs. The most commonly used is a CURRENT ACCOUNT (sometimes called a CHEQUE ACCOUNT) whereby customers pay money into the account and can then draw on it. Customers can access their money by:

- Writing cheques
- Withdrawing cash at the counter or from Automatic Teller Machines (ATMs)
- Arranging automated payments from the account
- Using their debit card in a shop or over the phone

Many current accounts attract a (low) rate of interest on a positive balance.

A customer can also choose to save money at a higher interest rate by paying money into a DEPOSIT ACCOUNT. This will not normally have a cheque book or a debit card but will generally pay a higher rate of interest than a current account. Some deposit accounts pay even higher rates of interest but restrict the movement of funds, for example a withdrawal of money may require one month's notice.

Making payments

Banks have a duty to pay cheques that are correctly written out by customers provided they have enough funds in their account. If they do not have sufficient funds then banks may dishonour or return cheques unpaid. The person who took the cheque in settlement of a debt must then find another way to obtain payment from the bank's customer.

To overcome this uncertainty many banks, in return for a fee, will provide customers with a BANK DRAFT, which is essentially a non-cancellable cheque drawn on the bank rather than the customer's account. A bank draft gives the recipient of it complete confidence that they will receive payment when it is presented to the bank. It is therefore often used in large transactions between individuals, for instance when one person (A) buys a car from another (B): A hands B the draft and drives the car away, which B is happy to allow as B knows that the draft will be honoured by the bank on which it is drawn.

The banks also offer the service of making payments out of an account by other means such as standing orders, direct debits, BACS, CHAPS and other automated payments, including online transfers. The banks must collect payment for cheques that the customer pays into the bank account, and will accept transfers from other bank accounts.

Providing loans

Banks can provide loans to both personal and business customers, in a number of different ways.

Many current accounts have an agreed OVERDRAFT FACILITY whereby a customer can authorise payments for more than the balance on the account up to a certain amount and these will still be paid. A fairly high rate of interest is usually charged for this facility.

A further method by which banks (and other financial institutions) can provide short-term loans to customers is by issuing CREDIT CARDS. These allow customers to make purchases and to defer payment until some future time. The balance on the credit card does not have to be paid off each month, only a minimum sum is necessary. Any outstanding balances on these credit card accounts usually attract a very high rate of interest.

Banks can provide medium- to long-term LOANS to both personal and business customers with various terms and conditions and repayment terms.

Banks also provide MORTGAGES, which are long-term loans, eg over 25 years, in order for the customer to purchase a property. The mortgage is secured on the property. This means that if the loan is not repaid for some reason then the bank ultimately has an enforceable right to sell the property in order to get its money back.

Other services

Banks also provide a number of other services that can be of use to businesses:

- Provision of a nightsafe (so the business can deposit cash and cheques at the bank even after it has closed for the day)
- Supplying foreign currency
- Making safe custody boxes available for safekeeping of valuable items such as documents
- Investment advice
- Insurance products
- Corporate credit cards

Task 1

A sole trader is setting up in business with £50,000. He hopes that only £30,000 of this will be initially required for trading transactions and that the remainder can be saved for future growth. What type of bank account would be best suited for the remaining £20,000 for this trader?

THE CLEARING SYSTEM

If you write out a cheque then the eventual outcome of this is that the money will be paid out of your bank account by your bank and paid into the account of the payee of the cheque. However, in order for this to happen to the many thousands of cheques that are written each day a complex system is in operation. This CLEARING SYSTEM was set up by the major banks and it generally means that it takes three working days for a cheque paid into a bank account to clear into that account and therefore to be available as funds that can be drawn on.

HOW IT WORKS

Southfield Electrical banks with the First National Bank in Benham. It has recently written and sent out two cheques drawn on its bank account to suppliers:

- Cheque number 100362 to Harris Enterprises
- Cheque number 100363 to Simons Bros

Day 1

Harris Enterprises receives cheque 100362 and pays it into its own bank, the First National Bank branch in Winnish.

Simons Bros receives cheque 100363 and pays it into its own bank, the National Eastern Bank in Benham.

Each bank sorts all the cheques paid in that day by the bank on which each cheque is drawn, and they are processed and coded.

First National Bank, Winnish sends all the cheques paid in during the day, including 100362, to the First National Bank clearing department in London.

National Eastern Bank, Benham sends all the cheques paid in during the day, including 100363, to the National Eastern Bank clearing department in London.

Day 2

Both banks' clearing departments receive all the cheques paid into their branches the previous day and these sort them by the bank on which each cheque is drawn.

The First National Bank clearing department sends cheque 100362 directly to the Benham branch of First National Bank (where Southfield Electrical has its account).

The National Eastern Bank clearing department sends cheque 100363 to the Central Clearing House (CCH), as it is a cheque that has been drawn on another bank (First National Bank).

CCH arranges for the banks to swap cheques and agree any differences in value (known as operational balances) to be paid over the following day.

Cheque 100363 is then sent to the clearing department of the First National Bank in London and the clearing department sends it to the First National branch in Benham (where Southfield Electrical has its account).

Day 3

The Benham branch of First National Bank checks that cheques 100362 and 100363 are valid and then pays them out of Southfield's current account. The accounts of Harris Enterprises and Simons Bros, at (First National Bank, Winnish and National Eastern Bank, Benham respectively) are credited with cleared funds.

It is at this point that a cheque may be dishonoured by the paying bank (First National Bank, Benham in this case) because, for instance, there may be insufficient funds in the drawer's (Southfield) account. A dishonoured cheque is sent back to the payee's bank so that the payee can pursue payment in some

other way. For this reason dishonoured cheques are often called returned cheques.

The head offices of First National Bank and National Eastern Bank clear any operational balances outstanding between the two banks.

To summarise this long and complex process let us look at the journey that cheque number 100363 made in those three days.

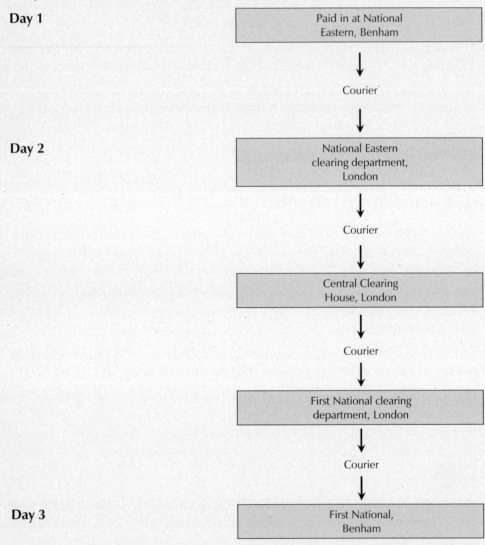

Day 1

Paid in at National Eastern, Benham

Courier

Day 2

National Eastern clearing department, London

Courier

Central Clearing House, London

Courier

First National clearing department, London

Courier

Day 3

First National, Benham

Cheque paid out of Southfield's account

Cleared funds paid into Simons Bros account

Operational balances between banks cleared

RETAINING BANKING DOCUMENTATION

We have seen throughout this text that, when dealing with its bank, a business will handle a large number of different types of document. They are all important and document retention should therefore be dealt with carefully, but for reasons of tax compliance and because they are used as primary documents which are recorded in the books of prime entry, the following documentation should be retained for at least six years:

- Cheque stubs
- Paying-in slip stubs
- Bank statements
- Standing order and direct debit schedules
- Instructions to make BACS and CHAPS payments

We have seen some of the details of these in Chapter 2. In this chapter we concentrate on checking payments received to ensure they are valid.

CHECKING PAYMENTS BY CHEQUE

In Chapter 2 we saw the types of check that a business should carry out when it receives a payment from a customer by cheque.

Cheques will be phased out as a payment method in the UK by 2018 but are currently still used in many transactions between individuals and, sometimes, between individuals and businesses.

When a customer sends in a cheque in payment of their debt it is important to check the details carefully:

- Check that there is a signature on the cheque and that this agrees with the account name printed on the cheque, if it is a personal cheque. This may be difficult however if the signature is unreadable, as is often the case!

- Check that the cheque has been completed properly in terms of payee name, the date, and that the words and figures agree with each other

CHECKING PAYMENTS BY CREDIT CARD

A further common method of paying for goods is by CREDIT CARD. A customer must apply to a credit card company for a credit card, and upon its issue a credit limit (which cannot be exceeded) is set for the customer. The customer can pay for goods and services with the credit card at outlets that accept credit card payments. At the end of each month the customer is sent a statement showing all of the purchases on the credit card for the month; the total outstanding on the credit card; the minimum payment required and the date by which payment

should reach the credit card company. The customer can then choose whether to pay off the full amount outstanding on the card or only part of it. Any unpaid outstanding amount will have interest charged on it which will appear on the next credit card statement.

A retailer which accepts payment by credit card will have to pay the credit card company a small percentage (normally about 1.25%) for the right to do so.

A typical credit card is shown below.

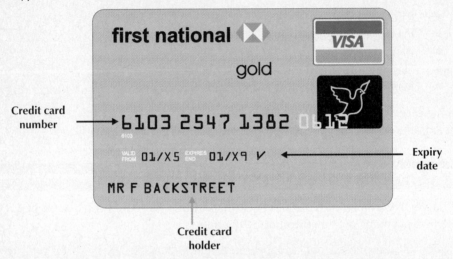

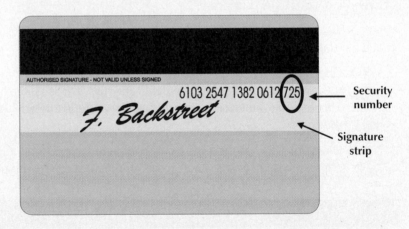

When accepting a credit card as payment the retailer will usually process it through an electronic swipe machine attached to the till, although some may still use a mechanical imprinter.

Electronic payment by credit card

On an electronic till the credit card is 'swiped' through the machine and the credit card details are read by the machine off the strip on the back of the card. These details are then transferred to the receipt produced by the till and the cardholder verifies the transaction by keying-in their personal identification number (PIN) or, rarely, by signing the slip.

Electronic till voucher

When credit cards are used in an electronic swipe machine the following checks should be carried out (most are carried out automatically by the machine):

- Run your finger over the signature strip to check that the card has not been tampered with

- Swipe the card through the machine – the machine will then automatically check that the card has not expired or is not stolen

- The goods details and total are entered into the swipe machine – if the machine is online with the credit card company the machine will automatically authorise the transaction and provide the authorisation code (it will also check that the customer has not exceeded the credit

card limit). If the machine is not online, or if the FLOOR LIMIT for how much the retailer can process in a single transaction is exceeded, then a telephone call will be required for an authorisation code

- The customer enters their PIN number into the keypad to confirm the transaction and their identity

- A two-part voucher or receipt is produced by the machine. The top copy of the voucher is given to the customer and the other copy is retained by the retailer

If an electronic swipe machine is used for credit card sales then normally the amount of the sale is automatically charged to the customer's credit card and credited to the retailer's account by electronic funds transfer at point of sale (EFTPOS), so there is no need to pay these vouchers into the bank.

Telephone payment by credit card

If a business takes credit card payments over the phone from customers it is important that the correct information is obtained from the customer. With reference to the credit card he or she should be asked for:

- The credit card account number embossed as a 16 digit number across the front of the card

- The expiry date on the card, for instance 05/12

- The exact name of the cardholder as embossed on the front of the card

- The last three digits of the number printed on the signature strip on the reverse of the card – this is the SECURITY NUMBER of the card

There is no need to ask for the 'valid from' date nor for the issue number which is printed on the front of the card in some cases.

It is completely inappropriate to ask the customer for either the credit limit on the credit card account or for the Personal Identification Number (PIN) which the customer uses when making cash withdrawals at ATMs or payments in shops. This is highly confidential information which the business has no right or need to know.

Mechanical imprinter payments by credit card

The mechanical imprinter is where the card is laid flat in the imprinter and the blank credit card voucher is placed on top of it. The embossed details on the card are then transferred onto the voucher by passing the top part of the imprinter over the receipt and card. This form of processing is now extremely rare.

Mechanical imprinter voucher

The procedure and checks that should be carried out when using a mechanical imprinter are as follows:

- Check that the signature strip has not been tampered with, and check any list of known lost and stolen cards that is available

- Place the card and voucher on the imprinter and pass the top of the imprinter over both to transfer the card details onto the voucher

- Enter the date, the type of goods or service being sold and the total amount of the sale on the voucher, checking that the floor limit for transactions is not exceeded

- The customer should be asked to check the amount on the voucher and to sign it – check that the signature is the same as that on the back of the card

- The top copy of the voucher is then given to the customer and the carbons removed from between the other copies which are retained by the retailer

We shall see a little later how these vouchers are paid into the bank by the business.

CHECKING PAYMENTS BY DEBIT CARD

Most banks provide their customers with a DEBIT CARD, eg Switch, Electron and Delta cards. These look very similar to credit cards but their purpose is very different. When a debit card is used to pay for a transaction, the amount of the

sale is automatically debited to the customer's bank account by EFTPOS and credited to the retailer's bank account.

The procedure for accepting a debit card as payment in an electronic transaction is similar to that for a credit card:

- The card should be checked to ensure that it has not been tampered with and that the date is before the expiry date on the card

- The card is swiped through the machine and the customer's bank account is checked to ensure that the funds are available

- The customer enters their PIN number into the retailer's keypad to verify their identity

- The machine provides a two-part receipt and the customer is given the top copy of the voucher while the retailer retains the other copy

If a business takes debit card payments over the phone from customers, the same information is required from the customer as for a credit card transaction: the debit card account number, the expiry date, the exact name of the cardholder on the front of the card and the security number. In addition, for some debit cards the issue number and 'valid from' date is required. It is inappropriate to ask the customer for any other information, particularly the PIN.

Task 2

What is the essential difference between a credit card and a debit card?

PAYING IN CASH AND CHEQUES TO THE BANK

Many businesses, and in particular retailers, receive payments from their customers in cash. As we saw in Chapter 2 cash and cheques are paid into the bank using a PAYING-IN SLIP. It is important that these receipts are paid in to the bank promptly for two reasons:

- Money kept on the premises is a security risk

- Money should be paid into the bank as soon as possible in order to increase the bank balance and earn more interest or reduce the overdraft and thereby the interest charged

When actually transporting cash to the bank, personal security must be considered. It might be advisable for two members of staff to take the money together or to employ a security firm if the amount of cash is very large. It is also advisable to change the route and timing of the bank visits on a regular basis.

BPP
LEARNING MEDIA

Most importantly, the details of bank paying-in visits must be treated with the highest confidentiality.

Often a business, particularly a retail business, will need to pay money into the bank when the bank itself is shut. Many bank branches provide a nightsafe for such eventualities. A nightsafe is normally a safe with access from the outer wall of the bank where the money and paying-in slip can be placed in a special wallet which travels down a chute into the bank itself.

PAYING IN CREDIT CARD VOUCHERS TO THE BANK

When a business makes sales which are paid for by credit card and a mechanical imprinter is used, the vouchers must be paid into the bank in just the same way as cheques. Before entering any credit card voucher details on the bank's paying-in slip a separate credit card voucher RETAILER SUMMARY must be completed.

This is shown below:

- Imprint the Summary with the retailer's card

- The back of the Summary must be completed first showing the amount of each voucher, and these amounts are then totalled

- The number and total of the sales vouchers are then entered onto the front of the Summary

- The number and total of any refund vouchers are also entered on the front of the Summary

- The Summary is then dated, totalled and signed

- The Summary is a three-part document and the top two copies are kept by the retailer, the bottom copy is placed in front of the sales vouchers and any refund vouchers and they are all placed in a clear plastic envelope

- The vouchers are then paid into the bank by including the total as part of the cheques total on the paying-in slip. The total of the vouchers must also be included in the cheque details on the back of the paying-in slip

	£	p	
1	23	50	
2	102	00	
3	62	50	
4	18	99	
5			
6			
7			
8			
9			
10			
11			
12			
13			
14			
15			
16			
17			
18			
19			
20			
Total	206	99	Carried Overleaf

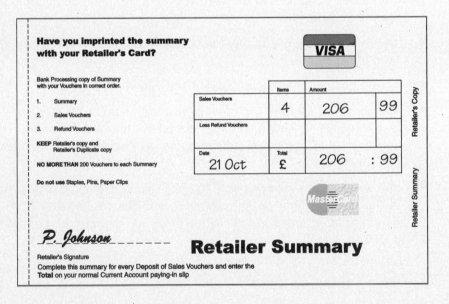

Have you imprinted the summary with your Retailer's Card?

VISA

Bank Processing copy of Summary
with your Vouchers in correct order.

1. Summary
2. Sales Vouchers
3. Refund Vouchers

KEEP Retailer's copy and
Retailer's Duplicate copy

NO MORE THAN 200 Vouchers to each Summary

Do not use Staples, Pins, Paper Clips

	Items	Amount	
Sales Vouchers	4	206	99
Less Refund Vouchers			
Date 21 Oct	Total £	206	: 99

MasterCard

Retailer's Copy

Retailer Summary

P. Johnson

Retailer's Signature

Retailer Summary

Complete this summary for every Deposit of Sales Vouchers and enter the
Total on your normal Current Account paying-in slip

Task 3

If money is paid into a bank current account this will appear as a debit/credit
on the bank statement.

CHECKING AUTOMATED PAYMENTS AND RECEIPTS

Automated payments by the business take the form of direct debits, standing orders and BACS or CHAPS payments. These should be agreed from the bank statement to the business's direct debit schedules, standing order schedules, and BACS/CHAPS instructions, and to remittance advices prepared by the business and sent to the supplier.

Automated receipts from customers should be agreed to remittance advices from the customer, plus the sales ledger account.

CHAPTER OVERVIEW

- Banks provide a variety of different types of account that customers can use such as current accounts and deposit accounts

- Banks have a duty to pay cheques that customers have correctly drawn up provided that there are enough funds in the customer's account

- Banks must honour a bank draft drawn on the bank by itself at its customer's request

- Banks provide overdraft facilities to customers, credit cards, loans and mortgages

- In the clearing system all cheques paid into banks in a day are sorted by bank, swapped between the banks and any differences paid from bank to bank – the system means that it takes three working days for a cheque to clear after being paid into a bank

- When a business accepts a credit card as payment this may be processed either through an electronic swipe machine or – rarely – through a mechanical imprinter. An electronic swipe machine will automatically check that the card has not expired/been stolen and, if it is online, it will also check that the customer's credit card limit has not been exceeded

- Payments by debit card are automatically debited to the customer's bank account and credited to the business's bank account

- Cheques and cash receipts should be paid into the bank promptly. Great care must be taken when taking large amounts of cash to the bank – ideally two people should be taking the money and using varying routes at different times of day

- Credit card vouchers, produced when using a mechanical imprinter, need to be paid into the bank on a paying-in slip using a credit card voucher Retailer Summary – the back of this should be completed with the total of each credit card voucher, the final total is then transferred to the front of the summary and it is dated, signed and totalled

- Automated payments by the business eg direct debits, standing orders, BACS/CHAPS payments should be checked from the bank statement to the business's direct debit and standing order schedule, BACS/CHAPS instructions and remittance advices.

- Automated receipts from customers should be agreed to the remittance advice from the customer and the sales ledger.

Keywords

Current account – a bank account designed to have money withdrawn by cheque or other methods on a regular basis

Deposit account – an account from which it is not intended to make regular withdrawals (a savings account)

Bank draft – non-cancellable cheque drawn on the bank rather than the customer's account

Overdraft facility – an agreement that the customer can withdraw more money from the account than they have in it, up to a certain limit

Credit card – a card which allows the customer to purchase goods and services now but gives them flexibility as to when they repay the credit card company

Loan – an advance from a bank on which interest will be charged and repayment conditions laid down

Mortgage – a long-term loan for purchase of a property under which the property serves as security for the loan

Clearing system – the system set up by the major banks to deal with the payment of cheques

Credit card security number – three digit security number printed at the signature ship on the reverse of a credit card

Floor limit – the amount up to which a business can process in a single credit card transaction

Debit card – a card which allows the customer to purchase goods and services where the sale is automatically debited to the customer's bank account and credited to the supplier's bank account

Retailer summary – a pre-printed document that must be filled in on the front and back detailing the credit card vouchers that are being paid into the bank

TEST YOUR LEARNING

Test 1

On a bank statement, would each of the following be described as a debit or a credit entry or balance?

	Debit entry/balance ✓	Credit entry/balance ✓
Money paid into the account		
Cheques paid out of the account		
An overdraft balance		

Test 2

Identify whether each of the statements below is True or False.

	True ✓	False ✓
A bank draft cannot be cancelled once it has been issued		
Any customer who pays with a debit card is taking out credit with its bank as a result		

ANSWERS TO CHAPTER TASKS

CHAPTER 1 Petty cash procedures

1 £4.80   VAT = £4.00 × 1.2   =   £4.80

2 VAT   = £9.36 × 20/120 =   £1.56

   Net amount   = £9.36 – 1.56   =   £7.80

3 Petty cash vouchers plus cash should equal imprest amount

   £103.69 + £36.31 = £140, this is below the imprest amount of £150 (ie too little cash)

   Possible reasons:

   ▪ Cash has been removed from the petty cash box without being supported by an authorised petty cash voucher

   ▪ Too much cash might have been given to a petty cash claimant and not noticed by either the petty cashier or the claimant

   ▪ A petty cash voucher may be missing (check the sequential numbering)

   ▪ A top-up has been recorded but the cash was not placed in the petty cash box

4 £41.30

CHAPTER 2 Maintaining the cash book

1 A credit

CHAPTER 3 Bank reconciliations

1 Debit side of the cash book

2 Credit side of the cash book

3 As an unpresented cheque

4 Credit

5 £1,441.93 debit balance

BPP
LEARNING MEDIA

CHAPTER 4   Introduction to control accounts

1   Debit Sales ledger control

    Credit Sales/VAT

2   Debit Purchases/VAT

    Credit Purchases ledger control

CHAPTER 5   Preparing and reconciling control accounts

1   Debit Irrecoverable debts expense

    Debit VAT control

    Credit Sales ledger control

2   The sales ledger control account

3   If the total of the discounts allowed column from the Cash Receipts Book of £300 was not posted for a period, this would be adjusted for in the sales ledger control account reconciliation by ~~adding £300 to~~/subtracting £300 from the SLCA balance/~~total of list of balances.~~

4   The purchases ledger control account

5   An invoice for £200 was entered into the individual account in the purchases ledger on the wrong side of the account. This would be adjusted for in the purchases ledger control account reconciliation by adding £400 to/~~subtracting £400 from the purchases ledger control account~~/the list of purchases ledger balances.

CHAPTER 6   The journal

1   £294.50 (400.00 – 69.00 – 34.00 – 2.50)

2   PAYE/NIC payable account = £143 (69 + 33 + 41)

    Wages expense account = £441 (400 + 41)

CHAPTER 7   Errors and the trial balance

1   A sales invoice recorded in the sales day book at £1,678 has been correctly recorded in the sales ledger control account but has been entered into the sales account as £1,768. This is a ~~single~~ entry/transposition-~~balancing/balance omission~~ error.

2   A commission error

3

Account name	Amount £	Debit	Credit
Bank	1,250		✓
Sales ledger control	1,250		✓
Suspense	2,500	✓	
Bank	1,250	✓	
Sales ledger control	1,250		✓

CHAPTER 8   The banking process

1   Deposit account

2   Debit cards immediately reduce the bank account balance of the customer. Credit is given for credit cards.

3   Credit

TEST YOUR LEARNING – ANSWERS

CHAPTER 1   Petty cash procedures

Test 1

1.1   An imprest petty cash system is one where the amount of the topped up petty cash float at the start of each period is:

Always the same

1.2   Amounts that have been paid out for authorised expenditure are represented in the petty cash box by

Petty cash vouchers

1.3   At the end of the period the total of the

Petty cash vouchers

in the petty cash box is the amount needed to restore the petty cash box to the imprest amount.

Test 2

PETTY CASH VOUCHER		
Number:	0624	
Date:	20 October	
	Details:	
Paper	£	4.50
Envelopes	£	2.35
Net	£	6.85
VAT	£	1.37
Total	£	8.22

221

				£
Paper VAT	=	£5.40 × 20/120	=	0.90
Envelopes VAT	=	£2.82 × 20/120	=	0.47
Total VAT				1.37
Paper net	=	£5.40 – £0.90	=	4.50
Envelopes net	=	£2.82 – £0.47	=	2.35

Test 3

£	89.46

Test 4

RECEIPTS			PAYMENTS								
Date	Details	Amount £	Date	Details	Voucher number	Total £	VAT £	Post £	Travel £	Sundry office £	Misc £
20 Oct	Bank	150.00	24 Oct	Train fare	771	14.00			14.00		
			24 Oct	Postage	772	18.60		18.60			
			24 Oct	Envelopes	773	16.80	2.80			14.00	
			24 Oct	Window cleaner	774	20.00					20.00
			24 Oct	Pens/paper	775	18.90	3.15			15.75	
			24 Oct	Postage	776	5.46		5.46			
			24 Oct	Taxi fare	777	9.60	1.60		8.00		
			24 Oct	Computer discs	778	28.20	4.70			23.50	
						131.56	12.25	24.06	22.00	53.25	20.00
			Balance c/d			18.44					
		150.00				150.00					
Balance b/d		18.44									
Bank top-up		131.56									

Test 5

Petty Cash Book

Debit side		Credit side					
Details	Amount £	Details	Amount £	VAT £	Postage £	Travel £	Motor expenses £
Balance b/f	180.00	Post Office	12.60		12.60		
		Motor Repair Workshop	72.60	12.10			60.50
		Great Eastern Trains	32.00			32.00	
		Balance c/d	62.80				
	180.00		180.00	12.10	12.60	32.00	60.50

Test 6

(a)

Petty cash voucher			Petty cash voucher		
Date: 14/09/XX Number: PC453			Date: 14/09/XX Number: PC454		
Carpet clean in office area			5 reams A4 printer paper		
Net	£	62.90	Net	£	14.50
VAT	£	12.58	VAT	£	2.90
Gross	£	75.48	Gross	£	17.40

(b)

Amount in petty cash box	£	79.45
Balance on petty cash account	£	78.60
Difference	£	0.85

(c)

Petty cash reimbursement		
Date: 30/09/20XX		
Amount required to restore the cash in the petty cash box	£	137.68

223

CHAPTER 2   Maintaining the cash book

Test 1

Date	Details	Discounts allowed £	Cash £	Bank £	VAT £	Cash sales £	Sales ledger £
23 Jan	Hoppers Ltd	16.86		545.14			545.14
23 Jan	Superior Products			116.70			116.70
24 Jan	Cash sales		128.4		21.41	107.05	
24 Jan	Esporta Leisure	11.36		367.20			367.20
25 Jan	Cash sales		86.4		14.40	72.00	
27 Jan	Body Perfect	21.86		706.64			706.64
27 Jan	Cash sales		58.8		9.80	49.00	
27 Jan	Langans Beauty			267.90			267.90
		50.08	273.6	2,003.58	45.61	228.05	2,003.58

Cross-cast check:

	£
Sales ledger	2,003.58
Cash sales	228.05
VAT	45.61
Total	2,277.24
Cash receipts	273.66
Bank receipts	2,003.58
	2,277.24

Test 2

Double entry for discounts allowed:

DR   Discounts allowed account

CR   Sales ledger control account

Test 3

Date	Details	Cheque No	Discounts received £	Cash £	Bank £	VAT £	Cash purchases £	Purchases ledger £
23 Jan	Trenter Ltd	002144	28.47		1,110.09			1,110.09
23 Jan	Cash purchase			105.60		17.60	88.00	
24 Jan	W J Jones	002145			246.75			246.75
24 Jan	P J Phillips	002146			789.60			789.60
24 Jan	Cash purchase			125.40		20.90	104.50	
25 Jan	Packing Supp	002147	8.04		305.45			305.45
26 Jan	O & P Ltd	002148	18.72		703.87			703.87
27 Jan	Cash purchase			96.00		16.00	80.00	
			55.23	327.00	3,155.76	54.50	272.50	3,155.76

Cross-cast check:

	£
Purchases ledger	3,155.76
Cash purchases	272.50
VAT	54.50
Total	3,482.76
Cash payments	327.00
Cheque payments	3,155.76
	3,482.76

Test 4

Cash balance:

Balance b/f	142.60
Cash received	273.66
Cash paid	(327.00)
Cash banked	(50.00)
Balance c/d	39.26

Bank balance:

Balance b/f (overdraft)	(1,290.00)
Cheques received	2,003.58
Cheques paid	(3,155.76)
Cash banked	50.00
Balance c/d	(2,392.18)

Test 5

(a) **Cash Book – Credit Side**

Details	Discounts £	Cash £	Bank £	VAT £	Purchases ledger £	Cash purchases £	Marketing £
Balance b/f			3,295				
Klimt Supplies		90		15		75	
Patel Trading		342		57		285	
TWE Ltd		83				83	
Western Industries	80		4,278		4,278		
Mountebank Co			564	94			470
Total	80	515	8,137	166	4,278	443	470

(b) **Cash Book – Debit Side**

Details	Discounts £	Cash £	Bank £	Sales ledger £
Balance b/f		792		
Vantage Ltd			1,278	1,278
Marbles Co	15		2,183	2,183
Total	15	792	3,461	3,461

(c)

£	277

(d)

£	–4,676

(e)   Bank balance calculated in (d) above: credit balance

	✓
Debit	
Credit	✓

CHAPTER 3   Bank reconciliations

Test 1

Cash Book – Debit Side

Date	Details	Ref	Discounts allowed £	Bank £	Sales ledger £
30/11	Burser Ltd	SL14	6.49	147.89	147.89
30/11	Crawley Partners	SL23	18.79	448.36	448.36
30/11	Breon & Co	SL15		273.37	273.37
30/11	Kogart Supplies	SL06	42.67	552.68	552.68
30/11	Alex & Bros	SL09		273.46	273.46
30/11	Minicar Ltd	SL22		194.68	194.68

Cash Book – Credit Side

Date	Details	Ref	Discounts received £	Bank £	Purchases ledger £	Sundry £
27/11	SO Loan Fin Rep	ML23		250.00		250.00
30/11	Waterloo Partners 001367	PL21	12.47	336.47	336.47	
30/11	Central Supplies 001368	PL16		169.36	169.36	
30/11	Gen Lon Trade 001369	PL23	10.58	268.38	268.38	
30/11	Eye of the Tiger 001370	PL19		84.50	84.50	
30/11	Chare & Cope 001371	PL27	19.86	447.39	447.39	

Test 2

Cash Book – Debit Side

Date	Details	Ref	Discounts allowed £	Bank £	Sales ledger £
30/11	Burser Ltd	SL14	6.49	147.89✓	147.89
30/11	Crawley Partners	SL23	18.79	448.36✓	448.36
30/11	Breon & Co	SL15		273.37	273.37
30/11	Kogart Supplies	SL06	42.67	552.68✓	552.68
30/11	Alex & Bros	SL09		273.46	273.46
30/11	Minicar Ltd	SL22		194.68	194.68

Cash Book – Credit Side

Date	Details	Ref	Discounts received £	Bank £	Purchases ledger £	Sundry £
27/11	SO Loan Fin Rep	ML23		250.00✓		250.00
30/11	Waterloo Part 001367	PL21	12.47	336.47✓	336.47	
30/11	Central Supp 001368	PL16		169.36	169.36	
30/11	Gen Lon Tr 001369	PL23	10.58	268.38	268.38	
30/11	Eye of the Tig 001370	PL19		84.50	84.50	
30/11	Chare & Cope 001371	PL27	19.86	447.39	447.39	

STATEMENT

NATIONAL DIRECT

THAMES TRADERS

CHEQUE ACCOUNT

Account number: 15-20-40 10267432

Date	Sheet 136	Paid out	Paid in	Balance
23.11	Balance b/f			1,489.65 CR
26.11	Bank Giro Credit - Burser Ltd		52.00	1,541.65 CR
27.11	SO-Loan Finance Repayment	250.00 ✓		1,291.65 CR
28.11	Cheque No 001367	336.47 ✓		
	Credit		147.89 ✓	1,103.07 CR
29.11	Cheque No 001368	196.36		
	Credit		448.36 ✓	1,355.07 CR
30.11	Credit		552.68 ✓	
	Bank charges	34.53		1,873.22 CR

Unticked items in the cash book

- The entries in the debit side of the cash book are cheques that have been paid into the bank but have not yet cleared – they will be agreed to subsequent bank statements

- Cheque no. 001368 – this cheque appeared as £169.36 in the cash book but as £196.36 in the bank statement – this should be checked to the original cheque stub and documentation and if the bank is correct the cash book must be adjusted

- The remaining cheque payments in the cash book have not yet cleared the banking system and they will be checked to subsequent bank statements

Unticked items in the bank statement

- 26/11 bank giro credit from Burser Ltd – this has not been entered into the cash book yet so it must therefore be adjusted to reflect this

- 29/11 – cheque no. 001368 – as has already been noted, this has been incorrectly entered into the cash book and must be adjusted for

- 30/11 – bank charges – these have not been entered into the cash book and this must be adjusted for

Test 3

Cash Book – Debit Side

Date	Details	Ref	Discounts allowed	Bank	Sales ledger
			£	£	£
30/11	Burser Ltd	SL14	6.49	147.89✓	147.89
30/11	Crawley Partners	SL23	18.79	448.36✓	448.36
30/11	Breon & Co	SL15		273.37	273.37
30/11	Kogart Supplies	SL06	42.67	552.68✓	552.68
30/11	Alex & Bros	SL09		273.46	273.46
30/11	Minicar Ltd	SL22		194.68	194.68
30/11	Burser Ltd BGC	SL14		52.00✓	52.00
			67.95	1,942.44	1,942.44

Cash Book – Credit Side

Date	Details	Ref	Discounts received £	Bank £	Purchases ledger £	Sundry £
27/11	SO Loan Fin Rep	ML23		250.00✓		250.00
30/11	Waterloo Part 001367	PL21	12.47	336.47✓	336.47	
30/11	Central Supp 001368	PL16		169.36✓	169.36	
30/11	Gen Lon Tr 001369	PL23	10.58	268.38	268.38	
30/11	Eye of the Tig 001370	PL19		84.50	84.50	
30/11	Chare & Cope 001371	PL27	19.86	447.39	447.39	
30/11	Adjustment to 001368	PL16		27.00✓	27.00	
30/11	Bank charges	GL		34.53✓		34.53
			42.91	1,617.63	1,333.10	284.53

Note that the amount £169.36 (cheque no. 1368) can now be ticked because the adjustment of £27 means that both entries total the amount (£196.36) ticked on the bank statement.

Test 4

	£
Opening balance	1,489.65
Add: receipts for the period	1,942.44
Less: payments for the period	(1,617.63)
Bank account trial balance figure at 30 November	1,814.46

Test 5

Bank reconciliation statement as at 30 November

	£
Balance per bank statement	1,873.22
Add:	
Breon & Co	273.37
Alex & Bros	273.46
Minicar Ltd	194.68
Total to add:	741.51
Less:	
001369	268.38
001370	84.50
001371	447.39
Total to subtract:	800.27)
Balance as per cash book	1,814.46

Test 6

Cash Book

Date 20XX	Details	Bank £	Date 20XX	Cheque number	Details	Bank £
01 Feb	Balance b/f	6,230	01 Feb	003252	Jeggers Ltd	2,567
20 Feb	Straightens Co	2,228	01 Feb	003253	Short & Fell	333
21 Feb	Plumpers	925	01 Feb	003254	Rastop Ltd	1,006
22 Feb	Eastern Supplies	1,743	01 Feb	003255	A & D Trading	966
09 Feb	Branthill Co	1,559	02 Feb	003256	Jesmond Warr	2,309
			02 Feb	003257	Nistral Ltd	3,775
			13 Feb	003258	Simpsons	449
			13 Feb		AxDC	250
			18 Feb		Trust Insurance	325
			20 Feb		Bank charges	14
			22 Feb		Interest charge	56
			23 Feb		Balance c/d	635
		12,685				12,685
24 Feb	Balance b/d	635				

Bank reconciliation statement as at 23 Feb 20XX

Balance per bank statement		£	725
Add:			
Name:	Plumpers	£	925
Name:	Eastern Supplies	£	1,743
Total to add		£	2,668
Less:			
Name:	Jesmond Warr	£	2,309
Name:	Simpsons	£	449
Total to subtract		£	2,758
Balance as per cash book		£	635

CHAPTER 4   Introduction to control accounts

Test 1

	Bank DR/CR	SLCA DR/CR	PLCA DR/CR	VAT DR/CR	Sales DR/CR	Purchases returns DR/CR	Discounts received DR/CR	Discounts allowed DR/CR
Gross sales		DR		CR	CR			
Gross purchases returns			DR	CR		CR		
Discounts allowed		CR						DR
Discounts received			DR				CR	
Gross payments from cash customers	DR			CR	CR			
Payments to credit suppliers	CR		DR					

Test 2

General ledger

Sales ledger control account

	£		£
Balance b/f	1,216.26	Bank	1,078.97
Sales	1,636.20	Discounts allowed	8.73
		Balance c/d	1,764.76
	2,852.46		2,852.46
Balance b/d	1,764.76		

Sales ledger

Virgo Partners

	£		£
Balance b/f	227.58	CB	117.38
SDB	96.72		
SDB	214.44	Balance c/d	421.36
	538.74		538.74
Balance b/d	421.36		

McGowan & Sons

	£		£
Balance b/f	552.73	CB	552.73
SDB	595.08	Balance c/d	595.08
	1,147.81		1,147.81
Balance b/d	595.08		

J J Westrope

	£		£
Balance b/f	317.59	CRB	308.86
SDB	167.40	CRB – discount	8.73
SDB	277.32	Balance c/d	444.72
	762.31		762.31
Balance b/d	444.72		

Jacks Ltd

	£		£
Balance b/f	118.36	CRB	100.00
SDB	107.64		
SDB	177.60	Balance c/d	303.60
	403.60		403.60
Balance b/d	303.60		

Reconciliation

	£
Sales ledger control account balance as at 31 May	1,764.76
Total of sales ledger accounts as at 31 May (see workings)	1,764.76
Difference	0

Workings

	£
Virgo Partners	421.36
McGowan & Sons	595.08
J J Westrope	444.72
Jacks Ltd	303.60
Total	1,764.76

Test 3

General ledger

Purchases ledger control account

	£		£
Bank	959.39	Balance b/f	839.46
Discounts received	30.07	Purchases	1,606.92
Balance c/d	1,456.92		
	2,446.38		2,446.38
		Balance b/d	1,456.92

Purchases ledger

Jenkins Suppliers

	£		£
CB	423.89	Balance b/f	441.56
CB – discounts	17.67	PDB	219.96
Balance c/d	671.28	PDB	451.32
	1,112.84		1,112.84
		Balance b/d	671.28

Kilnfarm Paper

	£		£
CB	150.00	Balance b/f	150.00
CB	150.00	PDB	153.12
Balance c/d	156.24	PDB	153.12
	456.24		456.24
		Balance b/d	156.24

Barnfield Ltd

	£		£
CB	235.50	Balance b/f	247.90
CB – discounts	12.40	PDB	317.16
Balance c/d	629.40	PDB	312.24
	877.30		877.30
		Balance b/d	629.40

Reconciliation

	£
Purchases ledger control account balance as at 31 May	1,456.92
Total of purchases ledger accounts as at 31 May (see workings)	1,456.92
Difference	0

Workings

	£
Jenkins Suppliers	671.28
Kilnfarm Paper	156.24
Barnfield Ltd	629.40
Purchases ledger control account balance	1,456.92

CHAPTER 5   Preparing and reconciling control accounts

Test 1

Sales ledger control account

	£		£
Balance b/f	16,339	Sales returns	3,446
Sales	50,926	Bank	47,612
Bank (dishonoured cheque)	366	Discounts allowed	1,658
		Irrecoverable debts	500
		Balance c/d	14,415
	67,631		67,631

Test 2

Purchases ledger control account

	£		£
Purchases returns	2,568	Balance b/f	12,587
Bank	38,227	Purchases	40,827
Discounts received	998		
Balance c/d	11,621		
	53,414		53,414

Test 3

Sales ledger control account

	£		£
Balance b/f	41,774	Sales returns	450
Sales	100	Irrecoverable debts	210
		Balance c/d	41,214
	41,874		41,874
Balance b/d	41,214		

	£
Original total of list of balances	41,586
Less: invoice misposted (769 – 679)	(90)
Less: discount (2 × 16)	(32)
Less: credit balance included as a debit balance (2 × 125)	(250)
Amended list of balances	41,214
Amended control account balance	41,214

Test 4

Purchases ledger control account

	£		£
Discount received	267	Balance b/f	38,694
		Purchases returns	300
Balance c/d	38,997	Bank (3,415 – 3,145)	270
	39,264		39,264
		Balance b/d	38,997

	£
Original total of list of balances	39,741
Less: settlement discount omitted	(267)
Less: credit note adjustment (210 – 120)	(90)
Less: debit balance omitted	(187)
Less: credit balance misstated	(200)
Amended list of balances	38,997
Amended control account balance	38,997

Test 5

(a)

Details	Amount £	Debit ✓	Credit ✓
Amount due to credit suppliers at 1 August	42,394		✓
Payments to credit suppliers	39,876	✓	
Purchases on credit	31,243		✓
Purchases returned to credit suppliers	1,266	✓	
Discounts received	501	✓	

(b)

	✓
Dr £ 31,994	
Cr £ 31,994	✓
Dr £ 34,526	
Cr £ 34,526	
Dr £ 32,996	
Cr £ 32,996	

(c)

	£
Purchases ledger control account balance as at 31 August	31,994
Total of purchases ledger accounts as at 31 August	32,190
Difference	196

. (d)

	✓
A debit balance in the subsidiary ledger may have been included as a credit balance when calculating the total of the list of balances	✓
A credit balance in the subsidiary ledger may have been included as a debit balance when calculating the total of the list of balances	
A credit note may have been omitted from the purchases returns day book total	
Discounts received may only have been entered in the subsidiary ledger	

Test 6

(a)

VAT control

Details	Amount £	Details	Amount £
Purchases	14,368	Sales	29,072
Sales returns	858	Cash sales	332
		Purchases returns	488

(b)

	✓
Yes	
No	✓

The amount is owing **to** HMRC, not from HMRC.

CHAPTER 6   The journal

Test 1

Account name	Amount £	Debit	Credit
Capital	7,500		✓
Trade receivables or Sales ledger control account	2,000	✓	
Trade payables or Purchases ledger control account	2,500		✓
Bank	8,000	✓	

Test 2

	Statutory deduction ✓	Non-statutory deduction ✓
Pension contributions		✓
Income tax	✓	
Employee's NIC	✓	
Trade union fees		✓

Test 3

(a)

£	1,642.84

Workings

	£
Gross pay £27,000/12	2,250.00
PAYE income tax	(418.16)
Employee's NIC	(189.00)
Net pay	1,642.84

(b)

Wages control account

	£		£
Bank	1,642.84	Wages expense	2,250.00
PAYE/NIC payable	418.16	Wages expense	274.50
PAYE/NIC payable	189.00		
PAYE/NIC payable	274.50		

Wages expense account

	£		£
Wages control	2,250.00		
Wages control	274.50		

PAYE/NIC payable account

	£		£
		Wages control	418.
		Wages control	189.
		Wages control	274.

Bank account

	£		£
		Wages control	1,642.

Test 4

(a)

Account name	Amount £	Debit ✓	Credit ✓
Irrecoverable debts	1,290	✓	
VAT	258	✓	
Sales ledger control	1,548		✓

(b)

Account name	Amount £	Debit ✓	Credit ✓
Capital	18,410		✓
Cash at bank	3,270	✓	
Heat and light	300	✓	
Loan from bank	5,000		✓
Machinery	10,000	✓	
Motor vehicle	7,800	✓	
Petty cash	200	✓	
Rent	1,300	✓	
Stationery	190	✓	
Vehicle expenses	350	✓	
Journal to record the opening entries of new business			

Test 5

(a)

Account name	Amount £	Debit ✓	Credit ✓
Wages expense	13,776	✓	
Wages control	13,776		✓

(b)

Account name	Amount £	Debit ✓	Credit ✓
Wages control	3,698	✓	
HM Revenue and Customs	3,698		✓

(c)

Account name	Amount £	Debit ✓	Credit ✓
Wages control	9,978	✓	
Bank	9,978		✓

(d)

Account name	Amount £	Debit ✓	Credit ✓
Wages control	100	✓	
Loan	100		✓

CHAPTER 7   Errors and the trial balance

Test 1

Error of originality entry (transposition error)

Test 2

Error of reversal of entries

Test 3

Error of commission

Test 4

Transposition error

The difference between the two figures (£270) is exactly divisible by 9 so the error may be in one of the balances in the trial balance.

Test 5

| £ | 2,121 | Credit balance/~~Debit balance~~ |

Test 6

Account name	Amount £	Debit ✓	Credit ✓
(a) Bank	3,250		✓
SLCA	2,350	✓	
Suspense account	900	✓	
Cash at bank	3,250	✓	
SLCA	3,250		✓
(b) Suspense account	1,000	✓	
Discounts allowed	1,000		✓
(c) Discounts received	450		✓
PLCA	450	✓	
PLCA	450	✓	
Discounts received	450		✓
(d) Suspense	1,088	✓	
PLCA	1,088		✓
PLCA	1,088	✓	
Purchases returns	1,088		✓

Suspense account

	£		£
(a) Bank	900	Balance b/d (184,266 – 181,278)	2,988
(b) Discounts allowed	1,000		
(d) PLCA	1,088		
	2,988		2,988

Test 7

(a)

Account name	Amount £	Debit ✓	Credit ✓
Suspense	9,247	✓	

(b)

Error in the general ledger	Error disclosed by the trial balance ✓	Error NOT disclosed by the trial balance ✓
Calculating the balance on a ledger account incorrectly by £100	✓	
Recording a supplier's credit note for £800 at £80 in the purchases returns day book		✓
Forgetting to include the £200 balance on the petty cash book in the trial balance	✓	
Making the debit entry for a cash sale of £150 but not the credit entry	✓	
Failing to record a petty cash purchase of food for £20 (no VAT)		✓
For a purchase of stationery on credit, debiting the PLCA and crediting the stationery account		✓

Test 8

(a) (i)

Account name	Amount £	Debit ✓	Credit ✓
Purchases	4,945		✓

(ii)

Account name	Amount £	Debit ✓	Credit ✓
Purchases	3,945	✓	

(iii)

Account name	Amount £	Debit ✓	Credit ✓
Suspense	1,000	✓	

(b) (i)

Account name	Amount £	Debit ✓	Credit ✓
Purchases	980	✓	
Purchases ledger control	980		✓

(ii)

Account name	Amount £	Debit ✓	Credit ✓
Purchases	980	✓	
Purchases ledger control	980		✓

Test 9

Purchases

Details	Amount £	Details	Amount £
		Suspense	256

Motor expenses

Details	Amount £	Details	Amount £
Suspense	893		

Suspense

Details	Amount £	Details	Amount £
Balance b/d	637	Motor expenses	893
Purchases	256		

Discounts received

Details	Amount £	Details	Amount £
		Discounts allowed	149

Discounts allowed

Details	Amount £	Details	Amount £
Discounts received	149		

Test 10

	Balances extracted on 31 March £	Balances at 1 April	
		Debit £	Credit £
Machinery	52,910	52,910	
Fixtures and fittings	17,835	17,835	
Computers	9,920	9,920	
Cash at bank	2,367	2,367	
Petty cash	250	250	
Sales ledger control	115,438	115,438	
Purchases ledger control	34,290		35,618
VAT owing to HM Revenue and Customs	2,337		2,337
Capital	52,254		52,254
Sales	270,256		270,256
Purchases	78,309	78,309	
Purchases returns	3,203		3,203
Wages	54,219	54,219	
Maintenance expenses	3,445	3,445	
Administration expenses	10,254	10,254	
Marketing expenses	6,287	6,287	
Premises expenses	15,244	15,244	
Discounts received	4,278		4,278
Discounts allowed	1,288	1,468	
Suspense account (credit balance)	1,148		
Totals		367,946	367,946

CHAPTER 8   The banking process

Test 1

	Debit entry/balance ✓	Credit entry/balance ✓
Money paid into the account		✓
Cheques paid out of the account	✓	
An overdraft balance	✓	

Test 2

	True ✓	False ✓
A bank draft cannot be cancelled once it has been issued	✓	
Any customer who pays with a debit card is taking out credit with its bank as a result		✓

INDEX

Notes

Notes

Notes

Notes

Notes

Notes

REVIEW FORM

How have you used this Text?
(Tick one box only)

☐ Home study

☐ On a course_____

☐ Other _____

Why did you decide to purchase this Text?
(Tick one box only)

☐ Have used BPP Texts in the past

☐ Recommendation by friend/colleague

☐ Recommendation by a college lecturer

☐ Saw advertising

☐ Other _____

During the past six months do you recall seeing/receiving either of the following?
(Tick as many boxes as are relevant)

☐ Our advertisement in Accounting Technician

☐ Our Publishing Catalogue

Which (if any) aspects of our advertising do you think are useful?
(Tick as many boxes as are relevant)

☐ Prices and publication dates of new editions

☐ Information on Text content

☐ Details of our free online offering

☐ None of the above

Your ratings, comments and suggestions would be appreciated on the following areas of this Text.

	Very useful	Useful	Not useful
Introductory section	☐	☐	☐
Quality of explanations	☐	☐	☐
How it works	☐	☐	☐
Chapter tasks	☐	☐	☐
Chapter Overviews	☐	☐	☐
Test your learning	☐	☐	☐
Index	☐	☐	☐

	Excellent	Good	Adequate	Poor
Overall opinion of this Text	☐	☐	☐	☐

Do you intend to continue using BPP Products?   ☐ Yes   ☐ No

Please note any further comments and suggestions/errors on the reverse of this page. The author of this edition can be e-mailed at: paulsutcliffe@bpp.com

Please return to: Paul Sutcliffe, Senior Publishing Manager, BPP Learning Media Ltd, FREEPOST, London, W12 8BR.

REVIEW FORM (continued)

TELL US WHAT YOU THINK

Please note any further comments and suggestions/errors below.

The U205 Health and Disease Course Team

The following members of the Open University teaching staff and external consultants have collaborated with the authors in writing this book, or have commented extensively on it during its production. We accept collective responsibility for its overall academic and teaching content.

Basiro Davey (Course Team Chair, Lecturer in Health Studies, Biology)

Gerald Elliott (Professor of Bio-physics, Physics)

Alastair Gray (Senior Research Associate, Centre for Socio-legal Studies, Wolfson College, Oxford, and Senior Lecturer in Health Economics, London School of Hygiene and Tropical Medicine)

Marion Hall (Course Manager)

Kevin McConway (Senior Lecturer in Statistics)

Perry Morley (Senior Editor, Science)

Stephen Pattison (Senior Lecturer, School of Health and Social Welfare)

Clive Seale (Senior Lecturer in Medical Sociology, Department of Sociology, Goldsmiths' College, University of London)

The following people have contributed to the development of particular parts or aspects of this book.

Sylvia Abbey (course secretary)

Martin Brazier (cover design)

Sandra Budin (BBC production assistant)

Viki Burnage (course co-ordinator)

Gary Elliott (picture researcher, course assistant)

Verena Forster (course co-ordinator)

John Greenwood (librarian)

Pam Higgins (designer)

David Jones (Research Fellow, School of Health and Social Welfare, Open University) (critical reader)

David Kelleher (Reader, Department of Sociology, London Guildhall University) (critical reader)

Donald Lane (Consultant Physician, Churchill Hospital, Oxford) (critical reader)

Patti Langton (BBC producer)

Julian Leff (Professor of Social and Transcultural Psychiatry, Institute of Psychiatry, London) (critical reader)

Mike Levers (photographer)

Roland Littlewood (Professor of Psychiatry and Anthropology and Director, University College London Centre for Medical Anthropology, London, and Director, MRC Social and Community Psychiatry Unit, Institute of Psychiatry, London) (critical reader)

Jean Macqueen (indexer)

Rissa de la Paz (BBC producer)

Mercia Seminara (BBC production assistant)

Liz Sugden (BBC production assistant)

John Taylor (graphic artist)

Doreen Tucker (text processing compositor)

Patrick Wall (Professor of Physiology, Department of Physiology, UMDS St Thomas's, London) (critical reader)

Ian Williams (Consultant and Senior Lecturer in Genito-Urinary Medicine, University College London Medical School) (critical reader)

Simon Williams (Lecturer in Sociology, Department of Sociology, University of Warwick) (critical reader)

Darren Wycherley (BBC assistant producer)

Authors

The following people have acted as principal authors for the chapters listed below.

Chapters 1 and 8

Basiro Davey, Lecturer in Health Studies, Department of Biology, The Open University.

Chapters 2, 7 and 8

Clive Seale, Senior Lecturer in Medical Sociology, Department of Sociology, Goldsmiths' College, University of London.

Chapter 3

Gareth Williams, Reader in Sociology and Deputy Director, Public Health Research and Resource Centre, University of Salford; Ray Fitzpatrick, Fellow, Nuffield College, Oxford; Alex MacGregor, Senior Registrar in Rheumatology, Department of Rheumatology, Royal Free Hospital, London; and Alan S. Rigby, Senior Lecturer in Statistics and Epidemiology, Chartered Statistician, Department of Paediatrics, Sheffield Children's Hospital, University of Sheffield.

Chapter 4

Graham Hart, Assistant Director, MRC Medical Sociology Unit, Glasgow; and Tim Rhodes, Research Fellow, The Centre for Research on Drugs and Health Behaviour, Charing Cross and Westminster Medical School, University of London.

Chapter 5

Bill Bytheway, Associate Researcher, Centre for Ageing and Biographical Studies, The Open University; and Anna Furth, Lecturer in Biology, Department of Biology, The Open University.

Chapter 6

Jacqueline Atkinson, Senior Lecturer, Department of Public Health, University of Glasgow.

External assessors

Course assessor

Professor James McEwen, Henry Mechan Chair of Public Health and Head of Department of Public Health, University of Glasgow.

Book 8 assessor

Professor Michael Bury, Professor of Sociology, Department of Social Policy and Social Sciences, Royal Holloway University of London.

Acknowledgements

The Course Team and the authors wish to thank the following people who, as contributors to the first edition of this book, made a lasting impact on the structure and philosophy of the present volume.

Nick Black, David Boswell, Sean Murphy, Jennie Popay and Steven Rose.

The Open University Press, Celtic Court, 22 Ballmore, Buckingham, MK18 1XW.

First published 1985. This completely revised edition first published 1996.

Library of Congress Cataloging-in-Publication Data

Experiencing and explaining disease/edited by Basiro Davey & Clive Seale. — Rev. ed.

p. cm. — (Health and disease series, book 8)

Includes bibliographical references and index.

ISBN 0-335-19208-4 (pbk.)

1. Social medicine. 2. Sick—Psychology. 3. Medicine—Philosophy. 4. Medical care. I. Davey, Basiro. II. Seale, Clive. III. Series.

RA418.E96 1996

616'.001'9—dc20 95–44211

CIP

Edited, designed and typeset by the Open University.

Printed in the United Kingdom by Butler & Tanner Ltd, Frome and London.

ISBN 0 335 19208 4

This text forms part of an Open University Second Level Course. If you would like a copy of *Studying with the Open University*, please write to the Central Enquiry Service, PO Box 200, The Open University, Walton Hall, Milton Keynes, MK7 2YZ.

2.1

EXPERIENCING AND EXPLAINING DISEASE

Edited by Basiro Davey and Clive Seale

PUBLISHED BY THE OPEN UNIVERSITY PRESS
IN ASSOCIATION WITH THE OPEN UNIVERSITY

 OPEN UNIVERSITY PRESS

 The Open University   Health and Disease Series, Book 8

Contents

About this book

A note for the general reader

An understanding of any condition commonly identified as a disease, illness or disability (terms explored in this book) requires some basic knowledge of several disciplines. *Experiencing and Explaining Disease* is a multidisciplinary account of the major factors influencing the ways in which states of wellness or illness are explained by professionals and experienced by lay people. These explanations and experiences are not fixed, even for the same disease condition, but vary from person to person and between different times and places. They are profoundly affected by the state of scientific and medical knowledge, which may be comprehensive or negligible; by the political and economic climate of the society in which they occur; by the personal circumstances of the individuals caught up in the condition, either as patients, family or carers; and by the nature of the condition itself, for example whether it is contagious or disfiguring, self-limiting or chronically-disabling, readily identified or difficult to diagnose and treat.

This book contains eight chapters. The first is a general introduction to the major themes explored in the book. Chapter 2 discusses the concepts of stigma and normality as powerful forces in social interactions and examines their influence on the experience of disease. These two chapters are the foundation of the four case studies in Chapters 3–6, each focusing on a certain state of ill-health, commonly identified by doctors as a medically-defined disease, and yet each subject to conflicting interpretations and uncertainties.

Each of the conditions discussed in Chapters 3–6 includes an analysis of its incidence and prevalence in the population and its distribution between different groups (the domain of epidemiology and demography), together with a description of the underlying biology of the condition and its medical treatment, so far as these are known and understood. No less important is the sociological perspective, which sheds light on the experience of the condition by investigating the meanings attached to it by individuals and societies. The conditions are: rheumatoid arthritis (Chapter 3), HIV and AIDS (Chapter 4), asthma (Chapter 5) and schizophrenia (Chapter 6).

These diseases have been chosen to reflect the range of conditions affecting people in developed and developing countries in the 1990s. We have included a chronic degenerative condition that primarily affects people after middle age (rheumatoid arthritis); a virus infection that damages the immune system and increases susceptibility to other potentially fatal infections, and is predominantly found in young adults (HIV and AIDS); a respiratory condition that can be chronic but may involve acute life-threatening emergencies, particularly among children (asthma); and a mental disorder characterised by problems in the perception of reality that is the subject of prolonged controversy about its very existence as an organic disease (schizophrenia).

In Chapter 7, we widen the territory once again to consider pain and suffering—however caused—and its alleviation by medical treatment. Here we suggest that the themes apparent in the preceding case studies of identifiable diseases can be detected just as readily in the explanations and experiences apparent in more elusive and subjective states of pain and suffering. In Chapter 8, we revisit the main themes of the book to demonstrate that they can be generalised to a wide variety of states of ill-health and disability.

This book is designed so that it can be read on its own, like any other textbook, or studied as part of U205 *Health and Disease*, a second level course for Open University students. General readers do not need to make use of the study comments, learning objectives and other material inserted for OU students, although they may find these helpful. The text also contains references to a Reader of previously published material and specially commissioned articles,[1] prepared in association with the OU course: it is quite possible to follow the text without reading the articles referred to, although doing so will enhance your understanding of this book's contents. The book is fully indexed and referenced and contains an appendix of abbreviations and an annotated guide to further reading.

---

[1] *Health and Disease: A Reader* (Open University Press, second edition 1995).

A guide for OU students

Experiencing and Explaining Disease is the final book in the *Health and Disease* series and focuses primarily but not exclusively on the United Kingdom in the present decade. The content of the eight chapters is briefly described above and in more detail in Chapter 1. Note that Chapter 8 concludes with a short reflection on the series of eight books in the *Health and Disease* series, which—together with the audiovisual components, Reader articles and assignments—constitute the Open University's course U205.

In writing *Experiencing and Explaining Disease* the authors have built on the basic knowledge of the epidemiological, biological and sociological influences on health, illness and disability that you have already gained from your studies earlier in the academic year. The first four books in the series contain particularly relevant foundation material. Study comments, where appropriate, are given in a box at the start of chapters. These primarily direct you to important links to other components of the course, such as the other books in the course series, the Reader, and audiovisual components.

Major learning objectives are listed at the end of each chapter, along with self-assessment questions (SAQs) that will enable you to check that you have achieved those objectives. The text and the index display key terms by printing them in **bold** type; the index indicates (in bold) the page on which a definition or explanation of that term can be found, enabling you to look it up easily as an aid to revision as the course proceeds. Abbreviations are listed at the end of the book. There is also a list of further reading for those who wish to pursue aspects of study beyond the scope of this book.

The following table gives a more detailed breakdown to help you to pace your study. You need not follow it slavishly, but try not to let yourself fall behind. Depending on your background and experience, you may well find some parts of this book much more familiar and straightforward than others. If you find a section of the work difficult, do what you can at this stage, and then return to the material when you reach the end of the book.

There is no tutor-marked assignment (TMA) associated with this book because it falls too late in the academic year to enable marked scripts to be returned to you before the final examination.

Study Guide for Book 8 (total 40–48 hours, spread over 4 weeks).

1st week

Chapter 1   **Personal experiences, professional explanations**

Chapter 2   **Stigma and normality**, including *Reader* article by Goffman (1969), optional *Reader* articles by Sontag (1978) and Jeffrey (1979), and TV programme 'More than meets the eye'

2nd week

Chapter 3   **Rheumatoid arthritis**

Chapter 4   **HIV and AIDS**, including *Reader* article by Small (1995), and TV programme 'A future with AIDS'

3rd week

Chapter 5   **Asthma**, including *Reader* article by Nocon and Booth (1990), optional *Reader* articles by Macintyre and Oldman (1977) and Kelleher (1990) and audiotape 'Reflections on asthma'

Chapter 6   **Schizophrenia**, including *Reader* article by Littlewood and Lipsedge (1982), and audiotape 'Hearing voices'

4th week

Chapter 7   **Pain and suffering**, including *Reader* article by Macintyre and Oldman (1977), and audiotape 'Being in pain'

Chapter 8   **Experiencing and explaining disease: some conclusions**, including optional *Reader* articles by Meador (1994), Morris (1991) and Burton-Jones (1992), and audiotape 'Living with epilepsy'

Cover photographs

Background: Electron micrograph of a Human Immunodeficiency Virus (HIV), the causative agent of AIDS (magnified 200 000 times). Courtesy of the National Institute for Biological Standards and Control.

Middleground: X-rays of the hands of a person with chronic rheumatoid arthritis. Courtesy of Dr Alex MacGregor and Northwick Park Hospital, Harrow.

Foreground: Child using a nebuliser system to inhale drugs for the prevention and treatment of asthma. Courtesy of Medix Ltd.

Illness and disability pose problems of meaning as each individual seeks a unique and personal answer to the pressing questions 'Why me? Why now? What next?'. (Photo: Mike Levers)

1 Personal experiences, professional explanations

> *This chapter introduces the final book in the Health and Disease series. The connections between this chapter and the first book in the series,* Medical Knowledge: Doubt and Certainty, *are particularly strong. The author of this chapter, Basiro Davey, chairs the Course Team that produced this series; she is Lecturer in Health Studies in the Biology Department of the Open University.*

Introduction

Suppose for a moment that you develop a persistent cough, or notice intermittent pain in one leg, or find yourself regularly waking at 3 a.m. feeling troubled and unable to sleep—or imagine any other departure from your familiar physical, mental or emotional states. In Western industrialised societies, events such as these are overwhelmingly interpreted as possible symptoms of illness, indicators of an underlying pathological change in the structure or function of a specific part of the body which, with the help of modern medicine, can often be detected and restored to 'health'. In the past and in some other cultures today, alternative explanations might have been considered—witchcraft perhaps, or the phase of the moon, an imbalance in opposing energies in the body (such as *yin* and *yang*) or in the flow of the four humours which dominated European understanding of the human body from ancient Greece until at least the sixteenth century.

Those of you who are reading this book as the final part of an Open University course will recognise that this is where we began—on a journey around different under-standings of what constitutes health and illness, disability

and disease.[1] We hope you are convinced that these states are 'contested' rather than 'fixed', in that they are each capable of sustaining a range of meanings, within certain boundaries imposed by the culture in which the term is being used. The same apparent condition may carry quite different meanings in different times and places—for example, epilepsy is attributed to brain malfunction in some cultures but to demon possession in others. Clearly, the meanings attached to a condition can profoundly alter the experience of everyone who is affected by it.

In this book we revisit this territory from a multi-disciplinary perspective, drawing on a very wide range of personal and professional influences on the experience of ill-health, mental or physical disorder or disability. People experience these conditions not as isolated states, but in a social context influenced by (among many other influences) widely-known professional explanations of ill-health, generated by several distinct disciplines of knowledge. In trying to 'make sense' of an illness or disability, everyone in Western industrialised societies has very probably been influenced at some time by the following professional disciplines:

- *Biomedicine*, the system of medical knowledge based on scientific research into the biological structure and function of the human body, including the brain and mental processes;

- *Epidemiology*, the statistical study of the distribution of disease in human populations, from which hypotheses about the causes of disease can be derived;

- *Sociological studies* of health and illness, which investigate health issues in the context of human social relationships and interactions;

[1] Discussed in the first book in this series, *Medical Knowledge: Doubt and Certainty* (Open University Press, second edition 1994), Chapter 2.

- *Psychoanalytic theory*, which interprets human thoughts, feelings and actions as a dynamic interplay between conscious and unconscious mental processes;

- *Anthropological studies* of belief systems in traditional societies.

Each of these professional disciplines approaches the explanation of health and ill-health in different ways. One of the aims of this book is to illustrate their relative contributions and their interactions in case studies of four contrasting diseases—rheumatoid arthritis, AIDS, asthma and schizophrenia. Later in this chapter, we will justify this choice of case studies.

Grand narratives and personal narratives

The foregoing list of professional disciplines which have contributed to this book is more than simply a reminder of their distinctive domains of interest. It is also a way of introducing an important theme running through many of the following chapters—the existence of what social scientists refer to as **grand narratives**. This term can be applied to any system of knowledge and/or belief that has become institutionalised in a society and commands (or once commanded) widespread allegiance and respect from a large section of the population. Using this definition, the great religions of the world can be thought of as grand narratives, and so can the major political ideologies such as capitalism and socialism, nationalism and imperialism, among many other examples. They have all been generated and sustained by many people over long periods of time; one interpretation of them is 'collective stories' on a grand scale.

☐ Look back at the list of disciplines (on pp. 5–6) from which we have drawn professional explanations of disease and disability in writing this book. Which of them do you think most obviously qualify as 'grand narratives' in modern Western culture?

■ Biomedicine is the most compelling as a grand narrative, since the majority of the population of Western societies give it their allegiance and respect, the training and practice of biomedicine is highly institutionalised and constrained by law, and medical terms and images abound in the popular media. You might also have identified psychoanalytic theory as a grand narrative, given the widespread

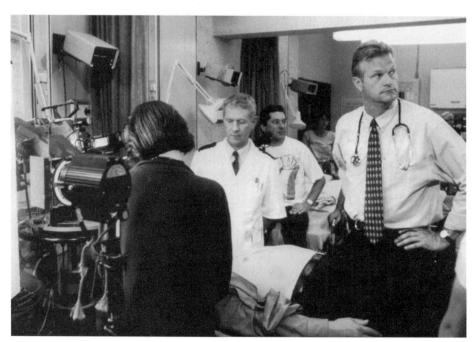

Biomedicine is one of the most powerful 'grand narratives' of the twentieth century, commanding widespread allegiance among lay people and unrivalled popularity as a source of news and entertainment. (Filming the BBC's long-running serial, 'Casualty'. Source: BBC Photograph Library)

The belief that events in the past unconsciously influence thoughts, feelings and actions in the present day is so widespread in Western society that psychoanalytic theory has achieved the status of a grand narrative. (Sigmund Freud; source: Freud Museum, London, A. W. Freud et al.)

and generally unquestioned belief in Western culture in the 'unconscious', the rise of psychoanalysis and psychotherapy as recognised professions, and the extent to which terms such as 'ego', 'repression', 'inferiority complex' and 'Freudian slip' crop up in everyday speech.

Grand narratives such as biomedicine and psychoanalytic theory are an important source of the knowledge and beliefs that lay people in Western cultures draw on when faced with an unexplained physical or mental symptom. To go back to the very start of this chapter, the person with the persistent cough will almost certainly consider biomedical or psychoanalytic ideas at some point in seeking an explanation for his or her symptoms, even if these ideas are later discarded in favour of more persuasive alternatives: for example, the cough may be attributed to bacteria infecting the lungs, inflammation due to cigarette smoke, or to a nervous manifestation of underlying anxieties. Other grand narratives may also contribute to the increasingly rich edifice of explanation growing in the person's mind: religious beliefs may lead some individuals to wonder if they are 'being tested by God', punished for transgressions or given a divine opportunity.

In the last 18 months I have found real peace of mind, a wonderful joy and a continuing deep contentment … In many ways I am glad to have weak legs because it makes me rely on God and I can use His strength … When I look back I can see how He helped and guided me. (Person with multiple sclerosis, quoted in Robinson, 1990, p. 1181)

Sociologists refer to the process of 'making up a meaningful story to explain my illness' as constructing a **personal illness narrative**, which is unique to that individual and which attempts to make sense of the illness as an understandable event occurring at that point in the person's life. The strands from which this story can be woven are extremely varied and grand narratives such as medicine and religion are only a part of the source material.

☐ Think back to a time in the past when you felt ill and try to recall the sources of information you drew on when deciding what your symptoms 'meant', what had caused them, how to treat them and whether to consult a health professional.

■ We can only guess, but they may have included previous contacts with 'healers' from orthodox or alternative traditions, reports in the news media, TV documentaries and dramas, conversations with friends and family, books and educational courses, 'folklore' about the possible causes of your condition, traditional remedies handed down from generation to generation, and so on.

Each personal account describes a dynamic state of **illness** (as distinct from 'wellness'), which incorporates a rich variety of information and a wealth of detail that the storyteller sees as important factors in their experience. The emerging narrative is unique because the 'ingredients' vary between individuals and because it tends to incorporate past events in that person's life which *now* come to seem significant in the light of present symptoms. For example, a recent walk home in the damp night air may suddenly seem important, prompting the narrator to reach further back to a childhood spent in a damp inner-city flat. Consider a fragment from the personal illness narrative of a woman who was ultimately diagnosed as having multiple sclerosis (MS):

> I lived at home with either my mother or my father being ill. I decided I had to leave because I was becoming ill, and did, but then my mother developed nephrosis in both her kidneys … I went back to look after her and after a while had an old-fashioned nervous break-down … I nursed her until she died … Sometime after I kept having peculiar symptoms but I thought it was probably all the stress I had been under … Then my husband insisted that I get medical advice, and later he was told I had MS, 4 months after we were married. (Quoted in Robinson, 1990, p. 1184)

In looking back over her life, she is reconsidering certain events and giving them a new meaning as they become woven into her explanation of 'Why me? Why now?'. The sociologist Gareth Williams (one of the authors of this book), refers to this process as *narrative reconstruction*; you will meet examples of it in later chapters.[2] Notice also that she has drawn on the 'grand narrative' of biomedicine when she says that her mother 'developed nephrosis in both her kidneys' and possibly also on a popular

version of psychoanalytic theory when she says she had 'an old-fashioned nervous breakdown'.

The purposes of constructing a personal illness narrative may be as obvious as they are varied: we feel in greater control of events if we can 'see where they came from'; thinking the sequence through may enable us to prevent the illness in the future or reduce its impact now; perhaps our story will help us to counter accusations of blame for our ill-health; or it may reinforce our faith in (for example) medicine or religion which will sustain us in a difficult future.

Variations on a theme

Within a certain culture and period there is some stability in the dominant themes that emerge in a wide variety of personal illness narratives, and some may even come to characterise a period: for example, 'stress' is an increasingly prevalent element in explanations of illness in the 1990s,[3] as illustrated by the last extract from the woman with multiple sclerosis. At the individual level, once a reasonably satisfactory personal account has been constructed, the dominant themes generally remain relatively stable, but variations may emerge over time and with different audiences: some themes in the narrative may be given more prominence in public settings where the storyteller has to establish his or her credentials among relative strangers, than they are in the private accounts told to close confidants.[4]

Discontinuities between our private beliefs, the views of the 'experts' we encounter and the 'common knowledge' about a condition that prevails in a society, help to sustain a tension between stability and variability in the meaning ascribed to an illness. If personal explanations of causes and symptoms integrate very easily with those of health professionals, then the stability of the personal narrative is reinforced. But what happens when the personal and professional perspectives are impossible to reconcile? Think for a moment of the dedicated smoker with a wheezy cough who wants to reject the medical assertion that smoking greatly increases the risk of bronchitis. Maintaining a personal narrative that excludes the role of cigarettes may be a tough proposition in today's anti-smoking culture.

---

[2]A television programme entitled 'Why me? Why now?' for Open University students accompanies *Medical Knowledge: Doubt and Certainty*, and explores the methods used by sociologists to analyse personal illness narratives. Research by Gareth Williams is featured in the programme.

[3]A discussion of stress and health, particularly among adults in the workplace, occurs in another book in this series, *Birth to Old Age: Health in Transition* (Open University Press, second edition 1995), Chapter 8.

[4]A discussion of public and private accounts occurs in another book in this series, *Studying Health and Disease* (Open University Press, second edition 1994), Chapter 3.

Certainty and uncertainty

The weight that most lay people commonly give to the opinions of health professionals in reaching a stable understanding of their illness is part of the pressure on doctors (in particular) to offer medical 'certainty' to their patients and sometimes to downplay 'uncertainty' as though it were an embarrassment. The **clinical method**, the process of reaching a medical diagnosis, amply illustrates the quest for certainty that characterises modern medicine.

A patient goes to see a doctor, who listens to the patient's 'story'—generally a cryptic version of the full illness narrative already constructed in the patient's mind, now reduced to a 'public account' containing those details the patient thinks will interest the doctor and convince him or her that the symptoms are genuine and worthy of medical attention. The **symptoms** are departures from physical or mental functioning that the patient is aware of and considers to be 'abnormal'. The doctor considers the story and discards anything that seems medically irrelevant. An examination follows, possibly leading to specialised diagnostic tests, as the doctor looks for additional **signs** of underlying pathology. Signs in medical jargon are abnormalities in the function or structure of the body that can only be detected by skilled medical examination or tests.[5] Patients report symptoms but are assumed to be unaware of signs until the news is revealed by their doctor.

The purpose of the clinical method just described is to reach a stable **diagnosis,** that is, to identify the specific underlying pathology in the patient's body that is producing the signs and symptoms, distinguish it reliably from other possible diagnoses, and label it correctly with the name of a medically recognised **disease**. In so doing, the doctor sets aside the inevitable variability in the precise details of *this* patient's signs and symptoms compared with that of every other patient to whom the same diagnostic label is attached. In reaching a diagnosis, the doctor is unlikely to consider the even greater range of variation in the 'personal' elements of each patient's story, which are generally discarded as medically irrelevant. The doctor's aim is to diagnose a *disease*, whereas the patient's is to achieve a personally meaningful understanding of the *illness*. As a consequence of these different agendas, the doctor is unlikely to be able to

[5]Signs and symptoms are defined in the discussion of the clinical method in *Medical Knowledge: Doubt and Certainty,* Chapter 7.

answer some of the patient's most pressing questions, such as 'Why me? Why now?'.

The doctor then attempts a **prognosis**, a prediction about the likely future course of the disease, given the available treatment. This is often another area of uncertainty and discontinuity between what the patient wants to know and what the doctor is able to say. Depending on the disease, the accuracy of prognosis can be extremely variable. Since all predictions are made on the basis of population averages, the doctor cannot know the extent to which this particular patient's future will reproduce the average pattern or vary markedly from it. The doctor is dealing in probabilities whereas the patient has a need for personal certainty. The greater the uncertainty about prognosis, the greater the tension between professional knowledge and personal experience that both doctor and patient have to reconcile. This leads us to the most important reason for choosing the four case studies named earlier as forming the core of this book.

Four case studies of disease

Everything that you have read thus far has been laying a foundation for what follows. Diseases that are characterised by uncertainty reveal the intensity of the struggle to 'make sense' of what is going on, not only among the patients and their family and friends, but also among the professionals of all the disciplines trying to define, treat, predict or prevent the disease.

With this in mind, we chose four highly contrasting diseases which have uncertainty as their common feature. They are: rheumatoid arthritis—a chronic, painful and permanently disabling condition, primarily affecting the joints (Chapter 3); HIV—a viral infection that commonly leads to other, ultimately fatal, infections and disorders collectively known as AIDS (Chapter 4); asthma—a respiratory condition that can involve acute, life-threatening emergencies, but may also be chronic or self-limiting (Chapter 5); and schizophrenia—a mental state characterised by thought disorders and problems in the perception of reality (Chapter 6). All four of these conditions illustrate the importance of drawing on contributions from biomedicine, epidemiology and sociology in attempting to reach an understanding of complex states of ill-health, despite the inevitable uncertainties.

All of these conditions can affect people of any age, although the onset of rheumatoid arthritis is commonest beyond middle age, whereas the other conditions are generally first diagnosed in younger adults or in children. They range from the acute to the chronic; all can lead to premature death, but there is a wide range in the fatality rates; all of them affect significant numbers of people around the world and cause considerable suffering. Four of the major physiological systems of the body are represented: the musculo-skeletal, immune, respiratory and nervous systems.

These four case studies also illustrate a sort of hierarchy in the professional status attached to certain diseases which is only dimly visible to people outside the professions. For example, rheumatology—the branch of medicine concerned with arthritis and other rheumatic conditions—has never been a 'fashionable' specialty, nor have these conditions attracted the huge amounts of research funding or the prestigious professorial appointments associated in recent years with HIV and AIDS. The focus on asthma seems to be rising in the 1990s, whereas it could be said that schizophrenia was attracting most attention in the 1960s and 1970s. This is but one example of the many ways in which the experience of health and disease can be affected by factors in the wider social fabric. You will encounter others in the course of this book.

The framework chapters

This is the first of four 'framework' chapters, which surround the case studies and set them in a wider context. Before commencing on the case studies, we want you to consider another important aspect of the tension between personal experiences of illness and professional explanations of disease. In Chapter 2, 'Stigma and normality', we examine the forces at work in a culture that often lead people to shun the 'sick' and identify themselves with the 'well'. Why is it that some diseases are so stigmatising that people who are affected by them must cope not only with the physical manifestations of their illness and its direct impact on their lives, but also with the rejection of those

who consider themselves 'normal'? In this book, AIDS and schizophrenia are examples of highly stigmatised conditions, whereas people with rheumatoid arthritis or asthma experience far less exclusion from 'normal' society.

Chapters 1 and 2 prepare the ground for Chapters 3–6, the disease case studies. Then we return to the wider arena in the last two framework chapters. Chapter 7, 'Pain and suffering', steps outside the constraints of a specific disease and examines the power of painful experiences, however caused, to disrupt our ability to participate in a meaningful world. Yet pain and suffering are not stable entities, but vary in their intensity and impact, almost from moment to moment. Chapter 7 considers the biological, cultural and personal factors that contribute most to the variability of our experience of pain and hence to our experience of disease. References back to the case studies begin to tie the main themes of the book together—a process completed in Chapter 8, 'Experiencing and explaining disease: some conclusions'.

Finally

It is the explicit intention of the authors of this book to take you into awkward territory, where definitions are contested and strategies are the subject of controversy, where personal experiences are often painful and the medical profession frequently finds itself unable to alter the course of a disease. We do not expect to provide simple answers to complex questions, for there are few enough. Our aim is to promote a greater understanding of the complexity of human health, disease, disability and illness, and thereby to strengthen the case for multidisciplinary and collaborative approaches to prevention and treatment.

2 *Stigma and normality*

Christ showing the marks of the crucifixion. Marks on the body have signified unusual status in many cultures since ancient times. (Source: Mansell Collection)

As Sicknesse is the greatest misery, so the greatest of sicknes is solitude; when the infectiousnes of the disease deterrs them who should assist, from comming; even the Phisician dares scarse come … it is Outlawry, an Excommunication upon the patient … (John Donne, 'Devotions upon emergent occasions', 1627, quoted in Sontag, 1991, p. 120)

Introduction

The term **stigma** was coined originally by the Greeks to describe the practice of branding slaves to indicate their status. Just as such marks on the body were once used to indicate inferiority or unusual status, so some illnesses have been used from time to time to mark people out as set apart from 'normal' people. Stigma involves the deliberate exclusion of certain categories of person, a type of inflicted social pain. However, just as some people specialise in caring for individuals with pain, so some make it their business to champion the cause of people who are stigmatised.

Several of the diseases that you will read about in this book have been used, at one time or another, as marks of stigma. Perhaps the best known of these currently is AIDS, where the people concerned have been subjected to a variety of discriminatory practices, but also have attracted a number of champions to their cause. Schizophrenia too—indeed mental illness generally—has often been the occasion for struggle over imputations of a discredited or shameful identity. The sociologist Erving Goffman, whose work on stigma will be discussed later in the chapter, has written an article called 'The insanity of place',[3] in which he explores differences between physical and mental illnesses. You should read this now and then consider the following questions.

---

[1]*Health and Disease: A Reader* (Open University Press, second edition, 1995).

[2]*Medical Knowledge: Doubt and Certainty*, Chapter 8.

[3]First published 1969; an edited extract appears in *Health and Disease: A Reader*.

☐ According to Goffman, how does mental illness differ from physical illness in its effect on a person's relationships with others?

■ With a physical illness, people are more likely to indicate to others that, but for their illness, they would be playing their normal part in family and work life. The symptoms of mental illness, on the other hand, are more likely to be construed as an *offence* against normal codes of behaviour.

☐ What is the effect of this in families?

■ Family members are likely to seek actively to define the person as mentally ill in order to validate their own view of normal family life. Factions may develop, where the 'patient' is watched and the patient may feel conspired against. Outsiders are drawn in to sustain a definition of the patient as ill. As Goffman puts it, 'The family is turned inside out'.

The illness conditions that give rise to stigma vary from one culture to another. At different times and in different cultures certain illnesses have been stigmatised that in other social contexts are unremarked upon. To understand why this is so it is necessary to explore the psycho-social forces that underlie the phenomenon. Particular stigmas depend on particular definitions of what it is to be normal. The roots of the desire to be normal, and the source of changing standards of normality are explored in the first section of the chapter.

We then turn to a detailed discussion of the problems faced by people suffering from stigmatised conditions.[4] There are different varieties of stigma, and Goffman's work is central in understanding how this variety affects interaction between people. Finally, the chapter considers the contribution of health care workers to stigma. For example, organised medicine can play a powerful role in creating and sustaining stigmatised identities; on the other hand, medicine has the capacity to challenge these identities. First, though, let us examine briefly the nature of normality, and the roots of the desire to be considered normal. This will involve a diversion into some more general considerations, before returning to the specific problems of illness.

[4]Open University students will find it useful to watch the television programme 'More than meets the eye' close to their study of this section. Please consult the Broadcast Notes before watching the programme.

Being normal

Normality as an agreement

Human social life is based upon fundamental agreements between people about what is to be counted as normal. This is reflected in even the most apparently routine interactions, as is demonstrated by the following sequence of talk between two people who have just seen each other:

S: (*waving his hand cheerily*) How are you?
E: How am I in regard to what? My health, my finance, my school work, my peace of mind, my …
S: (*red in the face and suddenly out of control*) Look! I was just trying to be polite. Frankly, I don't give a damn how you are.
(Adapted from Garfinkel, 1963, p. 222)

The American sociologist Harold Garfinkel conducted experiments, of which this was one, in which he deliberately ignored rules of normal conduct and observed the effects. The resultant disruption revealed the remarkable extent to which human social life depends on taken-for-granted assumptions about normal behaviour. Much humour depends on exploiting this fact.

☐ What causes the following interaction to be funny?

A: Where are you going?
B: I'm going quietly round the bend.
(Giddens, 1989, p. 96)

■ B has deliberately 'misunderstood' the normal meaning of A's question in order ironically to convey worries.

Norms of conduct can be as basic as sustaining mutual agreements about the meanings of words, or they may involve larger matters, such as conforming to a particular set of moral principles. The concept of **membership** is useful here. In recognising mutually agreed norms people are demonstrating their membership of the social group to which—at least for that moment—they belong. Naturally, the breaking of rules can threaten claims to membership. This may at times be deliberate, as in the following interaction between a parent and a teenager:

P: Where are you going?
T: Out.
P: What are you going to do?
T: Nothing.
(Giddens, 1989, p. 96)

The variability of social norms

The designation of a particular state as stigmatised involves drawing a boundary between membership and non-membership on the basis of conformity to standards of normality. These standards, which sociologists call **social norms**, influence whom we regard as a legitimate, creditable member of the group in which we claim membership and are constructed as a matter of tacit social agreement. People lay claim to their own membership, and police the claims of others according to standards which are in part 'handed down', and which are in part subject to negotiation and change. Inevitably, this means that definitions of what it is to be 'normal' vary across different social groups. Stigmatised qualities, as representations of the abnormal, must therefore also be variable.

For example, you will learn in Chapter 6 that there is variability in the social norms defining mental illness. Some people argue that the norms applied by Western psychiatrists to diagnose schizophrenia in African-Caribbean males are culturally inappropriate. What may be acceptable in West Indian culture as a form of religious possession, appears to some psychiatrists as schizophrenia.[5]

Although social norms are variable they are not, however, simply selected at random. The norms subscribed to in a particular society evolve over a long period of time, and reflect underlying social forces. For example, the way in which our modern habits, now interpreted as having a 'hygienic' rationale, have evolved over several centuries is shown in the following extracts from European books on manners, presented with dates of authorship:

Thirteenth century: When you blow your nose or cough, turn around so that nothing falls on the table.

1558: It does not befit a modest, honourable man to prepare to relieve nature in the presence of other people ... Similarly, he will not wash his hands on returning to decent society from private places, as the reason for his washing will arouse disagreeable thoughts in people.

1560: It is a far too dirty thing for a child to offer others something he has gnawed, or something he disdains to eat himself, unless it be to his servant ... he must not lift the meat to his

mouth now with one hand and now with the other ... he should always do so with his right hand, taking the bread or meat decently with three fingers only ...

1672: If everyone is eating from the same dish, you should take care not to put your hand in it before those of higher rank do so.

1714: Wherever you spit, you should put your foot on the saliva ... At the houses of the great, one spits into one's handkerchief.

1859: Spitting is at all times a disgusting habit, I need say nothing more than—never indulge in it. Beside being coarse and atrocious, it is very bad for the health.

(From various books on manners, quoted in Elias, 1978, pp. 91, 92, 131, 143, 154, 156)

All except the first and last of these extracts describe behaviour that today would be considered abnormal, marking out a person as socially inferior, blameworthy and in need of correction. Yet they are presented as models of good behaviour, whereby readers who followed them could gain acceptability in privileged social circles. It is easy to see that the direction to which these extracts point is towards modern standards, nowadays often justified on the grounds of hygiene. Yet they were formulated before there was a general acceptance that dirt contains germs that lead to disease, representing moments in historical negotiations about standards of behaviour.

These extracts were collected by a sociologist called Norbert Elias who was interested in the historical development of social norms, and in particular how these reflected what he came to call a **civilising process** (Elias, 1978, 1982). Elias describes how many aspects of 'manners' have changed, covering—in addition to the matters outlined above—attitudes to public nakedness, to sleeping in the same bed and towards defecating in the view of others, the use of forks, and taboos on the use of knives at table. Changes in the social norms governing all of these behaviours, he argues, have been in the same general direction: the threshold at which shame and disgust are elicited has shifted so that many behaviours once considered acceptable now give offence. Children undergo a personal 'civilising process' as part of their upbringing, the purpose of learning such 'manners' being to show sensitivity towards the feelings of others by encouraging a feeling of shame about certain bodily behaviours. Elias uses the concept of *sociogenesis* to summarise his belief that these mass psychological changes are social in origin, rather than the product of some innate change in human nature. He links the

[5]This argument is also proposed in an article by Roland Littlewood and Maurice Lipsedge, 'Ethnic minorities and the psychiatrist', in *Health and Disease: A Reader*, which Open University students will study with Chapter 6.

civilising process to the growing complexity of modern society compared with feudal medieval societies.

In the past, for example, power was gained and defended by force of arms, and there were no very powerful sources of central authority. As these developed, however, social advancement came increasingly to depend on skills of diplomacy and the calculation of likely consequences of actions, involving intensive study of others' feelings and prediction of their likely reactions. Whereas in the past, other people could be simply divided into enemies and friends, now all people were, potentially, both. Interpersonal relationships thus became vastly more complex. Cults of refined sensibility, which arose at first in courtly society, spread gradually to other social groups in the towns, resulting today in a degree of social stratification of manners which now indicate class distinctions.

'Manners' serve to indicate membership of particular groups, drawing boundary lines between those who belong and those who do not. They may be used deliberately to gain strategic advantage, as is seen in the social climber who, insecure of his or her position, invests considerable energy in demonstrating the inferiority of those who have not yet mastered rules of refined behaviour. Illness presents quite fundamental challenges to membership and normality which, if not *legitimised* by a medical label indicating that the person has a right to enter the *sick role*,[6] may be resented by people who expect the person to play a normal part in social life. Illness labels may also be used to designate inferiority in other people, bolstering the security of 'normals' in their own claims to membership. This is what is meant by the stigma of illness. Paradoxically, sick people may themselves be particularly concerned to draw firm boundaries between legitimate and illegitimate sickness in order to sustain the 'value' of the currency from which their own label is drawn. The parallel here is the social climber who displays a particular aptitude for exposing other social climbers.

Defending against anxiety

We turn now to the psychological roots of the desire to claim membership of a group. It is helpful to think of this as sustaining a sense of **ontological security**. 'Ontology' refers to the philosophical study of *being*. 'Ontological security' indicates a primary and basic sense of security

about being in the world, which underlies a person's capacity to engage in the business of living. For most of us, a basic sense of optimism about continuing in life is inculcated at a very early stage in human development by the experience of trust. This in turn generates the perception that, rather than living in a world of purposeless chaos, there is an order and a meaning to life. The sociologist Anthony Giddens describes this first stage in the formulation of self-identity as:

> ... a sort of emotional inoculation against existential anxieties—a protection against future threats and dangers which allows the individual to sustain hope and courage in the face of whatever debilitating circumstances she or he might later confront. (Giddens, 1991, p. 39)

Young children experience some fundamental anxieties that centre on trust: when a parent leaves the room, for example, the baby must 'trust' that he or she will return and often experiences difficulty in doing so. The psychic processes involved in dealing with these primary anxieties about one's place in the world are dealt with, in part, by a psychological mechanism known as **projection**, described here by Sigmund Freud as a:

> ... particular way of dealing with any internal excitations which produce too great an increase of unpleasure. There is a tendency to treat them as though they were acting, not from the inside, but from the outside, so that it may be possible to bring [a] shield ... into operation as a means of defence against them. (Freud, 1920, p. 32)

Psychoanalytic theory suggests that an individual's sense of self is made up of thoughts, wishes and feelings which are often in conflict with one another.[7] Angry feelings about the people whom we love, for example, produce an unpleasant contradiction between the two emotions, resulting in a sensation of guilt. This is an 'unpleasure' which some people deal with by blaming the loved person for creating the conflict, resulting in accusations of bad behaviour that the other person feels are false. Thus, in projection, uncomfortable parts of the self which, if acknowledged, would create unpleasant feelings about ourselves, are attributed to (projected onto) outside objects, commonly other people. These others then become 'bad' for causing our discomfort. To take the

---

[6]The sick role, and the role of doctors in guarding entry to it, is discussed in *Medical Knowledge: Doubt and Certainty*, Chapter 8. The sick role consists of a series of obligations which, it is argued, people who claim the right to be called 'sick' need to fulfil.

[7]This 'psychodynamic' view of the conscious and unconscious inner world is explored more fully in *Birth to Old Age: Health in Transition*, Chapter 6.

projection one stage further, we may imagine the other person feels aggression towards us; at its extreme, this can become paranoia. As a further twist, *good* parts of the self may also be projected into others, so that people come to **idealise** these others and imagine they have admirable qualities. Sometimes this is due to an over-compensation for hostile feelings towards the person thus idealised.

Sustaining membership through ritual

Ontological security in everyday social life is routinely threatened and repaired, most of the time occasioning no reflective thought at all. Garfinkel's experiments reveal the potential for chaos that exists from moment to moment, but which is hardly ever realised. This is because of the mundane nature of much social interaction and the ready availability of strategies for repair. Occasionally, however, major events occur which offer more serious threats to ontological security and require 'answers'. Chief among these are illness and death, which serve as frightening reminders of human fragility.

Stigma in relation to illness can be understood as a response to the threat it poses to ontological security. Firstly, an ontological 'offence' is experienced as the display of disease or deformity reminds the onlooker of the capacity of their own body or mind to deteriorate. Secondarily, as the 'unpleasure' that this provokes is experienced, the onlooker projects this bad feeling onto the ill or disfigured person, 'accusing' them of behaviour that has caused this discomfort or 'offence' to the onlooker. These accusations may involve the imputation of moral deficiencies in the person stigmatised. This, however, is secondary to the original ontological 'offence' of displaying disease.

For most of human history people have turned to religious explanations for answers to the major events that threaten ontological security. Religious rituals in their original forms were not just matters of affirming belief, but occasions where members of a social group gathered to generate emotional energy which bound them together in the face of potential threats. They involved the veneration of sacred objects or symbols, which were invested with the values of the community involved. Religious ceremonies were of particular importance at times when individuals were undergoing major transformations, such as birth, marriage or death, which threatened changes to the routine ordering of social life. They also became important when the group was threatened by an outside enemy. The night before a battle occasioned much praying, as did the beds of the sick, who were threatened by a different sort of enemy.

A notable feature of traditional societies, and of religious followings, is that they are apt to make firm divisions between people who are enemies and people who are friends. This leads to the formation of a distinct group or 'tribal' identity that serves to preserve *solidarity*, a feeling of togetherness in the face of threat. One of the peculiar features of the modern vantage point, where it is possible to survey a variety of groups and to review a series of religions, all of which may lay claim to represent the one true faith, is the possibility of seeing the apparent contradictions of the claims made by different social groups. These reveal a shared underlying motive.

Stigma and modern society

Modern societies differ from traditional societies in ways that make fixed definitions of normality difficult to sustain. A variety of systems of belief compete with each other for people's allegiance. Most obviously, commitment within a community or society to a single religious system is no longer widespread: religion becomes a matter of belief or non-belief, rather than a part of an unquestioned background assumption about the nature of the world. Science competes with religion, and there are many critics of science as well. In short, such *grand narratives*,[8] which make the individual's anxieties feel manageable (sometimes called *containing* the anxiety), and which explain to him or her how to behave, are less available in modern societies. This can contribute to the 'stress' that is so often described as characteristic of modern times.[9]

Additionally, everyday social life has become considerably more complex, involving most individuals in a large variety of social settings, all of which make different demands on appropriate behaviour. Thus modern conditions make unusually strong demands on people's capacity to tolerate differences. Particularly in middle-class circles (where the pacifying effect of the civilising process is, perhaps, at its most extreme) there is much talk of tolerance as a desirable social value, and eruptions of tribal enmity (for example, between rival football fans) are frequently characterised as 'primitive'. Psychotherapy exists, in part, to deal with the difficulties people have in managing the demanding pressures of tolerance.

Without the security provided by grand narratives, people are prone to project their difficulties onto others.

---

[8]Defined in Chapter 1 of this book.

[9]An analysis of 'role conflict' in producing stress appears in *Birth to Old Age: Health in Transition*, Chapter 8, and is relevant here.

New Age travellers: issues of tribal identity and the management of stigma are not just confined to matters of health and disease. Modern conditions make unusually strong demands on people's capacity to tolerate differences. (Photo: Roger Hutchings/Network)

At the same time, it is not always clear who these others should be. Grand narratives in traditional societies often serve to channel hostility towards 'safe' enemies—non-believers, people who believe in the 'wrong' things, the unhygienic, or simply strangers—who either live at a safe distance, or can be killed with impunity (and sometimes eaten!). Nowadays there are few enemies who are in this sense 'safe' for people to hate. The modern individual lives the life of a diplomat, whereas the traditional individual may be better characterised as a warrior.

This is not to say that opportunities for tribal enmity are entirely absent in modern society, or that grand narratives are unavailable to sustain them. The genocidal conflicts in Bosnia and Rwanda during the 1990s, and the violent politics of racial differences that occasionally erupt in the United Kingdom, are sufficient to remind us of the potential of grand narrative to identify 'safe' enemies to hate. However, in the usual run of everyday life in the United Kingdom diplomacy is better rewarded. On the one hand, because of the great variety of different social groups that continually present themselves, modern social conditions offer plentiful opportunities for categories of stigma to arise. On the other hand, these categories are also likely to be challenged. This may be followed by the negotiation of new categories of stigmatised identity.

The very fact that stigma can itself be a 'topic' for discussion and debate is a feature of modern social conditions which encourage us constantly to reflect on our attitudes. Indeed we gain university degrees for doing so! Because norms are not fixed matters but are constantly negotiated, those that define stigmatised individuals can at times be successfully challenged and overthrown. Sometimes such challenges come from the people who are stigmatised themselves, spurred on by the vicissitudes of managing this stigma—a trial to which we now turn our attention.

Managing stigma

The following was written by Paul Hunt, who lived and died with muscular dystrophy:

> … we are representatives of many of the things that they [the able-bodied] most fear—tragedy, loss, dark and the unknown. Involuntarily we walk, or more often we sit, in the valley of the shadow of death. Contact with us throws up in people's faces the fact of sickness and death in the world, which in themselves are an affront to all our aspirations and hopes. A deformed and paralysed body attacks everyone's sense of well-being and invincibility. People do not

want to acknowledge what disability affirms—that life is tragic and we shall all soon be dead. So they are inclined to avoid those who are sick or old, shying from the disturbing reminders of unwelcome reality. (Hunt, 1966, quoted by Shearer, 1981, in Black *et al.*, 1984, p. 276)

Individuals with stigmatising conditions face particular problems in managing their self-identities in social interaction. The sociologist Erving Goffman presented in 1968 an illuminating set of ideas that summarise these problems, and these have been elaborated by subsequent writers, examples of whose work will be used here. Goffman describes encounters between people with stigmas and 'normals' as 'one of the primal scenes in sociology' (Goffman, 1968, p. 24) because of his belief that the management of boundaries between normality and abnormality is central to the organisation of social life.

The major ceremonial moments referred to previously, such as religious events, are large-scale and dramatic enactments of group solidarity. Goffman's insight lies in his perception that the mundane events of everyday social interaction also constitute rituals. Showing deference to one's social superiors by an appropriate use of words or body language, greeting friends in the manner you and they expect, serve to affirm membership by demonstrating common understandings. Encounters with stigmatised individuals provide a series of threats to membership and ontological security, which are routinely patched up.

Here is a summary of the main terms and distinctions used by Goffman and others. All of these terms will be used again later in this book.

Virtual social identity and **actual social identity**: A *virtual social identity* is the character and attributes that 'normals' expect a person will possess; *actual social identity* is what is discovered about the attributes a person truly possesses. Stigma arises from a discrepancy between the two that is discrediting. Thus a person whose history of admissions to mental hospitals is revealed may experience rejection for causing such a discrepancy in the eyes of those who expected something else.

Discredited stigmas and **discreditable stigmas**: some stigmatised attributes are hidden from observers, such as being HIV-positive, and so the person is potentially *discreditable* if the attribute should eventually be revealed. Others, for example the advanced stages of rheumatoid arthritis, are obvious at first sight, immediately *discrediting* the person in the eyes of disapproving

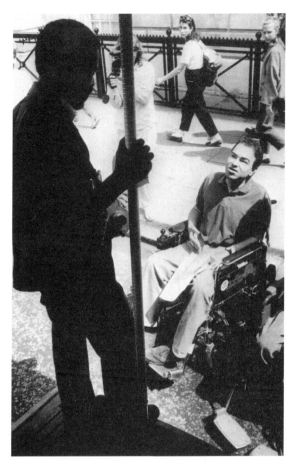

Is this a 'primal scene'? Goffman sees the management of boundaries between 'normality' and 'abnormality' as central to the organisation of social life. (Photo: Brenda Prince/Format)

others. Discreditable stigmas pose problems of managing the disclosure of information.

Passing and **covering**: These are strategies of information control relevant to discredited and discreditable stigmas. *Passing* involves the concealment of a 'discreditable' stigma (for example, a person concealing on an insurance form the fact of having had an HIV test); *covering* involves preventing a visible, 'discredited' stigma from looming large, as where a person with visual impairment wears dark glasses.

Master status: This refers to the 'spoiling' effect that a stigma has on other aspects of a person's identity. Once a stigma becomes known, many aspects of a person's behaviour come to be interpreted in that light. For example, if someone with a history of mental illness becomes angry, this is seen as a manifestation of the illness, which in another person might be interpreted as justified anger. Thus 'mentally ill' has become the person's *master status*. 'Secondary deviance' may then occur, whereby the person reacts to others' imputation of stigma by behaving in further deviant ways.

The own and **the wise**: These are two sets of sympathetic others, the *own* being the group of fellow sufferers (e.g. other HIV-positive people), the *wise* being 'normals' who by virtue of their special knowledge and sympathy for the condition become 'courtesy' members of the stigmatised group (for example, 'buddies' for people with AIDS).

Felt stigma and **enacted stigma**: Stigma may be experienced in acts of persecution or discrimination by others, in which case it is *enacted*. Alternatively, this enactment may be so feared by the stigmatised individual that he or she acts to avoid potential difficulties; this is known as *felt* stigma. Thus a person with epilepsy may avoid trying for job interviews, or proposing marriage, because he or she fears discrimination.

Additionally, stigmatising conditions can be broadly classified into three classes:

1   blemishes of the body, physical deformities like leprosy;

2   blemishes of the character or behaviour, like alcoholism or 'bad manners';

3   tribal stigma, gained by virtue of belonging to a particular social group, such as a religious or racial group.

☐ From your general knowledge, how does the stigmatisation of HIV and AIDS combine all the three classes listed above?

■ People with HIV or AIDS may: (i) exhibit visible signs of the disease such as severe weight loss or dark patches on the skin (Kaposi's sarcoma) which can be disfiguring; (ii) be blamed for bringing the virus upon themselves by behaviour others consider to be wrong; and (iii) suffer prejudice (*enacted stigma*) because of the association of HIV with groups already stigmatised, such as gay men, drug users or prostitutes.

Other conditions may be restricted to only one of these classes of stigma.

☐ Which stigmas are sometimes applied to blindness and mental illness?

■ Blindness attracts the first stigma—a blemish of the body. Mental illness attracts the second—a blemish of the character or behaviour.

Gerhard Nijhof, a sociologist from the Netherlands, interviewed people with Parkinson's disease, gathering stories of how they felt when in public places. This disease, which involves gradually increasing signs of stiffness, trembling and shaking, illustrates how a stigmatising condition can progress from one that is *discreditable* to one that is obvious to all, and therefore *discredited*.

I feel ashamed about the way I'm sitting here talking, totally different … Well, I don't talk any more when I am in a large group, because of the fact that the words come out so awkwardly, don't you think? … I stopped walking in the streets during the day, I found it very awkward to be so visibly in a bad condition … But it's specially with speaking that I have difficulties. I keep my mouth shut. When there are visitors, then my wife speaks. Yes, because I can't speak so well. I have the feeling that people notice. Isn't it? Don't you notice it?

You can take me to a restaurant. If not too difficult things are being served, then I can have dinner with you as usual, without people thinking: what is that old man there, sopping and messing around.

I was very good at disguising it. But one day I went to the hairdresser and he says, you must have a terrible back pain. I said, no, why? He said, you are walking very slowly. I said, I cannot walk fast at all. So then, yes, I was disguising it for myself. I found it terrible. Of course, you cannot hide anything. Whatever you wear, I mean, everybody sees it. You start to walk with difficulty, you start to act more crazily. I found that very hard. And, well, yes, the hanging over while walking, too. So it is definitely something you cannot disguise. Everybody sees it. You cannot say, as if it is a bad scar, I'm going to wear a dress. Everybody sees it.

Sometimes I have to sign my cheque. Then I think, these people must … think I have stolen the cheque … It's embarrassing.
(Nijhof, 1995, pp. 196–8, 198, 200)

These four examples illustrate the complex strategies of information control that some stigmatised individuals adopt to *pass* as 'normals'. Because they *felt* the stigma of their disease these people did all they could to prevent it being *enacted*. With such a progressive illness, however, strategies for passing as normal may become difficult. A degree of *covering* is only possible at the expense of forgoing things that others take for granted, such as appearing in the street, in restaurants, or even speaking.

Apart from the strain of passing as normal, once disclosed, a stigma can evoke reactions in others which indicate that disability has become an overwhelming *master status*, spreading beyond the confines of the original impairment:

> … the perceived failure to see may be generalised into a gestalt[10] of disability, so that the individual shouts at the blind as if they were deaf or attempts to lift them as if they were crippled. Those confronting the blind may have a whole range of belief that is anchored in the stereotype. (Gowman, quoted in Goffman, 1968, p. 16)

Sometimes, the reactions of others can cause great pain as stigma is *enacted*, as one person with epilepsy told sociologist Graham Scambler:

> This is what I've found, that whenever I tell anybody that I'm epileptic they don't want to know me at all. I've had friends here: as soon as they know I'm epileptic they don't want to know me at all. (Scambler and Hopkins, 1988, p. 166)

And another person with AIDS:

> The nurses are scared of me; the doctors wear masks and sometimes gloves. Even the priest doesn't seem too anxious to shake my hand. What the hell is this? I'm not a leper. Do they want to lock me up and shoot me? I've got no family, no friends. Where do I go? What do I do? God, this is horrible! Is He punishing me? The only thing I got going for me is that I'm not dying—at least, not yet. (Kleinman, 1988, p. 163)

The enactment of stigma can involve an exploitation of power over people whose stigma is such that they are defined as sub-human:

> A Dundee researcher has uncovered an American professor's proposals in the 1950s for radiation experiments on 'idiots and feeble minded children' … In May 1958 Donald M Pillsbury, professor of dermatology at the University of Pennsylvania, wrote … 'It would be our plan to give carefully calibrated ionising radiation in varying amounts to small areas of skin in human subjects…' the principal subjects would be 'idiots and feeble-minded children permanently committed to a home in New Jersey. An excellent rapport with the institution has been established and a number of experimental studies have been carried out there without incident …' [later he said] 'There would be no concern about the possible genetic effects; these individuals will never reproduce.' (*Times Higher Education Supplement*, 1995, p. 3)

Some conditions, however, attract *idealisation*, where people imagine that the affected person, by virtue of their experience, possesses special qualities of insight, or is unusually gifted.[11] These idealisations, to their recipient, can feel almost as inappropriate as the projection of negative qualities. Thus blind people are sometimes assumed to have special musical gifts, on grounds that deprivation of one sense must produce unusual sensitivity in others. One woman reported that she 'was asked to endorse a perfume, presumably because being sightless my sense of smell was super-discriminating' (Keitlen and Lobsenz, quoted in Goffman, 1968, p. 16). A blind writer described how other people expected him to have an unusually perceptive philosophy of life by virtue of his blindness. As a result:

> You develop a 'philosophy'. People seem to insist that you have one and they think you're kidding when you say you haven't. So you do your best to please and to strangers you encounter on trains, in restaurants, or on the subway who want to know what keeps you going, you give your little piece. You're a man of unusual discernment if you can realise that your philosophy is seldom one of your own devising but a reflection of the world's notions about blindness. (Chevigny, quoted in Goffman, 1968, p. 147)

[10]*Gestalt* is a German term referring to the perception of an organised whole that is more than the sum of its parts (for example, a melody as distinct from its separate notes).

[11]Susan Sontag in an article called 'Illness as metaphor', reprinted in *Health and Disease: A Reader,* discusses how tuberculosis attracted such idealisations in the nineteenth century. Open University students could usefully read this optional article.

One strategy that is available to stigmatised individuals is to form a life among their *own*, people who share the same stigma. While such befriending can be immensely helpful, it can also be experienced as unwelcome segregation, as the following example of a newly blind woman being shown around a facility for blind and partially-sighted people suggests:

> We visited the Braille library; the classrooms; the clubrooms where the blind members of the music and dramatic groups meet; the recreation hall where on festive occasions the blind dance with the blind; the cafeteria, where all the blind gather to eat together … I was expected to join this world. To give up my profession and to earn my living making mops … with other blind people … I became nauseated with fear as the picture grew in my mind. Never had I come upon such destructive segregation. (Keitlen, quoted in Goffman, 1968, p. 51)

The harmful effects of such segregation have been more widely recognised since Goffman wrote. Additionally, some conditions that attract stigma have, as Goffman puts it, attracted 'softer social labels' as where the word 'blind' is less often used to describe people with this difficulty; words like 'partially-sighted', 'unsighted' or 'visually impaired' have come into common usage. This reflects a growing awareness of the stigmatising, painful effect of labels such as 'blind'. Indeed, over-use of euphemisms to avoid bad feelings has now become a source of humour, as where short people are described as 'vertically challenged', fat people as 'circumferentially challenged'.

The desire to disavow stigmatising labels, or to ameliorate their stigmatising effects, can take the form of an assertive proclamation of human rights. Thus Mike Oliver, a sociologist involved in the promotion of the rights of people with disabilities, has argued against the view that disability constitutes a personal tragedy which, he says, is: 'one more attempt by the able-bodied to disable people with impairment' (when interviewed in 1985 for an audiotape associated with the first edition of this book). At the root of the disability-rights movement is a challenge to standards of normality in a bid to assert membership:

> Able-bodied professionals have tended to see these problems as stemming from the functional limitations of the impaired individual, whereas

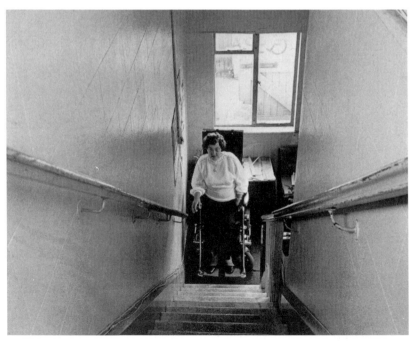

Is physical disability caused by bodily impairment, or by an environment that is geared to the needs of the able-bodied? (Photo: Suzanne Roden/Format)

disabled people have argued that they stem from the failure of physical and social environments to take account of the needs of particular individuals or groups. Is the problem of access to buildings caused by people not being able to walk or by the widespread social practice of having steps in buildings? (Oliver, 1993, p. 61)

This sort of argument has formed the basis of a vigorous political alliance, where the word 'disability' is itself regarded as a stigmatising label.

The position of 'normals' who regularly interact with stigmatised individuals is of some interest, and relevant to the consideration later in this chapter of the perspective of health care workers. It is the case that certain individuals become involved in the lives of people who are stigmatised, and come to identify strongly with their cause, sometimes taking part in the micropolitics[12] over labelling, and achieving as a result what Goffman calls a *courtesy* membership of the group. This is not, however, always an easy position:

> … a cult of the stigmatised can occur, the stigmaphobic response of the normal being countered by the stigmaphile response of the wise. The person with a courtesy stigma can in fact make both the stigmatised and the normal uncomfortable: by always being ready to carry a burden that is not 'really' theirs, they can confront everyone else with too much morality … (Goffman, 1968, p. 44)

Relations between stigmatised individuals and others, then, involve a complex acting out of interaction rituals, with claims and counterclaims to membership being made, judged and policed in circumstances where standards are fluid and ever-changing. The ontological security of all parties is continually at stake, with subtle shifts in the negotiation of norms blocking old channels of projection and at the same time offering new opportunities for the negotiation of stigmatised identities.

Viewed from the present day, where 'softer social labels' (to use Goffman's term) have become the norm, the categories used in the past reflect a simpler, cruder

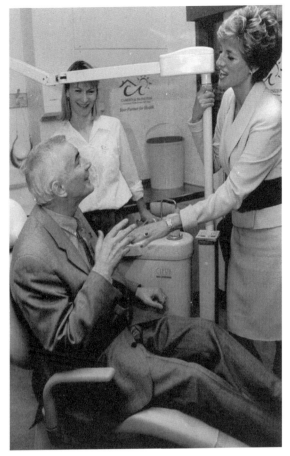

Princess Diana in a well-publicised handshake with a person with AIDS. In modern societies, tolerance is often promoted as a desirable social value and opinion leaders are often recruited as 'stigma champions'. (Photo: Popperfoto/Kevin Lamarque/WPA Reuter)

world. Then, the 'blind', the 'deaf', the 'poor', the 'feeble minded', 'retarded', 'mad', 'cripples', 'idiots' or 'bastards' were defined quite clearly and, often, permanently. It is probably the case that fixed categories like this are psychologically more easy to maintain for people who are *not* stigmatised—Goffman's so-called 'normals'. But the potentially devastating effects of such labels on the self-esteem of people who *are* thus stigmatised is now more evident. On the other hand, virtues which may now appear outdated, such as compassion, charity, pity and gratitude, were also probably expressed with less inhibition than is now the case. These may have softened the impact of stigma, while at the same time accepting and sustaining the boundaries on which it rested.

---

[12]A distinction is often made in sociology between 'micropolitics'—the political aspects of relationships between immediate social contacts (family, friends, workmates, club members, health professionals with whom there is direct personal contact, etc.), and 'macro-politics', involving wider social forces such as institutions, governments, political ideologies, etc.

The role of medicine

Medical labelling

If illness represents disorder in the body, medicine seeks to produce order. Medical knowledge, built up over centuries in the Western scientific tradition, categorises body parts, classifies diseases and seeks control over the disordered body through treatments designed to restore normal functioning. Medicine may have achieved its status as a grand narrative because it helps to give a sense of mastery and security in the face of apparently chaotic natural forces that otherwise threaten ontological security. Illness is a reminder of the temporary nature of bodily existence; medicine, in explaining and sometimes banishing disease, helps people 'forget' the limitations of their bodies.

A description of the normal body underlies scientific medicine,[13] and much medical research is devoted to establishing biological norms: blood pressure, temperature, sugar levels are some of the better known norms against which bodies are judged in investigations to establish disease.[14] People's experience of illness is inevitably permeated by medical ideas and practices, as Chapter 1 illustrated.

Diagnosis is a *dividing practice* in which the normal is separated from the abnormal, and the varieties of the abnormal are classified. Abnormal conditions are given **medical labels**, the delivery of which, if the label is considered stigmatising by the recipient, can cause shock, as revealed in this interview between Graham Scambler, a sociologist, and Mrs X:

> GS: How did you feel when he [the doctor] said it was epilepsy?
> Mrs X: I cried for two days. I think it was the word that frightened me more than anything.
> GS: Why was that?
> Mrs X: Oh, I just don't know. It was the way I felt I suppose. It's not a very nice word is it? I can't describe it really. I just can't describe how I felt.
> GS: It was something about this word 'epilepsy' that sparked that reaction off in you?
> Mrs X: Mm. Because, to me, when you tell people, they sort of shun you, that's the way I look at it. They, you know, they don't want to know; in fact my mother doesn't for one. If you go for a job and its on the form—and you've got

[13]See *Medical Knowledge: Doubt and Certainty*, Chapter 3.

[14]Biomedical research establishing norms is described in *Studying Health and Disease*, Chapter 8.

to put down 'yes', more often than not—you don't get the job, you know.
> GS: Have you actually found this, or is this something you understood would happen?
> Mrs X: I understood it would happen, because those who I work with don't know I have them [fits] anyway.
> GS: What made you think this sort of thing does happen to people with epilepsy?
> Mrs X: I don't really know, to be truthful. I just don't really know.
> (Scambler, 1984, pp. 212–3)

Here, the force of the stigma comes not from the doctor delivering the diagnosis, but from the speaker's own beliefs about the stigmatisation of people with epilepsy.

☐ Refer back to the earlier summary of terms and distinctions used by Goffman and others in discussing stigma. Which concept describes the process outlined above?

■ The concept of *felt stigma* describes how people may stigmatise themselves without the stigma necessarily being enacted by others.

Health care staff may, in fact, themselves be quite critical of the stigma attached to medical labels, even though they 'stick them on'. Indeed, health care workers sometimes achieve the status of stigma champions, wise to the distress involved in particular illnesses, negotiating acceptance of stigmatised groups by the wider community. In later chapters of this book, for example, you will see how certain sections of the medical establishment have struggled to counter prejudice against people with HIV or AIDS (Chapter 4). In the case of mental illness, community care to reintegrate people previously separated in asylums has been promoted by health workers (Chapter 6).

Indeed, medical settings may be havens of security and acceptance for people who are stigmatised. The word 'asylum', though it now has connotations of segregation and exclusion, was once used to mean a place of refuge for the persecuted. Indeed, some critics of the failures of community care policies for people with mental illness have argued for the restitution of asylums for those unable to look after themselves in a hostile 'community'. In the 1980s it was well known among people with HIV or AIDS that certain health centres in London hospitals offered confidential and sympathetic treatment not always available from general practitioners.

One strategy used by those seeking to ameliorate the conditions of people who are stigmatised is to question the system of knowledge that underlies stigmatising categories. This has been done, with some success at times, in an area where diseases are inherently difficult to define objectively, that of mental illness. Thus, in the 1960s, a movement arose that was known as **anti-psychiatry** (described more fully in Chapter 6 on schizophrenia), headed by a variety of doctors and academics such as the dissident psychiatrists Thomas Szasz in the USA and Ronald Laing in the United Kingdom. Their chief proposition was that mental illness either did not really exist or, if it did, it was a normal reaction to abnormal circumstances.

☐ Where have you seen this type of argument before in *this* chapter?

■ In the views expressed by groups campaigning against the stigmatisation of disability, where disability is conceived as the failure of others to provide an adequate environment for people with impairments.

An interesting and influential experiment took place in California in 1973, which demonstrated the arbitrary nature of psychiatric diagnosis. David Rosenhan and his colleagues conducted a study called 'On being sane in insane places', in which they sent eight sane research assistants to psychiatrists, faking mental illness. All were admitted to a mental hospital and, once there, behaved normally. Although other patients suspected they were frauds, none of the staff did, relying on the label given at admission to interpret their behaviour. Thus, the researchers' note-taking and their complaints of boredom were taken by staff to be signs of mental disturbance.

☐ What aspect of Goffman's analysis of stigma do these staff interpretations reflect?

■ Stigmatised individuals attract a *master status* whereby actions that are considered normal in other people are interpreted as reflecting their stigmatised condition.

The history of psychiatry is littered with disease categories that were once popular medical labels, but that are now discarded in favour of new ones.[15] This apparent inconsistency is encouraging for those who

[15]An example is 'hysteria', discussed in *Medical Knowledge: Doubt and Certainty*, Chapter 6.

wish to claim that the particular disease labels with which they are struggling are essentially arbitrary categories, of no lasting or objective importance. It is somewhat easier to mount such challenges in the arena of mental health than physical health, as the objective reality of mental conditions is harder to establish in the absence of physical pathology.

Additionally, some people may *seek* medical labels in order to disavow stigmatising labels emanating from non-medical sources. For example, the diagnosis of ME (myalgic encephalomyelitis, also known as post-viral fatigue syndrome), pre-menstrual tension and post-traumatic stress disorder may be helpful in countering imputations of malingering, irritability or weakness of character.

Typifications

At the same time, health care work is done by people who are as subject to all the usual pressures of negotiating their way through social situations as are the rest of the population. They may themselves subscribe to stigmatising prejudices, and may incorporate these within their work. For example, medical practice is not simply the objective application of medical knowledge, but occurs in particular social settings that encourage particular ways of seeing patients. This leads to a variety of informal pressures to place people in non-medical categories, the force of which may be equally stigmatising as that of a medical label.

☐ Can you think of some non-medical categories that might be used by health service workers when thinking about patients?

■ Here are a number of possible answers: elderly, stoical, complaining, hypochondriac, demanding, brave, tragic, caring, weak, patient, impatient, deserving.

One of the means by which people manage their interactions with each other is through **typifications**, the use of which serve to simplify the demands made on individuals in otherwise complex situations. Typification operates at a very basic level, helping, for example, to categorise objects so that weapons are divided from tools, food from non-food, and so on. In relation to people, typifications help to construct broad categories of person, so that the young may be divided from the old, male from female, pleasant from unpleasant, and so on.

When people are placed in demanding social settings, where they have to manage encounters with a large variety of people in short spaces of time—as is the case with much health work—the urge to typify people in order to simplify the mental difficulties of the task is strong. It is familiar, therefore, to hear of people in hospitals complaining of being treated 'like an object', or a 'number', envious comparisons being made with the more 'personal' service offered by private health care, where the demands on doctors' and nurses' time are not as pressing.

Informal models of 'typical' classes of patient very frequently emerge in health care settings, and are shared by staff. These may be local in character, and attract official disapproval, yet nevertheless help staff to further the aim of their organisation to run smoothly. Roger Jeffery in his article 'Normal rubbish' (first published in 1979)[16] describes how typification operated in busy casualty departments in three hospitals in an English city. People who had attempted suicide, drunks, tramps and people presenting with 'trivia' were categorised by staff as 'rubbish'. 'Good' patients, on the other hand, were those with 'genuine' medical conditions, preferably ones that were interesting, allowing doctors to practice their medical skills at a high level. 'Rubbish' patients were treated in a hostile fashion, made to wait for a long time or threatened with the police. 'Good' patients obtained prompt and courteous treatment.

Such typifications are not exclusive to hospital work. Gerry Stimson, a sociologist, studied the typifications of general practitioners (GPs) in the United Kingdom. He asked 453 GPs to write brief descriptions of patients who were 'least trouble' compared to those who were 'most trouble'. His analysis of the content of their replies revealed that certain characteristics distinguished the two groups of patients (adapted from Stimson, 1976):

Patients who are *least trouble* are: men, healthy, with specific symptoms that are organic/ physical, are easy to diagnose, can be treated, with medical problems, are easy to manage, get better, do not consult or can judge when to consult, are undemanding, do not take time, clearly present problems, have confidence in the doctor, accept limits to the doctor's skill, are grateful, want to get better or accept their illness, accept the judgement of the doctor, follow advice, are co-operative, intelligent, with common sense, can cope, are happy, settled, local,

adequate, busy or working and have good homes and circumstances.

Patients who are *most trouble* are: women, ill, with vague symptoms which are psychiatric or psychological, hard to diagnose and treat, originate in social problems, are hard to manage, do not get better, consult or cannot judge when to consult, are demanding, take up time, vaguely present problems, do not trust the doctor, do not accept limits to the doctor's skill, are ungrateful, do not want to get better or deny their illness, are critical of the doctor, do not follow advice, unco-operative, with low IQ, lack common sense, unhappy, unsettled, lonely, insecure, from elsewhere, inadequate, are idle or malingerers, have poor social circumstances.

It would be unfair to imply that all GPs subscribe to these stereotypes, or indeed that they are less sympathetic to 'trouble', 'rubbish' or 'problems' than to 'good' patients. Additionally, in the last twenty years the *consumerist* approach in the health service in the United Kingdom and elsewhere has encouraged health care workers to try harder not to stereotype patients in this way.[17] However, if such a picture still underlies health work, it is hardly surprising that consultations with doctors can be important moments for the defence of patients' 'moral reputations'. In talking about medical encounters after the event, people may also seek to display 'moral behaviour' in order to avoid stigma. Consider the following extracts from interviews with two mothers of young children:

> I went to the baby clinic every week. She would gain one pound one week and lose it the next. They said I was fussing unnecessarily. They said there were skinny and fat babies and I was fussing too much. I went to a doctor and he gave me some stuff and he said 'You're a young mother. Are you sure you won't put it in her ear instead of her mouth?'. It made me feel a fool.

> When she was born they told me she was perfectly all right. And I accepted it. I worried about her, which most mothers do you know—worry about their first child … She wouldn't eat and

---

[16]We recommend that Open University students should read this now if time is available. It is reprinted in *Health and Disease: A Reader*.

[17]Consumerism is discussed in another book in this series, *Dilemmas in Health Care* (Open University Press, 1993), Chapter 5.

different things. And so I kept taking her to the clinic. 'Nothing wrong with her my dear. You're just making yourself ... worrying unnecessarily' you see. (Quoted by Silverman, 1993, p. 109)

☐ What typifications are reported here?

■ The first extract suggests that the doctor has a rather disparaging view of the 'typical young mother'. The second extract does not reveal a medical typification, but the mother describes what she believes to be a generally held stereotype about first-time mothers as worriers, fitting the doctor's reported speech.

Commenting on these interviews, the sociologist Geoffrey Baruch (who interviewed the second person) argues that the mothers were seeking to display to the interviewer an identity as responsible parents, reporting the patronising treatment given them by medical staff as 'atrocity stories' in order to contrast this with their own 'moral behaviour' in being concerned about their children's welfare (Baruch, 1982).

☐ How does the concept of *membership* help in understanding what is going on here?

■ The women were claiming membership of the category of 'mothers who are concerned for their children's welfare', rejecting any imputation of a stigmatised identity as 'irresponsible'.

Medicine, then, may both sustain stigmatised identities and defend against stigma (as in the example given earlier of HIV clinics in London). By its most basic operation of diagnosis and classification, medical practice labels people with illnesses that may attract stigma from a variety of sources. Health care workers may be at the forefront of decrying such prejudice, providing a safe haven for people who are stigmatised and championing their cause. However, the conditions in which health care work is conducted can lead to typifications (such as 'good' or 'bad' patients) that may themselves be stigmatising. Aware of the force of such informal medical labelling, patients often seek to negotiate non-stigmatised identities both during health care and afterwards in discussing their experiences with others.

Conclusion

This chapter has approached the topic of stigma by first exploring the roots of the desire to be normal, identifying

this as a basic human need for security and membership that is fundamental to the organisation of social life. Illness is but one experience that threatens security, doing so because, ultimately, illness is a reminder of the limitations of bodily existence, and of eventual mortality. Claims to membership, which promote security, are based on agreed norms of behaviour. In both large-scale ritual events, and in small-scale interactions such as everyday conversation, claims to membership are made and judged between people. The exclusion of certain people in certain settings, if it is sustained and systematic, is called stigma, and is intimately linked to the attempts of the stigmatisers to maintain ontological security.

However, the effects upon those who are systematically stigmatised can be devastating, leading to a master status in which all actions are judged as emanating from a stigmatising condition. Covering up such conditions, trying to pass as if 'normal', or angry protestations against the unfairness of the whole process, are strategies available to people who are stigmatised. The damage done by stigma has become increasingly noticed in modern times as standards of 'civilised' conduct have developed, leading to a variety of attempts to negotiate and soften stigmatising labels. Permanently stigmatising categories are harder to maintain for any great length of time, as faith declines in the grand narratives that previously supported stigmatising categorisation, and as stigma champions arise to wage successful campaigns.

The final section dealt with the role of medicine and of health care workers in managing stigma, pointing out that categorisation and labelling is an essential activity in diagnosis, with potentially stigmatising consequences. Although health care settings can be a source of refuge and asylum for those stigmatised by the wider community, health care work itself can impose conditions where stigmatising typifications are created. In these circumstances, the moral identities of those seeking health care can be a matter of concern, and represent an underlying agenda in both medical consultations and in discussions of consultations after the event.

You will find the concepts used in this chapter useful in understanding people's experience of the illnesses described in the next four chapters, concerning rheumatoid arthritis, HIV and AIDS, asthma and schizophrenia. Some of these have attracted more stigma than others. All, to a greater or lesser extent, involve a search for a personal meaning for the disease, where you will find the concepts of *personal illness narrative* and *grand narrative* helpful. Chapter 7, on pain and suffering, will again take up some of themes raised in this chapter, by pointing out that stigma is a type of inflicted social pain.

OBJECTIVES FOR CHAPTER 2

When you have studied this chapter, you should be able to:

2.1 Discuss the psycho-social origins of the desire to be normal, and the part played by stigma and projection in maintaining the boundaries of membership.

2.2 Analyse the impact of stigmatising illnesses in modern social conditions, using key terms such as master status, passing, covering, discredited, discreditable, the own, the wise, felt and enacted stigma.

2.3 Describe the role played by medicine and health care workers in creating, defending against and managing stigma.

QUESTIONS FOR CHAPTER 2

Question 1 (*Objective 2.1*)

In 1897 the sociologist Emile Durkheim wrote in his study of the causes of suicide:

> ... great social disturbances and great popular wars rouse collective sentiments, stimulate partisan spirit and patriotism, political faith and national faith alike and, focusing activities on a single end, produce, at least for a time, a stronger integration of society ... [As people] come together to face the common danger, the individual thinks less of himself and more of the common cause. (Durkheim, 1897, quoted in Lukes, 1973, p. 209)

Durkheim found that the suicide rate declines in times of war. How might the concepts of stigma, ontological security, membership and projection be used to explain this? How does this large-scale phenomenon relate to small-scale interactions, such as conversations between able-bodied and disabled people?

Question 2 (*Objective 2.2*)

> Although I've been disabled since childhood, until the past few years I didn't know anyone else with a disability and in fact *avoided* knowing anyone with a disability. I had many of the same fears and anxieties which many of you who are currently able-bodied might feel about close association with anyone with a disability. I had ... rebelled against the prescribed role of dependence ... expected of disabled women. I became the 'exceptional' woman, the 'super-crip', noted for her independence. I refused to let my identity be shaped by my disability. I wanted to be known for *who* I am and not just by what I physically cannot do. (Galler, 1984, reprinted in Beattie *et al.,* 1993, p. 152–3)

What aspects of this account, by Roberta Galler, a woman who had had polio, illustrate the following concepts: master status, covering, discredited, the own, and enacted stigma?

Question 3 (*Objective 2.3*)

Here is a report from a conference of American doctors discussing the management of patients with pain:

> At the conclusion of a presentation on the experimental usefulness of [a test] for gauging pain tolerance, a physician in the audience stood to make the following comment: 'All of these lab experiments you've been talking about [are] a lot of hogwash. All of our patients are on disability [benefits] or on litigation, and they scream at the littlest pressure you apply. It seems like they hurt when you look at them [audience laughter] ... There is no validity when the patient has no motivation not to be in pain ...' (Kotarba and Seidel, 1984, p. 1396)

These doctors were also found to refer to patients complaining of pains that had no identifiable physical cause as 'compensation neurotics' (that is, complaining of pain in order to increase the chances of financial compensation) or 'problem pain patients'. Are these medical diagnoses or stigmatising typifications? What is the difference?

3 Rheumatoid arthritis

> *This chapter refers back to the role of antibodies and inflammation in the body's defence against infection, as discussed in* Human Biology and Health: An Evolutionary Approach, *Chapter 6. The television programme for Open University students, 'Why me? Why now?', associated with the first book in this series, uses rheumatoid arthritis to illustrate the relationship between lay and biomedical perspectives on the causes of the disease. If you videotaped it, you will find it useful to watch it again now, but in any case you should re-read the relevant sections of the Broadcast Notes.*
>
> *This chapter was written by Gareth Williams, Reader in Sociology, and Deputy Director, Public Health Research and Resource Centre, University of Salford; Ray Fitzpatrick, Fellow, Nuffield College, Oxford; Alex MacGregor, Senior Registrar in Rheumatology, Royal Free Hospital, London; and Alan S. Rigby, Senior Lecturer in Statistics and Epidemiology and Chartered Statistician, Department of Paediatrics, Sheffield Children's Hospital, University of Sheffield.*

Introduction

Of all the rheumatic disorders, rheumatoid arthritis is the condition that has been studied most extensively and over the longest period of time … It is frustrating, therefore, to have to acknowledge that all this effort has not led to commensurate enlightenment, and our appreciation of how and why this disease arises … remains rudimentary. (Wood and Badley, 1986, p. 63)

I was really in a terrible state at that time, really was. I couldn't do anything. I wasn't working, couldn't work. I had a job to get a mug of tea, cup of tea, or even a fork to my mouth, it was so bad … It started in my arms. My arms and shoulders are the worst. It is very difficult to describe to anybody what the pain is like. (Middle-aged man with rheumatoid arthritis, quoted in Williams, 1984a, p. 242)

Rheumatoid arthritis—commonly abbreviated to RA—is a disease of considerable significance for clinical medicine, public health and, most of all, the people who have to live with it day to day. Between 0.8 and 1 per cent of the population of the United Kingdom are thought to have RA—at least half a million people, each with a detailed personal narrative of pain, uncertainty about the future and changes in their relationships and other aspects of everyday life.

Like many chronic diseases, RA has many aspects. There are a variety of different ways of knowing about this complex condition, and these may give rise to different accounts of the nature of the disease—its aetiology, pathology, and consequences. The two quotations above illustrate the contrasting narratives of epidemiologists and people living long-term with the disease. For the laboratory scientists studying this puzzling condition, the causes of which remain uncertain, the story they tell is about genes, cells and viruses. Physicians treating RA may focus on levels of antibodies in the blood, inflammation of the joints and the latest drug trials or surgical interventions. Social researchers may seek to unravel the impact of the disease on personal lives and the role of society in alleviating or exacerbating its effects. All of these stories have a place in this chapter.

What is rheumatoid arthritis?

First, we will define what we mean by **rheumatoid arthritis**. As you will see, the definition depends very much on whom you ask and where you cast your gaze.

To a *rheumatologist*—a doctor specialising in rheumatology, the medical treatment of arthritis and rheumatism,[1] who may also conduct research—RA is a chronic inflammatory disease mainly affecting the joints, although every organ system in the body can become involved in the disease process. It is diagnosed on the basis of three groups of characteristic observations: *clinical features*—symptoms such as stiffness and physical signs such as symmetrical swelling in joints on both sides of the body, and X-rays showing erosion of the surface of the joints; *histological features*—findings on microscopic examination of involved tissues (*histo*, tissue), for example, infiltration of the lining of affected joints by large numbers of white cells usually engaged in the body's defences against infection; and *serological features*—principally the detection of a specific type of antibody called *rheumatoid factor* in the blood (*sero*, in the serum, or liquid fraction of blood).[2] We will return to the clinical picture of RA shortly, but it is important to emphasise at the outset that there is no single diagnostic test for the disease.

To the person affected by RA, the disease is not just the experience of pain or other common symptoms like fatigue and stiffness, nor is it simply a set of observable physical changes in the body. The illness reveals itself to the world over time in visibly swollen joints and loss of mobility as the disease process affects the soft tissue and bone. Other people can 'see' the RA, and it becomes, to a greater or lesser extent, part of the identity of the affected person, a chapter in his or her story. Moreover, RA is associated with considerable impairment in the functioning of the body's joints, and this interacts with the person's social and economic situation to create disability. The impairments produced by RA are often so severe and the provisions for affected people so meagre, that RA can be profoundly disabling.

---

[1] 'Arthritis' is the collective term for any disease or damage affecting the joints; 'rheumatism' has no precise definition but is widely used to describe any pain in and around bones, muscles and joints. There are about 200 different types of arthritis and rheumatism, which together are known as 'rheumatic diseases'.

[2] Inflammation is discussed as a normal part of the defence against infection in another book in this series, *Human Biology and Health: An Evolutionary Approach* (Open University Press, 1994), Chapter 6. Chronic inflammation occurs when this process is so prolonged and intense that formerly healthy tissues are damaged by it. White cells and antibodies are central components of the immune system; rheumatoid factor is an unusual antibody found in the blood of some—but not all—people with other signs of rheumatoid arthritis.

Uncertainty and rheumatoid arthritis

Another defining feature of RA is also a central theme of this book: it is fraught with *uncertainty* at all stages in its development, progression and treatment. The onset of symptoms typically occurs slowly over months or even years, but there are individuals who describe going from 'normal' to bed-ridden over the space of a few days. Symptoms fluctuate day to day, week to week, and month to month. Prediction of the course of the disease is difficult both for the person with RA and the professionals who deal with it. It disrupts domestic and working lives unpredictably and undermines long-term planning. There is no easy systematic relationship between the 'objective' severity of the disease and the 'subjective' disruptiveness of the illness and disability. RA usually affects people in middle age, but can occur at any age, and it is roughly three times as common in women as in men—yet the reasons for this distribution and the precipitating causes are uncertain.

These uncertainties greatly increase the likelihood that people with RA and the health professionals with whom they make contact will have sharply different expectations, hopes, agendas and stories within which the experience and understanding of RA is given meaning. We start to unravel these differences by building up a clinical description of the disease from the medical viewpoint, pointing to sources of diagnostic uncertainty, before assessing the consequences of this uncertainty from the patient's perspective. Then we return to the biomedical arena and describe the pathological processes occurring in the joints and organs of people affected by RA, before examining the difficulties that people experience in living with RA day to day. We explore its effects on activities, roles and relationships, and how these in turn are affected by public attitudes and social circumstances.

Next, we tackle another area of uncertainty: the question of what causes RA. In developing a greater understanding of this complex question, we draw on lay beliefs and personal illness narratives, and 'expert' knowledge from the disciplines of epidemiology and medical science. This leads to a discussion of how scientific knowledge about disease causation has influenced clinical strategies for disease management, and of the ways in which the patient's point of view has gradually become an increasingly regarded aspect of professional assessment of disability and of the outcome of medical and social interventions. Finally, as the backdrop to these personal and professional accounts, we refer to the history of RA as a disease category with attributes that have been 'socially constructed'.

The clinical picture of RA

There are many interesting aspects to the two case histories in Boxes 3.1 and 3.2, in addition to the fact that both involve women (RA is roughly three times more common in women than in men). What is immediately striking, and highly typical, is that there is no characteristic pattern of onset of RA. The onset may be *acute*, coming on explosively over a matter of days (Mrs J), or it may be *insidious*, with transient joint symptoms appearing and disappearing over a number of years before the presence of RA is recognised (Mrs P). The course of the disease also is one of relapse and remission, with no particular pattern to the timing and severity of episodes.

A number of characteristic clinical features point the physician to a diagnosis of RA. It involves inflammation of the *synovial membrane* lining the joints (see Figure 3.1), which is experienced by the patient as pain, stiffness and swelling. Characteristically, the stiffness increases when the joint has been at rest and is eased by movement. Stiffness is often felt most intensely in the morning and may last for several hours. Inflammation of the synovial membrane is recognised by the examining physician as a soft boggy feeling around affected joints, which are often warm. Excess fluid may be detected within the joint cavity.

Box 3.1

At the age of 55 years, Mrs J suddenly developed pain and swelling in her knee. She was referred to an orthopaedic surgeon who drained fluid from the knee and injected steroids. She had no further problem with the joint. However, six months later she developed problems with her hands. Over a few days, the knuckles swelled and were acutely painful. She had to remove her rings. She noticed in particular that her hands were stiff in the morning and that they tended to seize up if she rested them. In the next few days, her left ankle also became swollen and painful and she was unable to put her foot to the ground. A blood test showed the presence of unusual antibodies, collectively known as rheumatoid factor. X-rays of her hands showed that the bone at the edges of the joints in her hand and ankles was eroded. Her GP made the diagnosis of rheumatoid arthritis.[3]

---

[3]This is the first of several case histories illustrating the range of experience of rheumatoid arthritis, constructed from medical experience in rheumatology clinics; the details have been altered only in order to protect confidentiality.

Box 3.2

Mrs P, a 40-year-old woman who worked as a secretary, was referred to the rheumatology department of her local hospital with a history of a single episode of swelling of the hands and knuckles. When she was seen the swelling had virtually subsided and she could use her hands normally. The only abnormality found by the physician examining her joints was a mild swelling of the finger joints, producing a spindle-shaped appearance. Both hands were affected symmetrically. Her X-rays were normal. Blood tests were positive for rheumatoid factor. Thinking back, Mrs P remembered that she had had joint problems ten years earlier, shortly after the second of her two pregnancies, when her hands had been stiff. She had put this down to lifting her child. She also had 'tennis elbow' two years previously which her GP had told her had been due to typing.

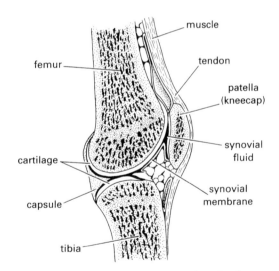

Figure 3.1 *Diagram of a 'side-on' section through a knee joint, showing normal anatomical features. Rheumatoid arthritis involves inflammation of the synovial membrane, leading to erosion of the cartilage covering the bones.*

Although any joint may be involved in the inflammatory process in RA, the small joints of the hands (the knuckles) and the wrists are involved most commonly. Certain joints are characteristically spared, most notably the small joints at the ends of all the fingers. A remarkable feature in RA is the frequency with which there is *symmetrical* joint involvement with joint areas on both sides of the body involved simultaneously.

The consequence of inflammation in the lining of joints occurring continuously over a period of months to years can be profound disability and chronic pain. As the chronic inflammatory process continues in the tissue lining the joints, the cartilaginous layer that overlies the bones becomes roughened and eroded. On X-rays, punched out areas called 'erosions' become visible

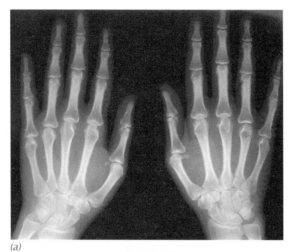

(a)

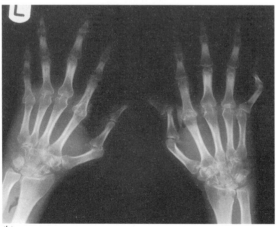

(b)

Figure 3.2 *X-ray photographs of the hands of a woman with rheumatoid arthritis (a) taken shortly after the onset of symptoms, showing normal alignment of bones, and (b) five years later, showing erosion of the surfaces of the bones and loss of alignment of the finger joints and thumbs (most obviously in the middle joint of the little finger of the right hand, and the wrist bones below it). (Photo: courtesy Dr Alex MacGregor, and Northwick Park Hospital, Harrow)*

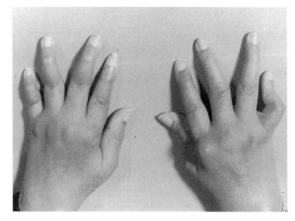

Figure 3.3 *The hands of the woman with chronic rheumatoid arthritis whose X-rays appear as Figure 3.2, photographed on the same day as X-ray (b). (Photo: courtesy Dr Alex MacGregor, and Northwick Park Hospital, Harrow)*

(Figure 3.2). Continuing erosion results in a loss of alignment of the bones in the joint as the normal direction of pull of tendons is altered (Figure 3.3). The joints themselves may dislocate.

Although joint involvement is the cardinal feature of RA, the disease may affect any of the body's organs. A *chronic inflammatory response* can become established in virtually any tissue. In up to 30 per cent of patients, lumps called *rheumatoid nodules* form when inflammation is localised, for example in the skin or lungs. Inflammation can also occur in the lining layers of the lungs, the heart and salivary glands, and more rarely in blood vessels, the eyes and peripheral nerves.

Another important feature of RA is the finding of particular *antibodies*—collectively termed **rheumatoid factor**—in the blood of approximately 80 per cent of affected individuals. The possible relevance of these antibodies to the progression of the disease is discussed in more detail later, but for the moment note that these antibodies are *not* present in 20 per cent of people who are subsequently diagnosed as having RA.

Diagnostic uncertainty

Rheumatoid arthritis, in common with so many rheumatic diseases, lacks a *single* uniquely identifying characteristic or biological hallmark that enables a doctor to diagnose the condition quickly and with absolute certainty—as the case history of Mrs P illustrates. Rather, a process of 'case ascertainment' goes on in which a range of features are investigated in combination. The most widely accepted basis for distinguishing RA as a clinical entity (illustrated in the case history of Mrs J) combines the detection of the clinical, histological and serological features, as described earlier.

One consequence of the lack of a single diagnostic test for RA is a degree of variation in methods of case ascertainment, which makes comparisons of epidemiological data from different sources somewhat problematic (a subject to which we return later in the chapter). Another, more pressing, consequence for the patient is the emotional effect of an often considerable delay in reaching a stable diagnosis of RA, which may be exacerbated by the tendency of signs and symptoms to 'wax and wane' over a prolonged period. Even when a diagnosis of RA has been reached, the uncertainties are not resolved. A number of the case histories given later in this chapter illustrate continuing uncertainty, both from the viewpoint of the clinician faced with deciding how best to treat individuals with such a variable condition, and for the patient trying to balance treatment benefits with possible adverse side-effects. We turn now to the experiences of the patients themselves.

Lay perspectives: the experience of uncertainty

In an early study of people with RA, Carolyn Wiener (1975) noted how the stock response of many doctors and nurses at that time—'You're going to have to learn to live with it'—was of little help to someone confronting the personal experience of living with an unstable, unpredictable, chronic disease. She argued that people with RA are constrained by two conflicting imperatives: the physical reality of variable pain and disability, and the social reality of daily life with all its pressures of time-keeping, relationships and the expectation of 'normality'.

For someone who develops RA, the early stages of the illness are fraught with uncertainty, particularly where (as in the vast majority of cases) symptoms are present for months or even years before they are finally diagnosed. It is often very difficult for people with early RA to know whether something is 'really' going wrong; and even when they are sure, it is often difficult to convince others, both relatives and professionals, that this is the case.

The phase of pre-diagnostic uncertainty can last for a considerable period—Mrs P's symptoms could be traced back to a possible first episode ten years earlier. The prime source of uncertainty in the early stages lies in the disease itself. Symptoms such as pain, joint stiffness and discomfort and more generalised fatigue are common enough, and a vague awareness may grow that everyday tasks cannot be performed as easily as before. The process of coming to terms with these symptoms and making some sense of them is far from straightforward. For people who have previously only experienced acute illness episodes, where they are ill and then well again, symptoms that appear and disappear over a prolonged period are difficult to understand. For the person who develops RA, difficulties can arise in understanding normal bodily processes:

> It was just my knee … [one man reported] … it just blew up for no reason. It wasn't painful to start with, just swollen … It was a funny shape and I thought 'what's going on here?' (Williams and Wood, 1988, p. 129)

The experience of uncertainty, however, does not exist in some kind of vacuum: the individual's response to bodily disorder and the way in which it is coped with depends to some extent on the person's background, understanding and experiences, as the case history in Box 3.3 illustrates.

Box 3.3

Mrs A was in her early 30s and a registered nurse. She had a sister and an aunt who were severely disabled as a result of RA. When she began to experience joint symptoms, she was immediately disturbed by what they might mean and, in a state of great anxiety and uncertainty, she was taken into hospital for tests. The hospital doctors kept her in for a week, during which her symptoms went into remission. Blood tests were taken but, according to her account, nothing was found, and she was informed that there was nothing wrong with her. The doctor said: 'You're a nurse, your sister's got this disease, your auntie's got this disease, you're thinking about it too much. We all have aches and pains, you know'. Mrs A reported 'I felt terrible. I came out of there with my tail between my legs and I came home'. Six months later she had a further spell of severe joint pain and quickly became too ill to care for either herself or her young daughter. She was readmitted to a different hospital where a rheumatologist diagnosed RA.

The experience of being labelled a 'malingerer' or a 'hypochondriac' is not uncommon amongst people in the early stages of many chronic diseases (a point already made in Chapter 2). The threat posed by these often vague symptoms may be compounded by the sometimes disbelieving response of close friends and relatives, who may insist that it is 'all in the mind'. The quality of the uncertainty changes once a diagnosis has been made. People often respond to the diagnosis of a serious disease with relief rather than horror. It seems to bring to an end a long process of 'unknowing' and provides a hook on which to hang the many troubling and strange symptoms:

> I thought I was going mental at the time … It came to the stage where I wasn't exactly glad that I had got arthritis, but at least there was really *something* that I was moaning about. (Williams, 1984a, p. 193)

Although the diagnosis of RA removes one dimension of uncertainty, there is then the problem of how to respond to a disease with symptoms that are literally there one day and gone the next. Some individuals come to doubt the original diagnosis when they experience a long remission, only to be knocked back again when the symptoms reappear. Moreover, not only is the disease unpredictable, it generates uncertainty in every aspect of a person's life. The person with RA is faced with having to accept the unpredictability of his or her body and its dictates, while continuing to respond to the demands and requirements of daily life.

Three major sources of uncertainty become part of life for the individual with RA and those close to them. The first can be summed up in the questions 'Why me?' and 'Why now?', which relate to the problem of cause (we return to this later). The second is raised by the question 'What should I do?' as the person addresses the problems of sustaining daily living, social roles and relationships. A third area of uncertainty is expressed as 'What will happen to me?', given the unpredictable outcome of RA. These uncertainties have a variety of implications for coping strategies and for the valued 'style of life' that someone is able to sustain in response to RA. These concerns are very similar to those of clinicians: 'What causes RA? What can we do for the patient? And what will influence the outcome?'.

Disease progression: the medical viewpoint

The course of RA is unpredictable and, although progression towards increasing disability fluctuates and periods of remission may occur, the affected joints often become intensely painful and their articulation can be profoundly impaired. Approximately two-thirds of patients with RA develop severe disability in a period of 15 years following its onset. The remainder have mild or moderate intermittent symptoms over a long period of time, sometimes with no apparent disability.

Not only is disruption of the joint architecture both painful and disabling, it may be life-threatening. In approximately one-third of patients with long-standing disease, the uppermost joint in the neck is involved in the inflammatory process. If instability and subsequent loss of alignment of the vertebrae occurs at this site, the bones themselves may press on the spinal cord within the spinal canal which, in 1 per cent of patients, leads to paralysis and possibly to death. A review of death rates among people with RA by two American rheumatic disease epidemiologists, Theodore Pincus and Lea Callahan (1986), shows that mortality is 50 per cent higher than in unaffected people, when all causes of death are combined. The commonest cause of death in RA is through infection, a consequence of the fact that the body's immune defences are impaired through the continuing process of chronic inflammation.

Chronic inflammation in major organ systems in RA can also lead to impaired function; for example, inflammation in the lungs causes breathlessness and respiratory failure; inflammation of the heart may cause heart failure, and inflammation in nerves can result in numbness, weakness and paralysis. The majority of people with long-term RA are anaemic, as the chronic inflammatory process inhibits the bone marrow's ability to produce red blood cells.

If these are the potential long-term consequences of RA for the patient's morbidity and mortality, what effects does the illness and disability have on everyday activities, social roles and personal relationships? We return to the experience of people with arthritis.

The impact and social consequences of RA

As we pointed out earlier, following a diagnosis of RA, people commonly ask themselves the question: 'What should I do?'. Pain, stiffness and fatigue interfere in incalculable ways with everyday life, from relatively simple activities such as getting out of bed to more complex formal and informal relationships with others. In this section of the chapter, three aspects of everyday life are examined: *activities of daily living*, *social roles*, and *dependency*. In reality, of course, these three aspects are closely interconnected, but for analytical purposes it helps to separate them.

Activities of daily living

In an in-depth study of living with RA, the sociologist David Locker (1983) interviewed 24 respondents who were severely disabled with RA and who had been affected for a number of years. Locker found that disability was often experienced as an accumulation of minor frustrations and difficulties—his respondents referred to the way in which it was the 'little things' that made life difficult and brought home the fact that they had disabilities. The everyday world becomes a world of obstacles.

Activities that for non-disabled people are more or less spontaneous, requiring no second thought, become matters of conscious deliberation for someone with RA:

> Last night I thought it's time to put that hot water bottle in. Well, I couldn't get the top out could I … so I thought there must be a way … so I put a screwdriver through the top and turned it round … Alright, it just needs a bit of thought and patience. (Williams, 1984a, p. 287)

The consequences of RA manifest themselves in relation to almost all areas of daily life: sleep and rest, walking and changing position, washing and bathing, dressing, mobility and housework. Locker's study established that it is only when it becomes difficult or impossible to do these things that people realise how significant the activities are. Moreover, both long-term planning and spontaneity are severely affected by the unpredictability of RA:

> Some days you feel ruddy marvellous and could jump over the moon, other days you're fit for nothing. (Locker, 1983, p. 18)

> You can't make arrangements, you've got to do things when you can. I never plan ahead, I can't, there's no good in planning ahead 'cause I just don't know how I am going to be from one day to the other. (Locker, 1983, p. 21)

RA obliterates the taken-for-granted trust in one's body (a component of *ontological security* discussed in Chapter 2), which is necessary for a person to make plans about 'what to do'.

☐ What sort of strategies do you think someone with RA would have to adopt to deal with difficulties in the activities of everyday life?

■ The strategies may involve getting others to help, doing tasks oneself but doing them differently, or finding a substitute for the activity that can no longer be done. (For example, David Locker found that people in his study started showering instead of

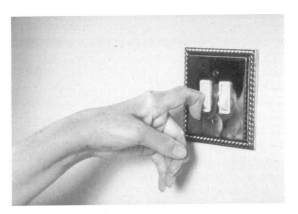

The everyday world can become a world of obstacles to a person with active rheumatoid arthritis. (Photos: courtesy of the Arthritis and Rheumatism Council)

bathing, or got adaptations to their bathroom which enabled them to go on bathing, or they had a wash instead and only bathed when visiting relatives who could help.)

However, it is not always easy to adapt: the impact of RA upon daily activities is mediated by a sense of what activities *ought* to be performed. Everyday life consists of moral imperatives that are difficult to resist, even where the experience of illness is severe and debilitating. People with RA sometimes define themselves as 'doers' who can no longer do things. The inability to open a tin of food is no problem if you have never wanted or needed to do this, or if there is somebody else there to do it for you. It is this wider aspect of the consequences of chronic illness that tends to be underplayed in most of the rehabilitation studies of activities of everyday life (Williams, 1987).

The impact of RA on individuals is seen particularly clearly in the context of paid work. Members of a specialist arthritis research centre in California (Yelin *et al.*, 1987) recruited a sample of individuals with RA and obtained data about their disease from their doctors. They interviewed the patients about their employment histories and showed that, of those individuals who were in work at the time of their diagnosis, 50 per cent stopped work within a decade. Such evidence is consistent with other studies in demonstrating how difficult it is to stay in employment following the onset of RA. However, the study also revealed how the specific *circumstances* of employment may determine whether or not the disease is associated with early retirement. The extent of the physical demands posed by the work, and the degree of control a worker could exert over the pace and content of the work, were better predictors of subsequent unemployment than were the person's disease characteristics. Such findings are powerful evidence of how the interaction between the disease and the social context ultimately shapes each individual's experiences of RA.

The importance of social roles

Tasks and activities are organised in terms of **social roles**.[4] While this is most clearly demonstrated in formal contexts such as paid work, social roles also structure activities and expectations in informal settings. Although the activities themselves may not seem particularly grand or important, their place within a role may accord them enormous significance. Where an activity is part of a caring role, the failure in this activity can have profound ramifications. For example, the tying of shoelaces involves a degree of manual dexterity that is a particular

---

[4]The concept of social roles is an important one in sociology; see for example Goffman, 1972. You have already studied an extract from an earlier article of Goffman's which deals with the breakdown of social roles in mental illness (see Chapter 2 of this book and *Health and Disease: A Reader*, second edition, 1995).

problem for many people with RA (Mason *et al.*, 1983). Sometimes it may be possible to make simple adaptations such as altering the type of footwear. However, when the person with RA is a parent, struggling alone to get children off to a school where they are required to wear lace-up shoes, the social effects run deep.

Other examples in which the meanings of activities vary with social role are provided by tasks associated with nurturing and homemaking, such as shopping and cooking. The importance of these tasks vary, among other things, with the position someone occupies in the domestic division of labour. In heterosexual couples in most industrialised countries, whereas a man may share in some domestic activities, the 'role responsibility' typically remains with the woman (Oakley, 1985), who—as we mentioned earlier—is roughly three times more likely to develop RA. As one woman with RA put it:

> If I am trying to do something [in the kitchen] and I get frustrated, I'll be cursing and [my husband] says: 'why do you try to do it? I'll do it for you if you ask me'. And I say: 'well I shouldn't have to ask you'. (Williams, 1987, p. 99)

The inability to prepare a meal can be a profoundly unsettling experience if it is a basic activity through which a woman feels her social role is delineated. As one woman put it: 'You feel a bit incomplete, I suppose', while another explained:

> I've got a guilt complex. I don't feel the children and my husband should do so much of my work, I feel I should take a bigger part. He will cook a meal sometimes if I've been really bad and I feel really guilty. (Williams, 1987, p. 99)

The problem for someone with RA, therefore, is not just one of an inability to perform certain *activities*, it is the failure in the performance of *social roles*. Cutting and peeling vegetables, cooking, putting food on the table, and washing-up can be seen both as discrete activities with which the symptoms of RA interfere, but they are also common parts of the ceremony of daily life. People with RA develop techniques and adaptations for undertaking specific activities but, rather than struggling to find new ways of doing things, it is sometimes possible to alter the overall division of labour and the expectations about who does what in the household. One woman, for example, in a study by Williams, offered her children payment for cleaning windows, helping to prepare meals, and doing the shopping. By redefining her role as supervisory and managerial rather than operational, she managed to maintain a sense of competent involvement in spite of her disabilities.

Difficulty in performing activities which are parts of the ceremony of daily life may be experienced as a failure in the performance of a social role. (Photo: courtesy of the Arthritis and Rheumatism Council)

The importance of social roles persists beyond the household. Although many people with RA have to give up work, others try to develop ways of adapting to the demands of their work:

> There were days when I couldn't really use a paintbrush in one hand. So I would get a piece of sandpaper and use the left hand and do a bit of sandpapering down for the next hour or so, ready for the next day … and I kept going. (Williams, 1984a, p. 344)

Compliance with sensible clinical recommendations (for example, to give up work) is often discussed as if it were an individual choice for patients, but it may simply not be practical for someone to comply:

> … it was necessity you see. My husband's only in a low wage bracket, and it did help pay the mortgage and keep things going properly here. (Williams and Wood, 1988, p. 130)

Failure to perform certain tasks is a major aspect of the experience of RA. These failures and the strategies used to offset them are often important in themselves, but they are particularly important in so far as they represent failures in the performance of social roles. It has been implicit in what has been said so far that this performance has implications for relationships of interdependence with others.

Dependence in relationships

The experience of disability is often described in terms of **dependence**—being dependent on others for help in meeting certain needs. Thus, dependence is generally but misleadingly defined as a property of *individuals* whose impairments prevent them from undertaking tasks and activities, such as washing and cooking, unaided. But individuals do not exist in isolation from society (however isolated they may sometimes feel). They are drawn into complex *social relationships* both with members of their informal networks and with agencies of the State—health services, social services and social security. However personal their experiences may be, those experiences are shaped by the features of economy, society and culture within which the person lives. Dependence is more accurately seen as a quality of *relationships in certain settings.*

The onset of RA disrupts the normal patterns of interdependence and reciprocity that are central to managing everyday life.[5] The severity of this disruption varies with the severity of the disease and the stability and robustness of the setting within which the person lives. One woman who had a severe and rapid onset of RA said:

> I just used to lie and shiver and couldn't move. Having got downstairs in the morning I used to spend most of the day wondering if my son and husband would get me back up there in the evening. (Williams, 1987, p. 100)

Studies of the experience of RA indicate that dependence gives rise to a great deal of anxiety and fear (Locker, 1983; Williams and Wood, 1988). Heavy dependency, such as that depicted by the woman above, is unusual and occasional. The experience of dependence is generally characterised by having to ask other people to do certain things, and having to wait for help. People with disabilities often state that they do not want 'to be a burden' or 'to interfere with' the lives of others by making demands. Discomfort comes both from the sense of depersonalisation that can follow from having things done for you, and from the feeling that certain tacit moral rules about what can be expected of others are being infringed. Drawing too freely upon the time of other family members is seen, literally, 'as taking liberties'. Very often people with RA feel that they do not want help unless they ask for it, but they are also reluctant to ask. As one woman put it:

> It's alright me saying I've got relations—my sister will come and tidy up and everything for me—but they have their own lives to live, they

---

[5]Dependence and reciprocity in relationships among people who develop physical impairments in later life are discussed in more depth in *Birth to Old Age: Health in Transition,* Chapter 11.

have their own families to see to. (Williams, 1987, p. 101)

This problem of dependence is felt more in some relationships than others. For example, in a study by Williams, a 30-year-old woman and her baby daughter were both being looked after by her mother who was in her mid-60s. This caused a double burden of guilt and anxiety: failure to discharge her own duties to her baby and imposing unfair demands on her mother. The feeling of concern about dependence for people with RA is felt most acutely in relationships with their children:

> I don't want to be a burden to my family that's the main thing. I'd hate to think that, because I've seen so many people be a burden to their children and I think it's most unfair. (Newman *et al.*, 1995, p. 44)

RA is a process, not a state. For some people, having struggled to do everything for themselves, there comes a point where they accept a change in their relationships:

> It would be about the middle of when I was ill that I began to settle for them [the family] to do things for me. (Newman *et al.*, 1995, p. 45)

However, making a 'settlement' such as this is always provisional. Living with chronic illness involves continual adjustment to changing aspects of the disease, alterations in the domestic situation, the varying availability of benefits and services, and changes in the wider economic and social situation.

Although this discussion of dependence in relationships has centred on the domestic arena, people with RA will often turn to resources in the public sphere in order to prevent the occurrence of problems of dependence on close relatives. For example, one woman, although having two sons living nearby, was helped in her bathing by the district nursing service, until the provision of a bath-seat released her from any dependence on others for taking a bath. The provision of simple aids and adaptations can transform personal and social relationships. As Gareth Williams (1993) has shown in a detailed case study of an elderly widow with RA, although dependence upon aids and adaptations can be uncomfortable, it may have fewer negative connotations than direct dependence on other people, be they relatives or statutory services. It also circumvents the complications of reciprocity and indebtedness.

☐ Although RA is not generally thought of as a 'stigmatising' condition, in the sense in which we applied that term to schizophrenia or AIDS in the discussion in Chapter 2, how might a person with RA experience stigma?

■ The ramifications of feelings of incompetence, failure to fulfil social roles or 'moral imperatives' concerning normal daily activities such as taking a bath, dependency on others, and the visible disfigurement of joints, all constitute a considerable threat to personal self-esteem and 'moral reputation'. Some people with RA may experience *felt stigma*, in which they withdraw from certain activities or avoid situations in which they fear others will discriminate against them or judge them negatively.

So far in this chapter, we have described the diagnosis of RA and its longer-term consequences from the medical and the lay perspectives. The clinical signs and symptoms have been discussed in the context of the personal and social features of the condition. We can now delve into another area of importance to both doctors and patients, and one in which similar uncertainties abound: what causes RA.

Lay beliefs about the causes of RA

Lay beliefs about illness are shaped by the culture and society of which they are a part and, consequently, their content and structure exhibit considerable variation. However, in almost all studies of **lay illness beliefs**, the issue of the *cause* of the illness is prominent.

Relatively little research has been done into lay beliefs about the causes of any form of arthritis. In one of the earliest studies, on osteoarthrosis (a degenerative form of arthritis that is particularly associated with ageing), an American social scientist, Ruth Elder, argued:

> The cause of arthritis symptoms … is unknown or, at best, controversial, and as a consequence official communications concerning it are limited. Thus a fertile field exists for the development of ideas derived from empirical experience and non-scientific beliefs about bodily functioning. (Elder, 1973, p. 29)

More than 20 years later the precipitating causes of arthritis remain obscure, and the 'fertile field' for the development of lay ideas persists. Some of these lay ideas are copies, elaborations, or corruptions of medical ideas, taken from direct encounters with doctors, nurses, and therapists, or gleaned from magazine articles or television programmes dealing with orthodox or alternative health care. Yet other ideas are based on everyday life, on observations of other people and conversations with friends.

The anthropologist Dennis Gray (1983) noted the wide variety of sources for beliefs about joint disease in his study of 104 'arthritis sufferers'. About three-quarters of their ideas about the cause of arthritis and rheumatism did not correspond with orthodox medical beliefs. Gareth Williams and his colleagues investigated lay beliefs about RA and also attempted to explain their logic and purpose (Williams, 1984a, b; 1986; Williams and Wood, 1986). This work is based upon in-depth interviews with a small number of people who had all had RA for at least five years since diagnosis. The wide variety of factors mentioned by respondents were grouped into 12 causal categories, displayed in rank order in Table 3.1.

The most significant aspect of lay beliefs in this study—invisible in a simple rank ordering like Table 3.1—is the way in which these factors were accounted for and 'weighted'. For example, where factors relating to occupation and a virus were both given particular emphasis, the individual identified their occupation as having made them *vulnerable* to symptoms, and a virus was seen as playing a *triggering* role. In some cases these beliefs amounted to formal 'models' which drew together the impact of a large number of factors existing over a long period. For example, Figure 3.4 shows the complex model of cause and effect developed by Mr A, who was in his early 60s, to explain the origins of his RA. Although he had had RA for about ten years, he traced it to the time he was in the army 40 years earlier, working in harsh physical conditions and under considerable psychological stress, combined with many years in the building trade, and a post-operative infection following surgery for stomach ulcers.

Table 3.1 Rank order of causal categories mentioned by 29 people who had all had rheumatoid arthritis for at least 5 years (respondents could choose more than one category)

Category	No. of respondents
stress/life crisis	12
heredity/genes	11
physical trauma	9
occupation	7
environment (including climate)	6
virus/germs	5
previous illness	3
ageing	3
personality type	3
wear and tear	2
divine influence	2
don't know	2

Source: Williams, G., 1986, Lay beliefs about the causes of rheumatoid arthritis: their implications for rehabilitation, *International Rehabilitation Medicine*, **8**(2), Table 3, p. 66.

Lay knowledge and narrative reconstruction

While medical explanations for diseases are related to a body of formal scientific knowledge, patients' views are woven out of the threads of their experiences, as Figure 3.4 illustrates. These experiences may include a strand of formal medical knowledge, but this is likely to be given no more weight than the information derived from friends, fellow-sufferers or the media.

The sociologist Mike Bury (1982) has described lay beliefs as a form of knowledge and understanding that

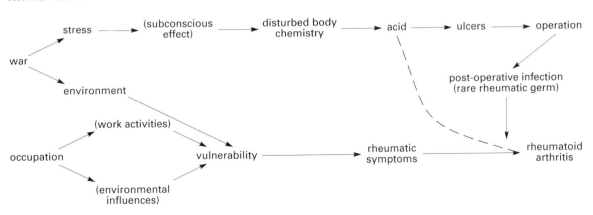

Figure 3.4 *Mr A's model for the development of his rheumatoid arthritis. (Source: Williams, G. and Wood, P., 1986, Common-sense beliefs about illness: a mediating role for the doctor, Lancet, **ii**, un-numbered diagram, p. 1436)*

enables people to re-establish some kind of meaning and cognitive order to cope with the 'biographical disruption' that chronic illness entails. (In Chapter 7 of this book you will learn about a related phenomenon—the ability of chronic pain to 'unmake the personal world' of the patient.)

Re-establishing meaning is not an event, but an ongoing endeavour. Gareth Williams (1984b) has analysed the process of **narrative reconstruction**, which occurs as people with RA seek to build a relationship between their experience of the illness and the details of their own lives. Narrative reconstruction leads to a coherent set of beliefs that are simultaneously *causal* and *teleological* (that is, framed in terms of purposes): thus, the reconstructed narrative seeks to answer 'Why me?' and 'Why now?' not only in terms of 'What caused me to become ill?' but also 'To what end or purpose have I become ill?'.

Narrative reconstruction is apparent in the following extract from a long interview with a 68-year-old man, who had had RA for over 20 years. He remembered World War II:

> I went to North Africa, Italy, Austria, through and home. But we was getting drowned through the night, in Italy and Africa mostly, at Christmas time. We was going to make a big push at Christmas, but the weather was so bad that they cancelled it, and we was up to our knees in mud. In Italy there were weeks when I never wore a pair of socks, it was a waste of time. We was on this brow here and you couldn't stand up during the day. We dug little slits and you was in that slit all day lying in the sun, can't move, and at night its throwing it down on you … and then they wonder why you're like this! (Williams and Wood, 1986, p. 1436)

Contained within this account is something much more than an explanation of what causes RA. He has reconstructed his narrative of wartime experience to explain 'why RA happened to *me*'. Other interviewees weave the cause of their RA into a narrative which emphasises the stresses of personal relationships and family life, as in this example from a middle-class woman in her 50s:

> I'm quite certain that it was stress that precipitated this. Not simply the stress of events that happened but the stress of suppressing myself while I was a mother and wife … There comes a time in your life when you think, you know, 'where have I got to? There's nothing left of me'. (Williams, 1984b, pp. 188–9)

The teleological aspect of personal illness narratives can be seen most clearly when a religious concept is invoked to make sense of what has happened in an individual's life.

> The Lord's so near and, you know, people say 'why you?' … and I [say] 'Look, I don't question the Lord, I don't ask … He knows why and that's good enough for me' … I've got the wonderful thing of having the Lord in my life. I've got such richness shall I say, such meaning. I've found the meaning of life, that's the way I look at it. My meaning is that I've found the joy in this life, and therefore for me to go through anything, it doesn't matter really, in one way, because I reckon that they are testing times. (Williams, 1984b, p. 193)

Lay beliefs such as those recounted here about RA can also be seen partly as attempts to understand the complexities of a disease that is inadequately understood within biomedicine. In the absence of a convincing medical explanation for 'Why me?' and 'Why now?', lay people are able to draw on a wide range of influences in constructing a narrative without direct contradiction from their doctors. Whether lay narratives are 'right' or 'wrong' in terms of biomedical knowledge, they clearly have a role in supporting someone attempting to live with RA. In the next two sections, we turn to the sources of 'expert knowledge' about the causes of rheumatoid arthritis, beginning with epidemiological studies.

Epidemiological knowledge

Arthritis and rheumatism as a whole are the biggest single source of disability in the United Kingdom and North American populations, and are among the main reasons for consultations with primary health care practitioners. A survey by the American epidemiologists L. S. Cunningham and Jennifer Kelsey (1984) of self-reported symptoms suggests that approximately 29 per cent of men and 32 per cent of women in the USA experience joint problems. This rises to 35 per cent and 51 per cent in people aged 55 or older. However, these estimates depend on individuals' own definitions of their symptoms and group together all forms of arthritis. Estimates of the prevalence of RA are much lower and vary considerably between populations. Caution must be exercised in interpreting apparent differences in the frequency of RA in different parts of the world.

□ Can you suggest why?

■ The absence of a characterising diagnostic feature for RA leads to variations in methods of case ascertainment based on several features of the condition (as discussed earlier in this chapter). This in turn leads to variations in disease classification and makes comparisons of data from different populations problematic. (For example, a case of rheumatoid arthritis in one population may be classified as inflammatory polyarthritis in another.)

Attempts at standardising the reporting of the disease have been made by the development of disease classification criteria, for example by the rheumatologist Frank Arnett and colleagues (1988) for the *American Rheumatism Association*. Their classification is based on evidence from three sources: clinical assessments, such as whether a joint is swollen; standard laboratory assays, such as the level of rheumatoid factor in the blood; and X-rays of the hands and feet. A minimum score on these criteria must be reached before a person is labelled as having RA for study purposes. By using standardised classifications such as these, it is possible to estimate the prevalence and incidence of RA in different populations.

Prevalence and incidence estimates[6]

In 1986, Philip Wood and Elizabeth Badley published a comprehensive review of the epidemiology of rheumatic disorders. They noted that surveys using more rigorous definitions of RA show a remarkable degree of convergence in estimates of *prevalence* in most Caucasian groups across different geographical areas, varying between 0.8 and 1.0 per cent (i.e. about one case per 100 population surveyed at a single time point). However, there is a marked excess in women, with estimates generally suggesting that three times as many women as men are affected. In both sexes, the prevalence of the disease increases with age, approaching 5 per cent in women and 2 per cent in men aged above 55 years.

There are few epidemiological surveys of the annual *incidence* of RA. Figure 3.5 shows the results of one of the few to be published on the trend in the United Kingdom, which was sharply downwards in the 1980s and approached 65 new cases per year per 100 000 population. Incidence (like prevalence) increases with age in all studies, but it has also been suggested that the number of severe cases is declining.

□ Why is the prevalence of RA so much greater than its incidence?

■ RA is a chronic disease lasting a long time, hence there are many more people with the disease at any one time than there are cases being newly diagnosed.

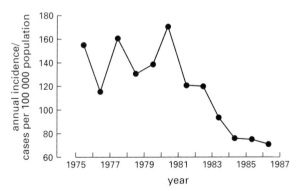

Figure 3.5 *Trends in annual incidence of RA among patients attending general practices in the United Kingdom in 1976–87 (all ages combined). (Source: Silman, A. J., 1988, Has the incidence of rheumatoid arthritis declined in the United Kingdom? British Journal of Rheumatology, 27, pp. 77–8)*

[6]Prevalence and incidence are defined and discussed in *Studying Health and Disease*, Chapter 7.

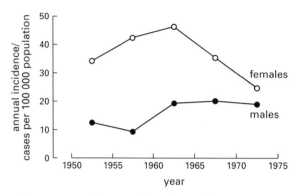

Figure 3.6 *Trends in annual incidence of rheumatoid arthritis in men and women in Olmstead County, Minnesota, USA, in 1950–74. (Source: Linos, A. et al., 1980, The epidemiology of rheumatoid arthritis in Rochester, Minnesota: a study of incidence, prevalence and mortality,* American Journal of Epidemiology, ***111**, pp. 87–98)*

□ Figure 3.6 shows a much earlier trend in the annual incidence of RA in both men and women in a study in the USA. Describe the trend and suggest what insight this research gave into the biology of the disease. (Hint: What 'revolution' in the 1960s affected women but not men?)

■ The incidence of RA fell by almost a half in women in the 1960s and early 1970s, whereas it rose by a small amount in men. It may have occurred to you that this period coincided with the rapid and widespread uptake of the oral contraceptive pill in women,[7] which has subsequently been shown to affect the occurrence of RA (discussed later in this chapter).

However, you should note that in the epidemiological study of any disease it is difficult to disentangle 'real' changes in frequency from changes in the way in which the disease is defined and diagnosed over time. (You will meet this problem again in the epidemiology of AIDS, asthma and schizophrenia—the case studies in Chapters 4, 5 and 6 of this book.)

Risk factors for rheumatoid arthritis

Epidemiological data on prevalence and incidence, such as the studies reviewed above, can provide valuable information about the patterns of RA in populations and

[7]As discussed in *Birth to Old Age: Health in Transition*, Chapter 7.

any associations with social and biological factors. These in turn suggest *possible* causal connections, but much more evidence is needed about the cause or causes of RA.

Ethnicity

There are some interesting ethnic variations in the frequency of RA. The prevalence in Asian populations is similar to that in Caucasians (Al-Rawi *et al.*, 1978), while in some American Indian groups it is reportedly much higher (Harvey *et al.*, 1981). In *urban* Black African populations the prevalence of RA is about the same as that reported in Caucasians (Solomon *et al.*, 1975), but in *rural* Black African populations it is about one-tenth of that in Caucasians (Brighton *et al.*, 1988).

□ What kinds of explanation do these variations suggest might be worth investigating?

■ In theory, reported ethnic variations in the prevalence of RA might be due to differences in susceptibility to RA arising from variations in genetic background, or to ethnic differences in the expression of symptoms, or to environmental effects associated with urbanisation.

The explanations are far from clear, but one of the authors of this chapter has attempted to investigate the role of urbanisation. Rheumatologist Alex MacGregor and his colleagues sent a postal questionnaire about the experience of RA to Afro-Caribbean and White respondents in a deprived, inner-city area of Manchester. MacGregor then examined those individuals who reported experiencing the disease. White respondents were found to have RA nearly three times more often than Afro-Caribbeans (MacGregor *et al.*, 1994). Such evidence makes urbanisation itself an unlikely causal factor in RA.

Social class

There have been occasional reports that the risk of developing RA is inversely related to income and occupational social class, but very few studies have examined the issue systematically. The majority of reports suggest that there is no overall relationship with social class (Lawrence, 1970; Jacob *et al.*, 1972), but interest has recently been revived by the work of Theodore Pincus and Lea Callahan in the USA (1994). They found an inverse relationship between 'educational level'—used as a 'proxy' for social class—and prevalence of RA in certain populations.

Age

The association of RA with age is two-fold: the risk of onset increases with age, and the disability associated with the disease increases over time. Incidence and prevalence increase with age in all studies, as shown, for example, in a survey conducted by Dugowson and colleagues (1991) of RA in women in Seattle, USA, in the period 1987–9. The incidence per 100 000 women aged 30–39 years was 16.5, but the incidence among 60–64-year-olds was 61.6. Although 'wear and tear' damage to joints tends to increase with age, and repair processes become less efficient, simple mechanical explanations cannot account for the chronic inflammation in major organs of the body as well as in the joints, nor for the presence of rheumatoid factor in the blood, which are characteristic features of RA. Biological explanations for these phenomena must be sought, as you will see in the next section.

Sex

Sex differences in the prevalence and incidence of RA are well established, but the underlying reasons are not well understood and represent an important challenge to research. The precise extent of the difference in prevalence is unclear, the often-quoted estimate of 3 : 1 being only the 'best guess'. However, Fleming and co-workers (1976) could find no differences in rates between men and women when patients were examined within a year of disease onset.

□ What does this finding suggest?

■ RA might have a similar incidence in men and women, but sex differences in prevalence appear over time. Perhaps there is more remission in men and the course of the disease is less severe.

A team of rheumatologists in Japan have observed that there are much smaller sex differences in rates of onset of RA after 60 years of age (Inoue *et al.*, 1987). Da Silva and Hall (1992) have suggested that the overall pattern of a much higher prevalence in women is due to an earlier age of onset in women, typically 45–64 years, and a more severe course of the disease. Much of the evidence does support the view that women experience RA in a more disabling form than men, but it is not consistent and there are variations depending on the measure of 'severity' used and which joints are studied.

Clearly, biological explanations for the observed sex differences in RA have been given great attention, and we will discuss them shortly, but the social and cultural influences of *gender* also need to be considered. Although these influences may not have a direct impact on the severity of the disease according to objective measures, there is evidence that gender does affect **illness behaviour**—the expression, perception and response to symptoms. However, findings from different studies are contradictory: Thompson and Pegley (1991) found that, at comparable levels of disease activity, disability for women was worse than for men, whereas another study by Deighton *et al.* (1992) found that sex differences in disability disappear after controlling for disease severity.

A related possibility is that aspects of *physical performance* that vary between men and women—for example, grip strength—result in greater disability for women after the onset of RA. Verbrugge and colleagues (1991) found that one of the biggest differences between men and women with arthritis is reported strength: similar tasks may thus pose greater challenges for women.

□ Can you think of another explanation for sex differences in disability, based on the discussion of social roles earlier in this chapter?

■ It may be that traditional social and domestic roles are more revealing of disability in women than they are in men. For example, the finely controlled movements required in some domestic tasks such as cooking and sewing might reveal a woman's inability to perform them, whereas men with RA may not attempt them.

However, the most compelling explanations for sex differences in the prevalence of RA have come from biomedical research, which has also shed light on possible underlying causes of the condition and the pathological processes involved in its progression.

Biological knowledge

In this section we start by describing biological research suggesting that hormones, genes and infectious organisms may play a part in triggering the onset of RA or in increasing a person's susceptibility to other—perhaps still unidentified—precipitating factors. We then describe what is known about the underlying pathological processes in RA, and evaluate the strongly-held view that RA is an *autoimmune disease*[8] in which chronic inflammation might be caused by inappropriate activity of the

[8]Autoimmune diseases and the possible mechanisms by which they are mediated are discussed in more detail in *Human Biology and Health: An Evolutionary Approach*, Chapter 6.

immune system against 'self'. Finally, we reflect on how more distant factors implicated by epidemiological studies of RA may be interacting with biological processes to cause the disease.

The role of hormones

The most obvious biological explanations for sex differences in the prevalence of RA relate to *sex hormones* such as testosterone and oestrogen. Hormonal influences could account for the common observation that women with RA experience temporary remission during pregnancy (Klipple and Cecere, 1989). Moreover, a study by Dutch epidemiologists provides evidence of a possible beneficial effect on RA of the oral contraceptive pill (Vandenbroucke *et al.*, 1982), as illustrated earlier in Figure 3.6. Two rheumatologists, Tim Spector and Marc Hochberg (1990), have suggested that oral contraceptives reduce the incidence of RA by postponing the onset of the disease, which occurs once the oral contraceptive has been stopped.

There are a variety of ways in which sex hormones might influence the causes or course of RA. There are, for example, many complex relationships between sex hormones and the immune system which, in turn, is directly involved in the production of chronic inflammation. However, overall research evidence on sex hormones and RA is contradictory and inconclusive. For example, elevated levels of a sex hormone in patients with RA may turn out to be a consequence rather than a cause of the disease (Da Silva and Hall, 1992).

Genetic inheritance

It has long been known that RA has a 'family connection'. Women who have a sister or mother affected by RA are two to four times more likely to develop the disease than those without such a history. Moreover, studies of affected twin pairs reveal that RA is up to five times more common in monozygotic (identical) twins than in dizygotic (non-identical) twins. However, a nationwide study of RA in twins in the United Kingdom, by Alan Silman, Alex MacGregor and colleagues, found the *concordance* in identical twins (i.e. the probability that if one twin develops RA, so will the other) was 15 per cent, but only 4 per cent in non-identical twin pairs (Silman *et al.*, 1994).

☐ What does this suggest about the importance of genetic inheritance in causing RA?

■ Concordance in identical twins is much higher than in non-identical twins, which indicates that a shared genetic component may be responsible for

their increased susceptibility to RA. However, the fact that concordance even in identical twins is so far below 100 per cent, despite their identical genes, indicates that environmental factors must have a major role in causing RA.

Although genetic susceptibility to RA is thought to be *polygenic* (that is, more than one gene is involved in disease predisposition), some strong associations with particular genes have been identified.[9] The most compelling evidence has come from studies by another of the authors of this chapter, Alan Rigby and his colleagues, who have investigated the association of RA with the presence of certain **HLA genes** (Rigby *et al.*, 1991; Rigby, 1992). Several alternative forms of these genes occur in humans, and one of them (known as *HLA-DR4*) occurs more frequently in people with RA than expected from its distribution in the population. But this gene cannot cause RA on its own because it is also found widely in non-affected people. The *HLA* genes are concerned with regulation of the immune system. As we said earlier, a breakdown in immunological regulation leading to an 'anti-self' (autoimmune) response in the joints is thought to be one of the precipitating factors in RA, and it is possible that there is a genetic component in this process.

Current knowledge about genetic aspects of RA is promising rather than revealing. As new technology increases the speed with which genetic associations with diseases can be found, there is hope that the genetic components of RA will be identified, leading to greater understanding of the disease processes and advances in treatment and perhaps even prevention. However, there are major scientific difficulties in applying such knowledge, particularly where the genetic component may be relatively small and outweighed by environmental factors (as the twin and *HLA* studies suggest). Moreover, there are serious ethical concerns about the effects on individuals of genetic knowledge about disease susceptibility.[10]

---

[9] The structures of genes and chromosomes, and the association of certain genes with disease susceptibility, are extensively discussed in *Human Biology and Health: An Evolutionary Approach*, Chapters 3, 4 and 9.

[10] The biological, ethical and social implications of the Human Genome Project, genetic screening and gene therapy are discussed extensively in *Human Biology and Health: An Evolutionary Approach*, Chapter 9, and in the associated television programme and audiotape band for Open University students.

A role for infection?

There is considerable uncertainty about the possible role of infectious organisms in RA (reviewed by Alan Silman, 1991). One of the most commonly studied viral agents is the *Epstein–Barr virus*, which is found in populations world-wide and has been implicated in many different diseases. Many studies have shown higher levels of antibodies to Epstein–Barr virus in RA patients, when compared to individuals without disease. Another candidate agent is *human parvovirus B19*, which has been isolated from the joints of individuals with an arthritis resembling RA. A third infectious agent, *Mycobacterium tuberculosis*, has been shown to produce a type of arthritis in laboratory animals that is similar to RA. But the flaw in all theories concerning infectious agents is a lack of specificity for the disease—not everyone who has RA can be shown to be infected with one of these organisms, and many infected people do not have RA.

☐ What does this suggest about the role of infectious agents in RA?

■ It seems highly unlikely that any of them are the single precipitating factor. Perhaps the best bet for the aetiology of RA is an infectious organism operating in a genetically susceptible host.

Multifactorial theories

Complex interactions between biological and environmental factors in the aetiology of RA are suggested by current research. In this respect, RA is similar to other chronic degenerative conditions, such as heart disease and cancers, in being *multifactorial* in origin. For example, it has been suggested that the apparent decline in incidence and severity in recent years may be due to changes in the biological nature of a viral agent, but it may also be related to the increased use of the oral contraceptive pill among women (look back at Figure 3.6).

Other factors (mainly anecdotal), such as the weather, diet and stress, have been implicated in multifactorial theories. Although symptoms of RA may vary with the weather, biochemical indicators of disease inflammation do not show similar changes. The relationship between diet and disease has been reviewed by Darlington and Ramsey (1993), and particular attention has been paid to the protective effect of diets high in fish oil. Many of these theories have not withstood rigorous scientific scrutiny, but they remain of interest—particularly to patients—and cannot be discounted.

Pathological processes in RA

Chronic inflammation is a central part of the disease process in RA. Microscopic examination of the *synovial membrane* of affected joints (refer back to Figure 3.1) reveals a thickened, swollen appearance. White cells of the types normally involved in producing inflammation at the site of an infection infiltrate the joint in huge numbers. Blood vessels become dilated and proliferate in the inflamed tissue, bringing more white cells to increase the inflammation.

Signalling molecules, known collectively as *cytokines*, are released into the joint by white cells participating in the inflammatory response. They promote the proliferation and activity of cells in their local environment. One particular cytokine, called *TNF-alpha*, predominates and may hold the key to a novel treatment for RA in the future (described in the next section).

The development of a chronic inflammatory response in normal tissue is the most compelling evidence that RA is an **autoimmune disease**. Autoimmunity implies that the disease process involves the loss of the immune system's normal tolerance to 'self' and the production of antibodies and other components of an immune response directed inappropriately against the body's own tissues. Unusual antibodies, known collectively as *rheumatoid factor*, can be found in the blood of about 80 per cent of individuals with RA. However, the precise role of rheumatoid factor in RA remains controversial. Conventionally, anti-self antibodies are seen as promoting and perpetuating an autoimmune disease, but a number of investigators have suggested that rheumatoid factor may have a *regulatory* role, limiting the degree of inflammation in RA (Levinson and Martin's 1988 review asked whether it is 'Dr Jekyll or Mr Hyde?'). Others have argued that the occurrence of rheumatoid factor is simply a by-product of inflammation.

It is, however, by no means certain that autoimmunity is the *cause* of RA—indeed, it might be a consequence. Inflammation in the joints may be triggered by an infection or by some as yet unknown factor, producing tissue damage which provokes the immune system into an inappropriate attack. Another possible mechanism is *antigenic mimicry*, in which parts of the structure of infectious organisms resemble components of 'self'. The *Epstein–Barr virus*, for example has proteins in its coat that resemble proteins in the cartilage lining of human joints. Hence, when the immune system sets up an attack on the infectious agent, it cannot avoid simultaneously attacking those similar components of the body's own tissues.

Problems with establishing causal processes

The epidemiology of RA implicates both genetic and environmental factors in the cause of the condition. What we have tried to indicate here is that while much recent work in immunology and cellular biology has been helpful in illuminating disease processes, 'true causes'—the events that initiate RA—remain elusive. A number of studies have indicated that RA may eventually comprise several distinct subsets, each with particular distinguishing clinical features. Alternatively, the clinical picture that is currently recognised as RA may represent a final common pathway for several aetiologically distinct chronic inflammatory processes.

Putting knowledge into practice: therapeutic strategies for RA

In view of the elusiveness of the cause or causes of RA, there is no adequate strategy for its prevention. The rationale for clinical management is based on the current understanding of the pathological processes involved. Chronic inflammation is established as the cause of joint destruction in RA, so suppression of inflammation by drugs remains the cornerstone of strategies aimed at treating the disease. We begin by briefly reviewing the major classes of drugs used in RA, their benefits, side-effects and limitations.

Drug treatments

One of the earliest and most effective methods of suppressing inflammation in RA was the use of *steroids* (synthetic forms of naturally occurring steroid hormones), introduced with dramatic effect in the 1940s. They abolished inflammation in patients in whom apparently irreversible disease had been present for decades. But it soon became clear to both clinicians and patients that the doses required to control RA produced many unwanted effects, including diabetes, high blood pressure, damage to blood vessels, and thinning of bone leading to collapse of vertebrae in the spine. In the 1990s, the precise place of steroids in the treatment of RA remains controversial. The use of steroids is generally limited to short courses or to injections directly into joints, which produce few adverse effects on the rest of the body.

Another effective class of drugs was the *salicylates* (aspirin), and for many years the long-term use of high-dose aspirin formed the mainstay of drug treatment for RA. This was, however, also associated with serious adverse effects, in particular a high frequency of gastro-intestinal complications including haemorrhage and perforation.

A number of drugs have since been developed which have similar properties to aspirin, with fewer adverse effects. These are broadly classed as *non-steroidal anti-inflammatory drugs* (or NSAIDs), and their use remains central in the day-to-day control of both pain and inflammation in the majority of patients with RA. They are not, however, believed to influence the long-term outcome of the disease. Despite their apparent superiority over aspirin, NSAIDs remain an important cause of morbidity from gastrointestinal haemorrhage and renal impairment. The risk is particularly high in elderly people.

A separate group of drugs, known collectively as *disease-modifying anti-rheumatic drugs* (or DMARDs), is used in RA to control the inflammatory process in the long term. They are believed to influence the rate of progression of disease, but the mechanisms of action of DMARDs are diverse and inadequately understood: most act directly on cells involved in the inflammatory process to suppress their activity. All DMARDs are associated with important and potentially serious toxicity, primarily affecting the bone marrow, liver and lungs, and their use necessitates careful monitoring.

Clearly, the benefits of drug treatments have to be weighed against the multiple risks of side-effects, but there are several problems in evaluating outcomes. Any benefit may take a considerable time to show; different measures of outcome will show different benefits; and what is a benefit in clinical terms may not be seen to be so by the patient. The relapsing and remitting course of the disease makes it difficult to be sure that an improvement is due to a given drug. In addition, the most potent drugs available for use in RA are frequently associated with the most adverse effects and are reserved until late in the disease—which makes their usefulness in early disease hard to evaluate. Drugs in combination may be more effective than agents used singly, yet few data are available. Finally, in assessing published reports, it is important to consider bias toward the publication of drug trials that show a positive rather than a negative outcome.

Given these limitations, it is perhaps not surprising that the available data on RA show no clear long-term effectiveness of any of the available drug treatments, and initially effective regimes are frequently discontinued because of adverse reactions. The majority of patients with a disease lasting 15 years will have changed drugs approximately three times.

New treatment strategies

A number of new treatments for RA are currently being developed, based on current understanding of the underlying biology of the disease. The most promising strategy to date is the use of synthetic antibodies directed against the signalling molecule, TNF-alpha. As mentioned earlier, TNF-alpha is a central mediator of inflammation in RA, so neutralising its activity could, in theory, suppress active disease. Initial trials are encouraging, though the results of its long-term use are awaited. Another strategy is to attempt to restore immunological *tolerance* to 'self' by giving carefully controlled doses of the proteins which may provoke anti-self reactions (in much the same way that people suffering from hay-fever are desensitised by receiving tiny repeated doses of pollens). The problem here is that the exact identity of the proteins that trigger the inflammation in RA remains unknown. (A review by Kingsley *et al.*, 1996, of therapeutic strategies involving the immune system is listed in the Further Reading section at the end of this book.)

New approaches also under development include *gene therapy*, in which genes are inserted directly into joints to correct defects in the function of cells there. Inhibitors of the *enzymes* responsible for 'digesting' away bone and cartilage in inflamed joints are also being researched.

Other medical and surgical interventions

Medical management of RA must include treating the 'whole body' manifestations of the disease, such as anaemia, and the involvement of major organs, such as the heart, lungs and kidneys. The consequences of persisting joint damage—joint destruction, muscle wasting and problems with locomotion—also have to be addressed. An important liaison in the management of RA is between rheumatologists, physiotherapists and orthopaedic surgeons, who specialise in joint surgery and have a crucial role in maintaining function and managing pain—as the case history in Box 3.4 illustrates.

Mr K's experience illustrates the advances in joint surgery and in the technological development of artificial joints in recent years. Physiotherapy also has a crucial role, in particular in preserving joint stability and muscle strength to prevent joint deformity and maintain function. Physiotherapists have an important part to play in the management of chronic pain through the use of techniques such as ultrasonic massage and weak electrical stimulation of affected areas. (Chapter 7 discusses pain-control techniques.)[11]

Box 3.4

Mr K, who has had RA for 40 years, has had numerous joint operations in that time, including replacements of both hips and knees, artificial joints in the small joints of his hands, and an artificial elbow and shoulder joint. His early operations relieved the pain in his joints, but they did not improve his joint function to any significant extent. However, the surgery performed on his hip in the last five years and on his shoulder two years ago has transformed his life and has enabled him to function at a level that he would not have previously imagined. Given the levels of disability he had previously experienced, he now leads a remarkably independent existence and manages his life by himself.

However, the use of surgery and physiotherapy is not routinely accepted everywhere. For example, the frequency and timing of surgical intervention show marked variations between centres. The long-term value of physiotherapy is also debated—indeed physiotherapy is used considerably less in the United Kingdom than in other European countries.

Unorthodox treatment strategies

As we described earlier, several theories about the causes of RA exist at the fringes of medical orthodoxy, and these have led to considerable uncertainty about the place of alternative treatments in the management of RA. The value of dietary modification is one such area of controversy. There is a widespread public perception that diet influences RA, but scientific data to confirm this are limited, although there is an indication that dietary fat content may influence disease activity. Some rheumatologists believe that allergy to foods such as cheese has a role and they prescribe exclusion diets in the treatment of RA. However, no data are available on the influence of dietary modification on the long-term outcome of the disease.

[11]For Open University students, an audiotape band on the work of a 'pain clinic' is associated with Chapter 7.

Many people with RA turn to a variety of complementary therapies, and most interest has focused on *homeopathy*. It is not clear whether the search for alternative treatments reflects the inefficacy of conventional medical management or the therapeutic potency of the alternatives. There are currently no adequate data suggesting the value of homeopathic remedies in RA but, given the difficulty in assessing the outcome of orthodox anti-inflammatory agents, it is unlikely that such data will become available unless new forms of evaluation and outcome assessment are devised.

Keeping the patient in view

RA affects all aspects of patients' lives. Doctors should take account of the patient's knowledge, circumstances, hopes and fears in order to arrive at strategies for medical management that are appropriate to the patient's present and future needs. Hip pain, for example, may not only impair walking but may affect sexual function, and this is an important consideration in planning hip surgery. A detailed occupational history is needed in planning and staging surgical procedures, which may require long periods off work to convalesce. Future hopes of pregnancy must be known when planning drug treatment in RA because it may impair fertility and may have to be stopped prior to conception.

The individual's response to his or her symptoms is another important component of the problem which the clinician has to consider when planning management strategies. Failure to understand the patient's experience can lead to situations like the one in Box 3.5.

Box 3.5

When Mrs L was referred as a new patient to the rheumatology clinic, she showed features of well-established RA with inflammation affecting her hands, wrists and elbows, and deformities of both wrists. During the consultation, she said she had attended hospital two years earlier when the symptoms had first developed. She remembered being told at that time that she had a chronic disease of the joints which would not get better without treatment. She was recommended to take a drug which she was told might affect the back of her eyes and could impair her eyesight. She did not take the drug or keep her follow-up appointment. She put up with the symptoms until increasing pain in her hands made her ask to be seen in the clinic again.

In order to manage the uncertainties being experienced by someone such as Mrs L, it is important to understand her point of view, to provide information in a manner and in a context that facilitates dialogue about the risks and benefits of different treatments, and to shape advice to her actual circumstances. There may be many months of trying various strategies before an adequate treatment regime is found, and this compounds the uncertainty of living with the symptoms of RA.

The unpredictable benefits of treatment, along with the psychological effects of having RA (such as depression and anxiety), may have important consequences for a patient's willingness to comply with lengthy spells of out-patient treatment, which place enormous demands on an individual's time and resources. Compliance is important from the doctor's viewpoint in order to make a realistic evaluation of the effectiveness of particular drug regimes, as measured in clinical or biochemical terms. However, what is 'effective' to a doctor will not necessarily be so for the patient. The doctor treating the person with RA has the difficult task of combining his or her abstract scientific understanding of the disease with the way in which it makes itself known in the body and the life of the individual patient.

Patients and their doctors have different expectations, hopes, agendas and stories within which the experience and understanding of RA are framed. As we indicated at the start of this chapter, the scientific story of RA—by epidemiologists, laboratory scientists and doctors—is only one of the stories to be told. The problems of treatment outcome and disease impact are central to the management of everyday life with RA, and are of growing importance within health services seeking to make their interventions more effective and more appropriate to patients' needs. In the next section of this chapter, we look at attempts to develop measures for evaluating the outcome of treatment and other interventions that do justice to the everyday experience of the person with RA.

Patient-provided measures of outcome

We have already discussed a variety of biological and clinical methods of assessing the severity and course of disease in RA, including blood tests and X-rays. Considerable efforts have also been made to assess the personal and social impact of RA. Standardised, precise and quantifiable questionnaires and interview-based assessments have been developed, which attempt to elicit the patient's own report of his or her disease and its personal consequences. This *patient-centred approach*[12] to measuring the course of RA is beginning to be used in basic research on the effectiveness of different therapies, as well as in the more routine provision and monitoring of care.

It is interesting to consider why efforts have been made to obtain and use assessments provided by patients—given that medicine is reputed to have strong 'reductionist' tendencies, i.e. a greater readiness to trust and be concerned with biologically-measured parameters of disease rather than with subjective evidence such as patients' reports. Whereas the patients' own perspectives are beginning to be regarded as of increasing interest in their own right, moves within health care in the 1990s to make it more sensitive to 'consumers' have opened up discussion and research on ways of using assessments provided by patients. Health services are increasingly being required to evaluate cost-effectiveness by devising and using **outcome measures**—systematic measures of the benefits of specific health-care interventions. Since the primary objectives of health-care for RA are to reduce pain, disability and disadvantages arising from the disease, so outcome measures should relate to these objectives. In turn, the objectives of health care have to relate to and derive from the main concerns of patients. It will already be clear to you that such apparently desirable reciprocity does not necessarily occur.

Another factor in the development of patient-provided outcome measures stems from the growing acceptance that the patient is uniquely placed to know the impact of disease upon him or her, and is also capable of providing reports with the same accuracy as is sought from conventional measures such as blood tests. If patients' personal experiences can be as reliably captured as biological processes, then they offer potentially powerful evidence of the benefits or side-effects of interventions.

The drive to find relevant as well as accurate measures of outcome ultimately stems from one crucial feature of all forms of intervention for RA. Beneficial effects—whether from drugs, surgery, psychological or complementary therapies—are invariably modest and therefore difficult to detect. This factor alone leads pharmaceutical companies, clinical researchers and indeed any agency interested in improving the care of individuals with RA, to search for more sensitive, appropriate and ultimately convincing measures of the outcomes of interventions. If such measures could be obtained directly from the patient via reliable, useful and practical methods, then traditional reservations about the weaknesses and 'softness' of subjective data will erode.

Questionnaires and the assessment of arthritis

A number of questionnaires have been developed that are completed by patients and intended to assess, with adequate accuracy, the personal and social consequences of RA. This kind of research has developed more extensively in rheumatology than almost any other area of medicine. Questionnaires on the impact of RA have been put to a wide variety of uses:

(i)   in a diverse range of clinical trials to assess the benefits to patients with RA of drugs, surgery, psychological therapies and alternative methods of providing care (e.g. in-patient versus out-patient care);

(ii)   to track the natural history of the disease in cohorts of patients with RA so that more precise statements can be provided about the usual range of progression of pain and disability over time;

(iii)   in medical audit and quality assurance in health care;[13]

(iv)   by clinicians in individual patient-care to detect and monitor problems in patients over time and to evaluate the impact of therapy.

To serve a useful and convincing role in such diverse contexts, questionnaires need to produce answers that match a clear set of requirements. They need to produce answers that are *reliable* (that is, answers that are consistent on repeated administration, provided no real change has occurred in the subject matter), and *valid*, (that is, the information provided does actually provide a measure of what the questionnaire purports to measure). In the context of health-care evaluation, a questionnaire needs to be *sensitive* to changes of importance to the patient over time. Finally it must be *acceptable* to the patient and *feasible* for use in the context intended.[14]

[12]Patient-centred approaches to health care in medical settings—particularly the clinical consultation—and the more traditional doctor-centred approaches are discussed in *Medical Knowledge: Doubt and Certainty*, Chapter 9, which includes an audiotape band on this subject for Open University students.

[13]Medical audit is a method of 'peer-review' among doctors of the outcomes of medical interventions; it is discussed with other methods of health-care evaluation, such as performance indicators, in *Dilemmas in Health Care*, Chapter 4.

[14]The design of questionnaires and issues of reliability and validity are discussed in more detail in *Studying Health and Disease*, Chapter 5.

Assessing disability and pain

The most widely used questionnaire in the assessment of RA is the *Health Assessment Questionnaire (HAQ)*, devised by Fries *et al.* (1982). The core of the HAQ consists of 20 simple questionnaire items asking individuals to assess their degree of difficulty with various tasks (for example, 'Are you able to cut your meat?'). The answers produce scores for an individual in eight aspects of daily life: dressing and grooming, rising from a chair or bed, eating, walking, hygiene, reach, grip and activities (for example, getting in and out of a car). The average of the eight scores is used as a summary *Disability Index*. The questionnaire performs very well against the criteria outlined above: respondents give consistent answers and find it easy and quick to complete, and it also has substantial validity.

☐ How would you test the validity of a questionnaire such as this one?[15]

■ By direct observation of patients to corroborate their questionnaire responses.

A group of general practitioners in Glasgow directly observed a sample of their RA patients perform the eight areas assessed by the HAQ, and scored what they estimated to be the patients' degree of difficulty (Sullivan *et al.*, 1987). Patients then also completed the HAQ themselves. There was a very high level of agreement between the two sets of evaluations. The HAQ is also a very practical tool for tracking the natural history of the disease. Two rheumatologists (Wolfe and Cathey, 1991) followed up a series of their patients with RA in a Kansas clinic over a twelve-year period. They showed a steady progressive deterioration in HAQ Disability Index scores over the period of the study. Moreover the best predictor of the extent of deterioration in disability was the patients' own answers to the HAQ at the beginning of the study.

As you have seen, pain is also a central feature of RA. Pain is a more obviously personal and, in measurement terms, subjective phenomenon. (It is the subject of Chapter 7 of this book.) The HAQ uses a simple technique to assess pain, inviting individuals to mark a position that represents their degree of pain on a linear scale. Simple measures such as this have proved just as useful as more sophisticated methods in which, for example, detailed account is taken of the vocabulary patients select to describe their pain (an example of the latter appears as Table 7.1 in Chapter 7). Another widely used questionnaire in RA—the *Arthritis Impact Measurement Scales (AIMS)* (Meenan *et al.*, 1980)—asks about the frequency and severity of pain, summing the answers to a single scale.

Consistency between different outcome measures is essential, if results from different studies are to be compared. Ray Fitzpatrick (another of the authors of this chapter) and his colleagues asked patients with RA to complete the AIMS and several other similar questionnaires on a single occasion. There was less consistency between different questionnaires in scoring pain than there was in scoring disability (Fitzpatrick *et al.*, 1992). It is essential to include measures of pain despite such measurement problems, because it is not possible to predict from a knowledge of the severity of their disease the degree of pain that someone with RA experiences. Indeed, when a group of rheumatologists from Missouri assessed their patients with RA for pain, they found that older age, lower income and various psychological measures of distress and helplessness were all better predictors of pain than conventional laboratory and clinical measures of disease severity (Parker *et al.*, 1988).

Assessing social aspects

Many questionnaires given to patients with RA also attempt to provide standardised assessment of its social aspects. As you already know, RA can have wide-ranging effects on the individual's social world, including problems of employment, loss of contact and diminished quality of relationships. However, it may be difficult within the confines of a short set of simple items in a questionnaire to capture all relevant aspects of individuals' social lives. The AIMS questionnaire emphasises the impact of RA in reducing the ability to maintain contact with friends and relatives, whether by visits or telephone. Other questionnaires focus on the individual's sense of being isolated and a burden to others.

☐ Why might two different questionnaires produce somewhat different impressions of the impact of RA, even if completed by a single group of patients?

■ The questionnaires may differ in which aspects of daily life they emphasise. Thus, the social dimension may be defined in one questionnaire as activities like maintaining contact with friends, and in another questionnaire as anxieties like feeling a burden to others.

---

[15]Think back to *Studying Health and Disease*, Chapter 5.

It has been shown that if patients with RA complete several different questionnaires, there is little agreement in the picture portrayed by the various social assessments (Fitzpatrick *et al.*, 1992).

Another problem has been identified by a group working in a specialist arthritis research unit in Connecticut (Reisine *et al.*, 1987). They claim that a fundamental bias exists in all questionnaires on social aspects, which tend to assess the impact of RA on household activities such as cooking and washing, but neglect what the authors term 'nurturant functions'. These functions include childcare, caring for other household members who are sick, and maintaining the family's social relations with the outside world.

☐ Think back to the earlier section on 'Activities of daily living'. What do you think might be the result of the questionnaire bias that Reisine *et al.* identified?

■ It is argued that 'nurturant functions' are more relevant to the lives of many women. Thus, existing questionnaires may have a gender bias that systematically underestimates the degree of impact of RA on women.

Problems of definition and emphasis also arise in attempting to assess the psychological consequences of RA systematically. There is evidence that individuals with RA have increased levels of serious psychological symptoms such as anxiety and depression and, for this reason, questionnaires such as the AIMS give most attention to such experiences. However, others would argue that the most important psychological problems for patients with RA are far more common, if less severe, symptoms such as feeling out of control and losing autonomy.

Personalised assessments

It should be clear to you from the previous discussion that it is very difficult to identify a standard list of questionnaire items that is suitable for assessing the impact of RA on everyone with the disorder. Not only does RA have a very diverse range of possible consequences for everyday life, individuals will vary enormously in their concerns and priorities.

A group of rheumatologists in Ontario have tackled this problem by devising a personalised method of assessing the impact of RA, which attempts to be sensitive to variations between individuals (Tugwell *et al.*, 1987).

Instead of asking patients a standard set of questions, they are invited to identify for themselves the areas and activities in their lives that are most affected, and that they would regard as the highest priority for improvement by means of therapy. Patients would therefore identify a list of personal priorities and then rate the degree of improvement or deterioration that occurred in relation to this list in subsequent assessments. The priorities most commonly selected by patients are not surprising: walking and housework. However, some patients selected activities that are rarely if ever assessed in conventionally-formatted questionnaires: for example, getting to church or the pub or playing golf.

This method has subsequently been used by the group in a double-blind randomised trial of the benefits of methotrexate, a slow-acting anti-rheumatic drug (Tugwell *et al.*, 1990). Eliciting and measuring patients' personal priorities proved more sensitive to the therapeutic benefits of the drug than either the doctors' traditional clinical measures, or a patient-completed questionnaire about disability with conventional standard questions asked of all respondents. However, this personalised approach to patients' problems requires an interview which, for the large-scale studies usually required for trials of new therapies, is not as feasible as a self-completed questionnaire.

There is still no consensus about the most sensitive and useful method of assessing the broader consequences for individuals of having chronic diseases like RA. Although it may be argued that attempts to simplify the diversity of individuals' personal experiences into quantitative forms are inevitably flawed, the purposes of such efforts should be kept in mind—to go beyond narrow measures of outcome to identify broader benefits. The use of questionnaires of the kind described here is becoming widespread in assessing the advantages and disadvantages of the many drugs now in use for patients with RA.

Research is still needed to discover what aspects of health care or social interventions can improve the well-being of patients with chronic disease, but some clues are emerging. A group of rheumatologists, social workers and psychologists set up a randomised trial to evaluate the benefits to patients of providing multi-disciplinary team care, compared with more usual management by a hospital doctor alone (Ahlmen *et al.*, 1988). After one year there were significant advantages to patients cared for by a team in terms of walking and psychological well-being, as measured by simple patient-completed questionnaires. It will increasingly be necessary to examine benefits of all forms of care—social as well as medical—by methods that reflect patients' perceptions as much as possible. You should now be aware of the potential as well as the pitfalls of current methods of including the patient in such assessments.

In the final section of this chapter, we stand back from the personal and professional narratives of RA, and briefly consider the impact on those narratives of the social history of arthritis in the twentieth century.

An historical footnote

There is little literature on public attitudes or societal reactions to arthritis, beyond Badley and Wood's study in 1979. This is in sharp contrast to AIDS, schizophrenia, or even asthma—as you will see in the case studies in later chapters of this book. Sex, drugs, madness, and children 'gasping for breath' have greater cultural resonance than middle-aged or elderly women and men living quietly alone in chronic pain. Nonetheless, all forms of arthritis, including RA, do have a *social history*. The historian, David Cantor, has done some important work in unpicking the threads of that history by looking at the wider social context in which the diagnosis and treatment of arthritis developed (Cantor, 1991, 1992, 1993).

Many times in earlier books in this series, it has been demonstrated that diseases are not stable and timeless entities. At least some aspects of every disease are not so much revealed as 'produced' by the social and cultural processes of analysis and interpretation.[16] The history of RA illustrates this rather well. In common with many other diseases, progress towards discovering the distinct nature of RA is often portrayed as a difficult but fundamentally unproblematic 'discovery of the facts'. But the history of RA has in fact been much more complex, and reveals something about attitudes to arthritic disorders in general. In particular, as David Cantor has shown, images of arthritis were bound up with the politics of industry and empire in Britain in the early twentieth century.

The history of professional and public attitudes to arthritis and rheumatism in general, and RA in particular, cannot be understood without analysing the factors influencing two developments. The first is the gradual emergence of a medical speciality—*rheumatology*—

---

[16]The main discussion of health, disease, disability and health-related behaviours as 'socially constructed' can be found in *Medical Knowledge: Doubt and Certainty*, Chapter 7, but see also *Birth to Old Age: Health in Transition*, Chapters 1, 9 and 10.

dealing with the treatment of arthritis and rheumatism, and the second is the establishment of research into these conditions. Both these developments affected the perceived importance of arthritis and rheumatism in society, and their status in relation to other organised interests such as the government, medical charities and the pharmaceutical industry. For example, public interest in arthritis and rheumatism clearly took off in the inter-war period in Britain as a result of concern about a number of social factors: the costs of these diseases to the National Health Insurance scheme set up by Lloyd George in 1911; their effects on 'national efficiency'; concern about infant and child welfare (particularly the impact of rheumatic heart disease); the revival of spa economies during World War I, and the inter-war growth of medical hydrology (medicinal use of spa and other waters).

Many of these concerns were given a further push by the socio-economic problems of the 1930s. With government reluctance to increase spending on health care, doctors turned to philanthropy for support. It was during this period that the major rheumatological research charity, the *Empire Rheumatism Council*, was set up. The early donations to this charity came predominantly from industrialists and businessmen concerned about the impact of rheumatic diseases on the efficiency and productivity of the workforce.

These developments had a significant impact on the development of rheumatology, and thus upon the development of knowledge about—and therapeutic intervention for—rheumatic diseases. At the time of the instigation of the NHS in 1948, rheumatology was a small and insignificant specialty. The Empire Rheumatism Council (later the *Arthritis and Rheumatism Council for Research*, or ARC) came to play an important role in encouraging research, and engaging in negotiations with the then Ministry of Health over the position of rheumatology in the health service. Rheumatology is now a medical specialty, with its own hierarchies of prestige, its conference circuit and its journals and newsletters. Although it cannot call forth public beneficence on the scale of cancer or heart disease, charities representing arthritis and rheumatism are consistently in the income 'top twenty'.

The present-day Arthritis and Rheumatism Council for Research exists to finance and organise research into the causes and means of treatment of rheumatic diseases, to encourage teaching about the diseases, and to stimulate public bodies to provide treatment. In 1994, ARC spent £16.7 million on these objectives, providing the major source of support for rheumatology research through institutes, research units, research grants and fellowships. It supports university appointments and has endowed a number of Chairs of Rheumatology. Its income is made up of donations and legacies and the work of more than 1 000 fund-raising branches throughout the country. The ARC thus plays a crucial role in the management of public attitudes to RA and other related diseases. It lies at the heart of a network of national and regional structures which link the general public, business, the medical profession and government. At times of economic and political uncertainty over the direction of health services, and when many worthy causes are competing for public attention, the intelligent construction and representation of the impact of a disease like RA play an important role in influencing public attitudes and hence funding.

In concluding the chapter with this historical footnote, we seek to remind you that RA—like all diseases—has a social history which can have a profound impact on the way a disease is perceived in society. In turn, the 'public image' of arthritis and rheumatism affects the experience of people who have these conditions, both directly through the availability of specialist medical help and research funding, and indirectly through the attitudes of others. For example, arthritis and rheumatism have not received much attention from the media and, in conse-

quence, the personal narratives of people who have RA have been neglected and individual lives are rendered invisible. RA often leads to physical impairments which can become severely disabling in a society that offers inadequate support. Partly through the activity of charities such as ARC, the 'public profile' of RA is beginning to rise and the patient's viewpoint is gradually being incorporated in the evaluation of treatment and social services.

People with RA often feel distressed about becoming a burden on their families or failing to fulfil their social roles, but their 'moral reputation' in society is preserved and they are seen as genuinely in pain and disabled through no fault of their own, once the diagnosis has been confirmed. They are not overtly stigmatised or actively discriminated against, except inasmuch as they experience the disadvantages in employment, housing and social security that are a common feature of the lives of all disabled people. As you will see at the start of the next chapter in this book, people with HIV infection or AIDS have a different experience of stigmatisation and discrimination, which flows from the social history of these conditions.

Objectives and self-assessment questions for Chapter 3 appear overleaf.

OBJECTIVES FOR CHAPTER 3

When you have studied this chapter, you should be able to:

3.1 Discuss the social and personal consequences of RA in terms of: the effects of uncertainty; difficulties in the performance of the activities of daily living and the fulfilment of social roles; and loss of autonomy and increasing dependence on others.

3.2 Review current biomedical knowledge of the pathological processes involved in RA, and the main strategies for its medical management, pointing to potential sources of difficulty for doctor and patient.

3.3 Discuss a range of theories about the causes of RA, drawing on epidemiological and biomedical research, and pointing to areas of continuing uncertainty.

3.4 Illustrate the complexity and significance of lay knowledge about RA and the ways in which it differs from professional knowledge.

3.5 Discuss the strengths and limitations of using patient-provided measures of outcome for assessing the impact of RA and the costs and benefits of treatment.

QUESTIONS FOR CHAPTER 3

Question 1 (*Objective 3.1*)

Why is it important to include the performance of social roles in any assessment of the experience of RA?

Question 2 (*Objective 3.2*)

Why is it so difficult to decide whether a drug treatment for RA is having a beneficial effect on the patient?

Question 3 (*Objective 3.3*)

What do you see as the major problems in identifying causes in RA?

Question 4 (*Objective 3.4*)

Read the following extract from an interview with a woman in her 50s. She was asked what she thought had caused her RA. What characteristic features of lay illness beliefs can you identify in this account?

> Well, if you live in your own body for a long time, you're a fool if you don't take note of what is happening to it. I think that you can make naive diagnoses which are quite wrong. But I think that at the back of your head, certainly at the back of my head, I have feelings that this is so, and I'm quite certain that it was stress that precipitated this … Not simply the stress of events that happened but the stress perhaps of suppressing myself while I was a mother and wife—not 'women's libby' but there comes a time in your life when you think, you know, 'where have I got to? There's nothing left of me.' … And then on top of that feeling of … not really discontent, but rather confusion about identity … to have various physical things happen like, you know, my daughter … I'm quite certain that the last straw was my husband's illness. So, I'm sure it was stress induced. I think that while my head kept going my body stopped. (Williams, 1986, pp. 188–9)

Question 5 (*Objective 3.5*)

There are two quite distinct approaches to assessing the personal consequences of health problems such as RA: (a) ask a standard set of questions of everyone, and (b) ask individuals to identify their own personal priorities and concerns. Give one strength and one weakness of each of these contrasting approaches.

4 HIV and AIDS

> *This chapter builds on material in earlier books in this series, most notably: the epidemiology of AIDS, in* World Health and Disease; *the interaction between the immune system and pathogenic organisms, in* Human Biology and Health: An Evolutionary Approach; *public health and primary health care strategies against infectious diseases, in* Caring for Health: History and Diversity; *and innovations in health care, screening and disease prevention, in* Dilemmas in Health Care.[1] *During your study of this chapter you will be asked to read an article by Neil Small, entitled 'Living with HIV and AIDS' which appears in the Reader.[2] A television programme, 'A future with AIDS', which focuses on outreach projects in Zambia, Brazil and India, is also highly relevant.*
>
> *The authors of this chapter are Graham Hart, Assistant Director of the MRC Medical Sociology Unit, University of Glasgow, and Tim Rhodes, Research Fellow at The Centre for Research on Drugs and Health Behaviour, Charing Cross and Westminster Medical School, University of London. Basiro Davey, from the Open University, and Ian Williams, from the University College London Medical School, contributed material on the biology of HIV and AIDS.*

Individual experiences, social responses

Unlike many other diseases of the twentieth century, HIV infection and AIDS have had a high media and public profile. **AIDS (acquired immune deficiency syndrome**) has been the subject of an unprecedented level of news stories, television and radio documentaries, advertising, and political and ethical debate. The risk of infection with **HIV** (the **human immunodeficiency virus**, which causes AIDS) has affected individuals' perceptions of sexual safety and has brought the most private of behaviours into the public domain.

Earlier chapters in this book (and others in this series) have emphasised that individual experiences of health, illness and risk are, to some extent, given meaning through social perceptions and actions towards those affected. This is particularly the case with HIV and AIDS. The meanings attached to these conditions are not simply dependent on 'expert' knowledge of the biology of HIV infection or the epidemiology of HIV transmission: they are also dependent upon what our HIV status communicates to others about who we are and how we behave. The public representation of AIDS thus speaks volumes about our private lives, which in turn has an impact upon our subjective experience.

This chapter illustrates how individual experiences are influenced by the ways in which social, ethical and political forces define and categorise HIV infection and AIDS. This endeavour demands a multi-disciplinary approach which brings together biological, epidemiological, historical, psychological and sociological perspectives on the discovery, spread and prevention of HIV.

Disease consequent upon infection with HIV (known collectively as **HIV-disease**), of which AIDS is the end-point, provides a good example of a health problem which is experienced in vastly differing ways according to the political and cultural contexts of those affected. However, the physical manifestations of HIV infection are relatively consistent. A person may feel perfectly healthy for months or years and, if untested, be completely unaware that they are infected with HIV. Symptoms begin with a series of skin, chest, mouth or stomach problems, many of which are the result of **opportunistic infections** by organisms that the immune system normally keeps in check. Individually, these infections cause varying degrees of discomfort but, together, they indicate increasingly deficient immune function. Episodes of more serious and debilitating illnesses occur,

[1] *World Health and Disease* (1993); *Human Biology and Health: An Evolutionary Approach* (1994); *Caring for Health: History and Diversity* (second edition, 1993); *Dilemmas in Health Care* (1993).

[2] *Health and Disease: A Reader* (second edition, 1995).

Panels from the AIDS Memorial Quilt, made to commemorate people who have died from AIDS in the United Kingdom. (Reproduced by kind permission of the NAMES Project (UK); photo by Estyn Williams-Hulbert)

until the person becomes unable to fend off any further challenge and dies—often from an infection which, in anyone with a healthy immune system, would never have arisen as a problem.

The experience of HIV and AIDS is not limited to those who are directly affected by the virus. The consumers of health services, the media and political organisations, medical establishments, pharmaceutical companies and national governments all have something to say about the subject. People at risk of HIV infection or AIDS, and the political groupings and self-help movements of which many are a part, also have strong views on individual, social and political responses to HIV-disease. All of this has both direct and indirect consequences for the men, women and children affected by HIV or AIDS, as well as knock-on effects for those who care for or work with them. These contrasting narratives are reflected in this chapter. We begin with a brief history of the HIV epidemic, which touches on all the themes that will be discussed in more detail in later sections.

A brief history of HIV and AIDS

In the late 1990s we have now entered the second decade of AIDS—distance enough to examine the history of medical and social responses to the HIV epidemic. Not only have medical discoveries helped to shape social and policy responses to HIV and AIDS, but the social and political climates have influenced the course of medical and scientific endeavour.

Socio-medical history

The identification of AIDS began at the Centers for Disease Control in Atlanta, which receive morbidity and mortality reports from throughout the USA. In early 1981, reports came of previously healthy young gay and bisexual men suffering from unexplained weight loss and an uncommon pneumonia, caused by a single-celled organism known as *Pneumocystis carinii*, commonly found in humans but rarely causing symptoms. At about the same time, deaths were reported in other gay men from *Kaposi's sarcoma*—a rare, slow-developing and usually benign tumour seen in older men from Mediterranean and African countries, which is possibly caused by a herpes-like virus. Other deaths from usually innocuous infections were recorded, the biological factor common to them all being a major deficiency in the patient's immune system. It was evident that these were opportunistic infections.

The condition was initially termed *gay-related immunodeficiency disease (GRID)*, more colloquially known as 'gay cancer'. A 'lay epidemiology' was generated in which the immunodeficiency syndrome became inextricably linked with gay men—an association that has had major implications for social and public responses to the disease.

As time passed, epidemiologists identified members of non-gay populations with opportunistic infections as a consequence of immunodeficiency. For most researchers this negated early thoughts that they were investigating an *autoimmune* disease.[3] In the early 1980s, it had been proposed that the immune system of some gay men had automatically 'self-destructed' as a consequence of repeated exposure to sexual infections and/or drug misuse. It is important to note that while almost all mainstream medical opinion in the 1990s asserts that HIV-disease is *not* the result of autoimmune activity, there remains a small number of scientists who argue that HIV does not cause AIDS and that the observed immunodeficiency is, in fact, the outcome of 'immune overload'. These individuals ignore the substantial body of scientific evidence unequivocally linking HIV infection with subsequent immunodeficiency. This does not deny that the presence of other factors—such as drug use, other infections or malnutrition—may speed up the immunodeficiency once a person is HIV infected.

Despite its inability to explain the world-wide distribution of HIV-disease, the minority view that 'lifestyle' causes AIDS continues to attract media attention, perhaps because it questions accepted scientific research or provides the preferred explanation of the AIDS epidemic for religious evangelists and the 'moral right'. This illustrates, once again, how interpretations of medical knowledge can be influenced by social responses.[4]

The emergence of the disease in non-gay groups gave support to the theory that the breakdown in immune function was caused by a single transmissible agent, possibly interacting with other factors. The syndrome was found first in people with *haemophilia* (a genetically-determined inability to form blood clots) who had received injections of Factor VIII, a clotting agent prepared from donated blood; then it was detected in recipients of blood transfusions and donated organs, and among injecting drug users. Later it was found that the male and female sexual partners of people in these 'at risk' groups, and the babies of 'at risk' mothers, could also be affected. Immunodeficiency syndrome was thus identified as being caused by an agent transmitted by blood-to-blood contact (e.g. via Factor VIII or from mother to unborn baby), or semen-to-blood contact (via unprotected penetrative sex).

The condition was renamed 'acquired immune deficiency syndrome': *acquired* because it is not inherited by

genetic transmission, but requires contact with an infectious agent; *immune deficiency* because this is the consequence of infection; and *syndrome* because the cluster of symptoms that indicate AIDS may vary from person to person, depending on the nature of HIV-disease that develops.

The race to identify the cause of AIDS began in laboratories around the world. In 1984, when many thousands of people had been diagnosed with AIDS world-wide, Luc Montagnier of the Pasteur Institute in France and Robert Gallo of the National Institutes of Health in the USA claimed, independently of each other, to have identified the virus that causes AIDS. Each gave their virus a different name, and it was not until 1986 that an international committee of eminent virologists renamed it 'human immunodeficiency virus (HIV)'.

The discovery of HIV was not without its political problems. Gallo had been sent a sample of the French virus by Montagnier, ostensibly as part of a collaborative venture to develop a kit for blood testing. Such a kit, designed to detect *antibodies*[5] to HIV in the blood, was subsequently patented exclusively by Gallo and colleagues in the USA. Montagnier accused Gallo of using the French virus to develop the American test kit, and a heated debate ensued. Subsequent genetic analysis confirmed that the Gallo virus was, in fact, the Montagnier virus, although Gallo has maintained that its 'appropriation' was accidental. The Pasteur Institute began legal proceedings claiming compensation for $20 million lost income from the sale of the blood-testing kits.

The personal and legal battle over the discovery of HIV is indicative of the wider social context of many contemporary scientific discoveries. The Gallo–Montagnier dispute over ownership and reward associated with the discovery of HIV has since become the subject of several books (e.g. Shilts, 1987; Connor and Kingman, 1989), and a major feature film (*And The Band Played On*). It is an early instance of what Cindy Patton—an American activist and lecturer—has termed the 'AIDS industry', in which scientific discovery tends to be characterised as much by the quest for personal or financial gain as for health gain (Patton, 1990).

---

[3]The status of rheumatoid arthritis as an autoimmune disease has already been discussed in Chapter 3 of this book; the immunological basis of autoimmune diseases is described in more detail in *Human Biology and Health: An Evolutionary Approach*, Chapter 6.

[4]The influence of social context on medical knowledge is discussed in *Medical Knowledge: Doubt and Certainty*.

[5]Antibodies are specialised proteins made by the immune system in response to an infection; those made in response to HIV infection can only bind to HIV. The test kit contains a known sample of HIV with which some serum (liquid fraction of the blood) is mixed. If antibodies in the serum are able to bind to HIV in the test kit, this is taken as evidence of HIV infection and the person is said to be 'HIV-positive'. Antibodies are discussed in greater detail in *Human Biology and Health: An Evolutionary Approach*, Chapter 6.

Socio-political history

Gay men are a socially marginalised and stigmatised population, in part because of medicine's role in defining homosexuality as a 'social disease' in the past. Early medical and societal responses to HIV and AIDS represented homosexuality itself—rather than infection—as the source and cause of fatal illness. With the advent of AIDS, the 'social problem' of homosexuality was once again articulated as a 'medical problem', but it resurrected a potent socio-political history common to other sexually-associated diseases or 'evils' of the past, such as syphilis and prostitution.

The social historian, Jeffrey Weeks (1989, 1990), has argued that most Western developed countries in past times have associated homosexuality with sin, sickness and disease. Past epidemics or 'plagues', particularly where sexual transmission is a factor, have also been viewed as signs of decay in moral standards and a threat to the 'public good'. Responses to homosexuality, illicit drug use, sexually-transmitted disease and prostitution have all been characterised by largely punitive measures of containment which were designed to protect the 'public' from these scourges. Responses to the HIV epidemic draw on earlier perceptions of marginalised populations and activities. As noted by Jeffrey Weeks:

> AIDS has a medico-moral history already partly written for it: a history of civilisation-threatening plagues, offering a repertoire of responses and remedies, from mass hysteria to moral panic to prejudice and the threat of compulsory quarantine. (Weeks, 1990, p. 134)

Each society therefore builds upon its underlying cultural history when responding to new diseases, particularly when these are seen to be characterised by an aspect of medical uncertainty and a threat to the integrity of the body politic. As tabloid newspaper reporting in the United Kingdom in the late 1980s and early 1990s strongly indicates, being a gay man or an injecting drug user was stigmatised as morally corrupt and HIV was represented as 'just rewards'.

> AIDS is a homosexual, drug related disease. They and they alone are responsible for people dying of AIDS. (Sun, January, 1990)

> The message to be learned—that the Department of Health should now be urgently propagating—is that active homosexuals are potentially murderers and that the act of buggery kills. (Daily Mail, 21 July, 1989)

Responses to the HIV epidemic are also influenced by the social and political conditions of the times and places in which it has occurred. A brief examination of AIDS-related policy in the United Kingdom and USA illustrates this point. The HIV epidemic emerged at a time when the political climate was dominated by conservative politicians emphasising the central importance of the family and 'family values'. The Reagan and Bush presidencies in the USA and the Thatcher governments in the United Kingdom wished to strengthen the family unit as a symbol of national identity and pride, and to counteract the perceived economic (and sexual) permissiveness of previous decades. The writer and activist Simon Watney has documented how initial government responses to HIV and AIDS emphasised the threat of 'promiscuity' and 'otherness' to the stability of the family and 'normality' (Watney, 1989a).

There was effectively no AIDS-related policy in the United Kingdom until 1984, despite warnings made by gay organisations that an epidemic was imminent. Government policy at this time was to contain the virus by recommending that gay men should not donate blood. The emphasis was on preventing the 'leakage' of HIV from populations of gay men to 'innocent' others, such as people with haemophilia. It was not until July 1985 that all blood donations began to be screened. A policy of virus containment continued throughout 1985, when Kenneth Clarke, then Secretary of State for Health, made further guarantees about the purity of donated blood, and introduced regulations (despite strong medical opposition) under the Public Health (Control of Diseases) Act 1984 to detain people with AIDS in hospital.

According to an analysis by Simon Watney, it was not until 1986, when hundreds of gay men had already died, that central allocations of funds to primary HIV prevention were made (Watney, 1987). These funds were directed almost exclusively to government-sponsored mass media advertising about AIDS, which tended to emphasise warnings about the dangers of sexual promiscuity ('the more partners, the greater the risk'), rather than actively promoting safer sex and condom use. Watney argues that almost all government-sponsored mass media advertising on AIDS since that time has aimed to address the uninfected 'general public' with warnings of the dangers of homosexuality, drug misuse and sexual promiscuity (an example appears in Figure 4.7 later in this chapter). In short, AIDS came to symbolise social and political concerns of the time about the fragility of the family unit and of sexual moral standards.

Later policies initiated by the Thatcher governments of the 1980s reinforced the ideal of the protected family unit. Section 28 of the Local Government Act 1988 made the 'promotion' of homosexuality in schools illegal and as a result introduced questions as to whether, and to what extent, sex education was legally able to refer to homosexuality. Public funding of a national survey of sexual lifestyles was vetoed because the survey was thought to be unnecessarily intrusive,[6] while an advertising campaign targeting heterosexuals was halted for being too sexually explicit (see Figure 4.8 later in this chapter). Government-initiated AIDS policies thus have as much to say about the ideological and political climate of the time as they do about the practical imperatives of preventing HIV-disease.

In the later 1980s and 1990s, biological knowledge about HIV and AIDS has undergone a huge increase, largely due to unprecedented levels of research funding. We review the central findings of this research effort in the next section: you may be intrigued by how little it has altered public perceptions of the disease in the United Kingdom or public and political responses to it.

The biology of HIV and AIDS

There are two major types of HIV. By far the most common is HIV-1 (see Figure 4.1), which was identified in the mid-1980s and is the cause of the epidemic worldwide. A second virus, HIV-2, has since been isolated from some people with AIDS in parts of West Africa and, although it differs in the structure of its proteins and genes from HIV-1, it has similar biological properties. In this chapter, the term 'HIV' refers to HIV-1.

HIV is a relatively fragile virus, which cannot survive for more than a few days outside the body (except in laboratory cultures). It is readily killed by the temperatures reached in the hot wash cycle of an ordinary washing machine, and infected blood spills can be safely dealt with by mopping up with weak domestic bleach. Contrary to early popular belief, it is not *contagious*—it cannot be transmitted by ordinary social contact such as shaking hands or hugging, nor by handling plates, cups and cutlery used by an infected person.

HIV replication

As the biological properties of HIV were unravelled in the late 1980s, the progression to AIDS began to be understood. HIV shares the property common to all viruses of 'hijacking' the chemical processes of the cells that it

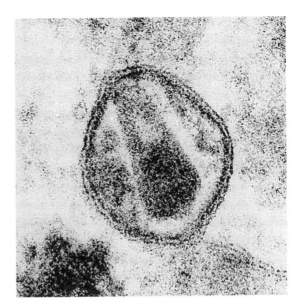

Figure 4.1 *Electron micrograph of the most common type of human immunodeficiency virus (HIV-1), magnified 200 000 times. Note the 'knobbly' outer envelope of the virus particle, and the thimble-shaped inner core (Photo: courtesy of the National Institute for Biological Standards and Control)*

infects and instructing them to make new virus particles.[7] HIV belongs to a small group of viruses, known as **retroviruses**, which store their genetic material in a strand of RNA (ribonucleic acid). Plate 1 (facing page 60) shows the infection cycle of HIV and its manner of replication: start at stage 1 (top left) and follow the cycle clockwise to stage 5. When you have studied the plate and its caption, turn back to this page and answer the following question. (Plate 2 should be referred to when you are studying Chapter 6 on schizophrenia.)

☐ Retro means 'backwards'. On the basis of Plate 1, can you explain why HIV is termed a *retrovirus*?

■ The normal sequence of transcription of genes is from DNA into RNA; retroviruses transcribe RNA into DNA (this is called reverse transcription).[8]

---

[6]This survey was subsequently conducted with funding from the Wellcome Trust; the organisation derives some of its income from the pharmaceutical company which manufactures Zidovudine (also known as AZT), a drug used in the treatment of HIV infection. Some of the results of the survey are discussed in *Birth to Old Age: Health in Transition*, Chapter 7.

[7]The details of how viruses replicate are given in *Human Biology and Health: An Evolutionary Approach*, Chapters 3 and 6.

[8]The transcription of the coded instructions contained in DNA into a corresponding code in messenger RNA (mRNA) is described in detail in *Human Biology and Health: An Evolutionary Approach*, Chapter 3. The chapter also deals with mutation, the principal process by which the code can change its sequence.

The viral genes may remain 'hidden' in the host-cell DNA for months or years, where they can no longer be detected by the person's immune system, which responds only to partly assembled or intact virus particles. However, there is a growing acceptance of the view that activation of viral genes occurs very quickly, in at least some infected cells. When the viral genes are activated, the host cell becomes a 'factory' entirely devoted to the manufacture of thousands of new virus particles, which 'bud' from its surface (see Figure 4.2). When a huge shower of mature virus particles is released, the host cell dies in the process, and the immune system is temporarily swamped by viruses so many more cells become infected. It has been estimated that in a person with an active HIV infection, at least a *billion* new virus particles are produced each day. Research to discover the mechanisms by which the viral genes are activated is being pursued in the hope that some way can be found to suppress them permanently.

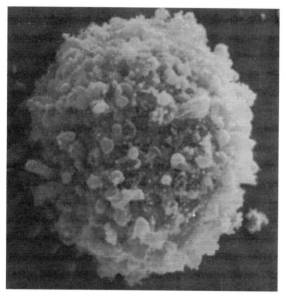

Figure 4.2 *Scanning electron micrograph of a human white cell infected with HIV, magnified 7 500 times. Thousands of small spherical virus particles can be seen 'budding' from the surface of the cell. As they are released the cell is destroyed. (Reproduced by kind permission of the British Medical Association Board of Science and Education)*

HIV can show marked variation in the 'fine details' of the molecules in its surface envelope and core proteins because there is a very high rate of *mutation* in the genes that contain the coded instructions for their manufacture. As a result of these changes in the coding sequence of HIV genes, many different variants of HIV occur, and more

than one variant can often be detected within the same person. A comparison of the variants isolated from different individuals can help to 'map' the transmission of infection from person to person (the greater the differences between variants isolated from two people, the lower the likelihood that HIV has been transmitted between them). The high mutation rate may hold the key to the ability of HIV to 'escape' from the body's immune response to virus infection, as you will see below.

Effect of HIV on the body

HIV appears to 'select' the immune system as its target, but in reality it can bind to and subsequently enter only those cells that carry specific receptors on their surface membrane, which exactly 'fit' the shape of a molecule called 'GP120' on the envelope of the virus (see Plate 1, stages 1 and 2). The main receptor to which GP120 can bind is known as 'CD4', which is found on various cells in the human body, but most notably on the **helper T cells**.[9] These cells are members of the white cell population circulating in the lymphatic system, bloodstream and tissues, which together constitute the immune system.[10] The chronic infection of helper T cells by HIV leads to a progressive decline in their number (see Figure 4.3), although all the mechanisms by which this occurs are not yet fully understood.

☐ What effect would a decline in the number of helper T cells have on the immune system as a whole and on the health of the affected person?

■ It would gradually compromise the ability of the immune system to function effectively, because helper T cells are responsible for stimulating all the other components of the immune system to a level of activity adequate to eliminate infection. A person with a declining population of helper T cells is susceptible to opportunistic infections.

Following infection with HIV, some people develop a 'flu or glandular fever-like illness as the virus begins an initial

[9]GP120 and CD4. If you are interested in biochemical nomenclature: GP stands for 'glycoprotein' (i.e. a protein with sugars attached) and 120 refers to the mass of the molecule; CD stands for 'cluster of differentiation' (i.e. a molecule appearing on a cell's surface at a certain stage in its development); there are many different CD molecules, each distinguished by a number.

[10]The role of helper T cells in the immune response to infection is discussed in *Human Biology and Health: An Evolutionary Approach*, Chapter 6.

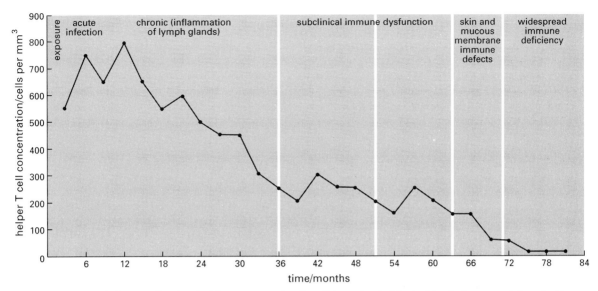

Figure 4.3 *Decline in helper T cells (identified by presence of surface CD4 molecules) in the blood of a person infected with HIV during progression through various stages of HIV-disease to widespread immune deficiency (AIDS) and death 83 months after infection. 'Subclinical immune dysfunction' refers to defects in the immune system which did not lead to overt symptoms. (Source: Scientific American, 1988, 259(4), October, p. 74)*

phase of unchecked proliferation, but most show no symptoms at all. However, the immune system soon detects the virus and mounts a vigorous immune response against it, which usually produces a dramatic fall in virus 'load' in the body—greater than any that is subsequently achieved through medical treatment. The most easily-detected sign of an immune response is the appearance of antibodies against HIV in the blood and saliva, usually within three months of infection. The first appearance of these antibodies is termed **sero-conversion** because the serum converts from being negative for antibodies to being antibody-positive. The immune system also generates huge numbers of *cytotoxic* cells, which attack and kill any of the body's own cells engaged in making new HIV particles.

There typically follows a period of several years in which the virus spreads through the immune system without causing symptoms—a key aspect of its life history that was unsuspected until the early 1990s, when the discovery (by Embretson *et al.*, 1993 and Pantaleo *et al.*, 1993) caused a revolution in biomedical models of HIV-disease. It is now generally believed that—in the first few years of HIV infection—the ability of the virus to proliferate and damage the helper T cells is just about held in check by the ability of the immune system to kill new virus particles as fast as they are being made (the interaction is reviewed by Martin Nowak and Andrew McMichael, 1995).

However, the immune response against HIV is not enough to eradicate all of the virus particles, with their immense potential for proliferation and mutation. New variants arising as a result of mutation are able to 'escape' from the immune system because it takes about three weeks before an adequate immune response can be generated against each new variant. Billions of new virus particles can be made during that time, and increasing numbers of helper T cells can become fatally infected. As the helper T cells decline, so the balance of survival shifts towards the virus and away from its human host.

The average time taken to develop symptoms of HIV-disease, which gradually progresses to AIDS, is 8–10 years from first infection, but the variation is considerable: it can be as short as 2–3 years, and people have survived 15 years or more without developing symptoms. Whether some HIV-infected people will live normal lifespans without ever progressing to AIDS remains to be seen. People who do not know that they are HIV-infected can transmit the virus to others during the long *latent period* before symptoms appear. This ensures that a 'pool' of HIV survives in the population, even though the virus causes such a high fatality rate in the people it infects.[11]

[11]The mutual adaptations co-evolved by pathogens and their hosts, which ensure the survival of both populations even though many individuals die, are discussed in *Human Biology and Health: An Evolutionary Approach*, Chapter 5.

In addition to helper T cells, two other kinds of white cells—*macrophages* and *monocytes*—carry the CD4 receptor molecule and so can be readily infected by HIV. They are thought to act as a major reservoir of infection and are responsible for other manifestations of AIDS, in particular the *dementia syndrome* which occurs in 10–20 per cent of people with AIDS. Infected macrophages and monocytes can migrate into brain tissue and lead to damage which results in symptoms such as impairment of thought processes (cognition), memory loss, fits, behavioural change and movement disorders.

The ability of HIV to proliferate in white cells ensures that it is abundant in the bloodstream, semen and mucus in sexual organs, and is therefore readily transmitted from person to person during unprotected penetrative sex (i.e. without a condom). The penis and vagina are in close abrasive contact with each other in penetrative heterosexual sex, and the rectum can suffer abrasions to its delicate lining by penetration during anal sex. Tiny 'breaks' in blood vessels in these organs can allow transmission of the virus from person to person.

HIV has also been identified in cells of other types such as those of skin, lung, kidneys, bone marrow and gut, so mechanisms (as yet unknown) exist that enable it to infect cells that do not carry the CD4 receptor. The variety of clinical manifestations of AIDS, and the variation in time of progression from initial infection to HIV-disease, may be due to the variants of HIV that have been generated, which cells they can infect, and to individual differences in each person's immune responsiveness. Some variants may be more prone to multiply than others, and some may cause more damage to host cells.

Study of long-term survivors with continuing HIV infection has important consequences for treatment and vaccine development because it may help to identify specific factors that regulate viral replication and maintain a protective immune response. A few individuals who are known to have been exposed to HIV may even have developed natural immunity which has eradicated it altogether. Study of their immune responses by research groups around the world (reviewed by Sarah Rowland-Jones and Andrew McMichael, 1995; and by Gene Shearer and Mario Clerici, 1996) may shed light on effective strategies for establishing immunity in others.

Treatment and vaccine design

The sharply rising number of people infected with HIV, and the progress of the epidemic in the developed world, have stimulated extensive research programmes to produce treatments and vaccines. The ability of HIV to form a DNA copy of its own genetic material has been exploited in the development of anti-HIV drugs such as Zidovudine (AZT), which resembles one of the chemical structures that make up DNA. It becomes incorporated into the new viral DNA as it is transcribed from the viral RNA, thereby terminating this important step in HIV replication. Although some studies have shown that Zidovudine can slow down the progression of symptoms in people with AIDS, it is not a cure and can have serious toxic side-effects. More recently it has been given to HIV-infected people before they develop AIDS, but the effect on progression to disease symptoms is transient and in the long term there is no difference between patients treated and not treated (Concorde Coordinating Committee, 1994). Laboratory tests have also shown that HIV can develop resistance to Zidovudine, raising further concerns about its possible long-term efficacy. Trials of combinations of therapy, and the use of new drugs that act on different parts of the virus replication cycle may, in time, overcome these problems.

Better clinical monitoring of patients has also led to the early preventative use of antibiotics in people who seem most at risk of developing opportunistic bacterial infections. The 1990s also saw advances in treating infections from opportunistic viruses commonly found among people with HIV-disease. These therapies have helped to improve the average survival of patients whose disease has reached the criteria for an AIDS diagnosis from just a few months in the early 1980s, to two years by the early 1990s. It is hoped that continued research into the biology of HIV-disease and AIDS will further the development of effective treatment strategies but, despite recent progress, low-cost, safe, freely-available and effective drugs remain many years away.

Equally important is the development of **vaccines** against HIV. A vaccine works by 'priming' the immune system with inactivated or harmless samples of infectious pathogens. White cells identify parts of the pathogen's structure as targets and direct increasingly effective responses against them. If subsequent exposure to 'live' pathogens occurs, the immune response to the previously-recognised parts of the pathogen is so rapid that the infection may be eliminated before symptoms occur. However, the constant generation of new variants of HIV poses a huge problem for vaccine design.

☐ Can you explain why?

■ By mutation, HIV genes are constantly changing their structures so, in order to 'prime' an effective immune response, a vaccine would have to contain samples of all known variants and any that might be generated in the future.

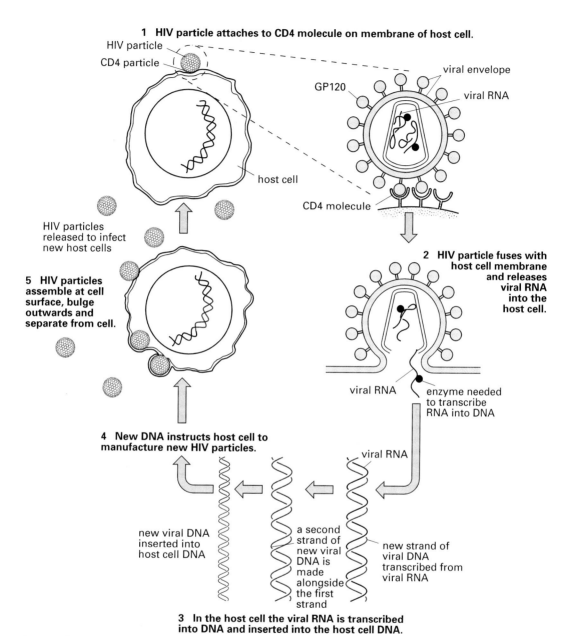

1 HIV particle attaches to CD4 molecule on membrane of host cell.

HIV particle

CD4 particle

viral envelope

GP120

viral RNA

host cell

CD4 molecule

HIV particles released to infect new host cells

2 HIV particle fuses with host cell membrane and releases viral RNA into the host cell.

5 HIV particles assemble at cell surface, bulge outwards and separate from cell.

viral RNA

enzyme needed to transcribe RNA into DNA

4 New DNA instructs host cell to manufacture new HIV particles.

viral RNA

new viral DNA inserted into host cell DNA

a second strand of new viral DNA is made alongside the first strand

new strand of viral DNA transcribed from viral RNA

3 In the host cell the viral RNA is transcribed into DNA and inserted into the host cell DNA.

Plate 1 *The cycle of infection and replication of the human immunodeficiency virus (HIV). The virus primarily infects human cells that have a particular surface receptor (CD4), to which the virus binds via a molecule called GP120 (stages 1 and 2 are further discussed later in Chapter 4). On entry to a host cell, the viral genes are transcribed into a new strand of viral DNA (deoxyribonucleic acid), using an enzyme (reverse transcriptase) common to all retroviruses. This new strand of viral DNA then replicates to form a double helix, which is inserted into the DNA of the host cell (stages 3 and 4). Once this has occurred, a variable period of 'dormancy' may elapse before progression to stage 5 and further virus replication occurs. (This diagram is not to scale.)*

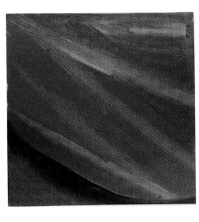

18 May, 1991: 'My mind seemed to be thought broadcasting very severely and it was beyond my will to do anything about it. I summed this up by painting my brain as an enormous mouth, acting independently of me.'

23 April 1991: 'I had come to the conclusion that most people around me had some extra sensory perception ability which gave them access to my mind … I was like a blind man. Hence the crosses on the eyes. They also let me know verbally what they had picked up from my thoughts.'

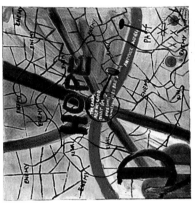

19 July 1991: There is no diary entry for this day. This painting was on his easel when Bryan Charnley committed suicide on 29 July 1991.

12 July 1991: There is no diary entry for this day. The words under 'HOPE' are adapted from a Bob Dylan song; they read THE CARDS ARE NO GOOD THAT I'M HOLDING UNLESS THEY ARE FROM ANOTHER WORLD.

20 April 1991: 'Very paranoid. The person upstairs was reading my mind and speaking back to me to keep me in a sort of ego crucifixion … The large rabbit ear is because I was confused and extremely sensitive to human voices, like a wild animal.'

24 May 1991: 'Perhaps a broken heart is the cause of it all. Certainly it hurts … The spiders legs on the right are to express my inhibitions and the feeling that comes over me as my thoughts surface and broadcast. Scary. I feel all the time now that I am getting nearer to a more acute expression of my schizophrenia.'

Plate 2 Six faces of schizophrenia: from a series of seventeen self-portraits made by Bryan Charnley between 11 April and 19 July 1991; the notes in quotation marks are taken from his diary. (Reproduced by kind permission of Terence Charnley, the artist's brother.)

An even more fundamental difficulty must also be overcome. In order to be effective in protecting people against HIV, a vaccine would have to be capable of eliciting an immune response of such potency that thereafter no 'live' virus particles could survive long enough in the bloodstream to infect host cells. No other vaccine has to achieve 100 per cent protection because the immune system remains intact during other infections and can later 'mop up' any pathogens that initially evaded detection. But HIV infects the immune system itself, so even a few surviving virus particles could ultimately lead to the gradual collapse of all the mechanisms of the immune response.

The massive genetic variability of HIV and the lack of a fully-protective immune response means that a breakthrough is thought to be some years in the future. Research in the 1990s on the closely-related *simian immunodeficiency virus* (*SIV*), which infects monkeys, has succeeded in generating a vaccine against SIV, raising hopes that an effective HIV vaccine may also be an achievable goal. To this end, clinical trials in humans are taking place, but it will be many years before these have been fully evaluated.

> This is the time to rethink the vaccine because the first avenues we explored were wrong ... I am not saying that there will not be a vaccine, but in any case it will take a long time and it will not solve every problem. We have to foresee living with the virus for a long time to come. (Luc Montagnier, interviewed by *The Times*, 12 March 1994)

The subsequent availability of any vaccine may be determined more by cost, acceptability and political considerations than by clinical effectiveness.

The epidemiology of HIV and AIDS

Biological research may hold the best prospect for containing HIV and AIDS in the future, but the most important discoveries about the 'natural' history of HIV infection in the 1980s were made through epidemiological research. The insights this generated into transmission routes are the basis of current strategies to prevent the spread of HIV.

Risk behaviours

Once the prevalence and distribution of HIV-disease were systematically being recorded, it became possible to identify and monitor the key **risk behaviours**—actions which have the potential to transmit HIV from person to person. Even before the identification of the virus,

retrospective case–control studies[12] had determined that particular sexual behaviours carried greater relative risks for AIDS than others. For example, gay men with multiple sexual partners were found to be more at risk than those with one partner, while gay men who reported a consistent preference for receptive anal intercourse were at higher risk than those who reported that they usually had penetrative anal intercourse or oral sex.

☐ What do these findings suggest?

■ The increased risk associated with multiple partners suggests that a sexually-transmitted infection is involved, since the greater the number of partners the higher the chance of meeting one who is already infected. The increased risk of receptive anal sex suggests that a semen-to-blood infection may be involved, transmitted through abrasions in the delicate lining of the rectum.

With the advent of widespread HIV antibody-testing in 1985, it became possible to identify and monitor other behaviours that carried a risk of HIV transmission, including vaginal sexual intercourse, both from male to female and female to male. Injecting drug users were identified as being at higher risk of HIV than drug users who had never injected or shared equipment—pointing to blood-to-blood transmission via shared needles and syringes. As the epidemic continued, some newborn babies of mothers with HIV infection were found to be HIV-positive, helping to establish that blood-to-blood transmission of the virus could occur across the placenta or at the time of birth.[13]

Table 4.1 (*overleaf*) shows the cumulative reported numbers of men, women and children in the United Kingdom up to December 1995 who were diagnosed with AIDS and HIV infection—categorised by likely route of HIV transmission. As you can see, HIV infection is primarily a sexually-transmitted disease, and one that disproportionately affects men—over 85 per cent of cases are in adult males, compared with 13 per cent in women. Later in this section we discuss limitations on interpreting what this table can tell us about the epidemiology of HIV and AIDS.

---

[12]Case–control studies are discussed in *Studying Health and Disease*, Chapter 8.

[13]Some initially HIV-positive babies are, in fact, free from infection and simply carry their mother's antibodies to HIV which 'leak' across the placenta. These maternal antibodies disintegrate within a few months so the babies become HIV-negative and remain free from infection.

Table 4.1 Exposure categories of AIDS cases and of HIV-1 infected persons: cumulative totals, United Kingdom to 31 December 1995

How HIV infection was probably acquired	Male		Female		Total			
	AIDS	HIV-1	AIDS	HIV-1	AIDS	(%)	HIV-1[1]	(%)
Sexual intercourse								
between men[2]	8 617	15 620		—	8 617	(73)	15 620	(61)
between men and women								
'high risk' partner[3]	41	104	133	468	174	(1)	572	(2)
other partner abroad[4]	705	1 801	505	1 642	1 210	(10)	3 450	(13)
other partner UK	79	145	69	241	148	(1)	386	(2)
under investigation	29	115	9	127	38	(<1)	243	(1)
Injecting drug use	493	1 952	212	880	705	(6)	2 837	(11)
Blood								
blood factor (e.g. haemophiliacs)	554	1 226	6	11	560	(5)	1 237	(5)
blood/tissue transfer (e.g. transfusion)	42	80	72	88	114	(1)	171	(1)
Mother to infant	88	166	94	168	182	(2)	336	(1)
Other/undetermined	102	673	22	128	124	(1)	837	(3)
Total	10 750	21 882	1 122	3 753	11 872	(100)	25 689	(100)

[1]HIV includes 54 reports with sex not stated. [2]Includes 196 AIDS cases and 362 HIV infections in men who have also injected drugs. [3]Includes men and women who had sex with injecting drug users, or with those infected through blood treatment/transfusion, and women who had sex with bisexual men. [4]Includes individuals without other identified risks who come from, or have lived in, countries where the major route of HIV-1 transmission is through heterosexual intercourse. (Source: Public Health Laboratory Service AIDS Centre and the Scottish Centre for Infection and Environmental Health, 1996, *AIDS/HIV Quarterly Surveillance Tables: Data to end December 1995*, PHLS, London)

The prevalence of HIV and AIDS

On the basis of epidemiological measurements of the prevalence of HIV and AIDS, it has become possible to map the course of the epidemic and to predict future outbreaks. Estimating prevalence and monitoring the geographical and population distribution of HIV are of pivotal importance in planning health care resources for affected people and targeting health education to prevent further HIV spread. Although the benefits of continued prevalence mapping are clear, it is important to recognise the limitations of HIV prevalence estimates.

Global estimates

Epidemiological uncertainties are most apparent when making global estimates of the extent and rate of spread of HIV. The World Health Organisation estimated that the cumulative global total by mid-1994 was 985 119 people with AIDS, from 104 countries (WHO, 1995, p. 111).

Nearly 42 per cent of those with AIDS were reported from the USA. Yet few people believe that these figures represent an accurate picture of the size or extent of the AIDS epidemic.

Epidemiological estimates are based on cases *reported* to central or national disease surveillance centres. The number of reported HIV and AIDS cases is thought to be considerably lower than the 'true' prevalence because of under-reporting, which affects all countries, but is most apparent in those developing countries where HIV prevalence is relatively high. Even in the USA, where disease surveillance is well organised and well resourced, there is thought to be an 11 per cent underestimate of AIDS diagnoses.

☐ Can you suggest some reasons why HIV and AIDS prevalence estimates from developing countries are so uncertain?

■ Many developing countries lack infrastructures and resources for monitoring and surveillance of diseases, or for HIV testing; nor do they have adequate resources to care for people with HIV-disease or AIDS. This gives people little incentive to come forward for testing or treatment. In developing countries, the majority of people with HIV infection are probably unaware of their HIV-positive status and thus go unreported.

Estimating the extent of the global HIV epidemic is vital for directing appropriate resources to countries most in need of HIV-prevention programmes. By mid-1994, WHO estimated that there was a global total of 16 million people infected with HIV, of whom over 10 million were in Sub-Saharan Africa, 2.5 million in South East Asia, and three million in the Americas (WHO, 1995, p. 112). Predictions suggest that, by the year 2000, well over one million people will develop AIDS annually—over half of them in Africa and a quarter in Asia (Sattaur, 1991). Once again, it is important to recognise the fragility and uncer-tainty of these predictions because they are based on limited and often inaccurate evidence.

The global transmission characteristics of the HIV epidemic are monitored by WHO. Figure 4.4 shows the predominant modes of transmission throughout the world.

In Europe, the transmission characteristics of the epidemic are still emerging, particularly in Central and Eastern European countries. In Northern Europe the predominant transmission route has been sexual, primarily among men who have sex with men. The exceptions to this are Scotland and Ireland where, as in the countries of Southern Europe and Poland, most transmission has occurred via injecting drug use. In Romania most HIV infection appears to have occurred in health-care settings, particularly to babies and young children, by repeated use of unsterilised needles. The epidemiology of HIV infection in the countries of the former Soviet Union remains unclear, but a rapid increase is predicted as travel restrictions are lifted.

Figure 4.4   *Global patterns of HIV infection and AIDS using the WHO classification. The majority of cases in Pattern I countries (e.g. USA) are among male homosexuals and injecting drug users; in Pattern II countries (e.g. in Central and East Africa) heterosexual transmission is most common; Pattern I/II countries (e.g. in South America) are homosexual male, bisexual and heterosexual transmission and through injecting drug use; Pattern III countries (e.g. the former USSR) have either too few cases or insufficient evidence to identify predominant modes of transmission. (Source: Adapted from Public Health Laboratory Service, 1991,* Communicable Disease Report, **1***(4), 29 March, PHLS, London)*

United Kingdom estimates

Like the USA, Canada and Australia, the United Kingdom has a relatively robust system of HIV reporting and surveillance. Despite this, uncertainties remain. Table 4.1 (earlier) showed a cumulative total of 25 689 people with HIV infection reported in the United Kingdom by the end of December 1995. These reports are of named individuals who have usually requested, or been advised to have, an HIV-antibody test. Others may have been tested without consent and then given their result. The prevalence and transmission characteristics shown in Table 4.1 give a limited epidemiological picture of the 'true' extent and nature of the HIV epidemic in the United Kingdom.

☐ What are the main sources of uncertainty in the data in Table 4.1?

■ Three problems may have occurred to you (there are others). First, and most importantly, cases are only reported when people with HIV infection come forward for testing. Many infected people have not been HIV tested and are unaware of their HIV-positive status. Second, there are doubts about the *representativeness* of people who come into contact with HIV testing and reporting centres: they may differ in some important respects from those not in contact with services. Third, there may be confusion in determining which transmission route resulted in infection (for example, among gay men who also inject drugs), or where transmission routes are unknown (3 per cent of cases are 'other/undetermined').

Furthermore, cumulative totals of people with HIV give little indication of *prevalence*: they are *numbers* of people infected via different transmission routes, not the *proportion* or rate of infected people within a specific population. Table 4.1 gives no indication, for example, of the proportion of gay men or injecting drug users who are HIV-positive.

☐ How could accurate measures of HIV prevalence be obtained, and what problems can you foresee in carrying them out?

■ One method would be to undertake mass HIV-screening programmes of the general population, but this raises serious ethical and political questions (discussed later in this chapter). Another method would be to survey representative samples of specific populations, but data collection problems are particularly acute when the populations under study are 'hard-to-reach' (e.g. injecting drug users).

Most HIV-prevalence estimates for injecting drug users are based on data from people in contact with treatment programmes. A comparison of injecting drug users in contact and not in contact with services in London found that HIV prevalence is higher among those with no service contact. A review of research studies compiled by Tim Rhodes (1994), one of the authors of this chapter, concluded that treatment-based reports may underestimate the 'true' HIV prevalence among drug-injecting populations.

Changing definitions of AIDS

The only feature common to everyone diagnosed with AIDS is an underlying immunodeficiency. The list of AIDS-associated diseases has undergone a number of revisions since 1982, when it was first defined. Diagnostic changes have introduced further uncertainties in mapping the epidemiology of AIDS, because the way in which AIDS is defined clearly influences the numbers of people diagnosed. An example occurred when the types of pneumonia considered to be symptomatic of AIDS were expanded to include those associated with micro-organisms other than *Pneumocystis carinii*. As a consequence, the number of injecting drug users diagnosed with AIDS increased sharply, because many had tubercular pneumonias. Conversely, women's groups have argued that the exclusion of conditions such as vaginal warts, recurrent candidiasis (thrush) and cervical cancer, all of which may be related to a deficient immune response, has led to a gross underestimate of AIDS among women.

Laboratory definitions of AIDS include the demonstration of HIV infection, coupled with a collapse in the numbers of helper T cells in the blood. Uncertainty about even this definition arose (briefly but hysterically) at the Eighth International AIDS Conference in Amsterdam in 1992, when a few cases of people with very low numbers of helper T cells without HIV infection were reported. Intensive research has so far failed to find either a new 'mystery' virus or evidence that AIDS can develop in the absence of HIV infection (Fauci, 1993).

Just as there are major sources of uncertainty in estimating the prevalence of HIV and AIDS in different populations, so similar uncertainties surround the extents of risk behaviour and behaviour change. The uncertainties stem in part from the limitations of epidemiological methods as tools for assessing complex behaviours and the individual and social forces that shape them, as the next section illustrates.

Investigating risk behaviour

Most epidemiological assessments of the extent of risk behaviour usually focus on the behaviour of *individuals*, reported in large-scale surveys of the general population, or within specific groups. These methods have two main limitations.

The first is that epidemiological estimates of the frequency and type of risk behaviour in individuals generally ignore the interaction *between* individuals at risk. Because HIV transmission is behavioural, its spread is not random or uniform but subject to much variation between individuals and groups. It is not simply the level of each person's risk behaviour that determines the course of transmission, but the level of risk of the people with whom those individuals mix, and whether they act riskily with others already connected to a pool of infection. This in part explains why, in the early 1990s, HIV-prevalence rates were as high as 50 per cent among drug injectors in Edinburgh, yet less than 2 per cent in Glasgow, even though the cities are only 40 miles apart. Future research thus needs to assess the interactive behaviour of socially or geographically bounded groups, rather than simply providing cross-sectional survey data on individuals.

The second limitation of many epidemiological surveys also stems from the tendency to concentrate on measures of *individual* risk behaviour. Such research often fails to account for the influence of social factors in explaining HIV-related risk behaviour and behaviour change. Of key significance in determining the actions of individuals are *social norms* (Chapter 2)—what others consider to be acceptable and normal behaviour. Studies by Graham Hart and Mary Boulton (1995) and by Tim Rhodes (1995) have shown that perceptions of HIV risk and risk behaviour are not simply dependent on individual knowledge, beliefs and attitudes, but are influenced by the opinions of others and the situational and social contexts in which such behaviour occurs.

For example, social norms have been shown to affect individual attempts to maintain **sexual safety** in terms of HIV risk in sexual encounters. A number of studies have shown that condom use is more likely within heterosexual and gay relationships when their use is endorsed by partners, close friends and peers (Friedman *et al.*, 1991; Kippax *et al.*, 1992). Conversely, a combination of love, trust and intimacy are all associated with the non-use of condoms in gay relationships, and this social norm

appears to have greater importance than sexual safety (McLean *et al.*, 1994). Qualitative research among heterosexual men and women also illustrates how social norms about gender role and 'appropriate' sexual behaviour may influence whether unsafe sex occurs. A group of feminist sociologists (Holland *et al.*, 1991) have described how women may have less power or control than men in negotiating condom use in sexual encounters—especially in new sexual encounters.

The influence of social norms can also be demonstrated in individual drug users' attempts at minimising the risks associated with injecting. Many studies have revealed community-wide changes among networks of injecting drug users away from risk behaviours. For example, Jill Burt and Gerry Stimson (1993) have shown that it is no longer the norm among groups of drug injectors to share another's needle or syringe. Because social norms are currently supportive of safer injecting behaviour, it is increasingly difficult for individual drug users to borrow or lend used syringes, even in situations where availability of equipment is scarce. However, in certain social situations or relationships, different norms may exist. Qualitative research by Neil McKeganey and Marina Barnard (1992) in the working-class drug culture of Glasgow has shown that needle sharing may still occur because there exists a wider *community norm* of reciprocity and 'sharing'. Drug users are in great part no different from the people around them in being willing to share what they own.

Later in this chapter, we return to this discussion in the context of HIV prevention. If interventions are to change individual risk behaviours, they may also need to bring about changes in the social contexts that influence why and how people behave in a certain way. This highlights the need for combining epidemiological approaches that monitor the physical dynamics of epidemic spread, with psycho-social approaches that seek to understand the social dynamics of risk behaviour. The next section shows how the experience of testing for HIV also depends on social as well as individual responses.

The experience of testing for HIV

As soon as the antibody test became commercially available, blood testing for HIV began. HIV testing and the receiving of negative and positive results have benefits as well as drawbacks, with implications not only for individuals who are tested but also for public health.

Experiences in developed countries

The major benefit to the majority of people tested is the relief at finding that they are HIV-negative. The benefits to people found to be HIV-positive—even in the developed world—are more uncertain, but they can at least be medically monitored and, at the earliest sign of symptoms, receive treatment. There are few, if any, other benefits to the HIV-positive individual apart from the knowledge that they can in future avoid infecting their sexual or drug-using partners. In virtually every other way, a positive test result is 'bad news'. Open University students should now turn to the Reader article 'Living with HIV and AIDS' by Neil Small,[14] and then answer the following question.

☐ How would you sum up the range of reactions to testing HIV-positive which the article illustrates?

■ Common features of the accounts quoted are the fear of death and the uncertainty about the future, but one person believed her positive test result would prolong her life because it made her give up drugs, and another felt relief that 'at least I had some time'. Some people referred to the stigmatisation and rejection they expect to encounter; others to the friendship and understanding they actually received. There is a determination to 'live with' HIV and get on with the practicalities of childcare and applying for tax rebates which don't stop 'just because you're hurting'.

Although a minority of individuals have remained HIV-positive and in good health for over a decade, the main variable associated with progression to HIV-disease and AIDS is time: the longer the time elapsed since infection, the greater the likelihood of developing AIDS. It is not surprising then that disclosure of HIV-positive status frequently results in depression and anxiety and occasionally in suicide. People infected with HIV have to face the probability that they will progress to a disease for which at present there is no cure.

The ways in which individuals experience HIV testing are also influenced by social responses to AIDS. As a WHO report summarised:

Adverse social consequences to [testing] can be profound (sometimes even if the results are negative), and may include social isolation, economic loss, cancellation of insurance, and restriction of opportunities for employment, schooling, housing, health care and social services. These potentially destructive outcomes lend special urgency to the issues of confidentiality and informed consent prior to testing. (WHO, 1988, p. 228)

Three related features of common social responses to people with HIV are of key importance in increasing the fear and anxiety associated with testing positive, namely: perceptions of *contagion*; implications of *reduced lifespan*; and *stigmatisation*. All of them lead to discrimination of the kinds outlined by WHO.

HIV is often popularly believed to be contagious—that is, readily transmitted in the course of ordinary social contact. While this is not the case, such beliefs have resulted in people with HIV being socially isolated. Fear of contagion has led to children with HIV or haemophilia being excluded from school, often against the wishes of their parents. HIV-positive people have been dismissed from employment as a result of pressure from work colleagues or employers, or denied health care, particularly where invasive procedures such as surgical or dental treatment are involved. As the historian Richard Davenport-Hines has written of press reporting on the communicability of HIV:

Stories of theatre cleaners who ... boycotted gay actors, or of schools which boycotted public swimming pools where gay men swam ... are usually published with denials that HIV can be transmitted by casual contact, but their focus nevertheless engenders rather than allays fear, stimulating anxiety rather than alleviating it. (Davenport-Hines, 1990, p. 331)

The knowledge that a positive HIV test usually indicates a reduced lifespan has major financial and economic implications. There have been cases where insurance policies of HIV-positive people were cancelled, and in most developed countries it is virtually impossible for a person with HIV to buy life insurance, obtain a mortgage or other similar financial services. Often, having an HIV *test* (even if the result is negative), or being advised to have one by a doctor, is sufficient for certain insurance companies to refuse services, because this is seen to indicate a higher than normal risk of HIV. In addition, many employers are reluctant to take on a person with HIV, despite the fact that there may be many years before the development of HIV-related illness.

[14]In *Health and Disease: A Reader* (second edition, 1995).

People with HIV are often stigmatised in everyday social life. As we noted at the beginning of this chapter (and in Chapter 2), the initial emergence of HIV infection among populations who are marginalised as 'other' in society has resulted in HIV-positivity being seen as a symbol of 'abnormality'. HIV infection has been used as biological ammunition or proof that a person has wilfully behaved in socially or morally unacceptable ways. In this respect, a positive HIV test can be treated as 'just' punishment for pursuing 'wrong' lifestyles or behaviour.

Although all people with HIV are potentially subject to stigmatisation, the media have made exceptions and identified some groups as the 'innocent victims' of HIV-disease. People with haemophilia who contracted HIV from infected Factor VIII, and children infected while in the womb have been given this status; it has also been extended to heterosexuals who have not injected drugs or had multiple sexual partners. The underlying message is that these individuals do not 'deserve' to be HIV-positive and are 'victims' of the otherness to which all are under threat. Their initial experience of testing HIV-positive may be no less distressing than for members of stigmatised groups, such as gay men, but the level of social concern for their welfare has been much greater.

An example is the disclosure in November 1991 of HIV-positivity by Earvin ('Magic') Johnson—a young, black, basketball star, worshipped by millions of American fans. His announcement generated enormous support, including a personal message of sympathy from President Bush. Johnson's heterosexuality (and therefore comparative 'innocence') was what fuelled the sympathy—despite the fact that he had, in his own words, 'accommodated as many women' as he could. For the first time many young people had to face the reality of the risk of HIV infection from heterosexual intercourse.

Experiences in developing countries

In developing countries, fear of contagion, premature death and stigmatisation also affect individual experiences of HIV testing and an HIV-positive diagnosis. Aspects of the wider social and political context also have a major impact, particularly the lack of medical resources which often means that medical help is scarce. As described by 'Mary' from Zimbabwe, who was first diagnosed in 1987:

> We went to the general hospital and he explained that you are HIV-positive. I was so confused, I asked him, 'What does that mean?' He said that if you are HIV-positive, you have

got the virus of AIDS. Nobody helped me. They said, 'You are HIV-positive, but by 1995 you will die because it's a very dangerous virus which kills people'. I wrote it down, that in 1995 I will be dead. (Quoted in Richardson and Bolle, 1992, pp. 46–7)

In most developing countries, the scarcity of testing means that only a minority of those infected with HIV will be aware of it before the onset of symptoms. As described by 'Imrat', interviewed here five years after his HIV status was confirmed:

> I was losing weight and had diarrhoea and terrible 'flu. Two months after, I was still losing weight. The doctor put us to another doctor, who said that we'll probably have to run an AIDS test. In Malaysia at that time, AIDS did not exist, nobody talked about it … So the first thing I told the doctor, 'Look', I said, 'as far as I'm concerned we Malaysians don't get AIDS'. I went for the test, and one week after, the results came back positive. The only knowledge I had at that time was if you have AIDS you die—you have no hopes. I was confused, depressed, really terrified. I said that's it, I probably have a month or two to live. (Quoted in Richardson and Bolle, 1992, p. 55)

The experience of testing positive for HIV in the developing countries has to be seen in the context of the wide range of health problems facing inadequately resourced economies. In 1987 an editorial in the *Lancet* entitled 'AIDS in Africa' noted that:

> HIV-related morbidity and mortality are not among the major health concerns when placed in the context of the million deaths from malaria that are estimated to occur in Africa annually, and the even larger number of deaths from diarrhoea and respiratory infections. Among adults, tuberculosis is a much greater burden. (*Lancet*, 1987, p. 193)

The major infectious diseases in developing countries are both preventable and treatable, and yet millions of people still die from them. HIV infection, although preventable, cannot yet be cured: even if someone could get to the general hospital of the nearest town or city, little treatment would be available. Health-care systems that cannot meet the needs of those with curable diseases cannot 'waste' resources on incurable ones. However, we now know that many cases of respiratory infections and tuberculosis (though not the majority) are the consequence of immunodeficiency caused by 'hidden' HIV infection.

Yet there are personal and organisational efforts to fight the spread of HIV in both developing and developed countries, and some of these initiatives have made the experience of testing HIV-positive less frightening for some individuals. 'Jennifer' from Uganda illustrates this practical approach:

> I had five babies—three died and two are still alive. My husband divorced me. I was diagnosed HIV-positive when I had my fifth baby. I started attending the day centre for comfort because my baby had died. I learned tailoring, handicrafts, sharing experiences with existing clients and helping where needed. The whole sense of death from AIDS disappeared. I made up my mind to plan for the future of my children … Through counselling, the AIDS organisation discovered that we HIV-positive mothers have a common financial problem. A club was formed to meet our needs and from discussions, income-generating activities were suggested. These are handicrafts, poultry farming and breadmaking. (Quoted in Richardson and Bolle, 1992, p. 83)

Personal experiences of receiving an HIV-positive result—usually as a result of a voluntarily undertaken test—give some insight into the concerns surrounding mass screening of the population for HIV.

Mass screening for HIV

Once the antibody test for HIV became available, there was soon demand for screening of the population on a far wider scale than voluntary testing could achieve. The question of mass screening for HIV raises major political and ethical questions.

Mass screening in the United Kingdom

Demands for mass screening for HIV in the United Kingdom have taken two forms. One option is for **anonymous mass screening**, in which a large sample of the population are tested when routine blood samples are taken for other medical purposes (e.g. during antenatal checks). Such screening programmes are 'anonymous' because test results cannot be traced back to individuals. Tests are generally made without the person's informed consent.

☐ What practical benefits and drawbacks can you suggest might result from large-scale anonymous screening for HIV?

■ Screening on this scale would provide important data on the prevalence and dynamics of HIV spread among populations who may not otherwise come forward for an HIV test. This should enable more accurate planning of prevention, education and treatment services and predictions of future spread. The practical drawbacks are that the sample may not be representative, and that HIV-positive individuals are not identified and thus cannot be given treatment or counselled to prevent transmitting HIV.

There are also ethical objections in that most anonymous screening is undertaken without informed consent; conversely, where consent is obtained it may raise unanswered concerns about their HIV status among the people tested.

The second option is **named mass screening** for HIV, in which positive tests are traced back to an individual. Advocates of named screening have argued that anonymous testing denies protection to 'the public' from contact with infected people. Although never considered a viable option by governments in the United Kingdom, some commentators in the early years of the epidemic demanded *compulsory* named screening of the whole population to protect the 'innocent' from the 'guilty':

> My concern is the moral issue as to whether we are entitled to expose innocent citizens to the danger of infection. If it indeed transpires that there are considerable numbers of carriers, this minority may seek security by deliberately spreading the contagion to escape what they experience as discrimination. (Lord Jakobivits, former Chief Rabbi, quoted in the *Independent*, 24 November 1987)

> It is more important to protect the lives of those who might innocently or accidentally catch the disease than to protect the reputation of those who have caught the disease through their own self-indulgence. (*Daily Express*, 30 August 1985)

In the United Kingdom, there is no legal basis for undertaking compulsory testing of individuals or mass screening of the population. Michael Adler, a leading physician specialising in genito-urinary medicine and adviser to successive British governments on AIDS issues, has consistently argued against compulsory testing—in part because this may lead to an *increase* in the spread of HIV infection.

☐ How might this come about?

■ Compulsory testing could result in HIV being 'driven underground' because those most at risk of infection might seek to avoid the adverse social and economic consequences of a positive test result. They would then be denied access to medical and health education services and, in the absence of these, might not take the precautions necessary to prevent transmitting HIV to others.

The medical profession has rejected compulsory screening as 'ethically unacceptable and a gross interference with civil liberties' (BMA, 1987). It is also impractical. Since there is a three-month incubation period between initial infection and the appearance of detectable antibodies in the blood, screening would have to be regularly repeated on all negative results so as to confirm HIV status. Policy in the United Kingdom in the 1990s is to encourage people to come forward voluntarily for counselling and HIV testing in confidence. Anonymous screening of routinely collected blood samples has been undertaken in selected hospitals and health centres, and in 1992 the government agreed that *voluntary* named screening could be offered to all pregnant women (Department of Health, 1992).

Mass screening in other countries

Even within Europe, there have been very different political responses to HIV screening. For example, in Sweden, statutes were introduced that allowed compulsory screening of named individuals (not mass screening of the population), identification of infected people and forcible detainment on a secure island in the Baltic archipelago of anyone thought to be infecting others. In Bavaria, Southern Germany, prostitutes and others suspected of being infected (including gay and bisexual men, prisoners and refugees) were compulsorily tested and could be imprisoned.

In Cuba, there is no organised mass compulsory screening, but blood taken during the course of routine clinical contact with primary health services or hospitals is tested for HIV without patients' consent. The Cuban government's initial response to those found to be HIV-positive was to 'encourage' them to enter state-run sanatoria, where they were expected to live until an affordable cure became available. Most such sanatoria

are now reportedly closed and community care has taken the place of confinement.

Some countries require visitors and guest workers to have an HIV test. In a global survey of migration and travel policies relating to HIV, the medical ethicists Margaret Duckett and Andrew Orkin asked 166 countries to provide data on their policies (Duckett and Orkin, 1989). The following examples from that period illustrate the diversity. Cuba reported testing people who were planning to stay longer than three months, so students, foreign workers and immigrants were all tested on arrival; the policy was to repatriate foreign nationals if found to be infected. Cyprus tested students only if they were African, and foreign workers only if they were 'cabaret artists'; those found to be HIV-positive were not granted long-stay permits. In contrast, Jamaica adopted the WHO principle that AIDS-related travel restrictions are ineffective as a public-health measure, and Zimbabwe reported a deliberate policy of non-discrimination.

In the USA in the 1980s and 1990s, the armed forces compulsorily test recruits and personnel on active duty, and immigrants must also undergo testing. Many applicants for US citizenship have lived and worked for many years in the country, sometimes illegally, but if found to be infected they can be deported. However, it is in travel restrictions that the USA has had its most unwanted media exposure. People with HIV-disease, at any stage from HIV infection with no symptoms to AIDS, fall within the regulations covering medical examination of aliens. HIV is one of the infections categorised as 'dangerous and contagious', and carriers may be excluded from entry into the USA. If permitted entry, people with HIV-disease are legally obliged to carry documentation to this effect.

The diversity of national policies on HIV screening among indigenous and visiting individuals illustrates the advantages and disadvantages associated with the surveillance of disease. Although it is almost universally accepted by researchers and practitioners in the field that compulsory screening methods carry with them a host of ethical, political and social problems, such methods exist in both developed and developing countries. It can be argued that some practices contravene basic human rights, or reinforce inaccurate notions of HIV as contagious. Once again, this illustrates how individual experiences of HIV testing and HIV-positivity are influenced by social and political responses.

However, it is important to recognise that people are not merely passive recipients of imposed meanings and practices, against which they cannot argue—as the next section illustrates.

Community action: preventing the spread of HIV

The history of HIV and AIDS is marked by people taking collective action, independently of governments or health organisations, to prevent the spread of HIV and to resist stigmatisation or discrimination. Here we discuss community responses to HIV prevention among two of the populations most affected by HIV and AIDS in developed countries: gay men, and injecting drug users; and a third group—sex workers—taking a world-wide view.

Gay men

In the absence of a cure or vaccine, the only way in which people can prevent HIV infection is to minimise their risk behaviour. Gay men—the first identified group affected by AIDS in developed countries—responded rapidly with **community action** initiatives: setting up organisations to distribute what little information there was to others in the gay communities, and putting pressure on governments, the medical establishment and pharmaceutical companies to take the epidemic seriously. In the major American and European cities this happened within the first two years of the recognition of AIDS and preceded any organised medical response.

In New York, the *Gay Men's Health Crisis* (*GMHC*), formed by a group of mainly white middle-class gay men, including the writers Larry Kramer and Edmund White, started producing leaflets in the early 1980s describing the first symptoms of AIDS and recommending changes to sexual behaviour (such as monogamy) that might prevent infection. In the United Kingdom, in response to the insensitive treatment of Terrence Higgins by hospital staff prior to his death from AIDS in 1982, some of his friends set up the *Terrence Higgins Trust*. The Trust produced guidelines on how to avoid infection on the basis of epidemiological information about risk factors.

Volunteers distributed health education information to men in gay bars and clubs, warning of the dangers of unprotected penetrative sex. Initially doctors had simply told gay men to stop having sex altogether, but subsequently modified this advice to the avoidance of anal intercourse. Supported by a gay press strongly committed to fighting the disease, gay communities introduced the concept of 'safer sex', which advocated, among other things, the use of condoms when having penetrative sex. Gay men were able to mobilise rapidly because of the progress they had achieved in community and civil rights action associated with the 'gay liberation' movement during the 1970s.

Two examples of HIV-prevention initiatives that encouraged community action are *Gay Heroes* in the USA, and *Men who have Sex With Men Action in the Community* (*MESMAC*) in the United Kingdom. Both these projects share a commitment to involving the men they target as participants in **peer-education programmes**, which aim to encourage mutual responsibility and support for sexual safety and HIV-risk reduction. They have promoted a collective response within gay communities, rather than attempting to change the beliefs and opinions of individuals.

Evaluations of these projects (by psychiatrist Jeffrey Kelly *et al.*, 1992; and by Alan Prout and Katie Deverell, 1995) show that the most effective advocates for change in the gay community are gay men themselves. In using peers as educators and employing 'opinion leaders' within specific networks or groups of gay men, these projects aim to make significant advances over conventional health education approaches, which tend to rely on the provision of information alone as the basis for behaviour change. **Information-giving approaches** assume that once individuals are given accurate information they will change their behaviour to minimise risk.[15] The limitations of information-giving approaches in preventing the spread of HIV and AIDS have been documented by social researchers Hilary Homans and Peter Aggleton (1988).

☐ Why do you think that community action and peer-education initiatives can be more effective than information-giving approaches in bringing about behaviour change? (Think back to the psycho-social research on risk behaviour discussed earlier in this chapter.)

■ Such initiatives build on research showing that the most effective means of changing the ways in which individuals think and behave is to change social and peer-group norms. Information-giving may not change individual behaviours if what is considered to be socially-acceptable behaviour within the peer group has not changed.

[15]A more detailed discussion of information-giving approaches to health education and disease prevention appears in *Dilemmas in Health Care*, Chapter 9.

Evidence of the effectiveness of community action can be seen in Figure 4.5, which shows the prevalence of rectal *gonorrhoea* among men and women (a 'marker' of recent unprotected anal sex), and Figure 4.6, which shows similar data for acute hepatitis B (a blood-borne infection which can be sexually-transmitted) and HIV among gay men.

☐ The first United Kingdom government-sponsored HIV-prevention campaign occurred in 1986. What can you conclude from Figures 4.5 and 4.6 about the response of gay men to the earliest reports of AIDS?

■ The rates of sexually-transmitted infection among gay and bisexual men had *already* fallen sharply before campaigns began in 1986, and continued to decline until about 1989. This highlights the effectiveness of the rapid mobilisation within gay communities towards self-help and the advocating of safer sex.

However, new diagnoses of sexually-transmitted infection began increasing in about 1990, before the downward trend was re-established. American researchers have attempted to explain the increase by suggesting that gay men were 'relapsing', that is returning (even if only occasionally) to risky sexual behaviour in the belief that they were no longer at risk. The *relapse thesis* has become prominent in preventive programmes in the USA and the focus of much recent research, but it suffers from a number of problems. Some new diagnoses in the 1990s will be among men who are not relapsing but actually *beginning* their sexual lives by having unsafe sex, often because they are young and consider AIDS to be a disease of older men. And men who never changed their behaviour and continued to have unsafe sex may have delayed coming forward for testing until about 1990, encouraged by improvements in treatment. The concept of 'relapse' has also been criticised for its negative association with disease progression and 'moral back-sliding'.

Injecting drug users

It has been less common for injecting drug users to organise themselves on a community basis to prevent HIV infection than has been the case with gay men. This is for two related reasons. First, there was an existing infrastructure for community action and organisation among gay men. In contrast there is little evidence of a collective or community identity among populations of drug

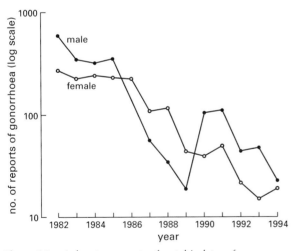

Figure 4.5 *Laboratory reports of rectal isolates of gonorrhoea* (Neisseria gonorrhoeae) *from males and females aged 15 years or over, in England and Wales. (Sources: 1982–91 from Evans, B. G. et al., 1993, Sexually transmitted diseases and HIV-1 infection among homosexual men in England and Wales, British Medical Journal, **306**, pp. 426–8, Figure 2; 1992–4 from PHLS Communicable Disease Surveillance Centre: unpublished Quarterly Surveillance Tables)*

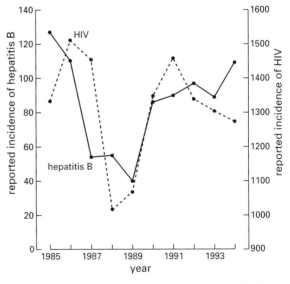

Figure 4.6 *Newly diagnosed reports of acute hepatitis B and HIV-1 infections in men who have sex with men, in England and Wales. (Data from PHLS AIDS Centre, Communicable Disease Surveillance Centre, and Scottish Centre for Infection and Environmental Health: unpublished Quarterly Surveillance Tables No. 29, September 1995)*

injectors. Second, injecting drug users have less collective power, in part because of a lack of cohesiveness and the absence of external support for an illegal activity, but also because of the everyday demands of drug-using lifestyles and their generally low economic and social status.

Despite these obstacles, drug injectors have also made significant changes in behaviour to prevent HIV transmission. Research by Tim Rhodes (1994) has shown that the proportions of drug injectors who report sharing used needles and syringes has continued to decline over time. HIV prevalence among injecting populations in the United Kingdom stabilised in the early 1990s.

However, there have been few changes in the sexual behaviour of drug injectors and their sexual partners. A review of research by Rhodes *et al.* (1996) shows that levels of sexual risk behaviour among drug injectors are almost identical to those reported among heterosexual populations as a whole. This points to the importance of wider social norms which endorse unsafe sexual behaviour among heterosexuals—a key problem for future HIV-prevention initiatives. In the context of a peer-group norm which endorses safer drug use but unsafe sex, the sexual transmission of HIV is likely to increase among drug injectors and their sexual partners.

The cornerstone of HIV-prevention initiatives targeted at drug injectors has been the **syringe exchange**—an agency where used syringes are exchanged for sterile ones. A government-sponsored pilot scheme was established in the United Kingdom in 1987. An evaluation conducted by medical sociologist Gerry Stimson showed a reduction in sharing and other risk behaviours among syringe-exchange attenders (Stimson, 1989). Evaluations of syringe exchanges world-wide have confirmed this finding, with little evidence that providing free sterile syringes has increased the prevalence of drug injecting, or the frequency of drug use among current injectors. Conversely, studies in the USA (Watters, 1996) show higher rates of HIV prevalence among drug injectors in states where syringe exchange has been prohibited by laws penalising possession of injecting equipment.

Despite their relative lack of cohesiveness as a 'community', drug injectors have nonetheless established some community action initiatives. One of the first of these, the *Junkiebonden* (Junkies' Union), was established initially as a civil rights action group in the early 1980s in Amsterdam. This organisation helped set up the first syringe exchange in the Netherlands in 1984, at the time as a measure to prevent hepatitis B infection. In New York, the *Association for Drug Abuse Prevention and Treatment (ADAPT)* combined the self-help efforts of

drug injectors with the expertise and support of health professionals, to lobby for more accessible drug treatment and service provision.

An important development in HIV-prevention initiatives aimed at drug injectors has been the use of **outreach projects**, which employ peer educators (in this case, drug users themselves) to get in touch with individuals who would otherwise remain out of contact with treatment and helping services. In the USA, the *National Institute of Drug Abuse (NIDA)* commissioned outreach projects in over 50 cities, and such projects have become an established feature of prevention work among drug injectors in the United Kingdom.

☐ What do you think are the main problems for community action approaches among injecting drug users?

■ The lack of a community identity among drug-using populations means there is little infrastructure for raising resources and organisational support for such initiatives. Drug injectors may avoid participation for fear of criminal prosecution. There has been opposition to initiatives such as needle exchanges from people who see them as encouraging drug use.

Despite these problems, community action initiatives are among the most effective means of preventing the spread of HIV among injecting drug users.

Sex workers and their clients

In developing countries, HIV has spread mainly by heterosexual transmission. However, almost all studies show that HIV infection among prostitutes is more likely to be associated with a history of injecting drug use than with unprotected sex with clients. The majority of prostitutes report consistently high rates of condom use in commercial sexual encounters. But condom use has been found to be less likely among prostitutes who use or inject drugs, in part because clients may seek out drug-using prostitutes and offer to pay more for unprotected sex.

Fewer prostitutes report using condoms with their private partners than with their paying partners. Sophie Day, an anthropologist, and Helen Ward, an epidemiologist, have studied this distinction between private relationships and 'work' or 'business' among women prostitutes in London. Their research indicates that these women are most at risk of HIV infection from their boyfriends, particularly if any of the latter are injecting drug users (Day and Ward, 1991).

In some parts of the world, condom use is less consistent between prostitutes and their clients. For example, high levels of HIV infection are associated with sex work in Thailand, despite there being little evidence of injecting drug use among sex workers. The owners and managers of sex-work brothels, bars and saunas have been encouraged by health workers to introduce condoms, but competition for customers is intense and many fear that men who dislike condoms will go elsewhere.

Female prostitutes in developing countries are rarely able to insist that their clients use condoms because of their financial dependence on prostitution: many send earnings back to families engaged in subsistence farming.[16] As in developed countries, unprotected sex often carries a higher fee, as well as a higher health risk. Condoms may also be unaffordable or unobtainable.

In both developing and developed countries a number of exceptional female prostitutes have organised collective action to protect the health of their co-workers: for example, in Nairobi, they have played a major role in encouraging clients to use condoms. In other countries, women sex workers have engaged in political lobbying in an attempt to legalise prostitution and hence improve prostitutes' access to health services and improve the 'occupational safety' of sex work. Self-help and peer initiatives, such as *Red Thread* in Amsterdam and *Call Off Your Old Tired Ethics* in California (*COYOTE*), argue that prostitutes themselves are only marginally able to create safer working conditions and to promote safer sex within these conditions. They campaign for wider social and political change as a foundation on which to build HIV-prevention activities.

Perhaps the biggest obstacle to creating safer working conditions for prostitutes, as far as the risk of HIV is concerned, is the behaviour of those who purchase sex services. As we noted above, it is relatively common for clients of prostitutes to demand unprotected sex and not uncommon for some prostitutes to provide such services at higher prices. Yet there have been relatively few attempts to research or educate the clients of prostitutes. Two exceptions are shown in the television programme mentioned earlier—one in India, where long-distance lorry drivers have been targeted, and another in Zambia, employing peer educators in rural villages where male migrant workers return after having sex with prostitutes in the cities. Both of these initiatives are examples of outreach projects.

[16] The television programme associated with this chapter for Open University students, 'A future with AIDS', illustrates this dilemma among women sex workers in India, and among children living rough on the streets of Rio de Janeiro, some of whom earn money from sexual services.

However, despite research evidence that prostitutes are at greater risk from their clients than their clients are from them, the general tendency has been to view prostitutes as vectors of disease. HIV-prevention initiatives among sex workers are likely to be more effective if it is recognised that safer sex is an activity negotiated between two people. Attempts to encourage safer sex among prostitutes also requires the compliance of clients.

Limitations of HIV-prevention strategies

We have already argued that the main limitation of most national (as opposed to peer and community-based) HIV-prevention initiatives is that they target individuals and give information and advice about HIV risk and behaviour change, without encouraging changes in the social 'norms' that predispose individuals to act riskily.

The arena of sexual safety illustrates this point. A notable feature of health education campaigns promoting safer sex in heterosexual relationships is that they target information on both men and women—recognising that safer sex is the outcome of a negotiation between two people and not simply a matter of individual choice. Yet such campaigns have generally ignored the imbalance in power relations between men and women.

☐ What effect is this likely to have on sexual safety?

■ Women may have less power or control than men in negotiating the use of condoms. The same imbalance of power applies to negotiating non-penetrative sexual activity.

A team of feminist social researchers who studied the sexual behaviour of young women in Manchester and London, argue that:

> Condoms are not neutral objects about which a straightforward decision can be made on health grounds. The idea that women are free to choose the most rational form of protection ignores the nature of the systematic inequalities in the social relationships between women and men. (Holland *et al.*, 1991, p. 129)

These inequalities suggest the need for changes in gender roles and social norms about 'appropriate' sexual behaviour, which influence the ability of women to exercise power in negotiating safety in sexual encounters. In some developing countries, for example, outreach projects are attempting to change the social norms governing condom use in rural communities, where women are at increased risk of HIV if they have unprotected sex with husbands who may purchase sexual services while working away from home.[17]

There has been persistent criticism of information-giving and mass-media prevention campaigns in the United Kingdom, which were viewed as too little, too late—particularly among gay communities. Most government-sponsored campaigns in the 1980s were aimed at the population as a whole, without reference to those groups whose behaviour put them at most risk. Even when later advertisements were targeted at the popula-

tions most affected, they often carried stigmatising messages (as in Figure 4.7).

A further limitation of mass health education and advertising campaigns is that they have been politically constrained in their ability to present sexual activity as healthy and pleasurable or to offer *practical* safer sex advice. Government policies promoting the sanctity of monogamy and the family over 'sexual promiscuity' or sexual diversity have tended to generate campaigns associating sex with danger, death and disease.

The linking of sex and health is in itself problematic in a cultural context which endows sex with meanings which are far from healthy. (Holland *et al.*, 1991, p. 129)

[17]A discussion of gender roles and sexual safety occurs in the television programme 'A future with AIDS', for students of the Open University.

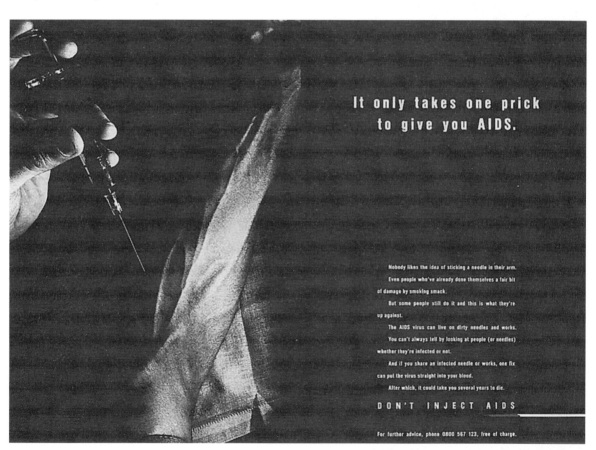

Figure 4.7   *In 1987 this poster broke new ground in government campaigns by warning about the danger of HIV infection associated with injecting drug use, and by using the vernacular of drug users ('smack' is heroin and 'works' are needles/syringes). The image of a dirty arm with needle poised over it and the use of innuendo in the slogan 'It only takes one prick to give you AIDS' reinforces negative attitudes to injecting drug users and the association of AIDS with a stigmatised group. (Reproduced by permission of the Controller of Her Majesty's Stationery Office; Crown Copyright)*

Government-sponsored slogans such as 'Don't Die of Ignorance' are in sharp contrast to campaigns designed by gay organisations, such as the Terrence Higgins Trust, with slogans such as 'Safer Sex: Keep It Up!' and 'Love Sexy, Love Safe' (Figure 4.8).

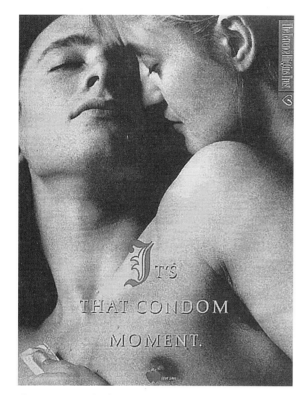

Figure 4.8 *In the late 1980s, the success of the Terrence Higgins Trust's campaigns to educate gay men about safer sex encouraged the British government to give them a grant for a similar campaign aimed at heterosexuals. Their posters promoted images of loving and erotic sex easily made safer by the use of condoms or alternatives to penetrative sex. The grant was withdrawn in 1993. (Poster reproduced by kind permission of the Terrence Higgins Trust)*

The limitations associated with HIV-prevention initiatives in developing countries are inextricably linked to the lack of funding, infrastructure and technological resources. And, because HIV infection is one of many public health problems, resources are often better spent on other primary prevention or health-care initiatives. Overseas aid aims to assist developing countries in implementing HIV-prevention work, but such interventions have not always been sensitive to local culture and circumstances, though some have utilised the skills of local healers in

addition to orthodox health-care workers.[18] In rural areas, where literacy levels are low and there is a culture based on oral traditions, written and visual messages may have little or no effect, whereas story-telling, drama and radio may be more effective means of communication.[19]

In some cultures, it may be necessary to attempt wider socio-cultural change before HIV-prevention initiatives are possible. These changes may be extremely difficult, for example where social norms endorse polygamy or where fertility is highly prized. This points to the importance of integrating approaches that encourage changes in individual knowledge and attitudes with those that encourage community-wide changes in socio-cultural norms about sex and sexuality.

The experience of HIV-disease

The experience of HIV-disease is characterised by personal struggle (see the Reader article by Neil Small[20])—not only in adapting to profound biological and medical changes, but also against stigmatisation and discrimination. Individual experiences of HIV-disease interact with social, organisational and political responses.

Personal responses

We have already commented that representations of HIV-disease in the media reflect wider social responses to HIV and AIDS, and that these have often characterised affected people either as 'innocent victims' or as 'guilty and deserving' their illness. Popular discourses on the subject of HIV and AIDS generally discriminate between 'us' and 'them', the healthy and the ill, the living and the dying. As a consequence, the personal experience of HIV-disease involves a constant struggle against such stigmatisation. People with HIV-disease are generally represented as 'suffering' or 'dying' from AIDS, rather than as individuals who—like 'Paul' and 'Peter Phoenix'—are living with an illness.

[18]Examples occur in two television programmes for Open University students (both were associated with earlier books in this course): 'Health and disease in Zimbabwe' and 'Zimbabwe: Health for all?' illustrate different aspects of government-sponsored HIV-prevention and treatment projects which centre on traditional healers.

[19]Examples from Zambia, Brazil and India appear in the television programme 'A future with AIDS'.

[20]See also Richardson and Bolle (1992) in the 'References' list at the end of this book.

Just because you've got AIDS doesn't mean you're any different … I'm living with AIDS. I try to normalise my life in some respects [he was planning to walk up a mountain the next summer]. It's not necessarily the quantity of your life, it's the quality that matters. ('Paul', quoted by Silverman in Aggleton *et al.*, 1989, pp. 112–3)

My feet itch, my chest itches, I have warts on my face, and my weight is about ten pounds below what it ought to be. I have no energy, my legs don't work right, I am subject to periodic depressions, and my friends and colleagues don't know what is wrong with me. But I am alive, working every day, enjoying the closeness of a loving wife and family. I do not feel like a dead or dying man. I feel very much alive. ('Peter Phoenix', quoted in *Living with AIDS*, 1989, p. 92)

Media associations of HIV-disease with death and dying can be potent: for example, in the 1980s the *Sun* newspaper's AIDS stories carried a logo of a skull. Simon Watney (1989b) reported that a colleague had written an article for the *Nursing Times* describing the experience of a woman 'living with AIDS'. By the time the piece was printed her words had been 'corrected' to a woman 'dying from AIDS'. The power vested in media institutions is such that people living with HIV-disease often have little control over how they are represented and seen by others. Personal experiences are often misrepresented, either to 'sell stories' or to promote a view of people with HIV as vectors of contagion. Evidence that this view exists can be found in the least expected of places:

Here we are at an international AIDS conference. Yesterday a woman came up to me and said, 'May I have two minutes of your time? I'm asking doctors how they feel about treating AIDS patients'. And I said, 'Well, actually I'm not a doctor. I'm an AIDS patient', and as she was shaking hands, her hand whipped away, she took two steps backward, and the look of horror on her face was absolutely diabolical. (Reported by Farmer and Kleinman, in *Living with AIDS*, 1989, pp. 136–7)

People with HIV often feel 'disempowered', as Andrew Hunt—a British researcher who recently died of AIDS—experienced:

I was diagnosed with AIDS in the middle of 1990. At the time there were a lot of well

meaning people offering advice and support, bandying about words like 'empowerment', 'being positive' and 'regaining control'. To me, at that stage in a state of shock and disbelief mingling with fits of anger and feelings of self contempt, such phrases appeared bland in the extreme. They were just words, too abstract to be applied to me. It took a long time to begin to understand what empowerment means and how to be positive and to regain control: they are concepts which inform a way of living and reacting. (Hunt, 1992, p. 353)

The stigmatisation associated with HIV-disease means that many people feel unable to talk openly about their diagnosis. Public figures such as Freddy Mercury, Rock Hudson, Liberace and Brad Davis kept their diagnosis and experience of living with HIV secret. In a recent study of the subjective experience of living with HIV, Daniele Carricaburu and Janine Pierret (1995) found that a key consideration was 'whether or not to tell others about being HIV-positive, whom to tell, and when' (p. 71). One reason that people often give for not telling others about their HIV-positive status is that they do not want to be treated as 'different'. In short, concealment is a strategy to ensure that you are 'treated like anyone else'—a strategy for avoiding the adverse consequences of stigma which the sociologist Erving Goffman termed *passing* (Chapter 2).

I don't want the others to look at me differently. I don't want any condescension, and even less, pity. I want to have the same relations with people, especially since, for now, there's no need to talk about it. (Quoted in Carricaburu and Pierret, 1995, p. 73)

If a person chooses to tell others—even if they are close friends who are knowledgeable about HIV-disease—this may nonetheless encourage a change in the way he or she is viewed and in the way others interact. Keeping silent in fear of such a change in relationships is an example of what Goffman called *felt stigma*:

… telling my friends would change their attitude, whether they wanted it to change or not. Not that they're going to think of me as being a sick person, a potential fatality. But inevitably, in their subconscious, something will change. (Carricaburu and Pierret, 1995, p. 73)

In terms of the everyday experience of 'managing' a stigmatised illness, a person's decision not to reveal their

HIV-positive status may become more and more difficult over time. Non-disclosure becomes particularly stressful when it becomes visible to others that one is ill:

> If I fall sick, I'll probably change my mind. But for the time being, it's my secret, and I'm keeping it. (Carricaburu and Pierret, 1995, p. 73)

Few research studies have systematically documented people's subjective experiences of living with HIV-disease: most have focused on the psychological impact of receiving an HIV-positive diagnosis and its implications for risk reduction. The work of Carricaburu and Pierret (1995) is a rare exception, since it illuminates the impact that HIV has on the management of a range of aspects of everyday living, including sexuality. For many people living with HIV, it feels easier not to think about the possibilities of meeting new sexual partners or having a sexual relationship. Knowing oneself to be HIV-positive introduces added 'delicacy' into the negotiation of new and existing sexual relationships. It is in part for this reason that some, but by no means all, people living with HIV may decide to become sexually abstinent.

> I've never had a sexual relationship, but I hope I'll not end up an old bachelor … She'd have to accept my being haemophilic and, in addition, my being HIV-positive. That's a lot! I don't think it's possible. (Carricaburu and Pierret, 1995, p. 74)

> I feel sexual impulses towards someone, automatically I think, 'Is it worth it?' … I couldn't even conceive of myself going all out to have a sexual experience. It doesn't even cross my mind. What crosses my mind is 'safety first' before the pleasure … Sex is a really big thing. It's a really big obstacle to overcome. (Quoted in Rhodes *et al.*, 1995, p. 92)

> For four years now, I've stopped having sex, having full sexual relations. I vaguely allow myself to masturbate now and then. (Quoted in Carricaburu and Pierret, 1995, p. 74)

Very little research has been published about the subjective experiences of being ill with HIV-disease, or of receiving medical help or treatment. This aspect of living with HIV in countries such as the United Kingdom and the USA has been illuminated primarily by the 'stories' of individuals, often told in television documentaries. While these can generate greater empathy and understanding, the lack of systematic research makes it difficult to gain generalisable insights which could lead to improvements in care.

In many cases, people with HIV-disease in developing countries, particularly in Africa, have somewhat different symptoms to those in the developed world, most frequently involving severe weight loss, weakness and eventual death. In most African countries, AIDS is called 'slim disease', no doubt with a certain degree of grim irony. There are other tangible burdens—a newspaper report tells of the concerns of one Ugandan woman:

> Gertrude Nakinganda smiles at her approaching death. 'This is how it is', she tells the health workers, taking in with a simple gesture her bare room, mattress on the ground, and her wasted body. She manages a joke: 'It's good you came now—next week you will not find me'. The health workers ask after her children. 'They are as you see them. They look after me, cook, fetch water'. Gertrude has eight children and no one to support her. Unable to leave her bed, she worries over her children's future. 'I tell my daughter to study hard and ignore the loving business. But I am worried for my children when I die. Will you help them?'. (Anthony Swift, *Guardian*, 23 April 1992)

With an estimated 500 000 'AIDS orphans' by the mid-1990s, Uganda faces a situation in which childcare responsibilities fall to grandparents, other children and voluntary and state agencies. Living with AIDS can therefore also involve living with its consequences for an entire generation.

Organisational responses

In the developed world, people with HIV-disease have been supported mainly through voluntary and self-help groups. In San Francisco, the *Shanti Project* has, since the earliest days of AIDS in that city, provided food parcels, respite care and accommodation to people with AIDS. In the United Kingdom, the Terrence Higgins Trust and similar organisations such as *Body Positive* and *Positively Women* have offered 'buddying' services. Buddies are volunteers who provide practical and emotional support to people with AIDS:

> I got involved with the buddy system, being a buddy with people who have full blown AIDS and are really sick. I had people close to me die in my arms. That was tough, because that was seeing my own mortality and saying it's a matter of time, my time will come. This could be me at some time down the line. But the pain they were

suffering, they had to deal with that themselves. I wanted to help, but you have to do that alone. ('Winston', quoted in Richardson and Bolle, 1992, pp. 85–6)

Few buddies are able to continue beyond their second or third person with AIDS, but buddying remains an invaluable service, and is a model of informal care which is being considered by other agencies serving people with life-threatening diseases.

However, there are tensions within organisations committed to health education, care and support of people with HIV-disease. These tensions are rooted in the increased 'professionalisation' of AIDS services and organisations. This has been one outcome of what Cindy Patton (1990) has called the 'AIDS industry'. Initially, most organisational responses were characterised by self-help projects among people with HIV-disease and their friends, relations and peers. In the 1980s, there was an unusual degree of involvement of those affected with HIV-disease in the running and organisation of services. People with HIV became 'experts' on their condition and their doctors had to listen. As Simon Mansfield, an AIDS specialist at St Stephen's Hospital, London, noted:

> We are being challenged by our patients to justify what we are doing on scientific, ethical and human grounds and this has just not happened before. AIDS is bringing the age of consumerism to medicine. This has its attendant difficulties, but it is necessary. It is something which should have happened long ago. (Quoted in the *Guardian*, 10 December 1991)

But, as organisational responses to HIV became increasingly professionalised as part of the growing 'AIDS industry', so participation from those most affected by HIV has been reduced. The distancing process has been enhanced by the increasing bureaucratisation of health services in the 1990s. The direction and organisation of service delivery have increasingly moved into the hands of health-service professionals, and have become less influenced by the ideas and suggestions of those who actually live with HIV-disease.

The growing divide between personal experiences and organisational responses has created tension and conflict: most notably in the suspicion that financial or commercial gain for the 'AIDS industry' has begun to outweigh the potential for health gain of individuals. The development, availability and price of anti-viral treatments for people with HIV-disease have provoked heated debate. In the USA, the radical activist organisation *AIDS*

Coalition to Unleash Power (*ACT-UP*) has repeatedly criticised what they see as over-pricing of anti-viral drugs to slow down the development of HIV-disease. ACT-UP favour high-profile demonstration as their method of community action. They have targeted drug companies such as Burroughs–Wellcome (now Glaxo–Wellcome plc) who produce Zidovudine (AZT), accusing them of prioritising financial gain over provision of health care.

This is a complex issue. The drug companies point to the huge costs of research and development necessary to bring a licensed drug 'to market'. Yet a study of the effect of Zidovudine on survival in Maryland noted that a large number of people with AIDS did not receive therapy, despite its availability, because of an inability to pay (Moore *et al.*, 1991). The system of fee-for-service medicine and the widespread lack of health insurance among people on low incomes in the USA must also be considered.[21] And it is important to note that individual and activist demands for better availability of anti-viral treatments are made in the context of limited scientific evidence of their effectiveness. If a drug company does develop a truly effective treatment for HIV-disease, or a vaccine that prevents HIV infection, how will it be priced and who will be able to afford it? Some would argue that it is only the potential for huge profits that drives on the research that will, one day, deliver such a breakthrough.

It is not only people with HIV who may gain from an expanding AIDS industry, but the many professionals and organisations who work within it. AIDS has generated numerous biomedical research programmes, arguably diverting funds from other health problems and from basic science. Biomedical and social scientists have benefited from apparently new research money, as have the evaluators of health services. Writers, drug companies and market researchers all have gained, either personally or financially, from an AIDS industry which serves every conceivable dimension of the epidemic. It has generated conferences, publications, central and local government funding, charitable and private income, and commercial profits. As a multi-million-pound health-care industry it cannot be ignored when attempting to understand and explain the interplay between individual and social responses to HIV-disease.

---

[21]International comparisons of how health services are financed, and the consequences of this for access and availability of health care, are discussed in *Caring for Health: History and Diversity*, Chapter 9.

Conclusions

The discussion in this chapter leads to three interlinked conclusions.

Individual experiences, social responses

The personal experience of HIV-disease is inextricably linked to its social construction in everyday life. Social responses to HIV infection have, to a large extent, viewed infection as an outcome of involvement in dangerous and morally-suspect lifestyles and behaviour, and have resulted in stigmatisation and discrimination. These social responses are rooted in the history of dealing with social and public health problems of the past. The epidemiological links between HIV-disease and homosexuality, drug use, prostitution and sexual 'promiscuity' have had a potent influence on how people with HIV are viewed. Individual experiences of HIV infection and HIV-disease depend not just on the biological condition of the body, but also on the prevailing scientific, social and political framework. This is why attempts to understand and explain HIV-disease demand a multidisciplinary approach.

Individual change, social change

The ways in which individuals think and behave are influenced by the social and cultural contexts in which they live. Behaviour change as a strategy for HIV prevention relies not only on individual knowledge and attitudes about HIV risk, but also on changes in peer-group and population norms about what is 'normal' behaviour.

Behaviour change is also influenced by wider health and legal policies and by the political context in which health care is organised. Policies such as travel restrictions which aim to protect the 'public health' of the majority, while discriminating against people with HIV, the management of HIV testing, and health education policies, all affect the degree to which individuals at risk of HIV-disease have control over their lives.

Individual attempts at behaviour change and individual access to health care and treatment are strongly influenced by the resources and funding available. The extent to which change can occur is often shaped by personal economic disadvantage, and—in developing countries—by the need to balance the financial and human costs of diverting scarce resources from one social or health problem to another. How much developed countries are prepared to invest in making treatment and care available to people with HIV depends on political as well as economic considerations.

Individual costs, social costs

Individuals with HIV-disease clearly experience costs to their health. They also experience 'costs' in everyday life, such as financial hardship associated with loss of employment, and the social isolation arising from stigmatisation. As HIV and AIDS become more 'normalised', the public health costs of care and treatment become clearer. Even in developed countries, such as the USA, where the costs of treating people with HIV are higher than in any other country, the economic implications of AIDS and the impossibility of meeting such costs within existing health-care budgets are being recognised. The cost of enhancing the quality of life for people living with HIV-disease are already being balanced against the escalating cost of providing effective prevention and treatment services. As noted by health-policy analysts Patricia Day and Rudolf Klein:

> If AIDS turns out to be just another killer disease, governments may no longer be able to use fear to justify the allocation of additional resources to study, prevent, and treat it. AIDS already resembles a chronic disease or a severe disability because of its claims on long-term care as well as acute services and its relatively high cost per case. New treatments that increase survival time after infection would make it even more obviously a chronic problem. (Quoted in *Living with AIDS*, 1989, p. 110)

In summary, the meanings of HIV and AIDS are not merely derived from the professional explanations of biological and medical science; like the other case studies in this book, they are also social, cultural and political products. Whether you are female or male, gay or heterosexual, with or without children, have used drugs or not; whether you live in downtown San Francisco, on a council estate in Edinburgh, or in a village in Uganda—social responses will have a marked influence on all our personal experiences of the risk of HIV and HIV-disease.

Objectives and self-assessment questions for Chapter 4 appear overleaf.

OBJECTIVES FOR CHAPTER 4

When you have studied this chapter, you should be able to:

4.1 Summarise the main contributions that epidemiological and biomedical research have made to the understanding of HIV and AIDS, and point to the implications for prediction, prevention and treatment of the remaining uncertainties in professional knowledge.

4.2 Illustrate how national responses such as government policies, mass advertising campaigns, and media representations of HIV infection and AIDS, can influence individual experiences of HIV risk and HIV-disease.

4.3 Discuss the advantages and limitations associated with a range of HIV-prevention initiatives to reduce the risk of infection in developing and developed countries.

4.4 Give examples of social, ethical, economic and political issues raised by different approaches to HIV testing and HIV screening.

QUESTIONS FOR CHAPTER 4

Question 1 (*Objective 4.1*)

What features of the biology of HIV have contributed to the lack of successful treatments or effective vaccines more than a decade after it was identified?

Question 2 (*Objective 4.2*)

Chapter 2 referred to the philosophical concept of 'ontological security' and the psychoanalytic concept of 'projection'. How might these concepts help to explain why advertising campaigns aimed at preventing HIV and AIDS have tended to distinguish between 'normals' and stigmatised 'others'? What historical and political forces may also be operating?

Question 3 (*Objective 4.3*)

What are the strengths and limitations of providing information on HIV prevention (e.g. in leaflets) to individuals? What combination of factors is likely to be most effective in getting people to change their HIV risk behaviour?

Question 4 (*Objective 4.4*)

Describe the relative merits and drawbacks of voluntary and compulsory named HIV testing, including the practical and ethical consequences of each approach.

5 Asthma

This chapter refers to the discussion of hyper-sensitivity (which used asthma as one example) in an earlier book in this series, Human Biology and Health: An Evolutionary Approach.[1] During your study of this chapter, you will be asked to read an article in the Reader by Andrew Nocon and Tim Booth, entitled 'The social impact of childhood asthma',[2] and listen to an audiotape band entitled 'Reflections on asthma'.[3] Two optional Reader articles, one by Sally Macintyre and David Oldman entitled 'Coping with migraine', and one by David Kelleher entitled 'Coming to terms with diabetes', are also recommended if you have time.

This chapter was written by Bill Bytheway, Associate Researcher at the Centre for Ageing and Biographical Studies, and Anna Furth, Lecturer in the Department of Biology—both at the Open University. Basiro Davey contributed some original material.

Introduction

Four-year-old Peter has just started school. His asthma began two years ago, two months after his father left home. Symptoms now often follow the onset of a cold but other factors also trigger them off, especially pollen, smoke and the smell of pigs or paints. They are also sparked off if he becomes upset or excited.

During the past year his asthma has been under better control and the amount of drugs he takes has been reduced. His hospital has provided a home nebuliser, which helps to avoid hospital admissions.

Peter's asthma means that he cannot have the pets he would like. He does sometimes have problems when out walking or in sport at school—but his asthma does not prevent him from joining in. However, he has to avoid bonfires and has to stay indoors on bonfire night. Even the smoke from candles on a birthday cake can trigger him off.

Peter's mother previously had to take time off work to look after him and lost money as a result. She now has a part-time job but still has to accompany him and take along his nebuliser when he goes on school trips. Peter's asthma means more housework for her, mainly in the form of regular wet-dusting.

A child using a nebuliser at home. The machine has an electric pump which delivers anti-asthmatic drugs as a fine spray, inhaled via a face-mask. (Photo: courtesy of Medix, Ltd.)

[1] *Human Biology and Health: An Evolutionary Approach*, Chapter 10.

[2] *Health and Disease: A Reader* (second edition, 1995).

[3] This audiotape band has been specially recorded for students of the Open University.

The asthma now only tends to worry her when Peter has a bad attack. Nevertheless, she continues to feel angry with her ex-husband for having contributed, however unwittingly, to its onset, with all the resultant suffering that it has caused her and her son.

While Peter's asthma is no longer severe, it still places some restrictions on what he is able to do. It continues to have a mild social impact on his own life and that of his family. (Nocon and Booth, 1990, pp. 60–1)

This account is taken from a research study carried out by Andrew Nocon and Tim Booth in 1990 (a longer extract from their report appears in the Reader for students of the Open University, and is referred to later in this chapter). They investigated a sample of 50 patients who had all been admitted to a Sheffield hospital in 1989 with a primary diagnosis of asthma. Nearly two-thirds of the sample were school-age children or younger; parents were interviewed where the child was under 10 years old. The aim of the research was to illuminate the social impact of asthma on the lives of the patients and other members of their families. Inevitably, it also shed light on *lay beliefs* about what causes asthmatic attacks.

☐ What clues about the possible causes of Peter's asthmatic attacks can you distinguish in the account above?

■ Five groups of causes can be identified. *Emotional upset*: his mother believes that the asthma is partly a response to Peter's father leaving home, and notes that it can be sparked off if he gets upset or excited. *Chemicals*: smoke provokes a particularly strong reaction, and paints are also mentioned. *Animal and plant material*: the smell of pigs, and pollen. (The reference to 'wet-dusting' contains a clue to house-mites in domestic dust as a trigger.) *Exercise*: walking and sports occasionally cause problems. *Infection*: he often gets an asthma attack with the onset of a cold. All of these factors have been implicated in asthma at various times in its history.

Asthma is a disease that most people know something about, but one that is still poorly understood and difficult to diagnose consistently. In medical terms, **asthma** can briefly be described as a constriction of the airways

due to inflammation and the build-up of mucus in the lungs. The typical symptoms are breathlessness, wheezing, coughing (especially at night), and tightness in the chest (especially on waking up). It tends to be a chronic condition, punctuated by occasional acute episodes in which the respiratory constriction can become so severe that it causes great distress and requires immediate medical intervention.

A fundamental question about Peter's asthma is whether or not it is an inherent part of his biological make-up: was he *born* asthmatic? Or is it something that has developed since he was born and that has an *external* cause which could have been prevented? Did his asthma really begin two years ago when his father left home, and are these two events causally related? Like the disorders in the other case studies in this book, asthma is associated with considerable uncertainty about its medical definition and its underlying causes.

We tend to think of asthma as a 'modern' condition—an impression reinforced by the widespread media attention on atmospheric pollution as the cause of an asthma 'epidemic' which is popularly believed to be taking place in the 1990s. Yet asthma has a long history in which doctors and society at large have held widely varying views about its nature. In this respect it is typical of many other diseases.

The history of scientific explanations for asthma

In ancient Greece, the physician Galen taught that asthma was not an entity in itself: it was no more than a symptom of disordered bodily *humours*.[4] This view was dominant up until the sixteenth century, when the idea developed that asthma was an *attack* upon the body, and hence one that was subject to cure. Initially, medical attention centred upon the abdomen as the source of asthma, and it was only in the eighteenth century that attention shifted to the chest. In the course of most of the nineteenth century the idea that asthma was due to *nervous spasm* of the airways was popular. The theory that it was due to peculiarities in the bronchial mucus began to gain ground, but the growing debate was then overtaken by early research on the immune system,

---

[4]Humoral theory and its continuing influence on medical thought and practice, even in the twentieth century, is discussed in *Medical Knowledge: Doubt and Certainty*, Chapters 2 and 3.

which suggested that asthma was closely related to *allergies*. In the 1930s, the connection with emotion was proposed and the idea that asthma was perhaps primarily a *psychosomatic* condition became fashionable.

By the 1990s, psychosomatic theories of asthma had largely been discounted in medical thought, but they remain powerful in lay beliefs—as Peter's case history illustrates. The trend of scientific opinion is towards an explanation of asthma as a nervous spasm of the airways, accompanied by inflammation, and triggered by (among other possibilities) allergic reactions to material in the atmosphere. Air quality has become a major issue in the *social history* of asthma at the end of the twentieth century. Before we examine the features of present-day scientific understanding of asthma, however, it is worth reflecting for a moment on the assertion that it is—at least partly—a *socially constructed* phenomenon.[5] This is most readily demonstrated by examining scientific and public views of asthma in the past.

John Gabbay, a medical historian and sociologist who has specialised in public health issues, undertook a study of the history of asthma (Gabbay, 1982). His analysis centred on *A Treatise of the Asthma*—the classic work of Sir John Floyer (1649–1734), published in 1698. For Gabbay, a critical feature of Floyer's work and that of several other early scientists, is that they had personal experience of asthma. Floyer focused upon abdominal symptoms as much as those in the chest, and ascribed pain in his gut to his asthma. He tried to make full use of 'sensible' (or sensory) observation, a growing priority in medical research at that time, but he was also anxious to confirm the truth of the ancient doctrines he had been taught. As a result, he interpreted what he observed in terms of traditional theories involving, for example, *defluxion* (the deposit of humours on selected organs) and *inciding* (medicines cutting through the humours). Floyer's commitment to humoral theory, roughly 1 500 years after it had been developed, was consistent with prevailing religious and political beliefs.

This glimpse into the past alerts us to the need for caution in accepting current scientific knowledge about asthma as necessarily the last word on the subject.

Far from medical knowledge about asthma having consisted of proven, timeless, objective facts, it has appeared under scrutiny to be composed of limited interpretations of the complex phenomena of illness. (Gabbay, 1982, p. 43)

The essence of Gabbay's argument is that medical knowledge has to be viewed in its *social context*. He argues that researchers such as Floyer change, and continue to change, the meaning of asthma. To social constructionists, it is an illusion to assume that medical research has simply led to an accumulation of knowledge about the inherent nature of any disease. According to this argument, diseases cannot exist independently of the social context which constantly shapes the direction and interpretation of medical knowledge.

Extending this hypothesis to the twentieth century, one can note the decline in the importance of *anatomy* in modern medicine and the rise of *pharmacology* (the use of medical drugs). This is reflected in the growing significance of medication in the process leading up to the diagnosis of asthma: at the extreme, asthma is what people have who benefit from anti-asthmatic medication. The manufacturers of inhalers and nebulisers are increasingly providing diagnostic aids that are shaping the way in which doctors think about and diagnose asthma.

Similarly, as you study the rest of this chapter, it will become apparent that people with asthma in the 1990s are being 'reconstructed' as victims of rising atmospheric pollution—a conclusion for which there is both scientific support and considerable uncertainty. In the atmosphere of alarm created by media attention, lay anxiety and scientific concern, other explanations may be denied breathing space!

The meanings of asthma

When you read an account of asthma such as Peter's, it is easy to assume that everyone knows what the word itself represents. It is part of the common vocabulary. Lay knowledge of asthma—in common with that of all diseases and disorders—is based partly on medical knowledge acquired through direct contact with health professionals, and from educational media. It also draws heavily upon the personal narratives of family and friends who have experienced it, and who then develop explanations for its occurrence. These explanations are influenced by the particular emphasis placed on news stories about asthma. Thus, asthma is both an *illness* with

[5]The idea that diseases are 'constructed' rather than 'revealed' by medical science is discussed in *Medical Knowledge: Doubt and Certainty*, Chapters 7 and 8.

a distinct social identity and a medically-defined *disease* category. Peters' mother obtains a medical name for his experience of illness, which legitimates it as a recognised disease.[6]

☐ Can you identify clues that a medical view of asthma as a disease has been incorporated into the account of Peter's asthma, which you read earlier?

■ His asthma has *symptoms* and occasionally these lead to *attacks*. His asthma is being *controlled* through the use of *drugs* and a *nebuliser*.

The doctor's diagnosis that Peter has asthma provides a link between Peter's personal experience of his illness (including the way those concerned for him talk about it), and the expert scientific knowledge of the doctor about this disease entity and the interventions presently available to treat it. Despite relatively successful treatment, Peter's asthma continues to have an impact on the life of his family. So, in addition to its medical meaning, asthma also has a personal and social meaning. People with asthma and their families often make strenuous efforts to cope with its effects and strive to live normal lives—not always with support from others. The restrictions that asthma can impose may be met with intolerance, and there may sometimes be doubt about its recognition as a 'legitimate' illness, as you will see later in this chapter.

☐ What different meanings do you think 'asthma' might have for Peter, his mother and his doctor?

■ Peter is only four. He will be learning the meaning of all sorts of words. 'Asthma' may mean that he feels special, different from other children. To his mother, the word might mean the anxiety of seeing Peter struggling for breath, or giving him his medication and getting him to use his nebuliser. It also means vigilance: no bonfires, and no candles on his birthday cake. His asthma is no longer a constant worry, but it still poses a threat to her son's life. It also means a loss of income, extra housework and a restriction upon her own lifestyle. For the doctor, Peter's asthma is a disease, much the same as many other patients have. It has been diagnosed through standard procedures, has involved referral to hospital, and it requires treatment based on drugs, nebulisers and effective preventive action.

[6]The distinction between illness and disease is discussed in Chapter 1 of this book, and in *Medical Knowledge: Doubt and Certainty*, Chapter 2.

Thus, even in Peter's four-year-old world, his asthma can have several meanings. Similarly, in the world of medicine and academic research, the concept of 'asthma' is understood differently by clinicians, epidemiologists, biologists and medical historians. All of these different meanings of asthma are represented in this chapter. Our next step is to examine the uncertainties about the epidemiology of asthma.

The epidemiology of asthma

The epidemiological study of asthma generates data on its incidence and prevalence, its distribution in different groups in populations—both within and between countries—and the extent of mortality and morbidity. It reveals statistical associations with other factors that might possibly contribute either to the underlying causes of asthma or to triggering an attack in someone who is already asthmatic. In this respect it is no different from rheumatoid arthritis (RA) and HIV-disease (Chapters 3 and 4).

However, unlike RA and HIV-disease, asthma is a rapidly-fluctuating condition. People who describe themselves as 'asthmatic' are not in a constant state of breathlessness and wheezing, but alternate between taking medication and other preventive action and trying to cope with an attack. Although taking preventive action might be considered a form of suffering, it is normally having an asthma attack that is thought of as 'suffering from asthma'. So, in answer to the question commonly posed in surveys: 'Have you suffered from asthma in the last twelve months?', most positive replies will reflect the occurrence of attacks rather than the background shortness of breath that is a characteristic of many asthmatic people.

The fluctuating nature of asthma contributes to difficulties with its diagnosis and measurement, and hence to the reliability and comparability of epidemiological data from different sources. In the discussion that follows, we have concentrated on asthma in Western industrialised countries, particularly the United Kingdom. The difficulties of collecting reliable data, even from countries with well-developed health-care systems, mean that very little is known about the epidemiology of asthma in the Third World.

Mortality

An important element in the experience of asthma is the fear of death. A serious asthmatic attack would be distressing enough if recovery were guaranteed, but the thought that it could be life-threatening makes it all the more stressful for the affected person and anyone else who is present. According to the Office of Population Censuses and Surveys, 1 699 people died of asthma in England and Wales in 1993 (OPCS, 1995a). This is equivalent to a mortality rate of close to 3.5 deaths per 100 000 population per annum.

However, some doubt has been expressed about the reliability of estimates based on cause of death as recorded on death certificates. For example, consider the comments of W. Berrill, a consultant physician practising in West Cumberland Hospital:

> In the 14 years since 1978, during which I have been the only consultant physician in respiratory medicine in West Cumbria, there should, according to [the national] statistics, have been at least 70 deaths from asthma and yet I know of very few, having personal knowledge of only three. (Berrill, 1993, p. 193)

In order to test his doubts about the national statistics, Berrill set about retrieving the case notes of the 40 West Cumbrian patients who were registered as having died of asthma between 1980 and 1989. He was able to re-evaluate 21 sets of case notes, and found objective evidence of asthma for only 6 of these patients. For 12 others there was clear evidence, in his view, of an alternative cause of death. He concluded that:

> Many older patients who probably neither had asthma nor died of asthma may be being entered into the statistics for asthma mortality because of inappropriate use of the word asthma on death certificates, diagnostic transfer, or coding changes. (Berrill, 1993, p. 194)

Berrill's comments touch on an important area of uncertainty in asthma epidemiology. If there are doubts about the true mortality rate in a particular location, how can we be sure if it varies geographically or if it is changing at the national level over time? Peter Burney, at the United Medical and Dental Schools of Guy's and St Thomas's Hospitals in London, found a *rising* trend in asthma mortality in England and Wales in successive birth cohorts since the 1940s; this became more evident from the mid-1970s to the mid-1980s in the age-group 5–34 years (Burney, 1986 and 1988). Conversely, H. R. Anderson, at St George's Hospital Medical School in London, found a *falling* trend in asthma mortality since 1958 in children aged 0–4, and since 1968 in 5–14-year-olds (Anderson, 1989). The definition of what constitutes 'asthma' and how it is best measured lie at the heart of this apparent contradiction.

Morbidity

The cost of asthma to the patient is not measured simply in terms of the threat to life. Around two million people in the United Kingdom are estimated to be suffering from asthma and requiring medical treatment. A number of small-scale studies have investigated the effects of asthma morbidity on the activities of daily living.

For example, Kevin Jones, a GP, coordinated a study covering three general practices in the Southampton area (Jones *et al.*, 1992), which focused on the restrictions that asthma places upon people's lives. A random sample of 296 patients with an asthma diagnosis were surveyed (5.8 per cent of everyone registered with the three practices). Some of the results are shown in Table 5.1. Just over half of the patients surveyed suffered attacks of wheezing during the night, and just under half had a 'wheezy or asthmatic condition' at least once a week. Nearly one in three had stayed off work or school at least once in the past year as a result of asthma.

Table 5.1 The morbidity of asthma in 296 patients in three general practices in the Southampton area, England, in 1990

	Percentage of all asthmatic patients
attacks of wheezing during the night	51
a wheezy or asthmatic condition at least once a week	49
stayed off work or school at least once in past year	31
avoids at least some activities between attacks	23
asthma interrupts daily life at least monthly	11
everyday activities affected at least 'quite a lot' in past year	10

Source: Jones, K. P., Bain, D. J. G., Middleton, M. and Mullee, M. A. (1992) Correlates of asthma morbidity in primary care, *British Medical Journal*, **304**, Table II, p. 362.

A study in Nottingham, based on a survey of 4 750 primary school children, found that 5.9 per cent had been diagnosed as having asthma and that 7.0 per cent had lost time from school because of wheezing (Hill *et al.*, 1989). The researchers noted an increased willingness to use the diagnostic label of asthma in wheezy children, but claim their research indicates that it is still being under-diagnosed.

We identified 96 children (2.5 per cent of respondents) in whom wheezing was sufficiently troublesome for them to lose time from school but who were receiving no medication for asthma. It would seem likely ... that some if not most of these children have asthma and would benefit from specific treatment. (Hill *et al.*, 1989, p. 250)

The studies by Jones and by Hill both revealed asthma morbidity as a significant health problem. However, the definition of what morbidity can be ascribed to asthma and what to other conditions is not a straightforward matter, as the earlier discussion of mortality illustrated.

Defining asthma

The question 'Does this person have asthma?' is generally addressed by two quite distinct approaches to a definition. Distinguishing between the two is fundamental to understanding the uncertainties about the epidemiology of asthma.

The *clinical* approach to defining the condition leads to estimates of **doctor-diagnosed asthma**. Like rheumatoid arthritis (Chapter 3), asthma lacks a single defining diagnostic characteristic, so clinical judgement is an important variable. A patient may have periodically consulted a doctor for breathlessness and wheeze for years before an asthma diagnosis is given, whereas another may be diagnosed as asthmatic at the first consultation. Both these patients might have had a different experience with a different doctor. To some extent the diagnosis is based upon standard tests, but it also depends upon the patient's history, including previous diagnoses—perhaps by other doctors. It can also depend upon how the patient responds to medication that is known to relieve the symptoms of asthma; the doctor may only reach an asthma diagnosis when the patient's condition has considerably improved as a result of treatment.

By contrast, the *scientific* approach to defining asthma is based on standard measurements of lung function in samples of the population. The simplest property to measure is **peak flow**—the fastest rate at which air can be pushed out of the lungs on a forced outbreath. Peak flow is usually expressed in litres per minute (l min^{-1}), and is measured with a *peak-flow meter* like the one in Figure 5.1. There are now standard charts showing 'normal' peak flow for men and women of different ages, and children of different heights. A peak flow which fails to reach a certain threshold is one of the indicators of **scientifically-defined asthma**.

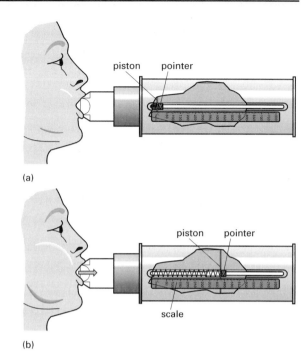

(a)

(b)

Figure 5.1 *Diagram to show the operation of a peak-flow meter at (a) the beginning, and (b) the end, of a forced outbreath. The outbreath forces the piston towards the end of the cylinder, pushing the pointer in front of it. When the person stops blowing, the piston falls back (pulled by the spring), leaving the pointer where its new position can be read from a scale calibrated in litres per minute.*

A child blowing into a peak-flow meter (of a different design from that shown in Figure 5.1) as part of a community project to estimate the extent of asthma in Welsh schoolchildren. (Photo: Duncan Williams)

☐ What are the main strengths and limitations of these two approaches to defining asthma?

■ Epidemiological data derived from doctor-diagnosed asthma may be subject to substantial variations as a result of differences in clinical judgement, whereas the scientific approach relies on standardised tests which should generate reproducible results. However, the strength of medical diagnosis is that it takes account of many aspects of the person's condition, including their history, and the effects on their daily lives (as Table 5.1 illustrates), whereas the scientific approach ignores actual morbidity. (Another way of representing this comparison is to suggest that doctor-diagnosed measures of asthma are likely to be less *reliable* but more *valid* than scientifically-defined asthma.[7])

Estimating prevalence

The definition of asthma used in any survey of prevalence clearly affects the outcome, and hence the explanations that are generated for patterns in the distribution of the condition. Epidemiologists want measures that help them to decide (for example) whether children in the area where Peter lives are more likely to suffer from asthma than children in other areas. The question of whether Peter himself has asthma is of secondary importance. What is critical are standardised measures which are suitable for comparative analysis and can be reproduced in further research.

☐ Imagine you work in a local primary health care team and you want to estimate the prevalence of asthma in your area. List several different sources of information that could help you.

■ Here are some sources you might consider: self-reported or 'parent-reported' asthma, based on responses to a questionnaire; clinical diagnosis by a doctor recorded in case notes; admission to, or discharge from, a hospital or a specialist unit; lung-function tests carried out for research purposes; post-mortem examination of the lungs.

Each of these sources of information has its own strengths and limitations, and it is important to bear this in mind when considering prevalence estimates.

[7]Reliability and validity are technical terms in experimental research, which are discussed in *Studying Health and Disease*, Chapter 5.

☐ Prevalence is usually expressed as the number of people in a defined population who have a certain disease or disability at a certain *point* in time (e.g. a chosen day), divided by the total number of people in that population at that point. Can you suggest why this method of calculating the prevalence of asthma is unsatisfactory and how this problem might be overcome?[8]

■ A substantial proportion of asthmatic people will not be experiencing symptoms at the designated time point, so estimates of *point prevalence* could underestimate the burden of asthma in the population. It is more accurate to estimate *period prevalence*, i.e. the number of people experiencing symptoms of asthma or receiving treatment for it in a given period (e.g. a year), divided by the number of people in the population at risk during that period. (Note: *Incidence* refers to the number experiencing symptoms for the *first time* in a given period, usually a year.)

Consider Table 5.2, which presents some national statistics regarding the period prevalence of asthma by age and sex. These rates are based on 'periods of sickness' during which the patient was both experiencing the symptoms of asthma and consulting a GP.

Table 5.2 Prevalence rates of asthma (per 1 000 person-years at risk*), determined from general practice statistics, in England and Wales, 1991–2. (Rates have been rounded up or down to nearest whole number.)

Age/ years	0–4	5–14	15–24	25–44	45–64	65–74	75–84	85+
male	99	86	40	26	26	37	36	27
female	72	64	46	33	34	41	33	18

*Some people surveyed were only on their doctor's register for part of the year covered by the study, so they were standardised in terms of 'person-years at risk', e.g. 6 months' registration = 0.5 person-year at risk. (Data derived from: McCormick, A., Fleming, D. and Charlton, J., 1995, *Morbidity Statistics from General Practice: Fourth National Study, 1991–92.* Series MB5, No. 3, Table 2P, p. 50, HMSO, London)

[8]This question has already been raised in *Human Biology and Health: An Evolutionary Approach*, Chapter 10.

□ Briefly summarise the main patterns in the data in Table 5.2.

■ Asthma is more prevalent in children than in adults, and prevalence rates are substantially higher among boys than girls; but middle-aged women experience slightly more asthma than middle-aged men. The prevalence of asthma appears to decline in people aged over 85 years.

To some extent these data reflect the *life course* of asthma. There is some doubt, however, as to whether or not asthma in childhood is the same as asthma in middle age. One view is that children typically 'grow out' of their asthma in their teens and that late-onset asthma is triggered by other causes. However, research in Australia, which tracked children with asthma at age 7 until they were 28 years old, has shown that:

... wheezing recurs in early adult life, suggesting that the prognosis for those with mild asthma may not be as favourable as popularly thought. (Kelly *et al.*, 1987, p. 1062)

Although some people who had childhood asthma may be 'cured', some may be avoiding asthma attacks in adulthood only through effective preventive action. Conversely, it could be argued that late-onset asthma may not reflect an asthma-free childhood, but is a recurrence of earlier problems which had not been diagnosed as asthma. Indeed, it may be changes in diagnostic criteria—not the patient's condition—that have led to asthma being diagnosed only in adulthood.

The uncertainties we have raised regarding the definition and measurement of asthma are an essential background to one of the leading public health questions of the 1990s—is asthma increasing?

Is asthma increasing?

Stephen Holgate, MRC Clinical Professor at the University of Southampton, begins a review of research on asthma with the simple statement: 'Asthma is on the increase' (Holgate, 1994, p. 20). The statistics showing an increase in the incidence of asthma are impressive. Data from GPs reported to the Royal College of General Practitioners and analysed by Frances Drever of the Office of Population Censuses and Surveys (OPCS) indicate a substantial rise in the 1980s and early 1990s in newly-diagnosed episodes of asthma (Figure 5.2).

E. A. Mitchell undertook an analysis of statistics from the Hospital In-Patient Enquiry (HIPE), conducted annually for England and Wales (Mitchell, 1985). He found that hospital admission rates for asthma for children aged 0–4 years increased by 124 per cent between 1980 and 1985. On a broader time-scale, he found a six-fold increase in admission rates had occurred between 1957 and 1981 for 0–14-year-olds.[9]

[9]Similar data are presented for 5–14-year-olds in 1958–86, in a study by Anderson, 1989 reported in *Human Biology and Health: An Evolutionary Approach*, Figure 10.1, Chapter 10.

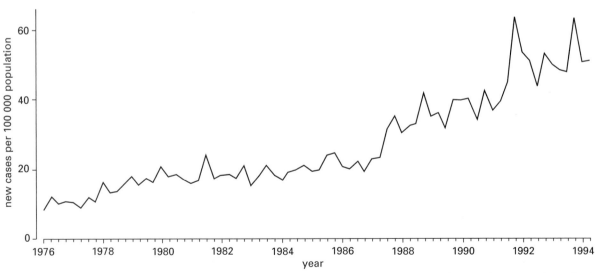

Figure 5.2 *Newly diagnosed episodes of asthma reported each week (per 100 000 population) in the period 1976–94, for England and Wales. (Source: Drever, F., 1994, Asthma: the changing scene, Population Trends, **78**, Figure 3, p. 45)*

The basis of the HIPE statistics was changed in 1986, from a national to a regional system, so it has not been possible to continue this method of monitoring the national trend. However, a research team based in Cambridge decided to update Mitchell's analysis using regional data for East Anglia and Wales (Hyndman *et al.*, 1994). They reported that the upward trend in East Anglian hospital admission rates *ended* around 1985, and that a similar rise in Wales was followed by a *fall* after 1988. A decline in hospital admissions seems to be reflected in England as a whole, according to data on 'finished consultant episodes' for asthma in NHS hospitals, published by the Department of Health (1994a and b). In 1988–9 the number was 113 928, falling to 93 277 in 1990–1, a decline of 18 per cent.

☐ In the light of the discussion so far, can you suggest three possible explanations for the rising trend in hospital admissions for asthma in England and Wales until the mid-1980s, followed by a fall?

■ The following may have occurred to you:

(a) Most obviously, there may have been a genuine rise and fall in the prevalence and severity of asthma requiring hospitalisation.

(b) The definition of what constitutes asthma may have been getting 'broader' until the mid-1980s, so patients with wheeze were more likely to be admitted with a diagnosis of asthma; if the definition later 'narrowed' again, similar patients may have been admitted under other diagnoses. (Epidemiologists call this process *diagnostic transfers*.)

(c) Some of the rise in hospital admissions for asthma could have been due to a shift in medical practice away from primary care; more recently, this trend may have reversed, as an increasing number of GPs treat asthma in the community. (A factor may have been the development of new drug treatments, which initially were only available in hospitals, but then became available from general practices.)

These explanations are not mutually exclusive: all may have had an influence. The research discussed here illustrates some of the difficulties in establishing whether there have been genuine changes in the severity or prevalence of asthma and, if so, what the underlying causes might be.

The apparent increase in the prevalence of asthma in children has generated the widest concern. One reason for this concern is that the effect of asthma on child development may have long-term implications for later life. Patrick Phelan, Professor of Paediatrics at the University of Melbourne, notes:

> The increase in the prevalence of asthma in children may well have serious implications for adults, as 40 per cent of children with infrequent trivial wheeze and 70–90 per cent of those with more troublesome asthma continue to have symptoms in mid-adult life … If the increase in the prevalence in children continues into adult life this will create substantial health problems and may well have important economic consequences through time off work and the cost of treatment. (Phelan, 1994, p. 1585)

Four studies of childhood asthma from Australia and the United Kingdom were the basis of concerns in the early 1990s and thus deserve close scrutiny.

The first was undertaken by respiratory physician Colin Robertson and colleagues (including Patrick Phelan), in Melbourne, Australia (Robertson *et al.*, 1991). Parents completed a questionnaire on respiratory symptoms for 3 324 children aged 7 years in 1990. The questions focused on the history of asthma and wheezing over the previous 12 months. Results were compared with a survey of children aged 7 years that was undertaken 26 years previously, in 1964. The two 'diagnostic' questions were: 'Has your child ever had asthma?' and 'Has your child ever had wheezing with bronchitis or cold?' In 1964, 19.1 per cent of parents responded positively to either or both these questions, compared with 45.7 per cent in 1990—an increase in 'parent-diagnosed' prevalence of 141 per cent.

A second Australian study based in Sydney was undertaken by Jennifer Peat and colleagues (Peat *et al.*, 1994). They compared two similar-sized towns in New South Wales: Belmont is on the coast and is humid, whereas Wagga Wagga is inland and dry. A random sample of 1 487 children aged 8–12 years when studied in 1982 was compared with 1 668 children of the same ages in 1992. Peat's team first compared the rates of doctor-diagnosed asthma, the use of asthma drugs, and occurrence of 'recent wheezing' as reported in questionnaires completed by parents. The team then identified children with more severe asthma by comparing their peak-flow measurement before and after exposure to histamine—one of the chemicals released during an asthmatic attack. (We will discuss the biological basis of asthma later in this chapter; for the moment, you should note that 'airway hyper-responsiveness' refers to the tendency of the airways in asthmatic people to constrict even when exposed to a low dose of a trigger such as histamine.) From results such as those shown in Table 5.3, Peat and colleagues concluded that the prevalence of asthma in children has 'increased dramatically' over the decade, even when comparing children living in towns with very different climates (Peat *et al.*, 1994, p. 1594).

Table 5.3 Prevalence rates of five indicators of asthma (percentages) among 8–12 -year-olds in two New South Wales towns, 1982 and 1992

	Belmont		Wagga Wagga	
	1982 %	1992 %	1982 %	1992 %
doctor-diagnosed asthma	9.1	37.7	12.9	29.7
use of asthma drugs	9.6	28.3	8.5	32.5
wheeze in previous 12 months (parent reports)	10.4	27.6	15.5	23.1
airway hyper-responsiveness	9.1	19.8	11.7	18.1
both wheeze and hyper-responsiveness	4.5	12.0	6.6	9.4
total number of children (= 100%)	718	873	769	795

Derived from: Peat, J. K., van den Berg, R. H., Green, W. F. *et al.*, 1994, Changing prevalence of asthma in Australian children, *British Medical Journal*, **308**, Table I, p. 1592, and Table II, p. 1593.

The third study is by Anderson, Butland and Strachan (1994), who are based at St George's Hospital in London. They analysed responses to a questionnaire which was first completed in 1978 by the parents of all children then aged 7.5–8.5 years living in Croydon (4 763 children); the survey was repeated in 1991 for the same age-group (3 786 children). The researchers found that the prevalence of attacks of wheezing or asthma over the previous 12 months (as reported by the parents) had increased by 16 per cent between the two surveys. When they looked at prevalence only over the previous month, they found an increase of 78 per cent in wheezing episodes, 51 per cent for any kind of wheezing (episodic or non-episodic), and 81 per cent for waking at night with wheezing.

A fourth study, undertaken by Burney *et al.* (1990), who are based at St Thomas's Hospital in London, focused on children attending a representative sample of primary schools in 22 parts of England. The parents of 29 000 children aged 6–12 years completed a questionnaire on respiratory conditions at least once between 1973 and 1986. A sophisticated statistical analysis generated the following conclusion:

> There has been a true increase in morbidity that is not simply due to changes in diagnostic fashion. The increase is large enough to explain much if not all of the increase in admission to hospital and mortality. (Burney *et al.*, 1990, p. 1306)

Despite this evidence of a recent increase in childhood asthma, there remains some scepticism that it has been universal. Considerable variation exists between different locations: for example, prevalence rates of around 25 per cent have been reported in Australia, Fiji and Chile, in sharp contrast with rates of between 4 per cent and 7 per cent in Germany and Switzerland (Phelan, 1994). There are equally striking regional variations within many countries.

These findings have fostered a wider concern with local environments and, in particular, with the effects of air pollution—a subject we address shortly. But doubts about the reliability of the prevalence data themselves have centred on the fact that most research has drawn upon parent-reported or doctor-diagnosed asthma, rather than standardised scientific assessments of lung function. Some of the differences between populations, and over time, could arise from different *medical* perceptions of what constitutes asthma.

For example, a German study carried out in 1989–92 by Erika von Mutius and her colleagues compared respiratory disorders and allergies in over 3 000 children aged 9–10 years in the cities of Leipzig and Halle in former East Germany, with over 7 000 similar children in the West German city of Munich (von Mutius *et al.*, 1992 and 1994). The 'lifetime' prevalence of doctor-diagnosed asthma was lower in Leipzig and Halle (7.3 per cent of the children had ever been diagnosed asthmatic) than it was in Munich (9.3 per cent),. But the lifetime prevalence of recurrent wheezing (26.8 per cent in Leipzig and Halle; 17 per cent in Munich) and bronchitis (33.7 per cent in Leipzig and Halle; 15.9 per cent in Munich) showed the opposite pattern. The authors comment:

> Differences … may reflect differences in medical practice and diagnostic labelling in the formerly separated states. One could argue that some of the children with bronchitis in East Germany would have been labelled as having

asthma if they had lived in West Germany. Similarly, the higher prevalence of wheezing and cough could point towards an underdiagnosis of asthma in East Germany. (von Mutius *et al.*, 1994, p. 362)

☐ Table 5.3 (earlier) shows that the prevalence of doctor-diagnosed asthma in children in 1992 was *higher* than the prevalence of parent-reported 'wheeze in previous 12 months'. By contrast, in 1982, doctors diagnosed asthma *less* often than parents reported wheeze. In the light of the German study (above), what could this imply?

■ Some children who were diagnosed by doctors as asthmatic in 1992 had *not* been suffering from wheeze according to their parents. This suggests that, over time, wheezing may have become less important to doctors as a diagnostic sign of asthma. The increase in asthma diagnoses between 1982 and 1992 may partly be due to changes in diagnostic criteria (an interpretation that Peat and her colleagues acknowledge).

There may also have been changes in the lay perception of asthma, both in terms of what constitutes the condition and when doctors should be consulted. Increased consultation rates by parents who suspect their child has asthma might be expected to lead to increased rates of diagnosis. In some situations, certain groups of patients— and also types of families—may have greater confidence in the prospective benefits of consulting the doctor, or better access to medical care, than other groups. This may be one reason why 'better-off' children seem more likely to be diagnosed as having asthma, as in the case of the West German children described above. (An alternative, *biological* explanation for this apparent bias towards asthma in higher social class groups has also been proposed, and will be discussed later in this chapter. For the moment, we continue to focus on shifts in awareness as a contributory factor.)

Three aspects may have contributed to an increased awareness of childhood asthma in the 1990s:

1 Media coverage has ensured that both doctors and parents have become more aware and concerned about the possibility that environmental pollution is contributing to a rise in asthma.

2 The availability and marketing of nebulisers, inhalers and other aids are making treatment for asthma more visible to the wider public. These interventions appear to relieve distressing symptoms in many patients, raising awareness of the availability of effective treatment, and hence increasing consultation rates.

3 With the trend away from long-term hospitalisation for children, GPs and community nurses are becoming more actively involved in the management of asthma, increasing their awareness of the condition.

It is reasonable to suggest that these factors in combination could have led to a rise in the number of 'border-line' children who emerge from a medical consultation equipped with an inhaler and an asthma diagnosis. But changes in medical and lay cultures towards a greater diagnosis of asthma may also have been driven by an *actual* increase in the prevalence of the condition. Epidemiologists who have analysed mortality data, the use of health services, and standardised objective measures of lung function—in addition to doctor-diagnosed and self-reported rates of asthma—have concluded that there *has* been a genuine increase:

The study by Peat and colleagues is particularly important as it reports objective measurements whereas the other studies were based on responses to a questionnaire. It showed that airway hyper-responsiveness increased 1.4 fold to twofold. Although airway hyper-responsiveness is not equivalent to asthma … its increase supports the validity of the questionnaire completed by parents. (Phelan, 1994, p. 1584)

So, despite the complications that must be borne in mind when interpreting the epidemiological data, there is a general agreement that the prevalence of asthma has indeed increased in certain parts of the industrialised world—particularly among children—though not uniformly and not everywhere. There are unanswered questions about the magnitude of the true rise, and in some places (e.g. in the United Kingdom) the trend may have reversed in the 1990s, at least in terms of falling hospital admissions.

As we noted earlier, any increase in childhood asthma is most frequently attributed in the media to rising atmospheric pollution. Before we can examine the evidence for this claim, we must first consider the biological basis of asthma. What happens in the lungs of an asthmatic person when an attack occurs, and what causes this reaction?

The biology of asthma

The lungs in health

In normal breathing, the lungs are like a pair of bellows, drawing fresh air into the chest and pumping stale air out. Fresh air is needed to replenish the body's supply of oxygen—vital for the production of energy.[10] Air enters through the nose and mouth, and passes down the wind-pipe or *trachea* into the chest (see Figure 5.3). Here the trachea splits into two *bronchi*, one to each lung, and the bronchi subdivide into smaller and smaller tubes like the branches of a tree (it is often referred to as the 'respiratory tree'). The narrowest tubes are less than 1 mm in diameter and end in a cluster of tiny airsacs or **alveoli**.

The inside of the human lung resembles a sponge formed from millions of alveoli; if they were all laid out flat, they would cover a tennis court. The alveoli are bounded by a thin membrane surrounded by blood vessels. The membrane and blood-vessel wall is all that separates the inhaled air from the bloodstream. Oxygen molecules can diffuse easily from the oxygen-rich air to the blood, which has a lower oxygen concentration; molecules of the waste gas, carbon dioxide, move in the opposite direction and are expelled as the stale air is breathed out.[11]

The trachea and bronchi are large-diameter tubes and are supported by rings of cartilage to prevent them collapsing (you can feel the larger tracheal rings through the skin below your voicebox). However, the smallest airways have no rigid support, and are very easily constricted if the layer of smooth muscle that surrounds them goes into spasm. They are also easily blocked by mucus. Both these processes contribute to asthma, as you will see below.

Figure 5.4 (*opposite*) shows the three most important layers of the airway lining: the innermost layer or *epithelium*; the thick 'spongy' layer of connective tissue; and the outer layer of smooth muscle. The epithelium is a single sheet of closely-packed cylindrical cells, and has two features vital for lung function: cilia and mucus-secreting cells. *Cilia* are the tiny hairs that protrude into the cavity of the airway. By beating in unison they drive fluid up the airway lining towards the mouth (where it can

[10]The role of oxygen in energy production in living processes is discussed in *Human Biology and Health: An Evolutionary Approach*, Chapters 3 and 7.

[11]The passive diffusion of biological molecules (e.g. the dissolved gases, oxygen and carbon dioxide) along 'concentration gradients' is described in *Biology and Health: An Evolutionary Approach*, Chapter 3.

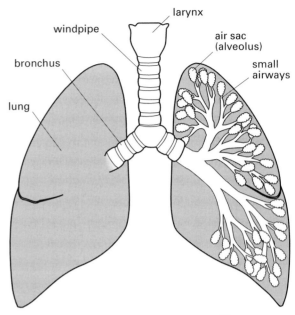

Figure 5.3 *Diagram to show basic structure of human airways: at the surface of the alveoli, oxygen and carbon dioxide are exchanged between the inhaled air and the bloodstream.*

be coughed up and spat out). Much of this fluid is the mucus secreted by specialised epithelial cells; it serves to protect the airway lining, and traps dust and other unwanted particles breathed in with the air.

The lungs in asthma

In people with asthma, the thin protective layer of mucus lining the airways tends to thicken, clogging up the narrow channel.

☐ What changes in the activity of the epithelial cells could cause this build-up?

■ Mucus accumulates when: (a) too much is secreted, and (b) the cilia beat less vigorously, failing to push the mucus towards the mouth. Both these effects are seen in the lungs of people with asthma.

The connective tissue layer between the epithelium and smooth muscle (Figure 5.4) contains very few cells, being composed mainly of water loosely held by a mesh of fibres. In asthma, this layer swells as fluid leaks out from blood vessels, and many different types of white cells are drawn out of the circulation and into the connective tissue. They include white cells involved in generating and sustaining *inflammation*. Nerve endings in the connective tissue may also have a role in making the airway lining excessively 'twitchy' in people with asthma.

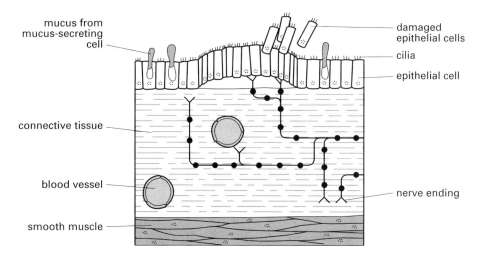

Figure 5.4 *Diagram to show the basic structure of the airway lining. (The functions of the three layers are described in the text.)*

The outer layer of the airways is a continuous sheet of smooth muscle fibres, surrounding all the airway tubes, including the smallest ones. The purpose of this smooth muscle layer is not known, and its contraction is involuntary (not controlled by conscious thought).

> ☐ What symptoms might a person feel if the smooth muscle layer contracted throughout the airways? (Medically this is termed **bronchoconstriction**.)
>
> ■ Breathlessness. Smooth muscle contraction tends to squeeze the airways shut, narrowing the passage so that air flows in and out only with difficulty—this contributes to the wheezy sound often characteristic of asthmatic breathing.

Even in mild asthma, the airway lining is permanently inflamed. A short-term (acute) inflammatory response is usually beneficial, a part of the body's defence against damage and infection, but asthma is the result of an excessive and inappropriate inflammation. If a minute piece of airway surface is pinched out by bronchoscopy (which involves inserting a narrow tube down into the lung), several signs of inflammation can be observed.[12]

[12]You will notice similarities between the description that follows and the processes involved in inflammation in the joints of people with rheumatoid arthritis, as described in Chapter 3. Note that the inflammation seen in lung tissue in asthma is not thought to be 'autoimmune' (i.e. an immune response inappropriately directed against the body's own tissues), in contrast to the inflammation in rheumatoid arthritis.

1   There is an accumulation of the types of white cell normally involved in an inflammatory response. Among the most important are the **mast cells** (which are also involved in hay fever and other allergies). They secrete a variety of signalling molecules (collectively termed *cytokines*) which coordinate and amplify the response, drawing in yet more inflammatory white cells. These cells also secrete inflammatory chemicals, including *bradykinin* (which stimulates nerve endings) and *histamine* (which stimulates smooth muscle contraction and leakage of plasma from blood vessels). Other inflammatory chemicals stimulate mucus secretion.

2   Patches of damaged epithelial cells are sloughed off, exposing some of the underlying nerve endings; this makes the lining excessively sensitive to stimulation.

3   In severe asthma, there may be more permanent changes. The connective tissue layer immediately under the epithelium thickens, as does the smooth muscle layer. More blood vessels are seen in the connective tissue and more mucus-secreting cells appear in the epithelium.

Taken together, these signs mean that asthmatic airways are predisposed to narrowing and filling up with fluid and mucus (see Figure 5.5, *overleaf*). The airways are characteristically **hyper-responsive**—excessively 'twitchy' and prone to contract and mount an inflammatory response to the mildest of triggers. The most common triggers—which would have little impact on the normal lung—are exercise, inhaled allergens, certain chemicals in the atmosphere, and respiratory infections, as the next section describes.

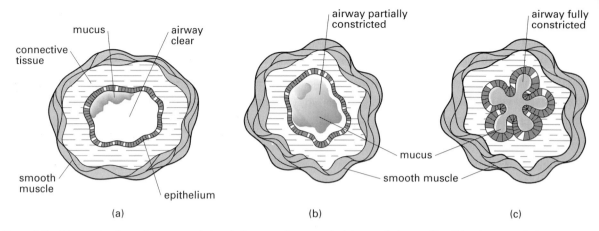

Figure 5.5 *Diagram to show airway constriction during an asthma attack: (a) normal airway; (b) mild asthma attack; (c) severe asthma attack, in which the air passage fills with mucus.*

The triggers of asthma

Considerably more is known about what *triggers* an asthma attack in a susceptible person than what causes someone to become susceptible in the first place. Clues to the underlying causes can be found by studying the biological processes that occur in asthmatic people.

Exercise

The asthma brought on by physical exercise is known as **exercise-induced asthma (EIA)**. It is seen particularly in children—who do a lot of running about in short bursts—and young adults interested in vigorous sport. It is quite common, particularly in people with no other signs of asthma, and is thought to be caused by the increased ventilation. Faster, deeper breathing can make the airway lining dry out, and this in itself can stimulate the underlying nerve endings and cause mast cells to release inflammatory chemicals.

☐ Would you expect any difference between running and swimming, as sports tending to cause EIA?

■ Swimming is less likely to cause EIA, because the air breathed in is more moist. Running, particularly in cold dry air, is a potent trigger for EIA.

Typically, a person who is prone to EIA feels fine for the first few minutes (see Figure 5.6 *opposite*), with the worst symptoms striking some six minutes into the exercise. However, the consequences of this acute response may still be felt several hours later. EIA can usually be avoided by inhaling preventive drugs *before* starting to exercise.

Allergens

Some people seem to be *genetically* predisposed to developing asthma—it is a condition that tends to 'run in families' (as the audiotape band associated with this chapter illustrates).[13] Susceptibility to asthma is strongly associated with a tendency to develop allergies such as hay fever, and allergic skin conditions such as eczema. People who are prone to allergies have an inherited tendency to over-react to intrinsically harmless substances known collectively as **allergens**.

The range of materials that can behave as allergens in a susceptible person is large: it includes certain synthetic chemicals, airborne particles of naturally-occurring substances such as animal 'dander' (fragments of fur and skin cells, most commonly from domestic pets), house-dust mites, plant pollens, and the spores of moulds and fungi. Once an individual is sensitised to a particular allergen, exposure even to very small quantities will invoke an allergic response which may, in turn, trigger an asthma attack.

The underlying cause of **allergic asthma** is the over-production of a type of antibody known as *IgE* (pronounced 'eye-gee-ee'). IgE has a particular role in the body's normal immune response to parasites. In allergic

[13]The audiotape band entitled 'Reflections on asthma' has been made for Open University students. You could usefully listen to it for the first time now, as a preview of many of the issues still to be discussed in this chapter, and play it a second time much later in the chapter, at the point indicated. However, if time is short, we suggest that you listen to it later, as a revision exercise. Please consult the Audiocassette Notes before playing the tape.

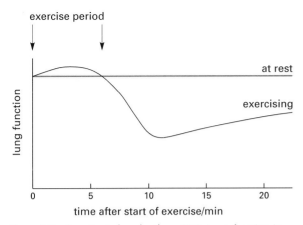

Figure 5.6 *Exercise-induced asthma (EIA). Lung function in terms of 'peak flow' in the same person at rest, and during and after a 6-minute exercise period. Note how lung function continues to fall beyond the end of the exercise period, and does not return to baseline for well over 20 minutes.*

people, molecules of IgE coat the outside of *mast cells*, a type of inflammatory cell mentioned earlier, which are particularly abundant in the lining of the respiratory system (Figure 5.7). Any substance capable of binding tightly to these IgE molecules will trigger the mast cells into releasing inflammatory chemicals. In most people, IgE molecules bind to parasites (and certain infectious organisms), so the resulting inflammation is beneficial.

People who have a tendency to over-produce IgE molecules which can bind to an allergen become

hypersensitive (highly sensitive) to its presence. Exposure to the allergen triggers a severe and prolonged inflammatory response, which—in the majority of sensitised individuals—causes the streaming nose and eyes, and wheezy breathing popularly known as 'hay fever'. In people with allergic asthma, this reaction can be severe enough to cause significant constriction of the airways and trigger an asthma attack. When the lungs respond in this way they are said to be *hyper-responsive*. It is probable that allergic reactions of this type are involved in most (perhaps all) cases of chronic asthma, but the biological basis of the condition is far from understood—for example, some people have high levels of IgE without developing asthma. There is also some uncertainty about the extent to which high IgE production is due entirely to inherited genes; early exposure to allergens and to infection may also play a part, as we discuss below.

A very common allergen involved in allergic asthma is the *house-dust mite*, the ubiquitous but microscopic animal that inhabits bedding, carpets, etc. It can be effectively removed by scrupulous vacuum cleaning or hot-water washing; regular freezing of teddy bears, pillows, etc. is also recommended to reduce the house-dust mite population. Other allergens like pollen dust and fungal spores are seasonal, and can sometimes be avoided by staying indoors, for example on days when the pollen count is high. But this avoiding action has social implications, of course, and may be an unacceptable restriction on lifestyle (a point we return to later).

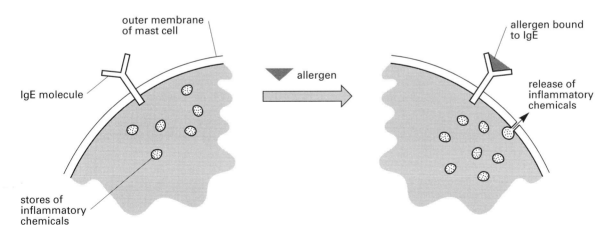

Figure 5.7 *Release of inflammatory chemicals by mast cells is mediated by molecules of the antibody, IgE. When IgE molecules bind to a mast cell and to an allergen, they influence events inside the cell. Inflammatory chemicals are stored in packets of membrane (vesicles), which fuse with the outer cell membrane, thus releasing inflammatory chemicals to the outside. (This diagram is not to scale; IgE molecules are actually much smaller than vesicles.)*

Considerable research interest has been directed towards determining whether a rise in exposures to naturally-occurring allergens in Western industrialised countries might be contributing to the increase in asthma prevalence discussed earlier. There are signs that it may have a significant role. For example, Jennifer Peat and her colleagues (whose comparison of two Australian towns was illustrated in Table 5.3) suggest that the explanation for the increase in asthma in New South Wales lies in increased exposure to airborne allergens, rather than to industrial pollutants (Peat *et al.*, 1994, p. 1595).

The same conclusion was drawn by Erika von Mutius and colleagues in their comparison of cities in former East and West Germany (von Mutius *et al.*, 1994). They tested children for sensitisation to common allergens and airway hyper-responsiveness to a blast of cold air. The West German children had a significantly higher prevalence of asthma *and* allergic reactions than the East German children, despite the fact that atmospheric pollution with sulphur dioxide and particles was significantly higher in the East than in the West German cities. The research team also found a greater exposure to 'domestic' allergens in West German children—principally animal dander and house-dust mites.

☐ Can you suggest a possible reason for this?

■ Before unification, West Germany had a higher living standard than East Germany; more families could afford to have pets, central heating, fitted carpets, etc.—ideal conditions for house-dust mites.

Less common chemical allergens primarily affect adults who encounter them at work. A person may gradually become sensitised to a range of materials including glues, dyes and sterilising agents, which eventually provoke *occupational asthma*. Avoiding exposure usually means leaving that form of work and perhaps losing one's livelihood, if no alternative occupation can be found.

Atmospheric pollution

The rising trend in asthma prevalence—until at least the mid-1980s—has coincided with significant changes in atmospheric pollution at 'street-level' in Western industrial nations. The two have frequently been linked in media reporting of asthma. The United Kingdom illustrates the major trends in air quality in the second half of the twentieth century.

The concentrations of *sulphur dioxide* and *'black smoke'* particles fell very sharply as a result of legislation such as the Clean Air Act 1956, which restricted the burning of coal fires and abolished the infamous post-war

'smogs'[14]. However, the concentrations of two gases—*nitrogen dioxide* and *ozone*—produced in vehicle exhaust fumes, have increased with the rise in traffic. So too has the concentration of minute airborne particles, invisible to the naked eye, which are collectively termed **PM$_{10}$**—(*Particulate Matter* less than *10* micrometres in diameter)[15]. In cities, these particles are most commonly emitted in diesel and other vehicle exhausts and industrial waste gases, whereas in rural areas they are primarily fragments of pollens and spores. PM$_{10}$ are so small that they can remain suspended in the atmosphere indefinitely; the smallest particles can penetrate deep into the narrowest branches of the respiratory tree.

More than 80 per cent of the minute particles suspended in the air in urban centres such as Greater London come from vehicle exhausts (Expert Panel on Air Quality Standards, 1995, p. 5) (Photo: David Rose © The Independent*)*

Many careful studies around the industrialised world have investigated the link between atmospheric pollution and respiratory diseases, including asthma. A common feature of their conclusions is that people who *already* have a respiratory disorder are most at risk from poor air quality. For example, a study in Manchester, by Higgins and co-workers (1995), showed that modest levels of sulphur dioxide or ozone—well *below* the limits recommended by the World Health Organisation's Air Quality Guidelines—can trigger respiratory problems in people

[14]The campaign to reduce urban air pollution in the 1950s is described in *Caring for Health: History and Diversity*, Chapter 6.

[15]One micrometre (abbreviated as 1 μm) is one-millionth of a metre.

with a history of asthma or another respiratory disorder—chronic obstructive airways disease (COAD). Mild exposure in these individuals coincided with a fall in their peak-flow readings; drugs to dilate the airways were used more often, and people with particularly 'twitchy' airways suffered wheeze and shortness of breath.

Pope and Dockery (1992) also showed a link between respiratory problems and PM_{10} emissions from a local steelmill in Utah, USA. This was true even for non-asthmatic children in the study, though asthmatic children were worse affected. Figure 5.8 illustrates the link between coughing in asthmatic children and two violations of permitted PM_{10} levels. The authors point out that *averaging* data from a large number of people may conceal *individual* cases of considerable distress, where children with particularly sensitive airways take a long time to recover from a pollution episode. Higgins and co-workers (1995) make a similar point: even small changes in lung function—when extrapolated over large populations—can add up to a considerable amount of illness.

Despite remaining scepticism from those with a vested interest in resisting measures to reduce street-level atmospheric pollution, the medical profession in the United Kingdom appears to be convinced of the link with respiratory symptoms in vulnerable individuals. An editorial in the *British Medical Journal* by Jon Ayres (1994), a consultant respiratory physician, suggested that doctors advise patients with asthma to take notice of poor air quality warnings, and take preventive action if necessary. This may include doubling the dosage of bronchodilating drugs and avoiding vigorous outdoor exercise (e.g. not running for a bus). Such restrictions on lifestyle extend the adverse experiences associated with asthma far beyond the immediate threat of an attack. The needs of society for transport and industry, which pollute the atmosphere, may be at odds with the needs of individuals to optimise their health and quality of life.

In 1994, the Parliamentary Office of Science and Technology in the United Kingdom issued a report, *Breathing in Our Cities*, which concluded that air pollution from traffic was contributing to the rise in asthma. Although a few studies have failed to find a link between pollutant gases and respiratory symptoms (Zwick *et al.*, 1991; Braun-Fahrländer *et al.*, 1992), the weight of evidence from epidemiological studies (primarily conducted in the USA) implicates PM_{10} levels as a potent trigger for asthma in urban settings. The Committee on the

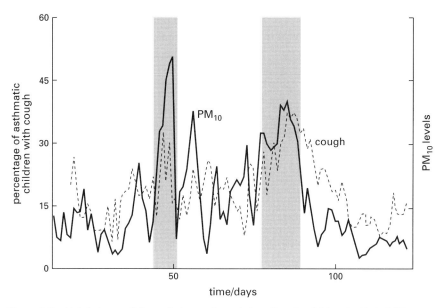

Figure 5.8 *Link between PM_{10} emission and cough in asthmatic children in Utah, USA between December 1990 and March 1991. Tone bars indicate two periods when emissions from a local steelmill violated regulations and PM_{10} levels rose above 'standard' concentrations. (Data from Pope, C. A. and Dockery, W., 1992, Acute health effects of PM_{10} pollution on symptomatic and asymptomatic children,* American Review of Respiratory Diseases, **145**, Figure 1, p. 1124)

Medical Effects of Air Pollutants, an expert panel set up by the Department of Health in the United Kingdom, reported in 1995:

> There is clear evidence of associations between concentrations of particles, similar to those encountered currently in the UK, and changes in a number of indicators of damage to health. These range from changes in lung function through increased symptoms and days of restricted activity, to hospital admissions and mortality ... It is well established from the reported studies that people with pre-existing respiratory ... disorders are at most risk of acute effects from exposure to particles ... There is no evidence that healthy individuals are likely to experience acute effects on health as a result of exposure to concentrations of particles found in ambient air in the UK. (Committee on the Medical Effects of Air Pollutants, 1995, pp. 1, 2)

The Department of the Environment, the Department of Health and the Department of Transport (1995) accepted the Committee's findings and concluded that:

> ... reducing winter and summer peak levels of PM_{10} will be a priority ... The Government intends therefore to take early action to reduce emissions from vehicles in urban centres ... (DoE and DoH and DoT, 1995, p. 8)

However, it is worth noting that, for at least some individuals with lifelong asthma, urban atmospheric pollution seems to make no difference to their symptoms (as in the case of one of the speakers on the audiotape band for OU students associated with this chapter).

Infection

Susceptibility to the triggers for asthma described above is, not surprisingly, increased if the lungs are already inflamed by an infection. Parents of asthmatic children and adults with asthma are often advised to increase the dosage of anti-asthmatic drugs at the first sign of a common cold. However, limited exposure to respiratory infections in early life may *reduce* later susceptibility to asthma—if the tentative interpretations being made from certain research studies prove to be correct.

In 1989 an epidemiologist, David Strachan, reported an *inverse* association between the number of children in a household and the prevalence of hay fever (i.e. hay fever was *less* common in households with more children). The study was based on a national sample of

17 414 children who were all born in the same week in March 1958, and who have been followed up ever since.[16] Strachan speculated that early exposure to infection was greater in these households and that infection might, in some way, 'train' the juvenile immune system to recognise appropriate targets. As a consequence, these children might be less likely to react to inappropriate targets—allergens—as they grew up, and so be less susceptible to hay fever and perhaps also to asthma.

Erika von Mutius and colleagues (1994), whose comparison of East and West German children has already been discussed, make a similar point when drawing attention to the very different use of day-care by working mothers. In the early 1980s, around 70 per cent of East German children aged 1–3 years attended some form of day-care, in contrast with around 7 per cent of West German children. The researchers suggest that an earlier and more varied exposure to infection may contribute to the lower prevalence of asthma in East German children—who also have fewer and lower exposures to domestic allergens than their West German counterparts.

Thus far, the research in human populations has been based on epidemiological data and can do no more than suggest a causal hypothesis. But biological research in experimental animals has added weight to the idea that a tendency to develop allergies—and hence, allergic asthma—may be 'programmed' partly by inherited genes and partly by experiences in early life. An Australian biologist, Patrick Holt, whose research in animals has greatly contributed to this line of reasoning, has reviewed the available literature and sets out the argument as follows:

> Major improvements in public health and personal hygiene practices, changes in infectious disease management (especially the widespread use of antibiotics in pediatrics), reductions in average family sizes, and improvements in general living standards in the developed countries over the last 2–3 generations, have collectively lowered the overall level of exposure to microbial stimulation during infancy, resulting (at a population level) in slower postnatal maturation of the immune system and thus prolongation of the 'high risk' period for primary allergic sensitisation. (Holt, 1995, p. 1)

[16]This birth cohort is the basis of the National Child Development Study—one of several longitudinal cohort studies discussed in *Birth to Old Age: Health in Transition*, Chapter 14.

Holt's research on rats and mice has identified a 'window' in early postnatal development (the 'high risk' period referred to above) in which continuous exposure to allergens, coupled with low exposure to infectious organisms, seems to result in a permanent shift within the immune system. Thereafter the individual remains prone to develop allergies, particularly to *inhaled* allergens. The research of Erika von Mutius and colleagues (1992, 1994) is once again cited by Holt as relevant; the East German children had higher rates of respiratory infections, including bronchitis, than children in West Germany, but lower rates of asthma and allergies.

The role of infection in early life as a 'prompting' mechanism for the immune system is far from being fully understood or accepted, but it is certainly gaining ground as a factor in the aetiology of asthma. The social reconstruction of asthma as a disease of sheltered middle-class children may already be underway!

A multifactorial approach to causation

In conclusion, the foregoing discussion seems to point to an aetiology for asthma in which a number of different factors interact. There is agreement that a genetically determined tendency to over-produce IgE antibodies which bind to allergens is a key factor. Additionally, persistent exposure to domestic allergens coupled with low exposure to infections in early life may direct the immune system towards a lifelong hypersensitivity to allergens—particularly those in the atmosphere.

The hyper-responsive respiratory system of a sensitised person is rendered more vulnerable to asthmatic symptoms by exposures to triggers such as cold air, exercise, allergens, atmospheric pollutants or respiratory infections. These triggers may exacerbate each other: several studies have found that air pollution can enhance sensitivity to allergens (Molfino *et al.*, 1991; Anto, 1995). In everyday life, people are very likely to experience a mixture of triggers such as these.

The experience of asthma

Earlier in this chapter, we discussed a study of hospital admissions for asthma by Hyndman and colleagues (1994). They make the comment:

> Admissions to hospital are distressing events for patients and their families and account for considerable proportions of the direct and indirect costs of most diseases. (Hyndman *et al.*, 1994, p. 1598)

In this section of the chapter, we ask what it is like to *experience* asthma. In approaching this question, we focus on two perspectives: the experience of *symptoms* described by people who are asthmatic, and the *social impact* that asthma has on them and their families. The audiotape band for OU students 'Reflections on asthma' is particularly relevant to this discussion.

A conceptual model of the experience of asthma from first diagnosis onward has been developed by David Snadden and Judith Belle Brown (Figure 5.9). It is based on detailed qualitative research into the experience of asthma of seven adult patients registered with a rural practice in Ontario, Canada. The model suggests that, in the transition from diagnosis to full control, there is a move from fear to acceptance. Snadden and Belle Brown claim that this process is greatly helped by a 'mentoring relationship', where the mentor is someone experienced in coping with asthma with whom patient or parent can discuss their worries. In this way, the asthmatic person gains experience, knowledge and self-awareness, all of which contribute to a growing sense of control.

The process described by Snadden and Belle Brown extends over several years and, as the authors point out, may never be completed: the experience of coming to

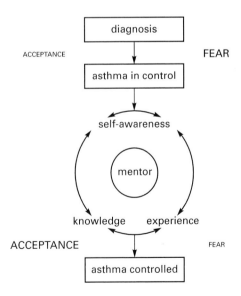

Figure 5.9 *A conceptual model of the experience of asthma. (Devised by Snadden, D. and Belle Brown, J., 1992, The experience of asthma, Social Science and Medicine, 34(12), p. 1358)*

terms with asthma is a *dynamic* process.[17] It begins with symptoms and confusion. The diagnosis of 'asthma' brings a temporary period of relief for the patient in knowing what is wrong, that it isn't 'nothing', and in believing that the doctor will know what to do about it:

> JK: It's nice to know that what I have is something. I don't like the idea of 'wait a minute, I'm having trouble breathing' and not knowing why. It's fine I can say it's asthma, that I'm asthmatic now. It's not all up in my head, I'm not dreaming this. (Snadden and Belle Brown, 1992, p. 1354)

This comment demonstrates the importance of there being a name, a medical label, that can be put to the condition. (This experience has already been discussed in Chapter 3 in relation to rheumatoid arthritis—another 'hard-to-diagnose' condition; we will return to it in Chapter 7, where failure to identify the cause of chronic pain poses similar problems of 'legitimacy' for patients.) The GP and anthropologist Cecil Helman (1990) has argued that doctors need to be able to organise their health work around a set of identifiable and largely familiar diseases and problems, procedures and treatments, which fit within accepted *medical narratives*. In the same way, people who have health problems need to organise their own 'health work' and develop *personal narratives* of their illness.

If individuals accept that they are asthmatic and that their health problem is not illusory, it generally makes it easier to collaborate with the doctor in treating the illness and in monitoring changes in their state of health. However, in accepting a medical label, the person also has to address the uncomfortable question of 'Why me?':

> ND: There was a lot of panic and anger about why me, because I have two sisters and neither one of them are affected. It's just me and I'm going like 'why me, why do I have to get dumped on with this?' and things like 'why can't it just be divided out between all three of us or

whatever, like why does it have to be me, that I have to get all these problems'. (Snadden and Belle Brown, 1992, p. 1355)

☐ The following comments are from four informants in Snadden and Belle Brown's study. What stage does each of them seem to have reached in the conceptual model shown in Figure 5.9?

> ND: I found it interfering with my life, that it would interfere with what I was doing, that it was going to put my life on hold and stop, that it was going to upset my husband and interfere with his job. (Snadden and Belle Brown, 1992, p. 1355)

> KM: You start to get tight and then all of a sudden you get thinking 'Gee, I can't breathe' and you're pumping on the puffers and it's not working, and then you start to hyperventilate, you start to get really excited, and then you see that's a bad thing if you get excited with asthma, you'll bring an attack on … Well I've been able to stop them myself, but the big thing is you've got to stay cool. (Snadden and Belle Brown, 1992, p. 1354)

> JK: What has helped me adjust? Understanding it more I guess, understanding that what I have can be controlled, not cured. It can be controlled so you can live a normal life. I worked as a counsellor at a day camp and we had asthmatic children. We had to go on a special course, the counsellors did, and they taught us things to do with the children. In the back of my head I've remembered them. It was just real simple exercises and I try doing them now. (Snadden and Belle Brown, 1992, p. 1355)

> AJ: I tend to keep it always in the back of my head. I am always conscious of what's going on in myself. I am always listening to my own breathing to see if I am whistling or wheezing or whatever. I guess it's subconscious but I know I do it a lot. (Snadden and Belle Brown, 1992, p. 1356)

■ ND is talking about the *self-awareness* that followed her first diagnosis; recognising the restrictions her asthma would place on her and her husband is a step towards eventual *acceptance*.

KM conveys something of the *fear* that asthmatic people have to cope with as they attempt

---

[17]It is helpful to compare the model developed by Snadden and Belle Brown with the stages described by Sally Macintyre and David Oldman in 'Coping with migraine' (originally published 1977). Open University students will study an edited extract in *Health and Disease: A Reader* (second edition, 1995) with Chapter 7 of this book, but could usefully read it now. Macintyre and Oldman suggest that people faced with migraine acquire knowledge of the disease in a series of discrete stages: experiencing the complaint, identifying it as migraine, and then acquiring a repertoire of methods of coping.

to *control* an attack, and also how they gain useful *knowledge* from *experience* of attacks in the past.

K also indicates the importance of *knowledge* as the source of her power to *control* her asthma, and the benefits of a *mentoring* relationship when she was trained to cope with asthmatic children. Both she and AJ show how important *self-awareness* is in *experiencing* and *accepting* the disease.

Experiential accounts such as these provide important insights into the personal worlds of people who are coping with illness.

Experiencing asthma in childhood

The account of Peter's asthma at the beginning of this chapter is taken from a research report on the *social impact* of asthma. For this reason it concentrates on the ways in which Peter's asthma complicates his life, for example by restricting what he is able to do at school and by imposing extra routine chores upon his mother. Echoing Snadden and Belle Brown's model, it also indicates something of the changing history of Peter's condition: the onset of asthma, the steps taken to control it, the acquisition of his nebuliser, the reduction in severity, and so on.

In order to obtain a broader view of the social dimension, you should now read the article in the Reader by Andrew Nocon and Tim Booth, entitled 'The social impact of childhood asthma'.

☐ As you do so, make out three lists of things that are mentioned:

(a) the apparent *causes* of asthma or asthmatic attacks;
(b) the *negative* outcomes of asthma;
(c) the *positive* outcomes of asthma.

■ Compare your lists with ours in Table 5.4.

Table 5.4 Apparent causes and social impact of asthma in a sample of 32 children who had all been admitted to a Sheffield hospital in the previous year

(a) Causes of asthma or asthmatic attacks	(b) Negative outcomes of asthma	(c) Positive outcomes of asthma
exercise	difficulty keeping up with friends, walking uphill, running, sports	a more health-conscious approach to food
allergies to animals, foods, plants	restrictions on certain trips, visits, activities, public transport, etc.	household members gave up smoking
smoke in atmosphere, especially from cigarettes	withdrawal from some activities (e.g. riding, parties, keeping pets, cancelled holidays)	families brought closer together, everyone 'helps out', parents share worries
feather bedding, carpeting	child absent from school, loses friends, gets 'picked on'	greater appreciation of the asthmatic child
cold air, cold water	parent takes time off work, loses or changes job, delays finding job	appreciation of siblings' help and concern
excitement, getting over-tired	family loses income, incurs extra expenses	inhaler makes asthmatic child feel special
	family suffers sleep loss, worry, exhaustion, tension, anger	
	parents have to do extra cleaning	
	parents feel guilty about causing/failing to prevent asthma	
	behavioural problems in asthmatic child or jealous sibling	
	dispute with school about supervision of medication	

Derived from Nocon, A. and Booth, T. (1990) *The Social Impact of Asthma*, Department of Sociological Studies, University of Sheffield; and edited extract (1995) The social impact of childhood asthma, pp. 83–8 in Davey, B., Gray, A. and Seale, C. (eds) *Health and Disease: A Reader*, 2nd edn, Open University Press, Buckingham.

It is clear from Nocon and Booth's research that, overall, childhood asthma places considerable strains upon the family, but some positive outcomes were also mentioned. The parents of asthmatic children (like the adult asthmatic patients studied by Snadden and Belle Brown) were fearful, anxious and angry, particularly in the period immediately following the onset of the condition or subsequent attacks. Many, however, were gaining experience and knowledge in the treatment of their child's asthma. A few said they 'had now learned to live with it'. Most were making changes in their lives by studying the circumstances in which attacks occurred, and by following the advice of their doctors on bedding, pets, smoking, food, etc. A few, in the light of experience, were making their own decisions *not* to implement suggested changes: retaining normal carpeting and bedding, and keeping the family cat, for example.

The parents of an asthmatic child, however, are constantly taxed by the problem of deciding whether or not to call the doctor. The doctor may say: 'Call me if you're in any doubt', but the parents know that doctors too live under pressure and they fear being criticised for 'wasting the doctor's time'. As one of the speakers in the audiotape band for OU students associated with this chapter says:

> … you obviously don't want to turn up at casualty with a fairly healthy baby and say 'Well, we thought he was a bit wheezy' when there's obviously nothing wrong with him. So you leave it as long as you dare, and then suddenly it seems to get worse and you can't do anything about it. (David Riley, interviewed for the audiotape band 'Reflections on asthma')

Most of the children interviewed by Nocon and Booth were not seriously affected by their asthma, and seemed less concerned than their parents. A problem that three of them faced was sustaining their parents' trust; these children were said to 'use' their asthma to their own advantage. This raises questions about the legitimacy of the illness and the degree of tolerance that others show towards it.

Legitimacy, tolerance and stigmatisation

People with uncontrolled asthma may, not surprisingly, be anxious or depressed. Emotional stress can make the symptoms worse, as is the case for many illnesses (for example, this could be why Peter's asthma appeared to be brought on by his father leaving home). But the current view is that asthma is not a psychosomatic condition.

How should people with asthma behave if their illness is to be considered *legitimate* and therefore *tolerated* by others? Judgements such as these normally involve a wide range of other people: for example, in the case of asthmatic children, their parents, siblings, relatives, friends, teachers, nurses and doctors may all have a say in the matter. These 'others' may play an important part in the process of accepting and controlling the condition but, conversely, their reaction can aggravate the negative impact of the illness on the child and the family. In Nocon and Booth's report we are told of the teacher who is sympathetic but doesn't have time to supervise medication, and the aunt who refuses to look after the child because she fears she couldn't cope with an attack. It is also implicit in references to parents dealing with the Benefits Agency and trying to claim allowances for taking time off work.

☐ Snadden and Belle Brown's research reveals something of the challenge that the person with asthma has in *managing* the appearance and presentation of their attacks to others. What clues can be discerned about this in the interview extracts given earlier?

■ JK prefers to say that her problem is asthma rather than 'having trouble breathing'. She implies that people will be more understanding if her condition is legitimated by a medical label. However, she may still face intolerance, given the restrictions ND reports as a consequence of her asthma; ND fears that an attack may upset her husband and interfere with what he is doing.

Problems in inter-personal trust, legitimacy and tolerance are discussed by the sociologist Simon Williams (1993), in his study of adults with COAD (chronic obstructive airways disease). What is critical, he argues, is the perception by others of the 'limits of tolerance'—the extent to which others can tolerate the failure of the person with the chronic disease to do what is required of them. The illness will be tolerated only if it does not impose 'unreasonable' burdens upon others. Perceptions of this limit may vary greatly between individuals and over time. For example, in one workplace, a person who is sometimes unable to work through chronic breathlessness may feel enormously indebted to the tolerance and help of colleagues; whereas, in another, there may be a strong sense of grievance that employment was terminated after only a brief absence through sickness. It is not difficult to think of parallel situations regarding the limits of tolerance in the home, at school and in the use of health services.

Gay Becker and colleagues studied how 95 adults with asthma, living in California, coped with the need for urgent care (Becker *et al.*, 1993). The majority indicated that they wanted to manage their asthma unassisted; they wanted to be self-reliant and to be in control of their illness. When this was no longer possible, they had to *negotiate* access to appropriate medical treatment. The researchers concluded:

> Individuals who have asthma are caught in a bind created by extremely narrow definitions of appropriate symptoms in the delivery of health care in the emergency department: they must not delay too long or seek help too soon. ... the fear that health professionals might create additional danger through their ignorance of the complexities of the medical treatment of asthma, thereby endangering the individual's life, creates sustained efforts to avoid such interactions. Yet resistance to using the health care system puts individuals at increased risk of death, should efforts to manage an episode alone fail. The juxtaposition of these concerns creates a constant push-pull dynamic, as individuals struggle to make decisions about emergency department use that will provide relief, ensure autonomy, deter the experience of stigma, and diminish the threat of death. (Becker *et al.*, 1993, p. 311)

This dilemma is echoed by David Riley, the parent of an asthmatic child, interviewed for the audiotape band for OU students associated with this chapter, when he says: 'Even though we know what the condition's like, I think we've left it too late on all occasions'.

The problem of legitimacy is experienced most acutely by those who are on the borderline of being asthmatic. There is a cultural assumption that one either does or does not have a disease. If a doctor says you have a certain disease, then it is difficult for anyone else (other than another doctor) to dispute that you do indeed have it. The implications of this diagnosis are fairly straightforward in the case of acute illness. As the sociologist Talcott Parsons (1951) argued in his theory of the *sick role*, people are normally expected to cooperate fully in efforts to get them 'better' again and, as a consequence, they acquire certain rights as being legitimately sick.[18]

---

[18]Talcott Parsons, sick role 'politics' and negotiations about the legitimacy of an illness are all discussed in *Medical Knowledge: Doubt and Certainty*, Chapter 8.

□ What difficulties do you foresee in applying this reciprocal agreement to a chronic episodic illness such as asthma?

■ Asthma intermittently 'attacks' and only marginally disables most of the time, so a question mark often hangs over the asthmatic person's right to present themselves as 'ill', to be excused from normal duties and to expect support from others.

Much of the potential *stigma* of asthma stems from the need to be ever-conscious of the importance of treatment and the need to avoid unnecessary risks. Asthmatic children have, in the past, sometimes been misunderstood at school by teachers and classmates. The stigma of being 'no good' at sport, frequently 'excused' from games, or absent altogether, can be made worse by people in authority over the child who do not understand the biological rationale of asthma treatment, nor the legitimacy of exercise-induced asthma. An instruction to 'see how long you can do without your inhaler' may mean that the asthmatic child suffers a build-up of otherwise avoidable symptoms, which can then take days to disappear. Teachers may get exasperated when seemingly fit adolescents start gasping for breath after only ten minutes' exercise. Being excused from games, but labelled as a 'neurotic who doesn't really like sport anyway', is hardly helpful. Parents have sometimes faced a struggle to persuade sceptical teachers and others of the legitimacy of the asthmatic child's needs, despite the evidence of medically-prescribed treatment for asthma.

□ Comparing Becker's study with that of Nocon and Booth, what do you think is the main *similarity* in the way in which the management of asthmatic attacks is negotiated by asthmatic adults and by the parents of asthmatic children?

■ They face a common dilemma in deciding when to deal with an attack themselves and when to seek medical help; wait too long and the consequences could be life-threatening, but seek help too soon or too often and risk being stigmatised as someone who 'over-reacts' and wastes precious medical time.

Research on the experience of asthma has shown the importance that parents and patients place upon obtaining and managing appropriate treatments, and developing and implementing strategies for minimising the threat of asthmatic attacks. It is to a discussion of treatment and prevention that this chapter now turns.

Treating and preventing asthma

Medical treatment

An initial difficulty for the clinician in deciding how to treat asthma is that it can be confused with bronchitis or other recurring respiratory infections, particularly in children. In older people, mild heart failure and emphysema (inflammation of the lining of the chest wall) can also give similar symptoms. To obscure diagnosis further, the lungs may be behaving normally at the time of investigation, so the case history becomes particularly important.

As you already know, the typical symptoms of asthma are breathlessness, wheezing, coughing (especially at night), and tightness in the chest (especially on waking up). These symptoms are not relieved by antibiotics because the underlying cause of the hyper-responsiveness and constriction of the airways is inflammation, not infection. A quantitative measure of lung function greatly aids in diagnosing and monitoring asthma; the simplest property to measure is *peak flow*, as shown in Figure 5.1 earlier.

The medical treatment of asthma has changed markedly over the past 15 years. The underlying pathology is now better understood, drugs have improved in effectiveness and selectivity, and inhalers and nebulisers are more widely available. Asthma medication involves two groups of drugs, known respectively as *relievers* and *preventers*. They offer two very different approaches to asthma therapy.

Use of relievers

The relievers are a group of drugs that usually give instant relief from asthmatic symptoms by acting as *bronchodilators*.

☐ Why should a bronchodilator relieve the feeling of breathlessness?

■ *Bronchodilation* is the opposite of *bronchoconstriction*; it reverses the narrowing of airway tubes brought about by contraction of the underlying smooth muscle (shown earlier in Figure 5.5b).

Figure 5.10 shows peak flow, as a measure of lung function, in an asthmatic person before and after inhaling a bronchodilator. Even with good medication, the peak flow in someone with asthma may not be more than 80 per cent of normal.

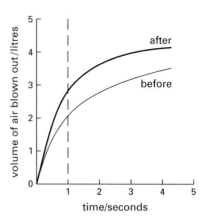

Figure 5.10 *Effect of inhaling a bronchodilator on the lung function of an asthmatic person. The dashed line indicates the response after 1 second.*

The most widely used bronchodilators are the β_2-*agonists* ('β_2' is pronounced 'beta-two') developed in the 1960s. As 'agonists' they mimic the effect of a natural hormone— in this case, adrenalin—which stimulates relaxation of smooth muscle. The drug binds to special receptor molecules in smooth muscle, stimulating the muscle fibres to relax. The term 'β_2' indicates that binding is only to the β_2-receptors of lung smooth muscle, and not to the rather similar receptors of heart muscle. The early bronchodilators were less specific, and could cause heart palpitations as a side-effect. Large doses of β_2-agonists may still give mild palpitations.

The commonest β_2-agonists are *salbutamol* (marketed as Ventolin) and *terbutaline* (marketed as Bricanyl), the benefits of which last up to six hours. By far the most effective way to administer these short-acting bronchodilators is by *inhaler* (Figure 5.11a and photograph), preferably with a spacer between the mouth and the drug canister (Figure 5.11b). When the canister is pushed down into the inhaler, a measured quantity of drug solution spurts out of the sidearm in a fine spray, which is inhaled directly into the lungs. Having a spacer increases the proportion of active drug reaching the lungs; less falls at the back of the throat, to be lost by swallowing. An asthmatic person will feel instant relief on inhaling the reliever drug, provided the asthmatic state is not so advanced that mucus and bronchial constriction together prevent the drug from reaching the site of action.

Longer-acting inhaled bronchodilators (such as *salmeterol*) were developed in the 1980s and are sometimes beneficial. The 'oldest' anti-asthmatic drug is *theophylline* (also found in tea), which was first

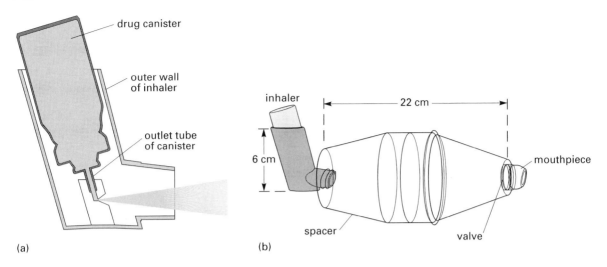

Figure 5.11 *Devices for inhaling bronchodilating drugs directly into the lungs. (a) Diagram of inhaler, showing outlet tube of drug canister resting on the valve inside the inhaler, and (b) inhaler used with spacer.*

prescribed in the 1930s and may still be used as a bronchodilator in the developed world. Theophylline is the most popular drug for treating asthma world-wide, simply because it is cheap. The great majority of asthma sufferers in the Third World cannot afford even the cheapest drugs, let alone the sophisticated new ones currently on trial in the West.

Bronchodilators may have other useful effects, such as speeding up the movement of cilia (the fine 'hairs' that sweep mucus through the airways, see Figure 5.4), and reducing the leakage of fluid from blood vessels in the connective-tissue layer of the lungs. But it is important to stress that they do not reduce the inflammatory reaction

Person using an inhaler of the type shown in Figure 5.11a. (Photo: Mike Levers)

underlying the symptoms of asthma. Since chronic inflammation is characteristic of all asthma, many people are advised to use preventers as well as relievers.

Use of preventers

Preventers are drugs that prevent, or at least suppress, the inflammatory reaction in asthmatic lungs. Since the symptoms are attacked at source, there is less need for bronchodilators. People with asthma who use a reliever drug more than once a day are now generally advised to take a regular course of a preventer drug instead. This requires forward planning, since the effects of most preventers are barely noticeable for several hours, and it may then be many days before the inflamed airways improve and the true benefit of therapy is felt.

The most effective preventer drugs are *steroids* (already discussed in the treatment of rheumatoid arthritis in Chapter 3). Just how they work is still not fully understood, but they inhibit the formation of inflammatory chemicals and cytokines, and block the leakage of fluid from blood vessels and the build-up of mucus in the lungs. Overall, inflammation is reduced and the airways are less twitchy. The commonest steroids used in inhalers are marketed as Pulmicort and Becotide. Some people with asthma have been reluctant to use steroids because of their known side-effects (reviewed briefly in Chapter 3). However, inhaled steroids are effective at much lower doses than those taken by mouth.

☐ Can you explain why?

105

■ Drugs given by mouth have to be at a high-enough concentration to overcome the diluting effect of being dissolved and absorbed into the bloodstream and carried round the body. Only a small proportion of the oral dose reaches the site of action, the lungs. Inhaled drugs are delivered direct to the lungs, so a much lower initial dose can achieve the same effect.

However, oral steroids can be used to provide higher and sustained treatment after a severe asthma attack. Taken as a short 'crash' course of seven to ten days, these doses cause few adverse effects as long as the drug is reduced gradually. Some people experience greater vulnerability to respiratory infections and sores in the mouth if inhaled steroid treatment is prolonged.

Treatment of life-threatening asthma

Exposure to high concentrations of trigger substances in the air, or a severe infection, can occasionally bring on acute symptoms of breathlessness in someone with asthma. In the most serious cases, the airways may become completely constricted and blocked (as in Figure 5.5c earlier), so the person is no longer even wheezing. 'Blueing' of the lips occurs as the oxygen content of the bloodstream falls, and immediate emergency treatment—usually in hospital—is essential. Oxygen and large doses of bronchodilator may be given through a mask, as well as steroids to reduce the inflammation.

The use of preventers in accordance with medical instructions has reduced the probability of suffering such a major asthma attack. Except for the comparatively few people with 'brittle' asthma (characterised by sudden deterioration interspersed with symptom-free periods), emergency treatment can usually be avoided. People with chronic asthma are generally advised to increase their normal dose of preventer drug at the first sign of wheezing, or even in anticipation that it might be triggered, for example by the start of a cold or 'flu. Treatment is always more effective if given *before* the inflammation builds up.

Educated use of a peak-flow meter is also advised, as lung function may fall so gradually that people who have learned to 'live with' their asthma sometimes do not realise how low their lung capacity has become. Self-management procedures worked out with medical advice often include instructions on what to do if peak-flow readings fall below normal; for example, a drop of 30 per cent might lead to a doubling of the preventer dose, whereas a drop of 60 per cent might be the signal to seek emergency treatment in hospital. People with even

moderate asthma are usually advised to travel with a peak-flow meter and oral steroids in their luggage.

In recent years, there has been increasing concern over 'avoidable' adult deaths from asthma. As we noted earlier, in 1993 in England and Wales, 1 699 fatalities occurred in which asthma was given on the death certificate as the primary cause of death. The British Thoracic Association estimated in 1982 that 86 per cent of asthma deaths were potentially preventable. Treatment and prevention of asthma are closely linked, illustrating the old saying 'prevention is better than cure'. At the individual level, this means sensible planning and self-monitoring. Prevention at the national level, for example by tackling the sources of potent triggers such as airborne particles, might be even more beneficial, but the difficulties in achieving significant improvements are obvious.

Organising routine treatment and providing support

The person with prime responsibility for the management and administration of treatment for asthma, on a day-to-day basis, is the patient, or parent or other adult caregiver. He or she has to take or medication in accordance with medical instructions, and decide when to consult a doctor and when emergency action is appropriate. This is not unusual in itself, since most illness conditions are self-treated.

☐ A particularly high level of responsibility for asthma treatment is carried by lay people. Can you explain why this is the case?

■ Asthmatic symptoms fluctuate in response to environmental triggers, which are themselves highly variable. Thus, the patient or parent has to judge whether to use a reliever or a preventer drug sporadically or routinely, how much medication to give and how soon, whether to increase the dose in anticipation of a certain trigger, what significance to place on self-administered peak-flow measurements, and finally when to seek medical help and with what degree of urgency.[19]

[19]Diabetes mellitus is one of the few other potentially life-threatening conditions with a similar level of personal responsibility for 'juggling' treatment, as a Reader article 'Coming to terms with diabetes' by David Kelleher (originally published in 1988) makes plain. Open University students could very usefully read this optional article in *Health and Disease: A Reader* (second edition, 1995).

The study by David Snadden and Judith Belle Brown (1992) demonstrated that patients with asthma can develop a sophisticated expertise in the management of their illness. They consult the doctor not just because they feel ill, but for more specific reasons, expressing particular concerns and having particular expectations of the action the doctor will take. Treatment is often based on an on-going collaboration between doctor and patient. This is consistent with a trend in Western medicine towards viewing the 'patient as an expert' who shares responsibility for treatment in partnership with health professionals[20].

However, when symptoms become acute, patients can be faced with a difficult dilemma, as illustrated in several of the research studies discussed earlier and in the audiotape band for OU students associated with this chapter. Anxieties about what to do for the best can affect a person's judgement. When Bonnie Sibbald (1988) studied 211 adults with asthma who were resident in Surrey, she found that those who suffered most morbidity were also the most likely to delay using their inhalers or summoning medical help. She argues that—rather than attempting to increase the patient's 'general knowledge' about asthma—education should be directed more to helping individuals to cope with the day-to-day demands of their illness. In particular, she suggests that people with more severe asthma should be taught the importance of speedy action in the event of an attack.

Routine medication is just one element of a wide range of adjustments that follow an asthma diagnosis. Often a system of support develops that is intended to ensure that the condition is well controlled and that the patient has as normal a life as possible. To this end, the advice and experience of other people with asthma have a particular value. Snadden and Belle Brown stressed the importance of a mentor (look back at Figure 5.9)—someone to whom the patient or parent can turn, who has direct experience of asthma. Nocon and Booth's respondents expressed a similar need, but with the emphasis on professional rather than lay help:

> When they were at their wits' end, parents wanted someone to talk to, someone who could sit and listen while they aired their grievances or anxieties ... this should be a professional person: they felt that other parents, for all their

understanding and helpfulness, might not preserve the same degree of confidentiality.
(Nocon and Booth, 1990, p. 52)

In the conclusion of their report, Nocon and Booth list eight areas in which people with asthma and or their carers would value assistance:

- more information about their own asthma;

- more information about the practical implications of asthma;

- counselling;

- practical help, including financial help;

- information about where to obtain help;

- increased awareness on the part of medical and nursing staff about the social impact of asthma;

- increased awareness in schools and workplaces about the nature of asthma and its management;

- increased public awareness.
(Derived from Nocon and Booth, 1990, pp. 65–6)

Nocon and Booth argue that much of the social organisation of support mechanisms, such as those listed above, can be developed by the members of local asthma societies.

Some GPs have encouraged people with asthma to engage in self-help and community groups, or have contributed to the education of asthma patients in group settings, as in the case of South Wales GP, Ajay Thapar (1996). Katy Gardner, another GP, whose practice is in the Granby/Toxteth district of Liverpool, regularly talks to groups of parents about childhood asthma. She also addresses some of their more local concerns, including housing, traffic pollution, use of health services and financial help, in collaboration with Steve Mumby, a welfare rights worker in a centre for unemployed people in Kirkby. Mumby has provided guidance to some of the parents of children with asthma concerning their eligibility for the care component of the Disability Living Allowance. In order to qualify, a child needs to be 'so severely disabled physically or mentally' that he or she requires attention or supervision from another person. The application form has questions regarding the care required during the day and the night, and ways to ensure that the child is kept safe.

☐ What extra care work do you think parents might have to undertake if they have a child with asthma?

---

[20]The 'patient-centred' approach to medical consultations is illustrated in *Medical Knowledge: Doubt and Certainty,* Chapter 9.

■ You probably thought of household chores aimed at reducing house-dust mites, e.g. vacuuming, wet-dusting, frequent changing of bedclothes, and freezing teddy bears! Steve Mumby (1994) lists the following—some of which may also have occurred to you: cleaning the nebuliser, measuring the peak-flow rate of the child, treating associated infections and sore mouths (an occasional side-effect of inhaled steroids), dealing with behavioural problems including sleepwalking, settling the child down at night, attending hospital, and responding to 'bleepers' which signal a possible emergency.

People who have asthma share many everyday challenges and questions about 'treatment' can extend to many areas of social life. By obtaining specialist advice, not just from doctors but also from experts in welfare rights, social services, etc., and by helping each other, people with asthma can do much to reduce the negative impact that the disease can have on the quality of life.

Open University students should now listen to the audiotape band entitled 'Reflections on asthma'.[21] A number of people describe their experiences of asthma and its treatment, and discuss the factors which—in their view—may contribute to the underlying causes of asthma or to triggering an asthma attack. This audiotape band and its associated notes provide a review and illustrations of all the issues presented thus far in this chapter. Even if you listened to it earlier, it will be helpful to do so again now.

Public concerns

Asthma—a national issue?

One of the reasons why asthma was selected as a case study for this book is that there has been considerable public concern about it in the 1990s. Asthma has become a national issue. To a large extent this concern has been part of a wider anxiety about atmospheric pollution and climate change. It is generally felt that polluted air must have damaging effects upon lungs, particularly the lungs of young children. Air quality is a major political issue involving international policies on power generation and transport, so it is important that the arguments are examined critically.

Earlier in this chapter, we reviewed some of the evidence that links air pollution with asthma, including the findings of the Committee on the Medical Effects of Air Pollutants which reported to the British government in 1995. The Committee's conclusion was that the levels of very small particles (PM_{10}) in the atmosphere are clearly associated with asthmatic attacks in people whose lungs are already hyper-responsive. In urban areas, the source of over 80 per cent of these particles is vehicle exhausts, particularly from diesel engines. In rural areas, the particles are primarily composed of airborne material from plants and animals. The evidence is less secure, but still indicative, that other pollutants in the atmosphere— primarily nitrous oxide, sulphur dioxide and ozone—also contribute to asthmatic attacks and exacerbate other respiratory conditions such as COAD.

However, there is considerable uncertainty about whether poor air quality *causes* asthma to develop in people who would not otherwise have suffered from it. Scientific and medical opinion generally favours the view that asthma is an *allergic* condition that is *aggravated* by inhaled pollutants, not caused by them. This is in marked contrast to much media publicity which has presented traffic pollution as 'the' cause of asthma. Consider, for example, the following description of a one-year-old girl's sudden asthma attack, written by Geoffrey Lean in the *Independent on Sunday* ('Gasping for breath', 1993, 10 October, p. 19). Over a period of five months she had twice been rushed into hospital. Her parents were now fearful that 'next time their daughter might lose her fight for breath'. Lean describes her as:

> … the latest statistic in a neglected epidemic that is sweeping through Britain's children … Almost everyone has a victim of the asthma epidemic in their family … this issue is likely to prove a political time-bomb. Tick by tick, evidence is accumulating from little noticed scientific studies all over the world that one of the main factors behind the epidemic is the growth in the use of private cars. (Lean, 1993, p. 19)

The journalist then claims that a quarter of the children at a Surrey school have asthma, and continues:

> Most parents blame the nearby M25 motorway and say the situation has got dramatically worse in the past five years. (Lean, 1993, p. 19)

[21]This audiotape band has been recorded for students studying this book as part of an Open University course. You should consult the Audiocassette Notes before listening to the tape and afterwards attempt the questions posed in the Notes.

This article is typical of the mass-media stories in recent years that have focused on asthma and air pollution. It uses emotive language to promote public concern, and encourages its readers to 'blame' asthma exclusively on one source (traffic) rather than engage with the complex story of multifactorial causes. Some clinicians feel that this alarmist approach is distressing for people with asthma and their families and does little to foster objective debate. Too great an emphasis on one piece of the asthma 'puzzle' could reduce funding and research into other contributory factors, and even perhaps distort legislation.

Yet it is undoubtedly also the case that traffic pollution was a neglected issue until the media chose to bring the link with asthma into the limelight. The Parliamentary Office of Science and Technology's 1994 report, *Breathing in our Cities* (mentioned earlier), notes that the Medical Research Council's Air Pollution Unit was closed in the early 1980s. It will be interesting to see what follows from the acceptance of the British government in 1995 that PM_{10} levels must be reduced because of their threat to health.

Local action in South Wales

Even if air pollution turns out to be an 'aggravator' rather than a cause of asthma, this does not reduce its potency as a threat to the quality of life—and perhaps to life itself—for asthmatic people in areas of high atmospheric pollution. The identification and diagnosis of asthma is of particular concern to populations living in polluted areas and, in some, this concern has led to local action by residents, GPs and other health professionals. A closer examination of one such community—in South Wales—illustrates the way in which local concern generates the collection of particular kinds of information. This process, in turn, fosters a rather different view of asthma from the one promoted in the national media.

The coal-mining industry of South Wales has always been associated with respiratory illness among the miners. With the demise of the deep mines, however, attention has shifted to other concerns. In 1988, Mark Temple, a GP practising in Glynneath, made representations to a Public Enquiry regarding proposals to extend a local open-cast mining site. He argued that dust from the site could cause an increase in asthma in the local population. Despite his and other objections, the mine was given the go-ahead.

Because of Welsh Office concern with NHS drug-prescription costs, the Glynneath practice had been auditing its treatment of new asthma episodes since 1983. Thus, it was able to monitor the impact of the mining operations when they started in October 1990. Temple recorded an increase in new episodes of asthma from a weekly average of 4.4, before mining began, to 7.9 episodes per week afterwards. Alan Sykes, a statistician, helped Temple analyse the data, which they published in the *British Medical Journal* (BMJ) in August 1992. They concluded:

> Our findings are prima facie evidence to support the practice's concern about the risks to the general population from the open cast coal site. The results of this small study give cause for national concern in view of the current increasing trend towards open cast mining in Britain. (Temple and Sykes, 1992, p. 397)

The study was subject to immediate and vigorous criticism, which the authors answered without retracting or qualifying their conclusion. The exchanges, although confined to the pages of the BMJ, had a major impact locally in Glynneath. Publication of the research in a prestigious medical journal was seen in itself as authoritative evidence of a cause for concern. The study received attention in the local press and the views of councillors were quoted. Other GPs became concerned. For example, Duncan Williams, whose South Wales practice is also adjacent to large open-cast mine-workings, began liaising with local primary schools in order to develop a longitudinal study of respiratory problems in young children (Williams and Griffiths, 1996).

In December 1992, West Glamorgan County Council (in its role as the Mineral Planning Authority responsible for approving applications for further open-cast developments) wrote to West Glamorgan Health Authority to propose that research into the issue should be launched. It cited the study by Temple and Sykes, and several national studies undertaken by British Coal and the Institute of Occupational Medicine. It also had at hand the report of Professor Alwyn Smith, the Medical Assessor to the Public Inquiry in Glynneath which preceded the commencement of open-cast mining. All these authorities, with the exception of Temple and Sykes, were *sceptical* that there was a link between open-cast mining dust and asthma. Even so, the Health Authority agreed that research would be valuable.

A substantial project proposal was drawn up, involving most of the concerned agencies: the Health

Authority, the County Council, the four Borough Councils, British Coal, and Temple and Sykes. The Welsh Office refused to provide financial support, but British Coal agreed to provide equivalent funding to that of the other authorities and to accept the findings regardless of outcome—subject to the Institute of Occupational Medicine being represented on the steering committee.

The proposal was accepted, and the project was launched in January 1995. It is based in four primary schools in West Glamorgan—one in a rural setting, one in the centre of Swansea, and two in Glynneath. The local Environmental Health Departments are monitoring the quality of the air in all three areas over a six-month period, and the Health Authority is monitoring the lung function of all children aged 7 or 8 years in the four schools over two six-week periods, one in winter and one in summer.

Children at one of four primary schools participating in a research project to monitor lung function and air quality in South Wales. (Photo: Duncan Williams)

Meantime, however, while these plans were being drawn up, the decline of the local deep-mine industry had led to a rise in coal stocks accumulating at local docks. People in Port Tennant live close to Swansea Harbour. Alerted by the Glynneath campaign to the possible connection between dust and asthma, they formed the *Coal Off the Docks Action Committee (CODAC)*. A spokesman for CODAC told the *South Wales Evening Post* that they were becoming increasingly concerned about the rise in asthma and bronchitis.

> People have had enough and will no longer be fobbed off. Now, increasingly, we are getting reports of children and fit men and women

suffering from asthma. It is very disturbing ... [A worried mother claimed] '... every other house in Port Tennant is home to someone with asthma. They call us The Puffers. They really ought to call us Asthma City.' (*South Wales Evening Post*, 24 June 1994)

There are 45 children in the local marching band. The newspaper reported that about a third of them were suffering from asthma and that, during marching displays, helpers were on hand with inhalers in case the children ran out of puff. Another mother is quoted:

> When I was in Danygraig School 40 years ago there was only one child with asthma but today there are dozens of children carrying pumps to school. (*South Wales Evening Post*, 24 June 1994)

The newspaper's editorial commented:

> The health of our children, elderly and indeed everyone in those parts of the city affected comes before the business of importing coal. The economic cost of stopping the trade must be weighed against the risk of asthma and other dust-related diseases becoming endemic because of the fall-out from the coal mountains. (*South Wales Evening Post*, 24 June 1994)

Although it will certainly be interesting to read the results of the research project when they become available, and to follow the CODAC campaign, what this example of local action demonstrates is how quickly ideas about a *cause* of asthma can develop within a local area. In the space of six years, the concern of one GP has led to the launching of a major research project—one, incidentally, that has attracted interest from other cities in the United Kingdom—and to a sharp rise in public consciousness of a possible causal link between dust and asthma. It is reasonable to suppose that many doctors and nurses in the area will have begun to think differently about identifying and explaining asthma, about treating and advising patients, and about how the risks to the local population might be reduced (Williams and Griffiths, 1996).

Conclusion

In this chapter we have reviewed some of the current literature on asthma. It seems to us that a full understanding of asthma is frustrated by one important paradox. In short, whereas there is no ambiguity for the person who regularly suffers from asthmatic attacks, the disease itself becomes enigmatic when you try to study its occurrence within a population. Asthma has proved to be an elusive phenomenon to identify and define, for a number of reasons.

First, asthma takes time to diagnose and then is often totally controlled by treatment. Many people who could be described as 'asthmatic' because they routinely take anti-asthma medication, rarely or never suffer an asthma attack. As a result, the numbers of people recorded as having asthma may be under-represented in epidemiological studies.

Second, for every person who unambiguously has asthma and who needs to take regular medication, there are several who are close to the borderline. As a result, epidemiological data are extremely sensitive to how the line is drawn between the 'nearly asthmatic' and the 'just asthmatic'. Minor fluctuations in what is defined as asthma can have a major impact on prevalence estimates.

Third, the growing global concern with the environment and, in particular, with atmospheric pollution, has put asthma in the limelight. Increasingly, asthma prevalence rates are used as an indicator of air quality. The linking of asthma with air pollution is inevitably changing the way that doctors, scientists and lay people define and identify the condition. These perceptual changes may already have contributed to the apparent rise in asthma prevalence in urban environments.

As a consequence of the points made above, the extent to which asthma rates are indeed rising is uncertain. Greater awareness of asthma among health professionals may have uncovered formerly undiagnosed cases, or it may have changed the diagnostic criteria they use. People living close to major sources of pollution in the 1990s have readily learnt to diagnose 'asthma' in their community. The widespread availability of inhalers has increased the public profile of the condition still further.

Even though the prevalence of asthma may not be increasing in quite the straightforward and consistent way that is so often assumed, air pollution is bad news for people with asthma. It might not actually *cause* people to become asthmatic in the first place but, for those who are predisposed to asthma, the damage that pollution can do to the lungs may be the cause of much of their *suffering* from asthma.

Scientific attention seems to be shifting away from the disease and its *treatment* to the environment and *prevention* of the disease. Will asthma in the twenty-first century be reconstructed as a disease of relative affluence? Or will the present-day emphasis on atmospheric pollution as the cause of asthma achieve the status of scientific as well as popular 'fact'?

OBJECTIVES FOR CHAPTER 5

When you have studied this chapter, you should be able to:

5.1   Critically evaluate and discuss epidemiological evidence relating to the prevalence of asthma and interpret the findings of new studies.

5.2   Describe the effect that asthma has upon the respiratory system, the ways in which an asthmatic attack might be triggered, and the different kinds of medical treatments available to people with asthma.

5.3   Describe some of the anxieties and the problems that people with asthma and their carers may experience.

5.4   Critically discuss the argument that air pollution causes asthma.

QUESTIONS FOR CHAPTER 5

Question 1 (*Objective 5.1*)

A number of longitudinal studies cited in this chapter estimated the prevalence of asthma in children on the basis of their parents' responses to a questionnaire. What reservation must be borne in mind when concluding, from studies such as these, that childhood asthma has risen over time? If you were designing a research study, how would you go about increasing your confidence that you could detect genuine changes in prevalence rates?

Question 2 (*Objective 5.1*)

What similarities and differences are there between the concepts and methods used by professional researchers to collect epidemiological data on trends in asthma prevalence, and the kinds of evidence that lay people draw on to make judgements about asthma trends?

In considering this question, look at two sources of lay accounts:

(a)   The reports quoted earlier from the *South Wales Evening Post* article on the CODAC (Coal Off the Docks Action Committee) campaign in Port Tennant; and

(b)   part of an article by Steve Mumby, a welfare rights worker at a centre for unemployed people in Liverpool, describing how he came to be conscious of asthma as an important local issue:

> A co-worker, herself a grandmother of a child with asthma, pointed out to me how many of the children in the area suffered from asthma. Once we started asking about it on a routine basis, we soon found that about half the parents coming through the door had children with the condition. (Mumby, 1994, p. 5)

Question 3 (*Objective 5.2*)

What are 'relievers' and 'preventers', and how do these drugs affect the lungs of a person who has asthma?

Question 4 (*Objective 5.3*)

What sources of financial difficulty might be experienced in a family where an adult or child is severely affected by asthma?

Question 5 (*Objective 5.4*)

What light do the comparative studies of children in former East and West Germany (von Mutius *et al.*, 1992, 1994) shed on the question of whether atmospheric pollution causes childhood asthma? What important questions are raised but left unanswered by this research?

6 *Schizophrenia*

Early in your study of this chapter you will be asked to listen to an audiotape band entitled 'Hearing voices'. Later in the chapter you will read an article in the Reader,[1] 'Ethnic minorities and the psychiatrist' by Roland Littlewood and Maurice Lipsedge. This chapter builds on the discussion of the social construction of disease categories and the consequences for diagnostic uncertainty which is a major theme of the first book in this series, Medical Knowledge: Doubt and Certainty. This chapter was written by Jacqueline Atkinson, a psychologist and Senior Lecturer in the Department of Public Health, University of Glasgow.

Introduction

Schizophrenia probably causes more disquiet than any other disorder. It is found in all societies and, when using the same diagnostic criteria, at very similar rates. In acute episodes it resembles what has traditionally been described as 'madness'. It can be a one-off episode or a severely debilitating life-long condition. At one time, schizophrenia filled more hospital beds than any other illness, but most patients now spend most of their life in the community and are treated there—a policy that has received almost as much criticism as previous institution-alisation did. Its cause is unknown but hotly pursued, spanning genetics and family communication, brain structure and function, viruses and allergies, social pressures and political views. Schizophrenia is a battleground on which the ideological wars surrounding mental illness are fought, with myths and prejudices, disputed facts and opinions raised to the level of doctrine. But it is, most of all, a personal experience. No one approaches a subject like schizophrenia neutrally.

□ What is likely to influence your understanding of schizophrenia?

■ A wide variety of factors are possible, including: the type of experience you have of it (for example, do you or does anyone you know have a diagnosis of schizophrenia?); your academic or professional background (for example, do you see yourself primarily as a scientist, a social scientist or a student of the humanities, are you a nurse or a social worker?); information you have gained from the media (for example, portrayals of schizophrenia in newspapers, books, films and television).

A person diagnosed as having schizophrenia will have a different view from the psychiatrist who makes the diagnosis. Family members—whether carers or not—will have yet another perspective, as will the person whose only experience comes from newspaper articles on yet another 'mental patient' attacking a stranger. For most people their only understanding of schizophrenia comes from the media and, as you will see later, this can be a highly misleading picture.

□ Write down a list of words you associate with schizophrenia and a second list of what you think the symptoms are. (This is not intended as a test of knowledge, and will be returned to at the end of the chapter.)

Some of the debates over schizophrenia are a microcosm of wider debates surrounding the nature of science. Science exists in a social context and some people believe the 'facts' that scientists uncover are socially constructed, reflecting the way scientists work rather than objective truth.[2] Most people engaged in research on schizophrenia are probably psychiatrists, and it can be argued that they are dependent on schizophrenia being an accepted disease classification for the status and

---

[1]*Health and Disease: A Reader* (second edition, 1995).

[2]The social constructionist view of medical knowledge is discussed in *Medical Knowledge: Doubt and Certainty*, Chapter 7.

power of their profession. Following this line of argument, the psychologist Mary Boyle points out:

> Psychiatrists may not be as free to imagine alternative accounts of bizarre behaviour as were, say, physicists to imagine alternatives to Newton's theory. (Boyle, 1994, p. 403)

Whilst this may be true, similar arguments can be applied to others who have built their reputations (and thus, in part at least, their jobs) on attacking the medical concept of schizophrenia.

As you read this chapter you will be encouraged to consider the implications of different views of schizophrenia, since these influence decisions about treatment and management, the kinds of services provided and the wider social view of mental illness. For example, you will learn that there are variable criteria for deciding whether a person should be diagnosed as having schizophrenia. In the USA, diagnostic criteria have important implications because a formal diagnosis is necessary to get insurance coverage. The advice given to politicians and service planners is never neutral; prejudices and assumptions play as much a part as facts, as will be seen later in the chapter in the discussion of community care in the United Kingdom. No one can say with absolute certainty what schizophrenia is, what causes it, or how to cure it. There is no single answer to the questions that schizophrenia poses.

Schizophrenia: a personal experience

First-hand accounts of people diagnosed as having schizophrenia probably bring us nearer to understanding what 'schizophrenia' means than anything else. Many experiences show similarity over time, but care should be taken to put reported events—particularly concerning treatment and diagnosis—in their historical context. As you will see later in this chapter, these aspects have changed considerably over time.

The first description is from the audiotape band 'Hearing voices', to which you should now listen.[3] In it you will hear an account given by Ron Coleman, who describes his experiences of psychiatric services, as well as a self-help group called *Hearing Voices*, after he was diagnosed as having schizophrenia.

[3]This audiotape has been recorded for Open University students studying this book as part of an undergraduate course. You should consult the Audiocassette Notes before playing the tape.

□ In Chapter 2 the creation of *softer social labels* to counteract stigma was described. How does Ron Coleman's experience reflect this?

■ He was labelled 'schizophrenic' by people in the formal health care system. When he joined the Hearing Voices group he experienced the change of status to that of 'voice hearer' as helpful. For him, it marked a change towards acceptance by other people.

The stigma experienced by the person diagnosed as having schizophrenia can be distressing, as can the experience of psychiatric services. The experiences defined as symptoms of schizophrenia are also distressing and frequently frightening, as the following account by Mary Barnes suggests:

> When I was bad, time seemed endless. To be able to think that in two, four, six hours, the feeling would lift, was not possible. It was so awful at the time, that there didn't seem to be any before or after. The only possibility was to live one moment at a time. When really bad, I never spoke, knowing the only safe thing was to be very still, going into a sort of half-sleep, stupor state … people might try to talk to me, I knew better than to attempt to reply. Though I might moan or groan. It just had to lift before I could move, without stirring it worse … It, my anger, always did lift. But when caught in its grip I was still, immobile, dead. To me, at this time, IT coming out was very dangerous, it might kill anyone … To suffer myself, to stem my own rebellion, was the fight that at times became so intense within me that I hardly knew how to live with myself. (Barnes and Berke, 1971, pp. 129–30)

Plate 2, facing page 61 of this book, gives the most compelling insight into the experiences of a person who has struggled with the symptoms of schizophrenia for over twenty years. It shows six self-portraits from a series of seventeen, painted by the artist Bryan Charnley between 11 April and 19 July 1991. The notes below each painting are from his diary. He began cutting back on his medication, knowing that he could expect a return of the symptoms of his schizophrenia (diagnosed in 1971), but wanting to work on a series of self-portraits *with* his illness rather than *in spite of* it. On 29 April he wrote:

> The doctors just prescribe more and more drugs when the patient comes up with something he can't handle. What I think is interesting is that

the drugs, no matter how high the dosage had no effect. What made the change was rational insight, the truth. The beauty of truth. The doctors of course will mutter the drugs just began to take effect but I do not believe this for an instant. I believe instead that the answer to my condition is rational insight but the doctors seem unwilling, or unable to help me here. Certainly many different schizophrenias exist and some cannot be attacked by rational insight for reason has broken down but why should everybody be lumped in the same druggy boat? I am overwhelmed by things I cannot understand. Understanding what was going on, the truth of the situation, would bring release. (Extract from Bryan Charnley's diary, 29 April 1991, by courtesy of his brother, Terence Charnley)

The impact of schizophrenia extends beyond the individual to the family and can have a devastating effect on those who live with, or care for, the person involved. This is illustrated in an account by Anne Deveson who is a writer, broadcaster and film-maker. Her son, Jonathan, diagnosed as having schizophrenia, died of a drug overdose in 1986 at the age of 24. She writes of her experience:

That same day I went to the Magistrate's Court to make application in person for the restraining order. I had to explain my reason for needing one. The magistrate looked at me over his glasses and said, 'But can't the boy get help? Why isn't he in hospital?' I said tartly that I wished that he would ask the hospital that same question. As I left the court, the police told me that because Jonathan did not have any fixed address, they might be unable to serve the order, which would mean it could not be enforced.

I returned to South Terrace alone, and felt the most terrible desolation. Georgia and Joshua had both been forced to leave home. Security guards were watching the house. Jonathan was still crazy. And I was helpless and frightened.

Sometimes I slept at the house out of bravura: I would not be turned out of my own home. But I would wake in the night at the slightest rustle outside. The security guards' torches would flicker through my bedroom window and startle me so I would sit upright,

pretending that I wasn't alarmed. Once, when the moon was flying high and I had been woken by a possum—or was it a cat? or was it my errant son?—I marched through the house in my bare feet shouting, 'Go away, Jonathan, go away! Leave me alone, Jonathan, leave me alone.' As I clambered back into bed I thought ironically of all those statements about mothers who clung to their children and would not cut the umbilical cord. God, I'd cut it, burn it, blow it up —anything to get rid of this burden that would never give me peace, and which left me so exhausted I did not know how I could face each day.

… February 1986. I began this year with a sense of profound melancholia. I felt haunted by the need to find some way of stopping Jonathan's deterioration but, because of my heavy work-load, I had little time to start another round of 'saving Jonathan'. It may sound foolish to write about 'saving Jonathan' after all those other abortive attempts but Jonathan needed saving.

… Now, so many years later when people say, 'But I don't know how you stood it', the answer is that you stand it because you have no option. You do hang on, precariously, to any small ledges of hope. You cling with your fingernails, with your breath tightly held, and you cling, you bloody well cling. (Deveson, 1992, pp. 175, 245–7)

These passages give some indication of how devastating schizophrenia can be, not only to individuals but also to their families, but it would be wrong to suggest that the experience is always wholly bad.

Mark Vonnegut, son of the novelist Kurt Vonnegut, Jr., was hospitalised in 1971, in Vancouver, with a diagnosis of schizophrenia. His book about his experience closes thus:

As well as being one of the worst things that can happen to a human being, schizophrenia can also be one of the richest and humanizing experiences life offers. Although it won't do much toward improving your condition, the ins and outs of your bout with schizophrenia are well worth figuring out. But if you concentrate on getting well for now, and come back to puzzling things out later, I guarantee you'll do a better job of it. Being crazy and being mistaken are not at all the same. The things in life that are upsetting you are more than likely things well worth being upset about. It is, however, possible to be upset without being crippled, and even to act effectively against those things ... There are great insights to be gained from schizophrenia, but remember that they won't do you or anyone else much good unless you recover. (Vonnegut, 1979, p. 274)

The perspectives of user groups

Experience with schizophrenia and the psychiatric services has led some people to write their story; it has led many more to become involved in the **user movement**, of which probably the best known organisation in Britain is *MIND* (*National Association for Mental Health*). There are many other national and local groups. **Empowerment** is a common goal for all, reflected in the emphasis in most organisations on issues of advocacy,[4] education and a right to define members' problems in their own way, including the use of their own 'labels'.

Labels may focus on a particular experience, as does the term 'voice hearer'. This does not replace a diagnosis, since everyone who hears voices would not receive a diagnosis of schizophrenia and everyone diagnosed as having schizophrenia does not hear voices. It does, however, remove the experience from the realm of medicine and offers other approaches to living with it. Other labels focus on current status, as does the term *survivor* (of the system or of the illness) used by the group *Survivors Speak Out*. Still others stay with the diagnosis (for example, the *Manic-Depression Fellowship*).

Mike Lawson, writing in 1991, when he was a director of *International Self-Advocacy Alliance*, vice-chair of MIND and an active member of Survivors Speak Out, reflects the political aspects common to much of the user movement:

> Power cannot be given, only advocacy and self-advocacy can ensure it is not taken away. Psychiatry is a sanctioned licence to remove power; self-advocacy and advocacy challenge and redress that imbalance. Power is essential to function and gain some autonomy and we regain our power through self-advocacy and advocacy ...

[4]Advocacy is discussed further in *Dilemmas in Health Care*, Chapter 5.

Reintegration does not mean to us taking on the values of the existing society. It means being able to function within that society, having a voice there, being heard and being able to work for change without persecution ... The focus is moving to the political systems that oppress us rather than the individual who responds to that oppression in ways that are seen as 'sick'. (Lawson, 1991, pp. 69, 79)

□ How does this compare with the politics of 'disability'? (Think back to Chapter 2.)

■ The disavowal of 'disability' as a stigmatising label has involved identifying the cause of disability as being the physical and social environment, rather than the physical impairments of 'disabled' individuals.

Ron Coleman, whom you heard on the audiotape band 'Hearing voices', has written from a slightly different position to that of Lawson:

> I now had an understanding of why the voices were there, I was learning to accept that the voices might never go ... I was still prone to being 'mad' at regular intervals and my life was still chaotic ... My great self-discovery was that I still acted like a schizophrenic, I had given up the drugs but not the character ... I was still a victim of my diagnosis ... I realised that from then on I would have to accept responsibility for my own life, that I had to give up being a victim ... I would find out all sorts of things about myself, including many that I would not like. For example, I discovered that I had used hospital as a bolt hole as soon as things got tough. I had also used my 'illness' as an excuse for some disgusting behaviour both on and off the ward. My illness was my power, it was the only power I had and, boy, did I learn to use it. (Coleman, 1995, p. 17)

□ How does Ron Coleman's position differ from that of Mike Lawson?

■ Lawson is concerned to change external 'oppression', which he sees as responsible for the persecution of the people he represents. Coleman (while the audiotape shows him to be critical of the psychiatric system) is also concerned to change himself.

The changes brought about by the purchaser–provider split in the NHS[5] mean that user organisations, notably MIND, are also now involved in providing services. This dual role poses a potential conflict of interests if a campaigning organisation is simultaneously highlighting the shortcomings of health and social service provision for users and carers, while bidding to the purchasers of those services for contracts of its own. Vociferous campaigning may not be acceptable in a service provider and, as charities, voluntary organisations are prohibited from any campaigning that is 'political'. Apparently straightforward projects may still be contentious: for example MIND's *Yellow Card* scheme, which encourages people taking prescribed drugs to report harmful effects to MIND, which will then pass this on to the Committee on Safety of Medicines. Doctors are supposed to report harmful effects through official 'yellow cards', but few returns are received, and MIND's scheme is intended to encourage awareness of such effects. It has, however, been criticised by some psychiatrists.

The *National Schizophrenia Fellowship (NSF)* also provides services, running many drop-in centres and some of the very few respite services for people with mental health problems and for their carers. It has been actively campaigning for better community services to be in place when hospital beds are closed. It differs from other user groups in that the NSF is an organisation predominately for carers. This has, at times, led to tensions between the NSF and some user groups. Throughout the world groups for carers of people diagnosed as having schizophrenia are found which take the NSF as their model.

SANE (Schizophrenia: A National Emergency) is neither part of the user nor carer movement. Started and run by the journalist Marjorie Wallace (Patron: HRH the Prince of Wales) it seeks to campaign in the media on various issues related to schizophrenia and mental illness. The organisation has repeatedly called for halts in the closure of mental hospitals, at least until more community services are in place. It also raises considerable sums for research and runs a telephone help line (Saneline). With no public funding (unlike, for example, both MIND and NSF) all its funds come from private donations, industry and commerce and fund-raising events. It was involved in a dispute with MIND over the nature of one of its campaigns which was seen as stigmatising people diagnosed as having schizophrenia.

[5]The purchaser–provider split, and the associated 1991 reforms to the United Kingdom health service, are discussed in *Caring for Health: History and Diversity*, Chapter 7.

As the views of consumers are increasingly sought by both providers and purchasers of health services, so user and carer organisations are solicited for their opinions. How representative their views are is open to debate, but since neither users nor carers are homogenous groups a variety of opinions should be expected. Both the personal experiences of individuals and the political perspectives of users' and carers' organisations demonstrate diversity. They all, however, have in common the experience of living in a world where orthodox medical and scientific views of schizophrenia exert a powerful influence over peoples' thinking—even if this ultimately leads some people to reject the medical viewpoint. For this reason, in the next two sections of this chapter we seek an understanding of the medical and scientific view of schizophrenia, starting with the contribution of epidemiology.

Schizophrenia: a world-wide experience

Throughout this chapter the unfolding story of schizophrenia is one of claim and counterclaim, and epidemiological studies of schizophrenia are no exception. Studies are complicated by the problems surrounding cross-cultural definitions of schizophrenia. International research is dominated by the *International Pilot Study of Schizophrenia (IPSS)* which began in 1968. It was organised by the World Health Organisation and first reported in 1973 (WHO, 1973). The IPSS studied 1202 patients in nine centres: Aarhus (Denmark), Agra (India), Cali (Colombia), Ibadan (Nigeria), London (United Kingdom), Moscow (then USSR), Prague (then Czechoslovakia), Taipei (Taiwan) and Washington DC (USA). Psychiatrists used an interview schedule called the *Present State Examination (PSE)* to interview and diagnose patients. The PSE is designed to ensure that patients are asked the same kinds of questions and the same significance is given to their responses. A computer program (called *Catego*) was developed to apply the same diagnostic rules to all information obtained by the psychiatrists, resulting in consistent diagnostic decisions.

One major and fairly controversial finding from this study was that the *core symptoms* of schizophrenia (discussed in the next section) are found with similar frequency throughout the world. Less surprising was the finding that there were differences in the way schizophrenia was diagnosed in different places. Since the PSE and Catego had been developed in London it was to be expected that there would be good agreement between British psychiatrists and the diagnostic program. In fact only two centres diagnosed schizophrenia substantially differently from the program—Washington and Moscow. Both diagnosed *more* people as having schizophrenia, but for different reasons.

In the 1970s, American psychiatry—including diagnostic practice—was heavily influenced by psycho-analysis and the **psychodynamic** approach. This approach emphasises drives and motives and describes non-observable, unconscious processes within the mind as having an active influence or control on current behaviour, thought and emotion.[6] Such *intra-psychic* functions are inferred from symptoms, and greater emphasis is given to them than to the symptoms themselves. The psychodynamic approach led to a much broader definition of schizophrenia in the USA than that used in the United Kingdom. Many of the patients diagnosed as having schizophrenia in Washington would have been labelled 'neurotic' in London.

In contrast, in Moscow an approach to schizophre-nia had developed which emphasised the course of the illness and the level of *social adjustment* between epi-sodes more than the symptoms themselves. Thus the social component of the illness played a significant part in the diagnostic process in Moscow which was not evident elsewhere. Clearly, there are opportunities for abuse of this emphasis in societies where deviations from the cultural norm are poorly tolerated. However, the IPSS only looked at diagnostic practice in Moscow, in clinicians trained in one particular school of psychiatry. There was evidence that elsewhere (Leningrad, now St Petersburg, for example) diagnostic practice was much closer to that in Britain.

Diagnostic practice has since changed in the USA, with the use of observable symptoms advocated, rather than psychodynamic concepts. The American Psychiatric Association in 1980 announced this official change with the publication of a new classification system for mental disorder (the most recent version of this system, known as DSM IV, is described later). However, it takes time for diagnostic practices to change in the clinical setting and this, plus the time involved both to carry out and publish research, means that care must be taken when extrapolating from American data to British circum-stances—particularly before about the mid-1980s.

The second major finding subsequently to come out of the IPSS, which caused initial surprise, was that the course of schizophrenia, or its outcome, was better in what were described as the 'developing' countries

compared with the 'developed'. Subsequent research has confirmed this finding, and the WHO has sought to deter-mine the reasons (Jablensky *et al.*, 1992). The difference, it was concluded, was due to 'culture': less reliance on medication, less pressure in rural societies which have a place for people with mental illness in the work force, and the role and support of the extended family were all seen as important.

These findings have been challenged, however, by researchers who question the methodology and highlight the many inherent difficulties in measuring, translating and comparing 'cultures' (for example, the work of American psychiatrists Robert Edgerton and Alex Cohen, 1994). The heterogeneity of centres in both 'developed' and 'developing' countries is pointed out, along with the fact that many of the centres in the developing countries were predominately urban (the assumption usually being made that they are rural). Edgerton and Cohen suggest that gender can explain most of the differences in out-come. Gender is a good predictor of outcome almost everywhere, with women having a milder course to their illness and a better prognosis than men, but gender differ-ences are more than three times greater in developing countries. The explanation for this is unclear, but one possibility is that cultural factors may 'buffer' women from the most severe expressions of schizophrenia. Other studies point to family responses to the patient (Leff *et al.*, 1990), a topic that will be returned to later in this chapter.

Concentrating on the difference between Western and non-Western, or industrialised and non-industrialised countries, ignores the fact that everywhere schizophrenia can follow different courses with widely different outcomes. In industrialised societies approxi-mately 30 per cent of people diagnosed as having schizophrenia remain chronically disabled, which is the same percentage as typically reported in non-industrialised societies. Even for these patients there can be a levelling-off process and a degree of recovery. For people experiencing a first episode of schizophrenia, a quarter in the West recover and remain well compared with a half in developing countries.

The WHO study (Jablensky *et al.*, 1992) indicates rates of schizophrenia based on two definitions, the first being a *broad* definition (incorporating many symptoms), the second being *narrow* (incorporating fewer symp-toms). The centre studied in Britain was Nottingham. What the researchers called *morbid risk* (the likelihood of developing the condition between the ages of 15 and 54 years) was given as 0.8 per cent for males and females combined in Nottingham, using the broad definition (i.e. 8 people per 1 000 in this age-group can be expected to

---

[6]The psychodynamic approach is described further in *Birth to Old Age: Health in Transition*, Chapter 6.

Table 6.1 Morbid risk (%) for age 15–54 years by broad and narrow case definition for schizophrenia

	Broad definition			Narrow definition		
	male	female	male and female	male	female	male and female
Aarhus	0.68	0.51	0.59	0.33	0.20	0.27
Chandigarh (rural)	1.48	2.03	1.72	0.54	0.40	0.48
Chandigarh (urban)	1.04	1.21	1.10	0.22	0.42	0.30
Dublin	0.85	0.80	0.83	0.31	0.32	0.32
Honolulu	0.55	0.47	0.50	0.27	0.26	0.26
Moscow	1.08	1.17	1.13	0.39	0.54	0.47
Nagasaki	0.79	0.65	0.72	0.39	0.34	0.37
Nottingham	0.98	0.62	0.80	0.60	0.47	0.54

Source: Adapted from Jablensky *et al.* (1992) Schizophrenia: manifestation, incidence and course in different cultures, *Psychological Medicine*, monograph supplement 20.

develop schizophrenia). Further details of Nottingham and the other centres are given in Table 6.1.

☐ What do the data in Table 6.1 show?

■ Rates for males and females combined, using the broad definition, suggest that people are at the highest risk of developing schizophrenia in rural Chandigarh and at the lowest in Honolulu. The international differences are less marked for the narrow definition (in fact, they are only statistically significant for the broad definition). Far fewer people are diagnosed as schizophrenic under the narrow definition. Gender differences show a mixed pattern in different countries.

There are, then, some differences in rates between countries and between sexes, but more important is the impact of *definition* on numbers. This indicates how important it is to know the definition of schizophrenia being used before trying to compare or interpret data in schizophrenia research.

Schizophrenia in Britain

The low priority generally given to research in psychiatry is nowhere more evident than in the epidemiology of schizophrenia. Few large-scale studies have been conducted and methodological problems abound. The media frequently report that the lifetime risk of developing schizophrenia is 1 in 100. In fact it is slightly under

this and further translating this easily remembered statistic into meaningful prevalence estimates is beset with problems.

The OPCS (Office of Population Censuses and Surveys) carried out a series of surveys in 1993 and 1994 into psychiatric morbidity in Britain. The first report to be published (OPCS, 1995b) concerned 10 000 adults aged between 16 and 64 years, living in private households. Since the number of people diagnosed as having schizophrenia was small, people with this diagnosis were grouped together with people having other diagnoses of mental disorder, including *manic-depressive psychosis* and *schizo-affective disorder* (commonly termed *functional psychoses*). Together, this spectrum of related disorders had a yearly prevalence rate[7] of 4 per 1 000, with no difference between the sexes. Prevalence rates showed only small differences with age, but were highest in 30–34-year-old women and 55–64-year-old men.

Increased prevalence in men was associated with being widowed, being economically inactive (i.e. not seeking work) and living alone. Increased prevalence in women was associated with being divorced, unemployed (which includes those who are 'looking after the home or family') and being a lone parent. In both sexes, increased prevalence was associated with having educational qualifications of 'A' level or above, being in social

[7]In this study, prevalence was estimated during a *period* of a year (rather than a *point*, such as a day) because the prevalence of these disorders is so low. Period prevalence was discussed in Chapter 5.

class V, living in rented accommodation and living in a flat (which includes a room in a house or a bed-sit). Psychosis, along with most other disorders, was twice as prevalent in urban as in rural populations.

☐ Do these associations suggest that the factors identified by the OPCS *cause* psychoses?

■ No, an association does not prove causality. It is, of course, also possible that these factors are a *result* of mental illness.[8]

It is possible to trace changes in hospital admissions for schizophrenia over time in England by using Hospital Episode Statistics (HES), published annually by the Department of Health. The top section of Table 6.2 relates to the years 1988–93, and gives the annual number of 'ordinary admissions' to hospital of people diagnosed as having schizophrenia ('ordinary' means that the person was not detained compulsorily under the Mental Health Act), and (in thousands) the number of 'bed days' on which an ordinary-admission patient occupied a hospital bed. The middle section of Table 6.2 indicates how long people who were diagnosed with schizophrenia stayed in hospital in 1992–3. The bottom section of the Table shows the age distribution of those people.

☐ What do the data in Table 6.2 show?

■ Although the number of ordinary admissions remained fairly stable between 1988–9 and 1992–3, the number of bed days more than halved. The decline was extremely rapid at the beginning of the 1990s, falling by almost 14 million bed days in just two years. In 1992–3, about half (52 per cent) of hospital admissions were for 30 days or less, and the majority (61 per cent) were for people in younger (15–44) age-groups.

Additionally, of the total admissions in 1992–3, 60 per cent were males and 40 per cent were females. The shortening of bed stays reflects the impact of the care in the community policy in the 1990s (discussed later in this chapter), which encourages short stays in hospital before returning people to the community, or avoiding admission when possible.

[8]The difference between causal relationships and associations, and the issue of causal direction, are explored more fully in *Studying Health and Disease*, Chapters 5 and 8.

Table 6.2 NHS hospital use by people diagnosed with schizophrenia, England, various years between 1988 and 1993

Number of ordinary admissions, and bed days (thousands)

	1988–9	1989–90	1990–1	1991–2	1992–3
ordinary admissions	31 055	33 585	34 096	33 944	35 469
bed days (thousands)	23 068	24 291	17 691	10 458	10 674

Length of hospital stay, 1992–3

days in hospital	0–7	8–30	31–182	183–365	366+
per cent of patients (35 469 = 100%)	20	32	35	5	7

Admissions by patient's age, 1992–3

age/years	15–44	45–64	65–74	75+
per cent of patients (35 469 = 100%)	61	26	8	4

Source: Adapted from Department of Health, *Hospital Episode Statistics (HES)*, *1988–89*, Table 1, p. 13; *HES, 1989–90*, Table 1, p. 13; *HES, 1990–91*, Table 1, p. 13; *HES, 1991–92*, Table 1, p. 13; *HES, 1992–93*, Table 1, p. 13, Table 2, p. 39, Table 3.1, p. 46; all HMSO, London.

The difficulty of using such hospital activity statistics to draw conclusions about whether the incidence of schizophrenia is changing over time is illustrated by considering an apparently falling trend in first-admission rates for schizophrenia, reported in several studies from Western countries (Australia, England, New Zealand, Scotland). If true, this would have profound implications both for theories about the underlying causes of schizophrenia, and for the development and organisation of psychiatric services. There are, however, several methodological problems besetting such research which make it impossible to conclude that the incidence of schizophrenia is actually falling.

The major reason for uncertainty has already been discussed: changes in the diagnostic criteria for schizophrenia which have narrowed considerably over the last 20 years, making direct comparisons over time impossible. The second reason has to do with the recording of first admissions (typically used to determine incidence). For a variety of reasons a substantial and changing number of apparent first admissions are not true first admissions. For example, patients may receive a different diagnosis on first and subsequent admissions. Changes in admissions policy, including the use of hospitalisation generally, will also affect rates. If, for example, the average age of first admission to hospital rises, then first-admission rates will fall over time. It is therefore difficult to answer questions about trends in the rates of schizophrenia.

Cross-cultural diagnosis in the United Kingdom

Within multi-racial societies the influence of ethnicity on the diagnosis of schizophrenia has also been questioned. In the United Kingdom, African-Caribbean people have higher rates of psychosis than do the white population. The rate among African-Caribbeans born in the United Kingdom is even higher than for immigrants. Whether higher rates are found in other ethnic groups, for example the Asian population, is unresolved.

At this point, students of the Open University should read the article by Roland Littlewood, a psychiatrist, and Maurice Lipsedge, a consultant in psychological medicine, entitled 'Ethnic minorities and the psychiatrist', which appears in the Reader.[9] It was first published in 1982.

☐ What do Littlewood and Lipsedge suggest are the main reasons for over-diagnosis of severe psychiatric illness requiring hospitalisation among black people in the United Kingdom?

■ They emphasise cultural differences between doctor and patient, particularly where the doctor is white: the doctor may not understand the cultural relevance of the patient's experiences, or may discriminate against the patient in subtle ways, e.g. rejecting psychotherapy and out-patient treatment as unsuitable and prescribing anti-psychotic drugs and hospitalisation.

Although a misunderstanding of cultural beliefs and experiences may account for some of the increased rates of schizophrenia diagnosis in ethnic minorities, it does not account for all.

☐ What other explanations occur to you?

■ People from ethnic minorities are over-represented in lower social classes, and therefore

experience higher unemployment, poverty, poor housing and other forms of material deprivation;[10] together with the cumulative effects of living with racial discrimination, these factors may contribute to higher rates of schizophrenia.

Selective migration (the idea that people with a disposition to schizophrenia are more likely to migrate to countries such as the United Kingdom) has also been suggested as a possible contributory factor. Other reasons suggested include biological factors, such as obstetric complications and intra-uterine infections (which are also probably associated with lower social class), use of cannabis, and genetic factors.

A study in central Manchester by psychiatrist Philip Sugarman and geneticist David Craufurd (1994) assessed the role of genetic factors by studying the prevalence of schizophrenia among the relatives of patients from different ethnic groups. There was no significant difference between the lifetime risk of developing schizophrenia for parents of the African-Caribbean patients (8.9 per cent) and the white patients (8.4 per cent). The risk for siblings was, however, significantly different, with a risk for siblings of African-Caribbean patients of 15.9 per cent compared with 1.8 per cent for white siblings. Where African-Caribbean patients had been born in the United Kingdom, the risk in their siblings was even higher, at 27.3 per cent. These patterns support an environmental rather than a genetic explanation for ethnic differences in prevalence. The authors conclude:

> There is no evidence that genetic predisposition is any less important as an aetiological factor in black people than in the rest of the British population; nor do the results of the present study support the notion that schizophrenia is more common in the Afro-Caribbean community because of greater genetic vulnerability. (Sugarman and Craufurd, 1994, p. 479)

Environmental factors are clearly important, but their exact nature is uncertain.

☐ Consider the preceding discussion and the views of Littlewood and Lipsedge: sum up why there might be an over-representation of schizophrenia among people from ethnic minorities in the United Kingdom.

[9]*Health and Disease: A Reader* (second edition, 1995).

[10]See *World Health and Disease* (Open University Press, 1993), Chapter 9.

■ The cultural views of the majority will apply, and cultural differences may be lead to the labelling of behaviour that seems 'odd' as illness. The psychiatrist fits the patient's experience into that of Western medicine, which is compounded by the effects of indirect discrimination regarding treatment. If mental illness is related to material deprivation and hence to social class, since ethnic minorities are disproportionately represented in lower social classes, this will show itself in increased incidence of schizophrenia.

Epidemiologists who try to measure schizophrenia, then, are beset by many problems of definition. These arise for various reasons, notably the difficulties in agreeing stable diagnostic criteria that can be applied cross-culturally in an unbiased way, and the difficulties of interpreting trends in official statistics. Difficulties with diagnosis are also experienced by clinicians even when faced with a patient from the same culture and background as the doctor, and it is to clinical diagnosis that we now turn.

Schizophrenia: a clinical entity

Schizophrenia is both an individual experience and a defined clinical entity and, as such, can be understood as both an illness and a disease.[11] If we examine the concept historically we can say either that schizophrenia *itself* has changed or that the *description* of schizophrenia has changed: the two statements make different assumptions. In this section the way in which clinicians have attempted to describe schizophrenia as a disease will be outlined.

When the German psychiatrist Emile Kraepelin developed his classification of mental disorders at the end of the nineteenth century, he introduced the term *dementia praecox* to describe a severe, chronic, deteriorating condition (dementia) that started early in life (praecox). This concept of the disorder was redefined by the Swiss psychiatrist Eugen Bleuler in 1911 (translated 1950), who coined the term **schizophrenia** (from the Greek words for 'split mind' to signify a splitting off from reality). Bleuler altered Kraepelin's original description to reflect the observation that the outcome was not always negative, but the term has created the misleading public impression that people diagnosed as having schizophrenia switch between two 'personalities', one

apparently normal and the other violent. We return to the misrepresentation of schizophrenia in public opinion at the end of this chapter. Since Bleuler's time, the description of schizophrenia has undergone numerous revisions, and thus descriptions of the illness and research on it as a clinical entity must be put in an historical and geographical context.

Some people have taken the position that schizophrenia did not exist before industrialisation, claiming that schizophrenia is a modern illness caused by the pressures of modern living. This is, however, a rather extreme view. More likely schizophrenia did exist, as clear descriptions of psychoses exist in earlier centuries, but it could have been described differently and/or included in other conditions. Descriptions of the conditions that are now called catatonia and dementia, for example, have existed for much longer than these medical labels. It is not uncommon in other areas of medicine for apparently new diseases to emerge. For example, in the early 1980s, AIDS was diagnosed, apparently for the first time (as described in Chapter 4 of this book), but it had probably existed in Africa for decades as 'slim disease'.

There is clearly a necessity to describe a set of **core symptoms** which always indicate schizophrenia. Finding symptoms that are both necessary and sufficient to diagnose schizophrenia is no easy task.[12] Of importance today in diagnosing schizophrenia are two major classification systems, known as DSM IV and ICD–10. DSM IV is the *Diagnostic and Statistical Manual of Mental Disorders*, fourth revision (published by the American Psychiatric Association, 1994), and is the system developed in the USA. ICD–10 refers to the *International Classification of Diseases*, tenth revision, *Classification of Mental and Behavioural Disorders* (published by WHO, 1992), which is used more in Britain and elsewhere in Europe. For research purposes, however, DSM IV has proved to be more popular, although ICD–10 is intended to be used for cross-cultural work. Both systems describe schizophrenia as a disease in which aspects of the person's thinking, perception and personality become distorted, the central aspect of which is a distortion of reality. The person experiences difficulty in distinguishing between their internal subjective experiences and the external, 'real' or objective world, as their normal mental processes break down. ICD–10 describes this:

---

[11]The distinction between illness and disease was discussed in Chapter 1 of this book, and more extensively in *Medical Knowledge: Doubt and Certainty*, Chapter 2.

[12]Similar problems beset the diagnostic criteria for hysteria, as explained in *Medical Knowledge: Doubt and Certainty*, Chapter 6.

The disturbance involves the most basic functions that give the normal person a feeling of individuality, uniqueness and self-direction. (WHO, 1992, p. 86)

Disturbances of thought processes may involve individuals experiencing that their thoughts and feelings are known by others (*thought broadcast*), or that thoughts are put into or taken out of their mind without their control. This can give rise to explanatory delusions (e.g. supernatural forces at work) to make sense of what is going on. Disturbances of volition occur when the person experiences control (of thought, feeling or action) by some outside force—often expressed in statements such as 'I was made to …' Although **hallucinations** may occur in any of the senses, the most common are auditory hallucinations, often in the form of voices giving a running commentary on the person's behaviour or discussing the individual between themselves.

Persistent **delusions** may occur. A delusion is an unshakeable belief that is culturally inappropriate. It may be viewed as completely impossible, for example when a person describes him or herself as being controlled by rays from outer space, or more mundane and plausible, for example the mistaken belief in a partner's infidelity. The person may see him or herself as pivotal in all that is happening, and ordinary insignificant events have enormous personal meaning. Perceptual disturbances may make colours or sounds seem peculiarly vivid or altered in some way, and trivial features of objects, situations or concepts become more important than the whole. When peripheral and irrelevant features take over, the person's thinking looks to others to be vague, inconsistent, following a non-linear path (called *knight's move thinking*) and is generally obscure, resulting in incoherent or irrelevant speech. This can be compounded by the introduction of new words made up by the individual (*neologisms*), or even a new written language (Figure 6.1, *overleaf*). *Catatonic* behaviour, which includes bizarre movement disturbances, may be present. Inappropriate emotions may occur, for example laughing when sad or at serious moments. These make up the so-called **positive symptoms** of schizophrenia in that they add something by distorting normal experiences.

The **negative symptoms**, on the other hand, represent a *lack* of normal behaviour. They include apathy and lack of motivation which show themselves as loss of interest, aimlessness and what some family members may see as 'laziness'. Speech may be slow and lacking in content, and the individual becomes self-absorbed. The person may exhibit *emotional blunting* in that they no longer express the full range of human emotions. Not surprisingly all this can lead to social withdrawal and lowering of social performance. It is these negative symptoms, which are seen to alter the personality of the individual, which are possibly the most distressing for the person with the illness and their family and friends. Intellectual capacity is not affected, although performance may be, as a consequence of the behaviour described above and problems with concentration and memory.

A number of sub-types of schizophrenia have been described, of which the most common and best known is **paranoid schizophrenia**. The individual usually has one or more relatively stable, often paranoid, delusions, usually accompanied by auditory hallucinations and perceptual disturbances. In areas of life not affected by their delusion, individuals often continue to function normally. Common delusions are of persecution (anyone or everyone is out to get them—MI5, the CIA or the KGB, space aliens), exalted birth (Jesus, the Queen's child), special mission (to save the world, destroy certain groups of people), perception of bodily changes (part of their body is believed to be peculiarly formed, big or small) or jealousy. Their 'voices' usually threaten or give commands, and auditory hallucinations such as hearing whispering or laughing (at them) may occur. Other notable sub-types include *hebephrenic schizophrenia* in which disturbances of emotions are prominent, and *catatonic schizophrenia* which is characterised by psychomotor disturbances, often rigidity or immobility.

Schizophrenia need not follow a chronic or deteriorating course as was once believed inevitable. It varies from complete (or very nearly complete) recovery to a continuous illness, or the illness may involve episodic acute phases with a greater or lesser degree of deficit due to negative symptoms.

The description of schizophrenia as a clinical entity thus sets out to categorise a variety of behaviours as symptoms and to find in them some recognisable pattern, which can then be treated in a similar way to physical disorders. Once the core symptoms of schizophrenia have been defined, the question then arises whether it is both valid and reliable as a clinical entity. That there is no reliable relationship between a diagnosis of schizophrenia and any specific abnormality of brain structure or function or, come to that, any specific type of family functioning or dysfunctioning, makes many doubt its validity as a diagnosis. The clinical emphasis is on distinguishing symptoms from 'normal' experiences, but some people prefer to put such behaviours or experiences on a continuum from 'normal perception' to hallucinations.

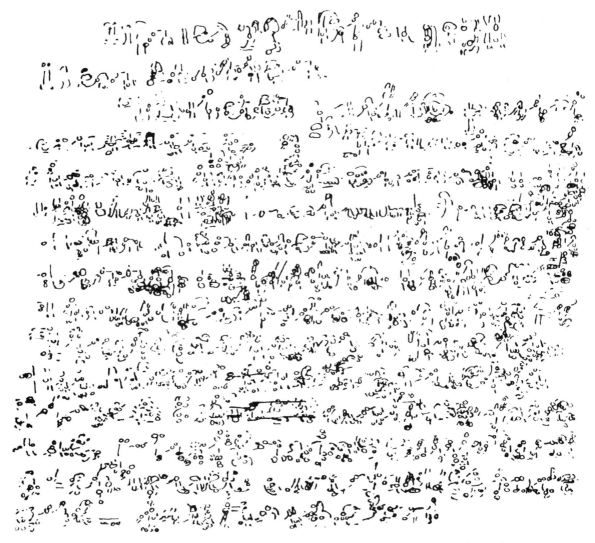

Figure 6.1 *Writing produced by a person diagnosed as having schizophrenia. (Source: Curran, D. and Partridge, M., 1969, Psychological Medicine, Churchill Livingstone)*

For example, what are otherwise 'schizophrenic symptoms' can be part of 'normal experience', albeit in abnormal situations. Being held hostage and deprivation of sleep, sensory stimuli, food or water are some of the circumstances in which people can experience schizophrenic-like symptoms, especially hallucinations and delusions.

Although there are persistent difficulties of definition and diagnosis, research continues from a variety of perspectives to try to explain what causes schizophrenia. These explanations are the subject of the next section.

Approaches to explaining schizophrenia

There are, across the world, thousands of researchers looking for the cause of schizophrenia. So far, although many theories have been proposed—the major contenders are discussed below—none explains everything about its aetiology. There are suggestions, hypotheses, 'facts' which seem to hold true for a while before being succeeded by new explanations and different 'facts'. People as diverse as geneticists and sociologists contribute their ideas. Other researchers look less for the cause, but concentrate on factors that seem to influence the course and outcome of the illness. Whatever the approach, care must be taken not to confuse statistical associations with evidence of causal connections.

The only point of general agreement at present is that there is no single cause, either of all schizophrenia or of schizophrenia in an individual, and that more research is needed.

Genetic approaches to explanation

The interest in the possible role of genes in schizophrenia has developed rapidly since the 1980s and caused considerable debate. Those who oppose a genetic view of mental illness point to the fact that the 'schizophrenic gene' has not yet been found. Proponents of the genetic explanation would argue that it may still exist; after all, Huntington's disease was recognised as a condition long before the defective gene associated with it was discovered. It is possible that several genes may interact in a multifactorial pathway, culminating in schizophrenia, which will be much more difficult to unravel than was the case for the classic 'single gene' disorders such as Huntington's disease.[13] It should already be obvious that the claims and counter-claims of protagonists and antagonists for genetic explanations can lead to circular arguments. How individuals see the evidence can depend on their views about broader debates concerning the relative influences of nature and nurture on human development.

Supporting the genetic theory is evidence that people who are close kin to someone diagnosed as having schizophrenia have a greater lifetime risk of developing the illness than the risk for the general population of just under 1 per cent. Risk estimates vary considerably between studies, but are higher for first degree relatives (brother, sister, child) than for more distant relatives, and higher still for identical twins or for a child where *both* parents have been diagnosed as having schizophrenia. Some studies put the risk for a person whose identical twin has schizophrenia as high as 50 per cent, but as research methodologies improve and become more rigorous, studies replicating this work show that the risk may be less than previously described. The problem of accurate diagnosis is particularly awkward for genetic linkage studies involving pedigree analysis

(of 'family trees'). Relatives of people diagnosed as having schizophrenia are at higher risk for a number of disorders similar to schizophrenia; the counting of these so-called *spectrum disorders* as schizophrenia may have increased the likelihood of researchers finding an apparent genetic linkage in these studies (Levinson and Mowry, 1991).

☐ Where else in this chapter have you seen the effect of broadening the definition of schizophrenia?

■ Table 6.1 (p. 119) showed that a broad definition (which includes spectrum disorders) can dramatically increase estimates of the prevalence of schizophrenia.

Other evidence supporting genetic explanations is the finding that adopted children have a risk of developing schizophrenia that correlates with the prevalence in their biological family of origin, rather than in their adoptive family. It is also argued, from clinical observation, that where siblings develop schizophrenia they do so at the same *age*, rather than at the same time, suggesting that innate developmental factors are operating. Additionally, it has been suggested that rather than there being a genetic *cause* of schizophrenia, there is a genetic *predisposition* to develop schizophrenia which is triggered by environmental factors.

Biomedical approaches to explanation

Possibly the best known biological explanation for schizophrenia focuses on the neurotransmitter **dopamine** and its possible overactivity in the brains of people diagnosed as having schizophrenia.[14] This theory arose because prolonged use of a dopamine derivative to treat people with Parkinson's disease produced symptoms akin to schizophrenia in some patients. Moreover, drugs that block dopamine reduce symptoms in most people with schizophrenia. However, the theory ignored the possibility that the artificial blocking of dopamine could cause the dopamine system to overcompensate by producing more dopamine and increasing the sensitivity of receptors. As a way of developing an hypothesis it is as sensible as suggesting that, because a headache can be relieved by aspirin, it is the lack of aspirin that causes the headache.

---

[13]Single-gene and multifactorial disorders are discussed in *Human Biology and Health: An Evolutionary Approach*, Chapters 4 and 9.

[14]Neurotransmitters are discussed further in *Human Biology and Health: An Evolutionary Approach*, Chapter 3.

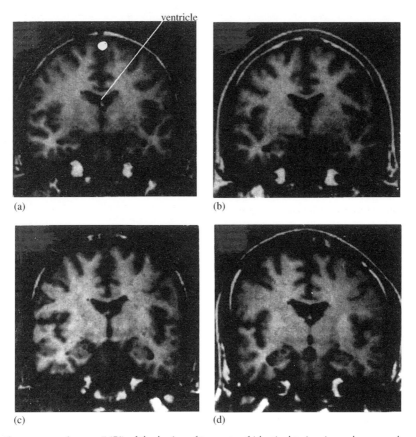

Figure 6.2 *Magnetic resonance images (MRI) of the brains of two sets of identical twins. In each case only one twin has a diagnosis of schizophrenia. The ventricles at the centre of the brain in the affected twins (b) and (d) are larger than those in the unaffected twins (a) and (c). (Source: Suddath, R. L. et al., 1990, Anatomical abnormalities in the brains of monozygotic twins discordant for schizophrenia, New England Journal of Medicine, **322**, p. 791)*

Over the last 15 years there has been major interest in the use of *imaging techniques* (principally computed tomography or CT scans, and magnetic resonance imaging, MRI[15]) to look at living, and thus functioning, brains. Previously the only way of examining the brain was at post-mortem. There is a body of evidence to show that a substantial number of people diagnosed as having schizophrenia, who are highly selected to meet research criteria, have abnormalities in the structure of their brains. There is an enlargement of the ventricles (fluid-filled cavities) at the centre of the brain (see Figure 6.2), with a corresponding decrease in the volume of nerve cells in the temporal lobes at the sides of the brain

[15]Imaging techniques in biomedical research and clinical diagnosis (including CT and MRI) are discussed further in *Studying Health and Disease,* Chapter 9.

(beneath the temples). The brains of some people diagnosed as having schizophrenia are less symmetrical than the brains of people without schizophrenia.

Taken together, these anatomical differences suggest an arrested development in the areas of the brain that are responsible for higher functioning, including verbal and non-verbal communication, social relationships, and monitoring and interpreting the environment. There is debate over when such brain abnormalities arise. Since some (but not all) of the patients have been on neuroleptic (anti-psychotic) drugs, it has been suggested that the brain changes may be due to their medication, but there is no evidence to support this. Other researchers have put forward the hypothesis that schizophrenia is a developmental problem, with brain abnormalities present at or before birth, and that it is the maturation of the brain at adolescence that triggers the psychotic symptoms.

Obstetric complications and birth trauma may also result in subtle brain damage from, for example, oxygen deprivation. An analysis of the British Perinatal Mortality survey data, by psychiatrists led by Professor Eve Johnstone, has indicated that people diagnosed as having schizophrenia are more likely to have a history of birth complications than expected from population data (Done *et al.*, 1991). An American study by Fuller Torrey and colleagues has shown that people diagnosed as having schizophrenia are also more likely than expected to be born in the winter months, and this has been linked with maternal exposure to influenza (Torrey *et al.*, 1993). Not all studies support these two sets of findings, but improvements in methodology and increasingly sophisticated research techniques may clarify the position.

Other biological theories that have been put forward in recent years include schizophrenia as a virus infection, an allergy and a vitamin deficiency. Lack of methodological rigor and replication bedevil these studies and there is currently little support for them.

Interpersonal and environmental approaches to explanation

Psychodynamic explanations for schizophrenia are focused on the upbringing of the child, as recollected by adults, rather than by direct observation of the parent–child relationship. The person most closely associated with this approach is the psychoanalyst Frieda Fromm-Reichmann who coined the term 'schizophrenogenic mother' (1948). The relationship between mother and child was seen as the heart of the problem, the mother usually being described as cold, hostile and rejecting. Attempts at explaining schizophrenia from this perspective led to a series of theories about the role of the family.

Thus, the 1950s and 1960s saw an upsurge of interest in the relationship between schizophrenia and family environment. Most of the research originated in the USA, of which the best known is that of the British-born anthropologist Gregory Bateson and his colleagues (Bateson *et al.*, 1956), who developed the theory of **double-bind relationships**. Schizophrenia was seen as developing because the child was put in a 'double bind', i.e. an intolerable situation of being given conflicting messages by a parent, so that whatever the child did would be wrong. This and other theories altered the description of schizophrenia, moving it away from being a 'disease', to a response by an individual to an intolerable or pathological environment. It had become a disorder of family communication and roles.

☐ The major and most common criticism of this body of work concerns cause and effect. How might these be confused?

■ Even if families of people diagnosed as having schizophrenia are different from other families, is this the cause of the illness or a result of living with someone who has schizophrenia? It may also be that the person diagnosed as having schizophrenia shows a number of behaviours seen by the family as 'odd' *before* the advent of the first acute episode, and so the child has been treated differently.

Anecdotally many parents report that the child who has been diagnosed as having schizophrenia was always 'different' or 'more difficult' when compared with siblings. Additionally, early family studies tended to concentrate on the mother to the exclusion of other relationships. Although most of the later theories include the role of the father, few address the issue of why 'this child' rather than another in the family should develop schizophrenia.

The psychodynamic and social-relationship approaches to explaining schizophrenia have been vaunted as being more concerned with the patient as a person than is the case with biomedical explanations. They have, however, had devastating consequences for a different group of people, namely the families of people with schizophrenia. Parents were blamed for causing their child's illness. Although some therapists tried to engage the family in therapy, in others the 'patient' was encouraged to loosen contact with the family. In some cases, visiting the patient in hospital was forbidden. A review by psychologist Jacqueline Atkinson (the author of this chapter) and Denise Coia, a psychiatrist (1995), revealed that there are still families who are deeply suspicious of professionals because of the way they were blamed for causing the illness, and there are professionals who are left with a lingering sense of unease about families and who thus dismiss them and their concerns.

The mid-1970s heralded what could be described as a minor revolution with respect to families and their relationship with schizophrenia. Two British researchers, Julian Leff, a psychiatrist, and Christine Vaughn, a clinical psychologist, decided to look at the way the expression of emotions in families affected the development of schizophrenia (Vaughn and Leff, 1976a, b). They developed the concept of **expressed emotion (EE)**—a measure of the emotional atmosphere in a family—and focused on two aspects: *critical comments* and *emotional over-involvement*, which includes over-protectiveness.

Assessing EE involves both the content of speech and non-verbal aspects. Thus, from examples given by Leff and Vaughn (1985), 'I wish he could hold down a job—any job would do' would not be rated as a critical comment unless a critical tone was also present. There must be a clear and unambiguous statement by the relative of dislike, disapproval or resentment of the behaviour of the person with schizophrenia or some characteristic, as in 'When I see her sitting all day long, it aggravates me. I figure she's decaying. And I don't like it.' Rejecting comments would include statements such as 'I washed my hands of her'. Over-involvement is detected by both the reported behaviour of the relative and their behaviour at interview. It includes exaggerated emotional responses, self-sacrificing and devoted behaviour, and extremely over-protective behaviour. A very clear version is given in this exchange:

> In response to the question 'Would you like her to have a boyfriend?' the mother replied, 'She's not interested in marriage, no. I don't really want her to marry, I would miss her. Anyway, marriages aren't very happy, are they? No, I'm happy to have her home; she would never listen to anybody else if not me.' (Leff and Vaughn, 1985, p. 55)

High levels of expressed emotion seem to contribute to increased relapse rates in people diagnosed as having schizophrenia, particularly when face-to-face contact in the family is high (more than 35 hours per week) and the person does not take medication. Interventions to reduce relapse have thus focused on all three aspects (EE, contact time and medication), although more attention has been paid to developing family interventions to reduce EE in relatives than to reduce contact. High expressed emotion is believed to be related to increased relapse through raising the stress levels to which the person diagnosed as having schizophrenia is exposed. Some studies measuring physiological arousal have also demonstrated this association.

Expressed emotion has been a very popular and powerful concept, particularly in Britain, but it is worth noting that not all families of a schizophrenic person show high EE, so interventions to reduce it are not universally applicable. Research has suggested that EE is not a stable trait, but that it fluctuates in families over time, and thus a measure of EE is only ever a 'snapshot' of the family. There is no clear evidence as to factors that influence changes in EE, and studies of fluctuations over time generally report a subsequent *decrease* in EE where high EE was initially recorded. These findings, combined with some

critics' perception of EE as a harking back to 'blaming the family', have led to suggestions that professionals should talk about high EE *settings* or environments and not high EE *families*. Recent research considering EE levels among staff and patients in residential settings echoes this point; high EE is not confined to relatives.

> ☐ Earlier you saw theories criticised on the grounds that they failed to disentangle cause and effect. How could this be applied to the work on EE?

> ■ As with other theories of family relationships, it is unclear whether high EE predates the development of schizophrenia or is a response to it. (This question has not been resolved, although reducing EE reduces relapse.)

Other explanations in this vein focus on the individual's social and physical environment, suggesting that the development of schizophrenia is related to the role of these factors in raising levels of stress. However, a recent review of the role of **life events**[16] in influencing schizophrenia, by psychiatrists Ross Norman and Ashak Malla in Canada (1993a, b), concludes that people with schizophrenia do *not* have higher levels of life events than people with other psychiatric disorders, and only minimally higher stressors than the general population. This suggests that life events are not a primary *cause* of schizophrenia. There is evidence, however, that life events are correlated with changes in symptoms over time among people who have already been diagnosed as having schizophrenia.

It is commonly believed that urban living is stressful and therefore more mental illness is found in cities. There might be several reasons why this should be so. On the one hand, environmental factors could directly cause schizophrenia: the disintegration of community structures could strengthen the tendency towards social isolation of the person with schizophrenia. On the other hand, it has been proposed that schizophrenia causes the individual to 'drift' into inner city areas where there is cheap bed-sit accommodation and a collection of other marginalised individuals amongst whom the person with schizophrenia is not stigmatised.[17]

---

[16]The impact on mental health of life events such as births, deaths and marriages, change of job or house, sudden major loss or other trauma, etc. are discussed briefly in *Studying Health and Disease*, Chapter 5.

[17]Social selection theories, of which this is an example, are discussed in more detail in *World Health and Disease*, Chapter 10.

An integrated approach to explanation

None of the individual theories reviewed so far is free of problems. As a consequence, an *integrated* approach has developed, which recognises the potential contributions of all these factors as well as their potential limitations. This has resulted in a **vulnerability model** of schizophrenia. Vulnerability to schizophrenia is conceived as a relatively permanent trait in the individual, almost certainly biological in origin. For schizophrenia to become manifest, however, levels of environmental stress are required to reach the threshold of each individual's level of vulnerability in order to trigger an episode. Thus, episodes of schizophrenia are temporary states when symptoms recur and are interspersed with periods of remission. Remission may be more or less complete; or negative symptoms may continue most of the time with episodes being more an exacerbation of positive symptoms.

This model is important for two reasons. First, it is a genuine attempt to unify biological and environmental factors in explaining schizophrenia. Second, it has encouraged health professionals to concentrate on factors that contribute to *relapse* rather than the traditional focus on the underlying *causes* of the condition. These are important developments with implications for clinical practice, redirecting activity towards finding interventions to prevent relapse, or initial episodes. This opens the way for more psycho-social interventions in schizophrenia and for seeing the treatment of schizophrenia as something other than the preserve of psychiatrists through medication. Biological vulnerability remains, however, a theoretical construct with no way (as yet) of measuring it directly.

Schizophrenia: a social and political entity

Although the approaches to explanation described above differ dramatically in their conceptualisation of schizophrenia, they do (by and large) agree that schizophrenia is at least a problem worthy of *medical* attention, even if not a true physical illness. Not everyone would agree with this. The 1960s and 1970s saw the rise of the **anti-psychiatry movement**, which denied the very existence of mental illness. In reality there were two distinct strands to this movement, linked only by a rejection of the medical model of psychiatry and treatment by drugs. The two people who are best known in this area (although both had strong objections to the 'anti-psychiatry' label) are Thomas Szasz, an American professor of psychiatry, and the late R. D. (Ronnie) Laing, a Glaswegian psychiatrist who became a cult figure in the 1970s.

Through a number of books, Szasz has systematically denied the existence of both neurotic and psychotic illness as disease states in the sense that measles or cancer are diseases. He argues that if there is no physical trauma or lesion, there is no physical illness or need for medical involvement. Szasz (1979) also believes that there are ethical and political questions to be answered in describing schizophrenia as either illness or disease. He questions whether the psychiatrist has the right to diagnose and treat someone who has not asked for it, and he also questions whether a diagnosis is an invasion of privacy. He sees the psychiatrist as relabelling the person's 'intimate personal possessions, such as their dreams and their opinions', in such a way that the person is redefined as a 'schizophrenic patient'.

Szasz is not opposed to what might be described as 'psychiatry between consenting adults', where there is clear freedom of choice to enter therapeutic relationships. Such relationships should be 'like ordinary contracts' of the type a person might have with an architect. What both parties agree is lawful, what one party rejects is unlawful. Thus 'treating' patients against their will, or even using everyday coercion, is unlawful. Szasz does not, however, suggest that anti-social behaviour is ignored or excused, but says that society already has other ways of dealing with this, through ethics, legal systems and politics.

If schizophrenia is not a disease, what is it? Szasz argues that behaviour labelled schizophrenic is merely anti-social behaviour, 'misbehaviour' or other unusual behaviour which society (or the individual) doesn't like or doesn't understand and then finds easier to deal with by labelling it as illness. If it is so labelled, people who display anti-social behaviour can be treated (involuntarily if necessary), constrained and controlled, and the medical label can stay with them all their lives. Szasz suggests that the 'psychotic and psychiatrist, are locked in an embrace of mutual coercion, confusion, and confirmation' (Szasz, 1979, p. 197).

Szasz seeks other, more 'everyday' explanations for behaviour defined as symptoms of mental illness. He prefers to describe 'thought disorder' as 'crazy talk' (1993), and then suggests that this is no different to the phenomenon of 'speaking in tongues', sometimes experienced in religious fervour. This interpretation is rejected by psychologists Richard Bentall and David Pilgrim (1993) who, although disputing schizophrenia as a discrete disease entity, point to a continuum of behaviour with psychotic symptoms lying at one extreme. They focus on the unintelligibility of such behaviour, and suggest that whether or not the negative valuing of some behaviour as 'illness' is appropriate, it should not stop attempts to understand it. The psychiatrist Julian Leff (1993) points out the inherent differences between speaking in tongues and the type of speech produced in schizophrenic disorder. The former are strings of sound which are not recognisable as language, the latter are recognisable words but in an order with no recognisable meaning. The former usually lasts a matter of minutes, possibly hours, whereas schizophrenic speech can last days, months, occasionally years. All three researchers are concerned that Szasz's views lead to the ignoring of human distress:

> ... Szasz's attempt to neatly mark off the manifestations of 'physical' and 'mental' illness is seriously misleading, mainly because it fails to provide a basis for helping people whose distress, however it is caused, might be relieved by physical or psychological interventions. (Bentall and Pilgrim, 1993, p. 75)

> Szasz's arguments ... are inhumane, since they deny the possibility of help for a condition which claims the life of one in ten sufferers. (Leff, 1993, p. 78)

If Szasz seeks to demolish 'the sacred symbol of psychiatry', Laing added to the mystique of schizophrenia. His early work, *The Divided Self* (1960), describes schizophrenia as a special strategy that a person invents in order to live in an unliveable situation, namely the family and a demand to be something other than oneself. Schizophrenia is then described not as a psychological problem of *intra*-personal functioning, but as a problem of *inter*-personal relationships. Up to this point, Laing is not too far removed from some of the family relationship theorists (such as Bateson) described earlier. But he then moves away from psychiatry altogether and declares schizophrenia to be 'a *political event*' (1967). He differs from Szasz in that, rather than labelling certain behaviours to be a problem for society, he labels society itself as being the problem. To Laing, schizophrenia is no longer a *breakdown* of a functioning person, but a *breakthrough* to a new, and more positive, state. If society is evil, then the mad are virtuous; if society is restrictive and coercive, then the insane are seeking new ways to experience reality and may have new insights to offer the rest of us.

There is a contradiction in Laing's views on the 'treatment' of people diagnosed as having schizophrenia. Szasz's position is that if there is no mental illness there is nothing to treat. Laing's 'otherness' of schizophrenia nevertheless requires 'something', if not to treat it, then to allow it full expression. In 1965, Laing helped to found the Philadelphia Association, its first action being to open Kingsley Hall as residential accommodation for people diagnosed as having schizophrenia, which allowed them to 'work through' their illness in their own way. Despite the claim that there were no differences between staff and patients this was not quite the case. When Mary Barnes, the most famous resident and advocate of Kingsley Hall, recounted her 'journey through madness' (an extract appeared earlier in this chapter), she clearly identified both her co-author as her psychiatrist and the pivotal role played by Laing (Barnes and Berke, 1971). The differences in lifestyle, status and responsibility between patient and staff are clear.

Both Laing and Szasz's views highlight the difficulty in abandoning the 'schizophrenia as illness' model. If people diagnosed as having schizophrenia are not 'ill', how are they to be treated? If they are no different from everybody else then there is no need to plead mitigating circumstances or lack of responsibility. They can be sent to prison for committing unlawful acts in the same way as other criminals. How, though, to deal with behaviour which is troublesome to others (anti-social), but not sufficient to break the law or warrant a custodial sentence? If they don't work should they be subject to the same rules and regulations as other unemployed people? Whether treated by psychiatry or abandoned as 'not ill', such people will tend to be marginalised by society, both socially and economically.

In Italy in 1978, a group of psychiatrists from the far left, supported by the Communist Party, forced the government to repeal the Mental Health Laws and to stop any more admissions to mental hospitals. This was a neo-Marxist response to what was seen as the marginalisation of psychiatric patients (amongst others) by capitalist society. (A full account is given by Michael Donnelly, 1992.) The problems of re-integrating such patients into society when sufficient community resources are not provided is echoed by many of the difficulties in the development of community care in the United Kingdom.

Community care

The formal introduction of community care by the *NHS and Community Care Act*, 1990 (enacted April 1993) was the logical outcome of a movement which had been under way since the 1960s.[18] The result has been that most hospital treatment for schizophrenia is now for episodes when the patient is very acutely ill, and in-patient stays are usually between six and twelve weeks. A small minority of patients require longer-term hospital care and an even smaller number will be detained involuntarily under a section of the Mental Health Act. The local authority has leading responsibility for community care, but in practice the lead agency can be either social services or the health authority, depending on the area, and is responsible for purchasing services from both the statutory and voluntary sectors.

As a result, self-help organisations such as the National Schizophrenia Fellowship (NSF) and MIND have also become service providers. A variety of new services are offered, including drop-in centres, employment projects, support for carers, telephone help-lines, as well as traditional day centres and accommodation projects. The need for social and recreational facilities has been recognised, along with the more traditional 'therapeutic' services. Voluntary organisations are often able to provide innovative services responding directly to users' needs and normally have user or carer representatives on the board of management. Moving into service provision has, however, meant that the nature of the organisations is changing from small self-help groups relying on mutual support to multi-million pound businesses (Atkinson and Coia, 1995). But the policy of community care has enabled carers' organisations, such as the NSF in Britain and the *National Alliance of the Mentally Ill (NAMI)* in the USA, to reiterate their demands to be taken seriously as primary carers and to demand services.

Although most people probably accept that treating patients in the community is more appropriate than long-stay institutionalisation, there is concern that some people fall through the gaps in the various service provisions and there may be a need for some kind of safety net. The media highlight the problems of community care: people who cannot get the services or treatment they need, people who end up homeless, and people who perpetrate acts of violence on others. Probably the best known case is that of Jonathan Zito who was stabbed to death on the London Underground in December 1992 by Christopher Clunis, who was suffering from schizophrenia. Zito's wife, Jayne, has kept the names of both men, and the problems inherent in community care, in

the public eye through her campaigning work and the formation of the *Zito Trust*, which was set up in July 1994 with the aim of supporting people like her, whose lives have been affected by the failure of community care to prevent acts of violence by mentally-ill people.

When Ben Silcock went into the lion's den at London Zoo on 31 December 1992, the presence of a family with a video camera raised a personal tragedy to a media event. What was a gift for cartoonists became a trigger for Virginia Bottomley, then Secretary of State for Health, to suggest that the Mental Health Act needed to be reviewed and provision made for some form of community treatment or supervision order. Amid controversy, *supervision registers* were introduced in England in 1994. *The Mental Health (Patients in the Community) Act 1995*, to be enacted in 1996, introduces community supervision and community care orders, although it does not attempt to make treatment in the community compulsory.

This development has provoked criticism from both sides: there are those who say community supervision without compulsory treatment will not be successful, because it makes no provision for people who do not comply with their treatment; others view close supervision as an infringement of civil liberties. All agree, however, that it adds little to current guidelines which, if sufficiently resourced and implemented, would make the new proposals unnecessary. The new proposals, while emphasising the needs of the most-severely ill and targeting resources on them, do not supply any additional money, and there is concern that the less-severely ill people will be neglected. Issues of confidentiality are rife. Who is entitled to know who is on a register? What are the implications for the individual regarding issues such as insurance and travel visas? Are psychiatrists more likely to be sued if a patient on a register commits a violent act? Some also argue that there is no proper procedure for appeal against inclusion on a register.

Concern for the welfare of people with mental illness who end up homeless, or even in a lion's cage, is overlaid with a fear for public safety. The controversial question is whether there is a need for legislation to supervise and control people with mental illness living in the community. Mental health legislation has been described as both paternalistic and authoritarian, playing on both compassion and fear as it seeks to constrain those who are at risk to themselves (through self-harm or severe self-neglect) as well as to others. The benefits to society are weighed against the harm to the individual. Current law allows for people to be admitted to hospital involuntarily. Should something be done to constrain such people in the community?

---

[18]The history of community care policies in the United Kingdom is discussed in *Dilemmas in Health Care,* Chapter 8.

Prediction of being a danger (to self or others) is unreliable, the best predictor being previous dangerous behaviour. In a recent retrospective survey by Elizabeth King (1994) of 17 men diagnosed as having schizophrenia who committed suicide, only four had given any warning of their intention. People diagnosed as having schizophrenia are much more likely to harm themselves than others. A review by Caldwell and Gottesman (1990) suggests that between 10–13 per cent of such people kill themselves and that suicide is the most common cause of premature death in this group.

There are no data showing the percentage of people diagnosed as having schizophrenia who commit murder, but the statistics indicate that the numbers do not reach those for suicide. The *Confidential Inquiry into Homicides and Suicides by Mentally Ill People* (Steering Committee, 1994) was funded by the Department of Health and set up by Stephen Dorrell, then Parliamentary Under Secretary for State. William Boyd, a psychiatrist, was appointed its Director. Its preliminary report observes that only 34 per cent of mentally ill people who committed murder had been in contact with the psychiatric services in the previous 12 months. In an 18-month period, 100 cases of murder by mentally ill people were identified. Of the 75 for whom a diagnosis was available, 27 (36 per cent) had a diagnosis of schizophrenia and a further 20 (27 per cent) had a diagnosis of either paranoid psychosis or psychosis. For a variety of reasons only 22 cases could be investigated further: of these, two murders were of strangers and 13 were of family members.

Treating schizophrenia

If diagnosing schizophrenia is controversial, then treating it is equally so, and it is important to separate reality from myth and from the past. For many people, psychiatric treatment is summed up by the film *One Flew Over the Cuckoo's Nest*, which includes heavy and forced medication, the use of surgery to affect psychological states (*psychosurgery*), controlling, insensitive or brutal staff, locked wards and long periods of hospitalisation. Although it might be a very powerful indictment of the worst of psychiatric treatment, the book by Ken Kesey on which the film was based was published in 1962 and relates to the psychiatric hospitals of the 1950s. The buildings may have remained the same, but many of the procedures and management strategies have since changed.

Psychosurgery is now extremely rare: in the United Kingdom it requires more than one medical opinion and cannot be performed without the patient's consent, even if he or she is an involuntary patient detained under the Mental Health Act. It is used mainly for severe, intractable depression and obsessive compulsive disorders. *Electroconvulsive therapy* (*ECT*) is infrequently used for people diagnosed as having schizophrenia, and then only for severe depressive symptoms or catatonic states. This is not to say that there are no longer, and never will be, any unpleasant staff or involuntary medication, but it is not the norm. Nor is it the norm for most patients with schizophrenia to be kept in hospital for long periods of time, nor in locked wards.

Medication is the primary source of treatment for people diagnosed as having schizophrenia and, for most patients, forms the foundation of the treatment plan on which other interventions are built. Although important, drugs are rarely successful alone; other interventions are equally useful and will be discussed in what follows.

Medication

The 1950s saw a revolution in the treatment of schizophrenia with the introduction of the *neuroleptic* (or anti-psychotic) *drugs* (for example, chlorpromazine or Largactil). These drugs form a diverse group of chemical compounds, but are normally grouped together because of their clinical effect. They are used with all types of psychosis, not just schizophrenia. The typical neuroleptics block dopamine neurotransmission which, as you saw earlier, is part of the evidence for the dopamine hypothesis of the aetiology of schizophrenia. They are used to treat the *positive* symptoms of schizophrenia (see earlier), but do not affect the *negative* symptoms and are not curative. They bring about a marked decrease in acute symptoms in 60–70 per cent of patients, and often a shorter period of chronic symptoms. The long-term course and outcome of schizophrenia is probably improved when treated by *maintenance* neuroleptics (designed to maintain patients in a reasonable state of mental health), but there remain some questions about this. Patients who have a slow onset of illness show less improvement.

The neuroleptics have harmful side-effects. These include unwanted, involuntary movements and twitches (mimicking Parkinson's disease), particularly of the mouth and tongue, and a 'restlessness' which is muscular in origin rather than psychological. *Dysphoria* is a distressing subjective state common among people on neuroleptics, who describe themselves as being generally 'ill-at-ease'. Some of these effects are irreversible.

The harmful effects of neuroleptics can generally be managed by giving the lowest appropriate dose of the drug, together with anti-Parkinsonian medication. However, the impact of the harmful side-effects of these drugs on some patients should not be underestimated and this contributes to reluctance to take them. Other reasons for refusing them include an unwillingness or inability to accept the illness or a general dislike of continued medication. Most patients who take neuroleptics do so for long periods to help prevent recurrences of the illness and to manage 'florid symptoms' (symptoms that are particularly visible).

Compliance with instructions to take medication can be low in schizophrenia, but this is also true of other long-term conditions and some acute illnesses as well. The reluctance of many people to finish a prescribed course of antibiotics because they are 'feeling better' is well known.

Following the introduction of the neuroleptics, the next stage of the revolution in drug therapy for schizophrenia was the introduction in the late 1960s of the long-acting *depot phenothiazines* (for example, fluphenazine decanoate or Modecate). These slow-release drugs are given by injection every two to four weeks, usually by a community psychiatric nurse, either at an out-patient clinic or at the patient's home. Although some patients are grateful not to have to remember to take their medication, others have seen the depot medications as depriving them of responsibility and choice.

During the 1980s, a new generation of drugs was introduced—the so-called *atypical anti-psychotic drugs*, sometimes also called 'novel', because they are chemically unlike the previous anti-psychotic drugs. Their definition is vague, they come from a number of different pharmacological groups and many are still under development. Clozapine (Clozaril) is the first of these to be used widely, particularly for people diagnosed with chronic schizophrenia who are 'drug resistant' (i.e. have not responded to other anti-psychotic medications). It underwent trials in Europe in the mid-1970s, but was withdrawn in the USA (it had never been available in the United Kingdom) when several patients developed a potentially-fatal blood condition (agranulocytosis). However, a double-blind trial[19] in the 1980s (Kane *et al.*, 1988) demonstrated its superiority over chlorpromazine

for 'drug resistant' patients, and it was reintroduced in the USA and licensed in the United Kingdom. However, it is restricted to patients who do not respond to other types of medication and is only given under close supervision.

The atypical anti-psychotic drugs have fewer harmful effects than the older neuroleptics (for example, they do not produce *dysphoria*), and they have some beneficial effects on the *negative* symptoms of schizophrenia, unlike the older drugs.

Current drugs, then, have great potential in the control of symptoms of schizophrenia, but also have a number of drawbacks. Compliance is often poor, the effects are inconsistent and a substantial group of patients derive little benefit from medication or believe the harmful effects outweigh the potential benefits. The neurological and psychological aspects of these drug side-effects may make rehabilitation more difficult and may, indeed, be the very signs that mark someone out as being 'a psychiatric patient'. Despite the problem of agranulocytosis with clozapine, the fact that many otherwise 'drug resistant' patients respond positively to it means that the new atypical anti-psychotics do hold out some hope for improvements in drug therapy.

Psycho-social interventions

As you have seen, drug therapy is aimed predominantly at the *positive* symptoms of schizophrenia. Although positive symptoms are distressing and incapacitating, it is often the more chronic *negative* symptoms that are most handicapping and disabling in terms of people enjoying a reasonable quality of life. Most **psycho-social interventions** are thus aimed at preventing deterioration and teaching empowering strategies such as new skills to manage the illness or aid daily living and rehabilitation—both social and vocational—and restoring skills lost through illness. Many of these interventions come under the general heading of **behavioural programmes**.

Behavioural programmes directed at improving social skills have expanded considerably from the early 1970s, and now encompass a wide repertoire of interventions and outcomes. They tend to have names such as 'training in community living' or 'survival skills workshops'. Many are unstructured, but the most successful are tailored to the special needs of their members and use specific behavioural techniques, such as those developed by Robert Liberman, a Californian-based psychiatrist.

Liberman has probably done the most to develop what is now generally termed 'skills training' for severely mentally-ill people. He advocates a *modular* approach:

---

[19]Double-blind trials to establish the efficacy of new drugs compared with existing treatments are discussed in *Studying Health and Disease*, Chapter 8.

each module is divided into a number of skills areas, and the same methods of instruction are used in each module. These include the use of manuals, video-assisted modelling, role-playing and rehearsal, problem-solving and exercises in 'real-life' situations. Since people with schizophrenia are believed to have cognitive dysfunctions that interfere with learning, there is an emphasis on repetition and 'over-learning' (i.e. learning beyond the level at which knowledge or skills will be applied, to allow for some 'fall back' of performance). Modules in Liberman's latest programme include Medication Management, Symptom Management, Recreation for Leisure, and Grooming and Hygiene. Liberman contends that strict adherence to the full programme is necessary for patients to show improvements and generalisation of skills to new situations. To this end a training programme for trainers has been provided (Liberman *et al.*, 1993).

Other types of psycho-social interventions include various group therapies, stress management, problem solving and specific behavioural and cognitive techniques to manage particular problems or symptoms, for example, auditory hallucinations. Empowerment is a key goal.

Running in parallel with, or as part of, many of these interventions are **educational programmes**, which give people information about their illness and its management. This is very often a central part of programmes aimed at getting patients to comply with their medication. Programmes vary in the balance they achieve between 'coercing' participants into becoming 'better patients', and giving the necessary information to enable participants to exercise informed choice and greater responsibility in the management of their condition.

An educational approach can simply mean giving people (carers as well as people diagnosed as having schizophrenia) information about schizophrenia, often relating this to coping strategies or medication compliance. It can also be used in a much wider sense whereby an 'educational approach' is contrasted with a 'therapeutic approach'. The educational approach looks at 'skill deficit' and people previously defined as 'patients' or 'clients' become students, learners or participants; 'therapists' become teachers, tutors or group leaders. In an effort to promote the 'student' image, manuals or workbooks are often used. **Psycho-education**, it has been suggested, expands these educational approaches to include social and psychological support and possibly counselling (Atkinson and Coia, 1995).

Although the majority of psycho-social interventions show positive outcomes for participants, these can be fairly short-lived unless some form of ongoing intervention or support is provided. For many patients, learning daily living and social skills is not a one-off, all-or-nothing intervention, but something that requires continued support and encouragement to use, if they are not to be overtaken by negative symptoms again. Many programmes report a variety of unexpected benefits which were not formally assessed: these include participants becoming generally more assertive, responsive and responsible as the groups progress. This may be due as much to the style of the intervention as the skills being taught. Changes in the behaviour and attitudes of therapists are often observed, or reported by the therapists, and these allow patients to take more initiative themselves.

Although the results of these interventions are encouraging, only a minority of people diagnosed as having chronic schizophrenia are involved in such programmes. This leads some to argue that much more attention needs to be paid to finding ways of engaging the most withdrawn, apathetic and negative patients in something that has meaning and relevance to them.

Family interventions

Despite the interest in the family's role in the development and course of schizophrenia, until the 1980s little effort was put into involving the family in therapy or other interventions. Where schizophrenia had been redefined as a problem in family communication or roles, then family therapy was offered with the aim of treating the dysfunctional family rather than the individual patient. Other family approaches, such as Laing's (described earlier), sought to distance the 'patient' from the family.

□ What factors (described in this chapter) may have led to the increasing interest in involving families in interventions?

■ Three factors have contributed, namely: research on levels of expressed emotion in families and its correlation with relapse; the rise of the self-help movement and carer organisations; and the policy of community care, which relies on families as informal carers.

Psycho-education forms the backbone of **family interventions**, whether they are group- or individual-based. Families showing critical high expressed emotion (EE) behaviour tend to have negative attitudes to schizophrenia and also to the patient, who is often held to be to 'blame' for his or her illness. Such families tend to believe that the patient could behave differently if he or she wanted to. Indeed it may be that it is these beliefs, rather than high EE as such, that are central to effective family interventions. Those involved in psycho-education, therefore, try to understand the family members' beliefs and work with them. The evidence shows that simply presenting information or 'facts' is not enough to change beliefs or behaviour. Amongst other aspects, families are helped to understand what *is* and, importantly, what is *not* within the voluntary control of the person with schizophrenia, how their behaviour may influence outcome, and the role and function of other treatment and management interventions (Leff and Vaughn, 1985).

Not all family intervention programmes are the same. Thus a slightly different approach is taken by psychiatrist Ian Falloon and his colleagues (1993), who use problem-solving techniques with families, focusing on stress management to influence the family environment.

Family-based interventions usually take *relapse* by the person diagnosed as having schizophrenia as their primary outcome measure, and there is good evidence that these programmes do reduce relapse rates. Set against this, however, is the problem of encouraging family involvement. Take-up rates are often low and drop-out high, with families not always seeing the relevance of the interventions. Take-up rates are higher when families are approached at a time of crisis, either at first episode of schizophrenia or subsequent relapse. Family sessions based in the family's home also seem to maintain family involvement. Involving families as early as possible in the illness also seems to be important in contributing to success. This may be because the families are actively looking for help and information and have not yet become cynical about the services on offer or demoralised by their problems. (Other reasons are suggested in the article by Goffman associated with Chapter 2 of this book.)

Although carers' organisations frequently demand more involvement of relatives in management and decision-making, clearly the family intervention programmes currently on offer do not appeal to all families. Little attention has been paid to the views of people diagnosed as having schizophrenia whose families are involved in these programmes.

> ☐ What tensions do you think may arise if people diagnosed as having schizophrenia are not included in family intervention programmes?

> ■ They may feel marginalised or that their privacy is being invaded.

On the other hand, if relatives are acting as carers they may feel entitled to information and help that will make them more effective in that role. Some family intervention programmes do have elements that focus largely on the carer's problems and aim to reduce *their* stress rather than that of the person with schizophrenia. A greater emphasis on outcomes for carers rather than patients would alter the 'tone' of the programmes and might make them more acceptable.

Rather than an intervention to change them or help them cope better, what some families want, however, is something that removes the source of stress. This could be anything from a cure for schizophrenia to better day-care services, supported housing, appropriate vocational rehabilitation and sheltered employment opportunities.

Multi-intervention approach

Community care guidelines require all patients leaving hospital to have a *care programme* clearly drawn up, with an identified key worker, following a comprehensive assessment of needs. In reality this does not always happen. Areas that are often inadequate are housing and employment opportunities and alternatives to employment.

Therapies are often presented as either/or (e.g. medication or psycho-social intervention) and seen as tied to a particular view of schizophrenia. In reality this need not be so and a **multi-intervention approach** can be used. People advocating this approach argue that the belief that schizophrenia is a biologically-based illness does not preclude the need for psycho-social interventions along with drug therapy. The family does not have to cause or even contribute to schizophrenia to benefit from involvement in family programmes. What is important is to develop individual care programmes to suit individual needs.

Schizophrenia: public opinion and the media

As mentioned at the start of this chapter, for people who have no personal knowledge of schizophrenia the only source of information may be the media. For this reason, public opinion and media representations of schizophrenia may be tied together. There have been a number of studies in both the United Kingdom and the USA since the 1950s examining attitudes to people with mental illness, but very little specifically on schizophrenia. Overall, these studies suggest that people with mental illness are often stigmatised as dangerous and unpredictable because of the social embarrassment they cause.

□ Thinking back to Chapter 2, what psychological processes might be involved in forming these public perceptions?

■ It was argued that stigma is the result of the *projection* of fundamental anxieties onto the person thus stigmatised, who is perceived as presenting a threat to the *ontological security* of others.

There has been some evidence, however, that attitudes are changing towards greater acceptance. A study by a group of psychiatrists in England, led by Ian Brockington, showed overwhelmingly that in the early 1990s the public fear and intolerance of mentally-ill people had receded, although it remained in 'a substantial minority of the community' (Brockington *et al.*, 1993). However, this study was based on expressed attitudes during research interviews, not on observed behaviours, and people may have been motivated to present tolerant views because these were felt to be socially acceptable. Additionally, genuine 'good intentions' held in a state of comparative ignorance and inexperience may give way in the face of reality. For example, in Brockington's study, although two-thirds of those interviewed at first said they would be prepared to marry someone with a mental illness, this dropped to only 6 per cent after being shown descriptions of people with mental illness. It may be that responses after the description were closer to reality. Responses suggested that only between a third and half the population would live next door to, work with or join the same club as someone with a mental illness. Although on average older people were more intolerant than younger, the *most* intolerant group were those under 25 years.

How far the media shape attitudes and behaviour is a controversial issue, especially when applied to acts of violence. Despite some good, positive and sympathetic portrayals, the media's record on images of mental illness is generally unfavourable. A study of the tabloid press and television by the Glasgow University Media Group (1993a) categorised representations according to whether they concerned people with mental illness harming others, harming themselves, behaving in a comical way, or were largely sympathetic or critical (Figure 6.3). The researchers found the majority of both fictional and non-fictional representations concerned people with mental illness harming others. This is despite the reality that people with mental illness who harm anyone are more likely to harm themselves than others.

When the researchers examined the responses of audiences to media representations of mental illness, some worrying findings emerged (Glasgow University Media Group, 1993b). Unlike other areas, where personal experience outweighs media representations, in this case this did not seem to be true. People who had limited, but *positive*, experience of mental illness

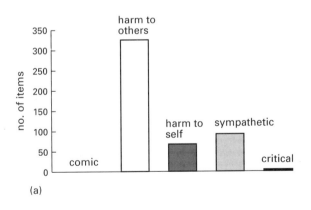

(a)

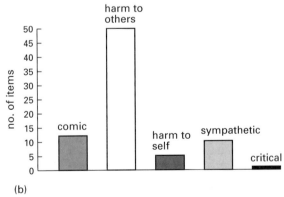

(b)

Figure 6.3 *(a) Fictional, and (b) non-fictional representations of mental illness. Analysis of television, newspapers and magazines during one month in 1993 showed that the greatest number of representations of people with mental illness involved them harming others. (Source: Glasgow University Media Group, 1993a,* Mass Media Representations of Mental Health/Illness. Report for the Health Education Board for Scotland, *Glasgow University Media Group, Glasgow, Appendix 3 and Appendix 4, pages unnumbered)*

CONTROVERSY: Mr Sissons and the new hostel. Campaigners condemned his 'Not In My Back Yard' attitude

Neighbours' fears over mentally ill patients

Plans to accommodate mentally ill people in the community can encounter opposition from local residents. (Sunday Express, 27 February, 1994, p. 7)

discounted or ignored their experience in the light of contradictory media messages. One woman, for example, who had done some voluntary work in a psychiatric hospital said:

> The actual people I met weren't violent—that I think they are violent, that comes from television, from plays and things … None of them were violent—but I remember being scared of them, because it was a mental hospital—it's not a very good attitude to have but it is the way things come across on TV, and films—you know, mental axe murderers and plays and things—the people I met weren't like that, but that is what I associate them with. (Glasgow University Media Group, 1993b, p. 32)

Concerns about the way in which mental illness is misrepresented in the media has led to groups as divergent as the Royal College of Psychiatrists and the *Schizophrenia Media Agency* (a user group) campaigning and working with the media to improve their reporting.

It is an interesting exercise, which you may like to try, to keep a note of all the references to mental illness in the newspapers you read, including the local ones, for a month. This can reveal a great deal about media

messages on mental illness. Removing the words 'mental patient' where crimes are reported can show that the story appears less 'newsworthy'. Such stories are often not followed up, and frequently newspapers only report that someone with a history of mental illness has been charged, not whether they were found guilty, or what happens to them.

Fictional portrayals of mental illness frequently mix reality with enough fantasy to make a good story. Schizophrenia is often misrepresented, even unrecognisable, especially in thrillers and horror films. The following description comes from the 1977 Warner Brothers film *Schizo*, for which the publicity poster, the video cover and the opening words read:

> When the left hand doesn't know who the right hand is killing, you're dealing with a SCHIZO … Schizophrenia, a mental disorder, sometimes known as multiple or split personality … an alternation between violent and contrasting behaviour patterns.

Most films that use 'schizophrenia' encourage the public to believe that it means 'split personality'—that the person is some kind of Jekyll and Hyde—or use the term as a description of anyone who is generally 'mad', or as a scaring-enough label in itself to generate fear in the audience. These are very useful concepts for a film producer, but a major handicap for anyone trying to set up supported housing in a community, let alone trying to live in such housing.

This is not to say that more positive portrayals of schizophrenia do not exist, but they are few and far between and more likely to come from made-for-television films than those for general release. *Promise*, made by TVM in 1986, starred James Garner as the brother of a man diagnosed as having schizophrenia. It won five Emmy and two Golden Globe awards. *Can You Hear Me Thinking?*, starring Judi Dench and Michael Williams, was made by the BBC in 1990 and offered a sympathetic view of a family shattered by the son's schizophrenia. On a critical note, as case histories, such films do not represent the full range of experiences of schizophrenia, by only presenting cases with poor outcomes. Thus in *Promise*, the man with schizophrenia goes to live in a group home because his brother cannot cope with him any more; it is suggested that he will have the opportunity for a better life there. In *Can You Hear Me Thinking?* the son commits suicide. However, both films try not to be sensationalist. By contrast, a more recent made-for-television film (released on Odyssey video in Britain in 1994) is *Out of Darkness*, produced by and starring Diana Ross. It has a somewhat unrealistically positive ending with the central character restored to health through Clozaril; it seems more like a drug advertisement than a realistic portrayal of outcome in schizophrenia.

There are some surprisingly good cameos of patients in films, but often used to comic effect, making use of the patient's delusions or hallucinations. Historically there are interesting portrayals, although they reflect diagnostic criteria and treatments that have now changed (as was pointed out in the earlier discussion of *One Flew over the Cuckoo's Nest*). *The Snake Pit* is a powerful and moving study of the asylums of the 1940s. *Family Life* describes schizophrenia from a Laingian point of view, while *I Never Promised You a Rose Garden*, based on the book of the same name by Hannah Green (1964), is based on Frieda Fromm-Reichmann's ideas. More commonly, however, the label 'schizophrenia' is thrown into the plot to explain why someone is violent, kills or is otherwise anti-social or beyond understanding. Despite some portrayals of schizophrenia in the media that aid understanding, the majority are misleading and invite ridicule or fear.

Conclusions

☐ Go back to the list of words you wrote down at the beginning of this chapter which you associated with schizophrenia, and your list of its symptoms. What, if anything, has changed?

Depending on your point of view, schizophrenia is either a clearly defined mental illness or a vague concept which keeps slipping away. Some people believe passionately that it is a biological disease with its roots in brain abnormalities. Other people believe, equally passionately, that as an entity it does not exist and that so-called 'psychotic behaviours' have other explanations. Some say that the family environment is central—others that the family environment is largely irrelevant; some that drugs are fundamental to management; others that drugs cause more problems than they solve. Yet others argue that people with schizophrenia often can't help their actions and therefore need to be protected or controlled; this is countered with the argument that people with schizophrenia should have all the rights of other citizens and accept the responsibilities that come with them.

Schizophrenia remains a confusing and tantalising chimera for researchers and a potentially devastating experience for those who have it or care about someone who has it. Whatever our views and beliefs we should not lose sight of the distress of people with schizophrenia—whether through the condition, or their treatment in 'the system'. Maybe the best way to end is to repeat the (very) old joke, first told to the author of this chapter by a patient over twenty years ago:

Schizophrenia? I'm in two minds about it.

OBJECTIVES FOR CHAPTER 6

When you have studied this chapter, you should be able to:

6.1 Describe the symptoms and prognosis of schizophrenia and distinguish a clinical diagnosis from lay descriptions.

6.2 Discuss the problems encountered in comparing people diagnosed as having schizophrenia across time and between geographical locations.

6.3 Describe the different approaches to explaining the causes of schizophrenia and how they are reflected in different approaches to treatment.

6.4 Discuss the issues involved in treating people diagnosed as having schizophrenia either in the community or in hospitals.

6.5 Recognise the influence of individual perspectives and experiences, and media representations, on personal and public attitudes to schizophrenia.

QUESTIONS FOR CHAPTER 6

Question 1 (*Objective 6.1*)

Distinguish between the *positive* and *negative* symptoms of schizophrenia. How do they compare with lay descriptions of the condition?

Question 2 (*Objective 6.2*)

Is schizophrenia an illness of Western industrialised countries? What evidence is there to shed light on this question, and what are the reasons for interpreting epidemiological data with caution?

Question 3 (*Objective 6.3*)

Do beliefs about the causes of schizophrenia necessarily determine which treatments are appropriate?

Question 4 (*Objective 6.4*)

Mental health laws in the United Kingdom allow for the compulsory detention and treatment in hospital of persons considered to be a danger to themselves or others by virtue of their mental illness. Imagine that, following the example of radical psychiatrists in Italy in the 1970s, a group of professionals in the United Kingdom proposes that these laws should be abolished. Others argue in favour of closing mental hospitals. What arguments could be made for and against these developments?

Question 5 (*Objectives 6.1 and 6.5*)

One of your closest friends comes to tell you he or she has just got engaged to someone who has been diagnosed as having schizophrenia. They are looking for your support. What factors would you try to take into account when discussing the possible prognosis? What misconceptions about schizophrenia might you have to dispel?

7 Pain and suffering

During your study of this chapter you will be asked to read an article, contained in the Reader,[1] by Sally Macintyre and David Oldman called 'Coping with migraine'. Students of the Open University will also be asked to listen to an audiotape entitled 'Being in pain'. This chapter was written by Clive Seale, Senior Lecturer in Medical Sociology at Goldsmiths' College, University of London.

Introduction

A doctor administered a lethal injection to an elderly dying woman to end her suffering, Winchester crown court was told yesterday … Mrs Boyes was suffering from severe rheumatoid arthritis … By August 16 she was seriously ill, suffering great pain and discomfort which was not relieved by large doses of pain killers … [she] had no reasonable prospects of ever living an independent life again … on August 10 she told her youngest son she had had enough and did not want to carry on … The drugs were not controlling her pain and once she screamed out and was severely distressed. [The prosecution said] 'By this time … Dr Cox himself was considerably affected by the condition of his patient and decided he must bring her suffering to an end.' … Staff nurse Christina Eeles said … that on the morning Mrs Boyes died Dr Cox had been distressed at the pain she was suffering. She had screamed with pain. The screams had sounded like those of a wounded animal. (*Guardian*, 1992, 11 September, p. 2)

This is a depiction of almost unimaginably severe pain, and the effect that this had on people who[1] felt responsible for alleviating it. In everyday life, pain and

[1] *Health and Disease: A Reader* (second edition, 1995).

suffering are rarely experienced so severely, or with such a devastating loss of hope. Many pains are quite minor, easily 'treated' by words of sympathy or simple medical remedies, so that they become part of a routine background of minor troubles. This chapter will consider some extreme examples of pain and suffering because, rather like the experiments conducted by Harold Garfinkel to disrupt 'normality', which you saw in Chapter 2, these reveal underlying strategies for *repairing reality* that are usually taken for granted. In particular, we focus on the experience of **chronic pain**. This type of pain—which continues long after 'normal' **acute pain** has gone away—makes people's routine strategies for dealing with pain and suffering fragile (and therefore visible). The place of medicine in people's attempts to alleviate and understand the meaning of suffering will also be illuminated by this method.

This chapter marks a return to the wider framework of this book. During its course you will be invited to reflect back on the case studies of rheumatoid arthritis, HIV and AIDS, asthma and schizophrenia, which all demonstrate varieties of human suffering and the varying success of medicine in its alleviation. In particular, rheumatoid arthritis shows the disruptive effect of chronic *physical* pain. Pain, though, can also be *social*, as in the stigma of AIDS and a variety of other stigmatised conditions (discussed in Chapter 2), and *emotional*, as in the fears and anxieties associated with asthma. Schizophrenia exerts a profoundly disruptive effect on mental processes, with consequences for social and emotional pain. For the purposes of this chapter physical, emotional and social pain will be discussed as three components of the broader phenomenon of human suffering.

The chapter begins by proposing that the experience of pain has the potential to 'unmake' the usual capacity of people to participate in a meaningful world. Medical treatments are then depicted as helping people to construct *personal illness narratives* (as well as giving physical relief), which enable them to repair the damage by giving a meaning and an explanation for pain. Different theories of pain are summarised to illustrate how biological explanations can contribute to medical narratives. A **medical narrative** can be loosely defined as a coherent 'story' about the causes, consequences or treatment of a health problem, which is generally accepted within the medical profession as a reasonable description of 'the way things are'. Medical narratives are passed on directly to patients by doctors, but often have a far wider currency as a result of the publicity they get in the media. Because they have the support of a powerful social institution—medicine—these narratives carry great weight and often dominate the personal narratives that people construct to explain their illness or distress. Some medical narratives encompass more dimensions of the experience of suffering than others, as you will see later in this chapter. The chapter ends by reviewing historical and cross-cultural evidence about variability in experiences and explanations for pain and suffering.

The making and unmaking of the world[2]

Human social life can be understood in part as a continuous, jointly organised struggle to 'forget' the crude fact that as individuals all our thoughts, our hopes, our plans and our participation in culture depend in the last analysis on the physical integrity of our bodies. The experience of illness, then, is a reminder of the limitations of bodily existence and often involves a sense of **marginality**, where people are forced to retire from this joint human endeavour.

 □ Can you think of examples of marginality from the earlier case studies?

 ■ Rheumatoid arthritis often stops people from taking part in social activities that require physical mobility; the social stigma of AIDS can exclude groups already marginalised by sexual stigmas; asthma can make children feel 'different' at school; the disruption of thoughts and emotions in schizophrenia places many sufferers outside 'normal' social participation.

Not all of the above examples are directly caused by physical limitations. For example, the degree to which schizophrenia is a physical disease excites great controversy. The excluding effect of stigma can be understood as a type of *inflicted* social pain that sometimes builds an additional layer of suffering onto the experience

of illness. Yet all of these situations demonstrate how illness can separate a person from others so that, in the words of the American sociologist Richard Hilbert, whose work with chronic pain sufferers will be described later:

 … [they are] continuously approaching the amorphous frontier of non-membership. They are falling out of culture. (Hilbert, 1984, p. 375)

To be 'in culture' means sharing a world of meaning with others. People's understanding of who they are is a matter of constant negotiation, seen starkly in the struggles over self-identity that occur in adolescence.[3] Provisional self-interpretations are tested out and validated in the external social world through continuing 'conversations' with others. In such conversations—which may literally be the experience of face-to-face talk, but which can also be interaction with cultural products such as the media, books, art, music and so on—people seek to construct meaningful *narratives* of the self.

 □ What role do personal illness narratives play in the experience of rheumatoid arthritis?

 ■ Through 'narrative reconstruction', people with rheumatoid arthritis construct explanations of why they have the disease, drawing on events and circumstances in their lives that seem significant. This process helps them to deal with their uncertainties about its daily course, including variations in their experience of pain. Such personal illness narratives draw on both lay and scientific accounts.

The process of constructing and reconstructing narratives of the self can be understood as a **world-making activity**, contributing to *ontological security* (see Chapter 2) by repairing damage from encounters with threats to existence. In order to maintain a sense of optimism and purpose about continuing in life, people need 'explanations' for suffering. Religion, in its origins, provided a structure of explanations that people could readily appropriate into their own internal world-making activity. Religious explanations are known as *theodicies*, as they seek to justify suffering as the will of God (*theo*, God; *-dicy*, justice). In modern times, many people turn to science (and particularly medicine) for explanations that are alternative to those of religion. Most obviously,

---

[2]These terms are taken from Scarry, E. (1985) *The Body in Pain: The Making and Unmaking of the World,* Oxford University Press, Oxford.

[3]An account of adolescence along these lines is given in *Birth to Old Age: Health in Transition*, Chapter 6.

theodicies and scientific explanations seek to provide explanations for death, the ultimate marginal situation, intimately linked with the limitations of bodily existence, where the individual's falling out of culture is complete. Theodicies that explain death can be understood as attempts to re-make a fractured world.

Theodicies also enable the surrender of the self to society. Rituals, in which allegiance to particular theodicies is enacted, whether religious or medical, transform an *individual* event into an episode in the history of *society*, thereby asserting a connectedness of the individual with others and giving continuity between generations. As the sociologist Peter Berger has put it, a type of 'sheltering canopy' covers 'even those experiences that may reduce the individual to howling animality' (Berger, 1973, p. 63).

Marginal experiences, such as that of illness, disrupt world-making activity and contribute to the **unmaking of the world**. The experience of physical pain, for example, means that the body ceases to be a vehicle for the expression of the self, as it is when it is draped with fashionable clothes, or used to indicate emotions ('body language'), or shaped by diet or exercise to indicate 'health' or 'fitness'. Pain makes the body strange, and the self 'watches' the body which is now acting *against* it. This is illustrated in the words of one sufferer from chronic pain:

> … [there are] those moments too when I think it's … I'm outside myself, this whole thing I've got to deal with is ah, a decayed mass of tissue that's just not any good, and I, I'm almost looking at it that way again; as if my mind were separated … I guess. I don't feel integrated. I don't feel like a whole person. (Good, 1994, p. 123)

At the extreme, such self-estrangement can lead to a collapse of ontological security and to self-destructive acts.

In acts of world making, people collectively create structures of meaning. Thus they agree to designate certain people as having a particular expertise, and to interpret certain actions as an exercise of that expertise. When meanings are routinely agreed by large numbers of people they 'thicken' and 'harden', so becoming *objectified* in social institutions such as the church, education and medicine. These interpretations are then reflected back to people to supply them with meanings that appear 'given' and are handed down through childhood socialisation as 'truths'. Most obviously, this is the case with the institution of religion in traditional societies.

But science and, in particular medicine, now provide people with institutionalised meanings for dealing with pain and suffering. Medicine in these terms can be understood as a *grand narrative* (Chapter 1), in which patients are offered opportunities to be scripted into a jointly produced 'story'.

□ The 'story' offered by medicine to the sufferer is not always a welcome one. Can you think of any examples of this from the book so far?

■ The medical narrative of rheumatoid arthritis may, on occasion, contain the message 'You'll just have to learn to live with it' (Chapter 3). The diagnosis of epilepsy may be deeply disturbing, as it can carry stigmatising connotations (Chapter 2). People diagnosed as having schizophrenia may resist the label, preferring softer social labels such as that of 'voice hearer'; they may also resist genetic explanations in favour of environmental causes that offer greater hope of personal control over the condition (Chapter 6).

Thinking of medicine as a 'narrative' does not imply a relativist position, where narratives can be constructed with no reference to whether they accurately describe an independently existing reality. Medical narratives may be concerned with technical measures that have real physical impact, alleviating certain pains very effectively (for example, the simple act of carrying an inhaler at all times can relieve the fear of an asthma attack). Additionally, medical narratives can be experienced as both helpful and unhelpful by sufferers. This is illustrated towards the end of the following discussion of the experience of chronic pain.

The experience of pain

Pain occurs in many varieties, ranging from the transient mild pain of a knock or a scratch, to the acute pains of childbirth or toothache. A common feature of *acute* pain is that those who suffer it expect that it will eventually go away. This is often because pain is linked to the idea of tissue damage: once the physical damage heals, it is thought, pain will disappear. However, in *chronic* pain this expectation is violated. This situation is outside the realm of most people's experience, although there are some chronic pains, such as low back pain, which are experienced by a significant proportion of the population. Here, pain may persist without obvious tissue damage or, as in rheumatoid arthritis, recur or intensify for no apparent reason. Unlike acute pain, which may be interpreted as a 'warning' to change behaviour in order to avoid further pain, chronic pain appears to serve no such useful purpose. It therefore poses significant problems of meaning to sufferers.

Additionally, one of the key problems facing the person with pain is to communicate its nature to others. Language is the means by which people place their subjective thoughts into culture and jointly engage in world-making activity. Pain is often expressed in primitive, pre-linguistic groans, cries and shrieks. To place the subjective experience of pain in culture, a common language for communicating pain experience must be created. Here again, the chronic pain sufferer is faced with particular problems, as the legitimacy of a pain without an identifiable physical cause may be questioned by others.

> Some people thought it was a joke, they thought I was just trying to get [something] over on everybody. Like my father, he didn't really think I had that much pain. (Hilbert, 1984, p. 367)

Variations in the experience of pain from day to day are subjectively experienced for reasons that may be mysterious; for people who live with or treat a person with chronic pain, the language of the sufferer is their only evidence for the existence of pain. Managing the disclosure of pain therefore has certain parallels with the problems experienced by those managing the disclosure of invisible stigmas.

Chronic pain and the 'unmaking' of the world

Richard Hilbert interviewed 22 people with chronic pain in order to gain an understanding of the problems they faced. When pains began, people initially used their existing knowledge of 'normal' acute pain to interpret the experience. It was only when the pain did not go away that they realised they were facing a qualitatively different experience, as in these two examples:

> I'm an athlete and a coach and very active, and so I was used to pain, and thought 'Well, I just kind of injured my tailbone a little bit'. And I thought it'd go away. I never *dreamed* what it would end up being.

> When my leg went numb in March of '77, then … it really hit me. I almost flipped out, in a sense, because I knew that there it was again, and it would be like a sore tooth. It would never go away. That's when it really threw me in an emotional turmoil—[a] crisis. (Hilbert, 1984, p. 367)

The lack of an adequate explanation was profoundly disturbing:

> I honestly don't know what it is. And *that's* pretty frustrating a lot of times. Just the fact that *I* don't know what it is, you know. I've been frustrated with that. Well, what *is* this goddamn thing? Why do I *have* these headaches? (Hilbert, 1984, p. 368)

'Brian', interviewed by Byron Good, an American anthropologist, describes the world-destroying qualities of his pain:

> Sometimes, if I had to visualise it, it would seem as though there there's a ah … a demon, a monster, something very … horrible lurking around banging the insides of my body, ripping it apart. And ah, I'm containing it, or I'm trying to contain it, so that no one else can see it, so that no one else can be disturbed by it. Because it's scaring the daylights out of me, and I'd assume that … gee, if anybody had to, had to look at this, that … they'd avoid me like the plague. So I redouble my efforts to … say … I'm gonna be perfectly contained about this whole thing. And maybe the less I do, the less I make myself known, and the less I … venture out … or display any, any initiative, then I won't let the, this junk out. It seems like there's something very, very terrible happening. I have no control over it. (Good, 1994, pp. 121–2)

There are striking similarities between this account and those of the people with schizophrenia you read about in Chapter 6. Like those who hear voices from inside, so Brian's pain is personified as an internal demon or monster that he is trying to contain. He expresses the fear of stigma if his efforts at containment fail and the monster is revealed to others. Hilbert's respondents made similar points about the difficulties of containment and in judging when and how much to reveal:

> When you're with somebody else and you really want to participate with them and get to know them or whatever … you would like to be able to give whoever the guy is your total attention for five minutes, and if in fact your attention is somewhere else you're going to end up … being a little anti-social. You know, I don't … go out much.

> They act like I've done something to them, like I've lied to them somehow. Like somehow I've done something wrong to them. (Hilbert, 1984, pp. 371–2)

☐ Think back to the explanation of the psychological roots of stigma in Chapter 2. In what sense might the complainer of chronic pain be 'doing something wrong' to those around him or her?

■ In Chapter 2 it was argued that the desire to be 'normal' was linked to the preservation of a basic sense of security (*ontological security*) about being in the world. People with deformities, or who stand outside 'normality', can be experienced as threatening to the security of others, and are therefore stigmatised. Chronic pain sufferers demonstrate an abnormal pain experience, for which onlookers may have no resources to find an adequate explanation, thereby provoking deep anxieties.

People experiencing conditions characterised by chronic pain, then, are potentially isolated, marginalised without resources to make sense of their condition, and unable to find others with whom to share their experience. Once again, you should remember that this depicts the extreme end of an extreme condition. Not all pains are like this, else it would be hard to imagine any of us continuing optimistically for long! The purpose of describing such an extreme is to show starkly what lies beneath more minor sufferings and their treatments, where the 'fall from culture' hardly begins before powerful reparative work occurs. Even for people with extreme troubles, there exists a variety of opportunities to pull back from despair and remake their worlds. It is to this that we now turn.

The remaking of the world

One view of healing is that it is devoted to the removal of suffering. This may be achieved by straightforward technical means that, for example, anaesthetise pain or remove its cause. This understanding masks another feature of healing, which is brought into sharp relief when technical means are inadequate, as in chronic pain. Here, healing can be understood as the search for an adequate *narrative* (by the healer as well as the patient) with which to bestow meaning on suffering. As Byron Good has put it:

> One of the central efforts in healing is to symbolise the source of suffering, to find an image around which a narrative can take shape. (Good, 1994, p. 128)

The pursuit of relief and the search for meaning go hand in hand, and the sufferer and the medical system may play a part in both. The case of Brian, interviewed by Byron Good, shows a succession of searches for an adequate narrative. Two were offered to Brian by the medical system. One focused on the physical level:

> Three successive physicians, treating him for congestion and pain in his ears and head, heard a clicking and popping sound in his jaw, suggested he might be suffering from 'temporomandibular joint disorder' or TMJ, and recommended restorative dentistry ... Thus began a reinterpretation of all of his pain ... 'I was a little sceptical at first ... [but then] I began to think this is something that may have a physical basis.' (Good, 1994, p. 120)

Another narrative emphasised psychological causation:

> I spent a period of three months when I was two years of age [in an orphanage] ... it might have just come in right at that time ... that stripped me of any parental attachment ... [it was] something that damaged my feelings in the process. (Good, 1994, p. 119)

Both surgery and psychotherapy, however, failed to alleviate the pain, and by their failure indicated to Brian their inadequacy as narratives. When interviewed, Brian found relief in art-work which:

> For him, it seems, is a symbolic form of world making ... when language fails as a medium of self extension ... 'there are times when I ... can find expression in the art ... If I have a shrieking person inside me, someone that's yelling and screaming and trying to get out, sometimes I don't do it concretely. You know, I don't do it verbally ... it comes out in the painting'. (Good, 1994, p. 129)

Pain and suffering have frequently inspired artists such as Edvard Munch, an expressionist painter who sought to convey basic features of the human condition in his work. To this end, many of his themes drew on images of illness, suffering and death, as in his famous painting 'The Scream' (Figure 7.1a). The use of non-verbal imagery as a means of communicating experiences of pain and suffering has also been encouraged in hospices, where patients seek to depict their feelings about terminal cancer (Figure 7.1b–d).

Figure 7.1 *Images of pain and suffering. (a) 'The Scream' by Edvard Munch; (b)–(d) Images produced or selected by people seeking to depict pain in terminal cancer. (Photos: (a) J. Lathion, © Nasjonalgalleriet, Oslo courtesy of The Munch Museum/The Munch-Ellingsen Group/DACS 1996; (b), (c) and (d) St Christopher's Hospice, London)*

Figure 7.1b was drawn by Mr H. Y., who

> … depicts his pain surrounding him totally as he lies stretched out on his bed. He described the whorled figure to us as the 'knotted muscles' of tension. He is cut off from the world by it. [His pain was subsequently relieved in a hospice.] (Saunders, 1978, p. 10)

Figure 7.1c was drawn by Mrs E. S., who felt 'constantly at the mercy of some kind of demolition squad' (Saunders and Baines, 1983, p. 12). Figure 7.1d is a photograph of a medieval tapestry given to Saunders and Baines by a patient who said: 'This is what my illness feels like to me'.

The moment of diagnosis can be of intense importance to people experiencing inexplicable illness, because of its potential to include the experience in a powerful institutionalised narrative. A medically-sanctioned explanation in the case of one person interviewed by Hilbert, for example, was crucial in reassuring him that he was experiencing his body 'correctly':

> When the doctor called me in and told me what I had, I remember, I was so *delighted* to know that I had something that I didn't even hear what he said … Even if they'd have told me I had *cancer*, I wouldn't have cared. Really! I had just got to the point where I was desperate to be told that I had something. Cause I *knew there was something wrong* but I didn't know *what*. And the doctors couldn't find anything. And that's really hell … It meant there was nothing wrong with my head. That I wasn't a—you know—a hypochondriac, that I wasn't imagining all this stuff, because I was beginning to *believe* it. (Hilbert, 1984, p. 368)

In the case of pain, whether a patient has 'something' or 'nothing' can thus be of crucial importance in the sufferer's search for an adequate narrative giving meaning to their personal experience. The history of medical knowledge, however, shows that it constantly changes, with new divisions of disease categories replacing old ones, and shifting views about the relative importance of mind and body offer clinicians a changing basis for diagnostic labels.[4] In the case of chronic pain, there have been major shifts in the medical understanding of its nature. This means that a variety of medically sanctioned narratives are now available, some of them offering more opportunities than others to patients seeking to remake worlds disrupted by pain.

Medical narratives for pain

In this section two biological theories to explain the phenomenon of pain, and the implications of these for the construction of different medical narratives, will be outlined. The concept of *total pain*—developed in response to the needs of people with terminal cancer—will then be outlined as a narrative that contains elements derived from both medical and other sources.

[4]Changes in medical knowledge over time, and across cultures, are discussed in *Medical Knowledge: Doubt and Certainty* and *Caring for Health: History and Diversity*.

Specificity theory

The first of the two biological theories explaining pain is known as **specificity theory**, shown at its simplest in the ideas of the seventeenth-century philosopher René Descartes. Figure 7.2 shows his (1664) concept of the pain pathway.

Figure 7.2 *René Descartes' concept of the pain pathway, which he described thus: 'If for example fire (A) comes near the foot (B), the minute particles of this fire, which as you know move with great velocity, have the power to set in motion the spot of the skin of the foot which they touch, and by this means pulling upon the delicate thread (c c) which is attached to the spot of the skin, they open up at the same instant the pore (d e) against which the delicate thread ends, just as by pulling at one end of a rope one makes to strike at the same instant a bell which hangs at the other end.' (Source: Oeuvres des Descartes, 1664)*

With advances in microscopy and other laboratory techniques in the nineteenth century, this theory was developed in various ways. It starts from the basic assumption that pain is experienced because of *specific* messages sent from the *periphery* (e.g. nerve endings in the skin) to the *central nervous system* (the brain and spinal cord). In this model, the analogy of the nervous system as a 'hard-wired' electrical circuit, like a telephone exchange system, is appropriate. The brain—or rather a specific part of it designated the 'pain centre'—is depicted as receiving signals, which themselves travel along specific nerve fibres with sensory endings devoted to recording only sensations of pain, rather than (say) warmth, cold or touch.

Unfortunately for specificity theory, these ideas fail to fit some of the known facts about pain. Most dramatically, perhaps, clinical evidence suggests that cutting a nerve pathway does not always achieve the same effect as cutting off a telephone. The pain sensation commonly reasserts itself, as if emanating from the same troublesome location as before. Additionally, a given level of stimulus does not always have an exact correlation with a given level of experienced pain. For these and other reasons, alternative theories of pain developed during the nineteenth and early twentieth centuries. *Pattern theories*, for example, suggest that the central nervous system acts to summarise messages from a variety of sources before an individual experiences pain. Other theories stress the role of emotions in determining whether pain is felt, rather than regarding emotion as a purely reactive consequence of pain.

Specificity theory rests on a very firm distinction made by Descartes between the mind and the body (so-called *mind–body dualism*). Pain is designated as a bodily event, to which the mind reacts. Medical treatment based on specificity theory seeks to identify physical origins and pathways, and intervene in these to alleviate pain (as, for example, in the surgical procedures shown in Figure 7.3). When such treatments are successful, they reinforce the medical narrative of pain as a purely bodily event. However, a patient complaining of pains whose origin cannot be found in the body runs the risk of being designated at worst a malingerer, or at best someone with psychological disturbance. For malingerers, no medically-sanctioned narrative is made available. For those with psychological conditions, a specialist in mental disorders may be brought in. Patients whose pain is diagnosed as having a psychological origin may experience this as an unwelcome medical narrative, as it indicates to them that their experience of their bodies is 'wrong'.

Gate-control theory

Any comprehensive theory of pain needs to explain how it is that different sorts of pain are experienced (for example, short-term acute pain versus long-term chronic pain), but must also explain certain puzzling features of pain. Listed here are a number of such puzzles.

1   Pain can sometimes occur when there has been no apparent injury or it can continue long after an injury has apparently healed.

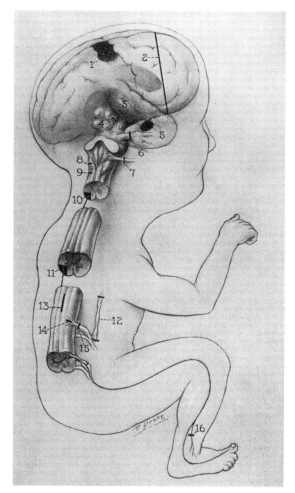

Figure 7.3 *Schematic diagram illustrating various surgical procedures designed to alleviate pain. Specificity theory has led surgeons to make interventions to block or cut physical pathways of pain. The numbers refer to points where the nerve pathways may be severed. (Source: MacCarty, C. S. and Drake, R. L., 1956, 'Neurosurgical procedures for the control of pain',* Proceedings of Staff Meetings of the Mayo Clinic, *31, facing p. 211)*

2   Extremely serious injuries are sometimes accompanied by no pain sensation.

3   Conversely, extreme pain can be experienced when only a light stimulus is applied.

4   The location of pain may differ from the location of damage (so-called *referred* pain).

5   Surgical intervention to cut or disable nerves transmitting pain sensations from a site of injury frequently fails to stop the experience of pain.

Most of us will not have had experience of the phenomena listed. They are, if you like, occasional oddities whose study has proven worthwhile in understanding the genesis of the more routine pains that most of us experience.

Gate-control theory, published originally by a psychologist, Ronald Melzack, and a neurophysiologist, Patrick Wall (Melzack and Wall, 1965), represented a major development of previous theories of pain. Although it has been modified in its details, and further theories proposing additional features have been developed since it was first published, there is broad agreement about it in general outline. It is based on extensive experimental evidence and detailed examination of the physical structures involved.

The theory—summarised in Figure 7.4—proposes that a mechanism in an area of the *spinal cord* acts like a gate (Figure 7.4a). Signals from peripheral sites of the body are transmitted to the spinal cord in the form of electrical impulses travelling along small-diameter *afferent* nerve fibres (afferent means 'conducting inwards'). The so-called 'gate' may be open to allow these impulses to stimulate *transmission* cells in the spinal cord, which then send impulses to the brain (the 'ascending pathway', Figure 7.4b). When the gate is 'open', the brain receives and records sensations of pain. Alternatively, the gate may be 'closed' either by electrical signals emanating from the brain (the 'descending pathway'), or by the action of large-diameter afferent nerve fibres that transmit other stimuli from the periphery (Figure 7.4c).

Gate-control theory has important implications for understanding how to relieve pain. Large-diameter afferent fibres (Figure 7.4c) are stimulated by gentle mechanical stimuli. Relief of pain obtained by, for example, rubbing a knocked knee may be due to the closing of the gate as large-diameter fibres are stimulated. This principle underlies *Transcutaneous Electrical Nerve Stimulation* (TENS), which is sometimes effective in giving pain relief by applying weak electrical stimulation to an affected area. It also helps in understanding how psychological treatments for pain may work. Mental events can be understood as sending signals down descending pathways from the brain which influence gate control.

☐ Which of the five puzzles of pain (listed earlier) are explained by gate-control theory?

■ The best candidate is puzzle 2. If the gate modifies the extent to which pain signals are transmitted to the brain, a closed gate could explain why some pains are not registered.

The other puzzles, however, are as yet less easy to understand. In order to explain them, more than this simplified version of the gate-control theory is needed, valuable though the basic concept is. The postulation of a gate opens up the possibility that the central nervous system has a degree of autonomy from the periphery in *creating* the perception of pain. In particular, the central nervous system performs a **summation** of a variety of stimuli from different sources, prioritising the perception of some stimuli and relegating others to a preconscious level. Thus, summation can be used to explain puzzle 2, by suggesting that in some contexts the perception of pain is not prioritised. Whether pain is experienced or not, and if so to what degree, is therefore influenced by what else is going on in the person's environment. Environment can be interpreted broadly, including both the immediate physical surroundings and the psychological and cultural climate of the individual. As Melzack and Wall state:

> The effects of mood, culture, experience and expectation fall into place as part of a unified and integrated system and not as mysteries to be pushed aside or assigned to a totally separate mechanism of the mind. (Melzack and Wall, 1988; reprinted 1991, pp. 182–3)

In addition, events in the spinal cord may, in certain circumstances, involve the abnormal stimulation of transmission cells, which continue to transmit electrical signals to the brain long after the original stimulation from the periphery has ceased. Abnormal stimulation can explain the persistence of pain without injury (puzzle 1), as well as the phenomenon of unusual sensitivity to mild stimuli (puzzle 3). Cutting peripheral nerves would not affect the transmission of signals from the transmission cells, thus explaining some (though not all) of the failures of such surgery (puzzle 5).

It is not the task of this chapter to present an in-depth study of the neurophysiology of pain, or indeed to claim that final explanations of the puzzles of pain have been reached. What is indicated here is simply an outline of some key ideas that have served to increase appreciation of the complexity of the phenomenon, while at the same time moving towards a more satisfactory explanation of some of its more puzzling aspects. In the course of this discussion, it will have become clear that modern *biological* theories of pain lead to a different *medical narrative* from specificity theory: they release us from the straight-jacket of seeing the body and mind as separate systems. Gate-control theory suggests that psychological phenomena are not simply *reactions to* pain, but play an

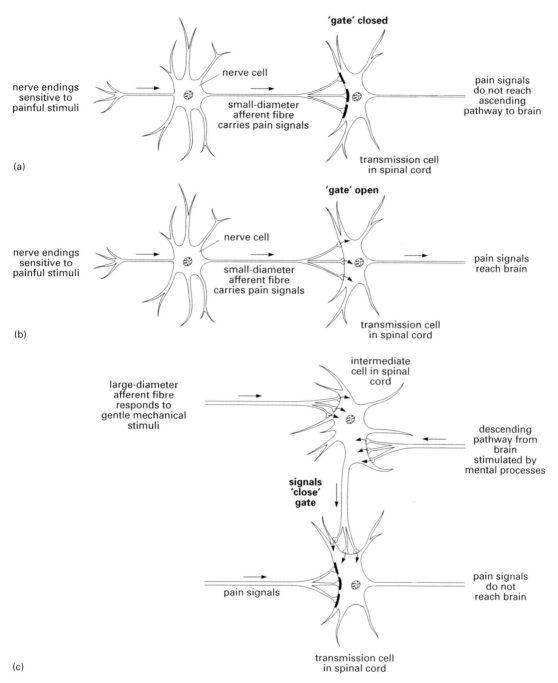

Figure 7.4 *The concept of gate control in the perception of pain. Diagram (a) shows the hypothetical 'gate' in the spinal cord closed, preventing the transmission of pain signals carried by small-diameter afferent fibres from the periphery to the brain. In (b) the 'gate' is open, and signals from the periphery stimulate transmission cells in the spinal cord to relay pain signals to the brain. Diagram (c) shows how the 'gate' may be closed by messages relayed by intermediate nerve cells, originating either from (i) large-diameter afferent fibres stimulated by gentle mechanical pressure in the periphery, or (ii) descending signals from the brain.*

important role in determining our subjective *experience of* pain. The new medical narrative allows for the influence of a large variety of external factors: the immediate physical environment, our evaluation of sources of threat and pleasure, our personalities, our conscious calculations about the consequences of courses of action, and indeed our cultural conditions. Matters that previously were relegated to the purely physical category of 'reflex' now appear to be amenable to a degree of influence from the conscious mind:

> If we pick up a hot cup of tea in an expensive cup we are not likely to simply drop the cup, but jerkily put it back on the table, and *then* nurse our hand. (Melzack and Wall, 1988, reprinted 1991, p. 193)

At this point, students of the Open University should listen to the audiotape 'Being in pain' which involves an interview with Patrick Wall about gate-control theory, and an account of the work of a pain clinic in Liverpool from the point of view of a doctor and some of the patients who attend it.[5] Then answer the following questions.

☐ What implications does gate-control theory have for the treatment of pain, according to Wall?

■ It explains the action of TENS and emphasises the importance of 'attitude', since mental processes influence the perception of pain.

☐ What features of pain are emphasised in the medical narrative adopted by the Liverpool pain management programme?

■ This programme emphasises psychological rather than medical or surgical treatment. Eric Ghadiali, the consultant neuropsychologist interviewed, distinguishes *cognitive, affective* and *behavioural* aspects of learning to live with pain. The programme seeks to help patients become more active and self-reliant in treating their own pain through understanding how to modify aspects of their lifestyle.

The concept of total pain

It should by now be clear that the delineation of a separate sphere of experience called 'physical pain', and its separation from emotional and social pain, are less easy to maintain in cases where pain is chronic. Just as this insight has arisen from study of rarer and more extreme

[5]Please consult the Audiocassette Notes before listening to this tape.

cases (such as people experiencing intractable pains or 'puzzles', such as a lack of pain where there is serious injury), so the concept of **total pain** and its alleviation derives from work with people at an extreme point in life: those with terminal illness. It represents a medical narrative which attempts to help people who are experiencing suffering at, perhaps, its most extreme.

Total pain is a concept used by some professionals associated with hospice care to describe the suffering that may be experienced as people approach death, and to provide a rationale for their treatment and care. Cicely Saunders and Mary Baines (1983), doctors working in St Christopher's Hospice, London, have distinguished four elements to total pain: physical, emotional, social and spiritual. Much effort in hospices has been devoted to investigating pharmacological and other methods for treating *physical* pain, for example advocating the use of high dosages of morphine without introducing irrelevant fears about drug dependency. In this respect, hospice care has drawn on the development of gate-control theory, and Patrick Wall is himself involved in the work of St Christopher's Hospice. However, hospices also seek to address other aspects of total pain.

Noting that a patient's mental distress is likely to be linked to his or her experience of physical pain, Saunders and Baines also observe that the effective treatment of one often relieves the other. Thus drug treatments for physical pain relieve mental distress; listening to people's fears and concerns in a sympathetic manner is also a means of addressing the *emotional* pain of dying, which can itself influence people's perceptions of their physical pain. By *social* pain, Saunders and Baines mean the distress of a dying person's family. Hospice care seeks to attend to their needs too, for example by providing specific services to help people with their bereavement. The identification of *spiritual* pain as a component reflects the religious background of some hospice practitioners, who seek also to maintain a religious narrative to give meaning to dying.

☐ How does the hospice account of 'total pain' compare with the definition of suffering as physical, social and emotional pain, given in the introduction to this chapter?

■ The principal differences are that the definition of social pain given earlier involved considerations of stigma as a wider social phenomenon, rather than of immediate family responses to impending bereavement, and the spiritual dimension was not mentioned.

In fact, hospice care has sometimes been characterised as treating the *pain of stigma*. Hospices arose partly in response to the stigmatisation of dying people in hospitals, who were (and perhaps still are) often discharged, avoided or shut away in side rooms because they represented failure for curatively oriented medical practice. Hospice care, in the context of this chapter, can be understood as an attempt to write a narrative of treatment and care that not only relieves physical pain, but also stresses the values of emotional and social *accompaniment* at a time of life when people are dying—or, in the words we used earlier, making a complete exit from culture.[6]

Negotiating treatment

Treatment for pain can be understood as a matter of negotiation between the personal life-world of the patient, and the technical or scientific world of the doctor or other healer. The first task in this negotiation is to come to an agreed definition of the problem, which in the case of pain is dependent on the creation of a shared language to communicate about subjective experiences. Issues of personal as opposed to medical responsibility for controlling the pain underlie negotiations over treatment, as you will see shortly.

Communicating about pain

Christian Heath, a sociologist interested in the dynamics of medical consultations, has presented evidence to suggest that from one moment to another people's expression and experience of pain may be determined by the particular psycho-social context, in a way that is consistent with the theories outlined by Melzack and Wall. Heath (1989) made videotape recordings of several consultations in which patients' pains were a topic. Through detailed analysis of the minutiae of the interaction, including the timing of pauses, manipulation of painful parts by the doctor, and analysis of exactly when 'pain cries' were emitted in the sequence of talk, Heath demonstrated that these occur only at *socially appropriate* moments. Patients managed the twin task of giving emotional expressions to their pain so as to 'prove' that it is there, and of withholding these cries when a more objective information-giving stance is required by the doctor. The following is an extract from one of the

[6]Hospice care is discussed in *Birth to Old Age: Health in Transition*, Chapter 13.

consultations where the doctor has just finished taking a man's blood pressure:

> *Dr*: That's all right actually [5 second pause]. Just show me where that pain was will you?
> *P*: It's just there, just on that bone.
> *Dr*: Yes, yes, yes. Is it sort of like inside or just
> ...
> *P*: Seems on the inside — *oooh*
> *Dr*: Yes.
> *P*: *ooh*, it is there tender.
> *Dr*: Yes, yes.
> *P*: What is it doctor if you don't think that's a rude question, is it?
> *Dr*: Well I don't think it's a rude question. I mean I think it just you know I think it is probably pain from your heart.
> (Adapted from Heath, 1989, p. 120)

The first pain cry (*oooh*) is accompanied by the patient pointing towards his chest; neither he nor the doctor touched the chest. Clearly, the expression of pain occurs at the moment when it was 'required' by the ongoing interaction, that is to say, at the moment when it was needed as 'evidence'.

☐ What alternative explanations could there be for this precise timing of pain cries?

■ The patient could be expressing a pain he did not have, or exaggerating it; he could be restraining himself from expressing a severe pain and 'letting it out' when given permission to do so; or he could be subjectively experiencing the pain according to the moment-to-moment demands of the interaction.

One of the major difficulties in trying to understand pain is that we cannot know exactly how other people experience their pain. However, it is at least possible, given the theory of *gate control* and *summation* of a variety of stimuli arriving simultaneously, that the last interpretation is the correct one. The central nervous system may be capable of changing its priorities for the perception of pain according to quite subtle changes in the flow of a conversation—'allowing' the pain sensations to reach consciousness only at socially-appropriate moments.

A shared language for pain

It was stated earlier that pain is often expressed in pre-linguistic cries; the lack of a shared language for communicating varieties of pain experience contributes to the isolating effect of pain and allows stigmatising perceptions to develop. Significantly, the scientists who developed and elaborated the theory of gate control have also been prominent in attempts to construct linguistic devices that convey the subjective experience of pain in an accurate and valid way.

Figure 7.5 shows the McGill–Melzack Pain Questionnaire, developed to measure different qualities of the pain experience. Table 7.1 is based on careful research into the language used by people to describe different sources of pain. It shows how six different pain syndromes were associated with particular words, and it has proved successful in helping to communicate clinically relevant information. One study (Dubuisson and Melzack, 1976) showed that, on the basis of the words chosen by patients with eight different pain

Table 7.1 Descriptions characteristic of clinical pain syndromes

Menstrual pain (N = 25)	Arthritic pain (N = 16)	Labour pain (N = 11)	Disc disease pain (N = 10)	Toothache (N = 10)	Cancer pain (N = 8)
Sensory					
cramping (44%)	gnawing (38%)	pounding (37%)	throbbing (40%)	throbbing (50%)	shooting (50%)
aching (44%)	aching (50%)	shooting (46%)	shooting (50%)	boring (40%)	sharp (50%)
		stabbing (37%)	stabbing (40%)	sharp (50%)	gnawing (50%)
		sharp (64%)	sharp (60%)		burning (50%)
		cramping (82%)	cramping (40%)		heavy (50%)
		aching (46%)	aching (40%)		
			heavy (40%)		
			tender (50%)		
Affective					
tiring (44%)	exhausting (50%)	tiring (37%)	tiring (46%)	sickening (40%)	exhausting (50%)
sickening (50%)		exhausting (46%)	exhausting (40%)		
		fearful (36%)			
Evaluative					
	annoying (38%)	intense (46%)	unbearable (40%)	annoying (50%)	unbearable (50%)
Temporal					
constant (56%)	constant (44%)	rhythmic (91%)	constant (80%)	constant (60%)	constant (100%)
	rhythmic (56%)		rhythmic (70%)	rhythmic (40%)	rhythmic (88%)

Note that only those words chosen by more than one-third of the patients are listed (N = number of patients), and the percentage of patients who chose each word is shown below the word. The word 'rhythmic' is one of three words ('rhythmic/periodic/intermittent') used in different versions of the McGill–Melzack Pain Questionnaire (Melzack, 1975). (Source: Melzack, R. and Wall, P. D., 1988, *The Challenge of Pain*, reprinted 1991, p. 42)

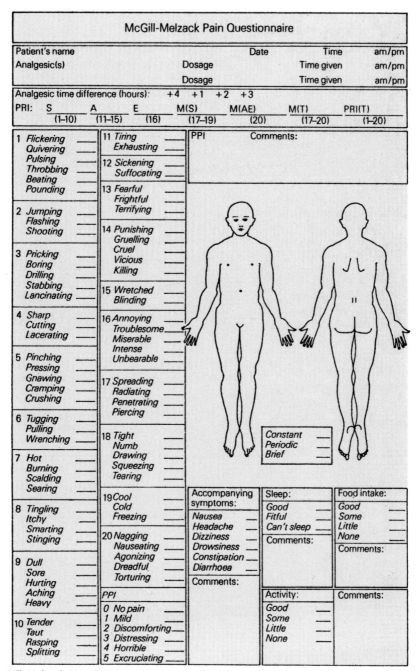

Figure 7.5   *The McGill–Melzack Pain Questionnaire. From each of the applicable sections, the sufferer chooses the word that best describes the current feelings and sensations evoked by the pain. The questionnaire allows people to assess separately various sub-classes of pain, e.g. sensory (S: numbers 1–10), affective (A: 11–15), evaluative (E: number 16) and miscellaneous (M: 17–20) categories. From the individual responses, a Pain Rating Index (PRI) can be calculated, based on the numerical values previously ascribed to each word. The Present Pain Index (PPI) is a single assessment of overall pain severity. (Source: based on the original version of the McGill–Melzack Pain Questionnaire described in Melzack, 1975, and reproduced in Melzack and Wall, 1988, p. 40)*

syndromes, a computer was able to identify correctly the cause of the pain in 77 per cent of cases. When the sex of the patients and the location of the pain were included, all cases were correctly classified.

As confidence in the validity of instruments such as those shown in Figure 7.5 and Table 7.1 grows in medical settings, so confidence increases in the ability to convey hitherto incommunicable experiences. This has the potential to combat the isolation experienced by people with chronic pain by offering a shared language. However, the limitations of using measures of pain devised by 'outsiders' rather than determined by patients themselves must be borne in mind, as the discussion of rheumatoid arthritis (Chapter 3) made clear.

Taking responsibility

Although medicine offers powerful institutionally based narratives for people experiencing pain and suffering, people are not simply 'written into' such narratives as if they were passive recipients of a 'script'. People actively *appropriate* medical narratives, sometimes choosing between a variety of conflicting scripts in negotiation with various medical practitioners.

> ☐ Which conflicting scripts for people with chronic pain (such as Brian, interviewed by Byron Good) have been reviewed in this chapter?
>
> ■ Specificity theory and gate-control theory offer people (through their interaction with doctors and others who 'represent' these narratives) different scripts in terms of their explanations and treatments for chronic pain. Locating pain as having a physical or psychological cause involves a choice between scripts; each at various times was accepted by Brian as he sought an explanation for his chronic pain.

The issue of personal responsibility is a theme that runs through many negotiations between doctors and patients with pain. Medical settings may initially be approached by patients with the expectation that the doctor will take responsibility for seeking a solution to their pain. Sometimes this may literally involve 'writing a script', as when the doctor issues a drug prescription. However, in many cases the interaction that proceeds is not as simple as that. To explore these issues you should now read the article by Sally Macintyre and David Oldman, 'Coping with migraine'.[7]

[7]An edited extract from Macintyre and Oldman (1977) appears in *Health and Disease: A Reader* (second edition, 1995).

> ☐ What treatments were experienced by Sally Macintyre?
>
> ■ She lists a variety of treatments: at first she used a drug to handle the migraine attacks. She was reluctant to accept psychological therapies as they threatened her feelings about herself. Eventually, Valium helped with her anxieties about attacks and helped her to begin to modify aspects of her life, such as her diet and the wearing of dark glasses. She now regards herself as an 'expert' in using her GP as a resource for her to manage her own treatment.

> ☐ What treatments were experienced by David Oldman?
>
> ■ His mother treated his migraine attacks with the home remedies of bed rest, a dark room and a hot water bottle. With varying degrees of success, he sought to build this pattern of withdrawal into his life to control attacks. Like Sally Macintyre, he too selectively uses drugs obtained from his doctor.

Sally Macintyre, in particular, describes her experiences with doctors as a series of negotiations over treatments, some being acceptable to her, others being unacceptable. David Oldman appears to have had a somewhat easier time in reaching an eventual position which, as in the case of Sally Macintyre, displays a strong sense of personal responsibility for controlling the illness. Both can be seen as having appropriated elements of medical narratives in writing a personal narrative that gives meaning to, and offers a degree of control over their pains.

Stoicism

The emphasis in hospice care and in pain clinics on recognising and treating pain in others involves the construction of medical narratives which emphasise sensitivity to the subjective experience of those affected. Heightened sensitivity of this type ('empathy') is commonly characterised as a caring or compassionate approach in modern culture and attracts considerable approval, so it may be seen as a widespread *social value*. However, the institutionalised promotion of care and compassion, involving an encouragement to speak and care about suffering, is a relatively recent historical phenomenon—at least on the large scale represented

(a)

(b)

Figure 7.6 *The annual hook-swinging ceremony practised in remote Indian villages. Left: Two steel hooks thrust into the small of the back of the 'celebrant', who is decked with garlands. The celebrant is later taken to a special cart which has upright timbers and a cross-beam. Right: The celebrant hanging on to the ropes as the cart is moved to each village. After he has blessed each child and farm field in a village, he swings free, suspended only by the hooks. The crowds cheer at each swing. The celebrant, during the ceremony, is in a state of exaltation and shows no sign of pain. (Source: Kosambi, D. D., 1967, 'Living prehistory in India', Scientific American, 216, pp. 110–111)*

by the construction of systems of health care. The alternative value of **stoicism** is one which was more widespread in the past, and may be characteristic of some traditional cultures today. In common parlance, it is associated with the 'stiff upper lip' and avoidance of resort to medicine.

There is evidence to suggest cross-cultural and historical variability in people's tolerance to pain and suffering. Cross-cultural aspects are illustrated, once again, by some rather dramatic examples (Figure 7.6). Indian fakirs appear to be able to induce a state of hypnotic analgesia when they walk across beds of hot coals or lie on nails; piercing the body with knives and skewers is occasionally displayed on stage, involving a similar state of mind. Certain ritual occasions induce in individuals, who have reached a sufficiently trance-like state, an ability to tolerate damage that would normally cause intense pain.

It is likely that in the past there were higher levels of stoicism. This is demonstrated by the discovery, in a variety of archaeological sites, of skulls with holes cut

into the top associated with a fairly common operation done in the past, described here by Melzack and Wall:

In East Africa, men and women undergo an operation—entirely without anaesthetics or pain-relieving drugs—called 'trepanation', in which the scalp and underlying muscles are cut in order to expose a large area of the skull. The skull is then scraped by the doktari [doctor] as the man or woman sits calmly, without flinching or grimacing, holding a pan under the chin to catch the dripping blood. Films of this procedure are extraordinary to watch because of the discomfort they induce in the observers, which is in striking contrast to the apparent lack of discomfort in the people undergoing the operation. There is no reason to believe that these people are physiologically different in any way. Rather, the operation is accepted by their culture as a procedure that brings relief of chronic pain. (Melzack and Wall, 1988, p. 17)

☐ In Chapter 2 you saw that Elias argued that a 'civilising process' had made people more sensitive to, and more ashamed of, bodily functions. How might this theory be applied to historical changes in perceptions of pain?

■ The same process may have made people more sensitive to pain. Whereas pain was not remarked upon before, now it is a focus of attention. Sensitivity to others' pains, institutionalised in the activities of health care workers, may have increased sensitivity to one's own pains.

If such a change has occurred, gate-control theory would suggest that subjective experiences of pain would have been *less* common in the past for a given level of physical stimulus. Stoicism is another word for effective mental control over pain sensation, not simply a suppression of the desire to express distress. In the terms used earlier in this chapter, stoicism involves effective resistance to the unmaking of the world by pain. This means that higher levels of injury can be tolerated before the remaking of the world by religious, medical or other narratives becomes necessary.

The encouragement in modern culture towards a heightened sensitivity to pain leads on the one hand to its widespread discussion and inclusion in medical narratives, and on the other to a decreased tolerance for pain. This lack of tolerance leads to dependence on technical methods for killing pain. The philosopher and theologian Ivan Illich (1976) develops this argument, saying that Western *medicalised*[8] culture is one where the general problem of human suffering has increasingly been interpreted as simply a matter of *physical* pain. The solution to pain in such a culture is to provide an anaesthetic for the slightest occasion and make remedies for pain available as commodities. Pain relief has come to be regarded as a right. Thus, Illich argues, we live in an 'anaesthetic society' in which we flee from pain by trying to kill it as soon as it appears.

Melzack and Wall, for example, although their theory allows for approaches that involve learning to live with pain, otherwise represent the sort of view of which Illich is critical: they consider it to be an appropriate goal to move towards a pain-free world:

There is no question that our new understanding is leading to our goal of abolishing pain … The challenges before us are clear: to conquer

pain and suffering in all their forms … [We must] combine all the available resources to allow the nervous system to move toward a normal, pain-free mode of operation. (Melzack and Wall, 1988, reprinted 1991, pp. 213, 273, 295)

Even if this were possible, it is debatable whether such a world would be a very pleasant place in which to live. John Hick (1977), a theologian, contemplated just such a world as proposed by the eighteenth-century philosopher David Hume. In opposition to Hume, Hick points out that pain is a warning signal that is essential for our survival in the material environment. Occasional cases of people who are congenitally unable to feel pain reveal that these individuals lead very dangerous lives, frequently damaging themselves very seriously. In addition, the removal of pain would radically alter the nature of human existence. As Hick argues, 'A soft unchallenging world would be inhabited by a soft unchallenged race of men [sic]' (p. 307).

The alternative, which Illich believes is characteristic of societies that have not experienced medicalisation, is to *include* pain as a part of the 'performance of suffering'. Pain is seen as an inevitable part of life, albeit unpleasant, but one that paradoxically means that the pleasures of life are experienced more fully when they occur. Illich also harks back nostalgically to a time when pain was contained in a religious narrative, making it more easy to accept.

It is undoubtedly the case that responses to 'normal' acute pain in Western culture generally take the form outlined by Illich. However, this chapter has demonstrated that, in the case of chronic pain and the 'total pain' of dying, new medical narratives are now available that stress on the one hand the acknowledgement and acceptance of pain and suffering, and on the other, the goal of eradicating it.

Conclusion

This chapter has demonstrated the value of an interdisciplinary approach to understanding the experience of pain and suffering. In so doing, a picture of pain as both a physiological and a psycho-social experience has emerged, and its position in the spectrum of distress commonly referred to as 'suffering' has been explored.

Central to the experience of pain is the search for an explanation that will turn the perception of chaos and the experience of isolation into one of order and inclusion in social life. Medical efforts have been depicted as institutionalised narratives, which can be drawn upon with

---

[8]Medicalisation, and the contribution of Ivan Illich to the debate about its impact, are discussed in *Medical Knowledge: Doubt and Certainty.*

varying degrees of success by people experiencing pain and suffering. Recent shifts in medical thinking have created more all-embracing narratives with a greater potential for inclusion and healing of hitherto mysterious conditions.

At the same time, these broader medical narratives, seen in gate-control theory and its associated treatments and in hospice care, can be understood as part of a wider historical process in which the modern experience of illness and care is located. Modern conditions encourage us to pay great attention to suffering, particularly suffering of the body, and paradoxically this may mean that we increase the likelihood that we will find it overwhelming and seek relief in 'anaesthetics'. The tension between killing pain, suffering pain, and learning to live with it is central to the modern experience of illness.

OBJECTIVES FOR CHAPTER 7

When you have studied this chapter, you should be able to:

7.1 Demonstrate how and why people who are suffering physical, emotional and social pain seek to give their experience meaning and legitimate it in the eyes of others.

7.2 Explain the role of medical narratives in attempts made by people to give suffering a meaning, drawing on biomedical theories of pain as examples.

7.3 Distinguish the specifically modern aspects of pain and suffering in Western culture from those that seem to have been current in earlier times.

QUESTIONS FOR CHAPTER 7

Question 1 (Objective 7.1)

Small children with quite minor scratches often cry inconsolably until a plaster is applied by a sympathetic adult, at which point their attention may then switch to more pleasurable activity. How could the concepts of 'making' and 'unmaking' the world help to explain this? What component of suffering is appealed to by the adult who says 'Don't make such a fuss: it's only a scratch'?

Question 2 (Objective 7.2)

Richard Hilbert concludes his study of people with chronic pains by stating:

> The mere addition of 'chronic pain syndrome' to the lexicon of sufferers is a treatment of sorts. (Hilbert, 1984, p. 376)

Why might the mere naming of a syndrome by medicine be tantamount to treating it?

Question 3 (Objective 7.3)

The diaries of the Reverend Ralph Josselin (1616–1683) discuss health and illness in his family over a forty-year period. The sociologist Deborah Lupton notes:

> They were unwell, or at least uncomfortable, most of the time, due to continual colds and occasional bouts of ague, eye and skin disorders, and in the case of Josselin's wife Jane, fifteen pregnancies and at least five miscarriages. Of the ten live births to the Josselins, five children predeceased their father. Worms, rickets, boils, measles and smallpox were suffered by the children, while Ralph Josselin himself suffered pain, swelling and ulceration in his left leg for the eleven years before his death, and inflammation of the navel for almost four years … While there were expectations that people sick enough to be confined to bed should stay in bed, be waited on and take medicine if required, it was expected that people well enough to be out of bed should bear their discomfort and carry on with their normal duties … [the family] almost never consulted physicians and surgeons, but relied on their own knowledge or that of others such as friends, nurses and part-time healers for treatment … the Josselins believed that God's will was of the ultimate importance in determining the outcome of an illness. (Lupton, 1994, p. 82, summarising a study of the diaries made by Beier, 1985)

How does the modern experience of pain and suffering in Western culture differ from this?

8

Experiencing and explaining disease: some conclusions

At the end of this chapter, as a revision exercise, you will be asked to listen to an audiotape band, 'Living with epilepsy' which has been recorded for Open University students. If you have time while reading this chapter, three optional articles in the Reader would enhance your understanding of the major themes of this book—they are: 'Tangled feelings: an account of Alzheimer's disease' by Julia Burton-Jones; 'The last well person' by Clifton Meador; and 'Pride against prejudice: "lives not worth living"' by Jenny Morris.[1]

This chapter was written by Clive Seale, Senior Lecturer in Medical Sociology at Goldsmiths' College, University of London, and Basiro Davey, Lecturer in Health Studies in the Biology Department, The Open University. This final chapter also marks the conclusion of the 'Health and Disease' series, so the authors briefly look back over the territory covered by students of the Open University course, of which this is the last of eight books.

Introduction

This book has described certain consistent features of the *experience* of illness and disability, and of the dominant *explanations* for disease in both lay and professional accounts. Every chapter has pointed to ways in which the experiential and explanatory domains interact and exert profound influences upon each other. In assembling material for this book, the authors have drawn on the findings of a variety of academic disciplines, including biology, epidemiology, clinical medicine and the social and behavioural sciences. We have also incorporated personal anecdotes, fragments of news reporting, advertising, and portrayals of illness in the entertainment media.

In this final chapter, we summarise the main themes of the book, which—for the sake of clarity—we have organised under two headings: 'Doubt and certainty' and 'Inclusion and exclusion'. Other methods of grouping the material are possible and, indeed, other interpretations of 'what this book is about' may have occurred to you as you read it—an outcome that we warmly welcome. Health and illness, disease and disability are not fixed entities, as we noted in Chapter 1, and each of us adds to the fluidity of meaning attached to these terms. However, we suggest that the major themes identified in this book have a certain universality: they can be found at different times and in different places and cultures, wherever humans experience ill-health and attempt to explain and alleviate pain and suffering. We reinforce this assertion by noting—briefly—the expression of these themes in accounts of illness, disease or disabling states other than those already discussed in earlier chapters of this book.

At the very end of this chapter, we offer a few concluding remarks for the *Health and Disease* series as a whole.

Doubt and certainty

It is no accident that the 'label' we have chosen to stand for one group of themes in this final book in the series, is also in the title of its first book.[2] Doubt and certainty—and the tension between them—have helped to link the

---

[1] *Health and Disease: A Reader* (second edition, 1995).

[2] *Medical Knowledge: Doubt and Certainty* (second edition, 1994).

various books in the series as they spanned huge distances of time, space and culture.

Personal knowledge

In this book, Chapter 2 brought the tension between doubt and certainty in our personal worlds to the foreground. It argued that any doubts about continuing in existence pose such a threat to the human psyche that we act—individually and collectively—to create an illusion of certainty. Illness, according to social theorists such as Anthony Giddens, undermines our *ontological security*, as well as disrupting the familiar mental and physical states we associate with 'normal' health. Recourse to the *grand narratives* of orthodox medical treatment, traditional therapies, prayer, psychoanalysis, or whatever else holds out hope of a cure, is prompted by the desire to banish threatening doubts and restore a degree of certainty and control, as well as by the desire to be free from pain and disability.

Part of the experience of illness and injury is the need to answer the questions we have posed throughout this book: 'Why me? Why now? What next?' They arise even for a trivial illness, a common cold for example—was it due to staying out too late in cold air, or getting stressed at work, or was it just our bad luck to encounter another 'bug' doing the rounds, which a couple of days' rest will resolve? Finding answers to these existential questions takes on real urgency when the illness is chronic, severely disabling, incurable, or potentially fatal, as several case studies in this book have illustrated. The search for certainty in a world 'unmade' by such an illness typically leads to the construction of a *personal illness narrative*, a meaningful story which explains the illness. Such narratives often involve the reconstruction and reinterpretation of past events, now seen to be part of the underlying history of the present state.

In schizophrenia, where the condition affects thought processing itself, reaching a satisfactory personal construction of the illness may be a particularly difficult task. Questions of 'Why me?', 'Why now?' may be 'answered' in ways that others find unbelievable—for example, 'voices' may be heard as real or emanating from sources that appear to others to be 'imaginary'.

Professionals who seem able to offer authoritative explanations for an illness are likely to be sought as allies in constructing a meaningful personal narrative. Medical knowledge and the treatment practices associated with it contribute to a grand narrative about human suffering, which ill people draw upon to give meaning to a potentially chaotic and mysterious process. It helps to 'remake

the shattered world' if a *medical label* can be tied to a person's symptoms, investing them with a reassuring legitimacy. Several of the people who have figured in this book expressed relief at being told by a doctor that they had an identifiable disease. The anxiety that one may be thought a 'malingerer' or 'hypochondriac' is relieved by a medical diagnosis, which can restore the patient's *moral reputation*.

The ability of medicine to do all these things helps to explain its power as a cultural icon in modern industrialised societies. The 'moral' aspect is particularly apparent when a medical diagnosis is applied to someone with a mental illness. As the Reader article by Goffman[3] and the chapter on schizophrenia show, mental illness presents a basic threat to *social norms* of conduct, which others often find more difficult to condone than in the case of deviations from the norm due to a physical illness.

But illness is more than a matter of abstract psychology and social constructs. It faces us with pressing physical realities. Common to all the conditions described in this book is the experience of uncertainty about the progression of the disease, and its likely consequences for an individual's life. Rheumatoid arthritis (RA), HIV-disease, asthma and schizophrenia are all relatively unstable, fluctuating or episodic conditions, and affected people face a daily uncertainty about the severity of their symptoms. There may be long periods of remission, followed by unpredicted relapse. As one of the people with HIV says in Neil Small's article in the Reader:[4]

> One of the cruellest ruses of the virus is letting you think the good times are the real times. (Quoted by Small, in Davey, Gray and Seale, 1995, p. 103)

Uncertainty, then, preoccupies many people with the conditions reviewed in this book. It also concerns their friends and families. The impact of illness extends beyond that of the person designated as 'sufferer', affecting the lives of others too. Parents of a child with severe asthma can agonise over whether to call a doctor to a bout of wheezing in the night; holidays may be cancelled, pets denied to siblings; broken sleep and worry become routine. Perhaps most powerfully in the case of a person with schizophrenia, others in their social circle may suffer too;

---

[3]'The insanity of place' in *Health and Disease: A Reader*, was referred to in Chapter 2 of this book.

[4]'Living with HIV and AIDS' in *Health and Disease: A Reader*, was referred to in Chapter 4 of this book.

their uncertainties and anxieties have come increasingly to be seen as a part of the experience of illness. This is graphically illustrated in 'Tangled feelings: an account of Alzheimer's disease', in the Reader, in which a researcher, Julia Burton-Jones (1992), recounts the story of Tom's struggle to look after his wife, Dot, as her ability to cope with the activities of daily living deteriorates.[5]

But most illness episodes do not rob the affected person of the ability to cope, at least to some degree. People are not usually the passive recipients of what a disease dictates, and uncertainty is actively counteracted with skills developed from past experiences of illness.

□ Can you recall an example from earlier in this book?

■ Sally Macintyre and David Oldman described how they came to deal with the uncertainty of migraines.[6] They built up expertise in self-care, recognising the signs of a coming attack and taking action at the appropriate time to pre-empt a worsening of symptoms.

But novel, fluctuating or puzzling symptoms raise doubts about 'What to do for the best?' It may be difficult to decide whether to seek medical help in determining whether the symptoms are serious or even 'real'. Delay may stem from anxiety about having one's worst fears confirmed, or out of a concern not to waste the doctor's time by 'making a fuss about nothing'. After all, most illness episodes resolve without medical help or are successfully self-treated. But delay may also mean that medical intervention comes too late to prevent an otherwise avoidable attack or deterioration of the condition—a dilemma acutely expressed in Chapter 5 by the parents of children with asthma. People with chronic ailments may worry that they will lose the goodwill of health professionals if they seek help too often, and may try to cope alone rather than risk the GP's heart sinking as they walk into the surgery again.

Part of the anxiety among lay people about whether they should seek professional help for an illness may arise from the common assumption that medicine is an exact science and that doctors deal in certainties. This book, along with others in this series, has sought to illustrate the tenuousness of this belief.

[5]This article in *Health and Disease: A Reader* is optional reading for Open University students.

[6]'Coping with migraine', in *Health and Disease: A Reader*, was referred to in Chapters 5 and 7 of this book.

Professional knowledge

The sphere of professional knowledge that has figured most prominently in our discussion of doubt and certainty is scientific medicine. This is not to deny the value of medical knowledge. In addition to establishing the legitimacy of an illness, a medical diagnosis holds out the hope of more tangible certainties for the patient. The doctor may be able to say what caused the condition, how it is likely to progress or be resolved by treatment, and what can be done to prevent it from occurring again. Medicine can be technically effective in reducing suffering, by alleviating pain or anxiety, or treating the underlying causes of the symptoms. Medicine on this level is a remarkable human achievement in which many health care workers are justifiably proud to play their part. But certain knowledge is relatively uncommon in modern medicine, as the disorders we chose as case studies for this book amply demonstrate.

□ What were the main areas of medical uncertainty highlighted in earlier chapters?

■ The disease processes themselves are generally well *described* in rheumatoid arthritis (RA), HIV-disease and asthma, but remain a mystery in schizophrenia and in many cases of chronic pain. The underlying *cause* of HIV-disease is known to be a virus, but there is considerable uncertainty about what 'triggers' the inflammation in RA and asthma, and what produces persistent pain in the absence of injury; the causes of schizophrenia are utterly obscure. All the conditions featured in this book have a *variable* course, sometimes progressing and at other times remitting, without any consistent explanation. Despite a medical consensus about the *range* of treatment options, there is still some disagreement about which therapies are most effective; none yet produce a *cure*, and available drugs and surgical interventions can have serious adverse *side-effects*. There are no *medical* strategies for preventing any of these conditions.

These uncertainties limit the extent to which medical knowledge can alleviate suffering, and they also reduce the power of medical narratives as sources of comfort and reassurance for patients. The principal doubts in scientific medicine stem from the inability of basic biological research to *explain* disease processes rather than simply describe them.

□ How does the example of AIDS illustrate a 'failure' of biological research (at least up to the mid-1990s and perhaps beyond) to supply vital medical knowledge?

■ The virus that causes AIDS was identified in 1984 and its mode of binding to host cells and replication within them has since been established. But despite this knowledge, over a decade later there has been little progress in developing protective vaccines or drugs against HIV itself. (The 'successes' have been new therapies to treat the consequent opportunistic infections, and social research and interventions to reduce the spread of HIV.)

This situation is in contrast to that of asthma. Biological knowledge about the mechanisms that lead to allergies, inflammation and bronchoconstriction has enabled treatment strategies to be devised, which enable most asthmatic people to live normal lives. However, there is continuing biological uncertainty about what causes asthma to develop in the first place, so, as yet, little can be done to prevent it.

Perhaps the most intriguing area of uncertainty in academic and professional knowledge concerns the *definition* of a disease entity, which reliably distinguishes it from the range of variation in 'normal' states of health and from other states of disease. The diagnostic criteria that, for example, distinguish asthma from 'wheezing' are necessarily imprecise: they may vary from one country to another, change over time, and be subject to disagreement between individual doctors.

Uncertainties about medical diagnoses can have a major effect on the epidemiology of a disease, raising doubts about the reliability, validity and hence the interpretation of published data. For example, as the list of opportunistic infections accepted as indicative of HIV-disease has grown, so larger numbers of individuals have been recorded as having AIDS. The numbers leapt when tubercular pneumonia was added to the list—a decision that increased the prevalence of recorded AIDS among Western drug injectors and some Third World populations, and fuelled doubts about the validity of estimates.

However, these difficulties should not be allowed to obscure the fact that a large degree of consensus about the signs and symptoms of a certain disease often exists, or can be achieved through collaboration.

☐ The published prevalence of schizophrenia in different countries has shown considerable variation in the past. What was the outcome when the same 'narrow' definition of schizophrenia was applied in several sites around the world?

■ Apparent differences in prevalence were greatly reduced and the rates became similar, even in countries with markedly different cultures. This finding casts doubt on the hypothesis that schizophrenia is a product of cultural pressures.

Epidemiologists have contributed to scientific understanding of the causes of many diseases, by demonstrating varying prevalence rates in particular subgroups within and between populations. This is most obviously illustrated by HIV and AIDS and their association with people exposed to sexual or blood-borne routes of infection. Epidemiological research on asthma is beginning to identify the environmental triggers for attacks (if not the underlying causes of susceptibility to these triggers).

☐ What insight into the underlying causes of RA has epidemiological research provided?

■ Demonstrating that prevalence is higher among women than men, but falls during pregnancy or with use of oral contraceptive pills, has strongly suggested a role for the female hormone oestrogen in the aetiology of RA.

However, considerable doubts about the causes of RA remain, and an equivalent uncertainty has been emphasised in other case studies in this book. For example, schizophrenia is one of many conditions in which the 'nature–nurture' debate has been fiercely contested in professional circles. In the 1990s, the majority view is that schizophrenia is a disorder of chemicals in the brain, rather than an expression of dysfunctional family relationships—a view that was more prominent in the 1970s. In the 21st century, a greater knowledge of human genetics may resurrect an interpretation of schizophrenia as an inherited condition—a belief that research in the 1980s failed to prove. For the moment, uncertainty prevails.

Inevitably, the dominant medical understanding of a disease at a particular time and place influences the treatments that are considered 'best practice', while relegating others to the 'fringe'. It is not always the case that medical knowledge accumulates and treatments are refined and improved on the basis of scientific evidence. Medical 'fashions' can influence treatment strategies, and the wonder drug of one period can fall from favour, as occurred with steroids in the treatment of RA. There is no shortage of examples to demonstrate tension between doubt and certainty in all areas of professional knowledge about health and disease.

Public knowledge

Changes in the professional understanding of a certain disease have also had a major impact on what seems to be 'public knowledge' about it. As the earlier chapters in this book have illustrated, every disease has a *social history*, which has influenced the ways that health professionals, lay people, governments and the media think and write about it, fund and research it, treat and legislate to control or prevent it. For example, AIDS was originally publicised as an immune deficiency disorder among gay men, reputedly brought about by frequent sexually-transmitted infections, extensive use of 'social' drugs, and a high-stress 'fast-lane' lifestyle. This interpretation of AIDS persists in some quarters but, on world-wide epidemiological evidence, AIDS should be publicly understood as a heterosexual disease associated with poverty. Its social history continues to evolve.

External forces can change the importance of a disease in public perceptions in a relatively short period, as occurred with RA in the inter-war years in Britain. Anxieties about the basic fitness of troops in wartime and the returning workforce in peacetime have proved to be potent stimulators of biomedical research in a number of debilitating conditions, including RA. Thus, a disease can emerge from neglect to prominence on medical and governmental agendas, and be fundamentally altered in the eyes of the general public. A further example of a disease which may be undergoing social reconstruction is asthma—widely believed to be a consequence of rising atmospheric pollution in the 1980s and 1990s. It may turn out to have a different interpretation placed upon it in the next century, in which relative affluence has a more prominent explanatory role. What seems certain now, if media reporting of asthma is to be believed, may not remain so.

The assertion that all diseases are—at least in part—*socially constructed* should not be taken to mean that the pain and suffering they produce is not real. However, it does suggest that the *nature* of the social construction influences the experience of illness for those affected by it, as AIDS has convincingly demonstrated. The influence of society and culture extends beyond the boundaries of identifiable diseases into less-defined realms of pain and suffering. In Chapter 7, it was argued that there are *cultural thresholds* which have changed over time, altering the perception and meaning of pain, and reactions to it.

□ How has the meaning and hence the experience of physical pain changed in Western culture, according to the analysis in Chapter 7?

■ The accepted public understanding of pain in modern society is as a *bodily* state, produced by physical damage or malfunction, which a person cannot control and should not have to endure. In the past, people may have been more stoical about pain, and interpreted it in a wider *spiritual* framework which viewed some forms of suffering as potentially valuable.

Some commentators (for example, Ivan Illich) have argued that the boundaries of what is now considered 'unacceptable' discomfort or disability have become so widely drawn in Western culture that medicine—as the panacea for all ills—has achieved a dangerous level of power over human lives.[7] Clifton K. Meador, a physician from Nashville, Tennessee, predicts the extinction sometime in late 1998 of the 'The Last Well Person' (the title of his article, which appears in the Reader associated with this series).[8] This individual would once have been diagnosed as having an obsessive-compulsive neurosis, so concerned is he about the health implications of every aspect of his life, except for the fact that ' ... the diagnosis has had to be dropped. Obsession is no longer a disease, but an essential attribute of staying healthy' (Meador, 1994, p. 441). Meador begins his article by explaining how the idea of the last well person came to him.

Well people are disappearing ... I began to realize what was happening only a year ago, at a dinner party. Everyone there had something. Several had high cholesterol levels. One had 'borderline' anemia. Another had a suspicious Pap smear. Two others had abnormal treadmill-test results, and several were concerned about codependency. There were no well people. After that I began to look more carefully. I have not met a completely well person in months ... Why are they vanishing? The demands of the public for definitive wellness are colliding with the public's belief in a diagnostic system that can find only disease ... What is paradoxical about our awesome diagnostic power is that we

---

[7]The medicalisation thesis propounded by Illich, and its limitations, are discussed in *Medical Knowledge: Doubt and Certainty*, Chapter 8. An article by Illich, 'The epidemics of modern medicine', appears in *Health and Disease: A Reader*.

[8]This article can be found in *Health and Disease: A Reader* and is optional reading for Open University students, but is highly recommended as light relief!

do not have a test to distinguish a well person from a sick one. Wellness cannot be screened for … If the behaviour of doctors and the public continues unabated, eventually every well person will be labelled sick. (Meador, 1994, p. 440, reproduced in Davey, Gray and Seale, 1995, pp. 423–4)

Meador's vision of the future may be somewhat whimsical, but it illustrates the increasing sophistication of lay knowledge about medical matters, and its pervasiveness in modern culture. He sees patients as increasingly pressuring doctors to 'invent' more disease labels to attach to their physical and mental experiences. And although some ancient disease categories may be fading away (hysteria, for example[9]), the rate of acquisition of new ones may be exceeding the rate of loss. This process illustrates a growing uncertainty about what constitutes 'normal health' and where the line should be drawn between health and disease. It also brings us to the second constellation of themes identified in this book, under the general title of 'Inclusion and exclusion'.

Inclusion and exclusion

It seems to be a feature of human societies that a distinction is made between what is considered normal in terms of physical and mental functioning and emotional and spiritual well-being, and what falls outside this norm into the realm of illness or disability. There may be cultural differences in how the norm is constructed, and even within one culture there are likely to be differences between what is considered to be normal health for people of different ages. But the members of a society share a common understanding of what it means to be well or sick, able-bodied or physically-impaired. Of itself, this distinction need not form a barrier between people, but observation of contemporary societies and a study of human history show that it generally does. Something in the human psyche seems to draw a line between 'us' and 'them'. This tendency can be detected in acts of stigmatisation and discrimination against ill or disabled people, and also in the superiority attributed to 'expert' professional accounts of these states, from which the lay perspective is generally excluded.

Stigmatisation and discrimination

As we noted earlier, illness and disability are reminders of the fragility of our bodies and minds and of the

[9]*Medical Knowledge: Doubt and Certainty,* Chapter 6.

inevitability of death. People who are ill or disabled can provoke quite fundamental insecurities in others. The anxiety has to be coped with somehow, and two strategies were described in Chapter 2.

◻ What are they and what are their consequences?

■ One strategy is to assuage the anxiety by attempting to alleviate the suffering of ill or disabled people, to form an alliance with them, and to champion their right to be *included* in mainstream society. Another method of coping with the discomfort is by *projecting* the negative feelings onto those who seem to have aroused them. It is as though ill or disabled people have committed an offence—'the sick' are blamed for upsetting the ontological security of 'the well', and are rejected and *excluded* from society as a punishment.

The first strategy has led to substantial support for civil rights and other activist organisations committed to the welfare and *normalisation* of people with physical and mental illness or impairment. The second strategy leads to the *stigmatisation* of illness and disability, and *victim-blaming* of those who are affected by these conditions. They may experience active *discrimination* in many areas of life, such as employment, housing and insurance.

◻ On the basis of what you have read in this book, and from your own experience, what features of an illness or disability seem most likely to provoke these negative reactions?

■ Physical disfigurement, mental disability, high mortality rate, contagiousness, sexual route of transmission, high prevalence in an already stigmatised group, violent behaviour towards others.

These features were illustrated most powerfully in this book by HIV-disease and schizophrenia, although people in chronic pain also report a degree of stigmatisation. Additionally, the depiction of HIV-infected people who are also haemophiliac or heterosexual as 'innocent' victims reflects stigmatising assumptions that others are 'guilty'. Newspaper headlines and films often portray schizophrenic people as inherently dangerous predators who stalk innocent bystanders with murderous intent; in reality, self-harm and suicide are by far the most likely outcomes of violence by mentally-disturbed individuals. Even if non-violent, the actions of a person with a mental disturbance can seem deliberately to offend *social norms* and will often be met with rejection.

The exclusion of certain categories of ill or disabled people from mainstream society can, in its most extreme form, lead to the view that they should be excluded from life itself. A disabled-rights activist, Jenny Morris (1991), has written about the ease with which able-bodied people assume that someone with severe physical impairments has a 'life not worth living'.[10] She argues that the stigmatisation and discrimination experienced by severely handicapped people can be so great that their quality of life becomes too low to sustain with grace and dignity. If exclusion from everything that maintains the desire to live is prolonged, the person may conclude that their life is indeed not worth living. Morris cites several cases in the USA where a physically-handicapped person has applied to the courts for the right to assisted euthanasia, and though this right has been denied, the court ruled that the wish to die was rational given the level of disability. Morris asks:

> The question is, in such a context, is the wish to die a so-called rational response to physical disability? Or is it a desperate response to isolated oppression? (Morris, quoted in Davey, Gray and Seale, 1995, p. 109)

One response to the excluding power of stigmatisation is to create a new society of people who have an illness or handicap in common (the *own*), together with their 'stigma champions' (the *wise*). Within this alternative social circle, the 'abnormal' becomes the norm. Self-help groups exist for a wide range of conditions, including all those illustrated in this book. They not only help their members cope with the activities of daily living, but also develop and present to outsiders a less stigmatising message about the condition. For example, people with facial disfigurements have formed a powerful alliance called 'Changing Faces' to help overcome stigma.[11] One self-help group for people with schizophrenia (featured in Chapter 6) refers to its members as 'voice hearers', supplying them with a less-stigmatising social label for their condition which acknowledges the reality of their experiences.

People are often referred to by the *medical label* that a doctor has applied to them: a person's individuality and uniqueness may be subsumed beneath a term such as 'schizophrenic' or 'asthmatic'. It is as though the person becomes equated with the disease and everything is viewed through this filter—a phenomenon that Erving Goffman saw as the disease assuming a *master status*. Medical labels have frequently been challenged as stigmatising in themselves, and this charge has extended to some of the explanations for certain diseases that have been provided by scientific research. Medicine may be an ally in the search for recovery and for personal meaning in the face of illness, but it also supplies powerful professional narratives which can be experienced as stigmatising.

This process could be illustrated by any of the conditions discussed in this book, but schizophrenia offers an instructive example. People who are diagnosed as schizophrenic may find particular medical explanations for the condition deeply stigmatising.

□ Suggest how a genetic explanation for schizophrenia might be received, and contrast this with the effects of locating the causes of the condition in family interactions.

■ The attribution of schizophrenia to faulty genes could induce feelings of inferiority and helplessness that nothing can ever be done to alter one's inheritance; the parents of schizophrenic children may suffer shame that they 'passed on' the condition. Alternatively, the family of a schizophrenic person may be deeply offended by theories that their ways of relating to each other have driven one of them to a mental breakdown; they may prefer a genetic explanation which 'absolves' them from direct blame.

Many illnesses are not considered particularly stigmatising by people on the outside looking in. The clearest examples in this book are RA and asthma. But affected individuals may experience what is known as *felt stigma*—an expectation or anxiety that others may be repelled or rejecting, despite seeing no outward signs of discrimination. People may also feel shame if they are unable to fulfil the tasks normally associated with their *social role*, or perform the usual activities of self-care such as washing and dressing. There may be a retreat from the world as illness threatens the capacity to participate in 'normal' social life, often forcing people to reconsider their relationships and re-order their lives.

In the modern world, relationships have increasingly come to depend on forward planning. Maintaining plans is made very difficult by chronic illness. An arrangement to see friends may have to be cancelled at the last minute,

---

[10]Students of the Open University can read her article 'Pride against prejudice: "lives not worth living"' in *Health and Disease: A Reader*, if you have time.

[11]The Open University television programme 'More than meets the eye', associated with Chapter 2 of this book, focused on people with facial disfigurements.

making particular demands on their tolerance. People with unpredictable or disabling conditions, and their carers, may experience a shrinking set of social contacts as a result of their apparent inconsistency and inability to reciprocate.

> By far the hardest thing about caring for a wife with Alzheimer's disease, says Tom, is the loneliness … At weekends, he can spend hours exchanging no words with anyone … [A friend] comes round for a chat on Saturdays … Other friends, though, do not come any more. (Burton-Jones, in Davey, Gray and Seale, 1995, p. 81)

This common experience can result in unwelcome feelings of dependency on those contacts who do 'make an effort' to maintain the relationship. Casual acquaintanceship is hard to sustain, and the person becomes reliant on family and old friends, with all the attendant embarrassment about becoming a 'burden' on those who are under most obligation to care. The chronically ill or disabled person is usually only too well aware of the extra workload and social discrimination that may be falling on his or her carers.

And finally, as we have illustrated many times, inadequacies in the formal support mechanisms provided by the health and social services, in employment and in other aspects of daily life, are a form of discrimination themselves. They often mean that chronically ill or handicapped people are further disabled and excluded from mainstream society.

Lay accounts and professional accounts

A basic analytic distinction which has run through this book (and others in the series) is between *illness* and *disease*, as described here by the medical anthropologist, Leon Eisenberg:

> To state it flatly, patients suffer 'illnesses', physicians diagnose and treat 'diseases' … illnesses are *experiences* of disvalued changes in states of being and in social function; diseases, in the scientific paradigm of modern medicine, are *abnormalities* in the *structure* and *function* of body organs and systems. (Eisenberg, 1977, p. 11)

This distinction marks the boundary between the *lay* and *professional* sectors of health care. The medical and scientific view of disease can be seen as a sort of parallel system to that of lay peoples' constructions of illness, but they do not have equal status.

Scientific medicine is supposed to be based on consistent and objective measurement under carefully controlled conditions; the possibility of bias is reduced to the minimum by the selection of random or representative samples of experimental subjects and controls, the use of placebos where appropriate, and the evaluation of outcome by people who are 'blind' to which subjects received which intervention.[12] Practitioners of all the professional disciplines represented in this book— epidemiologists, clinicians and medical scientists, sociologists, psychologists, and so on—strive to acquire knowledge about health and disease through the application of scientific research methods.

Against this literally 'disciplined' approach, the accumulation of hearsay and folklore, personal anecdotes, media reporting and TV dramas, which contributes to many lay accounts of illness, presents a striking contrast. The usage made by lay people of professional, disease-based explanations and treatments can be highly selective; they are intermingled with ideas and remedies from many other sources. Although the richness of lay narratives of illness and the importance of strategies for self-care have not been lost on sociologists and anthropologists, the lay perspective is frequently excluded from consideration by medical practitioners and other health care workers. When a person is transformed into a patient, his or her beliefs are generally seen as irrelevant distractions, unless they coincide with the medical model and can be manipulated to encourage compliance with treatment.

Yet the assumed superiority of professional over lay accounts denies what we established earlier: that medical knowledge, even in the well-developed scientific context of Western societies, contains rather more doubts than certainties. Medical treatments sometimes do not work, or are harmful. The narrative provided by medicine can itself be stigmatising and serve to exclude people from society.

Until relatively recently in the history of scientific medicine, the patient was not acknowledged as an 'expert' in his or her own illness, and was excluded from participation or negotiation in most aspects of medical care. This situation is gradually changing: medical schools now have at least some classes on the syllabus in communication skills, social awareness and patients' rights, and practitioners are increasingly advocating

---

[12]These and other aspects of scientific research methodology, including clinical trials, are discussed in several chapters of *Studying Health and Disease* (second edition, 1994).

patient-centred medicine. Researchers have begun to devise *patient-derived* outcome measures for evaluating interventions to alleviate arthritis, which are based on criteria provided by patients. Thus, instead of imposed criteria such as 'can walk upstairs unaided', people can set highly individual criteria of their own: for example 'can take my dog for a walk again' or 'can lift my grandson onto my lap'. The success or failure of any intervention is then judged against these criteria by the person receiving the treatment, rather than by the doctor who prescribed it.

Medical sociologists have also been involved in systematic measurement of the psycho-social impact of disease, increasingly as part of multi-disciplinary teams that include health practitioners and patients. Considerable efforts have been made to evaluate the consequences of certain conditions—notably arthritis and HIV-disease—for peoples' relationships and social lives. In this respect, medicine has begun to explore the patients' varied world of *illness*, breaking somewhat from the narrower concern only with their *disease*.

Attempts to include lay people more actively in their health care are certainly increasing and may one day be commonplace. In the audiotape band associated with Chapter 6, Ron—a man who has suffered from schizophrenia for most of his life—recounts a shift from exclusion to inclusion in his experiences of treatment. He describes his feelings about being given a series of unwelcome forced injections early in his illness, and being locked on wards with nurses who would not talk to him about his voices for fear of 'colluding' with his delusions. He has since broken away from a view of himself as a victim of medical treatment, and has come to see psychiatrists as people who genuinely want to help him and who might be his allies. The change has been gradual, but Ron thinks it is due to a shift in attitudes among professionals in mental health care; they now listen more to the patient's perspective and can themselves learn from the people they treat. Significantly, Ron links this with a broader societal acceptance of mental illness, linked to a reduction in the stigma associated with mental disturbance and a greater recognition of common humanity.

Religion in European societies once exercised an all-pervasive influence on peoples' attempts to give meaning to fundamental existential questions of life, death and the purpose of suffering. Religion requires allegiance, trust and faith, rewarding these attributes with the promise that a meaningful life is possible for all, and punishing heretics with excommunication and exclusion. It can be argued that medicine in modern society exhibits somewhat similar characteristics, and plays a similar excluding or including role. It has been one of our aims in writing this book to bring the worlds of lay experience and professional explanations for health and disease closer together.

Conclusion to the series

You have now reached both the end of this book, and the end of the series of eight books that together form the *Health and Disease* course of study. This is, in a sense a ceremonial moment, marking the completion of a small phase in the lives of those of you who have studied all the books from beginning to end. This is the sort of moment when tourist guides shake hands and wait for their tip, head teachers stand up and say a few inspiring words, vice chancellors don their gowns and rustle in their pockets to look for last year's speech, and the audience shuffle restlessly because they know that whatever is said at such a moment is going to sound quite vacuous.

This is the nature of ceremony and ritual in modern society. It fails to command much respect or generate much emotion. But let us see what can be done nevertheless.

The first book in the course, *Medical Knowledge: Doubt and Certainty*, began by introducing the metaphor of a *journey* to evoke a sense of embarking on something new that might change your thinking about illness, medicine and health care. Another metaphor—this time derived from an academic source (as is appropriate to the sources we now hope you are using to think about health and disease)—is that of the **rite of passage**. This concept is derived from the work of an early anthropologist, Arnold van Gennep (1909), who coined the term to indicate the purpose of rituals that mark passages from one stage of life to the next in traditional societies.

Van Gennep noted that events like birth, initiation into adult status, marriage and death are often marked by a series of three types of ritual, starting with *rites of separation*. Here the person is removed from a previously occupied state. The first book of this course specifically set out to introduce doubt about some of the certainty with which medical knowledge is often associated. It introduced a series of critiques about the socially-constructed nature of medical knowledge, aimed at disrupting an unquestioning faith in the objectivity and beneficence of medical institutions. The purpose was to help you stand back from any assumptions you may have brought with you, in order to view the world of health and disease as *anthropologically strange*.

Van Gennep's second set of rites are known as *rites of transition*. The period in which these rites occur is characterised by confusion about right and wrong. It is a time when the loss of the previous status is felt as disturbing, and where new knowledge is actively sought in order to construct a new identity or understanding of the world. This is the point, in traditional societies, where instruction in the duties of new social roles are given by magicians, priests or healers. In a sense, this is the sort of experience we hope that you will have had as you studied subsequent books in this series.

The second book, *Studying Health and Disease*, was designed to give you an understanding of how academic 'narratives' of health and disease are constructed, showing you the methods used by researchers in different disciplines and pointing to their strengths and often neglected limitations. The third book, *World Health and Disease*, sought to help you gain a world-wide perspective on problems that you might hitherto have only considered in a British or European context. It also continued the exploration of historical trends in patterns of illness and the sources of inequalities in health experience between and within societies. The fourth book, *Human Biology and Health: An Evolutionary Approach*, invited you to explore biological understandings of health and disease in some depth, focusing particularly on the interaction of biological evolution and human culture. Such a perspective has rarely been attempted in biological texts.

Together, the first four books constitute the foundation on which an understanding of the last four books is built. The fifth book, *Birth to Old Age: Health in Transition*, involved you in a sequential consideration of the life course, in which the contribution of different academic disciplines to the understanding of health issues at each stage of life was emphasised. The realm of inner experience was given prominence, together with the influence of social construction in shaping how we feel about growing up and growing old.

Next came two books concerned with health care, starting with *Caring for Health: History and Diversity*. This historical account traced the development of the British health system from 1500 to the 1990s, but it also considered the world-wide influence of Western colonial powers on Third World health care issues, and the role of women as key providers of lay and nursing care. The seventh book, *Dilemmas in Health Care*, was concerned with present-day dilemmas in the organisation and delivery of health care through the National Health Service in the United Kingdom; the effect on the NHS of the historical legacy from past systems was stressed. In this final book, *Experiencing and Explaining Disease*, you have been invited to use the knowledge you have acquired to develop a new understanding of what it is to be ill and to explain and to treat disease.

What have we just done? The last few paragraphs have summarised the topics contained in eight books and suggested a framework in terms of rites of passage in which their study might be placed. This is the nature of ceremonial moments. They do not offer new knowledge, but act as invitations to the audience to review and reformulate what you know already. They help to crystallise tracts of experience. If you have read these books in sequence, with care and attention, this cryptic listing of their titles and contents will evoke some memories for you of the process you have been through, and may help you see it as a coherent sequence.

The authors of this text now stand aside to allow you to complete the final rite yourself—what van Gennep called a *rite of incorporation*. In this phase, individuals use their new knowledge to construct their own, personal understanding of the position they now have reached. We hope that studying these books will have enhanced your capacity to develop many new perspectives on matters of health and disease.

An objective and a revision exercise appear overleaf.

OBJECTIVE FOR CHAPTER 8

When you have studied this chapter, you should be able to:

8.1 Summarise the main themes of this book, using examples from earlier chapters to illustrate them, and interpret new material on relevant topics in terms of those themes.

REVISION EXERCISE FOR CHAPTER 8
(*Objective 8.1*)

Listen to the audiotape band entitled 'Living with epilepsy', which has been prepared for Open University students completing the course in *Health and Disease*. This tape presents part of an interview with Jill, a young woman who developed epilepsy in her teens, and her mother, Rose. They describe their experiences of the illness and of the reactions of others outside the family, including health professionals.

Interpret this material in terms of the themes of this book, identifying as many aspects as you can find on the tape. We suggest that you listen to the tape twice: first, straight through to get an overview, and second, using 'stop-start' to allow time to make notes. Decide before you begin whether to use the same 'headings' for groups of themes that we used in this chapter, or to reorganise the themes into another scheme of your own.

When you have finished this exercise, turn to the section at the end of this book entitled 'Answers to self-assessment questions', where you will find some notes on this revision exercise under Chapter 8.

Appendix

Table of abbreviations used in this book

Abbreviation	What it stands for
ACT-UP	AIDS Coalition to Unleash Power
ADAPT	Association for Drug Abuse Prevention and Treatment
AIDS	acquired immune deficiency syndrome
AIMS	Arthritis Impact Measurement Scales
ARC	Arthritis and Rheumatism Council for Research
AZT	3'-azido-3'-deoxythymidine (also known as Zidovudine)
BBC	British Broadcasting Corporation
CD	cluster of differentiation
COAD	chronic obstructive airways disease
CODAC	Coal Off the Docks Action Committee
COYOTE	Call Off Your Old Tired Ethics
CT	computed tomography
DMARDs	disease-modifying anti-rheumatic drugs
DNA	deoxyribonucleic acid
DSM IV	*Diagnostic and Statistical Manual of Mental Disorders*, 4th revision
ECT	electroconvulsive therapy
EE	expressed emotion
EIA	exercise-induced asthma
GMHC	Gay Men's Health Crisis
GP	general practitioner
GP120	glycoprotein 120
GRID	gay-related immunodeficiency disease
HAQ	Health Assessment Questionnaire
HES	Hospital Episode Statistics
HIPE	Hospital In-Patient Enquiry

Abbreviation	What it stands for
HIV	human immunodeficiency virus
ICD–10	*International Classification of Diseases, 10th revision, Classification of Mental and Behavioural Disorders*
IgE	immunoglobulin E
IPSS	International Pilot Study of Schizophrenia
ME	myalgic encephalomyelitis
MESMAC	Men who have Sex With Men Action in the Community
MIND	(National Association for Mental Health)
MRC	Medical Research Council
MRI	magnetic resonance imaging
NAMI	National Alliance of the Mentally Ill
NHS	National Health Service
NIDA	National Institute of Drug Abuse
NSAIDs	non-steroidal anti-inflammatory drugs
NSF	National Schizophrenia Fellowship
OPCS	Office of Population Censuses and Surveys
PSE	Present State Examination
RA	rheumatoid arthritis
RNA	ribonucleic acid
SANE	Schizophrenia: A National Emergency
SIV	simian immunodeficiency virus
T cell	thymus-derived lymphocyte
TENS	transcutaneous electrical nerve stimulation
TNF	tumour necrosis factor
WHO	World Health Organisation

References and further reading

References

Aggleton, P., Hart, G. and Davies, P. (eds) (1989) *AIDS: Social Representations, Social Practices*, Falmer Press, Lewes.

Ahlmen, M., Sullivan, M. and Bjelle, A. (1988) Team versus non-team outpatient care in rheumatoid arthritis, *Arthritis and Rheumatism*, **31**, pp. 471–9.

Al-Rawi, Z. S., Alazzawi, A. J., Alajili, F. M. *et al.* (1978) Rheumatoid arthritis in population samples in Iraq, *Annals of Rheumatic Diseases*, **37**, pp. 73–5.

American Psychiatric Association (1994) *Diagnostic and Statistical Manual of Mental Disorders*, American Psychiatric Association, Washington.

Anderson, H. R. (1989) Is the prevalence of asthma changing?, *Archives of Disease in Childhood*, **64**, pp. 172–5.

Anderson, H. R., Butland, B. K. and Strachan, D. P. (1994) Trends in prevalence and severity of childhood asthma, *British Medical Journal*, **308**, pp. 1600–4.

Anto, J. M. (1995) Asthma outbreaks: an opportunity for research?, *Thorax*, **50**, pp. 220–2.

Arnett, F. C., Edworthy, S. M., Bloch, D. A. *et al.* (1988) The American Rheumatism Association 1987 revised criteria for the classification of rheumatoid arthritis, *Arthritis and Rheumatism*, **31**, pp. 315–24.

Atkinson, J. M. and Coia, D. A. (1995) *Families Coping with Schizophrenia: A Practitioner's Guide to Family Groups*, Wiley, Chichester.

Ayres, J. (1994) Asthma and the atmosphere, *British Medical Journal*, **309**, pp. 619–20.

Badley, E. M. and Wood, P. H. N. (1979) Attitudes of the public to arthritis, *Annals of the Rheumatic Diseases*, **38**, pp. 97–100.

Barnes, M. and Berke, J. (1971) *Mary Barnes: Two Accounts of a Journey Through Madness*, McGibbon and Kee, London.

Baruch, G. (1982) *Moral tales: interviewing parents of congenitally ill children*, unpublished PhD thesis, University of London.

Bateson, G., Jackson, D. D., Haley, J. and Weakland, J. (1956) Towards a theory of schizophrenia, *Behavioural Science*, **1**, pp. 251–64.

Beattie, A., Gott, M., Jones, L. and Sidell, M. (eds) (1993) *Health and Wellbeing: a Reader*, Macmillan, Basingstoke.

Becker, G., Janson-Bjerklie, S., Benner, P., Slobin, K. and Ferketich, S. (1993) The dilemma of seeking urgent care: asthma episodes and emergency service use, *Social Science and Medicine*, **37**(3), pp. 305–13.

Beier, L. (1985) In sickness and in health: a seventeenth century family's experience, in Porter, R. (ed.) *Patients and Practitioners: Lay Perceptions of Medicine in Pre-industrial Society*, Cambridge University Press, Cambridge.

Bentall, R. and Pilgrim, D. (1993) Thomas Szasz, crazy talk and the myth of mental illness, *British Journal of Medical Psychology*, **66**, pp. 69–76.

Berger, P. (1973) *The Social Reality of Religion*, Penguin Books, Harmondsworth. (First published in 1969 as *The Sacred Canopy*, Faber and Faber.)

Berrill, W. T. (1993) Is the death rate from asthma exaggerated?, Evidence for West Cumbria, *British Medical Journal*, **306**, pp. 193–4.

Black, N., Boswell, D., Gray, A. Murphy, S. and Popay, J. (1984) *Health and Disease: A Reader*, 1st edn, Open University Press, Milton Keynes.

Bleuler, E. (1950) *Dementia Praecox, or the Group of Schizophrenias*, Zimkin, J. (trans.), International Universities Press, New York.

Boyle, M. (1994) Schizophrenia and the art of the soluble, *The Psychologist*, **7**, pp. 399–404.

Braun-Fahrländer, C., Ackerman-Liebruch, U., Schwartz, J. *et al.* (1992) Air pollution and respiratory symptoms in preschool children, *American Review of Respiratory Diseases*, **145**, pp. 42–7.

Brighton, S. W., Harpe, A. L., Staden, D. J. *et al.* (1988) The prevalence of rheumatoid arthritis in a rural African population, *Journal of Rheumatology*, **15**, pp. 405–8.

British Medical Association (1987) *Third BMA Statement on AIDS*, BMA, London.

British Thoracic Association (1982) Death from asthma in two regions of England, *British Medical Journal*, **285**, pp. 1251–5.

Brockington, I. F., Hall, P., Levings, J. and Murphy, C. (1993) The community's tolerance of the mentally ill, *British Journal of Psychiatry*, **162**, pp. 93–9.

Bryar, R. and Bytheway, B. (eds) (1996) *Changing Primary Health Care*, Blackwell Science, Oxford.

Burney, P. G. J. (1986) Asthma mortality in England and Wales: evidence for a further increase, 1974–84, *Lancet*, **ii**, pp. 323–6.

Burney, P. G. J. (1988) Asthma deaths in England and Wales 1931–85: evidence for a true increase in asthma mortality, *Journal of Epidemiology and Community Health*, **42**, pp. 316–20.

Burney, P. G. J., Chinn, S. and Rona, R. J. (1990) Has the prevalence of asthma increased in children? Evidence from a national study of health and growth, 1973–86, *British Medical Journal*, **300**, pp. 1306–10.

Burt, J. and Stimson, G. V. (1993) *Drug Injectors and HIV Risk Reduction: Strategies of Protection*, Health Education Authority, London.

Burton-Jones, J. (1992) *Caring for the Carers*, Scripture Union, London. An edited extract appears as 'Tangled feelings: an account of Alzheimer's disease' in Davey, B., Gray, A. and Seale, C. (eds) (1995) *Health and Disease: A Reader*, 2nd edn, Open University Press, Buckingham.

Bury, M. (1982) Chronic illness as biographical disruption, *Sociology of Health and Illness*, **4**, pp. 167–82.

Caldwell, C. B. and Gottesman, I. I. (1990) Schizophrenics kill themselves: a review of risk factors for suicide, *Schizophrenia Bulletin*, **16**, pp. 571–90.

Cantor, D. (1991) The aches of industry: philanthropy and rheumatism in inter-war Britain, in Barry, J. and Jones, C. (eds) *Medicine and Charity Before the Welfare State*, Routledge, London.

Cantor, D. (1992) Cortisone and the politics of drama, in Pickstone, J. V. (ed.) *Medical Innovations in Historical Perspective*, Macmillan, London.

Cantor, D. (1993) Cortisone and the politics of empire: imperialism and British medicine, 1918–1955, *Bulletin of Medical History*, **67**, pp. 463–93.

Carricaburu, D. and Pierret, J. (1995) From biographical disruption to biographical reinforcement: the case of HIV-positive men, *Sociology of Health and Illness*, 17, pp. 65–88.

Coleman, R. (1995) How I stopped being a victim, *Openmind*, **75**, p. 17.

Committee on the Medical Effects of Air Pollutants, and Department of Health (1995) *Non-Biological Particles and Health*, HMSO, London.

Concorde Coordinating Committee (1994) Concorde: MRC/ANRS randomised double-blind controlled trial of immediate and deferred Zidovudine in symptom-free HIV infection, *Lancet*, **343**, pp. 871–81.

Connor, S. and Kingman, S. (1989) *The Search For the Virus*, Penguin, Harmondsworth.

Cunningham, L. S. and Kelsey, J. L. (1984) Epidemiology and musculoskeletal impairments and associated disability, *American Journal of Public Health*, **74**, pp. 574–9.

Curran, D. and Partridge, M. (1969) *Psychological Medicine*, Churchill Livingstone.

Da Silva, J. A. and Hall, G. M. (1992) The effect of gender and sex hormones in rheumatoid arthritis, *Baillieres Clinical Rheumatology*, **6**, pp. 196–219.

Daily Express (1985) 30 August.

Daily Mail (1989) 'AIDS: straight talk is the way to save lives', 21 July.

Darlington, L. G. and Ramsey, N. W. (1993) Review of dietary therapy for rheumatoid arthritis (Editorial), *British Journal of Rheumatology*, **32**, pp. 507–14.

Davenport-Hines, R. (1990) *Sex, Death and Punishment: Attitudes to Sex and Sexuality in Britain since the Renaissance*, HarperCollins, London.

Davey, B., Gray, A. and Seale, C. (eds) (1995) *Health and Disease: A Reader*, 2nd edn, Open University Press, Buckingham.

Day, P. and Klein, R. (1989) in *Living with AIDS*, Daedalus, **118**(2), Spring.

Day, S. and Ward, H. (1991) The Praed Street project: a cohort of prostitute women in London, in Plant, M. (ed.) *AIDS, Drugs and Prostitution*, Routledge, London.

Deighton, C., Surtees, D. and Walker, D. (1992) Influence of the severity of rheumatoid arthritis on sex differences in Health Assessment Question Scores, *Annals of Rheumatic Diseases*, **51**, pp. 473–5.

Department of Health (1989, 1990, 1991, 1992, 1993) *Hospital Episode Statistics*, HMSO, London.

Department of the Environment, the Department of Health and the Department of Transport (1995) *Health Effects of Particles (The Government's Preliminary Response to the Reports of the Committee on the Medical Effects of Air Pollutants and the Expert Panel on Air Quality Standards)* November, DoE and DoH and DoT, London.

Department of Health (1992) *Guidelines for Offering Voluntary Named HIV Antibody Testing to Women receiving Antenatal Care* (PL/CO(92)5), Department of Health, London.

Department of Health (1994a) *Hospital Episode Statistics: Finished Consultant Episodes by Diagnosis, Operation and Specialty. England: Financial Year 1989–90*, Department of Health, London.

Department of Health (1994b) *Hospital Episode Statistics: Finished Consultant Episodes by Diagnosis, Operation and Specialty. England: Financial Year 1990–91*, Department of Health, London.

Descartes, R. (1664) *L'homme*, translated by Foster, M. (1901) *Lectures on the History of Physiology During the 16th, 17th and 18th Centuries*, Cambridge University Press, Cambridge.

Deveson, A. (1992) *Tell Me I'm Here*, Penguin, London.

Done, D. J., Johnstone, E. C., Frith, C. D. *et al.* (1991) Complications of pregnancy and delivery in relation to psychosis in adult life: data from the British perinatal mortality survey sample, *British Medical Journal*, **302**, pp. 1576–80.

Donnelly, M. (1992) *The Politics of Mental Health in Italy*, Routledge, London.

Drever, F. (1994) Asthma: the changing scene, *Population Trends*, **78**, pp. 44–6.

Dubuisson, D. and Melzack, R. (1976) Classification of clinical pain descriptions by multiple group discriminant analysis, *Experimental Neurology*, **51**, pp. 480–7.

Duckett, M. and Orkin, A. J. (1989) AIDS-related migration and travel policies and restrictions: a global survey, *AIDS*, **3** (supplement 1), pp. S231–52.

Dugowson, C. E., Koepsell, T. D., Voigt, L. F. *et al.* (1991) Rheumatoid arthritis in women: incidence rates in a group health co-operative, Seattle, Washington 1987–9, *Arthritis and Rheumatism*, **34**, pp. 1502–7.

Edgerton, R. B. and Cohen, A. (1994) Culture and schizophrenia: the DOSMD challenge, *British Journal of Psychiatry*, **164**, pp. 222–31.

Eisenberg, L. (1977) Disease and illness: distinctions between professional and popular ideas of sickness, *Culture, Medicine and Psychiatry*, **1**, pp. 9–23.

Elder, R. (1973) Social class and lay explanations for the etiology of arthritis, *Journal of Health and Social Behaviour*, **14**, pp. 28–38.

Elias, N. (1978) *The Civilizing Process: The History of Manners*, Blackwell, Oxford.

Elias, N. (1982) *The Civilizing Process: State Formation and Civilization*, Blackwell, Oxford.

Embretson, J., Zupancic, M., Ribas, J. *et al.* (1993) Massive covert infection of helper T lymphocytes and macrophages by HIV during the incubation period of AIDS, *Nature*, **362**, pp. 359–62.

Evans, B. G., Catchpole, M. A., Heptonstall, J. *et al.* (1993) Sexually transmitted diseases and HIV-1 infection among homosexual men in England and Wales, *British Medical Journal*, **306**, pp. 426–8.

Expert Panel on Air Quality Standards (1995) *Particles*, Department of the Environment, HMSO, London.

Falloon, I. R. H., Laporta, M., Fadden, G. and Graham-Hole, V. (1993) *Managing Stress in Families: Cognitive and Behavioural Strategies for Enhancing Coping Skills*, Routledge, London.

Fauci, A. S. (1993) CD4+ T-lymphocytopenia without HIV infection—no lights, no camera, just facts, *New England Journal of Medicine*, **328**(6), pp. 429–30.

Fitzpatrick, R., Ziebland, S., Jenkinson, C. and Mowat, A. (1992) A generic health status instrument in the assessment of rheumatoid arthritis, *British Journal of Rheumatology*, **31**, pp. 87–90.

Fleming, A., Crown, J. and Corbett, M. (1976) Early rheumatoid arthritis, *Annals of the Rheumatic Diseases*, **35**, pp. 357–60.

Freud, S. (1961, first published 1920) Beyond the pleasure principle, in *The Standard Edition of the Complete Works of Sigmund Freud*, Vol. 18, Hogarth Press, London.

Friedman, S. R., Jose, B., Neaigus, A. *et al.* (1991) Peer-mobilization and widespread condom use by drug injectors, Paper presented at *7th International Conference on AIDS*, June, Florence, Italy.

Fries, J., Spitz, P. and Young, D. (1982) The dimensions of health outcomes: the Health Assessment Questionnaire, disability and pain scales, *Journal of Rheumatology*, **9**, pp. 789–93.

Fromm-Reichmann, F. (1948) Notes on the development of treatment of schizophrenics by psychoanalytic psychotherapy, *Psychiatry*, **11**, pp. 263–73.

Gabbay, J. (1982) Asthma attacked? Tactics for the reconstruction of a disease concept, pp. 23–48 in Wright, P. and Treacher, A. (eds) *The Problem of Medical Knowledge*, Edinburgh University Press, Edinburgh.

Garfinkel, H. (1963) A conception of, and experiments with, 'trust' as a condition of stable concerted actions, in Harvey, O. J. (ed.) *Motivation and Social Interaction*, Ronald Press, New York.

Giddens, A. (1989) *Sociology*, Polity Press, Cambridge.

Giddens, A. (1991) *Modernity and Self-identity: Self and Society in the Late Modern Age*, Polity Press, Cambridge.

Glasgow University Media Group (1993a) *Mass Media Representations of Mental Health/Illness: Report for the Health Education Board for Scotland*, Glasgow University Media Group, Glasgow.

Glasgow University Media Group (1993b) *Media Representations of Mental Health/Illness: Audience Reception Study: Report for the Health Education Board for Scotland*, Glasgow University Media Group, Glasgow.

Goffman, E. (1968) *Stigma: Notes on the Management of Spoiled Identity*, Pelican Books, London.

Good, B. (1994) *Medicine, Rationality and Experience*, Cambridge University Press, Cambridge.

Gray, D. (1983) 'Arthritis': variation in beliefs about joint disease, *Medical Anthropology*, 7, pp. 29–46.

Green, H. (1964) *I Never Promised You A Rose Garden*, Victor Gollancz, London.

Guardian (1991) 10 December.

Guardian (1992) Doctor denies attempt to kill suffering patient, 11 September, p. 2.

Hart, G. and Boulton, M. (1995) Sexual behaviour in gay men: towards a sociology of risk, in Aggleton, P., Hart, G. and Davies, P. (eds) *AIDS: Safety, Sexuality and Risk*, Taylor and Francis, London.

Harvey, J., Lotze, M., Stevens, M. B. *et al.* (1981) Rheumatoid arthritis in Chippewa band. I: Pilot study of disease prevalence, *Arthritis and Rheumatism*, **24**, pp. 717–21.

Heath, C. (1989) Pain talk: the expression of suffering in the medical consultation, *Social Psychology Quarterly*, **52**(2), pp. 113–25.

Helman, C. (1990) *Culture, Health and Illness*, Wright, London.

Hick, J. (1977) *Evil and the God of Love*, Macmillan Press, London.

Higgins, B. G., Francis, H. C., Yates, C. J. *et al.* (1995) Effect of air pollution on symptoms and peak expiratory flow measurements in subjects with obstructive airways disease, *Thorax*, **50**, pp. 149–55.

Hilbert, R. (1984) The acultural dimensions of chronic pain: flawed reality construction and the problem of meaning, *Social Problems*, **31**(4), pp. 365–78.

Hill, R. A., Standen, P. J. and Tattersfield, A. E. (1989) Asthma, wheezing, and school absence in primary schools, *Archives of Disease in Childhood*, **64**, pp. 246–51.

Holgate, S. (1994) What's causing the worldwide rise in asthma?, *MRC News*, **63**, pp. 20–3.

Holland, J., Ramazanoglu, C., Scott, S., Sharpe, S. and Thompson, R. (1991) Between embarrassment and trust: young women and the diversity of condom use, in Aggleton, P., Hart, G. and Davies, P. (eds) *AIDS: Responses, Intervention and Care*, Falmer Press, Lewes.

Holt, P. G. (1995) Environmental factors and primary T-cell sensitisation to inhalant allergens in infancy: reappraisal of the role of infections and air pollution, *Pediatric Allergy and Immunology*, **6**, pp. 1–10.

Homans, H. and Aggleton, P. (1988) Health education and AIDS, in Aggleton, P. and Homans, H. (eds) *Social Aspects of AIDS*, Falmer Press, Lewes.

Hunt, A. (1992) Getting used to the wolves, *AIDS Care*, **4**, pp. 353–5.

Hyndman, S. J., Williams, D. R. R., Merrill, S. L. *et al.* (1994) Rates of admission to hospital for asthma, *British Medical Journal*, **308**, pp. 1596–600.

Illich, I. (1976) *Limits to Medicine; Medical Nemesis: the Expropriation of Health*, Penguin, Harmondsworth.

Independent (1987) 24 November.

Inoue, K., Shichikawa, K., Nishioka, J. *et al.* (1987) Older age onset rheumatoid arthritis with or without osteoarthritis, *Annals of Rheumatic Diseases*, **46**, pp. 908–11.

Jablensky, A., Sartorius, N., Ernberg, G. *et al.* (1992) Schizophrenia: manifestation, incidence and course in different cultures, *Psychological Medicine*, monograph supplement 20.

Jacob, D. L., Robinson, H. and Masi, A. T. (1972) A controlled home interview study of factors associated with early rheumatoid arthritis, *American Journal of Public Health*, **62**, pp. 1532–7.

Jeffery, R. (1979) Normal rubbish: deviant patients in casualty departments, *Sociology of Health and Illness*, **1**(1), pp. 90–108; an edited version appears in Davey, B., Gray, A. and Seale, C. (eds) (1995) *Health and Disease: A Reader*, 2nd edn, Open University Press, Buckingham.

Jones, K. P., Bain, D. J. G., Middleton, M. and Mullee, M. A. (1992) Correlates of asthma morbidity in primary care, *British Medical Journal*, **304**, pp. 361–4.

Kane, J., Honigfeld, G., Singer, J. and Meltzer, H. (1988) Clozapine for the treatment-resistant schizophrenic: a double-blind comparison with chlorpromazine, *Archives of General Psychiatry*, **45**, pp. 789–96.

Kelleher, D. (1988) Coming to terms with diabetes: coping strategies and non-compliance, in Anderson, R. and Bury, M. (eds) *Living with Chronic Illness*, Allen and Unwin, London. An edited extract entitled 'Coming to terms with diabetes' also appears in Davey, B., Gray, A. and Seale, C. (eds.) (1995) *Health and Disease: A Reader*, 2nd edn., Open University Press, Buckingham.

Kelly, J. A., St Lawrence, J. S., Stevenson, L. Y. *et al.* (1992) Community AIDS/HIV risk reduction: the effects of endorsements by popular people in three cities, *American Journal of Public Health*, **80**, pp. 1483–9.

Kelly, W. J. W., Hudson, I., Phelan, P. D. *et al.* (1987) Childhood asthma in adult life: a further study at 28 years of age, *British Medical Journal*, **294**, pp. 1059–62.

Kesey, K. (1962) *One Flew Over the Cuckoo's Nest*, Methuen, London.

King, E. (1994) Suicide in the mentally ill: an epidemiological sample and implications for clinicians, *British Journal of Psychiatry*, **165**, pp. 658–63.

Kingsley, G., Lanchbury, J. and Panayi, G. (1996) Immunotherapy in rheumatic disease: an idea whose time has come—or gone? *Immunology Today*, **17**(1), pp. 9–12.

Kippax, S., Crawford, J., Connell, B. *et al.* (1992) The importance of gay community in the prevention of HIV transmission: a study of Australian men who have sex with men, in Aggleton P., Davies P. and Hart, G. (eds) *AIDS: Rights, Risk and Reason*, Taylor and Francis, London.

Kleinman, A. (1988) *The Illness Narratives: Suffering, Healing and the Human Condition*, Basic Books, New York.

Klipple, G. L. and Cecere, F. A. (1989) Rheumatoid arthritis and pregnancy, *Rheumatic Disease Clinics of North America*, **15**, pp. 213–39.

Kosambi, D. D. (1967) Living prehistory in India, *Scientific American*, **216**(2), pp. 110–1.

Kotarba, J. and Seidel, J. (1984) Managing the problem patient: compliance or social control? *Social Science and Medicine*, **19**(12), pp. 1393–400.

Laing, R. D. (1960) *The Divided Self: A Study of Sanity, Madness and the Family*, Tavistock, London.

Laing, R. D. (1967) *The Politics of Experience*, Penguin, Harmondsworth.

Lancet (editorial) (1987) AIDS in Africa, (**ii**), pp. 192–4.

Lawrence, J. (1970) Rheumatoid arthritis—nature or nurture? *Annals of the Rheumatic Diseases*, **29**, pp. 357–9.

Lawson, M. (1991) A recipient's view, in Ramon, S. (ed.) *Beyond Community Care: Normalisation and Integration Work*, Macmillan, London.

Lean, G. (1993) Gasping for breath, *Independent on Sunday*, 10 October, p. 19.

Leff, J. (1993) Comment on crazy talk: thought disorder or psychiatric arrogance by Thomas Szasz, *British Journal of Medical Psychology*, **66**, pp. 77–8.

Leff, J. P. and Vaughn, C. E. (1985) *Expressed Emotion in Families: Its Significance for Mental Illness*, Guilford Press, New York.

Leff, J., Wig, N. N., Bendi, H. *et al.* (1990) Relatives' expressed emotion and the course of schizophrenia in Chandigarh: a two-year follow-up of a first-contact sample, *British Journal of Psychiatry*, **151**, pp. 166–73.

Levinson, A. I. and Martin, J. (1988) Rheumatoid factor: Dr Jekyll or Mr Hyde?, *British Journal of Rheumatology*, **27**, pp. 83–90.

Levinson, D. F. and Mowry, B. J. (1991) Defining the schizophrenic spectrum: issues for genetic linkage studies, *Schizophrenia Bulletin*, **17**, pp. 491–514.

Liberman, R. P., Wallace, C. J., Blackwell *et al.* (1993) Innovations in skill training for the seriously mentally ill: the UCLA Social and Independent Living Skills modules, *Innovations and Research*, **2**, pp. 43–60.

Linos, A., Worthington, J. W., O'Fallon, M. *et al.* (1980) The epidemiology of rheumatoid arthritis in Rochester, Minnesota: a study of incidence, prevalence and mortality, *American Journal of Epidemiology*, **111**, pp. 87–98.

Littlewood, R. and Lipsedge, M. (1982) *Aliens and Alienists: Ethnic Minorities and Psychiatry*, Penguin, Harmondsworth. An edited extract entitled 'Ethnic minorities and the psychiatrist' appears in Davey, B., Gray, A. and Seale, C., (eds) (1995) *Health and Disease: A Reader*, 2nd edn, Open University Press, Buckingham.

Living with AIDS (1989) *Daedalus*, **118**(2), Spring.

Locker, D. (1983) *Disability and Disadvantage: the Consequences of Chronic Illness*, Tavistock, London.

Lukes, S. (1973) *Emile Durkheim: His Life and Works*, Penguin, Harmondsworth.

Lupton, D. (1994) *Medicine as Culture: Illness, Disease and the Body in Western Societies*, Sage, London.

MacCarty, C. S. and Drake, R. L. (1956) Neurosurgical procedures for the control of pain, *Proceedings of Staff Meetings of the Mayo Clinic*, **31**, pp. 208–14.

MacGregor, A., Riste, L., Hazes, J. and Silman, A. (1994) Low prevalence of rheumatoid arthritis in Black Caribbeans compared with Whites in inner city Manchester, *Annals of the Rheumatic Diseases*, **53**, pp. 293–7.

Macintyre, S. and Oldman, D. (1977) Coping with migraine, in Davis, A. and Horobin, G. (eds) *Medical Encounters*, Croom Helm, London. An edited extract also entitled 'Coping with migraine' appears in Davey, B., Gray, A. and Seale, C. (eds) (1995) *Health and Disease: A Reader*, 2nd edn., Open University Press, Buckingham.

Mason, J., Weener, J., Gertman, P. and Meenan, R. (1983) Health status in chronic disease: a comparative study of rheumatoid arthritis, *Journal of Rheumatology*, **10**, pp. 763–8.

McCormick, A., Fleming, D. and Charlton, J. (1995) *Morbidity Statistics from General Practice: Fourth National Study, 1991–92. A Study carried out by the Royal College of General Practitioners, the Office of Population Censuses and Surveys, and the Department of Health*. Series MB5, no. 3, HMSO, London.

McKeganey, N. and Barnard, M. (1992) *AIDS, Drugs and Sexual Risk*, Open University Press, Buckingham.

McLean, J., Boulton, M., Brookes, M. *et al.* (1994) Regular partners and risky behaviour: why do gay men have unprotected sex? *AIDS Care*, **6**, pp. 331–41.

Meador, C. K. (1994) The last well person, *The New England Journal of Medicine*, **330**(6), pp. 440–1. Also reproduced in its entirety in Davey, B., Gray, A. and Seale, C. (eds) (1995) *Health and Disease: A Reader*, 2nd edn, Open University Press, Buckingham.

Meenan, R., Gertman, P. and Mason, J. (1980) Measuring health status in arthritis: the Arthritis Impact Measurement Scales, *Arthritis and Rheumatism*, **23**, pp. 146–52.

Melzack, R. (1975) The McGill pain questionnaire: major properties and scoring methods, *Pain*, **1**, pp. 277–99.

Melzack, R. and Wall, P. (1965) Pain mechanisms: a new theory, *Science*, **150**, pp. 971–9.

Melzack, R. and Wall, P. (1988) *The Challenge of Pain*, Penguin Books, Harmondsworth; reprinted 1991.

Mitchell, E. A. (1985) International trends in hospital admission rates for asthma, *Archives of Disease in Childhood*, **60**, pp. 376–8.

Molfino, N. A., Wright, S. C., Katz, I. *et al.* (1991) Effect of low concentration of ozone on inhaled allergen responses in asthmatic subjects, *Lancet*, **338**, pp. 199–203.

Moore, R. D., Hidalgo, J., Sugland, B. W. and Chaisson, R. E. (1991) Zidovudine and the natural history of the Acquired Immunodeficiency Syndrome, *New England Journal of Medicine*, **324**, pp. 1412–6.

Morris, J. (1991) *Pride Against Prejudice: A Personal Politics of Disability*, The Women's Press, London. An extract appears as 'Pride against prejudice: "lives not worth living"' in Davey, B., Gray, A. and Seale, C. (eds) (1995) *Health and Disease: A Reader*, 2nd edn, Open University Press, Buckingham.

Mumby, S. (1994) Clearing the air on asthma, *Health Matters*, **17**, p. 5.

Newman, S., Fitzpatrick, R. Revinson, T., Skevington, S. and Williams, G. (1995) *Understanding Rheumatoid Arthritis*, Routledge, London.

Nijhof, G. (1995) Parkinson's disease as a problem of shame in public appearance, *Sociology of Health and Illness*, **17**(2), pp. 193–205.

Nocon, A. and Booth, T. (1990) *The Social Impact of Asthma*, Joint Unit of Social Services Research, University of Sheffield, Sheffield. An edited extract appears as 'The social impact of childhood asthma', in Davey, B., Gray, A. and Seale, C. (eds) (1995) *Health and Disease: A Reader*, 2nd edn, Open University Press, Buckingham.

Norman, R. M. G. and Malla, A. K. (1993a) Stressful life events and schizophrenia. I: A review of the research, *British Journal of Psychiatry*, **162**, pp. 161–5.

Norman, R. M. G. and Malla, A. K. (1993b) Stressful life events and schizophrenia. II: Conceptual and methodological issues, *British Journal of Psychiatry*, **162**, pp. 166–74.

Nowak, M. A. and McMichael, A. J. (1995) How HIV defeats the immune system, *Scientific American*, August, pp. 42–9.

Oakley, A. (1985) *The Sociology of Housework* (2nd edn), Basil Blackwell, Oxford.

Oliver, M. (1993) Re-defining disability: a challenge to research, in Swain, J., Finkelstein, V., French, S. and Oliver, M. (eds) *Disabling Barriers—Enabling Environments*, Sage, London.

OPCS (1995a) *OPCS Monitor, DH2 Series, No. 20*, Office of Population Censuses and Surveys, HMSO, London.

OPCS (1995b) *OPCS Survey of Psychiatric Morbidity in Great Britain. Report 1. The Prevalence of Psychiatric Morbidity among Adults living in Private Households*, HMSO, London.

Pantaleo, G., Graziosi, C., Demarest, J. F. *et al.* (1993) HIV infection is active and progressive in lymphoid tissue during the clinically latent stage of disease, *Nature*, **362**, pp. 355–8.

Parker, J., Frank, R., Beck, N. *et al.* (1988) Pain in rheumatoid arthritis: relationship to demographic, medical and psychological factors, *Journal of Rheumatology*, **15**, pp. 433–7.

Parliamentary Office of Science and Technology (1994), *Breathing in our Cities*, Parliamentary Office of Science and Technology, London.

Parsons, T. (1951) *The Social System*, Free Press, Glencoe, Illinois.

Patton, C. (1990) *Inventing AIDS*, London, Routledge.

Peat, J. K., van den Berg, R. H., Green, W. F. *et al.* (1994) Changing prevalence of asthma in Australian children, *British Medical Journal*, **308**, pp. 1591–6.

Phelan, P. D. (1994) Asthma in children: epidemiology, *British Medical Journal*, **308**, pp. 1584–5.

PHLS AIDS Centre and the Scottish Centre for Infection and Environmental Health (1995 and 1996) *AIDS/HIV Quarterly Surveillance Tables: No. 26, Data to end September 1995* and *Data to end December 1995*, and unpublished *Quarterly Surveillance Tables: No. 29 to end September 1995* (personal communication), PHLS, London.

PHLS Communicable Disease Surveillance Centre (1991 and 1993) *Communicable Disease Report*, **1**(4) and **3**(4).

Pincus, T. and Callahan, L. F. (1986) Taking mortality in rheumatoid arthritis seriously—predictive markers, socio-economic status and comorbidity (Editorial), *Journal of Rheumatology*, **13**, pp. 841–5.

Pincus, T. and Callahan, L. F. (1994) Association of low formal education level and poor health status: behavioral, in addition to demographic and medical, explanations?, *Journal of Clinical Epidemiology*, **47**, pp. 355–61.

Pope, C. A. and Dockery, W. (1992) Acute health effects of PM_{10} pollution on symptomatic and asymptomatic children, *American Review of Respiratory Diseases*, **145**, pp. 1123–8.

Prout, A. and Deverell, K. (1995) *MESMAC—Working with Diversity, Building Communities*, HEA/Longman, London.

Reisine, S., Goodenow, C. and Grady, K. (1987) The impact of rheumatoid arthritis on the homemaker, *Social Science and Medicine*, **25**, pp. 89–95.

Rhodes, T. (1994) *Risk, Intervention and Change: HIV Prevention and Drug Use*, Health Education Authority, London.

Rhodes, T. (1995) Researching and theorising 'risk': notes on the social relations of risk in heroin users' lifestyles, in Aggleton, P., Hart, G. and Davies, P. (eds) *AIDS: Sexuality, Safety and Risk*, Taylor and Francis, London.

Rhodes, T., Quirk, A. and Stimson, G. V. (1995) *Sexual Safety in the Context of Drug Using Lifestyles*, Centre for Research on Drugs and Health Behaviour (CRDHB), London.

Rhodes, T., Stimson, G. V. and Quirk, A. (1996) Sex, drugs, intervention and research, *International Journal of the Addictions*, **31**, pp. 385–407.

Richardson, A. and Bolle, D. (1992) *Wise Before Their Time: People with AIDS and HIV Talk about their Lives*, HarperCollins, London.

Rigby, A. S. (1992) HLA haplotype sharing in rheumatoid arthritis sibships: risk estimates in siblings, *Scandinavian Journal of Rheumatology*, **21**, pp. 68–73.

Rigby, A. S., Silman, A. J., Voelm, L. *et al.* (1991) Investigating the HLA component in rheumatoid arthritis: an additive (dominant) mode is rejected, a recessive mode is preferred, *Genetic Epidemiology*, **8**, pp. 153–75.

Robertson, C. F., Heycock, E., Bishop, J. *et al.* (1991) Prevalence of asthma in Melbourne schoolchildren: changes over 26 years, *British Medical Journal*, **302**, pp. 1116–8.

Robinson, I. (1990) Personal narratives, social careers and medical courses: analysing life trajectories in autobiographies of people with multiple sclerosis, *Social Science and Medicine*, **30**(11), pp. 1171–86.

Rosenhan, D. L. (1973) On being sane in insane places, *Science*, **179**, pp. 250–8.

Rowland-Jones, S. L. and McMichael, A. (1995) Immune responses in HIV-exposed seronegatives: have they repelled the virus?, *Current Topics in Microbiological Immunology*, **7**, pp. 448–55.

Sattaur, O. (1991) India wakes up to AIDS, *New Scientist*, **2** November, pp. 25–9.

Saunders, C. M. (1978) *The Management of Terminal Disease*, Edward Arnold, London.

Saunders, C. M. and Baines, M. (1983) *Living with Dying: The Management of Terminal Disease*, Oxford University Press, Oxford.

Scambler, G. (1984) Perceiving and coping with stigmatizing illness, in Fitzpatrick, R., Hinton, J., Newman, S., Scambler, G. and Thompson, J. (eds) *The Experience of Illness*, Tavistock, London.

Scambler, G. and Hopkins, A. (1988) Accommodating epilepsy in families, in Anderson, R. and Bury, M. (eds) *Living with Chronic Illness: The Experience of Patients and their Families*, Unwin Hyman, London.

Scarry, E. (1985) *The Body in Pain: The Making and Unmaking of the World*, Oxford University Press, Oxford.

Shearer, A. (1981) *Disability: Whose Handicap?*, Basil Blackwell, Oxford. An edited extract also entitled 'Disability: whose handicap?' appears in Black, N., Boswell, D., Gray, A., Murphy, S. and Popay, J. (eds) (1984) *Health and Disease: A Reader*, 1st edn, Open University Press, Milton Keynes.

Shearer, G. M. and Clerici, M. (1996) Protective immunity against HIV infection: has nature done the experiment for us? *Immunology Today*, **17**(1), pp. 21–4.

Shilts, R. (1987) *And The Band Played On*, Penguin, Harmondsworth.

Sibbald, B. (1988) Patient self care in acute asthma, *Thorax*, **44**, pp. 97–101.

Silman, A. J. (1988) Has the incidence of rheumatoid arthritis declined in the United Kingdom? *British Journal of Rheumatology*, **27**, pp. 77–8.

Silman, A. J. (1991) Is rheumatoid arthritis an infectious disease? *British Medical Journal*, **303**, pp. 200–1.

Silman, A. J., MacGregor, A. J., Thomson, W. *et al.* (1994) Twin concordance rates for rheumatoid arthritis: results from a nationwide study, *British Journal of Rheumatology*, **32**, pp. 903–7.

Silverman, D. (1989) Making sense of a precipice: constituting identity in an HIV clinic, in Aggleton, P., Hart, G. and Davies, P. (eds), *AIDS: Social Representations, Social Practices*, Falmer Press, Lewes.

Silverman, D. (1993) *Interpreting Qualitative Data: Methods for Analysing Talk, Text and Interaction*, Sage, London.

Small, N. (1995) Living with HIV and AIDS, in Davey, B., Gray, A. and Seale, C. (eds) (1995) *Health and Disease: A Reader*, 2nd edn, Open University Press, Buckingham.

Snadden, D. and Belle Brown, J. (1992) The experience of asthma, *Social Science and Medicine*, **34**(12), pp. 1351–61.

Solomon, L., Robin, G., and Walkenburg, H. A. (1975) Rheumatoid arthritis in an urban South African negro population, *Annals of Rheumatic Diseases*, **34**, pp. 128–35.

Sontag, S. (1978) *Illness as Metaphor*, Penguin Books, Ltd. Chapter 4 is reprinted under the title 'Illness as metaphor' in Davey, B., Gray, A. and Seale, C. (eds) (1995) *Health and Disease: A Reader*, 2nd edn, Open University Press, Buckingham.

Sontag, S. (1991) *Illness as Metaphor: AIDS and its Metaphors*, Penguin, Harmondsworth.

South Wales Evening Post (1994) 24 June.

Spector, T. M. and Hochberg, M. C. (1990) The protective effect of the oral contraceptive pill on rheumatoid arthritis: an overview of the analytic epidemiological studies using meta-analysis, *Journal of Clinical Epidemiology*, **43**, pp. 1221–30.

Steering Committee of the Confidential Inquiry into Homicides by Mentally Ill People (1994) *A Preliminary Report on Homicide*, Steering Committee of the Confidential Inquiry into Homicides by Mentally Ill People, London.

Stimson, G. V. (1976) General practitioners' 'trouble' and types of patient, in Stacey, M. (ed.) *The Sociology of the National Health Service*, University of Keele Sociological Review, Monograph no. 22, University of Keele.

Stimson, G. V. (1989) Syringe exchange programmes for injecting drug users, *AIDS*, **5**, pp. 253–60.

Strachan, D. P. (1989) Hay fever, hygiene and household size, *British Medical Journal*, **299**, pp. 1258–9.

Suddath, R. L., Christison, G. W., Torrey, E. F. *et al.* (1990) Anatomical abnormalities in the brains of monozygotic twins discordant for schizophrenia, *New England Journal of Medicine*, **322**, pp. 789–94.

Sugarman, P. A. and Craufurd, D. (1994) Schizophrenia in the Afro-Caribbean community, *British Journal of Psychiatry*, **164**, pp. 474–80.

Sullivan, F., Eagers, R., Lynch, K. and Barber, J. (1987) Assessment of disability caused by rheumatic diseases in general practice, *Annals of Rheumatic Diseases*, **46**, pp. 598–600.

Sun (1990) January.

Swift, A. (1992) *Guardian*, 23 April.

Szasz, T. (1979) *Schizophrenia: The Sacred Symbol of Psychiatry*, Oxford University Press, Oxford.

Szasz, T. (1993) Crazy talk: thought disorder or psychiatric arrogance? *British Journal of Medical Psychology*, **66**, pp. 61–7.

Temple, J. M. F. and Sykes, A. M. (1992) Asthma and open cast mining, *British Medical Journal*, **305**, pp. 396–7.

Thapar, A. (1996) Education for asthma patients, in Bryar, R. and Bytheway, B. (eds) *Changing Primary Health Care*, Blackwell Science, Oxford.

The Times (1994) 12 March.

Thompson, P. W. and Pegley, F. S. (1991) A comparison of disability measured by the Stanford Health Assessment Questionnaire disability scales (HAQ) in male and female rheumatoid outpatients, *British Journal of Rheumatology*, **30**, pp. 298–300.

Times Higher Education Supplement (1995) Proof of plan for child radiation tests, 27 January, p. 3.

Torrey, E. F., Bowler, A. E., Rawlings, R. and Terrazas, A. (1993) Seasonality of schizophrenia and stillbirths, *Schizophrenia Bulletin*, **19**, pp. 557–62.

Tugwell, P., Bombardier, C., Buchanan, W. *et al.* (1987) The MACTAR Patient Preference Disability Questionnaire: an individualized functional priority approach to assessing improvement in physical disability in clinical trials in rheumatoid arthritis, *Journal of Rheumatology*, **14**, pp. 446–51.

Tugwell, P., Bombardier, C., Buchanan, W. *et al.* (1990) Methotrexate in rheumatoid arthritis: impact on quality of life assessed by traditional standard-item individualized patient preference health status questionnaires, *Archives of Internal Medicine*, **150**, pp. 59–62.

van Gennep, A. (1960) *The Rites of Passage*, University of Chicago Press, Chicago (first published 1909).

Vandenbroucke, J. P., Valkenberg, H. A., Boersma, J. W. *et al.* (1982) Oral contraceptives and rheumatoid arthritis: further evidence for a protective effect, *Lancet*, **ii** (8303), pp. 839–42.

Vaughn, C. E. and Leff, J. P. (1976a) The influence of family and social factors on the course of psychiatric illness, *British Journal of Psychiatry*, **129**, pp. 125–37.

Vaughn, C. E. and Leff, J. P. (1976b) The measurement of expressed emotion in the families of psychiatric patients, *British Journal of Social and Clinical Psychology*, **15**, pp. 157–66.

Verbrugge, L. M., Gates, D. M. and Ike, R. W. (1991) Risk factors for disability among US adults with arthritis, *Journal of Clinical Epidemiology*, **44**, pp. 167–82.

von Mutius, E., Fritzsch, C., Weiland, S. K. *et al.* (1992) Prevalence of asthma and allergic disorders among children in united Germany: a descriptive comparison, *British Medical Journal*, **305**, pp. 1395–9.

von Mutius, E., Martinez, F. D., Fritzsch, C. *et al.* (1994) Prevalence of asthma and atopy in two areas of West and East Germany, *American Journal of Respiratory and Critical Care Medicine*, **149**, pp. 358–64.

Vonnegut, M. (1979) *The Eden Express*, Bantam, New York.

Watney, S. (1987) *Policing Desire*, Comedia, London.

Watney, S. (1989a) The subject of AIDS, in Aggleton, P., Hart, G. and Davies, P. (eds), *AIDS: Social Representations, Social Practices*, Falmer Press, Lewes.

Watney, S. (1989b) Taking liberties: an introduction, in Carter, E. and Watney, S. (eds) *Taking Liberties: AIDS and Cultural Politics*, Serpent's Tail, London.

Watters, J. (1996) Americans and syringe exchange: routes of resistance, in Rhodes, T. and Hartnoll, R. (eds) *AIDS, Drugs and Prevention*, Routledge, London.

Weeks, J. (1989) AIDS: The intellectual agenda, in Aggleton, P., Hart, G. and Davies, P. (eds), *AIDS: Social Representations, Social Practices*, Falmer Press, Lewes.

Weeks, J. (1990) Post-modern AIDS?, in Gupta, S. (ed.) *Ecstatic Antibodies: Resisting the AIDS Mythologies*, Rivers Oram, London.

Wiener, C. (1975) The burden of rheumatoid arthritis: tolerating the uncertainty, *Social Science and Medicine*, **9**, pp. 97–104.

Williams, D. and Griffiths, B. (1996) A research project on childhood asthma based in general practice, in Bryar, R. and Bytheway, B. (eds) *Changing Primary Health Care*, Blackwell Science, Oxford.

Williams, G. (1984a) *Interpretation and Compromise: Coping with the Experience of Chronic Illness*, unpublished Ph.D. thesis, University of Manchester.

Williams, G. (1984b) The genesis of chronic illness: narrative reconstruction, *Sociology of Health and Illness*, **6**, pp. 175–200.

Williams, G. (1986) Lay beliefs about the causes of rheumatoid arthritis: their implications for rehabilitation, *International Rehabilitation Medicine*, **8**, pp. 65–8.

Williams, G. (1987) Disablement and the social context of daily activity, *International Disability Studies*, **9**, pp. 97–102.

Williams, G. (1993) Chronic illness and the pursuit of virtue in everyday life, in Radley, A. (ed.) *Worlds of Illness: Biographical and Cultural Perspectives on Health and Disease*, Routledge, London.

Williams, G. and Wood, P. (1986) Common-sense beliefs about illness: a mediating role for the doctor, *Lancet*, **ii**, pp. 1435–7.

Williams, G. and Wood, P. (1988) Coming to terms with chronic illness: the negotiation of autonomy in rheumatoid arthritis, *International Disability Studies*, **10**, pp. 128–32.

Williams, S. J. (1993) *Chronic Respiratory Illness*, Routledge, London.

Wolfe, F. and Cathey, M. (1991) The assessment and prediction of functional disability in rheumatoid arthritis, *Journal of Rheumatology*, **18**, pp. 1298–306.

Wood, P. and Badley, E. (1986) The epidemiology of individual rheumatic diseases, pp. 59–142 in Scott, J. T. (ed.) *Copeman's Textbook of the Rheumatic Diseases, Volume 1* (6th edition), Churchill Livingstone, London.

World Health Organisation (1973) *The International Pilot Study of Schizophrenia*, WHO, Geneva.

World Health Organisation (1988) Report on criteria for HIV screening programmes, in Pinching, A. J., Weiss, R. A., and Miller, D. (eds) *AIDS and HIV Infection: The Wider Perspective*, British Medical Bulletin, **44**(1) (whole issue).

World Health Organisation (1992) *The ICD-10 Classification of Mental and Behavioural Disorders: Clinical Descriptions and Diagnostic Guidelines*, WHO, Geneva.

World Health Organisation (1995) World Health Organisation Global Statistics, *AIDS Care*, **7**, pp. 111–2.

Yelin, E., Henke, C. and Epstein, W. (1987) The work dynamics of the person with rheumatoid arthritis, *Arthritis and Rheumatism*, **30**, pp. 507–12.

Zwick, H. *et al.* (1991) Effects of ozone on respiratory health, allergen sensitization and cellular immune system of children, *American Review of Respiratory Diseases*, **144**, pp. 1075–9.

Further reading

We have not suggested additional reading for Chapters 1 and 8 of this book, which can be enriched by any of the titles that follow.

Chapter 2

Goffman, E. (1968) *Stigma: Notes on the Management of Spoiled Identity*, Pelican Books, London (reprinted most recently in June 1995). This is Goffman's classic analysis of the consequences of stigma for peoples' management of their relationships with other people. Controlling the flow of information about stigmatising attributes becomes a central preoccupation for individuals as they seek to avoid unwelcome discrimination.

Williams, S. (1987) Goffman, interactionism and the management of stigma in everyday life, in Scambler, G. (ed.) *Sociological Theory and Medical Sociology*, Tavistock, London. In this chapter, Simon Williams outlines the key ideas of Goffman in a clear and concise way, and explains their relevance for the sociological study of health and illness. Although now out of print, this book is well worth obtaining through a public library.

Chapter 3

Newman, S., Fitzpatrick, R., Revenson, T., Skevington, S. and Williams, G. (1995) *Understanding Rheumatoid Arthritis*, Routledge, London. Two of the authors, Ray Fitzpatrick and Gareth Williams, are also co-authors of Chapter 3 of this book. The volume brings together the available evidence from sociology and psychology concerning the impact of rheumatoid arthritis on individuals and their families, and examines the processes whereby individuals cope and adjust to the problems raised by a chronic disease.

Although now out of print, four other books can be recommended to readers who are interested in the impact of arthritis on daily lives. They can still be obtained through public libraries. Hadler, N. M. and Gillings, D. B. (eds) (1986) *Arthritis in Society: The Impact of Musculoskeletal Diseases*, Butterworth, London (the chapter by Mike Bury, entitled 'Arthritis in the family: problems in adaptation and self-care' is particularly relevant); Locker, D. (1983) *Disability and Disadvantage: the Consequences of Chronic Illness*, Tavistock, London; Woodall, C. (1980) *A Disjointed Life*, Heinemann, London (an autobiography by Corbett Woodall, the former ITN newsreader); and La Fane, P. (1981) *It's a Lovely Day Outside*, Gollancz, London (an autobiography by Pamela La Fane).

Maddison, P. J., Isenberg, D. A., Woo, P. and Glass, D. N. (eds) (1993) *Oxford Textbook of Rheumatology*, Oxford University Press, Oxford. This comprehensive medical textbook is aimed at rheumatologists, but may be useful to anyone who is seeking more detailed clinical description and discussion, if you are familiar with the relevant medical terminology or can use a medical dictionary. (See, for example, the chapter by F. A. Wollheim, pp. 639–60, 'Rheumatoid arthritis—the clinical picture'.)

Medical information produced for a lay audience is available in the booklets published free by ARC, The Arthritis and Rheumatism Council for Research. Write to: Booklets, ARC Publications, PO Box 31, Newark, Nottinghamshire, NG24 2BS, for booklets on all forms of arthritis, including rheumatoid arthritis. Treatment and adaptations to cope with aspects of daily living, such as diet and driving, are also covered in ARC booklets and information sheets.

Silman, A. J. and Hochberg, M. C. (1993) *Epidemiology of the Rheumatic Diseases*, Oxford University Press, Oxford, is a specialist textbook for readers with a background in epidemiology. More accessible in academic terms, but harder to find (because it is out of print, so must be ordered through a library) is Wood, P. and Badley, E. (1986) The epidemiology of individual rheumatic disorders, pp. 59–142 in Scott, J. T. (ed.) *Copeman's Textbook of the Rheumatic Diseases, Volume 1* (6th edition), Churchill Livingstone, London.

Chapter 4

Aggleton, P. and Homans, H. (1988) *The Social Aspects of AIDS*, Falmer Press, London. This edited collection brings together a number of papers originally presented at the 1st UK Conference on the Social Aspects of AIDS. The book explores the impact of the HIV epidemic on sexuality, sexual behaviour and risk perception. It is especially useful as a resource to complement the discussion in Chapter 4 on media representations of sexuality and moral responses to dealing with AIDS.

Bloor, M. (1995) *The Sociology of HIV Transmission*, Sage, London. This is an excellent and readable book for those who wish to learn how medical sociology has contributed to an understanding of the HIV epidemic in the United Kingdom. Drawing on qualitative research among injecting drug users and men involved in prostitution, this book reviews the emergence of HIV infection in the UK and the policy response to HIV prevention. It also contains an extremely useful chapter on theories of risk behaviour which shows how different social science paradigms conceptualise risk. Strongly recommended for anyone who wishes to gain an understanding of models of health behaviour.

Carter, E. and Watney, S. (eds) (1989) *Taking Liberties: AIDS and Cultural Politics*, Serpent's Tail, London. This is an excellent book for an exploration of the cultural and sexual politics of HIV infection and AIDS. The book contains chapters from a range of commentators on media representations of HIV and AIDS, and on the construction of AIDS as a social and medical problem. There is an incisive chapter from Cindy Patton on the 'AIDS Industry', a good critique by Simon Watney on 'AIDS, Language and the Third World', and an excellent contribution by Judith Williamson, 'Every Virus Tells a Story', on the social meanings of AIDS reporting.

Fee, E. and Fox, D. (eds) (1992) *AIDS: The Making of a Chronic Disease*, University of California Press. This book shows how an appreciation of the past can assist in understanding the present. Drawing on a social history of how public health policy and interventions have responded in times of epidemic, a range of authors explore how historical inquiry can inform contemporary understandings of social and medical responses to HIV and AIDS. The book includes chapters on history and epidemics (Guenter Risse), enforcement of health (Roy Porter and Dorothy Porter), medical responses to sexually-transmitted disease (Allan Brandt, Elizabeth Fee), and the social construction of sexuality in the time of AIDS (Paula Treichler, Dennis Altman). It is recommended for anyone who wishes to deepen their understanding of public health responses in times of sexual epidemic.

Nowak, M. A. and McMichael, A. J. (1995) How HIV defeats the immune system, *Scientific American*, August, pp. 42–9. This clear and accessible account by two well-respected research biologists presents the rapidly-emerging 'evolutionary model' of how HIV escapes from the vigorous immune response that most infected people initially mount against it. The rapid rate of mutation of HIV genes is seen to be the key, presenting the immune system with a constantly 'moving target', which eventually increases to such numbers that the body's defences are overwhelmed. *Scientific American* is generally available in the Reference Section of most public libraries.

Rhodes, T. and Hartnoll, R. (eds) (1996) *AIDS, Drugs and Prevention*, Routledge, London. This book brings together a range of international contributions on the research, theory and practice of developing community-based HIV prevention. It aims to understand how social factors influence drug use and sexual behaviour, and explain why there is a need for community approaches to HIV prevention. Chapters from North American and British authors focus on: sexuality (Graham Hart, Sheila Henderson), prostitution (Marina Barnard), drug injecting (Robert Power, Steve Koester), sexual behaviour change (Tim Rhodes, Benny Jose), and community and activist HIV prevention (Cindy Patton, Wayne Wiebel, Jean-Paul Grund). It is recommended for anyone who wishes to understand more about the social context of risk behaviour and how interventions can bring about community and political change.

Chapter 5

Barnes, P. J. (1995) Air pollution and asthma: molecular mechanisms, *Molecular Medicine Today*, **1**(3), pp. 149–154. A review of the research literature linking air pollution with increased inflammation in the lungs. This article assumes some knowledge of medical biology; it presents a reasonably accessible analysis of the possible biological mechanisms by which certain pollutants (such as ozone and PM_{10}) could bring about changes in lung function. The author, Peter J. Barnes, is at the National Heart and Lung Institute, London. He has co-authored several books about asthma, including a small handbook for doctors: Barnes, P. J. and Godfrey, S. (1995), *Asthma*, Martin Dunitz Ltd., London, and a popular account for parents and patients: Barnes, P. J. and Newhouse, M. T. (1991) *Conquering Asthma: An Illustrated Guide to Understanding and Self Care for Adults and Children*, Manson Publishing Ltd., London.

Bryar, R. and Bytheway, B. (eds) (1996) *Changing Primary Health Care*, Blackwell Science, Oxford. Accounts of a series of projects intended to develop primary health care in the valleys of South Wales. As with many other illnesses, an increasing emphasis is being placed upon the role of GPs and community nurses in the treatment of asthma. Chapters by Ajay Thapar, and by Duncan Williams and Beth Griffiths, describe two local projects intended to improve the effectiveness of asthma care by the primary health care team.

Williams, S. J. (1993) *Chronic Respiratory Illness*, Routledge, London. In his analysis of the meaning, experience and impact of Chronic Obstructive Airways Disease (COAD), Simon Williams gives a clear insight into the effects on individuals and families of chronic respiratory diseases. No equivalent analysis has been published for asthma, but much of Williams' book is relevant to Chapter 5. He provides a comprehensive review of the sociological and psychological research and discusses some of the policy implications for health professionals.

Chapter 6

Ancill, R. J., Holliday, S. and Higenbottam, J. (1994) *Schizophrenia: Exploring the Spectrum of Psychosis*, Wiley, Chichester. This book covers a wide range of topics in schizophrenia, ranging from issues surrounding de-institutionalisation to new work on brain abnormalities and new therapeutic advances. It also covers such areas as substance abuse and schizophrenia, and schizophrenia in relation to stress, anxiety, depression and mood disturbance. The majority of authors are psychiatrists from a variety of backgrounds and countries, although the book is predominantly North American in focus.

Atkinson, J. M. and Coia, D. A. (1995) *Families Coping with Schizophrenia: A Practitioner's Guide to Family Groups*, Wiley, Chichester. Written by a psychologist and a psychiatrist, this book offers a background to the involvement of families in schizophrenia—both as carers, and in terms of family influences on the aetiology of schizophrenia. The authors examine the provision of services for carers, focusing particularly on the development of groups for relatives for both education and support, including the development of self-help groups throughout the world. The book draws heavily on the authors' own research and work in this area.

Bentall, R. P. (ed.) (1990) *Reconstructing Schizophrenia*, Routledge, London. This book challenges the concept of schizophrenia from biological, historical and social perspectives and presents new insights into the concept. The final chapters, however, look at psychological approaches to therapy. All the authors are psychologists working in the United Kingdom.

Jablensky, A., Sartorius, N., Ernberg, G. *et al.* (1992) Schizophrenia: manifestation, incidence and course in different cultures, *Psychological Medicine, monograph supplement 20*. This monograph recounts an international study by the WHO into schizophrenia throughout the world. It is interesting for its detailed description of the research, as well as the findings it presents. The authors discuss the conclusions that may be drawn from such work, along with many of the problems inherent in it.

Chapter 7

Bendelow, G. A. and Williams, S. (1995) Transcending the dualisms: towards a sociology of pain, *Sociology of Health and Illness*, **17**(2), pp. 139–65. This article reviews sociological perspectives on pain.

Halliday, T. (ed.) (1992) *The Senses and Communication*, The Open University, Milton Keynes. Chapter 5 of this book, which is part of the Open University course *Biology, Brain and Behaviour* (SD206), covers the biology and psychology of pain. (The book is available from Open University Educational Enterprises, Walton Hall, Milton Keynes MK7 6AA.)

Kleinman, A. (1988) *The Illness Narratives: Suffering, Healing and the Human Condition*, Basic Books, New York. An anthropological account of the meaning of illness and the role of medical care, discussing the idea of narrative in relation to both chronic pain and stigma.

Melzack, R. and Wall, P. (1988, reprinted 1991) *The Challenge of Pain*, Penguin Books, Harmondsworth. This accessible paperback, by the originators of 'gate control' theory, outlines the major biological theories of pain and their implications for treatment.

Answers to self-assessment questions

Chapter 2

1   Suicide is often due to a failure to sustain *ontological security*, the resultant despair and anxiety so overwhelming the individual that the only way to end the feeling is the complete anaesthesia of death. In wartime people group together against a common enemy, upon whom the bad feelings that might otherwise lead to suicide are *projected*. The enemy is a receptacle for fundamental insecurities and anxieties, and is thus *stigmatised* as evil. (Of course, the enemy may in fact *be* evil, but the psychological effect remains the same.) This promotes feelings of togetherness and security amongst the *membership* of both sides.

Everyday conversations depend on sustaining agreements about what counts as normality, part of which can involve drawing boundaries between normality and abnormality. People who are not of 'normal' appearance may threaten ontological security by reminding others of the limitations of their own bodily existence. However, unlike enmity in wartime, it is morally unacceptable in modern conditions to ascribe character defects to disabled people, although it is becoming increasingly acceptable to condemn prejudice and stigma. This enables a more egalitarian sharing of ontological security.

2   The account shows Roberta Galler seeking to disavow a *master status* as a disabled person ('I wanted to be known for *who* I am and not just by what I physically cannot do'). This was done by *covering* her *discredited* status ('I became the "exceptional" woman, the "super-crip", noted for her independence'). She avoided contact with others with disabilities (the *own*) because this threatened her own security. Such avoidance of people who are stigmatised is an example of *enacted* stigma.

3   'Compensation neurotic' is not a medical diagnosis, but is based on an evaluation of the moral character of patients as malingerers, complaining about pain for ulterior motives. This typification gives a stigmatised identity to the patient. The use of such a label may arise from the need of doctors to simplify their task by placing 'problems' into a single category that can then be ignored. 'Problem pain patient' may be a category serving a similar purpose, though it may simply be an initial attitude before diagnosis of the nature of the problem begins. Medical diagnosis involves categorisation and labelling, but not with a stigmatising intent. However, certain disease labels may subsequently attract stigma or arguably rest upon stigmatising assumptions, as the anti-psychiatrists claimed in the case of mental illness categories. Typifications, however, are more likely to be stigmatising from the outset, and by intent.

Chapter 3

1   Failure to perform the tasks associated with fulfilling customary social roles leads people to feel that their status and importance in the social arena has been damaged and that the quality of their relationships has been diminished. Difficulties of this kind may lead to depression, anxiety and social isolation, and to feelings of loss of control and self-worth.

2   Benefits have to be weighed against the multiple risks of side-effects, any benefit may take a considerable time to show, different measures of outcome will show different benefits, and what is a benefit in clinical terms may not be seen to be so by the patient. The relapsing and remitting course of the disease means that it is difficult to be sure that an improvement is due to a given drug. These factors combine to make the prolonged follow-up required for scientific evaluation very difficult to implement. Moreover, the unpredictable benefits of treatment and possible adverse side-effects, along with the psychological effects of having RA (such as depression and anxiety), may have important consequences for a patient's willingness to comply with lengthy spells of out-patient treatment, which place enormous demands on an individual's time and resources. Compliance is important for realistic evaluation of the effectiveness of particular drug regimes.

3   Much of the problem in studying the aetiology of RA arises from the nature of the disease itself. It has a relatively low incidence, an onset which is often insidious and difficult to fix to a given date, and a chronic 'waxing

and waning' course which is often modulated by years of drug treatment. Studying individuals remote in time from the onset of disease may provide little information about its original cause, or causes. A further problem is that RA as a disease entity remains incompletely clinically defined; there are variations between individuals in the speed of progression of the disease and in their physical, histological and serological features (e.g. approximately 20 per cent of RA patients do not have rheumatoid factor in their blood). Finally, as biological knowledge of the condition accumulates, the possibility becomes stronger that a number of different factors—genetic, infectious, hormonal, immunological—may all be involved in a complex causal interaction which may vary from person to person.

4 Several common features of lay illness beliefs are illustrated in this account, perhaps most obviously the emphasis on 'stress' as a cause of her illness. But you should also note that:

(a) She has developed a *personal* causal model of her illness, in which she identifies the interaction of stresses in her family life and her own personality and methods of coping with stress;

(b) Her account shows signs of *narrative reconstruction* in which past events and experiences, that were not considered to be significant at the time, have subsequently become incorporated into a meaningful story of why she became ill (e.g. 'I'm quite certain that the last straw was my husband's illness'.);

(c) She hints at a possible *teleological analysis* of her illness (i.e. does it have a purpose?), when she talks about suppressing her feelings, her personal identity and her aspirations ('Where have I got to? There's nothing left of me'). Although she does not make the point directly, she implies that the illness made her focus on herself as an individual after too many years of identifying herself as 'a mother and wife'.

5 (a) A strength of asking standardised questions is that answers from different studies are easier to compare and results are easier to analyse and report. A weakness is that some individuals' main concerns or difficulties are not reflected in the questions and are thus neglected in reports.

(b) Conversely, the strength of a personalised questionnaire is to maximise sensitivity to individuals' own personal concerns. The weakness is that such data are much more time-consuming to collect and harder to analyse and compare with other studies.

Chapter 4

1 Treatment of HIV is difficult because, like all viruses, it replicates inside the cells of its host, which gives it some protection from attack by drugs (and by the immune system). It preserves its genes from destruction by transcribing them into DNA and 'splicing' them into the DNA of the cell it infects. The viral genes are extremely difficult to identify in this location, and (as yet) impossible to search out and destroy. Drugs (such as Zidovudine/AZT) aimed at disrupting the synthesis of viral DNA, also disrupt the synthesis of new host-cell DNA, so they have serious adverse side-effects. Treatment strategies primarily control the opportunistic infections rather than HIV itself.

Treatment is also complicated by the huge numbers of virus particles involved in an active infection: about a billion new virus particles are produced each day—a formidable 'load' for any drug to eradicate. These huge numbers also swamp the host's immune defences. New cells become infected at a rate that eventually outstrips the immune system's ability to kill infected cells. A vaccine would have to be 100 per cent effective: that is, it would have to enhance the activity of the immune system to such a degree that every virus particle would be killed on entering the body *before* it had a chance to infect a host cell and begin replicating new viruses. Vaccine design is further complicated by the fact that HIV genes mutate very frequently, producing new variants. The mutants temporarily 'escape' from attack by the immune system, which is primed to attack the original strains. During the delay in which an immune response to the new mutant viruses builds up, more host cells can become infected and the cycle continues.

2 *Ontological security* refers to a basic sense of trust and optimism about personal survival. Perceived threats to that sense of security arouse great anxiety, which may be dealt with by *projecting* anger onto anyone who seems to have provoked it. These 'others' are thus excluded from the tribe of 'normals'. Mass advertising campaigns have tended to reinforce the 'otherness' of people infected with HIV, who are represented as threatening the lives of 'normal' people. There are historical precedents for this reaction in public responses to sexually-transmitted infections in the past (e.g. syphilis), and in the persistent association of homosexuality in most Western countries with sin, sickness and death. The political climate of the 1980s, when HIV was identified in the USA and the United Kingdom, was characterised by the promotion of 'family values', in opposition to the perceived social and economic excesses of the 1960s and 1970s. This political

agenda reinforced the representation of people with HIV as a threat to the 'moral order' of society.

3   The strengths of providing information to individuals about HIV risk and HIV transmission is that this may increase personal knowledge and understanding, which are essential requirements of HIV prevention. Individuals may change their risk behaviour on the basis of accurate information on how to protect themselves and/or their sexual partners.

However, there are two main limitations to information-giving strategies. First, informed individuals may not be in a position to act on the basis of their knowledge: they also require the means to introduce behaviour change. Injecting drug users, for example, may know that the sharing of syringes is risky, but may not be able to obtain new ones; safe-sex practices may be taught in places where condoms are not available or affordable.

Second, information to individuals may not be able to encourage behaviour change in the absence of reinforcement from a peer-group or the wider community. If, for example, it is not considered socially 'normal' or 'acceptable' to use condoms with a long-term sexual partner, this makes the negotiation of condom use—particularly by women—considerably more difficult.

This points to the need for a combination of HIV prevention strategies, which:
(a) encourage change in individuals' knowledge, beliefs and behaviour;
(b) encourage change in wider social norms which influence individuals' capabilities to reduce their risks; and
(c) provide the practical means to act on that knowledge.

4   Voluntary testing has the merit of enabling individuals who think they may be at risk of HIV to come forward when they feel they can cope with knowing the outcome. Since the great majority of test results are negative, testing provides reassurance for worried people. It is a confidential service which preserves the right to privacy of its clients; this not only respects a basic human right, but also encourages people to come forward who would not otherwise present for testing. A positive test result leads to counselling support for the individual, practical advice on how to prevent further transmission of HIV, and prompt treatment if symptoms appear. The drawbacks are that an unknown proportion of people who are at risk never present for voluntary testing, which not only compromises their health and perhaps that of their partners, but greatly reduces the accuracy of epidemiological estimates of HIV prevalence and rate of spread. This in turn

reduces the efficient targeting of prevention and treatment services.

Compulsory testing (either of the whole population or of specific groups) could, in theory, detect everyone who is HIV-positive, with consequent benefits in terms of prevention of further spread and accurate service planning. However, this potential may not be realised if (as has been predicted) compulsory testing drives at-risk individuals 'underground' to protect themselves from the negative social consequence of being identified as HIV-positive. HIV transmission could rise as a result of individuals keeping out of reach of services which might have enabled them to change risk behaviours. Compulsion also infringes civil liberty and denies the right to privacy. Mass testing of the whole population, or everyone in a subsection of the population would be immensely expensive.

Chapter 5

1   The problem with studies that rely solely on 'parent-reported' symptoms of asthma is that public awareness of asthma has been increasing over time. A questionnaire given to parents in the 1970s may have elicited fewer reports of (say) 'child wheezing at night' than parents reported a decade later, simply because parents have paid more attention in recent years to wheezing as a potential danger signal of asthma. This difficulty could be reduced by simultaneously collecting objective data on the children's lung function (e.g. by taking peak-flow measurements) and seeing if this correlates with parental reports. Studies that use scientifically-defined measures of asthma could also include an experimental intervention, such as measuring peak flow before and after the child inhaled a blast of cold air (as in the East and West German comparisons by Erika von Mutius and colleagues, 1992, 1994).

2   The accounts from CODAC and by Steve Mumby show that, in a very informal way, lay people have been using basic epidemiological concepts to support their concerns that asthma may be increasing among children. For example, they recognise the importance of making some estimate of the *prevalence* of asthma within a defined population (of 45 children in the Port Tennant marching band about a third of them suffered from asthma; about half the parents with children coming to the Liverpool centre had children with the condition). They are also taking note of whether prevalence has changed *over time*: ' … 40 years ago there was one child with asthma in the school but today there are dozens'. Steve Mumby indicates that he has been investigating the local prevalence in a way that strives to be *systematic*: ' …

we started asking about it on a routine basis'. Lay observations such as these have much in common with the 'spirit' of professional ones, but lack the power of academic research data which has been collected from representative samples of the population that are sufficiently large for rigorous statistical analysis. Moreover, lay assessments of what constitutes 'asthma' will have been based on a variety of evidence, some of it scientifically or medically corroborated, but some may simply be hearsay. It is worth noting, however, that a great deal of the professional epidemiological literature on the prevalence of childhood asthma has been based on lay evidence, in the form of parents' responses to questionnaires (see Question 1 above).

3   Reliever drugs merely relieve the symptoms of breathlessness by stimulating bronchodilation, but they do not affect the underlying inflammation. The most commonly-used drugs in Western asthma treatment are β_2-agonists such as Ventolin, which mimic the action of the hormone adrenalin in stimulating smooth muscle in the airways to relax. An asthmatic person will feel instant relief on inhaling the reliever drug, provided the asthmatic state is not so advanced that mucus and bronchial constriction together prevent the drug from reaching the site of action.

Preventers reduce the likelihood that bronchoconstriction will occur by inhibiting the underlying cause—the excessive inflammatory reaction in the airways. The most commonly-used preventers are *steroids*, which inhibit the release of cytokines and inflammatory chemicals such as histamine in the lungs. This reduces mucus production, the leakage of fluid and white cells from blood vessels, and the 'twitchiness' of the airway lining. Treatment with a preventer drug does not produce a benefit for several days, until the inflammation begins to subside. Thereafter, the need for a 'reliever' is reduced.

4   The most obvious source of financial difficulty is loss of income from employment: unpaid leave may have to be taken from work; a part-time or lower-paid job may have to be accepted, perhaps to avoid an occupational trigger for asthma; a parent may decide not to return to work in order to look after an asthmatic child; in extreme cases a job may be lost altogether. In addition, there may be extra expenses on heating, non-allergenic bedding, trips to the GP or hospital, etc.

5   The researchers found that atmospheric pollution—particularly the levels of sulphur dioxide and particulate matter—was considerably higher in the East German cities they studied than it was in Munich, in former West Germany. However, the East German children had lower rates of asthma than their West German counterparts, on the basis of medical diagnoses, parental reports and objective scientific assessments of lung function. This finding casts doubt on urban air quality as a *primary* cause of asthma in children. However, it leaves open the question of whether atmospheric pollution could be *interacting* with other factors to produce asthma: in particular, high exposure to domestic allergens and low exposure to infection in infancy were more clearly apparent among children in the West than in the East of the country. It also fails to address the possibility that at least some of the differences in rates between the two areas was due to differences in the diagnostic criteria that doctors use to distinguish asthma from other respiratory conditions.

Chapter 6

1   The main *positive* symptoms can be described under headings of distortions of thinking (e.g. thought broadcast, delusions, incoherent and irrelevant speech), distortions of perceptions (e.g. hallucinations), disturbances of volition (e.g. 'I was made to …') and disturbances of movement (e.g. catatonia). Disturbances of personality are usually a consequence of *negative* symptoms, such as withdrawal, apathy, loss of interest, emotional blunting, slow speech and self-absorption. Lay versions of schizophrenia usually emphasise unpredictability and violence, especially to others, but in reality, violence is uncommon and most frequently results in *self*-harm.

2   International comparisons are often invalid due to different criteria being applied to measure schizophrenia. However, the International Pilot Study of Schizophrenia (IPSS) tried to impose a stable definition, and found that the core symptoms of schizophrenia occur in similar frequency throughout the world. However, other evidence (see Table 6.1) suggests some international variation when a broad definition of schizophrenia is taken, with inhabitants of Chandigarh in India, for example, being at high risk of developing schizophrenia. These findings would contradict the view that schizophrenia is an 'illness of Western industrialised countries'. However, the *course* and the *outcome* of schizophrenia are better in 'developing' rather than 'developed' countries, possibly due to differences in social organisation and support — giving some credence to the statement in the question.

3   Treatments for schizophrenia largely aim to influence the *course* of the disease rather than its *cause*. Thus

psycho-social interventions to reduce high expressed emotion are aimed at preventing relapse. Drug treatments aim to control symptoms and reduce relapse rather than remove the original cause of the illness. Additionally, neither a belief that schizophrenia is largely the result of genetic make-up, nor a belief in environmental causes, detracts from the fact that patients and families may benefit from a variety of treatment interventions, as is illustrated by the *multi-intervention approach.*

4 Arguments in favour of retaining the compulsory detention and treatment laws would include the point that they protect the public and may help individuals who are unable to look after themselves. Closing mental hospitals in favour of community care may be a laudable aim, but it could be argued that—in the absence of adequate support 'in the community'—it may do more harm than good.

Arguments against retaining the laws might mirror Szasz's view that dangerous individuals should be dealt with under the criminal law. Protecting the individual from harm by compulsory supervision and treatment can be viewed as paternalism and an infringement of civil liberties, as well as undermining the autonomy of people with mental illness to take charge of their own lives. Long-term institutionalisation may disable people from coping in the community.

5 You might want to weigh up information such as how long ago the person was diagnosed and how they have coped since then; whether or not they are stabilised (with or without medication); other factors that contribute to a good prognosis (including being female, in employment, living in a developing country, living with a low 'expressed emotion' family); and whether other members of the person's family have been diagnosed as having schizophrenia or similar conditions. Schizophrenia is a variable condition and some people 'do well' in that they recover or are able to live a fairly 'normal' life. Depending on the circumstances, it might be possible to make some estimate of prognosis. You might want to dispel misconceptions about schizophrenia producing a 'split personality', with violent tendencies, if personal prejudice, deep-seated anxieties or media misrepresentations of the condition are powerfully expressed, even in the face of positive personal experience.

Chapter 7

1 Small children are inadequately socialised into institutionalised routines for defending against the insecurity engendered by pain, for which they depend on their parents or other caretakers. A minor injury can appear as a frightening event, posing problems about the physical integrity of the body that a small child is not yet able to confront. Parental attention 'remakes' this sudden fracturing (unmaking) of the world, the application of a plaster serving to 'explain' the injury to the child and restoring security. The adult who says 'it's only a scratch' is appealing to a concept of physical suffering, divorced from the emotional and social aspects addressed by the 'unnecessary' plaster.

2 It is profoundly disturbing to suffer from conditions where a physical cause is difficult to identify, where symptoms are hard to communicate, and for which neither lay views nor medical science have an explanation. People may experience difficulty in persuading others of the legitimacy of their complaint, and the lack of a commonly accepted meaning for their condition may produce fear and isolation. The naming of a condition by an authoritative source of knowledge such as medicine can therefore allay such anxieties and make people feel that their condition is shared and potentially within the bounds of normal human experience. This may happen even in the absence of any valid medical explanation or effective medical treatment.

3 The sort of suffering which the Josselins experienced would nowadays be regarded as exceptional and tragic in Western cultures, where there is more widespread recourse to organised medicine to kill pain and cure the source of suffering, and less reliance on religious explanations. There is less tolerance of discomfort and a greater expectation that medical knowledge can explain its origin. Nevertheless, there exist some causes of pain and suffering—such as chronic illness and death—for which medicine has no cure, and sometimes no adequate explanation. The 'answers' to these provided by modern medicine emphasise guided self-reliance, for example, as taught in the pain control clinic featured on the audiotape band.

Chapter 8

Notes on the revision exercise 'Living with epilepsy'

These notes are not meant to be an exhaustive analysis of everything that could have been said about the material on the audiotape band 'Living with epilepsy'. We have picked out a number of the ways in which it illustrates major themes of this book, as summarised in Chapter 8. You may well have noted others. We have used the same headings as in Chapter 8, but we warmly congratulate you if you developed your own scheme.

Doubt and certainty

(a) *Personal knowledge* Jill and Rose describe their confusion and anxiety when her symptoms began, as they tried to work out what was happening. Jill says 'I started to think "Well, maybe I'm going mad. My friends aren't having this happen to them."' When the diagnosis was finally made, mother and daughter expressed relief at the certainty: 'at least it had a label', which to some extent has protected Jill's 'moral reputation' by convincing people that her symptoms were real. Rose describes her daughter's terror of her symptoms in the first couple of years, in which the medical and practical implications of epilepsy were not explained to her. (You may be interested to know that in part of the interview which was not included in this tape, Jill briefly outlines her 'personal illness narrative', attributing her epilepsy to the after-effects of an operation to remove her appendix.)

(b) *Professional knowledge* No medical explanation has ever been found for why Jill became epileptic at the age of 15, and doctors don't seem to have been sure how to treat her condition, given the number of different drugs she has been prescribed.

(c) *Public knowledge* Jill's experience suggests that there is considerable inaccuracy in the public understanding of epilepsy; people have thought that she ought to look 'different' or that epilepsy is due to cancer or having a 'rotten' brain, and shown surprise that she has achieved a high educational standard (an Open University degree, followed by a Masters). Some have assumed that she is not safe to 'be with people'.

Inclusion and exclusion

(a) *Stigmatisation and discrimination* There are numerous examples of this theme on the tape. Onlookers assumed Jill was drunk or a drug addict (two other stigma-tised 'identities') when she was having an epileptic fit, or had anorexia when her medication caused sickness and weight-loss. She has been discriminated against in employment, losing a Saturday job in a sweet shop which she had held for years before her diagnosis, and being told she could sort jumble but not do voluntary work with children. She was eventually asked to leave school and be educated at home. Jill also describes her experience of the *master status*, in which everything about her becomes interpreted and understood in terms of her epilepsy. She asserts her identity: '*I'm* not epileptic. My *fits* are epileptic'.

(b) *Lay accounts and professional accounts* The dominance of professional accounts, and their power to stigmatise, is illustrated by the doctor who told Jill she would be considered 'possessed' in the USA. His list of famous but dead people who were also epileptic pushed her further into a marginalised group. Her treatment has been driven by the medical model of epilepsy as a *disease*, and does not appear to have included her as an equal partner in coping with the *illness*: 'To the medical profession it's just a condition. I was never given any help socially to adapt'. Medication originally increased her exclusion as a result of its side-effects, although it later enabled her to rejoin society. Exclusion from school and work meant Jill became isolated from her friends, and Rose also speaks of her isolation: 'All our lives were very restricted ... I didn't go outside the door, I couldn't leave her'. The lay account of epilepsy has also contributed to Jill's exclusion from society: her family were over-protective and held her back from developing a social life. She has since fought her way back to inclusion, and now runs the local branch of a self-help group which aims to increase public understanding of epilepsy and counteract the stigmatisation associated with it.

Acknowledgements

Grateful acknowledgement is made to the following sources for permission to reproduce material in this book:

Figures

Figures 3.2 and 3.3 courtesy Dr Alex MacGregor and Northwick Park Hospital, Harrow; *Figure 3.4* Williams, G. H. and Wood, P. H. N. (1986) Common sense beliefs about illness: a mediating role for the doctor, *Lancet,* **ii**, pp. 1435–1437, The Lancet Ltd; *Figure 3.5* Silman, A. J. (1988) Has the incidence of rheumatoid arthritis declined in the United Kingdom? *British Journal of Rheumatology,* **27**, pp. 77–78, Oxford University Press, by permission of Oxford University Press; *Figure 3.6* Linos, A., Worthington, J. W., O'Fallon, M. *et al.* (1980) The epidemiology of rheumatoid arthritis in Rochester, Minnesota: A study of incidence, prevalence and mortality, *American Journal of Epidemiology,* **111**, pp. 87–98, The John Hopkins University School of Hygiene and Public Health; *Figure 4.1* courtesy of the National Institute for Biological Standards and Control; *Figure 4.2* Reproduced by kind permission of the British Medical Association Scientific Affairs Department; *Figure 4.3* Worpole, I. (1988) from HIV infection: the clinical picture by Robert R. Redfield and Donald S. Burke, *Scientific American,* October 1988, International edition; *Figure 4.4* Adapted from Public Health Laboratory Service (1991) *Communicable Disease Report,* **1**(4), 29 March, PHLS, London; *Figure 4.5* Evans, B. G. *et al.* (1993) Sexually transmitted diseases and HIV-1 infection among homosexual men in England and Wales, *British Medical Journal,* **306**, pp. 426–8; and PHLS Communicable Disease Surveillance Centre: unpublished Quarterly Surveillance Tables; *Figure 4.6* PHLS Aids Centre, Communicable Disease Surveillance Centre, and Scottish Centre for Infection and Environmental Health: unpublished Quarterly Surveillance Tables No. 29, September 1995; *Figure 4.7* 'It only takes one prick to give you AIDS', © Crown Copyright. Reproduced with the permission of the Controller of Her Majesty's Stationery Office; *Figure 4.8* 'It's that condom moment', reproduced by permission of the Terrence Higgins Trust; *Figure 5.2* Drever, F. (1994) Trends in morbidity and mortality from asthma, *Population Trends,* **49**(78), Winter 1994, OPCS, © Crown Copyright. Reproduced with the permission of the Controller of Her Majesty's Stationery Office; *Figures 5.4, 5.6 and 5.10* Barnes, P. J. and Godfrey, S. (1975) *Asthma,* Martin Dunitz, London, pp. 2, 18 and 8; *Figure 5.5* Adapted from Barnes, P. J. and Newhouse, M. T. (1994) *Conquering Asthma,* pp. 29 and 85, Decker Periodicals; *Figure 5.8* Pope, C. A. and Dockery, D. W. (1992) Acute health effects of PM_{10} pollution on symptomatic and asymptomatic children, *American Review of Respiratory Diseases,* **145**, pp. 1123–1128, Figure 1, American Journal of Respiratory and Critical Care Medicine; *Figure 5.9* Reprinted from *Social Science and Medicine,* **34**(12), Snadden, D. and Brown, J. B. The experience of asthma, pp. 1351–1361. Copyright 1992, with kind permission from Elsevier Science Ltd, The Boulevard, Langford Lane, Kidlington OX5 1GB, UK; *Figure 6.1* Curran, D. and Partridge, M. (1969) *Psychological Medicine,* Churchill Livingstone; *Figure 6.2* Suddath, R. L. *et al.,* Anatomical abnormalities in the brains of monozygotic twins discordant for schizophrenia, *New England Journal of Medicine,* **322**(12), p. 791. Copyright 1990, Massachusetts Medical Society; *Figure 6.3(a) and (b)* Philo, G., Henderson, L. and McLaughlin, G. (1993) *Mass Media Representations of Mental Health/Illness,* Glasgow University Media Group; *Figure 7.1(a)* J. Lathion, © Nasjonalgalleriet, Oslo; courtesy of The Munch Museum/The Munch-Ellingsen Group/DACS 1996; *Figure 7.1 (b) and (c)* Saunders, C. M. (1978) *The Management of Terminal Disease,* Edward Arnold, by permission of Hodder Headline plc; *Figure 7.1 (d)* St Christopher's Hospice, London; *Figure 7.3* MacCarty, C. S. and Drake, R. L. (1956) Neurosurgical procedures for the control of pain, *Proceedings of Staff Meetings of the Mayo Clinic,* **31**, p. 211, as reported in Melzack, R. and Wall, D. (1988) *The Challenge of Pain,* Penguin Books Ltd, by permission of Professor Ronald Melzack; *Figure 7.5* Reading, A. E. (1989) in Wall, P. D. and Melzack, R. (eds) *Textbook of Pain,* Churchill Livingstone; *Figure 7.6* Kosambi, D. D. (1967) Living prehistory in India, *Scientific American,* **216**, pp. 110–111, © D. D. Kosambi.

Tables

Table 3.1 Williams, G. (1986) Lay beliefs about the causes of rheumatoid arthritis: their implications for rehabilitation, *International Rehabilitation Medicine* (now *Disability and Rehabilitation*), **8**(2), p. 66, Taylor and Francis; *Table 4.1* Unpublished Quarterly Surveillance Tables, 1995, Public Health Laboratory Service Communicable Disease Surveillance Centre; *Table 5.1* Jones, K. P., Bain, D. J. G., Middleton, M. and Mullee, M. A. (1992) Correlates of asthma morbidity in primary care, *British Medical Journal*, **304**, p. 362, British Medical Journal Publishing Group; *Table 5.2* OPCS (1979) Studies in medical and population subjects, *Morbidity Statistics from General Practice 1971–72*, **36**, © Crown Copyright. Reproduced with the permission of the Controller of Her Majesty's Stationery Office; *Table 5.3* Peat, J. K., van den Berg, R. H., Green, W. F. *et al.* (1994) Changing prevalence of asthma in Australian children, *British Medical Journal*, **308**, pp. 1591–1596, British Medical Journal Publishing Group; *Table 5.4* Derived from Nocon, A. and Booth, T. (1990) *The Social Impact of Asthma*, Department of Sociological Studies, University of Sheffield; and edited extract (1995) The social impact of childhood asthma, pp. 83–88 in Davey, B., Gray, A. and Seale, C. (eds), *Health and Disease: A Reader*, 2nd edn, Open University Press, Buckingham; *Table 6.1* Jablensky, A. *et al.* (1992) Schizophrenia: manifestations, incidence and course in different cultures, *Psychological Medicine: Monograph Supplement 20*, Table 3.2, Cambridge University Press; *Table 7.1* Melzack, R. and Wall, D. (1988) *The Challenge of Pain*, Penguin Books Ltd, by permission of Professor Ronald Melzack.

Un-numbered photographs/illustrations

p. 6 BBC Photographic Library; *p. 7* Freud Museum, London, A. W. Freud *et al.*; *p. 11* Mansell Collection; *p. 16* Roger Hutchings/Network; *p. 17* Brenda Prince/Format; *p. 20* Suzanne Roden/Format; *p. 21* Popperfoto/Kevin Lamarque/WPA Reuter; *pp. 33, 35* courtesy of the Arthritis and Rheumatism Council; *p. 54* Reproduced by kind permission of the NAMES Project (UK), photo by Estyn Williams-Hulbert; *p. 81* courtesy of Medix Ltd; *p. 86, 110* Duncan Williams; *p. 96* David Rose © *The Independent*; *p. 105* Mike Levers, OU; *p. 137 Sunday Express*, 27 February 1994, p. 7, Express News and Feature Services/Express Newspapers plc.

Colour Plates

Plate 2 Reproduced by kind permission of Terence Charnley, the artist's brother.

Index

Entries and page numbers in **bold type** refer to key words which are printed in **bold** in the text. Indexed information on pages indicated by *italics* is carried mainly or wholly in a figure or table.